The International

INDUCTIVE STUDY

NEW TESTAMENT

THE MODERN LANGUAGE NEW TESTAMENT

NEW BERKELEY VERSION

This unique study edition of the New Testament
was prepared by the Billy Graham Evangelistic Association,
with permission from Harvest House Publishers
and Hendrickson Publishers, Inc.

The study materials in *The International Inductive Study New Testament—The Modern Language New Testament/New Berkeley Version* are adapted with the permission of Harvest House Publishers and Precept Ministries from:

THE INTERNATIONAL INDUCTIVE STUDY BIBLE
© 1992, 1993 Precept Ministries
Published by Harvest House Publishers
1075 Arrowsmith
Eugene, Oregon 97402

Precept Ministries
7324 Noah Reid Road
Chattanooga, Tennessee 37421

Inductive study material in *The International Inductive Study New Testament* was compiled by K. Arthur and the staff of Precept Ministries.

The New Testament Scripture text in this publication is taken with permission from:

THE MODERN LANGUAGE BIBLE
The New Berkeley Version in Modern English
Revised Edition

Copyright © 1945, 1959, 1969 by
Hendrickson Publishers, Inc.

New Testament Section, Copyright © 1945 by Gerrit Verkuyl.
Revised Edition Copyright © 1969 by the Zondervan Publishing House.
Assigned 1990 to Hendrickson Publishers, Inc.

Hendrickson Publishers, Inc.
137 Summit Street
Peabody, Massachusetts 01961

ISBN 0-913367-27-3

Both *The Modern Language Bible/The New Berkeley Version* and *The International Inductive Study Bible* are available from Christian bookstores or from the publishers.

TABLE OF CONTENTS

BIBLE STUDY HELPS:

OREWORD

When my wife, Ruth, and I saw the inductive Bible studies that were prepared by Kay Arthur, we were thrilled. We found that the inductive approach helps readers of the Bible discover deeper truths that will strengthen them for their daily life. We wanted more people to have the opportunity to study God's Word in this way, and so it is a pleasure for us to commend to you *The International Inductive Study New Testament*.

These study materials, combined with a modern language New Testament that faithfully translates the original Greek, open God's message to us in a fresh way. This study New Testament will enable you to search the Scriptures for yourself, and you'll receive powerful thoughts from God that will stabilize and give direction to your life.

The Bible is the one sure guide in an unsure world. Let it be the firm foundation upon which your hope is built. Let it be the staff of life upon which your spirit is nourished. Let it be the sword of the Spirit which cuts away evil and fashions us in Christ's image and likeness.

Great Christians, including D. L. Moody and many others, marked in the pages of their Bibles the things God was teaching them. This volume can be for you a visible record of what God has impressed on your heart. And remember that your goal is not only to observe and interpret what God says, but also to apply it to your daily life.

As you read and study the inspired words of the New Testament, you will find that the principles of life and conduct that the Holy Spirit gave to the ancient writers are as fresh and meaningful today as they were to the people of Jesus' day.

Billy Graham
Minneapolis, Minnesota
December 1993

REFACE

The Berkeley Version gained for the late Dr. Gerrit Verkuyl a place among the first rank of translators of the Bible into modern English. Its growing readership since the initial publication of the New Testament in 1945 bears witness to his success in combining freshness of expression with fidelity to the original Greek.

This is not just another revision; it is a completely new translation. It exhibits a faithful rendering of the original texts into lively modern English. While some modern translations of the Scriptures tend to be paraphrases, this version aims to achieve plain, up-to-date expression which reflects as directly as possible the meaning of the Greek. As Professor F. F. Bruce says, *"The Berkeley Version* of the whole Bible (1959) is the most outstanding among recent translations of both Testaments sponsored by private groups" (*The Books and the Parchments*, Westwood, N.J.: Fleming H. Revell Company, 1963, pp. 236, 237).

Throughout this New Testament, language is employed according to its choicest current usage. Even mention of weights, measures and monetary values is made in modern terms, so that the reader does not need to be a linguist to understand the information. As far as possible this is a complete translation of every word in the New Testament. Brief notes, related to, but apart from, the inspired writings, clarify and give a sharper view of the message.

In response to suggestions offered over a 25-year period, the publishers appointed three experienced Bible scholars to revise The Berkeley New Testament, namely, E. Schuyler English, Litt.D., chairman; Frank E. Gaebelein, A.M., Litt.D.; and G. Henry Waterman, A.M., Ph.D. The present edition is the result of their work. While not a retranslation, the revision is a very extensive one. In making it, there was constant reference to the Greek. Recent findings of textual criticism were considered. Explanatory notes were not only revised but a great many new notes were added. Topical headings were in many cases rephrased.

This is still The Berkeley Version. It rests upon the foundation Dr. Verkuyl laid. Nevertheless, the numerous changes in the New Testament text, explanatory notes, and headings warrant calling this 1969 edition *The Modern Language Bible*—The New Berkeley Version in Modern English.

As this New Testament is again offered to the public, the publishers share Dr. Verkuyl's sentiments—

"With expectant joy and acknowledgment of our Father's sustaining grace we surrender the results of our endeavors to the readers of the Bible, supremely grateful to Him who first inspired its contents. We pray that this version may be instrumental in the fulfillment of God's purpose, a translation of His teachings into Christlike living. This will most amply reward our labors."

THE PUBLISHERS

WELCOME TO THE INTERNATIONAL INDUCTIVE STUDY NEW TESTAMENT

Do you long to know God? Do you yearn for a deep and abiding relationship with Him? Do you want to live the Christian life faithfully—and to know what He requires of you? If so, *The International Inductive Study New Testament* is designed for you.

God reveals Himself through His Word. Through it, He shows us how to live. Jesus made it clear: "Man shall not live on bread alone but on every command that proceeds from the mouth of God" (Matthew 4:4). And where do we find this divine bread? In the Scriptures.

As you study this New Testament with the help of the Holy Spirit, and live out the truths that God reveals to you, you will discover new stability, strength, and confidence. You will be able to say with the prophet Jeremiah: "Thy words were found, and I ate them, and Thy words were to me a joy and a rejoicing of my heart" (Jeremiah 15:16).

Today, many people are convinced they cannot know truth for themselves. A babble of voices surrounds us claiming to know and interpret God's truth for us. Which voices are right? Which are wrong? How can we discern the true from the counterfeit unless we spend time with God and His Word?

Most Christians have been encouraged to study the Word of God, yet many have never been shown how. Others even feel inadequate to do so because they are not ministers, seminary students or scholars. Nothing could be further from the truth.

In fact, if you want to satisfy your hunger and thirst to know God and His Word in a deeper way, you must do more than merely read Scripture and study what someone else has said about it. Just as no one else can eat and digest your food for you, so no one else can feed on God's Word for you. You must interact with the text yourself, absorbing its truths and letting God engrave His truth on your heart, mind and life.

That is the very heart of inductive study: seeing truth for yourself, discerning what it means, and applying that truth to your life. In His inspired Word, God has given us everything we need to know about life and godliness. But He doesn't stop there. He gives every believer a resident teacher—the Holy Spirit—who guides us into His truth.

The Bible is unlike any other book. It is supernatural. It is complete in itself. The Bible needs no other books or truths to supplement it. In inductive study the Bible becomes its own commentary, and it can be understood by any believer.

Anyone who will take the time can see and understand what God has given us in His Word and how it applies to us today.

How to Use the Inductive Study Approach

If you know there is more to the Word of God than you have discovered so far...

🍂 If you sense there must be concrete answers to the complexities of life...

🍂 If you want a bedrock faith that keeps you from being tossed around by conflicting philosophies in the world and the church...

🍂 If you want to be able to face the uncertainties of the future without fear...

...then *The International Inductive Study New Testament* is designed for you.

God's eternal, infallible Word is your guidebook for all of life, and inductive study gives you the key to understanding that guide.

Inductive study, a method anyone can use, involves three skills: *observation, interpretation,* and *application*.

OBSERVATION–Discover What It Says, teaches you to see precisely what the passage says. It is the basis for accurate interpretation and correct application. Observation answers the question: What does the passage say?

INTERPRETATION–Discover What It Means, answers the question: What does the passage mean?

APPLICATION–Discover How It Works, answers the question: What does it mean to me personally? What truths can I put into practice? What changes should I make in my life?

When you know what God says, what He means, and how to put His truths into practice, you will be equipped for every circumstance of life. Ultimately, the goal of personal Bible study is a transformed life and a deep and abiding relationship with Jesus Christ.

The following ten steps provide the basis for inductive study. As you take these steps, observation, interpretation, and application will sometimes happen simultaneously. God can give you insight at any point in your study, so be sensitive to His leading. When words or passages make an impression on you, stop for a moment and meditate on what God has shown you. Record your personal notes and insights in the margin so that you can remember what you've learned.

One of the most valuable aspects of the *IISNT* is its wide-margin format, which has been specifically designed to enable you to easily keep a record of what God personally reveals to you from His Word.

Some people are hesitant to mark in their Bibles, but this interactive New Testament has been designed with marking in mind.

As you study the New Testament chapter by chapter and book by book, you will grow in your ability to comprehend the whole counsel of God. In the future, you will be able to refer to your notes again and again as you study portions of Scripture and grow in your knowledge of Him.

OBSERVATION–Discover What It Says!

Step One

BEGIN WITH PRAYER

Prayer is often the missing element in Bible study. You are about to learn the most effective method of Bible study there is. Yet apart from the work of the Holy Spirit, that's all it will be—a method. It is the indwelling Holy Spirit who guides us into all truth, who takes the things of God and reveals them to us. Always ask God to teach you as you open the Scriptures.

Step Two

ASK THE "5 W'S AND AN H"

As you study any passage of Scripture, any book of the Bible, train yourself to constantly ask: *Who? What? When? Where? Why? How?* These questions are the building blocks of precise observation, which is essential for accurate interpretation. Many times Scripture is misinterpreted because the context isn't carefully observed.

When we rush into interpretation without laying the vital foundation of observation, our understanding becomes colored by our presuppositions—what we think, what we feel, or what other people have said. We must be careful not to distort the Scriptures to our own ruin (2 Peter 3:16).

Accurate answers to the following questions will help assure correct interpretation.

Who is speaking? Who is this about? Who are the main characters? For example, look at the sample passage from 1 Peter 5 (see back cover). In this chapter, "I" is speaking. Verse 1 tells us that "I" is a fellow elder, a witness of Christ's sufferings, and a sharer in the glory that is to be revealed. From reading this and previous chapters (the context), you recognize that the "I" is Peter, the author of this epistle.

And, *to whom is he speaking?* Verse 1 refers to "the elders," verse 5 to "the younger men," and verse 6 to "yourselves" (the recipients of the epistle).

What is the subject or event covered in the chapter? What do you learn about the people, the event, or the teaching from the text? What instructions are given? In 1 Peter 5:2-3, Peter instructs the elders to shepherd the flock and to be examples.

When do or will the events occur? When did or will something happen to a particular person, people, or nation? When is a key question in determining the progression of events. In 1 Peter 5:4, we learn that "with the appearing of the Chief Shepherd," the elders will receive their "never-fading crown of glory."

Where did or will this happen? Where was it said? In 1 Peter 5, the only reference to a place is in verse 13, where there is a greeting from "she who is at Babylon."

Why is something being said or mentioned? Why would or will this happen? Why at this time? Why this person? First Peter 5:12 explains why and how Peter wrote this epistle, establishing the book's purpose: to encourage and to testify that this is the true grace of God, that they may stand firm in it.

How will it happen? How is it to be done? How is it illustrated? In 1 Peter 5:2, note *how* the elders are to shepherd the flock: willingly and eagerly, "because God wants you to."

Every time you study a passage of the Scripture, you should keep the "5 W's and an H" in mind. Don't be concerned if you can't find the answer to each question every time. Remember, there are many types of literature in the Bible and not all the questions will apply. As you ask *what, when, who, where, why,* and *how,* make notes in the margin of your New Testament. Meditate on the truths God reveals to you. Think how they apply to you. This will keep your study from becoming an intellectual pursuit of knowledge for its own sake.

Step Three

MARK KEY WORDS AND PHRASES

A key word is one that is essential to the text. It might be a noun, a descriptive word, or an action that plays a part in conveying the author's message. A key word or phrase is one which, when removed, leaves the passage devoid of meaning. Often key words and phrases are repeated in order to convey the author's point or purpose for writing. They may be repeated throughout a chapter, a segment of a book, or the book as a whole. For example, notice that some form of the word *suffering* is used three times in 1 Peter 5.

As you mark key words, ask the same *who, what, when, where, why,* and *how*

questions of them as you did of the passage as a whole. For example, *who* suffers?, *what* caused the suffering?, etc. Key words can be marked in several ways:

🍂 *Through the use of symbols.*

🍂 *Through the use of colors.* Colored pencils and certain multicolored ballpoint pens with fine tips work best.

FAITH   HUMILITY   GRACE

🍂 *Through a combination of colors and symbols.* For an illustration of these markings, see the back cover of this New Testament.

The value of a distinctive marking system cannot be overestimated. Whichever system you choose, mark each key word the same way every time you observe it. Then, in future study, the visual impact of your marks will help you track key subjects and quickly identify significant truths throughout Scripture. To be sure that you are consistent, list key words, symbols, and color codes on an index card and use it as a bookmark in your New Testament.

Be sure to mark pronouns *(I, you, he, she, it, we, our,* and so on) and synonyms (words that have the same meaning in the context) the same way you mark the words to which they refer. For example, a synonym for the devil in 1 Peter 5:8 is "opponent." The pronoun "him" in verse 9 also refers to the devil. Notice how marking the synonym "opponent" for the devil gives additional insight into his nature.

Step Four

LOOK FOR LISTS

Making lists can be one of the most enlightening things you do as you study a section of Scripture. Lists reveal truths and highlight important concepts. The best way to discover lists in the text is to observe how a key word is described, note what is said about someone or something, or group related thoughts or instructions together. (You may want to develop your lists on a worksheet before transferring them to your New Testament.)

1 Peter 5:2,3 for example, contains a *simple list* instructing the elders how to shepherd their flock. You can number simple lists within the text for easy reference.

Topical lists capture a truth, quality, or characteristic of a specific subject throughout a passage. One way to discover a topical list is to follow a key word through a chapter and note what the text says about the word each time it is used. See the back cover for how a list could be made for the key word "suffering."

As you write your observations on suffering, you will begin to have a better and broader understanding of God's thoughts on this subject. You will learn that:

- Christ suffered
- Christians in the world are suffering
- the recipients of the letter may also endure suffering

You will also discover that God:

- equips
- stabilizes
- strengthens
- establishes those who suffer

The application value of lists such as these is immeasurable. The next time you endure suffering, you will be able to recall more quickly that:

- Christ suffered
- Others are suffering
- ultimately God will use suffering to strengthen your own life

Discovering truths that apply to your daily life is what makes lists such an important part of the inductive method.

Step Five

WATCH FOR CONTRASTS AND COMPARISONS

Contrasts and comparisons use highly descriptive language to drive home significant truths and vital lessons. The word pictures they paint make it easier to remember what you have learned.

A *contrast* is a comparison of things that are different or opposite, such as light/darkness or proud/humble. The word "but" often signifies that a contrast is being made. Note contrasts in the text or in the margin of your New Testament.

A *comparison* points out similarities and is often indicated by the use of words such as "like," "as," and "as it were." For example, Peter says in 1 Peter 5:8: "Your opponent, the devil, prowls around *like* a roaring lion." Highlight comparisons in a distinctive way in the text so that you will recognize them immediately when you return to the passage in the future.

Step Six

NOTE EXPRESSIONS OF TIME

The relationship of events in time often sheds light on the true meaning of the text. The timing of something can be observed in exact statements such as "on the tenth day of the eleventh month" or "at the Feast of Booths." These phrases can be indicated in the margin by drawing a simple clock face ⏱ or a similar symbol.

Time is also indicated by words such as *until, then, when,* and *after.* These words show the relationship of one statement or event to another. Marking them will help you see the sequence of events and lead to accurate interpretation of Scripture.

Step Seven

IDENTIFY TERMS OF CONCLUSION

Terms of conclusion usually follow an important sequence of thought and include words such as *wherefore, therefore, for this reason,* and *finally.* As the saying goes, when you see a "therefore" (or any term of conclusion), note what it is there for. You should be able to look through the preceding verses and summarize the message. For example, 1 Peter 5:6 says, "Humble yourselves, *therefore....*" If you will look, you will discover that you should humble yourself under the hand of God because God "sets Himself against the arrogant, but He grants grace to the humble."

Step Eight

DEVELOP CHAPTER THEMES

The theme of a chapter will center on the main person, event, teaching, or subject of that section of Scripture. Themes are often revealed by reviewing the key words and lists you developed. Try to express the theme as briefly as possible, using words found in the text.

Be humble/sober

5 Therefore, as a fellow elder and a witness of Christ's sufferings, a sharer, too, in the glory that is to be revealed, I appeal to the elders among you:

For example, possible themes for 1 Peter 5 might be *Exhortations to Elders, Younger Men, and the Suffering,* or *God Gives Grace to the Humble.* The point of observation is to answer the question: What does the passage say? The theme summarizes the answer. If needed, you can adjust your themes as your study deepens.

Step Nine

DISCOVER LESSONS FOR LIFE

In the process of observing the text and seeing how God instructed people and dealt with various individuals, the Holy Spirit will bring to your attention truths that God wants you to be aware of and live by in your own life. These "Lessons for Life" can be noted in the margin under the abbreviation "LFL," or you may wish to create a distinctive symbol to mark your Lessons for Life throughout your *IISNT.*

Step Ten

COMPLETE THE *AT A GLANCE* CHART

The AT A GLANCE chart, found at the end of every book in the *IISNT,* provides a compact visual summary of the book that you can return to again and again for easy reference. See the sample AT A GLANCE charts on the following pages.

❧ **Record the author of the book.** If the author is not mentioned by name, read the introduction for that book. If the author is not mentioned in either place, leave this space blank.

❧ **Record the date the book was written.** If the date of writing is known, it will be mentioned in the introduction that precedes each book.

~● **Record the key words.** If the key words are not already listed on the AT A GLANCE chart, you will find them listed in the THINGS TO DO section at the beginning of each book.

In order to notice subjects which run throughout the entire Bible, there are some key words or phrases you will want to consistently mark in a distinctive manner. Write these on a card, color code them in the way you intend to mark them throughout your New Testament, and use the card as a bookmark.

Some of the key words you will want to mark are listed below:

sin (wickedness, evil, iniquity)
covenant
death (die)
life (live)
repent
love
law
grace
believe (faith)
righteousness (righteous)
holy (holiness)
cry (cries, cried)
Babylon
nations
day of the Lord (that day)
Satan (any reference to the devil,
    spirits, demons, mediums)
any reference to:
    Jesus' first coming
    Jesus' second coming

~● **Copy the chapter themes** that you recorded at the beginning of each chapter. Because chapter divisions were added much later than the Bible was originally written, they do not always fall naturally in the text. Occasionally you will find a chapter with more than one theme. If this is true, record both themes.

~● **Look for and record segment divisions.** See if any of the chapters can be grouped under a common theme or a common event. This is called a *segment division.* Segment divisions help you see the framework of a book.

The number and types of segment divisions will vary. A book might be divided according to dates, geographical locations, major characters or events, topics, or doctrines.

When you gain a broad view of a book through its segment divisions, it is easier to understand its content and purpose. The sample AT A GLANCE chart for the book of John shows a number of ways this book could be divided. For example, on the last line under "Segment Divisions," you will notice "Structure of Book." This shows you how John presents his material to achieve his purpose for writing this gospel.

~● **Record the purpose of the book.** Discerning the author's purpose for writing and then keeping this purpose in mind while you study the text will help you handle the Word of God accurately. Unless the author specifically states his purpose for writing, as in 1 Peter 5:12 and John 20:21, you will have to discover it by other means:

1. Look for the main subjects covered in the book. These can often be recognized as you study the key repeated words.
2. Watch for any problems that are addressed. It may be that the author's purpose in writing was to deal with these problems.
3. Note exhortations and warnings that are given. These may be the reason for the book.
4. Observe what the author did *not* cover in his writing. When you know what the author covered and what was left unsaid, you are better able to narrow down the real purpose of the book.

Generally the instructions at the beginning of each book in your *IISNT* will help you understand how that book might be divided.

➤ **Record the main theme of the book.** Once you have listed the theme for each chapter, evaluated the author's purpose for writing, and observed the content of the book chapter by chapter and segment by segment, you will be prepared to determine the theme of the book. What one statement best describes the book as a whole?

_____

Once you have completed the ten steps of observation, you are ready to move into interpretation and application.

1 PETER AT A GLANCE

THEME OF 1 PETER: Suffering & Glory

SEGMENT
DIVISIONS

		CHAPTER THEMES
	1	Trials Prove your Faith - Be Holy
	2	You're Chosen: Follow Christ's Example - Submit
	3	
	4	
	5	

Author:
Peter
Date:
63 or 64 A.D.
Purpose:
To exhort to
stand firm
in true grace
Key Words:
suffering
(and all its
synonyms)
grace
glory
salvation
Jesus Christ
God
Holy Spirit
called
chosen
holy
(dedicated)

14

THEME OF JOHN: Eternal life through Jesus Christ, Son of God

SEGMENT DIVISIONS

Structure of Book	Written	Signs & miracles	Ministry	CHAPTER THEMES
Introduces Jesus as Son of God	That you may believe Jesus is the Christ, Son of God	water to wine	To Israel	1 Prologue – The Word / John the Baptist / Calling Disciples
				2 Wedding Cana / cleansing temple
		Heals noble-man's son		3 born again
Gives signs that prove Jesus is the Christ, Son of God				4 woman at well / nobleman
		Heals lame man		5 father / son
		Feeds 5,000		6 bread / feeding 5,000
		Walks on water		7 feast of tabernacles / thirst – drink
				8 adulterous woman / truth sets free
		Heals blind man		9 blind man
				10 sheep / shepherd
		Raises Lazarus from dead	To Disciples	11 raising Lazarus
	Your hour has come. Decision Time.			12 King on donkey / dinner at Bethany
	That you may have life			13 Last supper / washing – disciples
				14 Father's house / hearts be troubled
	Life that belongs to those who believe God			15 abide / vine & branches
				16 Holy Spirit / another comforter
				17 Lord's prayer / high-priestly prayer
Obtaining of that life by death & resurrection		Resurrection appearances	To All Mankind	18 arrest & trial
				19 crucifixion
				20 resurrection
Purpose of life: Love & follow			To Disciples	21 do you love Me?

Author:

John

Date:

about A.D. 85

Purpose:

That his readers would believe that Jesus is the Christ, God's son, & thus have eternal life

Key Words:

Signs / miracles
believe
life
judge
judgment
witness
true, truth
King
kingdom
love
works
commands
fruit
abide
ask

INTERPRETATION – Discover What It Means!

While observation leads to an accurate understanding of what the Word of God *says,* interpretation goes a step further and helps you understand what it *means.* When you accurately interpret the Word of God, you will be able to confidently put its truths into practice in your daily life.

Like many other people, you may have been taught a system of belief before you ever studied God's Word for yourself. Or you may have formed opinions of what the Bible teaches before you carefully examined the Scriptures. As you learn to handle God's Word accurately, you will be able to discern if what you believe is in agreement with Scripture. If this is your desire and you come to the Word of God with a teachable spirit, God will lead you and guide you into all truth.

As you seek to interpret the Bible accurately, the following guidelines will be helpful.

1. Remember that context rules.

The word *context* means "that which goes with the text." To understand the context you must be familiar with the Word of God. If you lay the solid foundation of observation, you will be prepared to consider each verse in the light of:

- the surrounding verses
- the book in which it is found
- the entire Word of God

As you study, ask yourself: Is my interpretation of a particular section of Scripture consistent with the theme, purpose, and structure of the book in which it is found? Is it consistent with other Scripture about the same subject, or is there a glaring difference? Am I considering the historic and cultural context of what is being said? Never take a Scripture out of its context to make it say what you want it to say. Discover what the author is saying; don't add to his meaning.

2. Always seek the full counsel of the Word of God.

When you know God's Word thoroughly, you will not accept a teaching simply because someone has used one or two isolated verses to support it. Those verses may have been taken out of context, or other important passages might have been overlooked or ignored that would have led to a different understanding. As you read the Bible regularly and extensively, and as you become more familiar with the whole counsel of God's Word, you will be able to discern whether a teaching is biblical or not.

Saturate yourself in the Word of God; it is your safeguard against wrong doctrine.

3. Remember that Scripture will never contradict Scripture.

The best interpretation of Scripture is Scripture. Remember, all Scripture is inspired by God; it is God-breathed. Therefore, Scripture will never contradict itself.

The Bible contains all the truth you will ever need for any situation in life.

Sometimes, however, you may find it difficult to reconcile two seemingly contradictory truths taught in Scripture. An example of this would be the sovereignty of God and the responsibility of man. When two or more truths that are clearly taught in the Word seem to be in conflict, remember that we as humans have finite minds. Don't take a teaching to an extreme that God doesn't. Simply humble your heart in faith and believe what God says, even if you can't fully understand or reconcile it at the moment.

4. Don't base your convictions on an obscure passage of Scripture.

An obscure passage is one in which the meaning is not easily understood. Because these passages are difficult to understand even when proper principles of interpretation are used, they should not be used as a basis for establishing doctrine.

5. Interpret Scripture literally.

The Bible is not a book of mysticism. God spoke to us that we might know truth. Therefore, take the Word of God at face value—in its natural, normal sense. Look first for the clear teaching of Scripture, not a hidden meaning. Understand and recognize figures of speech and interpret them accordingly.

Consider what is being said in the light of its literary style. For example, you will find more similes and metaphors in poetic and prophetic literature than in historical or biographical books. Interpret portions of Scripture according to their literary style.

Some literary styles in the New Testament are:

- Historical—Acts
- Prophetic—Revelation
- Biographic—Luke
- Didactic (teaching)—Romans
- Epistle (letter)—2 Timothy

6. Look for the single meaning of the passage.

Always try to understand what the author had in mind when you interpret a portion of the Bible. Don't twist verses to support a meaning that is not clearly taught. Unless the author of a particular book indicates that there is another meaning to what he says, let the passage speak for itself.

APPLICATION – Discover How It Works!

No matter how much you know *about* God's Word, if you don't apply what you learn, Scripture will never benefit your life. To be a hearer of the Word and not a doer is to deceive yourself (James 1:22–25). This is why application is so vital. Observation and interpretation are the "hearing" of God's Word. With *application,* you will be transformed into Christ's image. Application is the embracing of the truth, the "doing" of God's Word. It is this process which allows God to work in your life.

Second Timothy 3:16, 17 says: "All Scripture is inspired by God and is profitable for teaching, for reproof, for correction, for training in righteousness, so that the man of God may be well-fitted and adequately equipped for all good work." Here is the key to application: Apply Scripture in the light of its teaching, reproof, correction, and training for life.

Teaching (doctrine) is what the Word of God says on any particular subject. That teaching, whatever the subject, is always true. Therefore, everything that God says in His Bible about any given subject is absolute truth.

The first step in application is to find out what the Word of God says on any particular subject through accurate observation and correct interpretation of the text. Once you understand what the Word of God teaches, you are then obligated before God to accept that truth and to live by it. When you have adjusted any false concepts or teaching you may have believed, and embraced the truth revealed in God's Word, then you have *applied* what you have learned.

Reproof exposes areas in your thinking and behavior that do not align with God's Word. Reproof is finding out where you have thought wrongly or have not been doing what God says is right. The application of reproof is to accept it and agree with God, acknowledging where you are wrong in thought or in behavior. This is how you are set free from unbelief, from sin.

Correction is the next step in application, and often the most difficult. Many times we can see what is wrong, but we are reluctant to take the necessary steps to correct it. God has not left you without help or without answers in this step of correcting what is wrong. Sometimes the answers are difficult to find, but they are always there, and any child of God who wants to please his or her Father will be shown by the Spirit of God how to do so.

Many times correction comes by simply confessing and forsaking what is wrong. Other times, God gives very definite steps to take. An example of this is in Matthew 18:15–17, in which God tells us how to approach a brother when he sins. When you apply correction to your actions and attitudes, God will work in you to do His good pleasure (Philippians 2:13). Joy will follow obedience.

Training in righteousness: Although God's Word is profitable for reproof and correction, the Bible was also given to us as a handbook for living. As we spend time studying His Word,

God equips us through:

- teachings
- commands
- promises
- exhortations
- warnings
- and the lives of biblical characters and God's dealings with people

Scripture has everything you need to meet any and all situations of life, so that you "may be adequate, equipped for every good work." The most effective application takes place as you go before the Lord and talk with Him about those things that you have read, studied, seen, and heard.

INSIGHTS ON APPLYING SCRIPTURE

In applying Scripture to your life, the following questions may be helpful:

1. What does the passage teach? Is it general or specific? Does it apply only to specific people? To a cultural problem of the day? To a certain time in history? Has it been superseded by a broader teaching? For example, in the Old Testament, Jews were not allowed to eat certain foods or to wear a certain combination of materials. Are those prohibitions applicable to Christians today?

2. Does this section of Scripture expose any error in my beliefs or in my behavior? Are there any commandments that I have not obeyed? Are there any wrong attitudes or motives in my life that the Scriptures bring to light?

3. What is God's instruction to me as His child? Are there any new truths to be believed? Are there any new commandments to be acted upon? Are there any new insights I am to pursue? Are there any promises I am to embrace?

4. When applying Scripture, beware of the following:

- Applying cultural standards rather than biblical standards
- Attempting to strengthen a legitimate truth by using a Scripture incorrectly
- Applying Scripture out of prejudice from past training or teaching

One of the apostle Paul's concerns for Timothy, his son in the faith, was that Timothy learn to handle God's Word in a way that would please the Lord (2 Timothy 2:15). Someday we too will want to give a good account of our stewardship of God's Word. Did we handle it accurately? Were we gentle and reasonable about our faith, giving honor to those whom God has called to lead us, while at the same time searching Scripture ourselves to understand its truths? Did we allow God's living and active Word to change our lives?

Observation, interpretation, and application lead to *transformation*. This is the goal of our study of the Word of God. Through it we are changed from glory to glory into the image of Jesus.

GETTING STARTED

With this basic understanding of the inductive process, you are ready to begin a lifetime of personal Bible study. Prayerfully choose one of the New Testament's 27 books, and then begin your study.

As you begin, quickly read through the THINGS TO DO section for an overview, but don't let the instructions overwhelm you. Taken one by one, chapter by chapter, and book by book, they become very manageable.

The THINGS TO THINK ABOUT section encourages you to get alone with God to consider how the truths of the book apply to you.

Many of the books in the New Testament contain an OBSERVATIONS CHART on which to record information you are instructed to look for in the THINGS TO DO section.

Finally, each book of the New Testament ends with an AT A GLANCE chart, as discussed earlier.

As you study the Bible inductively, you will get to know God in a deep, exciting, and enlightening way—and "the people who know their God shall be steadfast and will accomplish notable feats" (Daniel 11:32b).

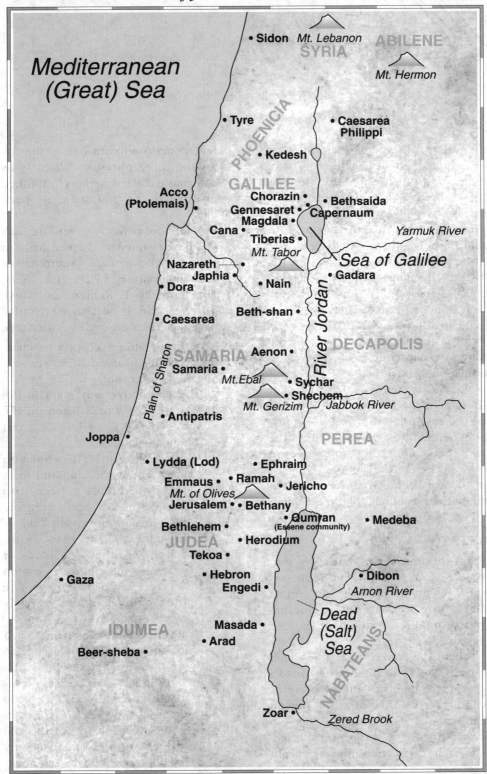

Bible Cities in the Time of Jesus

Mediterranean
(Great) Sea

• Sidon   *Mt. Lebanon*   ABILENE
SYRIA

Mt. Hermon

• Tyre   • Caesarea
Philippi

PHOENICIA   • Kedesh

Acco   GALILEE
(Ptolemais)   Chorazin •   • Bethsaida
Gennesaret •   • Capernaum
Magdala •
Cana •   *Yarmuk River*
Tiberias •
Nazareth   *Mt. Tabor*   Sea of Galilee
Japhia •   • Gadara
• Dora   • Nain
Beth-shan •   River Jordan
• Caesarea   DECAPOLIS

Plain of Sharon   SAMARIA   Aenon •
Samaria •
Mt. Ebal   • Sychar
• Shechem
Mt. Gerizim   *Jabbok River*
• Antipatris
PEREA
Joppa •
• Lydda (Lod)   • Ephraim
Emmaus •   • Ramah
Mt. of Olives   • Jericho
Jerusalem • •   • Bethany
Bethlehem •   • Qumran
(Essene community)   • Medeba
JUDEA   • Herodium
Tekoa •
• Gaza   • Hebron   • Dibon
Engedi •   *Arnon River*

IDUMEA   Masada •   Dead
• Arad   (Salt)
Sea
Beer-sheba •
NABATEANS

Zoar •   *Zered Brook*

MATTHEW

God promised Abraham that through his seed all the nations of the earth would be blessed (Genesis 12:3; 15:1-6). Where was this son of Abraham?

God promised Isaiah that a child would be born, a son would be given, and the government would rest on His shoulders. His name would be Wonderful, Counselor, Mighty God, Everlasting Father, Prince of Peace. There would be no end to the increase of His government or of peace. He would occupy the throne of David (Isaiah 9:6, 7). Where was this son of David?

No one knew until a baby's cry went up from Bethlehem Ephrathah. The Magi from the East arrived in Jerusalem saying, "Where is the newborn king of the Jews?" The One who was to be ruler in Israel (Micah 5:2), the son of David, the son of Abraham, had been born. Matthew tells us about Him, the King of the Jews.

THINGS TO DO

1. From the first verse Matthew's purpose is clear: to show that Jesus was the long-awaited King, the son of David, the Messiah whose coming was prophesied throughout the Old Testament.

   There is a pattern to Matthew that repeats itself and divides the Gospel into six segments. Matthew presents certain facts concerning the person and work of Jesus which he then follows with an account of Jesus' teaching. Each teaching account is brought to a conclusion with one of the following three phrases: "When Jesus had finished these sayings," "finished instructing," or "finished these parables."

   Therefore before you read through Matthew chapter by chapter, mark in a distinctive way each occurrence of a dividing phrase in 7:28; 11:1; 13:53; 19:1; and 26:1. Remember, these phrases conclude that particular teaching. Then the cycle begins again.

2. Now read Matthew chapter by chapter, keeping in mind these six segments. As you read:

   a. In a distinctive way mark in the text the key words listed on the MATTHEW AT A GLANCE chart following Matthew.

      1) List in the margin what you learn about the kingdom from the references where you marked the key words *king* and the *kingdom of heaven/God.*

      2) In addition to these key words, watch for other key words or phrases given in the observation section in "How to Use The International Inductive Study New Testament."

   b. Using the same color pencil each time, underline each reference to or quotation from an Old Testament prophecy which shows Jesus as the promised King. Then note in the margin how Jesus fulfills that prophecy. (You can spot the Old Testament quotes because they have a footnote and Old Testament reference at the bottom of the page.)

c. Watch for the events, works, or facts which demonstrate who Jesus Christ is. You may want to note these in the margin.

d. When you read Jesus' teaching on a particular subject, in the margin make a list of the main points covered in His teaching. If it is a prophetic teaching, pay attention to time phrases or indicators, including *then* and *when*. Watch for the progression of events.

e. Record the main theme or event of each chapter in the space just above the chapter number and on MATTHEW AT A GLANCE, following Matthew.

3. Chapters 26 through 28 give an account of the final events in the life of Jesus. Record the progression of events on the charts titled THE ARREST, TRIAL, AND CRUCIFIXION OF JESUS CHRIST and/or THE ACCOUNT OF JESUS' RESURREC- TION (both charts follow the Gospel of John). You may want to first record these insights on notebook paper and then transfer them to the charts. Note the chapter and verse of each insight for future reference.

a. When you record the circum- stances surrounding the resurrec- tion of Jesus Christ, also note any postresurrection appearances which are recorded in Matthew. After you do this for all four Gospels you will have comprehen- sive notes on all that took place.

b. As you do this, remember that Luke gives the consecutive order of events, and therefore, Luke becomes a plumb line for the other Gospel records.

4. A chart titled WHAT THE GOSPELS TEACH ABOUT THE KINGDOM OF GOD/THE KINGDOM OF HEAVEN is also after the Gospel of John. List and consolidate everything you learn from Matthew about the kingdom on a piece of notebook paper. Then trans- fer this to the chart. Be sure to note the chapter and verse for future refer- ence.

5. Complete MATTHEW AT A GLANCE. Under "Segment Divisions," record the theme of each segment of Matthew. There is also a blank line for any other segment divisions you might see.

THINGS TO THINK ABOUT

1. Have you bowed your knee to Jesus as King in your life? Read Matthew 7:21–27 and think about the difference between *merely hearing* something and *hearing and living accordingly*. Which best describes you?

2. Can you explain from Scripture to another person why Jesus is the King of the promised kingdom?

3. Do you realize that Jesus' final words to His disciples in Matthew 28:19, 20 are your responsibility also? What are you doing in order to fulfill His Great Com- mission? As you go, are you making dis- ciples? Are you teaching them to observe all that He has commanded?

Inside Herod's Temple

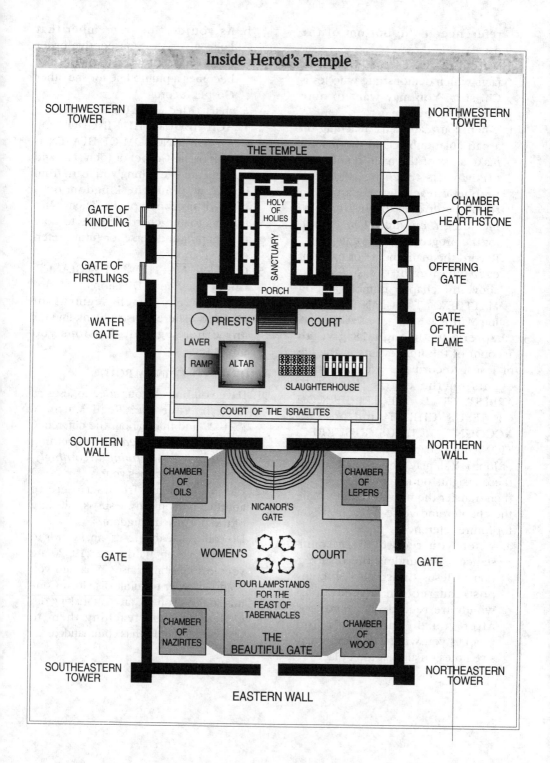

THE GOSPEL ACCORDING TO

MATTHEW

c. 5 B.C.

1 A BOOK OF THE GENEALOGY OF Jesus Christ, son of David, son of Abraham: ²Abraham was the father[a] of Isaac, Isaac of Jacob, Jacob of Judah and his brothers, ³Judah of Perez and Zerah by Tamar, Perez of Hezron, Hezron of Ram, ⁴Ram of Aminnadab, Aminnadab of Nahshon, and Nahshon of Salmon.

⁵ Salmon was the father of Boaz by Rahab, Boaz the father of Obed by Ruth, Obed of Jesse ⁶and Jesse of David the king.

David was the father of Solomon by Uriah's wife, ⁷Solomon of Rehoboam, Rehoboam of Abijah, Abijah of Asa, ⁸Asa of Jehoshaphat, Jehoshaphat of Joram, Joram of Uzziah, ⁹Uzziah of Jotham, Jotham of Ahaz, Ahaz of Hezekiah, ¹⁰Hezekiah of Manasseh, Manasseh of Amon, Amon of Josiah, ¹¹Josiah of Jeconiah and his brothers about the time of the Babylonian exile.

¹²After the Babylonian exile: Jeconiah was the father of Shealtiel, Shealtiel of Zerubbabel, ¹³Zerubbabel of Abiud, Abiud of Eliakim, Eliakim of Azor, ¹⁴Azor of Sadok, Sadok of Achim, Achim of Eliud, ¹⁵Eliud of Eleazar, Eleazar of Matthan, Matthan of Jacob, ¹⁶and Jacob of Joseph,[b] the husband of Mary,[c] of whom Jesus was born, who was surnamed Christ.[d]

¹⁷There are then altogether fourteen[e] generations from Abraham to David; also fourteen generations from David to the Babylonian exile, and fourteen generations from the Babylonian exile until the Christ.

¹⁸The birth of Jesus Christ came about this way: When His mother Mary was engaged to Joseph, before they came together she was found to be with child from the Holy Spirit. ¹⁹But as Joseph, her fiancé, was fair-minded and did not want to disgrace her publicly, he planned to break with her secretly.[f] ²⁰But while he was considering this, an angel of the Lord appeared to him in a dream and said, "Joseph, son of David, be not afraid to take Mary as your wife, for what is conceived in her is from the Holy

---

a) The Greek word rendered "was the father of" in vss. 1-16 has various meanings including *produce, originate* and *create*. The King James Version translates it "begat," which by implication denotes *was the father of*.

b) This genealogy, vss. 1-17, was that of Joseph, to whose care as a father Jesus was entrusted; that in Lk. 3:23-38 is of Mary, the mother of Jesus.

c) Four women named Mary are mentioned in the Gospels: (1) The mother of Jesus, Mat. 1:16, 18,20; 2:11; 13:55; Mk. 6:3; Lk. 1:27; 2:5. She is also specifically referred to without the use of her name in more than twenty other passages, e.g. Mk. 3:31; Lk. 1:43; Jn. 2:1; 6:42; 19:25, where she is called "the mother of Jesus," "His mother," etc. (2) The wife of Clopas and mother of James and Joses, Mat. 27:56; Mk. 15:40,47; Lk. 24:10; Jn. 19:25. (3) Mary of Bethany, the sister of Martha and Lazarus, Lk. 10:39; Jn. 11:1; 12:3. (4) Mary Magdalene, Mat. 27:56; 28:1; Mk. 15:40; 16:1; Lk. 8:2; 24:10; Jn. 19:25; 20:1.

d) *Christos*, meaning *Anointed*, is used in the Old Testament not in noun but adjective form when referring to priests and kings, but when referring to the prophesied Messiah it is used as a noun. In the New Testament it is applied to Jesus as Messiah.

e) To confine the list of Jesus' ancestors in each of the three periods to twice seven, and in the second period to stress the royalty of Christ's human ancestors, a number of them are purposely omitted. Frequently one is called a father who precedes his so-called son by several generations. Among the kings Ahaziah, Joash and Amaziah are omitted.

f) Mosaic law prescribed public accusation and death.

Spirit. 21She will give birth to a son and you are to call Him Jesus, for He will save His people from their sins."

22All this took place in fulfillment of what the Lord had said through the prophet,g 23"Behold! The virgin will be with child and shall bear a son, and will name Him Immanuel," which means, God with us.

24When Joseph awoke from his sleep he carried out what the angel commanded of the Lord. He took to him his wife 25but had no marital relations with her until she had given birth to a son, whom he called Jesus.

c. 4 B.C.

2 AFTER JESUS HAD BEEN BORN AT Bethlehemh in Judea during the reign of King Herod,i there arrived wise menj at Jerusalem from the east, 2inquiring, "Where is the newborn king of the Jews? For we saw His star in the east and we have come to worship Him."

3On hearing this, King Herod felt disturbed, and with him all Jerusalem, 4so he called together all the chief priests and scribesk of the people and inquired of them where the Christ should be born. 5They told him, "In Bethlehem of Judea; for so it is written by the prophet,l 6'And you, Bethlehem in the land of Judah, are by no means insignificant among Judah's rulers, for out of you a leader shall arise who will govern My people Israel.'"

7Herod then summoned the wise men for a private interview and ascertained from them just when the star appeared. 8As he sent them to Bethlehem he said, "Go and search carefully for the young Child, and when you have found Him, report to me so that I too may go and worship Him."

9After listening to the king they traveled on and, lo, the star they had seen in the east preceded them until it came and rested above the place where the young Child was. 10And on observing the star their joy was boundless.

11Entering the house, they saw the little Child with His mother, Mary,m and prostrating themselves they worshiped Him. And opening their treasure chests they offered Him presents: gold, frankincense and myrrh. 12Then, because of divine warning in a dream not to return to Herod, they went back to their own country by a different route.

13After they had left an angel of the Lord appeared to Joseph in a dream and said, "Rise! Take the Child and His mother and escape to Egypt. Stay there until I tell you, for Herod is about to search for the Child in order to murder Him." 14So he got up at night, took the Child and His mother and departed into Egypt 15where he remained until Herod's death, so that the Lord's word through the prophet became fulfilled,n "Out of Egypt I called My Son."

16When Herod perceived that he had been outwitted by the wise men he was furious and sent a detachment to murder all the male children in Bethlehem and its environs, those of two years and under, according to the time he had ascertained from the wise men. 17Then the saying of Jeremiah the prophet was fulfilled,o 18"A voice was heard in Ramah, weeping and great mourning; Rachel bewailing her children and refusing consolation because they are gone."

19But upon Herod's death an angel of the Lord appeared in a dream to Joseph in Egypt, 20saying, "Rise! Take the Child and His mother and go into the land of Israel, for those who were

---

g) Isa. 7:14. Observe how frequently in Matthew's Gospel attention is called to the fact that events recorded are in fulfillment of O.T. prophecies, e.g. ch. 2:15,17; 3:3; 4:14.
h) Bethlehem is situated five or six miles south of Jerusalem.
i) Herod the Great, who ruled from 37-4 B.C., was the father or ancestor of other Herods.
j) Magi, from *magus* meaning *great*, a Persian title that was used for teachers and wise men, in this instance astrologers.
k) The scribes were guardians of the law and teachers of the O.T. Scriptures. Most of the Pharisees were scribes. See note at Mat. 3:3. l) Mic. 5:2.
m) Mary and the Child were in a house, not a stable. Joseph is not mentioned as being there on this occasion. When on the fortieth day Joseph and Mary took the Child to the temple they offered the smallest allowable living thing, Lk. 2:24; *cf.* Lev. 12:8. The Magi arrived after that bringing rich gifts. Herod died in 4 B.C. Jesus had been born at least two months earlier.
n) Hos. 11:1, referring first to Israel and the Exodus; here to Jesus. o) Jer. 31:15; *cf.* Gen. 35:19.

seeking the Child's life are dead." [21]So he arose, took the Child and His mother and came into the land of Israel. [22]But when he heard that Archelaus[p] had succeeded his father, Herod, as ruler of Judea he was afraid to go there. However, by divine warning in a dream he withdrew to the Galilean region [23]where he arrived and settled in a town called Nazareth,[q] so that the prophetic utterance,[r] "He shall be called a Nazarene," might find fulfillment.

c. A.D. 26

3 IN THOSE DAYS JOHN THE BAPTIST appeared, proclaiming in the Judean desert, [2]"Repent, for the kingdom of heaven has come near!" [3]He is the one spoken of by the Prophet Isaiah,[s] "The voice of one calling out in the desert, Make ready the way of the Lord; straighten His paths."

[4]John himself had clothing made of camel's hair. He wore a leather belt around his waist and ate locusts and wild honey. [5]Then Jerusalem, all Judea and the entire Jordan region went out to him [6]and, on confession of their sins, were baptized by him in the Jordan River. [7]But when he noticed many of the Pharisees[t] and Sadducees[u] coming for his baptism, he said to them, "You viper brood, who warned you to flee from the approaching judgment? [8]Produce fruit in agreement with your repentance, [9]and do not fancy you can say to yourselves, 'We have Abraham for our father.' For I assure you that from these stones God can raise up children to Abraham.

[10]"The ax is already laid at the root of the trees; so every tree that fails to yield good fruit will be cut down and thrown into the fire. [11]Whereas I baptize you with water for repentance, the One who comes after me is so far superior to me that I am not fit to carry His sandals. He will baptize you with the Holy Spirit and with fire. [12]The winnowing fan is in His hand and He will thoroughly clean His threshing floor. His wheat He will store in the granary, but the chaff He will burn with fire that cannot be put out."

c. A.D. 27

[13]Then Jesus came from Galilee to John at the Jordan to be baptized by him, [14]but John tried to hinder Him, saying, "I need to be baptized by You, and why are You coming to me?" [15]Jesus replied to him, "Permit it to be so now, for so it is needful for us to fulfill all righteousness."[v] Then he allowed Him to come.

[16]At once after His baptism Jesus came up from the water and, behold, the heavens were opened and He saw the Spirit of God descending like a dove and lighting upon Him. [17]And a voice from heaven said, "This is My Son, the Beloved in whom I delight."

4 THEN JESUS WAS LED BY THE SPIRit into the desert[w] to be tempted by the devil; [2]and after fasting forty days and forty nights He was hungry. [3]The tempter approached Him and said to Him, "If You are the Son of God, command these stones to turn into loaves of bread. [4]But He replied, "It is written,[x] 'Man shall not live on bread alone but on every command that proceeds from the mouth of God.'"

[5]The devil then conducted Him to the holy city and had Him stand on the loftiest point of the temple, [6]saying

---

p) Archelaus reigned from 4 B.C. until A.D. 6, when he was deposed. In Hebrew fashion the fact that Joseph and Mary had previously lived in Nazareth is not mentioned.
q) Nazareth is located about halfway between the Mediterranean Sea to the west and the Sea of Galilee to the east. It is approximately sixty-five miles north of Jerusalem.
r) The name Nazareth comes from a Hebrew word, *nezer*, meaning shoot or branch. Christ is the Branch, Isa. 11:1; Jer. 23:5; Zech. 3:8; 6:12.　　s) Isa. 40:3; Mal. 3:1.
t) The Pharisees (Pharisee means *separatist*) were members of a religious party that was composed mostly of scribes (see note at ch. 2:4). The Pharisees were ritualists who held strictly to the letter of the Law but often departed from its spirit. They opposed the Lord Jesus Christ throughout His earthly ministry. During the final months of the life of Jesus on the earth they joined with their enemies, the Sadducees (see note below) to destroy Him.
u) The Sadducees, a religious party, were rationalists. They did not believe in the resurrection of the dead nor in angelic beings. Mk. 12:18; Acts 23:8.
v) That is, uprightness according to the Law. Jesus accepted the baptism of repentance; for although He was sinless He received baptism as representing sinful humanity.
w) A deserted place, not necessarily a sandy waste.　x) Deut. 8:3.

to Him, "If You are the Son of God, throw Yourself down; for it is written,[y] 'He will charge His angels concerning You and they will carry You on their hands so You may at no time stub Your foot against a stone.'" [7]Jesus replied to him, "Furthermore it is written,[z] 'You shall not test the Lord your God.'"

[8]Next the devil took Him to a very high mountain and showed Him all the kingdoms of the world and their splendor, [9]saying to Him, "All these I will give You if You will kneel and worship me." [10]Then Jesus said to him, "Begone, Satan; for it is written,[a] 'You shall worship the Lord your God and serve Him alone.'" [11]Then the devil left Him and lo, angels came and waited on Him.

c. A.D. 28

[12]When Jesus heard that John had been arrested He withdrew into Galilee. [13]Leaving Nazareth[b] He went and lived in Capernaum[c] by the sea in the country of Zebulon and Naphtali, [14]so that Isaiah's prophecy might be fulfilled,[d] [15]"Land of Zebulon and land of Naphtali, toward the sea beyond the Jordan, Galilee of the nations; [16]the people who sat in darkness saw a great light and on those who dwelt in the land of the shadow of death a light has dawned."

[17]From then on Jesus began to preach: "Repent, for the kingdom of heaven has drawn near." [18]And as He was walking by the Sea of Galilee, Jesus noticed two brothers, Simon, called Peter, and his brother Andrew, casting a net into the sea, for they were fishermen. [19]He said to them, "Come! Follow Me and I will make you fishers of men." [20]And at once they abandoned their nets and followed Him.

[21]Going a little further He saw two other brothers, James the son of Zebedee, and John his brother, in the boat with their father Zebedee, mending their nets, and He called them. [22]So, immediately they left the boat and their father and followed Him.[e]

[23]Jesus traversed all Galilee, teaching in their synagogues, announcing the good news of the kingdom and healing all kinds of disease and illness among the people. [24]Report about Him spread to all Syria and they brought to Him all who suffered from various ailments and pains — demoniacs, epileptics and paralytics. And He healed them.

[25]Great throngs followed Him out of Galilee, Decapolis, Jerusalem, Judea and beyond the Jordan.

5 SO, WHEN HE SAW THE CROWDS He went up on the hill; and when He was seated His disciples came to Him. [2]Opening His lips, He taught them:[f] [3]"Blessed are they who know their spiritual poverty, for theirs is the kingdom of heaven. [4]Blessed are they who mourn, for they shall be comforted. [5]Blessed are the gentle, for they shall inherit the earth. [6]Blessed are those who are hungry and thirsty for righteousness, for they shall be satisfied. [7]Blessed are the merciful, for they shall obtain mercy. [8]Blessed are the pure in heart, for they shall see God. [9]Blessed are the peacemakers, for they shall be called God's sons. [10]Blessed are those persecuted on account of righteousness, for theirs is the kingdom of heaven. [11]Blessed are you when they slander and persecute you and falsely accuse you of every wrong because of Me. [12]Be glad and supremely joyful because in heaven your reward is rich; for in the same way they persecuted the prophets who were before you.

[13]"You are the salt of the earth. But if the salt has lost its taste, with what

---

y) Ps. 91:11-12.   z) Deut. 6:16.   a) Deut. 6:13.   b) Lk. 4:16-30. See notes at Mat. 2:23.
c) Capernaum was situated on the northwestern shore of the Sea of Galilee.
d) Isa. 9:1-2.
e) John, Andrew, Peter and Nathanael (also known as Bartholomew) had begun to follow Jesus nearly a year earlier, Jn. 1:35-51; now they became His full-time disciples.
f) Chapters 5-7 contain the Sermon on the Mount, the best known of all sermons. In it our Lord declares His own divine standard of righteousness and thereby reveals how impossible it is for a man to be saved by the works of the Law. Consequently all men need a Redeemer. Here in the Sermon on the Mount is the basic expression of Christian ethics, reflected in the N.T. epistles as the pattern for Christan living. "Blessed" in vss. 3-11 means *happy*. See note at Lk. 6:20.

shall it be salted? It is thereafter good
for nothing but to be thrown out and
walked on by the people.[g]
14“You are the light of the world. A
city built on a hill cannot be hidden.
15Neither do they light a lamp and
place it under a grain measure, but on
a stand; then it shines for everyone in
the house. 16Similarly let your light
shine among the people, so that they
observe your good works and give
glory to your heavenly Father.[h]
17“Do not suppose that I came to annul the Law or the Prophets. I did not
come to abolish but to complete them;
18for I assure you, while heaven and
earth endure not one iota[i] or one pro-
jection of a letter will be dropped from
the Law until all is accomplished.
19Whoever, therefore, abolishes the
least significant of these commands and
so teaches the people, he shall be of
least significance in the kingdom of
heaven; but whoever shall observe and
teach them shall be prominent in the
kingdom of heaven. 20For I tell you
that unless your righteousness surpasses
that of the scribes and Pharisees, you
shall not at all enter into the kingdom
of heaven.
21“You have heard how men of
ancient times were told,[j] ‘Do not murder,’ and, ‘Whoever murders is liable
before the court.’ 22But I tell you that
anyone who is angry with his brother
[without cause][k] is liable before the
court, and whoever speaks abusively of[l]
his brother is liable before the Sanhedrin.[m] And whoever says ‘You fool!’ is
liable to the fires of hell.[n] 23So, when
you are offering your gift at the altar
and remember that your brother holds
something against you, 24leave your
gift there at the altar and go and become reconciled to your brother; then
come and offer your gift.
25“Come to terms with your opponent quickly while you are on the
way to court with him, else the opponent may hand you over to the judge
and the judge to the attendant, and
you will be thrown into prison. 26I
assure you that you will not get out
until you have paid the last penny.
27“You have heard that it was said,[o]
‘Do not commit adultery.’ 28But I tell
you that anyone who looks lustfully at
a woman has in his heart already committed adultery with her. 29If your
right eye causes you to sin, pluck it out
and throw it away from you. You had
better lose one of your members than
have your whole body cast into hell.
30And if your right hand causes you to
sin, cut it off and throw it away from
you. It is better to lose one of your
members than have your whole body
cast into hell.
31“It was also said,[p] ‘Whoever divorces his wife should give her a divorce certificate.’ 32But I tell you that
anyone who divorces his wife, except
for unfaithfulness, makes her commit
adultery, and whoever marries a di-
vorced woman commits adultery.
33“You have further heard how the
ancients were told,[q] ‘Do not swear falsely, but perform your oaths to the Lord.’
34But I tell you: Do not swear at all;
not by heaven, because it is God’s
throne; 35nor by the earth, because it
is His footstool; nor by Jerusalem, because it is the city of the great King.
36Neither swear by your head, because
you cannot make one hair white or
black. 37But let your word Yes be Yes
and your No, No. Anything beyond
this is from the evil one.
38“You have heard that it was said,[r]
‘An eye for an eye and a tooth for a
tooth.’ 39But I say to you, Do not resist injuries, but whoever strikes you
on the right cheek turn to him the
other as well. 40And if anyone wants

---

g) As salt is a preservative, so do Christians keep the world from being too wicked to exist.
h) The Christian characteristics suggested by Christ will, when practiced, distinguish disciples as lights amid darkness and will serve to illumine the darkness.
i) The iota is *i* in the Greek alphabet.
j) Ex. 20:13; 21:12,14. The Hebrew word rendered “kill” in the King James Version means *to commit murder*.
k) The words enclosed in brackets are not found in the majority of the most reliable ancient manuscripts. l) The Aramaic word *rhaka* used here in the original text means *empty, worthless.*
m) See note at Lk. 22:66. n) See note at Mk. 9:43.
o) Ex. 20:14. Adultery always involves at least one married person; fornication may relate to the unmarried. p) Deut. 24:1. q) Num. 30:2; Deut. 23:23. r) Ex. 21:24.

to sue you for your tunic, let him have your robe as well.[s] 41And whoever forces you to go one mile, go with him two miles. 42Give to the one who begs from you and do not refuse the borrower.

43"You have heard that it was said,[t] 'Love your neighbor and hate your enemy.' 44But I say to you, Love your enemy and pray for your persecutors, 45so that you may be sons of your heavenly Father;[u] for He makes His sun to rise on the evil and the good and He pours rain upon the just and the unjust. 46For if you love those who love you, what is your merit? Do not the tax collectors as much? 47And if you greet only your kin, how does your conduct excel? Do not even the pagans do the same? 48You, then, are to be perfect[v] as your heavenly Father is perfect.

6 "BE CAREFUL NOT TO PERFORM your good works publicly to be noticed by the people; else you forfeit reward from your Father who is in heaven. 2Thus, when you give charity, do not blow a trumpet ahead of you as the hypocrites do in the synagogues and in the streets to gain glory from men. I assure you, they have reward. 3But when you practice charity, your left hand must not know what your right is doing, 4so that your charity will be in secret. And your Father who sees in secret will reward you.

5"And when you pray, do not be like the hypocrites; for they love to pray standing in the synagogues and at the street corners to be seen by the people. I assure you, they have been paid in full. 6But you, when you pray, enter your inner room and with your door closed pray to your Father who is there in the secret place, and your Father who sees in secret will reward you.

7"When you pray do not repeat and repeat as the pagans do; for they imagine that for their much talking they will secure a hearing. 8Do not be like them, for your Father knows your need before you ask Him. 9This, then, is the way you should pray:

"Our Father who art in heaven, Thy name be kept holy. 10Thy kingdom come, Thy will be done on earth as in heaven.

11"Give us today our daily bread. 12And forgive us our debts[w] as we have forgiven our debtors. 13And lead us not into temptation but deliver us from the evil one. [For Thine is the kingdom and the power and the glory forever. Amen.][x]

14"For if you forgive others their trespasses, your heavenly Father will forgive you too; 15but if you do not forgive people, neither will your heavenly Father forgive your trespasses.

16"When you fast, do not be sad-faced like the hypocrites, for they disfigure their faces to show others their fasting. I assure you, they have received their full reward. 17But when you fast, anoint your head and wash your face, 18so that no one except your heavenly Father who is there in the secret place may notice your fasting. And your Father who sees in secret will reward you.

19Do not lay up for yourselves treasures on earth, where moth and rust destroy and where thieves dig through and steal. 20But lay up for yourselves treasures in heaven, where no moth or rust destroys and where thieves do not dig through and steal. 21For where your treasure is there will your heart be also.

22"The eye is the lamp of the body. If, then, your eye is sound, your whole body is illumined; 23but if your eye is defective your whole body is in the dark. If, then, the light within you grows dark — how dense a darkness!

24"No one can serve two masters, for he will either hate the one and love the other or support the one and

---

s) A tunic reached to the knees; a robe was a long outside garment which reached almost to the ankles.   t) Lev. 19:18; Deut. 23:3-6.
u) We show that we are God's sons by living His principles.
v) "Perfect" is from the Greek *teleios* meaning *complete, mature.*
w) Debts, or trespasses, in the sense of falling short of God's requirements.
x) The words enclosed in brackets are not found in the majority of the most reliable ancient manuscripts. They may have been added to the text here to make the prayer more appropriate for use in public worship. Certainly the last sentence is compatible with Scripture. *Cf.* I Chron. 29:11. In Luke's account of the Lord's Prayer, Lk. 11:2-4, this sentence is omitted.

treat the other with contempt. You cannot serve God and mammon.[y]

25"I tell you therefore, do not worry about your living — what you are to eat or drink, or about your body, what you are to wear. Is not the life more important than its nourishment and the body than its clothing? 26Look at the birds of the air, how they neither sow nor reap nor gather into barns, but your heavenly Father feeds them. Are not you more valuable than they?

27"Furthermore, who of you is able through worrying to add one moment to his life's course?[z] 28And why worry about clothes? Observe carefully how the field lilies grow. They neither toil nor spin, 29but I tell you that even Solomon in all his splendor was never dressed like one of these. 30But if God so clothes the grass of the field that exists today and is thrown into the furnace tomorrow, will He not more surely clothe you of little faith?

31"Do not, then, be anxious, saying, 'What shall we eat?' or 'What shall we drink?' or 'What are we to wear?' 32For on all these things pagans center their interest while your heavenly Father knows that you need them all. 33But you, seek first His kingdom and His righteousness and all these things will be added to you. 34Do not worry therefore, in view of tomorrow for tomorrow will have its own anxieties. Each day's peculiar troubles are sufficient for it.[a]

7 "DO NOT PASS JUDGMENT,[b] THAT you may not be judged; 2for the way you judge you will be judged and with what yardstick you measure you will be measured. 3But why notice the splinter in your brother's eye without taking notice of the beam in your own eye? 4Or how can you say to your brother, 'Let me extract that splinter from your eye,' when there is a beam in your own eye? 5You hypocrite! First get rid of that beam in your eye; then you will see clearly to extract the splinter from your brother's eye.

6"Do not give what is sacred to the dogs, so that they may not turn around and attack you; neither throw your pearls before the hogs, so that they may not trample them under their feet.

7"Ask and it will be given you; seek and you will find; knock and it will be opened to you. 8For everyone who asks receives, and the seeker finds, and to him who knocks it is opened. 9Who of you men whose son asks for a loaf of bread will give him a stone; 10or if he asks for fish, will give him a snake? 11If you then, evil as you are, know enough to give your children what is good, how much more surely will your heavenly Father give what is good to those who ask Him. 12Accordingly, whatever you would have people do for you, do the same for them; for this covers the Law and the Prophets.

13"Enter through the narrow gate; for wide is the gate and spacious the road that leads on to destruction, and many are those entering by it. 14Because narrow is the gate and contracted the road that leads on to life, and few are they who discover it.

15"Be wary of the false prophets who come to you in the guise of sheep while at heart they are voracious wolves. 16You will know them by the deeds they do. Do people gather grapes from thorns, or figs from thistles? 17So every healthy tree bears good fruit, but a rotten tree bears defective fruit. 18A good tree cannot bear bad fruit, nor can a bad tree bear good fruit. 19Every tree that fails to bear good fruit is felled and thrown into the fire. 20Similarly you will know people by the deeds they do.

21"Not everyone who says to Me, 'Lord, Lord!' will enter into the kingdom of heaven, but he who does the will of My Father in heaven. 22Many will say to Me on that Day, 'Lord, Lord, did we not prophesy in Your name and in Your name cast out demons and in Your name do many won-

---

y) Mammon is an Aramaic term. It refers to riches which, when trusted, stand in opposition to God, who alone is to be trusted.
z) "One moment to his life's course" could as well be translated "one cubit to his stature."
a) There is no abrogation in this passage of the commandment, "Six days you will labor and do all your work," Ex. 20:9. b) God alone knows motives behind words and deeds.

derful works?' 23Then I will frankly say to them, 'I never knew you. Get away from Me, you evil workers.'

24"Everyone, then, who listens to these sayings of Mine and puts them into practice will be like a thoughtful man who built his house on the rock. 25The rains came down, the floods rose, the winds blew and beat upon that house, but it never collapsed, for it was based on the rock. 26And everyone who hears these sayings of Mine and fails to practice them will be like a foolish man who built his house on the sand. 27The rains came down, the floods rose, the winds blew and beat upon that house and it collapsed. And the wreck of it was complete."

28It came about that when Jesus had finished these sayings, the crowds were amazed at His teaching, 29for He taught them as an authority and not like their scribes.c

8 WHEN HE HAD COME DOWN FROM the hill great crowds followed Him. 2And a leper came up and knelt before Him saying: "Lord, if You are willing, You are able to cleanse me." 3Reaching out His hand He touched him saying, "I am willing. Be cleansed." And instantly his leprosy was cleansed. 4Jesus told him, "See that you tell no one, but go, show yourself to the priest and offer the gift which Moses prescribedd as a witness to others."

5When He entered Capernaume a centurionf came to Him entreating Him, 6"Lord, my servant boy lies paralyzed at home, in great agony." 7He replied, "I will come and heal him." 8The centurion answered, "Lord, I am not fit to have You come under my roof; only speak the word and my boy will be healed. 9For I am personally under authority and have soldiers under me. To one I say, 'Go!' and he goes; to another, 'Come!' and he comes, and to my slave, 'Do this!' and he does it."

10As Jesus listened He marveled and said to those who were following Him, "I assure you, I have not found anyone in Israel with so much faith. 11And I tell you that many will come from east and west and will sitg at the table with Abraham, Isaac and Jacob in the kingdom of heaven, 12while the sons of the kingdom will be expelled into outer darkness. There will be weeping and grinding of teeth there."

13Then Jesus said to the centurion, "Go home. As you have believed, so let it be for you." And at that exact moment the serving boy was cured.

14When Jesus entered Peter's house He observed that his mother-in-law was bedridden with fever. 15So He touched her hand and the fever left her. She got up and waited on Him.

16In the evening they brought to Him many demoniacs and with a word He cast out the spirits and healed all who had diseases, 17so that the word spoken through the Prophet Isaiah might be fulfilled,h "He Himself took our weaknesses and carried away our diseases."

18Seeing a great crowd around Him, Jesus gave orders to cross to the other side. 19When a certain scribe approached and said to Him, "Teacher, I will follow You wherever You may go," 20Jesus told him, "The foxes have lairs and the wild birds have nests but the Son of Man has no place to lay His head."

21Another of the disciples said to Him, "Lord, permit me first to go and bury my father." 22But Jesus said to him, "Follow Me, and leave the dead to bury their own dead."i

23As He embarked, His disciples came along with Him. 24And a severe storm came up on the lake,j so that the boat was being swamped by the waves; but He lay sleeping. 25So they went to Him and roused Him, saying

---

c) The scribes quoted commentators in their teaching; Jesus did not need to do so. See note a ch. 2:4.   d) Lev. 14:3.   e) See note at ch. 4:13.
f) A military officer generally commanding 100 soldiers, although sometimes more.
g) See note at Mk. 2:15.   h) Isa. 53:4.
i) This may intimate that this man's relatives were spiritually dead; it certainly means that the inquirer must leave behind every interest that may be a hindrance.
j) Squalls from the canyon where the Jordan River entered the lake, i.e., the Sea of Galilee, were frequent and sudden. See note at Lk. 5:1.

"Lord, save us; we are perishing." [26]He said to them, "You of little faith! Why are you afraid?" Then standing up He rebuked the winds and the sea, and there was a great calm. [27]Amazed, the men exclaimed, "What kind of man is this that even the winds and the sea obey Him?"

[28]When He reached the other side in the Gadarene[k] country, two demoniacs coming out of the tombs met Him. So ferocious were they that no one could travel on that road. [29]They shouted: "Son of God, what business is it of Yours to bother us? Have You come here to torture us ahead of time?"

[30]Now at some distance from them a large herd of swine was feeding; [31]so the demons begged of Him, "If You expel us, send us into the herd of swine." [32]He said to them, "Go!" And they, coming out, entered into the swine and the whole herd rushed down the precipice into the sea and perished in the waters.

[33]The herdsmen fled, went off to town, and reported everything, including the affair of the demoniacs. [34]Then the whole town came out to meet Jesus and when they saw Him they begged of Him to move out of their district.

9 SO HE EMBARKED, CROSSED OVER and reached His own city. [2]There they carried to Him a paralytic on a couch. And seeing their faith Jesus said to the paralytic, "Cheer up, son, your sins are forgiven." [3]Some of the scribes then said to themselves, "This man blasphemes." [4]Jesus, knowing their thoughts, said, "Why do you think evil in your hearts? [5]For which is easier to say, Your sins are forgiven, or to say, Rise and walk? [6]But to let you know that the Son of Man has authority to forgive sins on the earth," He then said to the paralytic, "Rise, pick up your couch and go home." [7]Arising, he went home. [8]And when the crowds saw it they were awed, and they praised God who had granted such power to men.

[9]As Jesus passed on from there, He saw a man named Matthew sitting at the tax office and said to him, "Follow Me." So he arose and followed Him. [10]And as Jesus was sitting[l] at the table in the house[m] numerous tax collectors[n] and sinners came and sat at the table with Jesus and His disciples. [11]When the Pharisees noticed it, they said to His disciples, "Why does your teacher eat with tax collectors and sinners?" [12]But when He heard it He said, "The healthy have no need of a physician, but the sick. [13]But go and learn what this means,[o] 'I want mercy and not sacrifice.' For I did not come to call the righteous but sinners[p] to repentance."

[14]Then John's disciples came up to Him and said, "Why do we and the Pharisees fast, and Your disciples do not fast?" [15]Jesus answered them, "Can wedding guests mourn while the bridegroom is with them?[q] But the days are coming when the bridegroom will be taken from them, and then they will fast. [16]But no one sews a patch of unshrunk cloth on an old coat, for the patch would tear away from the coat and the tear become worse. [17]Neither do they pour new wine into old wineskins, else the wineskins burst, the wine is spilled and the skins are ruined. Instead they put new wine into new skins, and both are preserved."

[18]While He was still speaking to them about this, a ruler[r] came and knelt before Him, saying, "My daughter has just died; but come, place your hand on her and she will live." [19]Jesus rose and with His disciples followed him. [20]And a woman, who had for twelve years suffered from hemorrhages, came up behind Him and touched the fringe of His robe; [21]for she said to herself, "If I can only touch

---

k) See note at Mk. 5:1.
l) See note at Mk. 2:15.   m) This was the home of Matthew, also called Levi, Lk. 5:29.
n) Tax collectors as a class were despised by the Jews because, they themselves being Jews, were in the employ of the Roman government.   o) Hos. 6:6.
p) The sinners referred to here were specifically those Jews who considered themselves to be righteous and in no need of the Redeemer. They might be called the unchurched of their day, i.e., they neither attended the temple or synagogue, nor offered the sacrifices that were required by Mosaic Law.   q) Cf. Jn. 3:28-30.   r) Jairus, a ruler of the synagogue, Lk. 8:41.

His robe I will recover."[s] 22Jesus, turning and seeing her, said, "Cheer up, daughter, your faith has healed you." And the woman was well from that hour.

23On reaching the ruler's house and seeing the flute players and the noisy crowd, 24Jesus said, "Go out; for the girl is not dead but asleep." They laughed derisively at Him. 25But after the crowd had been expelled He went in and took her hand, and the girl rose up. 26The fame of it spread over all that country.

27While Jesus was walking away, two blind men followed Him, crying out, "Son of David, pity us!" 28Then when He had entered the house, the blind men came up to Him and Jesus said to them, "Do you believe I can do this?" They answered Him, "Yes, Lord." 29He then touched their eyes and said, "According to the measure of your faith it shall be to you." 30And their eyes were opened. Jesus charged them strictly, "See that no one learns of this." 31But they went out and spread His fame over that whole region.

32As they were leaving, a dumb man who was demon-possessed was brought to Him. 33And when the demon had been expelled, the dumb man spoke. Then the crowds marveled, saying, "The like was never seen in Israel." 34But the Pharisees said, "Through the ruler of the demons He casts out the demons."

35Jesus went among all the towns and the villages teaching in their synagogues announcing the good news of the kingdom and healing every disease and every illness. 36But as He looked at the multitudes He was filled with pity over them because they were like shepherdless sheep that are wearied and helpless. 37Then He said to His disciples, "The harvest is indeed abundant but the workers are few. 38There-fore pray the Lord of the harvest that He may send out workers into His harvest."

10 CALLING HIS TWELVE DISCIPLES to Him,[t] He gave them power over depraved spirits to cast them out, and to heal every disease and every malady. 2Now these are the names of the twelve apostles: [u]first, Simon, called Peter, and his brother Andrew; James, the son of Zebedee, and his brother John; 3Philip and Bartholomew;[v] Thomas and Matthew, the tax collector; James, the son of Alphaeus, and Thaddaeus;[w] 4Simon the Zealot, and Judas Iscariot, who also betrayed Him.

5These twelve Jesus sent out with the charge: "Do not go to the Gentiles nor enter a Samaritan[x] city, 6but rather go to the lost sheep of the house of Israel. 7And as you go, preach that the kingdom of heaven is at hand. 8Heal the sick; raise the dead; cleanse lepers; expel demons. Freely you have received; freely give. 9Provide neither gold, nor silver, nor copper to put in your belts, 10nor a bag for the journey; neither two coats, nor sandals, nor staff. For the worker deserves his support.

11"Whatever town or village you enter, inquire who in it is deserving and stay there until you leave the community. 12And as you enter the home, give your greetings, 13and if the home is deserving, let your peace come upon it; but if it is undeserving your peace will return to you. 14And where no one welcomes you or listens to your messages, leave that house or town and shake the dust off your feet. 15I assure you, the land of Sodom[y] and Gomorrah will fare better in the judgment day than that town.

16"Mind you, I am sending you out as sheep among wolves; therefore, be as subtle as serpents and as guileless as doves. 17And beware of men; for they

---

s) The healing power was in Christ, not in the robe, Lk. 8:46.
t) Selecting twelve from among His followers Jesus ordained them to apostleship, to be constantly with Him preparatory to His ascension.
u) "Apostle" comes from a Greek word that means *one who is sent,* i.e., a messenger.
v) Bartholomew is called Nathanael in John's Gospel, *cf.* Jn. 1:45-49. Observe how the apostles are paired; they did their visiting "two by two," Mk. 6:7.
w) Thaddaeus is called Judas, not Iscariot, in Jn. 14:22.   x) See note at Lk. 9:53.
y) See note at Lk. 10:12.

will deliver you to councils, and in their synagogues they will flog you; [18]and you will be haled before governors and kings on My account, to testify to them and to the Gentiles. [19]But when they hand you over, have no anxiety how or what to say, for it will be given you in that hour what to say; [20]for it is not you that speak but the Spirit of your Father speaking through you.

[21]"Brother shall betray brother to death, and the father his child. Children shall turn against parents and cause their death, [22]and you shall be hated by everyone on account of My name. But he who perseveres to the end shall be saved.

[23]"When they persecute you in one town, flee to the next; for I assure you that you will not have gone through the towns of Israel before the Son of Man comes.

[24]"A pupil is not above his teacher, nor a slave[z] above his master. [25]It suffices for the pupil to be like his teacher and for the slave to be like his master. If they have called the head of the house Beelzebul,[a] how much more its members. [26]Do not therefore fear them; for nothing is covered that shall not be uncovered, and hidden that shall not be made known. [27]What I tell you in the dark you must say in the light, and what you hear close to your ear you must herald from the housetops.

[28]"Do not be afraid of those who kill the body but cannot kill the soul; but rather fear Him[b] who is able to destroy both soul and body in hell. [29]Do not two sparrows sell for a penny? And not one of them falls to the ground apart from the will of your Father. [30]As for you, the hairs of your head are all numbered. [31]Have no fear, then; you are of more consequence than many sparrows.

[32]"Everyone, therefore, who shall acknowledge Me before men I will acknowledge before My Father who is in heaven; [33]but whoever disowns Me before men him will I also disown before My Father who is in heaven.

[34]"Do not suppose that I have come to bring peace on the earth. I have not come to bring peace, but a sword. [35]For I have come to bring division, a man against his father, a daughter against her mother, a daughter-in-law against her mother-in-law; [36]and a man's enemies will be those who belong to his own household. [37]He who loves father or mother more than Me is not worthy of Me, and he who loves son or daughter more than Me is not worthy of Me. [38]And he who does not take his cross and follow after Me is not worthy of Me. [39]Whoever finds his life will lose it, and whoever on My account loses his life will find it.

[40]"Whoever receives you receives Me, and whoever receives Me receives Him who sent Me. [41]Whoever receives a prophet because he is a prophet will receive the reward of a prophet, and whoever receives an upright man because he is upright will receive an upright man's reward. [42]And whoever gives one of these little ones but a cup of cold water to drink because he is a disciple, I assure you he will not lose his reward."

11 WHEN JESUS HAD FINISHED INstructing His twelve disciples He left there to teach and preach in their towns.

[2]Now when John heard in prison of Christ's activities, he sent and asked Him through his disciples, [3]"Are you the Coming One or should we look for someone else?" [4]Jesus replied to them, "Go and report to John what you hear and see: [5]the blind see, the lame walk, lepers are cleansed, the deaf hear, the dead are raised and the poor are evangelized. [6]And happy is anyone who does not lose his faith in Me."

[7]As they were leaving, Jesus began to say to the crowds about John, "What did you go out into the desert to gaze at? A reed swayed by the wind?[c] [8]What did you really go out to see? A man dressed in soft clothes? Wearers of soft clothes live in palaces. [9]What then did you go out to see? A prophet?

---

z) See note at ch. 13:27.   a) See note at Lk. 11:15.
b) The reference is not, as some suppose, to Satan but to God, who alone determines the final destiny of soul and body.   c) Although he was now perplexed, John the Baptist was no weakling.

Yes, I tell you, and far more than a prophet. [10]This is the one about whom it is written,[d] 'Behold, I send My messenger before Your face who shall prepare the road ahead of You.' [11]I assure you, none has arisen among those born of women greater than John the Baptist; yet the least in the kingdom of heaven is greater than he. [12]But from the time of John the Baptist until now the kingdom of heaven has endured violence, the violent seize it by force. [13]For until John all the Prophets and the Law prophesied. [14]If you will accept it, he himself is Elijah who was to come. [15]Whoever has ears, let him listen.

[16]"But to what shall I compare this generation? It is like children sitting in the market places and calling out to their playmates, [17]'We have played the flute for you and you have not danced; we have sung dirges to you and you did not beat the breast.' [18]For John came neither eating nor drinking and they say, 'He has a demon.' [19]The Son of Man came eating and drinking, and they say, 'Look! A glutton and wine drinker! A friend of tax collectors and sinners!' And still, wisdom is vindicated by her effects."[e]

[20]Then He began to reproach the towns in which most of His wonders had been wrought, because they did not repent: [21]"Alas for you, Chorazin![f] Alas for you, Bethsaida![g] Because if in Tyre and Sidon[h] the wonders had been done that were done in you, they would long ago have repented in sackcloth and ashes. [22]I tell you further, it will be more endurable in the Judgment Day for Tyre and Sidon than for you.

[23]"And you, Capernaum, will you be exalted to heaven? Brought down to hades[i] you will be. For if in Sodom the wonders had been done that were done in you, it would have remained to this day. [24]I tell you further, for the land of Sodom it will be more endurable in the Judgment Day than for you."

[25]At that time Jesus responded by saying: "I thank Thee, Father, Lord of heaven and earth, for hiding all this from the learned and intelligent and revealing it to babes.[j] [26]Yes, Father, for thus it was pleasing in Thy sight. [27]Everything has been handed over to Me from My Father, and no one really knows the Son except the Father, nor does anyone understand the Father except the Son and he to whom the Son wishes to reveal Him.

[28]"Come to Me all you who labor and are heavily burdened, and I will give you rest. [29]Take My yoke upon you and learn of Me, for I am gentle and humble of heart, and you will find rest for your souls; [30]for My yoke is easy and My burden is light."[k]

12 AT THAT TIME JESUS WALKED one Sabbath through the grain fields. His disciples were hungry and began to pluck heads of grain and to eat. [2]As the Pharisees observed it they said to Him, "Look! Your disciples are doing what is not lawful to be done on the Sabbath."[l] [3]But He replied, "Have you not read what David did[m] when he and his men were hungry, [4]how he entered the house of God and ate the loaves of presentation[n] which neither he nor his men, but only the priests, were allowed to eat? [5]Or have you never read[o] in the Law how on the Sabbath days the priests in the temple break the Sabbath and are blameless? [6]But I tell you that some-

---

d) Mal. 3:1.
e) Although John was evidently an ascetic and Jesus a companionable Man who attended dinners and weddings, the people generally did not respond heartily to either of them.
f) Chorazin was situated about four miles northwest of the northern tip of the Sea of Galilee.
g) See note at Mk. 3:22.
h) Tyre was a city on an island just off the western shore of the Mediterranean Sea and about twenty-five miles west of Caesarea Philippi (see note at ch. 16:13). Sidon, situated on the mainland, was twenty-two miles north of Tyre and fifty miles west of Damascus. Sidon was the principal city of ancient Phoenicia. Queen Jezebel had brought the sins and idolatry of Phoenicia into Israel, and this period remained a horrible memory for every Israelite.
i) The realm of the dead.   j) Infants, minors, uneducated and simple people.
k) Our Lord's message now goes beyond Israel with a gracious invitation to all men.
l) To pluck heads of grain was lawful, Deut. 23:24, but not on the Sabbath.   m) I Sam. 21:4,6.
n) This was the showbread, Ex. 25:30.   o) Num. 28:9.

thing greater than the temple is here. [7]And had you known what this means,[p] 'I want mercy and not sacrifice,' you would not have condemned the innocent. [8]For the Son of Man is Lord of the Sabbath."

[9]Leaving there He went into their synagogue. [10]And a man with a paralyzed hand was there; so, to incriminate Him, they asked Him, "Is it lawful to heal on the Sabbath?" [11]But He said to them, "Is there one of you with a single sheep who will not, if it falls into a pit on the Sabbath, take hold of it and lift it out? [12]How much more valuable, then, is a man than a sheep! Therefore it is lawful to do good on the Sabbath." [13]Then He said to the man, "Hold out your hand." He held it out and it was restored as healthy as the other. [14]But the Pharisees went away and devised a plot against Him so that they might destroy Him.

[15]Jesus, knowing this, withdrew from that place. Many followed Him and He healed them all [16]and charged them not to make Him known, [17]that what was said through Isaiah the prophet might be fulfilled,[q] [18]"Behold My Servant whom I have chosen, My Beloved in whom My soul delights; I will invest Him with My Spirit and He will announce justice to the nations. [19]He will not quarrel or shout, nor will anyone hear His voice in the streets. [20]He will not break a bruised reed; He will not extinguish a smoldering wick until He carries justice to victory. [21]And the nations will hope in His name."

[22]Then there was led to Him a blind and dumb demoniac, and He healed him, so that the dumb man both spoke and saw. [23]And all the crowds were amazed and said, "Is not this the Son of David?" [24]But when the Pharisees heard it, they said, "This fellow does not expel demons except through Beelzebul,[r] the ruler of demons."

[25]Reading their thoughts, He said to them, "Any kingdom that is divided against itself goes to ruin and any city or house that is divided against itself cannot stand. [26]If Satan expels Satan, he is divided against himself. How then will his kingdom stand? [27]Besides, if I cast out demons through Beelzebul, through whom do your sons cast them out? On this score they will be your judges. [28]But if I expel demons through the Spirit of God, then the kingdom of God has overtaken you.

[29]"How indeed can a person enter into a strong man's house and rob his belongings unless he first binds the strong man? After that he may rob his house. [30]Whoever is not with Me is against Me, and whoever is not gathering with Me scatters. [31]I tell you therefore: All sins and slanders are forgivable for men, but slander about the Spirit will not be forgiven. [32]If one should speak a word against the Son of Man he may be forgiven, but if he speaks against the Holy Spirit it will not be forgiven him either in this age or in the age to come.[s]

[33]"You either make both tree and fruit to be good, or you hold both tree and fruit to be rotten; for the tree is known by its fruit. [34]You brood of vipers, how can you speak good, evil as you are? For from the overflow of the heart the mouth speaks. [35]A good man brings out good things from good treasure in his heart, and a wicked man brings out bad things from bad treasure in his heart. [36]But I tell you that for every careless word spoken men shall be answerable in the Judgment Day. [37]For by your words you will be acquitted and by your words you will be condemned."

[38]Then some of the scribes and Pharisees replied to Him, "Teacher, we should like to see your token of proof." [39]And He answered them, "A wicked and disloyal generation craves a sign, and no sign will be given it except the sign of the Prophet Jonah. [40]For as Jonah was for three days and three nights in the belly of the sea-monster,[t] so will the Son of Man be three days and three nights in the heart of the earth. [41]The men of Nineveh will arise at the judgment along with this generation and will

---

p) Hos. 6:6; *cf.* Isa. 1:11; Mic. 6:8.   q) Isa. 42:1-4.   r) See note at Lk. 11:15.
s) No salvation is possible for one who continues to resist the call and influences of the Holy Spirit.   t) Jon. 1:17.

condemn it; for they repented at Jonah's preaching, and indeed something greater than Jonah is here. 42The Queen of the South[u] will rise at the judgment with this generation and condemn it; for she came from the ends of the earth to listen to Solomon's wisdom, and indeed something greater than Solomon is here.

43"When the unclean spirit goes out of a person he roams through dry places looking for rest and does not find it. 44Then he says, 'I will go back to the house I left,' and comes and finds it vacant, cleaned and orderly. 45He then goes out to bring along with him seven other spirits worse than himself, and they enter and live there. And the final condition of that person is worse than the first. So it will be with this wicked generation."

46While He was still speaking to the crowds His mother and brothers stood outside wanting to talk with Him. 47[Then someone told Him, "Your mother and Your brothers stand outside, wanting to speak to You."][v] 48But He replied to the one who told Him, "Who is My mother and who are My brothers?" 49And stretching out His hand to His disciples, He said, "Here are My mother and My brothers; 50for whoever does the will of My heavenly Father is My brother and sister and mother."[w]

13 THAT SAME DAY JESUS, LEAVING the house, sat by the seaside, 2and such great crowds gathered around Him that He stepped into a boat and sat down while the whole multitude stood on the beach. 3And He told them many things in parables, saying:[x] "A sower went out to sow 4and, in his sowing, some seed fell along the road and the birds came and ate them. 5Some fell on rocky soil, where they had little earth and sprang up quickly

because the soil was shallow; 6but with the rising sun they were scorched and, having no root, withered. 7Some fell among the thorns and the thorns grew up and choked them. 8But the rest fell on the good soil and bore a crop — some a hundredfold, some sixty and some thirty. 9Whoever has ears, let him listen."

10The disciples came up and said to Him, "Why do You speak to them in parables?" 11He answered, "It is granted you to know the secrets of the kingdom of heaven, but it is not granted them.[y] 12For whoever has will receive superabundantly, but whoever has not will be deprived of whatever he has. 13For this reason I speak to them in parables, because they look and see nothing; they listen and neither hear nor understand. 14On their part Isaiah's prophecy is fulfilled,[z] 'You will listen and listen but not at all understand; you will look and look but never see at all. 15For this people's heart has grown dull and with their ears they hear poorly; they have their eyes shut so that they may not see with their eyes, and hear with their ears, and understand with their hearts, and return and I would heal them.' 16But blessed are your eyes, for they see, and your ears, for they hear. 17For I assure you that many prophets and upright men have longed to see what you see and did not, and to hear what you are hearing and did not.

18"Listen, then, to the parable of the sower. 19When anyone hears the message of the kingdom and does not understand it, the evil one comes and snatches away what is sown in his heart. This represents the sowing along the road. 20But what was sown on rocky soil refers to the one who hears the word and at once accepts it gladly; 21but it takes no root in him; it does not last. Trouble or persecution arises

---

u) II Chron. 9:1-12.
v) Verse 47, enclosed in brackets, is not found in the majority of the most reliable ancient manuscripts.
w) Those who do God's will may have a relationship that is closer to the Lord Jesus than that of His own mother and brothers.
x) The parables of chapter 13 describe the influence of the Gospel in this present age, when not all the Word preached will be received in faith, and weeds will grow with the wheat until its end.
y) Not because of arbitrary judgment against them; but because they neglected divine grace they are themselves unresponsive soil.   z) Isa. 6:9-10.

on account of the message and at once he turns away from it. ²²And what was sown among thorns means one who listens to the message, but worldly cares and the enjoyment of wealth choke the word and it becomes unproductive. ²³But what was sown in good ground means one who listens and understands the message; he bears fruit and yields, some one a hundredfold, one sixty and one thirty."

²⁴He put before them another parable: "The kingdom of heaven is like a man who sowed good seed in his field, ²⁵but while men were asleep his enemy came and sowed weeds among the wheat and went away. ²⁶When the blade shot up and the wheat headed, the weeds appeared too. ²⁷The owner's slaves[a] went to him and said, 'Was not that good seed, sir, that you sowed in your field? Where then did the weeds come from?' ²⁸He said to them, 'An enemy has done this.' They asked him, 'Would you like then to have us go and weed them out?' ²⁹But he said, 'No, for in gathering up the weeds you might uproot the wheat along with them.[b] ³⁰Let them grow side by side until harvest time, and at harvest time I shall direct the reapers to collect the weeds first, bundle them up and burn them, but bring the grain into my barn.'"

³¹Another parable He presented to them: "The kingdom of heaven is like a mustard seed which a man took and sowed in his field. ³²It is the smallest of all seeds but when grown up it is bigger than any plant and becomes a tree, so that the birds of the air come and roost in its branches."

³³He told them another parable: "The kingdom of heaven is like yeast[c] which a woman took and buried in a bushel of flour until it was all raised."

³⁴Jesus said all this to the crowds in parables and never spoke to them except in parables, ³⁵so that the saying of the prophet was fulfilled:[d] "I will open my mouth in parables; I will express what has been hidden since the creation of the world."

³⁶Then leaving the multitudes He went indoors and His disciples came to Him saying, "Explain to us the parable of the weeds in the field." ³⁷He replied: "The sower of the good seed is the Son of Man. ³⁸The field is the world.[e] The good seed are the children of the kingdom, but the weeds are the children of the evil one. ³⁹The enemy who sowed them is the devil. The harvest is the end of the age. The reapers are the angels. ⁴⁰Just as the weeds are collected and burned up, so will it be at the end of the age. ⁴¹The Son of Man will send forth His angels and they will gather up out of His kingdom all those who offend and those who are guilty of lawlessness ⁴²and will cast them into the fiery furnace. There will be weeping and grinding of teeth there. ⁴³Then will the righteous radiate like the sun in their Father's kingdom. Whoever has ears, let him listen.

⁴⁴"The kingdom of heaven is like a treasure hidden in the field, which a man conceals after finding it. Then out of sheer gladness he goes out and sells everything he has and buys that field.

⁴⁵"Again, the kingdom of heaven is like a merchant looking for beautiful pearls. ⁴⁶Having found one pearl of exceptional value he went out and sold all he possessed and bought it.

⁴⁷"Once more, the kingdom of heaven is like a net cast in the sea which collected every kind of fish.

---

a) The Greek word *doulos* means *slave* and is so translated here and in many places throughout the N.T. Slavery was extremely prevalent in the Roman Empire; estimates of the proportion of slaves to free citizens range as high as three to one. Many slaves were people of education and culture who had been taken captive and enslaved during Roman conquests. Some were placed in positions of authority and were even entrusted with large financial responsibility, e.g. ch. 25:14-18 — these "domestic servants" were slaves, Gk. *doulous*. Social conditions have, of course, changed since the first century and today slavery is looked upon as unjustifiable and reprehensible. In this translation *doulos* in its different forms is variously rendered "slave," "bond-servant," or "servant," and, in several parables, "agent," e.g. ch. 18:23-35. In cases where the writers use the word in reference to themselves, e.g. Rom. 1:1; Jas. 1:1, it suggests their total commitment to their Lord. b) God alone sees into the hearts of men; thus He, rather than men, is able to distinguish the wheat from the weeds. Cf. ch. 7:1.   c) Or, leaven.   d) Ps. 78:2.
e) The Greek word here rendered "world," *kosmos*, means primarily *orderly arrangement*. It also denotes *universe, world,* and *inhabitants of the earth.* In this passage it alludes to those who dwell on the earth.

[48]When it was full they drew it to shore and, sitting down, they put the good ones into baskets and threw out the bad ones. [49]So will it be at the end of the age. The angels will come out and separate the wicked from the righteous [50]and will cast them into the fiery furnace; there will be wailing and grinding of teeth there.

[51]"Have you understood all this?" They answered Him, "Yes." [52]So He said to them, "Every teacher, therefore, who is versed in the kingdom of heaven is like the owner of a house who brings out of his storeroom new things and old."

[53]When Jesus had finished these parables, He went away from there [54]and, after arriving in His own home town, taught them in their synagogues in such a way that they were amazed, and said, "From where did this wisdom and these miracles of His come? [55]Is not this the carpenter's Son? Is not His mother called Mary, and His brothers James, Joses, Simon, and Judas? [56]And His sisters, are they not all with us? Where did He get all this?" [57]And they were offended at Him. But Jesus said to them, "A prophet is not without honor except in his own town and house." [58]And because of their unbelief He did not perform many miracles there.

14 AT THAT TIME THE Tetrarch Herod[f] heard of Jesus' fame [2]and said to his attendants, "This is John the Baptist. He is risen from the dead; therefore these powers are at work in him." [3]For Herod had arrested, bound and imprisoned John on account of Herodias,[g] the wife of his brother Philip, [4]because John had told him, "You have no right to have her." [5]He wished to kill him but was afraid of the people, for they considered him a prophet.

[6]At the occasion of Herod's birthday the daughter of Herodias danced before them and pleased Herod, [7]so he promised her on oath that he would give her whatever she might ask. [8]And, prompted by her mother, she said, "Give me here on a platter the head of John the Baptist." [9]The king was distressed; yet because of the oath and the guests he ordered it given, [10]and sent and beheaded John in prison. [11]His head was brought in on a platter and given to the girl, and she took it to her mother. [12]Then his disciples came, took up the body, buried it and went and told Jesus.

[13]When Jesus heard it, He withdrew by boat privately for a solitary place. When the throngs found that out, they followed Him afoot from the cities. [14]On landing He saw a great mass of people and felt deep sympathy for them and healed their sick.

[15]With the approach of evening the disciples came to Him, saying, "The place is solitary and the time is now advanced. Dismiss the crowds, so that they can go away to the villages and buy food for themselves." [16]But Jesus said to them, "They do not need to go away; you give them to eat." [17]They answered, "We have nothing here except five loaves and two fish." [18]He, however, said, "Bring those here to Me," [19]and ordered the people to sit[h] down on the grass. Taking the five loaves and two fish, and looking up toward heaven, He gave thanks and broke the loaves and handed them to His disciples, and the disciples to the people. [20]They all ate and were satisfied, and they picked up the fragments which were left over — twelve full baskets. [21]Not including the women and children there were five thousand men who ate.

[22]He immediately urged the disciples to embark and to sail ahead of Him to the other side while He dismissed the crowds. [23]And after He had dismissed the people He climbed the hill to pray. Evening had fallen and He was there alone. [24]But the boat was by that time a good distance from shore and was tossed by the waves, for the wind was contrary. [25]In the

---

f) Herod Antipas, one of the sons of Herod I, i.e., Herod the Great. A tetrarch was governor of one-fourth of a province. Herod Antipas is called King Herod in Mk. 6:14.
g) Granddaughter of Herod I and half-niece of Herod Antipas.
h) See note at Mk. 2:15.

fourth watch of the night[i] He approached them, walking on the sea. [26]And when the disciples saw Him walking on the sea, they exclaimed in terror, "It is a ghost!" and cried out from fear. [27]But He at once addressed them, "Cheer up! It is I; have no fear." [28]Peter answered Him, "Lord, if it is You, order me to come to You on the water." [29]He said, "Come." Peter got out of the boat and he walked on the water and came toward Jesus; [30]but looking at the wind he was afraid and, beginning to sink, he cried, "Lord, save me!" [31]Instantly Jesus reached out His hand and took hold of him, saying, "You of little faith! Why did you doubt?" [32]After they had gotten into the boat, the wind quieted. [33]Then those in the boat knelt before Him, saying, "Truly, You are the Son of God!"

[34]Having sailed across, they landed at Gennesaret[j] [35]and when the men of that place recognized Him, they sent into all that surrounding country and brought to Him all who suffered ailments. [36]They begged of Him that they might simply touch the fringe of His robe, and all who touched Him were completely healed.

15 THEN PHARISEES[k] AND SCRIBES[l] from Jerusalem approached Jesus with the remark, [2]"Why do Your disciples transgress the tradition of the elders? For they do not wash their hands before eating." [3]He replied to them, "Why do you transgress the command of God through your tradition? [4]For God has commanded,[m] 'Honor your father and mother,' and[n] 'He who curses father or mother must suffer death.' [5]But you say, 'Whoever says to his father or mother, "What you might get from me I make an offering," [6]he need not honor his father and his mother.'[o] So you have nullified the Word of God through your tradition. [7]You hypocrites, Isaiah rightly prophesied about you,[p] [8]'This people honors me with their lips, but their

heart is far away from Me. [9]Uselessly, they worship Me with their teaching of human commands.'"

[10]Summoning the people, He told them: "Listen and understand. [11]What enters the mouth does not pollute the person, but what comes out of the mouth pollutes a person."

[12]Then the disciples came and said to Him, "Are You aware that the Pharisees were shocked at hearing You say this?" [13]He replied, "Every plant that My heavenly Father has not planted will be uprooted. [14]Leave them alone; they are blind guides of the blind. But if one blind person leads another, they will both fall into a pit."

[15]Peter replied, "Explain the parable to us." [16]He said, "Even you do not understand? [17]Do you not know that whatever enters the mouth passes into the stomach and is purged? [18]But what comes out of the mouth comes from the heart; that pollutes a man. [19]For out of the heart come evil designs, murders, adulteries, sexual vices, thefts, lyings and slanders. [20]These pollute a person; but to eat with unwashed hands does not pollute a person."

[21]Leaving there, Jesus withdrew to the region of Tyre and Sidon. [22]Here a Canaanitish woman from those parts came out and cried, "Pity me, LORD, Son of David! My daughter is badly demon-possessed." [23]But He answered her never a word. Then His disciples came and urged Him, "Send her away, for she keeps shouting behind us." [24]But He replied, "I was sent only to the lost sheep of the house of Israel." [25]Then she approached and knelt before Him, saying, "Lord, help me!" [26]He answered, "It is not fair to take the children's bread and to throw it to the house dogs."[q] [27]But she said, "True, Lord, yet even the house dogs eat of the crumbs that fall from their master's table." [28]Then Jesus answered her, "O woman, your faith is great! Be it as you desire." And from that very moment her daughter was healed.

---

i) Between 3 and 6 A.M.
j) Located on the western shore of the Sea of Galilee between Capernaum and Magdala.
k) See note at ch. 3:7.   l) See note at ch. 2:4.   m) Ex. 20:12.   n) Lev. 20:9.
o) Property thus said to be dedicated as an offering released its donor from other responsibilities, e.g., to parents.   p) Isa. 29:13.   q) See note at Mk. 7:27.

29Moving away from there, Jesus went along the Sea of Galilee, climbed the hill and sat there. 30Great throngs came to Him. They brought along lame, blind, dumb, maimed and many others whom they laid at His feet, and He healed them; 31so that the crowd wondered when they saw the dumb speaking, the maimed sound in body, the lame walking, and the blind seeing. And they glorified the God of Israel.

32But Jesus called His disciples and said, "I feel deeply moved for the multitude because they have now stayed with Me three days and they have nothing to eat. I am not willing to send them away hungry, for they may faint on the road." 33The disciples said to Him, "Where are we to get loaves enough in the desert to satisfy such a crowd?" 34Jesus asked them, "How many loaves do you have?" They said, "Seven and a few small fish." 35He ordered the masses to sit[r] on the ground, 36took the seven loaves and the fish, gave thanks, broke them and handed them to the disciples, and the disciples to the crowds. 37They all ate and were satisfied; and the leftovers filled seven hampers. 38Four thousand men shared the eating, aside from women and children. 39Then, dismissing the crowds, He embarked and sailed to the Magadan region.[s]

16 THE PHARISEES AND SADDUcees[t] approached and, to test Him asked Him to show them a sign from heaven; 2but He replied, "[At eventide you say, 'Fair weather, for the sky is red,' 3and in the morning, 'A stormy day, for the sky is red and overcast.' You hypocrites, you can distinguish the face of the sky, but not the signs of the times].[u] 4A wicked and immoral generation seeks a sign and no sign shall be given it except the sign of Jonah.[v] Then He left them and went away.

5When the disciples had reached the other side, they had forgotten to bring along bread; 6and Jesus said to them, "Take heed and keep away from the yeast of the Pharisees and Sadducees." 7They discussed it among themselves, "We brought no bread." 8But Jesus, aware of it, said, "Why these discussions among yourselves, you of little faith? Because you brought no bread? 9Do you not understand even yet, neither remember the five loaves of the five thousand and how many baskets you took up, 10nor the seven loaves of the four thousand and how many hampers you took up? 11How is it you do not see that I was not talking to you about bread, but that you should be careful about the ferment of the Pharisees and Sadducees?" 12Then they realized that He did not tell them to beware of yeast in bread, but of the teaching of the Pharisees and Sadducees.

13When Jesus entered the region of Caesarea Philippi,[w] He asked His disciples, "Who do people say the Son of Man is?" 14They said, "Some say, John the Baptist; others, Elijah; others, Jeremiah, or one of the prophets." 15He asked them, "But you, who do you say I am?" 16Simon Peter answered, "You are the Christ, the Son of the living God." 17Jesus answered him, "Blessed are you, Simon, son of John, because it was not flesh and blood that revealed this to you but My heavenly Father. 18I also tell you that you are Peter,[x] and on this rock I will build My church,[y] and the gates of hades shall not prevail against her. 19I will give

---

r) See note at Mk. 2:15.
s) At a place on the western shore of the lake, probably near Magdala, the home of Mary Magdalene.   t) See notes at ch. 3:7.
u) The words that are enclosed in brackets in vss. 2-3 are not found in the majority of the most reliable ancient manuscripts.
v) Chapter 12:39; Jon. 1:17. Signs do not always soften stubborn hearts. Cf. Lk. 16:31.
w) Caesarea Philippi, now called Paneas, is situated about twenty-five miles north of the Sea of Galilee on one of the tributaries of the Jordan River. It was founded by Philip the Tetrarch, a son of Herod the Great.
x) From the Greek word *petros* meaning *a stone, a piece of rock.* The word "rock" in the next clause is a translation of *petra* meaning *a rock.*
y) The word "church" is translated from the Greek noun *ekklesia* which means *a called out group of people,* i.e., *an assembly.* In reading the N.T. one must distinguish whether the allusion is to the church as the whole body of believers in Christ, or to the church organization, i.e., a denomination or a local church.

you the keys of the kingdom of heaven; whatever you bind on earth will be bound in heaven, and whatever you allow on earth will be allowed in heaven."z 20Then He forbade the disciples to say to anyone, "He is the Christ."

21From then on Jesus began to show His disciples that He must go to Jerusalem and suffer much from the elders, priests and scribes, and be killed, and raised on the third day. 22Then Peter, leading Him aside, began to remonstrate with Him: "Mercy on You, Lord; this must never happen to You!" 23But, turning around, He said to Peter, "Get behind Me, Satan, you are a snare to Me; for you are not taking the divine view but man's." 24Then Jesus said to His disciples, "If anyone wants to walk after Me, he must deny himself, take up his cross and follow Me; 25for whoever wants to save his life shall lose it, but whoever loses his life for Me shall find it.

26"For what advantage will a man have if he acquires the whole world and forfeits his own life, or what will a man offer in exchange for his life? 27For the Son of Man is going to come in the glory of the Father with His angels, and then He shall reward each according to his deeds.a 28I assure you, there are some of those standing here who will not taste death until they see the Son of Man coming in His kingdom."

17 SIX DAYS LATER JESUS TOOK along Peter, James, and his brother John, and led them up a high mountain by themselves. 2In view of them He was transfigured: His face shone like the sun and His clothes became white as the light. 3Moses and Elijah also appeared to them as they conversed with Him. 4Then Peter addressed Jesus, "Lord, it is good that we are here. If You approve, I shall make here three booths, one for You, one for Moses and one for Elijah."

5While he was still talking, a bright cloud overshadowed themb and a voice from the cloud said, "This is My Beloved Son, in whom I am delighted; listen to Him." 6As the disciples heard it, they fell on their faces in great fear; 7but Jesus, coming forward, touched them and said, "Stand up and have no fear." 8And, raising their eyes, they saw no one except Jesus alone.

9As they were coming down from the mountain, Jesus commanded them, "Do not mention the vision to anyone until the Son of Man is raised from the dead." 10The disciples asked Him, "Why, then, do the scribes say that Elijah must first come?" 11He replied, Elijah will come indeed and will restore all things.c 12But I tell you that Elijah has already come and they did not recognize him, but have done to him as they pleased. In a similar way the Son of Man is about to suffer at their hands." 13Then the disciples realized that He was speaking to them of John the Baptist.d

14When they approached the crowd, a man came forward and knelt to Him, saying, 15"Lord, take pity on my son, for he is an epileptic and suffers badly; he often falls into the fire and often into the water. 16I brought him to Your disciples, but they had no power to cure him." 17Jesus replied, "O unbelieving and rebellious generation, how long shall I remain with you? How long shall I put up with you? Bring him here to Me." 18So Jesus rebuked the demon and it came out of him, and from that moment the boy was cured.

19Then the disciples came to Jesus privately and said, "Why did not we have power to expel it?" 20He said to them, "Because of your little faith. For I assure you, if you have faith the size of a mustard seed, you will say to this mountain, 'Move from here to there,' and it will move. And nothing shall be impossible for you. 21[But this kind does not go out except through prayer and fasting.]"e

---

z) What the Church teaches as taught by the Holy Spirit is acknowledged in heaven and serves to control human behavior. See the action of the church at Jerusalem, Acts 15.
a) Rev. 20:12-13; *cf.* Eph. 2:8-10.   b) *Cf.* Ex. 40:34.   c) Mal. 4:5-6.
d) Obviously John the Baptist was not a reincarnation of Elijah, for Elijah had just visited with Jesus; but John the Baptist came in the power of Elijah.
e) Verse 21, which is enclosed in brackets, is not found in the majority of the most reliable ancient manuscripts.

22While they were gathering in Galilee, Jesus said to them, "The Son of Man is about to be betrayed into the hands of men, 23and they will kill Him, and on the third day He will be raised." And they felt deeply distressed.

24When they arrived at Capernaum the tax collectors came to Peter and said, "Does not your teacher pay the tax?" 25He said, "Yes." And as he entered the house, Jesus forestalled him by saying, "What is your idea, Simon? From whom do the kings of the earth collect customs or taxes, from their sons or from foreigners?" 26When he said, "From foreigners," Jesus declared to him, "Then the sons are exempt. 27However, not to offend them, go to the sea, cast a hook and take the first fish you bring up, open its mouth and you will find a coin. Take it and pay them for Me and for yourself."

18 AT THAT TIME THE DISCIPLES came and asked Jesus, "Who really excels in the kingdom of heaven?" 2Calling a little child, He stood it in the midst of them 3and said, "I assure you, unless you are converted and become like little children, you will certainly not enter the kingdom of heaven. 4Whoever, then, humbles himself like this little child, he excels in the kingdom of heaven; 5and whoever receives one such child in My name, receives Me. 6But whoever is an occasion for stumbling to one of these little ones that believe in Me, it were better for him to have a millstone hung around his neck and to be drowned in the depth of the sea.

7"Alas for the world because of the occasions of stumbling. The occasions have to come, but woe to the person on whose account they occur. 8If your hand or your foot hinders you, cut it off and throw it from you; it is better for you to enter life maimed or crippled than to keep both hands or feet and to be thrown into eternal fire. 9If your eye hinders you, pluck it out and throw it from you; it is better for you to enter life with one eye, than having two eyes to be cast into the fires of hell. 10See to it that you do not despise one of these little ones; for I tell you, that their angels[f] in heaven are forever looking at the face of My heavenly Father.

11"[The Son of Man has come to save the lost.][g] 12How does this seem to you? If a man has a hundred sheep and one of them strays, does he not leave the ninety-nine on the mountains to go out in search of the stray one? 13And if he manages to find it, I assure you that he is happier over that one than over the ninety-nine that did not stray. 14So it is not the will of your heavenly Father that one of these little ones should be lost.

15"If your brother should do wrong against you, go and show him his fault privately; in case he listens, you have won your brother.[h] 16In case he does not listen, take one or two along, so that from the testimony of two or three witnesses the whole dispute may be settled.[i] 17If he refuses to listen to them, tell the church; and if he will not listen to the church, treat him like a pagan and a tax gatherer. 18I assure you, whatever you will bind on earth shall be bound in heaven, and whatever you allow on earth will be allowed in heaven.[j] 19Once more I assure you that if two of you are agreed on earth about anything for which you pray, it will be done for you by My heavenly Father. 20For where two or three have gathered in My name, I am there with them."

21Then Peter approached and said to Him, "Lord, how often shall my brother act amiss toward me and I forgive him? Up to seven times?" 22Jesus said to him, "I do not say, up to seven, but up to seventy times seven.

23"For this reason the kingdom of heaven may be compared to a king who planned to settle accounts with his agents.[k] 24As he began the settlement,

---

f) Our Lord here teaches angelic protection of individuals.
g) Verse 11, enclosed in brackets, is not found in the majority of the most reliable ancient manuscripts. h) Cf. Gal. 6:1. i) Deut. 19:15.
j) The Church should be diligent in the exercise of the disciplinary functions that Christ has committed to it. k) See note at ch. 13:27.

one was brought in who owed him twenty million dollars,[1] 25but as he had nothing to pay, his master ordered him to be sold, as well as his wife and children and everything he had, and to pay. 26Then the agent fell down and implored him, 'Have patience with me and I will pay you everything.' 27So, in pity for that agent his master released him and canceled his debt.

28"But as that agent was leaving he met one of his fellow agents, who owed him twenty-five dollars. Grabbing him by the throat, he said, 'Pay me what you owe!' 29Then his fellow agent fell down and implored him, 'Have patience with me and I will pay you.' 30But he refused, and went and threw him into prison until he should pay the debt.

31"When his fellow servants saw what was done they were greatly distressed, and they went and told their master everything that had occurred. 32Then his master summoned him and said to him: 'You contemptible slave! I canceled all that debt for you because you begged me. 33Should not you have had pity on your fellow servant as I had pity on you?' 34And angrily his master handed him over to the scourgers, until he should pay everything he owed him. 35And so will My heavenly Father do to you, if each of you does not heartily forgive his brother."

19 WHEN JESUS HAD COMPLETED these sayings, He left Galilee and entered the Judean territory across the Jordan. 2Large crowds followed Him and He healed them there.

3Then the Pharisees approached Him to test Him. They asked, "Is it right to divorce one's wife for every given reason?" 4He replied, "Have you not read that from the beginning the Creator made them male and female, 5and said,[m] On this account a man shall leave his father and mother and be joined to his wife, and the two shall be one flesh?' 6So they are no longer two but one flesh. What God then has joined, man must not separate." 7They said to Him, "Why then did Moses command[n] to give a divorce certificate and to dismiss her?" 8He answered them, "Due to your hard-heartedness Moses permitted you to divorce your wives, but it was not that way from the beginning. 9I tell you that whoever divorces his wife, except for unfaithfulness, and marries another commits adultery."

10The disciples said to Him, "If such is the case of a man with his wife, it is preferable not to marry." 11But He replied, "Not all people accept this saying, but only those to whom it is given; 12for some eunuchs are such from birth, some were made eunuchs by men, and some have made themselves eunuchs for the sake of the kingdom of heaven. Whoever is able to accept it, let him accept it."

13Then little children were brought to Him so that He might lay His hands on them and pray, and the disciples reproved them. 14But Jesus said, "Allow the little ones and do not stop them from coming to Me, for of this kind the kingdom of heaven is composed." 15And after laying His hands on them He went away from there.

c. A.D. 30

16Someone approached Him and said, "Teacher, what good deed shall I do to secure eternal life?" 17He said to him, "Why do you ask Me about goodness? Only One is good. But if you wish to enter into life, keep the commandments."[o] 18He inquired of Him, "Which?" Then Jesus said, "This: Do not commit murder;[p] do not commit adultery; do not steal; do not witness falsely; 19 honor your father and mother, and[q] love your neighbor as yourself."

---

1) How could a slave owe his master $20,000,000? Obviously this great sum is used to show that the man could not possibly have paid such a huge amount; it is contrasted with the reasonable figure that the second slave is said to have owed the first, namely $25. Even this was a large sum in N.T. times, equivalent to three and a half months' wages.
    The text reads "ten thousand talents" in vs. 24 and "a hundred denarii" in vs. 28. One silver talent equals about $2000; a denarius equals approximately twenty-five cents.
m) Christ substantiates the authenticity of the Genesis account of creation.
n) Christ affirms the Mosaic authorship of Deuteronomy.
o) Specifically the Ten Commandments, Ex. 20:1-17. p) See note at ch. 5:21. q) Lev. 19:18.

20The young man said to Him, "All these things I have observed. How do I still fall behind?" 21Jesus replied, "If you want to be complete, go and sell what you have and donate it to the needy, and you will have treasure in heaven; then come and follow Me." 22But the young man, on hearing that, went sadly away, for he had much property.

23Jesus remarked to His disciples, "I assure you, it will be difficult for a rich person to enter the kingdom of heaven. 24I say to you again, it is easier for a camel to pass through a needle's[r] eye than for a wealthy person to enter the kingdom of God." 25When the disciples heard this, they were utterly dumbfounded and said, "Who then can be saved?" 26But Jesus looked at them and said, "With men this is impossible, but with God all things are possible."

27Then Peter replied to Him, "We have left everything and have followed You. What then is there for us?" 28Jesus answered, "I assure you that your followers of Mine, in the new age, when the Son of Man will sit upon the throne of His glory, you too will sit on twelve thrones judging the twelve tribes of Israel.[s] 29Also everyone who has left houses or brothers or sisters or father or mother or children or fields on account of My name, will receive a hundred times over and will inherit eternal life. 30But many now first will be last, and the last will be first.

20 "FOR THE KINGDOM OF HEAVEN resembles an estate owner, who went out early in the morning to hire workmen for his vineyard,[t] 2and after agreeing with the workmen on twenty-five cents[u] a day, he sent them into his vineyard. 3At about nine o'clock he went out and saw other workmen standing in the market place unemployed, 4and said to them, 'You go into the vineyard, too, and I will pay you whatever is fair.' So they went. 5Going

out again at twelve and at three, he did the same thing. 6When he went out at five o'clock, he found others standing there and said to them, 'Why do you stand here idle all day?' 7They answered, 'Because nobody has hired us.' He said to them, 'You go out into the vineyard too.'

8"As evening fell the owner of the vineyard said to his foreman, 'Call the workmen and pay their wages, starting with the last and on to the first.' 9When those who began around five o'clock came, they got twenty-five cents each; 10and when the first workmen came they thought that they would get more, but they, too, got twenty-five cents each. 11On receiving it, they grumbled against the owner 12and said, 'These last have worked one hour and you have ranked them equal with us who endured the arduous toil and the scorching heat of the day.' 13But he answered one of them, 'Friend, I am not wronging you. Did you not agree with me on twenty-five cents? 14Take what is yours and go. I choose to pay this last one the same as you. 15Have I no right to do with my belongings as I please? Or do you look resentful because I am generous?' 16So the last will be first, and the first last."

17As Jesus was going up to Jerusalem, He took the Twelve aside and on the road said to them, 18"Take notice. We are going up to Jerusalem and the Son of Man will be betrayed to the chief priests and scribes. They will sentence Him to death, 19and hand Him over to the Gentiles to be mocked and scourged and crucified, and on the third day He will be raised."

20Then the mother of Zebedee's sons approached Him with her sons, kneeling and requesting something of Him. 21He said to her, "What do you wish?" She replied, "Command that these my two sons will sit one at Your right and one at Your left in Your kingdom." 22Jesus answered, "You do not know what you are asking. Can you drink the cup I am about to

---

r) See note at Mk. 10:24. s) Cf. Isa. 1:26. t) Cf. Isa. 5:7.
u) The actual coin was the denarius, worth in the mid-twentieth century about twenty-five cents. In the first century it had a much higher purchasing power than now and was a fair day's wage for a field hand.

drink?" They said to Him, "We can." [23]He told them, "You will indeed drink My cup[v] but to sit at My right and My left is not Mine to grant, but it is for those for whom it has been prepared by My Father."

[24]When the ten heard it, they were indignant at the two brothers, [25]but Jesus called them and said, "You know that the rulers of the Gentiles lord it over them, and their superiors oppress them, [26]but with you it is different: Whoever among you wants to be great must be your servant [27]and whoever would be first will be your slave, [28]just as the Son of Man did not come to be served but to serve, and to give His life a ransom for many."

[29]As they were leaving Jericho, a great throng followed Him. [30]And when two blind men who were sitting by the road heard that Jesus was passing, they shouted, "Lord, Son of David, take pity on us!" [31]The crowd rebuked them, demanding silence, but they shouted the louder, "Lord, take pity on us, O Son of David." [32]Then Jesus stopped, called them and said, "What do you want Me to do for you?" [33]They said, "Lord, we would have our eyes opened." [34]So Jesus took pity on them and touched their eyes and at once they received their sight and followed Him.

21 WHEN JESUS CAME NEAR JErusalem and reached Bethphage[w] at the Mount of Olives, He sent out two disciples, [2]saying to them, "Go to the village opposite you and immediately you will find a donkey hitched, and a colt with her. Unhitch them and bring them to Me. [3]Should anyone say anything to you, reply, 'The Lord needs them,' and without delay he will let them go." [4]This happened so that the saying of the prophet might be fulfilled,[x] [5]"Tell Zion's daughter, Behold, your king is coming to you, gentle and mounted on a donkey, even on a colt, the foal of a beast of burden."

[6]The disciples went and did as Jesus had directed them. [7]They brought the donkey and the colt and placed their coats on them, and He seated Himself on them. [8]Many of the multitude, too, spread their clothes on the road, while others cut branches from the trees and strewed them on the road. [9]And the crowds, some marching ahead[y] and some in the rear, shouted,[z] "Hosanna to the Son of David! Blessed is He who comes in the name of the Lord! Hosanna in the highest."

[10]When He entered Jerusalem, the whole city was agitated. "Who is this?" [11]they asked. The crowd replied, "This is the Prophet Jesus, from Nazareth in Galilee."

[12]Jesus entered the temple and expelled all who were buying and selling in its courts. He overturned the tables of the money changers and seats of those who sold doves, [13]and told them, "It is written,[a] 'My house shall be called a house of prayer,' but you are making it a robbers' den."

[14]The blind and the lame came to Him in the temple and He healed them. [15]But when the chief priests and the scribes noticed the wonderful things He did, and the children shouting in the temple, "Hosanna to the Son of David!" they were indignant [16]and said to Him, "Do You hear what they are saying?" Jesus answered, "Yes. Did you never read,[b] 'From the mouth of babes and nurslings Thou hast perfected praise?'" [17]And leaving them He went outside the city to Bethany,[c] and there He spent the night.

[18]In the early morning, as He re-

---

v) Both James and John would dedicate their lives to the Lord Jesus Christ. Part of the cup that they would drink would be martyrdom for James, Acts 12:1-3, and exile for John, Rev. 1:9. However, the request that they and their mother made of Jesus was essentially selfish.
w) "Bethphage" means *house of unripe figs.* See note at Lk. 19:29. x) Zech. 9:9.
y) They evidently came from Jerusalem to meet Jesus and became the van of the procession.
z) Ps. 118:25-26. "Hosanna" means *save now* or *salvation.* The expression is somewhat similar to "God save the king." a) Isa. 56:7; Jer. 7:11. b) Ps. 8:2.
c) "Bethany" means *house of depression* or *house of a wine press.* It was in Bethany, at the home of Mary, Martha and Lazarus, that Jesus was sometimes entertained. Bethany was also the home of Simon, the leper, ch. 26:6, and it was from Bethany that our Lord ascended to heaven, Lk. 24:50. It was at the foot of the Mount of Olives, not more than two miles from Jerusalem.

The Barren Fig Tree; the Vineyard

turned to the city, He felt hungry 19and, noticing a single fig tree by the roadside, walked to it and found on it nothing but leaves. He said to it, "Let there be no fruit from you any more forever." And instantly the fig tree withered. 20As the disciples observed it, they marveled and said, "How did the fig tree wither so quickly?" 21Jesus answered them, "I assure you, if you have faith and do not doubt, you will not only do what was done to the fig tree, but if you say to this mountain, 'Be lifted and thrown into the sea,' it will happen. 22And everything you ask in prayer you will obtain, if you believe."

23Upon his entering the temple, the chief priests and the elders of the people stepped up to Him during His teaching and said, "By what authority are You doing these things and who gave You this authority?" 24Jesus answered them, "Let Me ask you one question, too, and if you answer Me, then I will tell you by what authority I do these things: 25Where did John's baptism come from, from heaven or from men?" But they argued among themselves, "If we say 'From heaven,' He will say to us, 'Then why did you not believe him?' 26But if we say, 'From men,' we are afraid of the people, for they all consider John a prophet." 27So they answered Jesus, "We do not know." He said to them, "Neither do I tell you by what authority I do these things.

28"But how does this seem to you: A man had two sons and, going to the first, he said, 'Son, go out and work today in the vineyard.' 29He replied, 'I won't.' Afterward he felt sorry and went out. 30Going to the second, he said the same to him. He answered, 'I will, sir.' But he did not go. 31Which of the two did the father's will?" They said, "The first." Jesus said to them, "Truly I tell you, the tax gatherers and the prostitutes are en-

tering the kingdom of heaven ahead of you. 32For John came to you on a mission of righteousness and you did not believe him; but the tax gatherers and the prostitutes believed him, and although you saw that, yet you did not afterward repent and believe him.

33"Hear another parable:d There was an estate owner who planted a vineyard, hedged it in, dug out a wine press in it, built a watchtower and leased it to tenant farmers, then went abroad. 34When vintage time approached, he sent his agentse to the tenant farmers to collect his share; 35but the farmers took his agents and beat one, killed another, and stoned a third. 36Subsequently he sent other slaves more numerous than the first, whom they treated in the same way. 37Finally he sent them his son, saying, 'They will respect my son.' 38But when the tenant farmers saw his son, they said among themselves, 'This is the heir. Come on, let us kill him and get hold of his inheritance.' 39So they seized him, put him out of the vineyard, and killed him. 40When therefore the owner of the vineyard arrives, what will he do to those tenant farmers?"

41They answered, "He will put the wretches to a miserable death and will lease the vineyard to other tenant farmers, who will pay him his share each season." 42Jesus said to them, "Did you never read in the Scriptures,f 'The stoneg which the builders rejected has become the chief corner stone; this is the Lord's doing and it fills our eyes with wonder'? 43I tell you, therefore, that the kingdom of God will be taken from you and will be given to a people that produces its fruits. 44[Whoever falls on that stone will be smashed, and on whom it falls, he shall be pulverized.]"h

45When the chief priests and the Pharisees heard His parables, they knew He was talking about them,

---

d) Cf. Isa. 5:1-7.   e) See note at ch. 13:27.   f) Ps. 118:22-23.
g) A stone or a rock is frequently used in the Scriptures as a symbol of Christ. See Gen. 49:24; Deut. 32:4; Isa. 8:14-15; 28:16; Dan. 2:34; Rom. 9:32-33; I Cor. 1:23; 3:11; Eph. 2:19-22; I Pet. 2:3-8.
h) Verse 44, enclosed in brackets, is not found in the majority of the most reliable ancient manuscripts.

[46]and they wanted to arrest Him; but they were afraid of the crowds, since they considered Him to be a prophet.

22 JESUS AGAIN TALKED TO THEM in parables, saying,[i] [2]"The kingdom of heaven is similar to a king who prepared a wedding banquet for his son [3]and sent out his servants to notify those invited to the wedding, but they would not come. [4]Once more he sent other servants, saying, 'Tell those invited, "Look here! I have gotten my dinner ready, my steers and fatted beasts are killed, and everything is prepared. Come to the wedding." ' [5]But disregarding it, they went off — this one to his farm, that one to his trade, [6]and the rest, taking hold of his servants, ill-treated and killed them.

[7]"The king was infuriated. He dispatched his troops, destroyed those murderers, and burned their city. [8]He then told his servants, 'True, the banquet is ready, but the invited guests proved undeserving; [9]so go to the thoroughfares and invite to the wedding everyone you find.' [10]Those servants, as they went out on the roads, got together all whom they came across, both bad and good, and the wedding was fully supplied with guests.

[11]"But when the king came in to look the guests over, he noticed there a man not dressed in a wedding robe, [12]to whom he said, 'Friend, how did you enter here without a wedding robe?' But he was speechless.[j] [13]Then the king said to his domestic servants, 'Bind him hand and foot and throw him out into the outside darkness; there will be weeping and grinding of teeth.' [14]For many are called, but few are chosen."

[15]The Pharisees then went and plotted how they might entangle Him in His speech. [16]So they dispatched their disciples to Him, with the Herodians,[k] who said, "Teacher, we know that You are sincere and that You teach the way of God honestly. You are afraid of none and You court no one's favor. [17]Give us therefore Your opinion: Is it right to pay tax to Caesar or not?" [18]But Jesus saw through their malice and said, "Why do you test Me, you hypocrites? [19]Show Me a coin." And they brought him a coin.[l] [20]"Whose is this likeness and signature?" He asked them. [21]They said, "Caesar's." He told them, "Then pay Caesar what is due to Caesar, and God what is due to God." [22]As they listened, they marveled and went off and left Him.

[23]That same day Sadducees, who say there is no resurrection, approached Him and asked Him, [24]"Teacher, Moses said[m] if someone dies childless, his brother shall marry his widow and raise descendants for his brother. [25]Now there were seven brothers in our community, the first of whom married and died and, having no children, left his widow to his brother. [26]So the second, and the third, down to the seventh; [27]and, following them all, the woman died. [28]At the resurrection, then, whose wife will she be of the seven? For they all had her."

[29]Jesus answered them, "You are mistaken. You understand neither the Scriptures nor the power of God, [30]for in the resurrected state they neither marry nor are given in marriage, but are like angels in heaven. [31]And about the rising of the dead, have you never read what God said to you,[n] [32]'I am the God of Abraham, the God of Isaac, and the God of Jacob'? He is God, not of dead but living beings."

[33]As the crowds listened they were amazed at His teaching; [34]but when the Pharisees heard that He had silenced the Sadducees, they put their heads together [35]and one of them, a teacher of the Law, by way of testing Him, asked, [36]"Teacher! what is the

---

i) The parables of the final week of Christ's earthly ministry relate to His rejection by His own nation.
j) *Cf.* Rom. 3:19.
k) The Herodians were not a religious sect like the Pharisees and Sadducees (see notes at ch. 3:7) but a political party that supported the Herods. All three groups opposed Jesus, vss. 15-16, 23, 34-35.
l) The text reads "denarius," a coin equal to about twenty-five cents in mid-twentieth century U.S. currency. See notes at chs. 18:24 and 20:2.
m) A custom that predates even the Mosaic Law, *cf.* Gen. 38:8; Deut. 25:5-6.   n) Ex. 3:6.

great commandment in the Law?" [37]He said to him, "You shall love the Lord your God with your whole heart, with your whole soul, and with your whole mind. [38]This is the great and chief commandment. [39]The second is like it, 'You shall love your neighbor as yourself.' [40]On these two[o] commandments the whole Law and the Prophets depend."

[41]While the Pharisees were still together, Jesus questioned them, [42]"What is your idea about the Christ? Whose Son is He?" They said to Him, "David's." [43]He asked them, "How then does David in the Spirit call Him Lord, saying,[p] [44]'The LORD said to my Lord, Sit at My right hand until I put Thy enemies under Thy feet'? [45]If then David calls Him Lord, how is He his son?" [46]No one was able to answer Him a word; neither from that day did anyone presume to question Him any more.

23 THEN JESUS SAID TO THE crowds and to His disciples: [2]"The scribes[q] and the Pharisees are occupying Moses' seat; [3]therefore do and observe whatever they tell you, but do not behave as they do; for they talk and do not practice. [4]They tie up heavy loads and place them on the people's shoulders, but they themselves do not care to move them with their finger. [5]They conduct all their activities to be noticed by men. For they enlarge their phylacteries[r] and lengthen their fringes;[s] [6]they cherish the chief place at dinners and the best seats in the synagogues, [7]the greetings in the market places and to be called Rabbi[t] by men.

[8]"But you must not be called Rabbi, for one is your teacher and you are all brothers. [9]And call no one on earth your father, for one is your heavenly Father; [10]neither be called teachers, for you have one teacher — the Christ. [11]But he who is greatest among you will be your servant; [12]for whoever elevates himself shall be humbled, and whoever humbles himself shall be elevated.

[13]"Alas for you, scribes and Pharisees, hypocrites, because you shut the kingdom of heaven in people's faces; for neither do you enter[u] nor do you allow those entering to go in. [14][Alas for you, scribes and Pharisees, hypocrites, for as a pretext for your piety you pray long prayers, and you cheat widows out of their houses. For this you will receive greater judgment.][v] [15]Alas for you, scribes and Pharisees, hypocrites, for you traverse sea and land to make one proselyte and, when he becomes one, you make him a son of perdition twice worse than yourselves.

[16]"Alas for you, blind leaders, who say, 'If anyone swears by the temple, it means nothing; but if anyone swears by the temple's gold, he is bound by his oath.' [17]Blind fools! For which is greater, the gold, or the temple that renders the gold sacred? [18]Furthermore you say, 'If anyone swears by the altar, it means nothing; but if he swears by the offering upon it, he is bound by his oath.' [19]Blind ones, which is greater, the offering, or the altar that renders the offering sacred? [20]So one who swears by the altar, swears by it and by everything on it, [21]and one who swears by the temple, swears by it and by Him who occupies it, [22]and one who swears by heaven, swears by the throne of God and by Him who sits upon it.

[23]"Alas for you, scribes and Pharisees, hypocrites, because you tithe

---

o) Deut. 6:5; Lev. 19:18.
p) Ps. 110:1. This psalm, written by David about 1000 B.C., points to Christ, the Messiah, and is one of a number of Messianic psalms. q) See note at ch. 2:4.
r) A phylactery was a square calfskin box in which slips of parchment, bearing Scripture texts, namely Ex. 13:2-10, 11-17; Deut. 6:4-9; 11:13-22, were placed. The phylactery was worn either on the forehead or on the left arm below the elbow.
s) The Israelites sewed fringes on the borders of their garments as a reminder of God's commandments and that they were His chosen people, Num. 15:37-40.
t) "Rabbi," from the Hebrew word *rav* or *rab*, means *master, lord.*
u) In following the scribes and Pharisees, who were themselves lost, the people would not reach heaven.
v) Verse 14, enclosed in brackets, is not found in the majority of the most reliable ancient manuscripts.

mint, dill and cummin,ᵂ and you omit the weightier aspects of the Law — justice, mercy, and faith. These you ought to do without omitting the others. 24Blind leaders, who strain out the gnat but swallow the camel!

25"Alas for you, scribes and Pharisees, hypocrites; for you clean the outside of the cup and the plate, but inside they are full of extortion and self-indulgence. 26Blind Pharisees! First clean the inside of the cup and the plate so that its outside may be clean as well. 27Alas for you, scribes and Pharisees, hypocrites, for you resemble white-washed tombs which appear beautiful on the outside, but inside they are full of dead men's bones and every impurity. 28So you seem to men to be outwardly upright, but inside you are full of hypocrisy and lawlessness.

29"Alas for you, scribes and Pharisees, hypocrites, for you build the tombs of the prophets and you decorate the monuments of the righteous, 30and you say, 'Had we lived in the days of our fathers, we would not have had a part in shedding the blood of the prophets.' 31Thus you testify against yourselves; for you are the sons of the prophets' murderers. 32Fill up the measure of your fathers. 33Snakes! You viper brood! How will you escape the sentence to hell?ˣ

34"Therefore, take notice: I will send you prophets and sages and scribes, some of whom you will kill and crucify, and some of whom you will flog in your synagogues and persecute from town to town, 35so that there may come upon you all the righteous blood that has been shed on the earth, from the blood of righteous Abelʸ to the blood of Zechariahᶻ the son of Barachiah, whom you murdered between the temple and the altar. 36I assure you

that all this will come upon this generation.

37"O Jerusalem! Jerusalem! murdering the prophets and stoning those sent to you! How often have I wanted to gather your children as a hen gathers her chicks under her wings, but you were unwilling. 38See, your house is left forsaken; 39for I tell you that you will no longer see Me at all until you say, 'Blessed is He who comes in the name of the Lord.'"

24 LEAVING THE TEMPLE, JESUS went on His way; and His disciples came forward to point out to Him the temple buildings. 2And He said to them, "Do you not see all these things? I assure you, not one stone will be left here on another, that will not be thrown down."

3When He was seated on the Mount of Olives, the disciples came to Him privately and said, "Tell us, when will these things happen and what will be the sign of Your coming and of the end of the age?"ᵃ 4Jesus replied to them,ᵇ "See that none misleads you; 5for many will come in My name, saying, 'I am the Christ,' and will mislead many.

6"You will be hearing of wars and rumors of wars; see that you be not troubled; for they have to come, but that is not yet the end. 7For nation will rise against nation and kingdom against kingdom, and there will be famines and earthquakes in various places; 8all these are but the early pains of childbirth. 9Then they will hand you over to be persecuted, and they will kill you, and you will be hated by all the nations on account of My name. 10Many then will fall away and will betray one another and hate one another; 11and many false prophets will arise and will deceive

---

w) Dill (or anise) and cummin are herbs that are native of the Near East. Their aromatic seeds are used in flavoring.
x) This was a warning that they were at the point of killing their Messiah, thus following the murderous spirit of their fathers.   y) Gen. 4:1-8.
z) II Chron. 24:20-22. Doubtless Jehoiada was Zechariah's grandfather, whereas Barachiah was his father.
a) There are two questions really: (1) concerning the destruction of the temple, v. 2; and (2) about the Lord's return at the end of the age. The former is answered clearly in the parallel passage in Lk. 21:20, 24, and the latter in this chapter, vss. 4-33.
b) Beginning with the events that culminated with the destruction of Jerusalem, Jesus goes right on to foretell circumstances leading up to His return in judgment.

many [12]and, due to excessive lawlessness[c] the love of many will grow cold. [13]But he who endures to the end will be saved. [14]And this good news of the kingdom will be preached all over the world to testify to all the nations, and then the end will come.

[15]"When you, therefore, see the desolating abomination mentioned by the Prophet Daniel,[d] set up in the holy place — let the reader take note of this — [16]then those in Judea should flee to the mountains; [17]one on the roof must not go down to fetch things out of his house, [18]and one in the field must not turn back to pick up his coat. [19]But alas for those who are pregnant and those who are nursing children in those days!

[20]"Pray that your flight may not be in winter or on a Sabbath; [21]for then there will be such great tribulation as has never been experienced from the world's beginning until now,[e] nor ever will be. [22]If those days were not shortened, not a mortal could survive. However, for the sake of the elect, those days will be shortened.

[23]"If someone then tells you, 'Look! here is the Christ!' or, 'There He is!' do not believe him; [24]for false Messiahs and false prophets will arise and show great signs and wonders to mislead, if possible, even the elect. [25]Remember that I have forewarned you. [26]So, if they say to you, 'He is there in the desert,' do not go out; 'In these rooms here,' do not believe it. [27]For like the lightning that flashes from the east and shines to the west, so will the coming of the Son of Man be.[f] [28]Wherever there is a corpse the vultures will flock there.

[29]"Right after the tribulation of those days the sun will be darkened and the moon will not shed her light; the stars will fall from the sky and the forces of heaven will be shaken. [30]Then will the sign of the Son of Man be shown in the sky, and all the tribes of earth will mourn.[g] And they will see the Son of Man coming on the clouds of heaven[h] with great power and glory. [31]And He will send out His angels with a loud trumpet call, and they will gather His chosen from the four winds, from one end of heaven to the other.

[32]"Learn a lesson from the fig tree. As soon as her branch becomes tender and puts out leaves, you know that summer is near. [33]When you observe all these things, you know that He is so near, that He is at the door. [34]I assure you, all these things will take place before this present generation passes on.[i] [35]Heaven and earth will pass away, but My words will never pass away. [36]But no one knows about that day and hour; neither the angels in heaven, nor the Son but only the Father.

[37]"As were the days of Noah,[j] so will the coming of the Son of Man be; [38]for as in those days before the flood people ate and drank, married and were given in marriage until the day when Noah entered the ark, [39]and did not understand until the deluge came and swept them all away, so will the coming of the Son of Man be. [40]Then there will be two men in the field — one will be taken and one left; [41]two women will be grinding at the mill — one will be taken and one left.

[42]"Keep watch, therefore, because you do not know on what day your Lord is coming. [43]But of this be sure, if the owner of the house had known in which hour of the night the thief was coming, he would have kept awake and would not have allowed his house to be broken into. [44]Therefore you also be ready; for the Son of Man is coming at an hour when you do not expect Him.

[45]"Who, then, is the faithful and prudent slave,[k] whom the master has

---

c) Cf. II Thess. 2:7; II Tim. 3:1-5.
d) Dan. 9:27; 11:31; 12:11. One temple desecration had already occurred under Antiochus Epiphanes in 167 B.C.; the temple was destroyed in A.D. 70 under Titus; and this verse points to a future desecration by Antichrist of a rebuilt temple, Dan. 9:26-27. e) Dan. 12:1.
f) Cf. Rev. 19:11-16. g) Zech. 12:10-14; cf. Rev. 18:11, 19.
h) A cloud carried Christ up into heaven at His ascension, Acts 1:9-11.
i) The destruction of Jerusalem is a figure of the world's destruction at the return of the Lord.
j) Gen. 6:1—7:24. k) See note at ch. 13:27.

appointed in charge of his household to provide their sustenance at the proper time? 46Happy is that servant whom his master finds doing so when he arrives. 47I assure you, he will put him in charge of all his property.

48"But if that servant is wicked and says to himself, 'My master is delaying his coming,' 49and he starts to strike his fellow workers, and eats and drinks with the drunkards, 50that slave's master will arrive on a day when he does not expect him and at an hour he does not know 51and will scourge him till his flesh is cut and will put him with the hypocrites; there will be wailing and grinding of teeth there.

25 "THEN THE KINGDOM OF HEAVEN will be comparable to ten bridesmaids,1 who, taking their lamps, went out to meet the bridegroom.m 2Five of them were foolish and five were prudent. 3The foolish ones took lamps but took no oil along with them, 4but the prudent ones took along oil in the flasks with their lamps. 5And as the bridegroom delayed his coming they all grew drowsy and fell asleep.

6"But at midnight there came a shout, 'Here is the bridegroom; go out to meet him!' 7Then all those bridesmaids got up and trimmed their lamps. 8And the foolish said to the prudent, 'Give us some of your oil, for our lamps are going out.' 9But the prudent answered, 'No, indeed; there would not be enough for you and us; go to the dealers and buy for yourselves.'

10"Now while they went off to buy, the bridegroom came, and those who were ready went in with him to the marriage feast. And the door was shut. 11Afterward the rest of the bridesmaids came and said, 'Master, master, open up for us!' 12But he replied, 'I tell you

truly, I do not know you.' 13So keep watch; for you know neither the day nor the hour [when the Son of Man is coming].n

14"For it will be like that of a man going away, who summoned his domestic servants and committed to them his belongings: 15To one he gave ten thousand dollars;o to another, four thousand; and to a third, two thousand — to each according to his own ability; then he went away. 16At once the one with the ten thousand dollars went and did business with them and gained another ten thousand; 17so did the one with four thousand dollars gain another four thousand. 18But the one with two thousand dollars went and dug in the earth and hid his master's money.

19"After a long time the master of those servants came back and settled accounts with them. 20The one who had ten thousand dollars came forward and brought ten thousand dollars more, saying, 'Master, you entrusted to me ten thousand dollars; look, I have gained these other ten thousand.' 21His master said to him, 'Well done, good and faithful servant, you were trustworthy in a little, I will appoint you over much. Share the happiness of your master.' 22Then the one with four thousand dollars came and said, 'Master, you handed me four thousand dollars; see, I have gained four thousand dollars more.' 23The master said to him, 'Well done, good and faithful servant; you were trustworthty in a little, I will appoint you over much. Share the happiness of your master.'

24"But the one who had received two thousand dollars also came forward and said, 'Master, knowing you, that you are a harsh man, reaping where you never sowed and gathering where you did not winnow, 25I was in fear;

---

1) The Greek word rendered "bridesmaids" here and in the verses that follow is *parthenois*, a plural form of a noun which means specifically *virgin*. It is the precise word which is used to describe Mary, the mother of Jesus, in ch. 1:23, "Behold, the virgin will be with child." Obviously the girls of this parable would be virgins. Because of the context a modern equivalent is employed here.   m) Some translations, notably the Vulgate and Syriac, read "the bridegroom and the bride." n) The words enclosed in brackets are not found in the majority of the most reliable ancient manuscripts.
o) In vss. 15-28 the direct translation from the Greek text reads "five talents [*pente talanta*]," "two talents" and "one talent," and in vs. 29 "ten talents." A silver talent would be equivalent to about $2000 in mid-twentieth century U.S. currency, so that the figures given in this edition are approximately accurate.

so I went and buried the two thousand dollars in the ground; here you have what is yours.' 26His Master replied to him, 'Despicable and lazy slave! You knew that I reap where I did not sow and gather where I did not winnow? 27Then you should have invested my money with the bankers, and on my return I would have gotten my capital with interest. 28So, take the two thousand dollars away from him and give it to the one with the twenty thousand dollars. 29For to everyone who has will be given, and he will have more than plenty; but from him who is wanting will be taken even what he has.p 30Throw the useless slave into the outside darkness; there will be weeping and grinding of teeth there.'

31"When the Son of Man comes in His glory,q and all the angels with Him, then He will be seated on the throne of His glory, 32and all nationsr will be gathered before Him. And He will separate them from one another as a shepherd parts the sheep from the goats; 33and He will place the sheep at His right and the goats at His left.

34"The King will then say to those at His right, 'Come, My Father's blessed ones, inherit the kingdom that has been prepared for you from the foundation of the world; 35for I was hungry and you gave Me food; I was thirsty and you gave Me drink; I was a stranger and you entertained Me; 36naked, and you clothed Me; sick, and you looked after Me; in prison, and you visited Me.'

37"Then the righteous will answer Him, 'Lord, when did we see You hungry and nourished You, or thirsty and provided You drink? 38When did we see You a stranger and entertained You, or naked and provided You with clothing? 39When did we see You ill or in prison and visited You?' 40And the King will answer, 'I assure you, insofar as you did it to one of the least of these brothers of Mine, you did it to Me.'

41"Then will He say to those at His left, 'Begone from Me, accursed ones, to the everlasting fire prepared for the devil and his angels; 42for I was hungry and you did not feed Me; thirsty and you gave Me no drink; 43I was a stranger and you did not entertain Me; naked and you failed to clothe Me; ill and in prison and you did not come to see Me.' 44Then will they too answer, 'Lord, when did we see You hungry or thirsty or a stranger or naked or ill or in prison and did not serve You?' 45Then He will answer them, 'I assure you, insofar as you failed to do it to one of the least of these, you failed to do it to Me.' 46And they will go away into eternal punishment, but the righteous into eternal life."

26 WHEN JESUS HAD FINISHED ALL these words, He said to His disciples, 2"You know that after two days the Passover will be celebrated and the Son of Man will be handed over to be crucified." 3Then the chief priests and the elders of the people met at the palace of the high priest, Caiaphas by name, 4and plotted to arrest Jesus underhandedly and to kill Him. 5But they said, "Not during the Feast, else there might be a riot among the people."

6While Jesus was at Bethany in the house of Simon, the leper, 7a womans approached Him with an alabaster flask of very precious perfume and poured it on His head as He was seatedt at the table. 8Observing it, the disciples said indignantly, "Why this waste? 9This could have been sold at a good price and given to the poor." 10When Jesus heard it He said to them, "Why do you embarrass the woman? She has done something lovely for Me; 11for you always have the poor with you, but Me you do not have always. 12By pouring this perfume on My body she has prepared for My burial. 13I assure you that wherever this gospel is preached throughout the world, this

---

p) A basic spiritual principle — i.e., that those who have received most from God are held most responsible to Him.   q) Rev. 19:11-16.
r) This does not refer to nations in totality but to individuals among the Gentile nations. Each person who stands before the Lord on this occasion will be classed either as a sheep or a goat.
s) This was Mary, the sister of Martha and Lazarus, Jn. 12:3.   t) See note at Mk. 2:15.

that she has done will be mentioned to her memory."

¹⁴Then one of the Twelve, called Judas Iscariot, went to the chief priests ¹⁵and said, "What are you willing to give me and I will hand Him over to you?" And they offered him thirty pieces of silver.ᵘ ¹⁶From then on he watched for an opportunity to betray Him.

¹⁷On the first day of unleavened bread the disciples approached Jesus and said, "Where do You want us to prepare for You to eat the Passover?" ¹⁸He said, "Go into the city to so-and-so and tell him, 'The Teacher says, My time is near; I shall observe the Passover with My disciples at your house.'" ¹⁹So the disciples did as Jesus directed them and prepared the Passover.

²⁰As evening was falling, He sat at the table with the twelve disciples ²¹and, while they were eating, He said, "I tell you truly that one of you will betray Me." ²²Greatly distressed, they began to say to Him one after the other, "Surely it is not I, Lord?" ²³But He replied, "He who has dipped his hand with Me in the dish, he will betray Me. ²⁴The Son of Man will indeed go away as has been written of Him, but alas for that man by whom the Son of Man is betrayed. Better for that man had he never been born!" ²⁵Judas, who betrayed Him, said, "Surely it is not I, Rabbi?"ᵛ He said to him, "You have said it."

²⁶As they were eating, Jesus took bread, gave thanks, and broke it and gave it to the disciples, saying, "Take, eat,ʷ this is My body." ²⁷He also took the cup and, after giving thanks, gave it to them, saying, "All of you drink of it; ²⁸for this is My blood of the new covenant poured out for many for the forgiveness of sins. ²⁹I tell you, from now on I shall not drink of the product of the vine at all until that

day when I shall drink it new with you in My Father's kingdom."

³⁰When they had sung a hymn they went out to the Mount of Olives. ³¹Then Jesus said to them, "Tonight you will all desert Me; for it is written,ˣ 'I shall strike the shepherd and the sheep of the flock will be scattered.' ³²But after I am raised up I will precede you to Galilee."

³³Peter answered Him, "Though all the rest desert You, I will never desert You." ³⁴Jesus said to him, "I assure you, this night before a rooster crows, you will deny Me three times." ³⁵Peter said to Him, "Even if I must die with You, never will I deny You." And all the disciples spoke the same way.

³⁶Then Jesus came with them to a place called Gethsemane,ʸ and told the disciples, "Sit down here, while I go yonder and pray." ³⁷Taking along Peter and the two sons of Zebedee,ᶻ He began to feel grieved and deeply distressed. ³⁸Then He said to them, "My soul is mortally grieved; stay here and keep watch with Me." ³⁹And, moving forward a little, He fell on His face, praying, "My Father, if it be possible, let this cup pass from Me; however, not as I will but as Thou wilt."

⁴⁰When He came to the disciples, He found them fast asleep and said to Peter, "So you were not able to watch with Me for a single hour? ⁴¹Watch and pray, so that you may not fall into temptation; the spirit is willing, but the flesh is weak."

⁴²For a second time He went away and prayed, "My Father, if it cannot pass from Me without My drinking it, Thy will be done." ⁴³When He came back, again He found them asleep, for their eyes were heavy. So ⁴⁴He left them once more and went away the third time speaking the same words. ⁴⁵Then He came to the disciples and said to them, "Are you still sleeping

---

u) These pieces of silver were probably silver shekels equal, in mid-twentieth century U.S. currency, to a little more than one dollar per shekel. Judas' price for betraying Christ was from thirty to thirty-five dollars.
v) "Rabbi," a courteous title of address meaning *master, lord.* Judas apparently left after Jesus answered his question and did not share in the institution of the Lord's Supper.
w) *Cf.* I Cor. 11:23-29.
x) Zech. 13:7.
y) "Gethsemane" means *oil press.* It is situated east of Jerusalem on a slope of the Mount of Olives and across a brook called Kidron.   z) James and John, ch. 4:21.

and taking your rest? The hour has come, and the Son of Man is betrayed into the hands of sinners.[a] 46Arise, let us be going. Look, My betrayer is at hand."

47He was still speaking when Judas, one of the Twelve, came and with him a large mob from the chief priests and elders of the people, carrying swords and clubs. 48Now His betrayer had given them a signal, "Whom I kiss, He is the man. Seize Him." 49At once he went up to Jesus and said, "Greetings, Rabbi," and kissed Him. 50But Jesus said to him, "Friend, for what are you here?" Then they came forward, put their hands on Jesus, and arrested Him.

51One of Jesus' companions[b] put out his hand, drew his sword and, striking the high priest's slave, cut off his ear. 52Jesus then spoke to him, "Return your sword to its place, for all who draw the sword shall be destroyed by the sword. 53Or do you suppose I cannot appeal to My Father and at once He would provide Me with more than twelve legions[c] of angels? 54How, then, will the Scriptures be fulfilled that it must happen this way?"

55At the same time Jesus said to the crowds, "Have you come as against a robber, with swords and clubs to arrest Me? Daily I have sat in the temple teaching, and you never seized Me. 56But all this has occurred, so that the writings of the prophets may be fulfilled." Then all the disciples deserted Him and fled.

57Those who had arrested Jesus led Him away to Caiaphas, the high priest, where the scribes and the elders had gathered together. 58But Peter[d] followed Him from a distance as far as the high priest's courtyard and, stepping inside, sat down with the attendants to see the end. 59Now the chief priests and the entire Sanhedrin[e] looked for false testimony against Jesus,[f] in order that they might exe-cute Him; 60but although many false witnesses came forward, they found nothing. Finally two came forward, 61who said, "This fellow said, 'I have power to destroy God's temple and to build it again in three days.'"

62So the high priest stood up and said to Him, "Have You nothing to say? What about their evidence against You?" 63But Jesus was silent.[g] The high priest said to Him, "I charge You on oath by the living God that You tell us whether You are the Christ, the Son of God." 64Jesus said to him, "As you say. Besides, I tell you that short-ly you will see the Son of Man seated at the right hand of the Almighty and coming upon the clouds of heaven."

65Then the high priest tore his clothes, saying, "He has blasphemed! What further need do we have of wit-nesses? You have now heard His blas-phemy. 66What do you think?" They answered, "He deserves death!" 67Then they spat in His face[h] and struck Him with the fist.[i] Others slapped Him[j] 68saying, "Prophesy to us, Christ! Who struck You?"

69Now Peter was sitting outside in the courtyard and one slave girl came up to him, saying, "And you were with Jesus the Galilean." 70But before them all he made denial, "I do not know what you mean!" 71As he was going out into the entrance of the courtyard, another girl noticed him and said to those who were there, "This fellow was with Jesus the Nazarene." 72Again he denied it with an oath, "I do not know the man!" 73A little later the bystand-ers came up and said to Peter, "You certainly are one of them too, for your accent reveals it." 74Then he started to curse and to swear, "I do not know the man!" Then a rooster crowed. 75And Peter recollected the word that Jesus had spoken, "Before a rooster crows you will deny Me three times." And going outside he cried bitterly.[k]

---

a) This may mean the approaching crowd, v. 47, but it also refers to the Romans to whom He would be delivered, ch. 20:19.　b) Simon Peter, Jn. 18:10.
c) A Roman legion was composed of 5000 to 6000 men.　d) John followed also, Jn. 18:15-16.
e) See note at Lk. 22:66.　f) Cf. Ps. 35:11.
g) Isa. 53:7. See also Matt. 27:14.　h) Isa. 50:6; Zech. 13:7.　i) Cf. Isa. 52:14.　j) Cf. Mic. 5:1.
k) See note at Lk. 22:62.

27 AT DAWN ALL THE CHIEF priests and the elders of the people held consultation against Jesus in order to execute Him. [2]Having bound Him, they led Him away and handed Him over to Pilate, the governor.

[3]When Judas, His betrayer, saw that He was condemned, he felt remorse and returned the thirty pieces of silver to the chief priests and elders, [4]saying, "I sinned in betraying innocent blood." But they said, "What is that to us? You see to that yourself." [5]He then flung down the silver pieces in the temple, withdrew and, going off, hanged himself. [6]The chief priests picked up the money and said, "It is not right to put this in the treasury, since it is blood money." [7]So, after conferring, they bought with it the Potter's Field as a cemetery for strangers; [8]therefore that field is called to this day, "The Field of Blood." [9]Then the saying of Jeremiah the prophet was fulfilled,[1] "And I took the thirty pieces of silver, the price of the man on whom a price was set, whom Israel's sons had evaluated, [10]and gave them for the potter's field as the Lord directed me."

[11]But Jesus stood before the governor, and the governor questioned Him, "Are You the King of the Jews?" Jesus replied, "As you say." [12]And to the accusations of the chief priests and the elders against Him He made no reply. [13]Then Pilate said to Him, "Do You not hear how much they testify against You?" [14]But to the governor's great surprise He answered him never a word.

[15]Now it was customary for the governor to release at the feast one prisoner selected by the populace. [16]And at that time they held a notorious convict called Barabbas.[m] [17]So when they had assembled, Pilate said to them, "Whom do you want released to you, Barabbas or Jesus, who is called

Christ? [18]For he knew that they[n] had delivered Him out of envy.

[19]While he was seated on the tribunal, his wife sent him a message that said, "Have nothing to do with that innocent man, for I suffered a great deal today in a dream because of Him." [20]But the chief priests and elders persuaded the masses to ask for Barabbas and to have Jesus destroyed. [21]The governor answered them, "Which of the two shall I release to you?" They said, "Barabbas!" [22]Pilate asked them, "Then what shall I do with Jesus, who is called Christ?" They all said, "Let Him be crucified!" [23]Pilate said, "Why, what wrong has He done?" But they shouted all the more loudly, "Let Him be crucified!"

[24]When Pilate saw that he was accomplishing nothing but that instead a riot was brewing, he took water and washed his hands[o] before the crowd, saying, "I am innocent of the blood of this man; you yourselves see to it." [25]And all the people answered, "His blood be on us and our children." [26]He then released Barabbas to them; but Jesus he flogged and handed over to be crucified.

[27]Then the governor's soldiers took Jesus along into the palace and gathered the whole cohort[p] around Him. [28]They stripped Him and put a scarlet robe on Him; [29]they plaited a crown of thorns and placed it on His head, also a reed in His hand, and, kneeling before Him, they ridiculed Him, "Long live the King of the Jews!" [30]They spat on Him; they took the reed and struck Him on the head; [31]and after they had mocked Him, they took off the robe and put on His own clothes. Then they led Him away to be crucified.

[32]On the way out they found a Cyrenian called Simon,[q] whom they forced to carry His cross. [33]Arriving at a place called Golgotha, which means

l) Although the citation is attributed to Jeremiah, the reference is certainly to Zech. 11:12-13. In Jer. 18:1-4 and 19:1-3 allusion is made to a potter, but no prediction concerning a potter's field for burial is found there. Doubtless "Jeremiah" in vs. 9 is due to a copyist's error. To discover how low a value Judas placed upon Jesus, see Ex. 21:32, note. m) "Barabbas" means *son of the father*. n) "They" means the leaders and not the crowd; for it was to the leaders of the people that Pilate appealed.
o) It was customary in ancient times to wash one's hands before an audience when absolving oneself from guilt, Deut. 21:6-7. p) See note at Acts 10:1.
q) A Jew from North Africa, near Tripoli. His sons were Alexander and Rufus, Mk. 15:21. One of them may have become a Christian, *cf.* Rom. 16:13.

"Place of a Skull," [34]they gave Him wine to drink mixed with gall;[r] but after tasting it He would not drink it.

[35]And when they had crucified Him, they distributed His clothes among them by casting lots [so that the prophet's saying was fulfilled,[s] "They parted My garments among them, and over My vesture they cast lots"].[t] [36]And, sitting down, they watched Him there. [37]Over His head they placed the written charge against Him, THIS IS JESUS, THE KING OF THE JEWS.

[38]Then robbers were crucified along with Him, one to the right and one to the left.[u] [39]And those walking by insulted Him, wagging their heads and saying, [40]"You destroyer and reconstructor of the temple in three days, save Yourself if You are the Son of God, and come down from the cross!" [41]Similarly, the chief priests with the scribes and the elders scoffed at Him, [42]"He saved others but He cannot save Himself. Is He King of Israel? Let Him now come down from the cross and we will believe in Him. [43]He trusts in God? Let Him rescue Him now, if He wants Him; for He said, 'I am the Son of God.'" [44]The robbers, too, who were crucified with Him, leveled the same reproach at Him.

[45]From twelve o'clock, until three darkness lay on all the land; [46]and at about three o'clock Jesus cried out with a loud voice,[v] "Eli, Eli, lama sabachthani?" that is, "My God, My God, why hast Thou forsaken Me?"

[47]Some of the bystanders who heard it, said, "He is calling for Elijah." [48]And at once one of them ran, took a sponge, dipped it in vinegar and, putting it on a reed, offered it to Him to drink. [49]But the others said, "Hold on! Let us see if Elijah comes to save Him."

[50]Jesus, once more crying with a loud voice, dismissed His spirit. [51]And the veil of the temple was torn in two from top to bottom; the earth shook; the rocks were split; [52]the tombs were opened and many bodies of the buried saints were raised [53]and after His resurrection they left their tombs, entered the holy city and appeared to many.

[54]When the centurion and his men, who were watching Jesus, observed the earthquake and everything that happened, they were dreadfully frightened and said, "Truly, this was God's Son!" [55]There were also numerous women observing from a distance, those who had followed Jesus from Galilee rendering Him service, [56]including Mary Magdalene, and Mary the mother of James and Joses, and the mother of Zebedee's sons.

[57]With the coming of evening there came a rich man from Arimathea,[w] called Joseph, who was himself a disciple of Jesus. [58]He went to Pilate and requested the body of Jesus. Then Pilate gave orders to have it relinquished. [59]When Joseph had obtained the body, he wrapped it in clean linen [60]and laid it in his own new tomb,[x] which he had hewn out in the rock. Then, rolling a large stone in front of the opening of the tomb, he went away. [61]But Mary Magdalene was there and the other Mary[y] sitting opposite the tomb.

[62]The next day, that is the day after the preparation, the chief priests and the Pharisees gathered before Pilate [63]and said, "We remember, Sir, that this imposter said,[z] while He was still alive, 'After three days I will rise.' [64]Give orders, therefore, to have the tomb safeguarded until the third day, so His disciples may not come and steal Him and then tell the people, 'He is risen from the dead,' and the final fraud will be worse than the first." [65]Pilate said to them, "The guard is yours; go on and make it as secure as you can." [66]So they went and safeguarded the tomb, sealing the stone and setting a guard.

---

r) Ps. 69:21. s) Ps. 22:18.
t) The words enclosed in brackets are not found in the majority of the most reliable ancient manuscripts. u) Isa. 53:12. v) Ps. 22:1.
w) Arimathea was about twenty miles northwest of Jerusalem. In the O.T. the city is designated as Ramathain-Zophim or Ramah. x) Isa. 53:9. y) See note at ch. 1:16.
z) Chapters 16:21; 17:22-23; 20:17-19; *cf.* Jn. 2:19-22.

28 AFTER THE CLOSE OF THE SAB-bath, with the dawning of the first day of the week, came Mary Magdalene and the other Mary to look at the tomb. ²And a severe earthquake occurred; for an angel of the Lord came down from heaven and, approaching the stone, rolled it aside and sat on it. ³His appearance was like lightning and his clothing white as snow. ⁴The sentries shook for fear of him and became like corpses. ⁵But the angel said to the women, "Have no fear! I know you are looking for Jesus, who was crucified. ⁶He is not here; for He is risen just as He said. Come, see the place where He lay. ⁷And go, hasten to tell His disciples that He is risen from the dead and is preceding you into Galilee; there you will see Him. See, I have told you."

⁸Hastily they left the tomb, in fear and with great joy, and ran to tell the news to His disciples. ⁹And behold, Jesus met them, saying, "Rejoice!" Going up to Him they clasped His feet and knelt before Him. ¹⁰Jesus then said to them, "Have no fear. Go, tell My brothers to go to Galilee; and they shall see Me there."

¹¹While they were on their way some of the guard entered the city and reported to the chief priests everything that had occurred. ¹²They, deliberating in session with the elders, gave the soldiers considerable money, ¹³telling them, "Say 'His disciples came by night and stole Him while we were asleep.' ¹⁴And if this reaches the governor's ears, we will win him over and keep you out of trouble." ¹⁵So the guards accepted the money and did as they were instructed, and this story has been current among the Jews until the present day.

¹⁶But the eleven disciples went away to Galilee,ᵃ to the mountain to which Jesus had directed them. ¹⁷And when they saw Him they worshiped Him, but some were in doubt. ¹⁸Jesus came to them and He said, "All authority in heaven and on earth has been given Me. ¹⁹Go, therefore, and make disciples of all the nations, baptizing them in the name of the Father, and of the Son, and of the Holy Spirit, ²⁰teaching them to observe everything that I have commanded you. And, remember, I am with you all the days until the end of the age."ᵇ

---

a) Verses 7, 10; ch. 26:32.
b) The word "age" is from the Greek noun *aion* which means (1) *a lifetime,* the period of an individual's existence on earth; (2) *a segment of time,* such as the present age or the age to come; (3) *a very long time,* as the age of mankind; (4) *perpetuity of time,* eternity (especially in the plural); and (5) occasionally *the world, the universe.* Concepts (1), (2) and (4) all fit the context of Christ's promise.

THEME OF MATTHEW:

SEGMENT DIVISIONS

			CHAPTER THEMES
		1	
		2	
		3	
		4	
		5	
		6	
		7	
		8	
		9	
		10	
		11	
		12	
		13	
		14	
		15	
		16	
		17	
		18	
		19	
		20	
		21	
		22	
		23	
		24	
		25	
		26	
		27	
		28	

Author:

Date:

Purpose:

Key Words:

king
(kingdom,
kingdom of
heaven,
kingdom
of God)

fulfilled
(fulfillment,
accomplished)

mark every
reference to
the devil or
demons

covenant

$\mathcal{M}$ARK

$\mathcal{J}$esus was clearly born to be King of the Jews, as Matthew points out. However, the gospel was not just for the Jews; it was for the whole world. Before Jesus would reign as King of kings, He would be servant of all by dying for mankind. Mark tells of the works and authority of the One who came not to be served but to serve and to give His life as a ransom for many.

THINGS TO DO

Mark is a fast-paced Gospel which emphasizes the works of Jesus rather than the teachings of Jesus. Although Jesus is referred to as a teacher a number of times, Mark shows Jesus' power and authority through the works He does as He goes about His Father's business.

In reading this Gospel you will notice the repeated use of the word *immediately* (*without delay, at once, directly,* etc.) as Mark takes his reader from one event in the life of Jesus to another. These events and the works of Jesus show the reader Jesus' power and authority as the servant of God and man.

Chapters 1–13

Read through all of the instructions below before you begin working on chapters 1-13.

1. Although the emphasis in the Gospel of Mark is on the works of Jesus that show His divine power, Mark opens his Gospel by declaring the deity of Jesus Christ. He also gives an account of the events that took place prior to and in preparation for Jesus' ministry.

Read Mark 1:1-13 and list in the margin of the text the following:
   a. The facts that declare the deity of Jesus Christ.
   b. The events that took place in Jesus' life prior to His public ministry.
2. Now read Mark chapter by chapter, and in a distinctive way mark in the text the key words listed on the MARK AT A GLANCE chart following the Gospel of Mark.
   a. Record these key words on an index card and use it as a bookmark while you study this Gospel.
   b. Also underline in the text each geographical location, whether it is a city, a region, or a place such as the temple or the synagogue. Noting these will help in your overall understanding of these events in Jesus' life.
3. Chapters 1–3 cover events (including healings and miracles) that demonstrate Jesus' authority.
   a. As you look at each event, observe how it demonstrates Jesus' authority, how the people respond, and what Jesus has authority over.
   b. Record your insights in the margin by listing the event, then under that event noting how the people, religious leaders, disciples, and others responded. For example:

   Healing on Sabbath
   Pharisees counsel to destroy Him

   c. After you have recorded these demonstrations and responses, be sure to record the scope of Jesus' authority. For example, next to the illustration above, you might write, "Authority over Sabbath." Watch for Jesus' power over nature, demons, disease, and so on. Ask God to show you how this demonstration of Jesus' power declares His deity. Also, notice how these events portray Jesus as a servant.

d. Throughout these chapters, Jesus faces the accusations and rejection of the Jewish religious leaders of His day. Each time the scribes, Pharisees, or Sadducees accuse Jesus, He reasons with them. Note that conflict in the margin.

4. Also list in the margin the main points of Jesus' teachings, whether the teaching comes as a result of healing, casting out demons, working a miracle, or responding to a question from either the disciples or the multitude. Also note the response of those who hear the teaching.

5. Look at every reference you marked to the kingdom of God and do the following:

a. Note in the margin when Jesus increases His emphasis on the kingdom of God.

b. Underline every prediction of Jesus' death and resurrection and note how it coincides with Jesus' emphasis on the kingdom of God.

c. Observe that in the first part of Mark, Jesus defines the kingdom of God, then at chapter 9 the emphasis shifts to how to enter the kingdom.

d. Compile the *main* teachings from Mark about the kingdom of God on the chart titled WHAT THE GOSPELS TEACH ABOUT THE KINGDOM OF GOD/THE KINGDOM OF HEAVEN following the Gospel of John. It would be good

to do this on notebook paper first and then consolidate your insights and transfer them to the chart. Note the chapter and verse beside each insight for future reference.

6. After you finish reading and marking each chapter, record the theme of that chapter on MARK AT A GLANCE. Also record it in the text in the space just above the chapter number.

Chapters 14–16

1. When you read Mark's account of the trial, death, burial, and resurrection of Jesus Christ, record the progression of events on the appropriate charts: THE ARREST, TRIAL, AND CRUCIFIXION OF JESUS CHRIST and THE ACCOUNT OF JESUS' RESURRECTION (both of these charts are after the Gospel of John). Once again, do this on notebook paper before transferring the information to the chart and note the chapter and verse beside each insight.

a. When you record the circumstances surrounding the resurrection of Jesus Christ, also note any postresurrection appearances recorded in Mark. After you do this for all four Gospels you will have comprehensive notes on everything that took place at this time in our Lord's life.

b. As you do this, remember that because Luke gives the consecutive order of events, it is a plumb line for the other Gospel records.

2. Complete MARK AT A GLANCE. Fill in any segment divisions you have seen from studying the book.

THINGS TO THINK ABOUT

1. People often say that Mark shows the servant aspect of Jesus' ministry. Although the word *servant* is used only a few times, Mark 10:45 says that

Jesus "did not come to be served but to serve and to give His life a ransom for many." How like your Lord are you in that respect? Would others regard you as a servant? Or do they see you as having to be "number one"? What is it to be "number one" in God's eyes?

2. Jesus talks about discipleship in this Gospel. According to Jesus, what is required of disciples? Can you consider yourself a true disciple of Jesus Christ? Why? Think about Mark 8:34–36 and 10:28–31.
3. Can you say with Peter, "You are the Christ"? And will you listen to Jesus as the Father commands?

Jerusalem of the New Testament

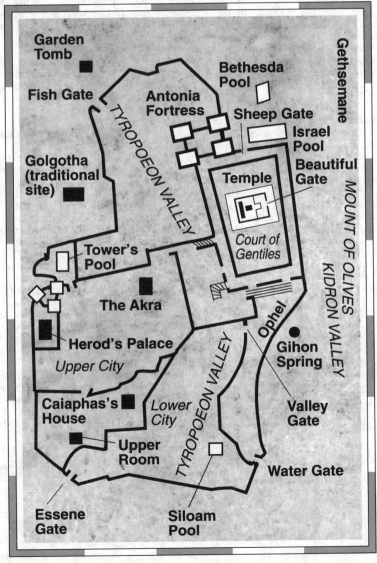

THE GOSPEL ACCORDING TO

MARK

1 THE BEGINNING OF THE GOOD news of Jesus Christ, the Son of God; [2]as it is written[a] in the Prophet Isaiah, "Behold, I send My messenger ahead of You, who shall prepare Your way; [3]a voice of one shouting in the desert, 'Make the Lord's way ready; make straight His paths!' "

c. A.D. 26

[4]John the Baptist appeared in the desert, preaching a baptism of repentance for the forgiveness of sins, [5]and all Judea and all the people of Jerusalem came out to him and were baptized by him in the Jordan River upon confessing their sins.

[6]John was dressed in clothing made of camel's hair, with a leather belt around his waist, and he ate locusts and wild honey. [7]He proclaimed, "After me comes One greater than I, the strings of whose sandals I am not worthy to stoop down and untie. [8]I have baptized you with water, but He will baptize you with the Holy Spirit."

c. A.D. 27

[9]In those days Jesus came from Nazareth[b] in Galilee and was baptized by John in the Jordan. [10]And the moment He came up from the water He saw the heavens parted and the Spirit, like a dove, coming down upon Him. [11]There also came a voice from heaven, "Thou art My Son, My Beloved; in Thee I am delighted."

[12]Without delay the Spirit drove Him into the desert [13]where He remained forty days, being tempted by Satan. He was with the wild beasts, and the angels waited on Him.

c. A.D. 28

[14]After John had been arrested Jesus went to Galilee, preaching the good news from God, [15]saying, "The time is completed and the kingdom of God is near; repent and believe in the good news."

[16]As he was passing along the Sea of Galilee He noticed Simon and his brother Andrew casting a net into the sea, for they were fisherman. [17]Jesus said[c] to them, "Come after Me and I will make you become fishers of men." [18]At once they left their nets and followed Him. [19]Going on a little, He saw James, the son of Zebedee, and his brother John, who were in their boat, mending the nets. [20]At once He called them and, leaving their father Zebedee in the boat with the hired hands, they went off after Him.

[21]They entered Capernaum[d] and the next Sabbath day He went to the synagogue and taught. [22]They marveled at His teaching, for He taught them as one who had authority and not as the scribes.[e]

[23]There was in their synagogue just then a man with an unclean spirit, who cried out, [24]"What business is it of Yours to bother us, Jesus You Nazarene? Have You come to destroy us? I know who You are, the Holy One of

---

a) Isa. 40:3; *cf.* Mal. 3:1.   b) See note at Matt. 2:23.
c) This was the second and permanent call, *cf.* John 1:35-51. Peter, Andrew, James, John and Nathanael (Bartholomew) may have helped Jesus on occasions prior to this.
d) See note at Matt. 4:13.   e) See note at Matt. 2:4.

God." 25Jesus rebuked him: "Silence! Get out of him!" 26The unclean spirit, throwing him into a spasm, cried out with a loud voice and came out of him. 27They were all amazed, so that they inquired among themselves, "What does this mean? A new teaching? With authority He orders even the unclean spirits and they obey Him!" 28And rapidly His fame spread in every direction through that whole Galilee region.

29Directly, from the synagogue they went with James and John to the house of Simon and Andrew; 30but Simon's mother-in-law was in bed with fever and at once they told Him about her. 31He went to help her, took her by the hand and helped her rise. The fever left her and she began to wait on them.

32In the evening at sunset they brought to Him all the sick and the demon-possessed 33until the whole city was gathered at the door. 34He cured many who were ill with various diseases and cast out many demons; but since the demons knew Him, He did not permit them to speak.

35Rising early in the morning long before daylight, He left and went out to a lonely spot and prayed there. 36Simon and his companions searched for Him, 37found Him and told Him, "They are all looking for You." 38He said to them, "Let us go elsewhere into the adjoining towns so that I may preach there too, because for this purpose I came." 39And He went preaching in their synagogues and casting out demons through all Galilee.

40A leper came to Him, begging of Him on his knees, "If you are willing, You can cleanse me." 41Deeply sympathetic, He reached out His hand and touched him, and said to him, "I am willing. Be cleansed." 42Immediately the leprosy left him and he was cleansed. 43Then and there He sent him off with the stern injunction, 44"Be careful to tell no one, but go and show yourself to the priest and offer what Moses has prescribed[f] for your purification, as a testimony to the people." 45But he went off and began to publish it so much and to spread the report so widely that Jesus could no longer enter a town openly, but stayed outside in lonely places. And from everywhere people came to Him.

2 SOME DAYS LATER HE RETURNED to Capernaum, and it was learned that He was at home. 2So many congregated that shortly there was no longer any room even at the door. He was preaching the word to them 3when they came and brought a paralytic to Him, carried by four men. 4And, being unable to get near Him on account of the crowd, they removed the roof above Him and through the opening lowered the couch on which the paralytic was lying.

5Observing their faith, Jesus said to the paralytic, "Son, your sins are forgiven you." 6But some of the scribes were sitting there with questions in their hearts, 7"Why does He talk this way? It is blasphemy. Who but God alone can forgive sins?" 8Perceiving at once in His spirit that they were reasoning that way to themselves, Jesus said to them, "Why do you question this way in your hearts? 9Which is easier, to tell the paralytic, 'Your sins are forgiven,' or to say, 'Rise, pick up your couch and walk off'? 10But to let you know that the Son of Man has authority to forgive sins on the earth," He said to the paralytic, 11"I tell you, rise, pick up your mat and go home." 12At once he arose, picked up his couch and went out in the presence of everyone, so that they were all amazed and glorified God, saying, "We have never seen anything like it before!" 13Then He went out again by the seaside, where the whole crowd came to Him, and He taught them.

14As He walked along He noticed Levi,[g] the son of Alpheus, sitting at the

---

f) Cf. Lev. 14:2-32. Under the Mosaic Law the priest performed some of the functions of a physician. Jesus, our great high priest before God, Heb. 4:14, is the great physician.
g) Levi is another name for Matthew. This is evident after comparing vss. 14-17 with the parallel passage at Matt. 9:9-13. No explanation is given in the N.T. as to why this man has two names, which was not uncommon among the Jews of that period, e.g., see note at ch. 2:25. Some suppose that like Simon, whom the Lord named Peter, and Saul, who later became Paul, Levi received the name Matthew after he became a Christian. He is always called Matthew in the lists of the apostles.

tax office, and said to him, "Follow Me." He arose and followed Him. [15]And so it was, as He sat[h] at the table at his house, that along with Jesus and His disciples, many tax collectors and sinners were seated there also; for many such were His followers. [16]The scribes, who were of the Pharisees,[i] who observed that He dined with sinners and tax collectors remarked to His disciples, "Why does He eat with tax collectors and sinners?" [17]On hearing it Jesus told them, "Not the well but the sick have need of a physician. I did not come to call the righteous but sinners."

[18]John's disciples and the Pharisees were observing a fast; so they[j] came and said to Him, "Why do John's disciples and the disciples of the Pharisees fast, but Your disciples do not fast?" [19]Jesus replied to them, "Can the wedding guests fast while the bridegroom is in their company? So long as the bridegroom is with them they cannot fast, [20]but a time will come when the bridegroom[k] will be taken from them, and then will be their day to fast. [21]No one sews a patch of unshrunken cloth on an old coat, for the new piece would tear away from the old and the tear become worse. [22]Neither does one pour new wine into old wineskins, for the wine would burst the skins, with both wine and skins ruined. But new wine goes into new skins."

[23]He happened on the Sabbath to pass through a wheat field and His disciples started to pick the heads of wheat. [24]The Pharisees said to Him, "See how they are doing what is not allowed on the Sabbath!" [25]He replied, "Have you never read[l] what David and his men did when they were hungry? [26]How in the days of Abiathar, the high priest, he went in-

to the house of God and ate the presentation loaves,[m] which none but the priests are allowed to eat, and shared with His companions?" [27]He said further to them, "The Sabbath was made for man's sake, not man for the Sabbath, [28]so that the Son of Man is Lord also of the Sabbath."

3 AGAIN HE ENTERED THE SYNA-gogue, and a man with a withered hand was there. [2]They watched Him, whether He would heal him on the Sabbath, so that they might accuse Him. [3]He told the man with the withered hand, "Stand there in the center." [4]Then He asked them, "Is it right to help or to hurt on the Sabbath; to save a life or to kill?" But they kept still. [5]Looking around at them angrily because He was vexed at their callousness of heart, He said to the man, "Hold out your hand." He held it out and his hand was restored. [6]And at once the Pharisees went out and plotted against Him with the Herodians[n] for the purpose of destroying Him.

[7]With His disciples Jesus retired to the seaside and a great many followed Him from Galilee and from Judea, [8]from Jerusalem, from Idumea, from beyond the Jordan, and from around Tyre and Sidon — a large number came to Him when they heard what He had done. [9]He told His disciples to have a little boat ready for Him, so that the throng might not press upon Him; [10]for He healed many, so that all who had ailments closed in on Him to touch Him. [11]And whenever the unclean spirits saw Him they fell down before Him, screaming, "You are the Son of God!" [12]But He charged them strictly not to make Him known.

[13]Then He went up the hill, summoned those whom He wanted, and

---

h) In N.T. times dining custom was different from what it now is. One did not sit down at a table to eat but reclined on a couch beside a table. While leaning on one elbow he used the other hand for eating. To accord with present-day usage the Greek words for "recline," "reclining" and "reclined" are rendered "sit," "sitting," "sat" and "seated" in this translation.
i) See note at Matt. 3:7.   j) "They" are the disciples of John the Baptist, Matt. 9:14.
k) Christ is pictured in the N.T. as the Bridegroom and His Church as His bride, *cf.* Eph. 5:25, 26; Rev. 19:7-9. In the same way the O.T. alludes to Jehovah as the Husband and Israel His wife, *cf.* Isa. 54:5; Jer. 31:32; Hos. 2: 16-23.
l) I Sam. 21:1-6. Abiathar is called Ahimelech in I Sam. 21:1; 22:9, 11, 20 and Ahiah in I Sam. 14:3, in accord with Hebrew practice of occasionally giving more than one name to an individual.
m) This was the showbread, Exod. 25:30.   n) See note at Matt. 22:16.

they came to Him. 14He appointed twelve to be with Him, that He might send them out to preach 15with power to [heal the sick and to]° expel demons. He appointed these twelve: 16Simon whom He called Peter; 17James, the son of Zebedee and John, the brother of James, whom He called Boanerges — that is Sons of Thunder; 18Andrew and Philip; Bartholomew and Matthew; Thomas and James, the son of Alpheus;ᵖ Thaddeus and Simon of Cana; 19and Judas Iscariot, who also betrayed Him.

20They entered a house, and again the crowd collected so that they could not even have a meal. 21When His relatives learned of it, they came out to seize Him, for they said, "He is deranged." 22But the scribes who had come down from Jerusalem said, "He has Beelzebul�q and through the ruler of demons He expels demons." 23So He called them to Him and said to them in parables, "How can Satan expel Satan? 24If a kingdom is divided against itself, that kingdom cannot last, 25and if a household is divided against itself, that household cannot last, 26and if Satan rebels against himself, he cannot stand but is about to come to an end. 27But no one can enter a strong man's house and plunder his property unless he first binds the strong man and then will loot his place.

28"I assure you that all the sins that the sons of men commit and all the blasphemies that they utter are pardonable, 29but whoever blasphemes against the Holy Spirit will have no forgiveness forever but is guilty of an eternal sin" — 30because they said, "He has an unclean spirit."

31His mother and His brothers came and, standing outside, sent messengers to call Him. 32A crowd was sitting around Him and they told Him, "Your mother and Your brothers are outside asking for You." 33He answered them, "Who are My mother and My brothers?" 34Looking at those sitting around

Him in a circle He said, "See! My mother and My brothers. 35Whoever does the will of God, that one is My brother and sister and mother."ʳ

4 AGAIN HE BEGAN TO TEACH BY the seaside, and so huge a crowd collected around Him that He got into a boat on the lake and sat in it, while all the people stayed on shore near the water. 2He taught them many lessons in parables, and told them in His teaching, 3"Listen! A sower went out to sow 4and, as he sowed, some seed fell along the road, and the birds came and ate it up. 5Other seed fell on rocky soil where it had little earth, and because it had no depth of soil it sprang up at once; 6but when the sun rose it got scorched, and because it had no root it withered. 7Other seed fell among the thorns, and the thorns grew up and choked it, so it yielded no crop. 8And other seed fell on the good soil and it sprang up and grew and yielded a crop — thirty, sixty, even a hundredfold." 9He added, "Whoever has ears which can hear, let him listen."

10When He was by Himself, those near Him, with the Twelve, inquired about the parables 11and He told them, "The secret of God's kingdom is committed to you; but to outsiders these matters all come in parables 12so thatˢ 'for all their seeing they may not perceive and for all their hearing they may not understand, so they may not turn about and be forgiven.'"

13He told them further, "If you do not understand this parable, how will you grasp all the parables? 14The sower sows the word. 15Those along the road are where the word is sown and, as soon as it is heard, Satan comes and snatches away the word that was sown in them. 16Similarly those seeds on rocky soil — they readily and gladly receive the word, 17but it takes no root in them; they last briefly. When trouble or persecution comes on account of the word at once they stumble and

---

o) The words enclosed in brackets are not found in the most reliable ancient manuscripts.
p) This Alpheus, the father of James, is apparently not identical with the father of Levi (Matthew), ch. 2:14. There is no reason to suppose that Matthew and James were brothers.
q) See note at Luke 11:15.
r) Relationship with Christ surpasses family ties no matter how close they may be. s) Isa. 6:9, 10.

fall. [18]Others are sown among thorns — they hear the word [19]but the world's cares and the delight of wealth and the passions for other interests enter in to choke the word and it becomes fruitless. [20]And those sown on good soil — they are the ones who hear and accept the word and they yield thirty, sixty, even a hundredfold."

[21]He said to them, "Is a lamp brought in so that it may stand under the peck measure or under the bed? Is it not put on the stand? [22]For nothing is hidden except to be shown and nothing kept secret except to be revealed. [23]Whoever has ears which can hear, let him listen."

[24]He further said to them: "Be careful what you hear. The measure you deal out to others will be dealt to you, with more added; [25]for to one who has shall be given, and one who has not shall be deprived of what he has."

[26]And He said, "The kingdom of God is as when a man scatters seed in the soil, [27]then sleeps at night and rises by day while the seed sprouts and springs up, he does not know how. [28]The soil produces of itself first the blade, then the head, then the mature wheat in the head; [29]and whenever the crop is ready, he puts in the sickle because harvest has come."

[30]He also said, "To what may we compare the kingdom of God or by what parable may we picture it? [31]It is like a mustard seed — smaller than any seed on earth, [32]yet, when planted, it springs up and grows to be larger than any plant, producing such large branches that the birds of the air can nest under its shelter."

[33]With many such parables He told them the word insofar as they could grasp it; [34]He spoke in parables only and explained everything to His disciples by themselves.

[35]At evening that same day, He said to them, "Let us cross to the other side." [36]So, leaving the crowd, they took Him along in the boat just as He was, and other boats accompanied Him. [37]A heavy squall of wind came up and the waves dashed into the boat so that the boat was filling, [38]while He was in the stern asleep on a pillow. They awoke Him and said to Him, "Teacher, do You not care that we are sinking?" [39]He rose up, rebuked the wind and said to the sea, "Silence! Be still!" Then the wind fell and there was great calm. [40]He said to them, "Why are you so afraid? Have you still no faith?" [41]They were terribly frightened and said to one another, "Who is this anyway? For even the wind and the sea obey Him!"

5 THEY ARRIVED AT THE OPPOSITE shore in the country of the Gerasenes.[t] [2]And no sooner had He disembarked than there met Him a man from the tombs, with an unclean spirit. [3]He made his home among the tombs and no one could ever bind him, even with chains; [4]for several times he had been bound in fetters and chains, but the chains were shattered and the fetters smashed by him. Nobody was strong enough to control him. [5]All the time, night and day, he remained among the tombs and in the mountains, shrieking and cutting himself with stones.

[6]When from a distance he noticed Jesus, he ran and knelt before Him, [7]crying with a loud voice, "What business is it of Yours Jesus, Son of God Most High? I adjure You to God, do not torment me." [8]For He was saying to him, "Unclean spirit, come out of the man!" [9]And was questioning him, "What is your name?" He answered, "My name is Legion,[u] for we are many." [10]Then he urgently begged Him not to send them out of the country.

[11]Now a large herd of swine was feeding there on the hillside; [12]and the demons besought Him, "Send us to the swine so that we may enter them!" [13]He permitted them, and the unclean spirits went out and entered the swine. Then the herd of about

---

t) Some other manuscripts read "Gadarenes," still others "Gergesenes." Gerasa was situated twenty miles due east of the Jordan River, approximately halfway between the Sea of Galilee and the Dead Sea. u) A Roman legion was composed of 5,000 to 6,000 men.

two thousand rushed headlong down the precipice into the lake and drowned in the lake. 14Those tending them fled and told the news in town and in the countryside, and the people came to see what had happened. 15They came to Jesus and saw the demoniac, who had been possessed of the legion, sitting down, dressed and sane, and they were filled with awe. 16Those who had seen it told them what had happened to the demoniac; also about the swine. 17Then they began to implore Him to leave their shores.

18As He was embarking the former demoniac requested that he might be with Jesus, but He did not let him. 19Instead He said to him, "Go back to your family and friends and tell them everything the Lord has done for you and the mercy He has shown you." 20And he went off and began to announce throughout the Decapolis[v] everything that Jesus had done for him, and all were astonished.

21When Jesus had crossed again to the other side, a great multitude massed around Him. He was on the shore 22when one of the synagogue directors, named Jairus, came and at sight of Him fell at His feet 23and strongly pleaded with Him, "My daughter is at the point of death. Come, place Your hands on her, that she may recover and live." 24And He went with him. A vast host followed Him and pressed upon Him.

25A woman too, who for twelve years 26had suffered hemorrhages and had been treated much by many physicians, spending all she had without improving but rather growing worse, 27when she heard about Jesus, came in the crowd behind and touched His robe, 28for she said, "If only I touch His robe, I shall be healed." 29At once her hemorrhage stopped, and she felt in her body that she was healed of her affliction.

30Then and there Jesus, conscious that power had gone from Him,[w]

turned around in the crowd and asked, "Who touched My clothes?" 31His disciples remarked to Him, "You see the crowd pressing You on all sides and You say, 'Who touched Me?'" 32But He looked around to see her who had done it. 33Then the woman, afraid and trembling because she knew what had happened to her, came and fell at His feet and told Him the whole truth. 34And He said to her, "Daughter, your faith has saved you; go in peace and be healed of your affliction."

35While He was still speaking there arrived those from the ruler's house who told him, "Your daughter is dead. Why trouble the Teacher further?" 36But Jesus, overhearing the spoken message, said to the ruler of the synagogue, "Have no fear; only believe." 37He permitted no one to accompany Him except Peter and James and James' brother John. 38Arriving at the ruler's house He observed the bedlam — loud weeping and wailing — 39and as He entered He said to them, "Why this turmoil and weeping? The child is not dead but asleep." 40They ridiculed Him; but He personally put them all out, took along the child's father and mother and those with Him, and entered the room where the child was. 41Then, taking the child's hand, He said to her, "Talitha koum," which means, "Little girl, I tell you, rise." 42And instantly the little girl got up and walked around. She was twelve. They were astonished beyond all expression, 43but He strictly charged them that no one should know it, and told them to give her something to eat.

6 LEAVING THERE, HE CAME TO HIS home town,[x] accompanied by His disciples; 2and on the Sabbath He began to teach in the synagogue. Many, when they heard Him, were utterly amazed, saying, "Where did He get all this? What wisdom has been given Him and what miracles are these that happen by His hands? 3Is not this the

---

v) The Decapolis (from *dekapolei* meaning *ten cities*) refers to a group of cities that were allied against common enemies. They were situated in the region between Damascus and the Arabian Desert and are generally listed as Scythopolis, Hippos, Gadara, Pella, Philadelphia, Gerasa, Dion, Canatha, Raphana and Damascus. w) Christ, not His robe, was the source of the power to heal. x) Nazareth. See note at Matt. 2:23.

carpenter, the son of Mary and the brother of James and Joses and Jude and Simon?[y] And do not His sisters live here with us?" And they took offense on His account.

[4]Jesus told them, "No prophet is without honor except in his own country and among his relatives and in his home." [5]And He could do no mighty work there, except that He laid hands on a few sick and healed them. [6]And He wondered at their unbelief. So He went around the nearby villages teaching, [7]and called the Twelve, whom He began to send out two by two, giving them authority over the unclean spirits [8]and directing them to take nothing for the trip except only a staff — no bread, no bag, not a penny in the belt — [9]to wear sandals and not to put on two coats.

[10]He further told them, "Wherever you enter a house, remain there until you leave the place. [11]And whatever community will neither receive you nor listen to you, when you leave there shake off the dust from under your feet for a witness against them. [Truly I tell you, it will be more endurable for Sodom[z] and Gomorrah in the Judgment Day than for that city.]"[a] [12]So they went out and preached that men should repent. [13]They expelled many demons; and many sick they anointed with oil and healed.

c. A.D. 29

[14]King Herod[b] heard of it, for Jesus' name had become well known, and he said, "John the Baptist is risen from the dead and therefore these miracles are being done by him." [15]Others said, "He is Elijah"; others again, "He is a prophet like one of the prophets of old." [16]But on hearing of Him, Herod asserted, "John, whom I beheaded, has risen from the dead." [17]For Herod himself had sent to arrest John and had confined him in prison, because of Herodias, his brother Philip's wife; for

he had married her. [18]For John had told Herod, "You have no right to have your brother's wife." [19]So Herodias held a grudge against him and wanted to execute him but was unable to do so; [20]for Herod stood in awe of John because he knew that he was an upright and holy[c] man. He protected him and, on hearing him, was perplexed; yet he enjoyed listening to him.

[21]An opportune time came, when on Herod's birthday, he gave a banquet to his nobles and commanders and prominent Galileans, [22]at which Herodias' daughter came in and danced. She pleased Herod and his guests. So the king said to the girl, "Ask whatever you want and I will give it to you." [23]Then he swore to her, "Whatever you ask me, I will give it to you up to half my kingdom." [24]She went out and asked her mother, "What shall I request?" "The head of John the Baptist," she replied. [25]She entered the hall and at once hastened to the king and made the request, "I want you to give me at once on a platter the head of John the Baptist."

[26]Although the king was extremely sorry, yet for the sake of his oaths and his guests he did not want to refuse her. [27]And at once the king dispatched a guardsman with orders to bring John's head. He went, beheaded him in prison, [28]brought his head on a platter and gave it to the girl; and the girl presented it to her mother. [29]And when his disciples heard of it, they came and took up his body and laid it in a tomb.

[30]The apostles gathered around Jesus and reported to Him everything they had done and taught. [31]Then He told them, "Come away to a solitary place and rest awhile." For so many were coming and going that they did not have time even to eat. [32]So they left in a boat for a lonely spot by themselves. [33]But the people saw them leaving and many recognized them, and from all

y) James became the leader of the Jerusalem church, cf. Acts 12:17; 15:13; 21:18, and was the author of the epistle bearing his name. Jude also wrote a N.T. epistle. All four men named in this verse were sons of Joseph and Mary. z) See note at Luke 10:12.
a) The words enclosed in brackets are not found in the majority of the most reliable ancient manuscripts. b) This was Herod Antipas, one of the sons of Herod the Great. cf. Matt. 14:1.
c) "Holy" is from the Greek hagios, which means to be revered, set apart for, dedicated to, consecrated to God.

the towns they ran there on foot and arrived ahead of them. [34]When Jesus landed, He saw a large crowd and was moved with pity over them because they were like sheep without a shepherd. And He began to teach them many things.

[35]As the hour grew late, His disciples came to Him and said, "This is a solitary place and now the hour is late; [36]dismiss them so that they may go to surrounding farms and villages and buy themselves something to eat." [37]But He answered them, "You give them to eat." They said, "Shall we go and buy fifty dollars worth of food and feed them?" [38]He asked them, "How many loaves do you have? Go and find out." When they had found out, they reported, "Five, and two fish."

[39]He then gave them all orders to sit[d] on the green grass by groups, [40]and they sat in groups of hundreds and fifties. [41]Taking the five loaves of bread and the two fish, and looking up toward heaven, He gave thanks and broke the bread and gave it to the disciples to set before the people. He also divided the two fish for them all. [42]They all ate and were fully satisfied.[e] [43]They picked up twelve full baskets of the broken pieces of bread and fish. [44]And there were five thousand men who partook of the food.

[45]Then without delay He urged His disciples to board the boat and to cross over to Beth-saida,[f] [46]while He dismissed the crowd and, after He had taken leave of them, went away to the mountain to pray.

[47]At nightfall the boat was in the middle of the sea and He alone on land. [48]Seeing them toiling hard at rowing because the wind was against them, He approached them around the fourth watch[g] of the night walking on the sea as if He meant to pass them. [49]But observing Him walking on the sea they supposed that it was a ghost and they cried out; [50]for they all saw Him and were terrified. But, speaking to them at once, He told them, "Take courage! It is I; have no fear." [51]He then climbed into the boat with them, and the wind fell. They were beside themselves with amazement; [52]for they failed to understand the meaning of the loaves — their hearts were dull.

[53]After crossing the lake they landed at Gennesaret[h] and docked. [54]But as soon as they disembarked the people recognized Him [55]and ran around that entire district and began to carry to Him on their couches, wherever they heard He was, all who had ailments. [56]And wherever He went, into village or town or country, they placed their sick in the market place and begged Him to let them touch if only the hem of His robe. And as many as touched Him were healed.

7 THEN THE PHARISEES AND SOME of the scribes who had come from Jerusalem, called on Him jointly, [2]having noticed some of His disciples eating their food with unclean, that is, unwashed hands. [3]For the Pharisees, and all the Jews who observe the traditions of the elders, do not eat without washing their hands up to the elbow, [4]and when they come from market they do not eat without washing. And there are numerous other rules which they follow traditionally, such as washing cups and pots and bronze utensils and beds.

[5]So the Pharisees and the scribes questioned Him, "Why do Your disciples behave contrary to the elders' tradition, but eat food with unclean hands?" [6]He told them, "Suitably did Isaiah prophesy about you hypocrites as it is written,[i] 'This people honor Me

---

d) See note at ch. 2:15.
e) Christ, who made all things, John 1:3, had power over nature as well as human life. The three miracles of this chapter (feeding the 5,000, walking on the water, and calming the sea) are among the most impressive miracles of this kind. It is significant that the first miracle (or *sign*, Gk. *sēmeion*) He performed, changing water into wine, John 2:11, was in the realm of nature.
f) See note at ch. 8:22.
g) The first watch was from 6 to 9 p.m.; the second, 9 p.m. to midnight; the third, midnight to 3 a.m.; and the fourth, 3 to 6 a.m.
h) Gennesaret was on the northwestern shore of the sea of Galilee.
i) Isa. 29:13; *cf.* Isa. 58:1-3; Ezek. 33:31.

with their lips; but their hearts are estranged from Me. [7]Vainly they worship Me, when teaching human regulations as doctrines.' [8]You let go of God's commandments to cling to human tradition."

[9]He added, "How well you frustrate the law of God to observe your own tradition. [10]For Moses said,[j] 'Honor your father and your mother' and[k] 'Whoever curses father or mother, let him be executed.' [11]But you say, 'If a man says to his father or mother, "What you would have received from me is Corban," that is to say consecrated to God, he is exempt,' [12]you no longer permit him to do anything for his father and mother. [13]Thus you annul God's word through your tradition which you have handed down. And you do many things of that kind."

[14]Calling the people to Him again, Jesus told them, "All of you listen to Me and understand. [15]Nothing entering a man from the outside can defile him, but the things that come out of the man render the person unclean. [16][If anyone has ears to hear, let him hear.]"[l]

[17]When He had gone indoors away from the crowd, His disciples questioned Him about the parable [18]and He said to them, "Are you, too, so lacking in comprehension? Do you not perceive that whatever enters from the outside cannot defile a person, [19]because it does not enter his heart but his stomach, and is eliminated?" In saying this He declared all foods to be clean. [20]He said further, "What comes out of the man defiles him; [21]for from within, out of a man's heart wicked thoughts emerge — unchastity, [22]theft, murder, adultery, greed, wickedness, deceit, licentiousness, vicious envy, blasphemy, pride, foolishness. [23]All these wicked things come from the inside and defile a man."

[24]Then He arose and left there for the district of Tyre[m] where He entered a house, not wanting anyone to know it; but He could not remain hidden. [25]Instead, a woman whose little daughter had an unclean spirit came as soon as she heard of Him and threw herself at His feet. [26]She was a Gentile, a native Syro-Phoenician, and she begged Him to expel the demon from her daughter. [27]He said to her, "First let the children be satisfied; for it is not fair to take the children's bread and to throw it to the house dogs."[n] [28]But she answered Him, "Yes, Lord, yet the house dogs under the table eat from the children's scraps." [29]He said to her, "For this thought go your way; the demon has gone out of your daughter." [30]And when she reached home she found the child lying on the bed and the demon expelled.

[31]Returning from the district of Tyre He passed through Sidon on to the Sea of Galilee and up the center of the Decapolis[o] region. [32]And they brought Him a deaf man who had an impediment in his speech, and begged Him to lay His hands on him. [33]Taking him by himself away from the crowd, He put His fingers into his ears and touched his tongue with saliva. [34]Then, looking up toward heaven, He sighed and said to him, "Ephphatha," that is, "Be opened." [35]And his ears were opened, and at once the obstruction of his tongue was loosed and he spoke clearly.

[36]He charged them to tell no one; but the more He charged them, the more widely they made it known. [37]They were immeasurably astonished, and exclaimed, "How well He has done everything! He even makes the deaf hear and the dumb speak."

8 IN THOSE DAYS ONCE AGAIN AN IMmense crowd gathered and had nothing to eat. So, summoning the disciples, He told them, [2]"I feel very sorry for these people because they have stayed with Me now for three days and

---

j) Exod. 20:12.   k) Exod. 21:17.
l) Verse 16, enclosed in brackets, is not found in the majority of the most reliable ancient manuscripts.   m) See note at Matt. 11:21.
n) The Greek word rendered "house dogs" is the plural form of *kunarion*, meaning *little dog* or *house dog*, any dog that might sit under a dining table hoping for scraps of food. There is another word for "dog," *kuōn*, which denotes an unclean kind of canine. This word is used in Matt. 7:6; Luke 16:21; II Pet. 2:22.   o) See note at ch. 5:20.

have nothing to eat. 3If I should send them home hungry, they would faint on the way, and some of them are from a considerable distance."

4His disciples answered Him, "Where in this desert can we secure bread to satisfy such a number?" 5He asked them, "How many loaves do you have?" They said, "Seven." 6So He instructed the crowd to sit down on the ground and, taking the seven loaves of bread, He gave thanks, broke them, gave them to His disciples to set before the people, and they set them before the crowd. 7They also had a few small fish, and when He had given thanks for them He told the disciples to set them before the crowd also. 8So they ate and were satisfied; and they picked up the leftovers, seven baskets full. 9About four thousand had eaten. He then dismissed them, 10and immediately embarking with His disciples, reached the region of Dalmanutha.[p]

11The Pharisees came out and began to dispute with Him. To test Him, they asked Him for a sign from heaven. 12Sighing deeply in His very soul, He said, "Why does this generation seek a sign? I assure you, no sign will be given to this generation." 13So He left them, embarked again and crossed to the other side.

14The disciples had forgotten to bring along bread, nor did they have more than a single loaf with them in the boat. 15Thus He cautioned them, "Look out. Beware of the yeast[q] of the Pharisees and of Herod's yeast." 16They remarked to one another, "It is because we have no bread." 17Aware of it, He said to them, "Why are you talking about having no bread? Do you still neither grasp nor understand? Is your heart calloused? 18Having eyes can you not see and having ears can you not hear? And do you not remember 19when I broke the five loaves for the five thousand, how many baskets you picked up full of leftovers?" They said to Him, "Twelve." 20"When there were seven loaves for the four thousand, how many baskets of leftovers did you pick up?" They said to Him, "Seven." 21And He said to them, "Do you still not understand?"

22They reached Bethsaida,[r] where they brought a blind man to Him and appealed to Him to touch him. 23So, taking hold of the blind man's hand, He led him out of the village; then after putting saliva on his eyes, He put His hands on him and asked him, "Do you see anything?" 24He looked up and said, "I see people, but they look like trees — walking around." 25Then again Jesus placed His hands on his eyes; and he looked steadily and was restored and saw everything distinctly. 26So Jesus sent him home saying, "Do not even enter the village."

27Jesus and His disciples went to the villages around Caesarea Philippi,[s] and on the way He asked His disciples, "Who do the people say that I am?" 28They said to Him, "John the Baptist; but others say, Elijah, and others, one of the prophets." 29He asked them, "But you, who do you say I am?" Peter answered Him, "You are the Christ."[t] 30And He charged them to tell no one this about Him.

31He then began to teach them that the Son of Man must suffer much and be rejected by the elders, the chief priests and the scribes, and be executed, and after three days rise again. 32He told them this without reservation. Then Peter, taking Him aside, began to remonstrate with Him; 33but turning round and looking at His disciples, He rebuked Peter, saying, "Get away from Me, Satan, for you are not taking God's viewpoint, but men's." 34Then, summoning the crowd as well as His disciples, He said to them, "If anyone wishes to come after Me, let him say 'No' to himself and take up his cross and follow Me. 35For whoever wishes to save his life will lose it; but

---

p) Dalmanutha, called Magadan in Matt. 15:39, was situated at the most western point of the Sea of Galilee. Josephus, the historian, identifies both names with Taricheae. q) Or, leaven.
r) Beth-saida was located on the northern shore of the Sea of Galilee, where the Jordan River flows into the sea, about nine miles from Capernaum. Beth-said means *house of fishing* or *hunting*. It was the home of Philip, Andrew and Peter, John 1:44. s) See note at Matt. 16:13.
t) This marks a high point in the Lord's teaching ministry. Toward this conviction He had patiently trained the Twelve.

whoever loses his life on behalf of Me and the gospel will save it. 36For what does it benefit a man to gain the whole world and forfeit his own life? 37For what will a man give in exchange for his life?

38"Should anyone in this immoral and sinful generation be ashamed of Me and of My teaching, of him the Son of Man will be ashamed, too, when He comes in His Father's glory with the holy angels."

9 HE ALSO SAID TO THEM, "I ASSURE you, there are some standing here who will not taste death until they have seen the kingdom of God come in power."

2Six days later Jesus took with Him Peter, James, and John and led them up a high mountainu alone by themselves, and in their presence He was changed in appearance. 3His clothes became a brilliant white, whiter than any bleacher on earth could bleach them. 4And there appeared to them Elijah and Moses, and they conversed with Jesus.

5Peter said to Jesus, "Rabbi,v it is good that we are here. Let us build three booths — one for You, one for Moses, and one for Elijah." 6For he did not know what to say, because they were awed.

7Then there came a cloud overshadowing them, and a voice came out of the cloud, "This is My Son, the Beloved; listen to Him." 8Suddenly, as they looked around, they no longer saw anyone with them except Jesus only. 9And as they were descending from the mountain He forbade them to divulge to anyone what they had seen until the Son of Man should rise from the dead. 10So they kept the matter secret among themselves, while discussing together what rising from the dead might mean.

11They asked Him, "Why do the scribes maintain that Elijah must first come?" 12He answered them, "Elijah is indeed to come first, to put everything in order; but how is it written of the Son of Man that He shall endure much suffering and be treated with contempt? 13I tell you, however, that Elijahw has come and they have treated him as they pleased, just as it has been written of him."

14When they reached the disciples they noticed a large crowd around them and scribes disputing with them. 15On seeing Him the whole multitude was awed and, running toward Him, they greeted Him. 16He asked them, "What are you discussing with them?" 17One of the crowd answered Him, "Teacher, I have brought You my son, who has a dumb spirit; 18whenever it gets hold of him, it throws him down — he foams at the mouth, he grinds his teeth and becomes rigid." I spoke to Your disciples to cast it out, but they could not."

19"O unbelieving generation!" He replied, "How long shall I be with you? How long shall I put up with you? Bring him to Me." 20So they brought him to Jesus. The spirit, on seeing Him, instantly threw the boy into convulsions, so that he fell on the ground and rolled over, foaming at the mouth. 21Then He asked his father, "How long has this gone on?" He said, "From early childhood. 22Often it has thrown him into fire and into water to destroy him; but if You can do anything, help us; take pity on us!"

23Jesus said to him, "'If You can do anything?' Everything is possible for the person who believes!"x 24At once the father of the boy exclaimed, "I believe. Help me because of my unbelief." 25Jesus, noticing that a mob was collecting, rebuked the unclean spirit, to whom He said, "Dumb and deaf spirit, I order you: Come out of him and never again enter into him." 26And, shrieking and throwing fit after fit, he came out. The boy looked like a

---

u) It does not seem likely that this was Mt. Tabor since Jesus was at that time northeast of the Sea of Galilee, whereas Mt. Tabor is southwest of the lake. The mountain may have been in the Anti-Lebanon range somewhere near Mt. Hermon.
v) "Rabbi," from the Hebrew word *rav* or *rab*, means *master, lord.* See note at 10:51.
w) John the Baptist, whose ministry was similar to that of Elijah, Matt. 11:13, 14.
x) What Jesus said in this situation stresses the role of believing and praying in the healing of this afflicted boy.

corpse, so that many declared that he was dead; 27but Jesus, taking him by the hand, raised him and he stood up.

28After He had gone indoors His disciples asked Him privately, "Why were we unable to cast it out?" 29He told them, "This kind cannot be expelled except through prayer."y

30Leaving there they passed through Galilee. He did not want anyone to know it 31because He was teaching His disciples, "The Son of Man will be delivered into human hands and they will execute Him and, when He is killed, He will rise again in three days." 32But they did not understand the saying and were afraid to question Him.

33They reached Capernaum and, when He arrived home, He asked them, "What were you arguing on the road?" 34But they kept still; for on the road they had argued with one another who was the greatest. 35Seating Himself He summoned the Twelve and told them, "If anyone wants to be first, let him be last of all and servant of all." 36Then taking a little child, He set him in the center of their circle, and taking him in His arms, said to them, 37"Whoever receives one of such children in My name receives Me, and whoever receives Me does not so much receive Me as Him who sent Me."

38John said to Him, "Teacher, we saw someone not in our company, expelling demons in Your name and we forbade him, because he was not one of us."z 39Jesus told him, "Do not forbid him; for there is no one who performs a miracle in My name who can soon speak evil of Me. 40He who is not against us is for us; 41for whoever gives you a cup of water to drink because you belong to Christ, I assure you that he will not miss his reward.

42"Whoever occasions the stumbling of one of these little ones who believe in Me, it would be better for him if, with a millstone hung around his neck, he had been cast into the sea. 43Should your hand occasion you to do wrong, cut it off; it is better for you to enter into life maimed than with both hands to be thrown into hell,a into the fire that cannot be put out. 44[Where their worm never ceases and the fire is not put out].b 45In case your foot occasions you to go wrong, cut it off; it is better for you to enter into life crippled than with two feet to be thrown into hell, 46[where their worm never ceases and their fire is not put out].b 47If your eye occasions you to stumble, tear it out; it is better for you to enter the kingdom of God with one eye than with two eyes to be thrown into hell, 48where their worm never ceases and the fire is not put out.

49"For everyone will be salted with fire. 50Salt is beneficial; but if the salt loses its saltiness, with what will it be seasoned? Have salt in yourselves and live together in peace."

10 HE LEFT THERE AND WENT TO the Judean region on the farther side of the Jordan. Again crowds flocked to Him and, as usual, He taught them. 2And there came Pharisees questioning Him, "Is it lawful for a man to divorce his wife?" — testing Him. 3He answered them, "What ruling did Moses give you?" 4They said,c "Moses permitted the writing of a divorce certificate and to divorce her." 5Jesus told them, "In view of your hardheartedness he wrote you this ruling, 6but from the beginning, from the time of creationd male and female He made them; 7Therefore shall a man leave his father and mother and shall cling to his wife, 8and the two shall be one flesh'; so that they are no longer

---

y) Some ancient manuscripts read "through prayer and fasting."
z) That this lesson on tolerance has not yet been learned has cost the kingdom of God great losses.
a) "Hell" is rendered here from the Greek noun *geenna*, from which the English word "Gehenna" is derived. Gehenna is sometimes used to denote the Valley of Hinnom, a place where human sacrifices were once made, Jer. 7:31. In this valley refuse was burned. Consequently fires were constantly going. The Israelites used the word "Gehenna" to express the eternal judgment of the wicked. Jesus employed it here and elsewhere, e.g., Matt. 5:22, to illustrate the consequence of sin. Cf. "lake of fire," Rev. 19:20.
b) Verses 44 and 46 are not found in the majority of the most reliable ancient manuscripts. They are identical with verse 48, which all the best manuscripts carry.
c) Deut. 24:1.   d) Gen. 1:27; 2:24.

two but one flesh. ⁹What God therefore has joined, let not man divide."

¹⁰When they were indoors the disciples questioned Him again on that subject, ¹¹and He told them, "Whoever divorces his wife and marries another, commits adultery against her, ¹²and if she divorces her husband and marries another, she commits adultery."

¹³They brought children for Him to touch, but the disciples reprimanded them. ¹⁴When Jesus noticed that, He was indignant and told them, "Permit the children to come to Me. Do not hinder them, for to their kind belongs the kingdom of God. ¹⁵I assure you, whoever fails to receive the kingdom of God like a little child, will not enter it at all." ¹⁶Then taking them in His arms He blessed them while He laid His hands on them.

c. A.D. 30

¹⁷As He was setting out on His journey a man came running to Him, who knelt before Him and asked, "Good Teacher, what shall I do to become heir to eternal life?" ¹⁸Jesus said to him, "Why do you call Me good? No one is good except One, even God. ¹⁹You know the commands:ᵉ 'Do not murder; Do not commit adultery; Do not steal; Do not witness falsely; Do not cheat; Honor your father and your mother.'"

²⁰He replied, "Teacher, I have observed all these things from my boyhood." ²¹Jesus, looking at him, prized him dearly and told him, "One thing you lack. Go and sell all you have and give to the poor, and you will have treasure in heaven; then come and follow Me." ²²At this saying he was appalled and went away saddened, for he possessed great wealth.

²³Looking around, Jesus said to His disciples, "How difficult it is for these possessing wealth to enter the kingdom of God!" ²⁴The disciples wondered at His remark; but Jesus spoke to them once more, "Children, how difficult it is [for those who trust in wealth]ᶠ to enter the kingdom of God. ²⁵It is easier for a camel to pass through a needle'sᵍ eye than for a wealthy person to enter the kingdom of God."

²⁶Astonished beyond words they said to themselves, "Who then can be saved?" ²⁷With His eyes upon them Jesus replied, "With men it is impossible but not with God; for everything is possible with God."

²⁸Peter began to say to Him, "Look, we have given up everything and have followed You." ²⁹Jesus said, "I assure you, there is no one who has left home or brothers or sisters or mother or father or children or fields on account of Me and the gospel, ³⁰but will receive a hundred times over now in this life homes and brothers and sisters and mothers and children and fields, along with persecutions, and in the future age eternal life. ³¹But many that are first will be last, and the last first."

³²They were on the road going up to Jerusalem with Jesus leading them, and as they followed they were in a daze and were apprehensive. Then summoning the Twelve, He began once more to tell them what was about to happen to Him, ³³"See, we are going up to Jerusalem and the Son of Man will be delivered to the chief priests and the scribes. They will condemn Him to death and will hand Him over to the Gentiles; ³⁴and they will mock Him, spit on Him, flog Him, and execute Him, and after three days He will rise again."

³⁵Then James and John, the sons of Zebedee, approached and said to Him, "Teacher, we want You to do for us what we ask." ³⁶And He said to them, "What do you want Me to do for you?" ³⁷They answered Him, "Grant us to be seated, one at Your right and one at Your left in Your glory." ³⁸But Jesus told them, "You do not know what you are asking. Are you able to drink the cup that I drink, or to undergo the baptism I am baptized with?" ³⁹They replied, "We are

---

e) Exod. 20:12-17.
f) The words in brackets are not found in the majority of the most reliable ancient manuscripts.
g) The Greek noun *raphis* means *a sewing needle,* such as that commonly used in a household. Nothing is impossible with God, vs. 27.

able." Then Jesus told them, "The cup that I drink you will drink, and with My baptism you will be baptized; [40]but to sit at My right or left is not Mine to grant, but is for those for whom it is reserved."

[41]When the other ten heard it, they began to be indignant at James and John, [42]but Jesus summoned them and said to them, "You know how those supposed to govern the Gentiles lord it over them, and their great men exert authority over them; [43]but this is not your way. Instead, whoever wants to be great among you will be your servant, [44]and whoever wants to be first among you will be everyone's slave. [45]For even the Son of Man did not come to be served but to serve and to give His life a ransom for many."

[46]They came to Jericho and, as He was leaving Jericho with His disciples and a great throng, Bartimaeus,[h] son of Timaeus, a blind beggar, was sitting by the roadside. [47]Hearing that it was Jesus of Nazareth, he began to cry out, "Jesus, son of David, take pity on me!" [48]Many ordered him to keep still; but he shouted the louder, "Son of David, take pity on me!" [49]Jesus stopped and said, "Call him." So they called to the blind man, "Have courage! Get up, He is calling you." [50]Throwing off his coat and springing to his feet, he went to Jesus. [51]In response, Jesus said to him, "What do you want Me to do for you?" The blind man replied, "Rabboni,[i] let me see again." [52]Jesus said to him, "Go, your faith has restored you." And instantly he recovered his sight and followed Him on the way.

11 WHEN THEY CAME NEAR JERUsalem, at Bethphage[j] and Bethany[k] by the Mount of Olives, He dispatched two of His disciples, [2]to whom He said, "Go to the village opposite you and, as soon as you enter it, you will find a tethered colt which no one has ever ridden; untie and fetch it. [3]If anyone says to you, 'What are you doing there?' you say, 'The Lord needs it, and He will send it back here without delay.'"

[4]They went away, found the colt tethered outside the door in the street and untied it. [5]Some of the bystanders there remarked to them, "What are you up to, untying the colt?" [6]So they answered just as Jesus had told them and they let them take it. [7]Then they brought the colt to Jesus, spread their clothes on it, and Jesus sat upon it. [8]Many also spread their garments on the road, and others leafy branches which they had cut from the fields. [9]Both those walking ahead and those behind shouted[l] "Hosanna! Blessed is He who comes in the name of the Lord! [10]Blessed is the coming kingdom of our father David! Hosanna in the highest!"

[11]He entered Jerusalem and went to the temple, where He observed everything and, as night was approaching, He went out to Bethany with the Twelve.

[12]The next morning, as they were leaving Bethany, He felt hungry [13]and, noticing a leafy fig tree at a distance, went to see whether He might find anything on it. But on reaching it He found nothing but leaves;[m] in fact, it was not the time for ripe figs. [14]And He addressed it, "May none eat fruit from you forevermore." And His disciples were listening.

[15]They reached Jerusalem and, on entering the temple, He began to expel the sellers and the buyers that were in the temple. He upset the tables of the money-changers and the stalls of those who sold doves, [16]and did not allow anyone to carry any goods through the temple.[n] [17]He taught them, "Is it not written,[o] 'My house

---

h) The prefix "bar" means *son of*, e.g., "Barjona" equals *son of John*. So Bartimaeus was the son of Timaeus.
i) "Rabboni" is a heightened and perhaps more intimate title or form of address than "Rabbi" (see note at Matt. 26:25). Rabbi, from the Hebrew word *rav* or *rab*, means *master, lord*. Rabboni denotes *my master, my lord*.
j) See note at Luke 19:29.   k) See note at Matt. 21:17.
l) Ps. 118:25, 26. "Hosanna" means *save now* or *salvation*. The expression is akin to "God save the king."   m) Normally as soon as the leaves begin to bud, early figs show.
n) That is, the temple courts.   o) Isa. 56:7; Jer. 7:11.

shall be called a house of prayer among all nations?' But you have made it a den of robbers."

18 The scribes and chief priests heard it and looked for ways to destroy Him; for they were afraid of Him, as all the people were amazed at His teaching. 19 With the fall of evening, He left the city.

20 And when they came along the next morning they noticed the fig tree withered to the roots. 21 Then Peter remembered and said to Him, "Rabbi, look! The fig tree You cursed is withered!" 22 Jesus answered them, "Have faith in God. 23 For I assure you, whoever says to this mountain, 'Be taken up and thrown into the sea,' and entertains no inner doubt but believes that what he says will happen, it shall be so for him.

24 "I tell you, therefore, whatever you ask in prayer, believe that you have received it and it will be yours. 25 And whenever you stand praying and you have a grievance against anyone, forgive him, so that your Father in heaven may forgive you your trespasses. 26 [But if you do not forgive, neither will your Father in heaven forgive your trespasses.]"[p]

27 Once more they entered Jerusalem and, while He was walking around in the temple, the chief priests and the scribes and the elders came to Him 28 and asked Him, "By what authority are You doing these things or who gave You this authority to do them?" 29 Jesus said to them, "I will ask you one question; you answer Me and I will tell you by what authority I do these things. 30 Was the baptism of John from heaven or from men? Answer Me."

31 They argued among themselves, "If we say, 'From heaven,' He will say, 'Why then did you not believe him?' 32 But if we say, 'From men — .' " They were afraid of the people, for everyone considered John to be a prophet; 33 so they answered Jesus, "We do not know." Jesus replied to them, "Neither do I tell you by what authority I do these things."

12 He began to address them in parables: "A man planted a vineyard, encircled it with a hedge, excavated a winepress, built a tower and leased it to tenant farmers, then went away. 2 At the proper season he sent an agent[q] to the workers to collect from them a share of the vineyard's yield, 3 but they took and flogged him and sent him off empty-handed. 4 Again he sent them another agent whom they wounded in the head and shamefully maltreated. 5 Once more he sent another, whom they killed, and many others — some they flogged and some they killed.

6 "Having still one, a son he dearly loved, he finally sent him to them, saying, 'They will respect my son.' 7 But those tenant farmers said among themselves, 'This is the heir. Come on, let us kill him and the inheritance will be ours.' 8 So they took and killed him and threw him outside the vineyard. 9 Now what will the owner of the vineyard do? He will come and put the tenants to death and lease the vineyard to others.

10 "Have you never read this Scripture,[r] 'The stone which the builders rejected has become the head of the corner; 11 this was the Lord's doing and it is wonderful to our eyes'?" 12 Then they looked for ways to arrest Him, but they were afraid of the people. For they knew He spoke the parable against them.[s] So they left Him and went away. 13 And they sent to Him some of the Pharisees and of the Herodians[t] to trap Him with a question. 14 Coming to Him, they said, "Teacher, we know that You are sincere and not partial to anyone; for You court no human favor but teach truly the way of God. Is it lawful to pay tax to Caesar or not? 15 Shall we pay or not pay?" But knowing their hypocrisy He said

---

p) Verse 26, enclosed in brackets, does not appear in the majority of the most reliable ancient manuscripts.
q) See note at Matt. 13:27.
r) Ps. 118: 22, 23.
s) Compare Isa. 5:1-7 where Israel is God's vineyard.
t) See note at Matt. 22:16.

to them, "Why do you test Me? Bring Me a coin,[u] so I may see it." [16]They brought one and He asked them, "Whose image and inscription is this?" They said "Caesar's." [17]Jesus told them, "Pay Caesar what belongs to Caesar, and God what belongs to God." And they greatly wondered at Him.

[18]Then the Sadducees,[v] who maintain that there is no resurrection, came to Him and asked, [19]"Teacher, Moses wrote[w] for us that if a man's brother dies, leaving behind a wife but no child, his brother should take the widow and raise offspring for his brother. [20]Now there were seven brothers, the first of whom took a wife and died without offspring. [21]Then the second married her and died without leaving offspring. [22]So the third and all seven, without leaving offspring. Last of all, the woman, too, died. [23]In the resurrection then, when they rise, whose wife shall she be? For the seven were married to her."

[24]Jesus said to them, "Are you not mistaken in this, since you know neither the Scriptures nor the power of God? [25]For when they rise from the dead they neither marry nor are given in marriage but are like the angels in heaven. [26]But in regard to the raising of the dead, have you not read in the book of Moses[x] how at the bush God said[y] to him, "I am the God of Abraham, the God of Isaac, and the God of Jacob'? [27]He is not the God of the dead but of the living.[z] You are much mistaken."

[28]Then one of the scribes, having listened to the discussion and aware that He had answered them well, came forward to question Him, "Which is the chief commandment of all?" [29]Jesus answered him, "The chief one is,[a] 'Hear, O Israel: The Lord our God is one Lord, [30]and you shall love the Lord your God with your whole heart, with your whole soul, with your whole mind, and with your whole strength.

[31]"The second is this,[b] 'You shall love your neighbor as yourself.' There is no other commandment greater than these."

[32]The scribe said to him, "Right, Teacher, You have said in truth that He is One and there is none beside Him, [33]and to love Him with all one's heart, with all one's mind, with all one's soul, and with all one's strength; also to love one's neighbor as oneself, is more than all burnt offerings and sacrifices." [34]Then Jesus, observing his intelligent response, said to him. "You are not far from the kingdom of God." After that, no one ventured any more to question Him.

[35]As Jesus was teaching in the temple, He said, "How can the scribes say that the Christ is David's son? [36]For David himself said through the Holy Spirit,[c] 'The LORD said to my Lord, "Sit at My right hand until I place your enemies for a footstool of your feet."' [37]David himself calls Him Lord; in what way then is He his son?" And the great throng listened to Him with delight.

[38]In the course of His teaching He said to them: "Beware of the scribes, who enjoy walking around in long robes to be greeted in the market places, [39]to have the front seats in the synagogues and the choice places at the banquets; [40]who prey upon the properties of widows, and pray long prayers for show. They shall receive severer sentence."

[41]Taking a seat opposite the treasury He watched how the people put money into the treasure chest. Many of the rich put in much; [42]but one poor

---

u) Probably this coin was a denarius, the smallest silver coin in circulation. It would be worth twenty-five cents in mid-twentieth century U.S. currency.
v) See note at Matt. 3:7.
w) Deut. 25:5, 6.
x) The Pentateuch, the first five books of the Old Testament, was considered and often referred to as The Law. These five books were also sometimes spoken of simply as "Moses." Jesus here affirms the Mosaic authorship of the Pentateuch, its historicity and inspiration.
y) Exod. 3:1-10.
z) God has a vital relationship with living persons. Abraham, Isaac and Jacob still live.
a) Deut. 6:4, 5.   b) Lev. 19:18.
c) Ps. 110:1. The interrogation recorded in vss. 35-37 shows that Jesus challenges both the head and the heart.

widow came and put in two mites, that is one-quarter of a cent[d] [43]Summoning His disciples, He told them, "I assure you that this poor widow has put in more than all those contributing to the treasury; [44]for they all contributed from their surpluses but she out of her poverty gave all she had— her whole living."

13 AS HE WAS LEAVING THE TEM-ple, one of His disciples said to Him, "Teacher, see what wonderful stones and buildings these are." [2]Jesus replied to him, "You see these great buildings? Not a stone shall be left on another, that shall not be torn down."

[3]As He sat on the Mount of Olives opposite the temple, Peter, James, John and Andrew asked Him privately, [4]"Tell us when this is to happen and what is the sign when all these things are to be accomplished!" [5]So Jesus began to tell them: "Look out that no one deceives you; [6]for many will come in My name saying, 'I am He,' and will mislead many. [7]But when you hear about wars and rumors of wars, be not alarmed; for it must be so, but the end is not yet. [8]For nation shall revolt against nation, and kingdom against kingdom; there will be earthquakes at various places; also famines — these are the first pains of childbirth.

[9]"Look out for yourselves; for they will deliver you to councils and you will be flogged in synagogues; you will stand before governors and kings for My sake and in order to testify to them. [10]And the gospel must first be preached to all the nations.

[11]"And when they arrest you and take you to court, do not worry beforehand what you will say, say whatever is given you in that hour, for it is not you who are speaking, but it is the Holy Spirit.

[12]"Brother will hand over brother for death, and father will hand over son; children will rise against their parents and have them put to death,

[13]and you will be hated by everyone, because of My name. But whoever perseveres to the end will be saved.

[14]"But when you see the desolating abomination set up where it should not be[e] — let the reader take notice — then let those in Judea flee to the mountains. [15]A person on the housetop should not go down or go inside to fetch anything out of his house, [16]and one in the field should not turn back to pick up his coat.

[17]"Alas for the pregnant and the nursing women in those days. [18]Pray that your flight may not be in winter; [19]for the misery of those days will be such as never was since the beginning of God's creation until now, neither ever will be. [20]And unless the Lord had shortened those days not a human being would survive; but because of the elect whom He has chosen He has shortened the days.

[21]"If anyone then tells you, 'Look, here is the Christ!' or, 'Look, there!' put no faith in it; [22]for false Christs and false prophets will arise and perform signs and wonders to lead astray, if possible, even the elect. [23]Be on your guard! I am forewarning you of it all.

[24]"But in those days, after that tribulation, the sun will be darkened and the moon will not shed her light, [25]the stars will be falling from heaven and the powers in the heavens will be shaken. [26]Then will they see the Son of Man coming in the clouds with great power and glory. [27]And then will He send out the angels and gather His chosen from the four winds, from the end of the earth to the end of heaven.

[28]"Learn this parable from the fig tree: Whenever its branch grows tender and it puts out leaves, you know that summer is near. [29]Similarly, when you see these things happen, you will know that He is near, at the door. [30]I assure you, the present generation will not pass on until all this takes place. [31]Heaven and earth will pass away, but My sayings will not pass away.

---

d) The Greek word rendered "one-quarter of a cent" is *kodrantēs*, meaning *farthing*. A mite, a small copper coin worth about one-eighth of a cent, takes its name from the Greek word *lepton*, which means *small, thin, light*.

e) This is prophetic of the desecration of the temple by the Romans, who destroyed it in A.D. 70. In 167 B.C. Antiochus Epiphanes offered swine on the temple altar. *Cf.* Dan. 9:27; 12:11.

32But about the exact date and hour no one knows, not even the angels in heaven, nor the Son, but only the Father. 33Be on guard; keep wide awake [and pray][f]; for you do not know the time. 3It is like a man leaving his home to go abroad, who authorizied his slaves[g] and assigned to each his work, with the sentinel appointed to watch. 35You, therefore, watch; for you have no idea when the Lord of the house will come — in the evening or at midnight or at the cockcrowing or in the morning, 36lest coming unexpectedly, He may find you sleeping. 37And what I say to you, I say to everyone, Watch!"

14 THE PASSOVER AND THE FEAST of Unleavened Bread were due two days later. The chief priests and the scribes were seeking a way to arrest Him through treachery and execute Him, 2for they said, "Not during the feast, lest there will be a mob disturbance."

3While He was at Bethany in the home of Simon the leper as He was sitting[h] at the table, a woman[i] came with an alabaster jar of pure nard perfume, very valuable and, breaking the jar, she poured the ointment on His head. 4But there were some who indignantly remarked to one another, "What use is this waste of ointment? 5This could have been sold for over seventy-five dollars[j] and given to the poor." And they censured her.

6But Jesus said, "Leave her alone. Why do you embarrass her? She has treated Me nobly. 7For you always have the poor with you, and whenever you wish, you can benefit them; but you will not always have Me. 8She has done what she could; she has prepared My body with perfume for burial. 9I assure you, wherever this gospel will be preached over the whole wide world, what she has done will be told as a memorial of her."

10Then Judas Iscariot, one of the Twelve, went off to the chief priests to betray Him to them; 11and when they learned of it, they were delighted and promised to pay him money. So he looked about how he might conveniently betray Him.

12On the first day of Unleavened Bread, when the Passover lamb was annually sacrificed, His disciples asked Him, "Where do You want us to go and prepare, so that You may eat the Passover?" 13Then He sent out two of His disciples[k] and told them, "Go into the city and a man will meet you, carrying a water pitcher; follow him. 14And wherever he enters, say to the proprietor, 'The Teacher says, "Where is My guest room where I am to eat the Passover with My disciples?"' 15He will show you a large upper room — furnishings and everything ready — there prepare for us."

16His disciples went out, came to the city and found it as He had told them. They prepared the Passover, 17and as evening fell He arrived with the Twelve. 18As they were sitting[l] and eating, Jesus said, "I tell you with certainty that one of you who is eating with Me will betray Me." 19They began to be greatly distressed, and they said to Him, one after another, "It is not I, is it?" 20He answered them, "It is one of the Twelve who is dipping with Me in the dish. 21The Son of Man is going the way that has been written of Him, but alas for that man by whom the Son of Man is betrayed. It were better for that man never to have been born."

22As the meal proceeded, He took bread, gave thanks and broke it, gave it to them, and said,[m] "Take it. This is My body." 23Also taking the cup and giving thanks, He gave it to them and they all drank of it. 24He said to them, "This is My blood of the covenant,[n] which is poured out for many. 25I assure you, I shall no more drink of the

---

f) The two words enclosed in brackets are not found in the majority of the most reliable ancient manuscripts.   g) See note at Matt. 13:27.   h) See note at ch. 2:15. i) Mary, the sister of Martha and Lazarus, John 12:3. j) The text reads "three hundred denarii." A denarius would be worth about twenty-five cents in mid-twientieth century U.S. currency.   k) Peter and John, Luke 22:8.   l) See note at ch. 2:15. m) *Cf.* I Cor. 11:23-29.   n) Some ancient manuscripts read "new covenant."

vintage until that day when I shall drink it new in the kingdom of God."

26With the singing of a hymn[o] they went out to the Mount of Olives. 27And Jesus said to them, "You will all turn away from Me, for it is written[p] 'I shall strike the shepherd and the sheep will be widely scattered.' 28But after My resurrection I will precede you into Galilee."

29Peter said to Him, "Even if all turn away from You, I will never!" 30Jesus told him, "Truly I tell you, during this very night, before the rooster crows twice, you will disown Me three times." 31But he asserted more insistently, "Even if I must die with You, never will I disown You." And so they all said.

32They came to a place called Gethsemane, and He told His disciples, "Be seated here while I pray." 33But He took along with Him Peter, James and John, and as He began to feel deeply alarmed and distressed, 34He said to them, "My soul is mortally grieved; stay here and watch." 35Going a little farther, He fell on the ground and prayed that, if possible, the impending hour might pass from Him. 36He said, "Abba,[q] Father, all things are possible with Thee. Remove this cup from Me. Not, however, what I will but what Thou wilt."

37He came and found them asleep, and said to Peter, "Simon, are you sleeping? Were you not able to watch for one hour? 38All of you watch and pray, so that you may not enter into temptation. The spirit is willing enough, but the flesh is weak."

39He left again and prayed, uttering the same words. 40Then He returned to find them asleep once more; for their eyes were heavy. And they did not know what excuse to give Him. 41He then came for the third time and said to them, "Sleeping and resting still? It is enough; the hour has come. The Son of Man is betrayed into the hands of sinners. 42Rise up; let us go. Look, My betrayer is near."

43At once, while He was still talking, Judas, one of the Twelve, approached and with him a great mob with swords and clubs, sent by the chief priests, scribes and elders. 44Now His betrayer had given them a signal: "The One whom I kiss is the One. Seize Him and lead Him safely away." 45So, as soon as he came, he stepped up to Him, said, "Rabbi,"[r] and kissed Him. 46Then they put their hands on Him and arrested Him.

47One[s] of those standing beside Him drew his sword, struck the high priest's slave and cut off his ear. 48And Jesus' response to them was: "Have you come out as against a robber, with swords and clubs to arrest Me? 49Daily I was with you in the temple teaching, and you did not seize Me. However, this[t] is happening so that the Scriptures may be fulfilled."

50And they all forsook Him and fled. 51But a certain youth[u] followed Him, wearing a linen cloth on his bare body, and when they seized him, 52he left the linen cloth behind and fled from them naked.

53They brought Jesus before the high priest, and all the chief priests and elders and scribes assembled. 54And Peter followed Him from a distance until he was inside the high priest's courtyard, where he sat down with the attendants and warmed himself by the fire.

55The chief priests and the entire Sanhedrin[v] searched for sufficient evidence against Jesus to execute Him, but failed to find it; 56for while many bore false witness against Him, their testimony did not agree. 57Some rose up to testify falsely against Him, 58"We heard Him say, 'I will break down this temple made by hands and in three days will build another made

---

o) This hymn would probably have been some such psalm as Ps. 112.
p) Zech. 13:7.
q) "Abba" (Aramaic) means *father*. Aramaic was the everyday language in Palestine in the first century.
r) That is, "Master." See note at ch. 10:51.
s) Simon Peter, John 18:10.   t) Isa. 53:7, 8.
u) It is probable that this was Mark himself.
v) See note at Luke 22:66.

without hands.'" ⁵⁹But even so their evidence did not agree. ⁶⁰Then the high priest stood up in the center and asked Jesus, "Are not You answering at all what these are testifying against You?" ⁶¹But He kept still and never answered at all.ʷ

Again the high priest questioned Him. He said, "Are You the Christ, the Son of the Blessed?" ⁶²Jesus said, "I am. And you will see the Son of Man seated at the right hand of the Almighty, and coming on the clouds of heaven." ⁶³Then the high priest, tearing his clothes, said, "What further need do we have of witnesses? ⁶⁴You have heard the blasphemy; how does it seem to you?" And they allˣ condemned Him as deserving death. ⁶⁵Some also started to spitʸ at Him and to blindfold Him and to hitᶻ Him with the fist and to say to Him, "Prophesy!" And the attendants took Him and slapped His face.

⁶⁶As Peter was below in the courtyard, one of the high priest's maids came and saw Peter warming himself. ⁶⁷She looked at him and accosted him, "You were with the Nazarene Jesus, too." ⁶⁸But he denied it: "I do not know or understand at all what you are talking about." Then he went outside to the entrance, and the rooster crowed. ⁶⁹Then the servant girl started again to tell the bystanders, "This fellow belongs to them." ⁷⁰Again he denied it. In a little while the bystanders once more told Peter, "Surely, you are one of them; for you are a Galilean."

⁷¹Then he commenced invoking a curse on himself as he swore, "I do not know the Man you mention." ⁷²And instantly for the second time the rooster crowed. Then Peter remembered how Jesus had told him, "Before the cock crows twice, you will disown Me three times." As he considered that, he wept audibly.

15 AS SOON AS MORNING DAWNED the chief priests formed a con-ference with the elders and scribes, including the entire Sanhedrin and, binding Jesus, they led Him off and handed Him over to Pilate. ²Pilate asked Him, "Are You the king of the Jews?" He answered him, "So you say." ³Then the chief priests accused Him of many things, ⁴but Pilate questioned Him again, "Have You no answer? See what they are charging against You." ⁵Still Jesus made no further reply, so that Pilate wondered.

⁶But at the feast he used to release to them one prisoner for whom they asked, ⁷and there was one named Barabbas, confined with the insurrectionists, who had committed murder in the uprising. ⁸The shouting mob proceeded to request the usual privilege for them. ⁹Pilate replied to them, "Do you want me to release to you the king of the Jews?" ¹⁰For he knew that out of envy the chief priests had delivered Him. ¹¹However, the chief priests stirred up the crowd to prefer that Barabbas be released for them. ¹²Then Pilate came back at them again, "Then what shall I do with the One you call king of the Jews?" ¹³But again they shouted, "Crucify Him!" ¹⁴Pilate asked them, "Why, what wrong did He commit?" But they cried out the more loudly, "Crucify Him!"

¹⁵So Pilate, wishing to satisfy the crowd, released Barabbas for them and, after flogging Jesus, gave Him over to be crucified. ¹⁶The soldiers led Him inside the hall, that is, the Praetorium,ᵃ where they mustered the entire cohort.ᵇ ¹⁷They dressed Him in purple, and crowned Him with a crown of thorns, which they had twisted; ¹⁸then they began to salute Him, "Long live the king of the Jews!" ¹⁹They further hit Him on the head with a reed, and spat at Him and with bended knees did Him homage. ²⁰After the mockery, they took the purple off Him and put on His own clothes; then they led Him out to crucify Him.

²¹They forced a certain passerby,

---

w) Isa. 53:7.
x) It does not seem likely that Joseph of Arimathea, Luke 23:50, 51, and Nicodemus, John 7:50-52, were present.   y) Isa. 50:6.   z) Cf. Isa. 52:14.
a) "Praetorium" was a name for Roman headquarters, whether in a military camp, a castle, or the governor's palace. Here it was probably Herod's palace.   b) See note at Acts 10:1.

Simon, a Cyrenian, the father of Alexander and Rufus,[c] who was coming from the country, to carry His cross.

22They led Him to the place called Golgotha, which means Place of a Skull, 23and offered Him a drink of wine, flavored with myrrh; but He refused it. 24And they crucified Him, and divided His clothes, over which they cast lots to determine each one's share. 25It was nine in the morning when they crucified Him. 26The inscription of His accusation was written on top, THE KING OF THE JEWS.

27With Him they crucified two robbers, one at His right and one at His left. 28[So the Scripture was fulfilled.[d] "He was counted with the lawless."][e] 29The passers-by reviled Him, shaking their heads and saying, "Aha, You who were going to destroy the temple and build it in three days! 30Save Yourself! Come down from the cross!" 31Similarly the chief priests, as they mocked between themselves and the scribes, said, "He saved others; Himself He cannot save. 32Let the Christ, the king of Israel, now come down from the cross, so that we may see and believe." And those crucified with Him reproached Him too.

33From twelve until three o'clock darkness settled over the whole country; 34and at three o'clock Jesus cried with a great voice, "Eli, Eli, lama sabachthani?" which means, "My God, My God, why hast Thou forsaken Me?"

35Some of the bystanders, as they heard it, said, "Notice, He is calling for Elijah." 36But one ran and soaked a sponge in vinegar, then fixed it to a reed and gave Him a drink, with the remark, "Hold on, let us see if Elijah comes to take Him down."

37But having uttered a strong cry, Jesus died. 38The temple veil was torn in two from top to bottom, 39and the centurion, who stood facing Him, seeing how He died in that way, exclaimed, "Truly this man was God's Son!" 40There were women also, looking on from a distance, among them Mary Magdalene, and Mary[f] the mother of James, the younger, and of Joses, and Salome[g] — 41the women who had been following Him and helping Him when He was in Galilee, and many others who came up with Him to Jerusalem.

42When evening had come,[h] since it was the day of preparation, that is the day before the Sabbath, 43Joseph of Arimathea, an honorable member of the Sanhedrin, who was personally awaiting the kingdom of God, came and boldly approached Pilate and asked for the body of Jesus. 44But Pilate wondered whether He was already dead; so he summoned the centurion and asked him if He had been dead for some time. 45When he had received this information from the centurion, he granted Joseph the body.

46He bought a linen sheet in which he wrapped the body after taking it down; then he laid Him in a tomb that was carved out of a rock and rolled a stone against the opening of the tomb; 47and Mary Magdalene and Mary the mother of Joses observed where He was laid.

16 AFTER THE SABBATH MARY Magdalene, and Mary the mother of James, and Salome bought spices, so that they might go and anoint Him. 2And very early in the morning at sunrise on the first day of the week they came to the tomb. 3They said among themselves, "Who will roll the stone from the mouth of the tomb for us?" 4But as they looked up, they saw that the stone — a very heavy one — had been rolled away.

5They entered the tomb and saw a young man sitting to the right, dressed in a white robe, and they were struck

---

c) Both sons became known to the church. A Rufus is mentioned in Rom. 16:13, who may have been this son of Simon the Cyrenian.
d) Isa. 53:12.
e) Verse 28, enclosed in brackets, is not found in the majority of the most reliable ancient manuscripts.
f) See note at Matt. 1:16.
g) Salome was Zebedee's wife, the mother of James and John, the apostles, Matt. 27:56; Mark 10:35.   h) The time was between 3 and 6 p.m.

with terror. 6But he said to them, "Do not be terrified. You are looking for Jesus the Nazarene, who was crucified. He is risen; He is not here; see the place where they laid Him. 7But go, tell His disciples and Peter that He precedes you into Galilee; there you will see Him, just as He told you."i 8Hurriedly they fled from the tomb, trembling and alarmed, and they spoke to no one, for they were afraid.

9[After Jesus had risen early the first day of the week, He appeared first to Mary of Magdala, from whom He had expelled seven demons. 10She went and told those who had accompanied Him, grieving and weeping as they were. 11When they heard that He was alive and had been seen by her, they did not believe it. 12But later on He appeared in a different form to two of them while they were walking into the country. 13They went and told the others; but neither did they believe them. 14Afterward He appeared to the Eleven as they satj at the table, and chided their unbelief and hardheartedness, because they did not believe those who had seen Him after He had risen.

15He also told them, "Go into the whole world and preach the gospel to every creature. 16He who believes and is baptized will be saved; but he who does not believe will be condemned. 17And these signs will follow those who believe: in My name they will expel demons; they will speak with new tongues; 18they will pick up snakes; and if they drink anything fatal it will not injure them in the least. They will lay hands on the sick and they will become well."

19So after the Lord had talked with them, He was received up into heaven and sat at the right hand of God. 20But they went out and preached everywhere; for the Lord was working with them and was confirming the message by the signs that followed.]k

---

i) Chapter 14:28.
j) See note at ch. 2:15.
k) Verses 9-20, enclosed in brackets, are not found in the majority of the most reliable manuscripts.

THEME OF MARK:

SEGMENT DIVISIONS

		CHAPTER THEMES
		1
		2
		3
		4
		5
		6
		7
		8
		9
		10
		11
		12
		13
		14
		15
		16

Author:

Date:

Purpose:

Key Words:

immediately
(without delay,
at once, etc.)

authority

kingdom of
God

mark every
reference to
the devil or
demons

covenant

LUKE

*I*n Matthew we see Jesus as King of the Jews. In Mark we see the Servant who came to give His life a ransom for many. Then Luke takes us consecutively through the days of the Son of Man. In this book we see the fulfillment of the things written about Him in the law of Moses, the Prophets, and the Psalms, things which no other Gospel tells us.

THINGS TO DO

1. Luke's purpose in writing is stated in Luke 1:1-4. Read it and then record his purpose on the LUKE AT A GLANCE chart following this Gospel.
2. As you read chapter by chapter, be sure to do the following:
   a. Mark in the text the key words listed on LUKE AT A GLANCE.
   b. Mark references to time with a symbol of your choice. The references will come in many different forms, from the mention of actual days or years to the naming of a Jewish feast, a chief priest, or a king. This part of your study will keep before you the timing and sequence of the events in Jesus' life. These are critical to Luke's purpose.
   c. It is also important to note where each event takes place. Underline every reference to places, cities, or regions. Locate these on the map before the Gospel of Matthew. Note in the margin *where* something occurs, along with *when* it occurs.

   d. List in the margin the main points covered in each chapter.
      1) As you list each event in the margin of the text, color code or mark it in a distinctive way so it can be recognized as an event. This will help you see at a glance the chronology of events in Luke. You can also consult the "Life of Christ" chart before the Gospel of John.
      2) As you note each event or teaching, pay attention to the setting and the response of those who are listening or participating in what is happening. In the margin, note their response. Watch where Jesus is, His relationships to people, what social events He is involved in, and what He expects from people.
   e. If Jesus tells a parable or tells of an incident such as the rich man and Lazarus dying (Luke 16), note what provokes Jesus to do so.
   f. Record the theme of each chapter in the space just above the chapter number and on LUKE AT A GLANCE. Do the same for the theme of the book as you complete the chart.
3. Record the facts concerning Jesus' betrayal, arrest, trial, crucifixion, resurrection, postresurrection appearances, and ascension on the appropriate charts: THE ARREST, TRIAL, AND CRUCIFIXION OF JESUS CHRIST and THE ACCOUNT OF JESUS' RESURRECTION following the Gospel of John. Note the

chapter and verse for each insight. Do this on notebook paper before you write it in your Bible. After you do this for all four Gospels you will have comprehensive notes on what took place at this time in our Lord's life.

4. Also following the Gospel of John you will find a chart titled WHAT THE GOSPELS TEACH ABOUT THE KINGDOM OF GOD/THE KINGDOM OF HEAVEN. Record on a piece of paper the information you glean from marking every reference to *the kingdom of God* in Luke. Then consolidate your findings and record them on the chart in your New Testament. After you study all the Gospels, you will have an overview of what the Gospels teach about the kingdom of God.

THINGS TO THINK ABOUT

1. Have you been slow of heart to believe all that Moses and the prophets wrote about Jesus Christ? Do you see Jesus as the Son of Man, the fulfillment of prophecy, the Christ, the Son of God? Have you bowed to Him as Lord of your life?

2. Jesus reached out to the hurting, the sinners, and the outcasts. He visited in their homes. He was available and accessible. What about you? Do you have compassion on these people? Are you wasting your life on self or are you investing in others? What did you learn from watching Christ's response to others that you can apply to your life?

3. If Jesus needed to withdraw often to a lonely place to pray, what about you? Is prayer a high priority in your life? Do you understand and incorporate the principles of prayer that Jesus taught in the Gospel of Luke?

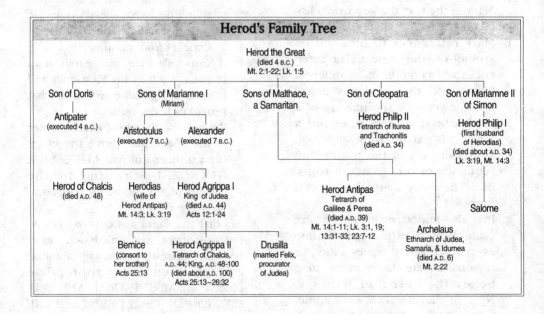

Herod's Family Tree

Herod the Great
(died 4 B.C.)
Mt. 2:1-22; Lk. 1:5

Son of Doris
Antipater
(executed 4 B.C.)

Sons of Mariamne I
(Miriam)
Aristobulus
(executed 7 B.C.)
Alexander
(executed 7 B.C.)

Sons of Malthace,
a Samaritan

Son of Cleopatra
Herod Philip II
Tetrarch of Iturea
and Trachonitis
(died A.D. 34)

Son of Mariamne II
of Simon
Herod Philip I
(first husband
of Herodias)
(died about A.D. 34)
Lk. 3:19, Mt. 14:3

Herod of Chalcis
(died A.D. 48)

Herodias
(wife of
Herod Antipas)
Mt. 14:3; Lk. 3:19

Herod Agrippa I
King of Judea
(died A.D. 44)
Acts 12:1-24

Herod Antipas
Tetrarch of
Galilee & Perea
(died A.D. 39)
Mt. 14:1-11; Lk. 3:1, 19;
13:31-33; 23:7-12

Salome

Bernice
(consort to
her brother)
Acts 25:13

Herod Agrippa II
Tetrarch of Chalcis,
A.D. 44; King, A.D. 48-100
(died about A.D. 100)
Acts 25:13–26:32

Drusilla
(married Felix,
procurator
of Judea)

Archelaus
Ethnarch of Judea,
Samaria, & Idumea
(died A.D. 6)
Mt. 2:22

THE GOSPEL ACCORDING TO

LUKE

1 NOW THAT MANY HAVE PUT THEIR hands to the composition of a narrative regarding the events that have certainly taken place among us, ²transmitted as they were to us by those who were from the first eyewitnesses and ministers of the Word, ³it seemed fitting for me as well, since I investigated accurately everything from its beginning, to write you in orderly fashion, most excellent Theophilus, ⁴so that you may know the certainty of the instructions you have received.

c. 6 B.C.

⁵In the days of Herod, the king of Judea, there was a certain priest named Zechariah, of the week of the priestly service[a] named after Abijah, and his wife Elizabeth, of Aaron's daughters. ⁶Both lived uprightly before God, blamelessly walking in accordance with all the commandments and injunctions of the Lord. ⁷They had no child because Elizabeth was barren, and both were getting up in years.

⁸Administering his priestly service before the Lord in the sequence of his series, as customary among the priests, ⁹it fell to him by lot to enter the Lord's temple for the burning of incense. ¹⁰And at the hour of incense the whole multitude of people were praying outside.

¹¹But an angel of the Lord appeared to him, standing to the right of the altar of incense, ¹²and when Zechariah saw him, he was troubled and fear got hold of him. ¹³But the angel said to him, "Have no fear, Zechariah, because your prayer has been heard. Your wife Elizabeth will bear you a son, whom you will call John. ¹⁴He will afford you joy and happiness and many will be glad at his birth, ¹⁵for he will be great before the Lord. He will drink no wine or liquor at all, and from his birth he will be filled with the Holy Spirit. ¹⁶Many of the sons of Israel will he turn to the Lord their God, ¹⁷before whom he shall go forth in the spirit and power of Elijah, to turn the hearts of the fathers to the children and the obstinate to the wisdom of the righteous, to prepare a people who are ready for the Lord."

¹⁸Then Zechariah said to the angel, "In what way can I be assured of this, for I am an old man and my wife is advanced in years?" ¹⁹The angel answered him, "I am Gabriel, who stands in the presence of God, and I was sent to speak to you and to announce these glad tidings to you. ²⁰Behold! You will be silent and unable to speak until the day when these things take place, because you did not believe my words, which will come true at the proper time."

²¹The people were waiting for Zechariah and wondering why he lingered in the temple; ²²but when he came out he could not speak to them, and they recognized that he had seen a vision in the temple, for he made signs to them and remained speechless. ²³And as soon

---

a) King David had assigned the priests to twenty-four divisions, each section to serve at the sanctuary for a week. The Abijah division was the eighth, I Chron. 24:10.

as his time of service was over, he went home.

c. 5 B.C.

24After those days his wife Elizabeth conceived and hid herself five months, saying, 25"In this way has the Lord treated me when He favored me to remove my humiliation among men."

26In the sixth month of Elizabeth's pregnancy the Angel Gabriel was sent by God to Nazareth,b a town of Galilee, 27to a virgin named Maryc who was engaged to Joseph, a descendant of David. 28The angel, as he approached her, said, "Greetings, favored one. The Lord is with you."

29But she was troubled at his message and reflected what sort of greeting this might be. 30The angel said to her, "Have no fear, Mary, for you have found favor with God. 31And lo, you will conceive in your womb and give birth to a son and you shall call Him Jesus. 32He will be great and will be called Son of the Highest, and the Lord God will give Him the throne of His father David. 33He will be king over the house of Jacob forever; there will be no end to His kingdom."

34Mary asked the angel, "How will this be, since I have no husband?" 35The angel answered her, "The Holy Spirit will come upon you and the power of the Highest will overshadow you; therefore that holy Offspring will be called the Son of God. 36Also your cousin Elizabeth is to be mother of a son in her old age, and this is now the sixth month with her who was called barren. 37For nothing is ever impossible with God." 38And Mary said, "Here I am, the Lord's bondslave. Let it be with me as you say." And the angel left her.

39After those days Mary got ready and hurried to the hill country to a town of Judah, 40arrived at the home of Zechariah, and greeted Elizabeth. 41And as Elizabeth listened to Mary's greeting, the babe leaped within her. Then, filled with the Holy Spirit,

42Elizabeth spoke with a loud voice, "Blessed are you among women and blessed is the fruit of your womb. 43And how did this happen to me, that my Lord's mother should visit me? 44Just think, when the voice of your greeting reached my ears the babe leaped within me for joy! 45And blessed is she who believed, because the things told her by the Lord will be accomplished."

46And Mary said,d "My soul magnifies the Lord 47and my spirit is glad in God my Savior, 48for He took notice of the lowliness of His bondslave. Consider, from now on all generations will call me blessed, 49for the Almighty has done great things for me. His name is holy 50and His mercy is to those who reverence Him through all generations. 51He exercised strength with His arm; He scattered the proud in their heart's imaginations; 52He dethroned princes and lifted up the lowly; 53the needy He supplied to the full with good things and the rich He sent away empty-handed. 54He sustained Israel, His servant, in remembrance of His mercy, 55as He spoke to our fathers, to Abraham and his descendents forever."

56And Mary stayed with her for about three months, and returned to her home. 57Now Elizabeth's time to give birth had come and she bore a son; 58and her neighbors and relatives heard what great mercy the Lord had granted her, and they shared her happiness. 59On the eighth day they came to circumcise the baby and were going to name him Zechariah, after his father. 60But his mother demurred, "No, he must instead be called John!" 61They argued with her, "None of your relatives bears that name." 62Then they motioned to his father, what he wanted him to be called 63and he, requesting a writing tablet, wrote, "His name is John." This surprised them all. 64And instantly his mouth was opened and his tongue was loosed, and he spoke in praise of God.

65A deep sense of awe came upon all

---

b) See note at Matt. 2:23.
c) See note on the four Marys in the Gospels, Matt. 1:16.
d) Mary knew the Hebrew Scriptures. That is evident from her free use of Hannah's song, I Sam. 21:1-8.

the neighbors, and these happenings became matters of conversation in the entire hill country of Judea. [66]All who learned of it kept it in mind. They said, "What kind of child will this be?" For the Lord's hand was with him.

[67]His father Zechariah was filled with the Holy Spirit and prophesied, [68]"Blessed be the Lord God of Israel, for He has looked with favor upon His people and has accomplished redemption for them. [69]He has raised up a powerful Savior for us in the house of David, His servant, [70]as He spoke by the mouth of His holy prophets from ancient times — [71]salvation from our enemies and from the hand of all who hate us. [72]To show the mercy that was promised our ancestors, and to remember His holy covenant, [73]He swore an oath to our father Abraham; [74]to grant us, being saved from our enemies, fearlessly to worship Him [75]in holiness and righteousness in His presence all our days.

[76]"And you, little one, will be called a prophet of the Highest; for you will go in advance of the Lord to prepare His way, [77]to bring to His people a knowledge of salvation by remission of their sins [78]through the tender mercies of our God, by which the light of dawn will beam on us from on high, [79]to shine on those sitting in darkness and in the shadow of death, to direct our feet into the path of peace."

[80]And the child grew and was spiritually strengthened, and was in solitary places until the time of his appearing to Israel.

2 IN THOSE DAYS AN ORDER WENT out from Caesar Augustus that a census should be taken of the whole world. [2]This registration first occurred while Quirinius was governor of Syria. [3]They all went to be registered, each to his own city, [4]and Joseph, too, went up from Galilee out of the city of Nazareth to Judea, to the city of David called Bethlehem,[e] because he was of the house and family of David, [5]to be registered with Mary, his betrothed wife, whose pregnancy was advanced.

[6]While they were there her days were completed to give birth, [7]and she bore her first-born Son, whom she wrapped in swaddling clothes and laid in a manger, because there was no room for them in the inn.

[8]There were in the same country shepherds, staying in the fields and keeping watch over their flock by night.[f] [9]And an angel of the Lord stood by them and the glory of the Lord shone around them, and they feared greatly.

[10]And the angel said to them, "Have no fear, for behold I announce to you good news of great joy that will be for all the people; [11]for today there was born for you in the city of David, a Savior, who is Christ the Lord. [12]And this is a token for you: you will find the baby wrapped in swaddling clothes and lying in a manger."

[13]And suddenly there was with the angel a multitude of the heavenly host, praising God and saying, [14]"Glory to God in the highest, and on earth peace among men in His favor!"

[15]As the angels went from them into heaven, the shepherds said to one another, "Let us go straight to Bethlehem, and let us see what has happened that the Lord has made known to us." [16]And hastily they went, found both Mary and Joseph, and saw the baby lying in the manger. [17]When they had seen the child they made known to others what had been told them regarding it, [18]and every one who heard it marveled at the things that were reported to them by the shepherds. [19]But Mary treasured those reports and thought them over in her heart. [20]And the shepherds went back, glorifying and praising God for everything they had heard and seen, just as it had been told them.

[21]When eight days were completed,[g] at His circumcision the name Jesus was given Him, as named by the angel before His conception in the womb.

---

e) See note at Matt. 2:1.
f) The precise month of the birth of Christ is uncertain.
g) Lev. 12:3.

c. 4 B.C.

22When the days for their purification according to the Law of Moses were completed,[h] they brought Him to Jerusalem to present Him to the Lord, 23as prescribed in the Law of the Lord,[i] "Every first-born male shall be called holy to the Lord," 24and to offer a sacrifice as mentioned in the Law of the Lord,[j] "A pair of turtle doves or two young pigeons."

25Now there was a man in Jerusalem, Simeon by name, an upright and devout man who was looking for the consolation of Israel.[k] The Holy Spirit was on him 26and it was divinely communicated to him by the Holy Spirit that he would not see death before he had seen the Lord's Christ. 27Moved by the Spirit he came into the temple and, when the parents brought in the child Jesus to perform the legal ritual for Him, 28he took Him up in his arms and thanked God, 29"Now let Your bond servant depart in peace, Lord, in agreement with Your word, 30for my eyes have seen Your salvation, 31which You have prepared before all the nations, 32a light for revelation to the Gentiles and a glory to Your people Israel."

33As His father and mother were wondering about the things spoken regarding Him, 34Simeon blessed them and said to His mother Mary, "See, this child is appointed for the falling and rising up of many in Israel and for a sign that will be opposed — 35And a sword shall pass through your own soul — so that the reasonings of many hearts may be revealed."

36There also was Anna, a daughter of Phanuel of the tribe of Asher, a prophetess advanced in years who had, after her girlhood, lived seven years with her husband, 37and was a widow of about eighty-four. She never left the temple but worshiped night and day in fastings and intercessions. 38She, too, came up that same hour and gave similar thanks to the Lord and talked about Him to all those looking for the redemption of Jerusalem.

39When they had finished everything according to the Law of the Lord, they went back to Galilee to their own city, Nazareth. 40And the child grew and became strong, filled with wisdom, and the grace of God rested upon Him.

c. A.D. 8

41Annually at the Passover Feast His parents traveled to Jerusalem. 42And when He was twelve they went up to Jerusalem according to the custom of the feast. 43When the days were ended and they returned, the boy Jesus remained behind in Jerusalem without His parents being aware of it. 44Supposing that He was in the caravan, they traveled a day, then looked for Him among relatives and acquaintances 45and, not finding Him, went back to Jerusalem in search of Him. 46The third day they found Him in the temple, sitting among the teachers, listening to them and asking them questions. 47And all who heard Him were astonished at His understanding and His answers.

48When His parents saw Him they were amazed, and His mother said to Him, "Child, why have You treated us this way? Your father and I have anxiously been looking for You." 49He said to them, "Why were you seeking Me? Did you not know that I ought to be in My Father's house?" 50But they did not understand the saying which He spoke to them.

51He went down with them to Nazareth and submitted Himself to them, and His mother treasured all these matters in her heart. 52And Jesus advanced in wisdom and in stature and in favor with God and men.

c. A.D. 26

3 IN THE FIFTEENTH YEAR OF TIBErius Caesar's reign,[l] when Pontius

---

h) Lev. 12:1, 2, 4.
i) Num. 8:17. "Holy" (Gk. *hagios*) equals *consecrated to*. The first-born male was to be consecrated to the Lord.
j) Lev. 12:6-8.
k) Simeon was looking for the coming of the Messiah, Israel's hope and comfort, Isa. 40:1-5; 61:1-3.
l) The reign of Tiberius began about A.D. 11-12.

Pilate was governor of Judea; Herod, tetrarch of Galilee; his brother Philip, tetrarch of Ituraea and of the Trachonitis region; and Lysanias, tetrarch of Abilene, [2]Annas and Caiaphas being high priests, the word of God came to John, the son of Zechariah, in the desert.

[3]Then he went into all the area on either side of the Jordan River, preaching a baptism of repentance for the forgiveness of sins, [4]as has been written in the book of messages of Isaiah the prophet,[m] "A voice of one shouting in the desert, Prepare the way of the Lord, make His paths straight. [5]Every ravine will be filled up and every mountain and hill will be leveled; the crooked paths will become straight and the rough ways smooth, [6]and all people will see the salvation of God."

[7]So he said to the crowds that came to be baptized by him, "Viper brood, who forewarned you to flee from the coming wrath? [8]Therefore produce fruits in keeping with your repentance, and do not begin to say within yourselves, 'We have Abraham as our father'; for I tell you that God can raise offspring to Abraham from these stones. [9]The ax is lying ready at the root of the trees, so that every tree that fails to produce good fruit will be felled and thrown into the fire."

[10]The crowds asked him, "Then what should we do?" [11]He answered them, "He who has two tunics should share with him who has none, and he who has food should behave similarly."

[12]The tax collectors also came to be baptized and said to him, "Teacher, what shall we do?" [13]To them he said, "Do not collect more than your appointed rate." [14]And when the soldiers asked him, "What shall we do?" he told them, "Do not extort money by intimidating or informing, but be content with your pay."

[15]As the people were in suspense and were all wondering in their hearts about John, whether he might perhaps be the Christ, [16]John answered them all, "I, it is true, baptize you with water, but One mightier than I is coming after me, whose sandal-strings I am not fit to unfasten. He will baptize you with the Holy Spirit and with fire. [17]His winnowing fan is in His hand and He will thoroughly clean up His threshing floor, storing the wheat in His granary and burning the chaff in fire that cannot be put out."

[18]With many another appeal, also, he preached to the people; [19]but when Herod the tetrarch was taken to task by him regarding Herodias, his brother Philip's wife, as well as about all the evils he had practiced, [20]he crowned all this by confining John in prison.

[21]When all the people were being baptized, Jesus too was baptized and, while He was praying, heaven was opened [22]and the Holy Spirit came down on Him, in bodily shape like a dove, and a voice came from heaven, "Thou art My Beloved Son; in Thee I am well pleased."

[23]And Jesus Himself, when He began His ministry, was about thirty years of age, being the son, as was supposed, of Joseph, the son of Heli,[n] [24]whose father and forefathers were Matthat, Levi, Melchi, Jannai, Joseph, [25]Mattathias, Amos, Nahum, Esli, Naggai, [26]Maath, Mattathias, Semein, Josech, Joda, [27]Joanan, Rhesa, Zerubbabel, Shealtiel, Neri, [28]Melchi, Addi, Cosam, Elmadam, Er, [29]Joshua, Eliezer, Jorim, Matthat, Levi, [30]Simeon, Judas, Joseph, Janam, Eliakim, [31]Melea, Menna, Mattatha, Nathan, David, [32]Jesse, Obed, Boaz, Salmon, Nahshon, [33]Aminadab, Arni, Hezron, Perez, Judah, [34]Jacob, Isaac, Abraham, Terah, Nahor, [35]Serug, Reu, Peleg, Eber, Shelah, [36]Cainan, Arphaxad, Shem, Noah, Lamech, [37]Methuselah, Enoch, Jared, Mahalaleel, Cainan, [38]Enos, Seth, Adam who was of God.

4 FILLED WITH THE HOLY SPIRIT, Jesus returned from the Jordan River and for forty days was guided about in the desert by the Spirit, [2]while being tested by the devil. He did not eat at all during those days and

---

m) Isa. 40:3-5.
n) Jesus was the grandson of Heli through Mary.

on their completion He was hungry. ³So the devil said to Him, "If You are the Son of God, tell this stone to become bread." ⁴Jesus answered him, "It is written,º 'Man shall not live on bread alone; [but by every expression of God].'"ᵖ ⁵Then leading Him up [to a high mountain],ᵖ the devil showed Him in an instant all the world's kingdoms and told Him, ⁶"All this authority and the splendor of them will I give You, for it has been handed over to me and I bestow it on whomever I please; ⁷so if You will worship me, it shall all be Yours." ⁸Jesus answered him, "It is written,q 'You shall worship the Lord your God and serve Him alone.'"

⁹Then he brought Him to Jerusalem and, placing Him on the summit of the temple, told Him, "If You are the Son of God, throw Yourself down from here, ¹⁰for it is written,ʳ 'He will give orders to His angels on your behalf to protect you,' ¹¹and 'They will carry you on their hands so that you may not stub your foot against a stone.'" ¹²Jesus answered him, "It is also written,ˢ 'You shall not test the Lord your God.'" ¹³So the devil, after bringing to completion every kind of temptation, left Him until a favorable time.

c. A.D. 28

¹⁴Jesus returned to Galilee in the power of the Spirit, and His fame spread over all the surrounding country. ¹⁵He taught in their synagogues and was lauded by everyone. ¹⁶He came to Nazareth,ᵗ where He had been brought up, and in agreement with His custom He went to the synagogue on the Sabbath and stood up to read. ¹⁷The book of the Prophet Isaiah was handed to Him and on opening the scroll He found the place where it was written,ᵘ ¹⁸"The Spirit of the Lord is upon Me, for He has anointed Me to preach the gospel to the poor; He

has sent Me to announce release to the captives and restoration of sight to the blind, to set free the downtrodden and ¹⁹to proclaim the year of the Lord's favor."ᵛ

²⁰Rolling up the scroll He handed it back to the attendant and sat down. The eyes of everyone in the synagogue were fixed on Him, ²¹and He began by telling them, "Today this Scripture is fulfilled in your hearing." ²²They all remarked about Him and wondered at the gracious words that flowed from His lips. They said, "Is not this Joseph's son?" ²³He said to them, "You will doubtless quote Me this proverb, 'Physician, heal Yourself.' Do in Your own hometown what we hear You did in Capernaum." ²⁴But He continued, "I assure you that no prophet is acceptable in his home town. ²⁵I tell you truly, in the days of Elijahʷ there were many widows in Israel, when for three years and six months the heaven was closed up and a severe famine visited all the land; ²⁶but to none of them was Elijah sent except to a widow at Sarepta of Sidon. ²⁷There were also many lepers in Israel in the time of Elishaˣ the prophet, and none of them was cured but Naaman the Syrian."

²⁸When the people in the synagogue heard this, they all felt deeply resentful. ²⁹They got up and expelled Him from the city and led Him to the brow of the hill on which the city was built, to hurl Him down; ³⁰but He made His way straight through their midst and went away.

³¹He came down to Capernaum,ʸ a city of Galilee, and taught them on the Sabbath. ³²They were overwhelmed with His teaching, for His message had authority. ³³And in the synagogue there was a man with an unclean demon's spirit, who cried out loudly, ³⁴"Ah, what business is it of Yours to bother us, Jesus of Nazareth? Have You come to destroy us? I know

---

o) Deut. 8:3.
p) The words in brackets are not found in the majority of the most reliable ancient manuscripts.
q) Deut. 6:13; 10:20.   r) Psa. 91:11, 12.   s) Deut. 6:16.
t) See note at Matt. 2:23.   u) Isa. 61:1, 2.
v) Compare this with the message sent to the bewildered John the Baptist while he was in prison, Matt. 11:4, 5.   w) I Kings 17:1-16; *cf.* James 5:17, 18.
x) II Kings 5:1-18.   y) See note at Matt. 4:13.

who You are — The Holy One of God."
³⁵But Jesus rebuked him, "Be still and get out of him!" Then throwing him to the floor in their midst, the demon came out of him without hurting him.

³⁶A sense of awe came over all of them and they remarked to one another, "What teaching this is! For with authority and power He gives orders to unclean spirits and they come out." ³⁷And a report about Him went out into every place in the surrounding country.

³⁸He then went from the synagogue to Simon's home; but Simon's mother-in-law was suffering from a high fever and they consulted Him about her. ³⁹Standing over her, He rebuked the fever and it left her. And at once she arose and began to wait on them.

⁴⁰At sunset all who had any who were ill with various diseases, brought them to Him and He laid hands on all of them and cured them. ⁴¹Even demons came out of many people, shouting, "You are the Son of God." But He rebuked them and did not allow them to speak, because they knew that He was the Christ.

⁴²At break of day He went out to a lonely spot, but the crowds were looking for Him and came to where He was and tried to keep Him from leaving them; ⁴³but He told them, "I must preach the good news of the kingdom of God to other towns as well, because for this purpose I was sent." ⁴⁴And He continued preaching in the synagogues of Judea.

5 AND AS THE PEOPLE WERE CROWDing Him to hear God's message, He noticed, while standing by the Lake of Gennesaret,^z ²two boats moored near the shore, but the fishermen had disembarked and were washing their nets. ³He stepped into one of the boats which belonged to Simon, and asked him to push out a little from the shore;

then when He had sat down He began to teach the crowd from the boat.

⁴When He had finished speaking, He told Simon, "Push out into the deep and lower your nets for a haul." ⁵Simon replied, "Master, all night we were working hard without catching a thing; however, at Your word, I will cast the nets." ⁶And when they did so, they enclosed such a shoal of fish that their nets started tearing. ⁷They signaled their partners in the other boat to come and help them, which they did, and they filled both boats until they almost sank. ⁸At the sight of it, Simon Peter fell at Jesus' knees and said, "Leave me, Lord, for I am a sinful man!"^a ⁹For amazement had gripped him and all his partners at the catch of fish they had made — ¹⁰so also with James and John, the sons of Zebedee, partners with Simon. And Jesus said to Simon, "Have no fear; from now on you will be catching men." ¹¹Then bringing the boats to shore, they left everything and followed Him.

¹²While He was in one of the towns, a man covered with leprosy saw Jesus and, falling on his face, begged of Him, "Lord, if You will, You can cleanse me." ¹³Reaching out His hand, Jesus touched him, saying, "I will; be cleansed." And immediately the leprosy left him. ¹⁴Jesus warned him to tell no one; but "Go, show yourself to the priest,"^b He said, "and make offerings for your purification as Moses prescribed, as evidence to the people." ¹⁵But word about Him spread even more, and large crowds gathered to listen and to be healed of their diseases. ¹⁶Jesus, however, habitually withdrew into the desert for prayer.

¹⁷One of those days He was teaching, and Pharisees^c and teachers of the law, who had come from every village of Galilee and from Judea and Jerusalem, were sitting there, and the power

---

z) The Lake of Gennesaret is another name for the Sea of Galilee. The same body of water is also called the Sea of Tiberius, John 6:1. In O.T. times it was known as the Sea of Chinnereth, Num. 34:11; Josh. 12:3; 13:27.
a) If he had not realized it before this, Peter was now beginning to understand that Jesus was more than a mere man.
b) In O.T. times part of the priestly function was to prescribe for the sick in accord with the Law of Moses, Lev. 14.
c) See note at Matt. 3:7.

of the Lord was present so that He healed people. [18]Then some men came carrying a paralytic on a couch and tried to bring him in and lay him before Jesus; [19]but as they found no way to carry him in because of the crowd, they went up on the roof and let him down through the tiles, couch and all, right in front of Jesus.

[20]Seeing their faith, He said, "Man, your sins are forgiven you." [21]The scribes[d] and the Pharisees began to reason, "Who is this, speaking blasphemies? Who is able to forgive sins except God alone?"[e] [22]Jesus, aware of their reasonings, said to them, "What are you deliberating in your minds? [23]Which is easier, to say: 'Your sins are forgiven,' or to say, 'Arise and walk'? [24]However, so that you may know that the Son of Man has authority on earth to forgive sins," He said to the paralytic, "I tell you, rise, pick up your couch and walk home." [25]At once he got up in their presence, picked up what he had been lying on and, praising God, went home. [26]Amazement gripped them all; they, too, praised God and, full of awe, said, "We have seen astounding things today."

[27]Going outdoors after this, He noticed a tax collector named Levi[f] sitting at the revenue office, and said to him, "Follow Me." [28]Rising up, he left everything and followed Him. [29]Then Levi gave Him a great banquet at his home, at which a large group of tax collectors and others sat[g] at the table together. [30]But the scribes and the Pharisees grumbled to His disciples, "Why do you eat and drink with tax collectors and sinners?" [31]Jesus answered them, "Healthy people do not need a physician, but those who are ill. [32]I have come, not to call the upright but sinners to repentance."

[33]And they said to Him, "John's disciples fast and pray frequently, as do those of the Pharisees as well; but Yours both eat and drink." [34]And Jesus said to them, "Can the wedding guests be made to fast while the bridegroom is with them? [35]But the time will come when the bridegroom will be taken from them, and in those days they will fast."

[36]And He spoke this parable to them: "No one patches an old garment with a patch taken from a new one, or else he will tear the new, and also the patch from the new will not match the old. [37]And no one pours new wine into old wineskins; otherwise the new wine will burst the skins and run out and the skins will be ruined. [38]But new wine should be put into fresh wineskins. [39]And no one, used to drinking old wine, wants new wine right away, for he says, 'The old is preferable.' "[h]

6 ON A SABBATH,[i] WHILE HE WAS passing through grainfields, His disciples picked the heads of grain, rubbed them in their hands and ate them. [2]But some of the Pharisees said, "Why do you practice what is not allowed on the Sabbath?" [3]Jesus answered them, "Have you never read[j] what David did when he and his companions were hungry, [4]how he entered the house of God and took and ate the loaves of presentation,[k] which none but the priests are allowed to eat, and he shared them with his companions?" [5]He said further, "The Son of Man is Lord of the Sabbath."

[6]On another Sabbath, as He went into the synagogue and taught, a man was present whose right hand was withered, [7]and the scribes and the Pharisees were watching Him whether He would cure him on the Sabbath, so that they might find something to accuse Him of. [8]But He knew their thoughts and said to the man with the

---

d) See note at Matt. 2.4.
e) The scribes and Pharisees were right in thinking that only Deity can forgive sins, and for them Jesus was no more than a mere man. And with Jesus the healing of men's souls was more important than the healing of their bodies.
f) Levi is the Matthew of ch. 6:15. See note at Mark 2:14.   g) See note at Mark 2:15.
h) This parable is Jesus' simple way of portraying the difficult change from the restrictions of the ceremonial Law to the liberty of the Gospel of grace.
i) Some ancient manuscripts read, "On the second Sabbath after the first."
j) I Sam. 21:1-7.   k) This was the showbread, Exod. 25:30.

withered hand, "Arise, and stand here in the center." And he got up and stood there.

[9]Then Jesus said to them, "I ask you, is it allowed to do good or to do evil on the Sabbath; to save a life or to destroy it?" [10]Then, looking around at all of them, He said to the man, "Hold out your hand." This he did, and his hand was fully restored. [11]But, maddened with anger, they discussed together what they might do to Jesus.

[12]In those days He went up into the hills to pray and was spending the entire night in prayer to God. [13]At daybreak He summoned His disciples and chose twelve of them whom He named apostles: [14]Simon whom He also called Peter, and his brother Andrew; James and John; Philip and Bartholomew; [15]Matthew and Thomas; James the son of Alphaeus and Simon called the Zealot; [16]Judas the son of James, and Judas Iscariot, who turned traitor against Him.

[17]With them He came down and stood on a level spot with a large throng of His disciples and a vast crowd of people from all over Judea and from Jerusalem and from the borders of Tyre and Sidon, who came to hear Him and to be cured of their diseases. [18]Those troubled with unclean spirits were healed also. [19]And the whole crowd tried to touch Him because power issued from Him and healed every one.

[20]Fixing His eyes on His disciples, He proceeded to say,[1] "Blessed[m] are you poor, for yours is the kingdom of God. [21]Blessed are you that are hungry now, for you will be satisfied. Blessed are you that weep now, for you will laugh. [22]Blessed are you when people hate you and exclude you and denounce and defame your name as wicked on account of the Son of Man. [23]Be glad at such a time and leap for joy, for in heaven your reward is rich.

Their fathers treated the prophets just that way.

[24]"Alas, however, for you who are wealthy,[n] for you have enjoyed your comfort. [25]Alas for you who are filled up now, for you will suffer hunger. Alas for you who laugh now, for you will mourn and weep. [26]Alas when everyone praises you, for their fathers treated the false prophets just that way.

[27]"But to you who are listening to Me I say, Love your enemies; treat well those who hate you; [28]bless those who curse you; pray for those who abuse you. [29]To him who hits you on the cheek, offer the other, and do not prevent the one who takes your coat from taking your tunic as well. [30]Give to everyone who asks you, and do not request your belongings back from him who took them. [31]Treat others exactly as you would like to have them treat you.

[32]"If you love only those who love you, what credit is that to you? For sinners, too, love those who love them. [33]And if you treat well those who treat you well, what credit is that to you? Sinners do that much. [34]And if you lend to those from whom you expect a return, what credit is that to you? Sinners lend to sinners as well, to get back an equal amount.

[35]"But love your enemies; do good and lend without prospect of return. Then your return will be rich; you will be sons of the Most High, for He is kind to the ungrateful and wicked. [36]Be merciful, just as your Father is merciful. [37]Do not judge and you will not be judged; do not condemn and you will not be condemned; pardon and you will be pardoned; [38]give and it will be given to you — good measure, pressed down, shaken together and running over will they pour into your lap. For with the yardstick you use for measuring, it in turn will be measured to you."

[39]And He told them a parable: "Can

---

1) In this passage, vss. 20-49, Luke records in somewhat different words a good part of the Sermon on the Mount, Matt. 5-7.

m) The Greek word *makarioi*, rendered "blessed" here and in the beatitudes as written in Matt 5:3-11, may also be translated "happy." It is significant that Jesus teaches that some of the very things that men consider cause for sorrow will bring His disciples blessing and happiness.

n) Such a reversal of conditions is vividly illustrated in the story of the rich man and Lazarus, Luke 16:19-31.

one blind person guide another? Will they not both stumble into a pit? 40A disciple is not above his teacher; but every well-trained student will be like his teacher.

41"And why do you notice the splinter in your brother's eye without being at all aware of the beam in your own eye? 42How can you say to your brother, 'Brother, let me extract the splinter from your eye,' without noticing the beam in your own eye? Hypocrites, first extract the beam from your eye and then you can clearly see to extract the splinter from your brother's eye.

43"For no good tree bears worthless fruit; neither does a worthless tree bear good fruit; 44for each tree is known by its own fruit. Accordingly, no figs are picked from thorns, nor are grapes gathered from a bramble bush. 45The good person expresses good from the good that is stored in his heart, and the evil person expresses evil from the evil that is stored in his heart. For from the abundance of the heart the mouth speaks.

46"Why do you call Me, 'Lord, Lord,' and do not do what I say? 47Whoever comes to Me and listens to My words and does them, I will show you whom he resembles. 48He resembles a man who built a house; he dug and went down deep and set the foundation on a rock. When the flood rose, the river rushed against that house but had no power to shake it, because it was securely built. 49But one who listens and does not do what I say resembles a man who built his house on the ground without a foundation, against which the river rushed and at once it fell, and the wreck of that house was terrible."

7 WHEN HE HAD FINISHED ALL HIS utterances in the hearing of the people, He entered Capernaum. 2There a centurion's slave,° who meant much to him, was ill to the point of death;

3but hearing about Jesus he sent Jewish elders to Him who begged Him to come and heal his slave. 4On reaching Jesus they urged Him strongly, "He deserves to have this done for him, 5for he loves our nation and has built us a synagogue." 6So Jesus went with them.

However, they were not far from the house when the centurion sent friends to tell Him, "Lord, take no further trouble; for I am not fit to have You under my roof, and for this reason 7I did not consider myself worthy of approaching You. Simply say the word and have my serving boy cured. 8For I am also a man under orders and I have soldiers under me and say to this one, 'Go,' and he goes, and to that one, 'Come,' and he comes, and to my slave, 'Do this,' and he does it."

9Jesus marveledp when He heard that and, turning to the crowd that followed Him, said to them, "I tell you, I have found no such faith, even in Israel."q 10The messengers then went back to the house and found the slave healed.

11Shortly afterward He visited a town called Nain, accompanied by His disciples and a large crowd. 12As He neared the city gate there was being carried out a dead man — an only son whose mother was a widow — and a large crowd from that city was with her. 13When the Lord saw her He felt sympathy for her and said to her, "Do not weep." 14Then going forward He touched the bier. The pallbearers stopped and He said, "Young man, I tell you arise." 15The lifeless one sat up and began to speak, and He presented him to his mother. 16Awe took hold of everyone; they gave God the glory and said, "A great prophet has arisen among us." and "God has cared for His people." 17This report about Jesus spread throughout Judea and all the surrounding country.

---

o) See note at Matt. 13:27. The centurion's slave was used as a domestic servant, vs. 7; cf. Matt. 8:6.
p) The N.T. records only two instances of Jesus' marveling — at the faith of the Roman officer, vss. 6-8; cf. Matt. 8:10, and at the unbelief of the people of His home town, Nazareth, Mark 6:6.
q) It is not unusual for those outside the place of highest privilege to display greater faith than those who should be closest to God.

18John's disciples reported all this to him. 19And John, summoning two of them, sent to ask the Lord, "Are You the Coming One, or should we look for someone else?" 20When the men reached Him, they said, "John the Baptist has sent us to You with the question, 'Are You the Coming One or should we look for someone else?'"

21Just then He was curing many of diseases and ailments and evil spirits; He also gave sight to many who were blind. 22And He answered them, "Go and tell John what you see and hear. The blind see; the lame walk; lepers are cleansed; the deaf hear; the dead are raised; the poor are evangelized, 23and blessed is he who does not turn away from Me."

24When John's messengers were gone, He began to address the throngs regarding John: "What did you go out to see in the desert? A reed swayed by the wind? 25Really, what did you go out to see? A man elegantly dressed? Of course those who are stylishly dressed and living in luxury dwell in palaces. 26Then what did you go out to see? A prophet? Yes, I tell you and far more than a prophet. 27It is he of whom it is written,r 'Behold, I send My messenger ahead of You, who will prepare the road before You.' 28I tell you no person born of woman is greater than John, and yet the least important in the kingdom of God is greater than he."s 29All the people, when they heard Him, even the tax collectors, acknowledged God as just, because they accepted John's baptism, 30but the Pharisees and the teachers of the Law rejected God's purpose for them by refusing baptism at his hand.

31"To what then shall I compare the men of this generation? What do they resemble? 32They are like children sitting in a market place and calling out to one another, 'We have played the flute for you and you would not dance;

we have sung you dirges and you would not weep.' 33For John the Baptist came neither dining nor wining and you say, 'He has a demon.' 34The Son of Man came eating and drinking, and you say, 'Look at a man, a glutton and a drunkard, a friend of tax collectors and sinners.' 35So is wisdom vindicated by all her children."t

36One of the Pharisees invited Him to dinner; so He went to the Pharisee's home and satu at the table. 37When a woman of the town, a sinner, learned that He was dining in the Pharisee's home, she brought an alabaster flask of perfume 38and, standing behind Him at His feet, weeping, began to wet His feet with her tears, then wiped them with the hair of her head, tenderly kissed His feet and anointed them with the perfume.v 39When His host, the Pharisee, saw it, he said to himself, "If this person were a prophet, He would know what kind of woman is touching Him; for she is devoted to sin." 40Jesus answered, "Simon, I have something to tell you." He said, "Teacher, go ahead and speak." 41"Two men were in debt to a moneylender; one owed him one hundred and twenty-five dollars and the other twelve dollars and a half.w 42As neither had anything to pay him, he generously canceled the debt of both. So which of them will love him more?" 43Simon replied, "I suppose the one for whom he canceled more." He said to him, "You have judged correctly." 44Then turning to the woman, He said to Simon, "You see this woman? As I entered your home you supplied no water for My feet but she has washed My feet with her tears and wiped them with her hair. 45You did not give Me a kiss, but she from the moment I came in has not stopped tenderly kissing My feet. 46You did not anoint My head with oil, but she has anointed My feet with perfume. 47So I tell you, her sins, many

---

r) Mal. 3:1.
s) The new covenant is richer than the old.
t) Wisdom is vindicated by those who accept and practice her suggestions.
u) See note at Mark 2:15.
v) Nowhere in the N.T. is it suggested that this was Mary Magdalene.
w) The text reads five hundred denarii and fifty (denarii). A denarius would be equivalent to about twenty-five cents in mid-twentieth century U.S. currency.

as they are, are forgiven, for she has greatly loved.[x] But the person who is forgiven little, loves little." 48 And He said to her, "Your sins are forgiven."

49Those at the table with Him began to say to themselves, "Who is this who even forgives sin?" 50But He said to the woman, "Your faith has saved you. Go in peace."

8 SUBSEQUENTLY HE TRAVELED from one town and village to another, preaching and telling the good news of the kingdom of God. The Twelve were with Him, 2and also certain women who had been healed of evil spirits and diseases — Mary called Magdalene, from whom seven demons had been expelled, 3and Joanna the wife of Chuza, Herod's steward, and Susanna, and many others who helped support them[y] out of their means.

4When a great throng was gathering and people resorted to Him from every town, He told them in a parable: 5"A sower went out to sow his seed and, as he sowed, some fell along the road and was walked on, and the birds of the air ate it. 6Other seed fell on the bedrock and sprouted, but then withered because it lacked moisture. 7Other seed fell among the thorns, and the thorns grew with it and choked it. 8Other seed fell on the good soil and grew up and yielded a hundredfold." Upon telling this, He called out, "He who has ears to hear, let him hear."

9And His disciples asked Him the meaning of this parable, 10and He said, "It is granted you to know the secrets of the kingdom of God, but I speak the rest in parables that[z] seeing they may not see, and hearing they may not hear. 11The parable's meaning is this: the seed is the word of God. 12Those along the road are people who hear; then the devil comes and carries away the word from their hearts, so that they may not believe and be saved. 13Those on the bedrock are people who hear the word and welcome it gladly, but they have no root; they believe for a while and in time of trial they fall away. 14What falls among the thorns are people who listen but, as they go on, the word is choked by worries and wealth and pleasures of life, so that they never mature. 15But the seed in the good soil are those who listen to the word and retain it in a good and well-disposed heart, and steadily bear fruit.

16"No one lights a lamp and hides it under a vessel or puts it under a couch; instead, he sets it on a stand so that people who enter the room may see the light. 17For nothing is hidden that will not be disclosed; nothing concealed that will not be known and brought to light. 18Look out, therefore, how you listen; for whoever has, will receive more, and from one who has nothing, what he fancies he possesses will be taken away."

19His mother and His brothers came to Him but could not get near Him because of the crowd. 20So it was told Him, "Your mother and your brothers are standing at the edge of the crowd, wanting to see you." 21But He replied to them, "My mother and My brothers are those who hear and practice the word of God."[a]

22One day He and His disciples got into a boat and He said to them, "Let us cross to the other side of the lake"; and they set sail. 23But as they were sailing He fell asleep. And a squall of wind came down on the lake, and they were shipping water and were in jeopardy. 24So they went and awakened Him, exclaiming, "Master, Master, we are perishing!" And He awoke and rebuked the wind and the surging of the water, and they ceased and there was a calm. 25Then He said to them, "Where is your faith?" But they, awed and

---

x) Whereas Simon, Jesus' host, seems not to have shown even the ordinary courtesies to his guest, this woman demonstrated her love for Him by her deeds.
y) Some ancient manuscripts read "him."
z) Cf. Deut. 29:3, 4; Isa. 6:9, 10; Acts 28: 26, 27.
a) Jesus taught that His family included not just His immediate relatives but all who are obedient to the Word of God. The door to closeness to Christ is the obedience of faith; all who submit themselves to the practice of the Word may be as near to Him as His own mother and brothers were.

amazed, said to one another, "Who is He, anyway, to give orders to winds and water and they obey Him?"

26They landed at the country of the Gerasenes,b which is opposite Galilee, 27and as He stepped out on the land a demon-possessed man, who came from the town, met Him. He had worn no clothes for a long time, nor did he live in a house, but in the tombs. 28Seeing Jesus, he cried out, threw himself in front of Him and shouted loudly, "What business is it of Yours to bother me, Jesus, Son of the Most High God? I beg of You, do not torture me." 29For He had ordered the unclean spirit to leave the man. Often it had seized him and, although he was securely fastened in chains and fetters, and guarded, he would snap the bonds and be driven by the demon into the desert.

30Jesus asked him, "What is your name?" He said, "Legion,"c because many demons had entered him. 31And they begged Him not to order them to go away into the abyss. 32But there was a huge herd of swine grazing on the hillside, and they asked Him to give them permission to enter them; which He allowed. 33Then the demons left the man and entered the swine and the drove rushed down the steep bank into the lake and were drowned.d

34When the herdsmen saw what had occurred they ran away and reported it in town and country. 35The people came out to see what had happened and, reaching Jesus, they found the man from whom the demons had gone, sitting at Jesus' feet dressed and sane—and they were frightened. 36Those who had seen how the demoniac had been healed then reported it to them; 37and all the Gerasenes and the people living around them requested Him to leave them; for they were thoroughly frightened. So He got into the boat and went back.

38The man whom the demons had left begged to accompany Him, but Jesus sent him away, saying, 39"Go back to your home and tell all that God has done for you." So he went and published all over the town what Jesus had done for him.

40At His return the crowd welcomed Jesus, for they were all looking for Him. 41And a man named Jairus, a ruler of the synagogue, came and fell at Jesus' feet and requested Him to come to his home 42because his only daughter, about twelve, was dying. But as He was going, the throngs pressed Him closely, 43and a woman who had suffered from hemorrhages for twelve years and had spent on doctors all she had, whom no one had been able to cure, 44came up behind Him and touched the hem of His robe. Immediately, her hemorrhage stopped. 45Jesus said, "Who touched Me?" When everyone denied it, Peter remarked, "Master, the crowds are all around and pressing you." 46But Jesus said, "Some one has touched Me, for I am conscious of power having gone out of Me."e 47When the woman saw that she had not escaped notice, she came trembling, fell before Him and confessed in the presence of all the people why she had touched Him and how she had been instantly cured. 48He said to her, "Daughter, cheer up. Your faith has healed you; go in peace."

49While He was still speaking, someone came from the home of the ruler of the synagogue and said, "Your daughter is dead. Do not trouble the Teacher any further." 50But when Jesus heard it, He replied, "Have no fear; simply believe and she will be healed."

51On reaching the house He allowed no one to enter with Him, except Peter, John, and James, and the child's father and mother. 52All the people were wailing and beating their breasts for her, but He said, "Stop wailing. She is not dead but asleep." But knowing that she was dead 53they laughed at Him. 54Grasping her hand, He

b) Some ancient manuscripts read "Gadarenes." See note at Mark 5:1.
c) A Roman legion was composed of 5,000-6,000 men.
d) The demons were homeless after all!
e) The healing of others was apparently a drain on Jesus' personal strength. It was the power of Christ, not His robe, that healed the woman.

called out, "Little girl, arise." [55]Her spirit returned and at once she arose, and He ordered that she be given something to eat. [56]Her parents were amazed; but He instructed them to tell no one what had happened.

9 CALLING THE TWELVE TOGETHER He gave them power and authority over all the demons and to heal diseases. [2]He sent them out· to preach the kingdom of God and to heal the sick. [3]He said to them, "Take nothing for the journey, neither staff, nor bag, nor money, nor an extra tunic. [4]Whatever home you enter, stay there and go out from there. [5]Where they do not welcome you, when you leave that town shake off the dust from your feet for a testimony against them." [6]So they went out from village to village preaching the gospel and healing everywhere.

[7]Now when Herod[f] the tetrarch heard of all the events that were occurring, he was at a loss because it was told by some that John had risen from the dead, [8]by others that Elijah had appeared, and by still others that one of the old prophets had come back to life. [9]But Herod said, "John I have beheaded; now who is this about whom I hear such things?" And he endeavored to see Him.

c. A.D. 29

[10]The apostles came back and reported to Jesus everything they had done. Then He took them and withdrew into privacy near a town called Beth-saida,[g] [11]but the crowds learned of it and followed Him. And, bidding them welcome, He spoke to them about the kingdom of God and healed those who needed healing.

[12]As the day began to decline, the Twelve came to Him and said, "Dismiss the multitude, so they may go into the surrounding villages and hamlets to lodge and to find food, for here we are in an isolated place." [13]But He

told them, "You give them to eat." They replied, "We have only five loaves and two fish[h]—unless we go and buy food for all these people." [14]For there were about five thousand men. But He told His disciples, "Have them sit[i] in rows of about fifty"— [15]which they did. They had them all sit down. [16]Then taking the five loaves and the two fish, and looking up toward heaven He gave thanks and broke them and gave them to the disciples to set before the crowd. [17]They all ate and were completely satisfied, and the leftovers were picked up — twelve baskets full.

[18]When He was praying by Himself the disciples joined Him. He asked them, "Who do the crowds say I am?" [19]They answered, "John the Baptist; but some say, Elijah, and others that one of the ancient prophets has risen." [20]Then He asked them, "But who do you say I am?" Peter answered, "The Christ of God." [21]Then He strictly forbade them to tell this to anyone, [22]and said, "The Son of Man has to suffer and will be rejected by the elders, chief priests, and scribes and be executed, and will rise from the dead on the third day."

[23]He told them all, "If anyone wants to come after Me, he must deny himself, take up his cross day by day and follow Me; [24]for whoever wants to save his life will lose it, but whoever loses his life on My account will save it. [25]For what will it benefit a person to gain the whole world and lose or forfeit himself? [26]For whoever is ashamed of Me and My teachings, of him the Son of Man will be ashamed when He comes in His own glory and His Father's and of the holy angels. [27]However, I tell you truly, some of those standing here will not taste death until they see the kingdom of God."[j]

[28]About eight days after these teachings He took along Peter, John, and James, and went up the mountain to

f) This was Herod Antipas, one of the sons of Herod the Great.   g) See note at Mark 8:22.
h) The five loaves of bread and the two fish were provided by a boy, John 6:9.
i) See note at Mark 2:15.
j) The transfiguration scene that would follow in about a week, vss. 28-36, would give Peter, James and John a glimpse of the glory of the kingdom.

pray. 29And while He was praying the appearance of His face underwent a change and His garments turned a dazzling white. 30And behold two men, Moses and Elijah 31appeared in glory and conversed with Him about His departurek which He was to accomplish at Jerusalem.

32Peter and his companions had been overcome by sleep, but when they awoke they saw His glory and the two men standing by Him. 33At their parting from Him Peter said to Jesus, "Master, it is good for us that we are here. Let us construct three booths, one for You, one for Moses, and one for Elijah," not knowing what he was saying. 34Even while he said it a cloud came and overshadowed them, and they were awe-struck as they entered the cloud. 35Then a voice came out of the cloud, that said, "This is My Son, My Chosen One,1 listen to Him." 36And when the voice had spoken, Jesus was found alone. At that time they kept still and told no one what they had seen.

37The next day, when they came down from the mountain, a great crowd met them 38and a man shouted from the crowd, "Teacher, I beg of You to take a look at my son, for he is my only child. 39A spirit seizes him and suddenly he shrieks; it convulses him till he foams at the mouth. It bruises him and hardly leaves him. 40I entreated your disciples to expel him, but they were not able." 41Jesus replied, "O faithless and perverse generation, how long must I still be with you and endure you? Bring your son here." 42And even while he was coming the demonm threw him down and convulsed him; but Jesus rebuked the unclean spirit, and cured the lad and presented him to his father.

43And all were overwhelmed at the majesty of God. While everyone was wondering at everything He was doing, He said to His disciples. 44"Let these teachings sink into your ear; for the Son of man is to be delivered into human hands." 45However, they did not understand this saying; it was kept hidden from them so that they might not grasp it, and they were afraid to question Him about this saying.

46Then there came up a discussion among them, who of them was greatest; 47and Jesus, aware of what occupied their minds, took a child, placed it by His side, 48and said to them, "Whoever receives this child in My name receives Me, and whoever receives Me, receives Him who sent Me. For the lowliest among you all, he is truly great."

49John made the remark, "Master, we saw someone expelling demons in Your name and we forbade him, because he does not follow along with us." 50Jesus told him, "Do not forbid him; for whoever is not against you is for you."n

51When the time of His ascension was nearing completion He set His face to go to Jerusalem. 52And He sent messengers ahead of Him. And they went and entered a Samaritan village to prepare for His arrival. 53But they would not receive Him because He was traveling with His face toward Jerusalem.o 54The disciples James and John, on observing this, said, "Lord, do you want us to command fire to come down from heaven and destroy them?" 55But He turned and rebuked

---

k) The Greek word rendered "departure" is the accusative form of *exodos*, from which the English word "exodus" is derived. *Exodos* is sometimes employed euphemistically to denote *decease,' death*, which is certainly the connotation here.

l) Some ancient manuscripts read "My Beloved."

m) According to Matt. 17:15 this boy was an epileptic. At the same time he was demon-possessed, for here it speaks of this. The epilepsy may have been caused by the demon. *Cf.* ch. 11:14; Mark 9:29.

n) One's own denomination or local church or other Christian activity must not be thought to be the only one that is faithful to the Lord.

o) The Samaritans and Jews had no dealings with one another, John 4:9. The Samaritans were still worshipping God at Shechem on Mt. Gerazim, Judg. 9:7; *cf.* John 4:20. Thus the people of the village in Samaria were displeased with Jesus, since He was journeying to Jerusalem, and would not receive Him.

them: "[You do not know your attitude. [56]The Son of Man did not come to destroy human lives but to save]."[p] And they journeyed on to another village.

[57]As they were traveling along the road someone said to Him, "I will follow You wherever You may go." [58]Jesus told him, "The foxes have holes and the birds have nests, but the Son of Man does not have a place to lay His head." [59]He said to another, "Follow Me." But he replied, "Allow me first to go and bury my father." [60]But He said to him, "Let the dead bury their own dead; you go and preach the kingdom of God." [61]Another also said, "I will follow You, Sir, but first allow me to say good-by to those at my home." [62]Jesus told him, "No one who puts his hand to the plow and looks back is fit for the kingdom of God."

10 AFTER THAT THE LORD commissioned seventy[q] others, whom He sent ahead of Him two by two into every town and community that He planned to visit, [2]and told them, "The harvest is rich but the workmen are few; therefore pray the Lord of the harvest to send out laborers into His harvest. [3]Go forth. Notice that I am sending you as lambs into the midst of wolves. [4]Carry no purse, or wallet, or sandals, neither stop to greet anyone formally along the road. [5]Whatever home you enter, first say, 'Peace be to this house.' [6]If a person who is worthy of this greeting lives there, your peace will settle down on him; but if not, it will return to you. [7]Stay at the same house, eating and drinking what they provide; for the workman deserves his wages. Do not move from house to house.

[8]"Whatever town you enter, if they welcome you, eat what is placed be-fore you. [9]Heal those who are ill there, and tell them, 'The kingdom of God has approached you.' [10]But whatever town you enter and they fail to welcome you, go out into its streets and say, [11]'Even the dust of your town that sticks to our feet, we wipe off in protest against you. Know this, how-ever, that the kingdom of God has approached you.' [12]I tell you, it will be more endurable on that Day[r] for Sodom[s] than for that town.

[13]"Alas for you, Chorazin![t] Alas for you, Beth-saida![u] For if the miracles had occurred in Tyre and Sidon[v] that were done in you, they would long since have been sitting repentant in sackcloth and ashes. [14]But it will be more endurable for Tyre and Sidon at the judgment than for you. [15]And you, Capernaum,[w] will you be lifted up to heaven? No! You will sink to hades.

[16]"Whoever listens to you, listens to Me, and whoever rejects you, re-jects Me. But whoever rejects Me, rejects Him who sent Me."

[17]With joy the seventy returned and said, "Lord, even the demons are subject to us in Your name." [18]He said to them, "I saw Satan fall from heaven like lightning.[x] [19]See, I have given you the authority to step on snakes and scorpions, and over all the power of the enemy, and nothing will at all hurt you. [20]However, do not rejoice because the spirits submit to you, but rejoice because your names are registered in heaven."

[21]At that time Jesus exulted in the Holy Spirit and said, "I praise Thee, Father, Lord of heaven and earth, be-cause Thou hast concealed this from the learned and intelligent and hast revealed it to babes. Yes, Father, for thus it was pleasing in Thy presence.[y] [22]Everything has been handed over to Me by My Father and no one knows

---

p) The words in brackets are not found in the majority of the most reliable ancient manuscripts.
q) Some of the best ancient manuscripts read "seventy-two" here and in vs. 17.
r) That is, the Judgment Day.
s) The wickedness of Sodom is proverbial, Gen. 19. Frequently in Scripture Gomorrah is linked with Sodom, e.g., Gen. 18:20; Matt. 10:15; Mark 6:11; II Pet. 2:6.
t) See note at Matt. 11:21.   u) See note at Mark 8:22.
v) See note at Matt. 11:21.   w) See note at Matt. 4:13.
x) Isa. 14:12-15; Rev. 12:7-17; cf. John 12:31; 16:11.
y) As thanksgiving was a leading element in our Lord's prayers and in those of the Apostle Paul, we should not neglect it.

who the Son is except the Father, nor who the Father is, except the Son and he to whom the Son chooses to reveal Him."

23Turning to them privately, He said, "Blessed[z] are the eyes that see what you see. 24For I tell you that many prophets and kings have longed to see what you see but they did not see it, and to hear what you hear but they did not hear it."

25Now a certain teacher of the Law got up to put Him to a thorough test. He asked, "Teacher, what shall I do to inherit eternal life?" 26Jesus asked him, "What is written in the Law? How do you read it?" 27The teacher of the Law answered, "You must love the Lord your God with your whole heart, your whole soul, your whole strength and your whole mind, and your neighbor as yourself." 28Jesus told him, "You have answered correctly. Do this and you will live."

29But he, wishing to absolve himself, asked Jesus, "And who is my neighbor?" 30Jesus replied, "A certain man was going down from Jerusalem to Jericho and fell among robbers, who stripped and pummeled him and ran off, leaving him half dead. 31Coincidentally, a certain priest was coming down that road and, seeing him, passed on the other side. 32In the same way, a Levite[a] arrived at the spot, and passed on the other side. 33Then a certain Samaritan[b] came there as he traveled, saw him, and took pity on him. 34Going to him, he bandaged his wounds, poured oil and wine into them, set him on his own donkey, took him to an inn and looked after him. 35The next morning he took out and handed the innkeeper fifty cents,[c] and said, 'Take care of him and whatever further expenses you incur I will refund when I come back.' 36Which of these three, do you think, was really neighbor to the one who fell among the robbers?"

37He said, "The one who was merciful to him." Then Jesus told him, "You go and do the same."

38During their travels He entered a certain village, where a woman named Martha welcomed Him to her home. 39She had a sister named Mary, who took a seat at the Lord's feet and listened to His teaching. 40But Martha got worried about much housework so, approaching Him, she said, "Lord, do You not care that my sister left me to do the work alone? Then tell her to help me." 41But the Lord answered her, "Martha, Martha, you are anxious and bothered about many matters, 42when there is need of but one thing. Mary has selected the good portion which will not be taken away from her."

11 He was praying in a certain place and, when He ceased, one of His disciples said to Him, "Lord, teach us to pray as John, too, taught his disciples." 2He said to them, "When you pray, say[d]: 'Father, Thy name be held holy. Thy kingdom come. 3Daily grant us our food for the coming day. 4And forgive us our sins; for we also forgive every one indebted to us. And bring us not into temptation.'"

5He further said to them, "Let us say that one of you has a friend to whom he goes at midnight and says, 'Friend, lend me three loaves of bread, 6since a friend of mine has arrived at my house from a trip and I have nothing to set before him,' 7and the one inside should answer him, 'Do not bother me. The door is already locked and my children are in bed with me. I cannot get up and give to you.' 8"I tell you, if he does not get up to give to him because he is his friend, he will rise on account of his brazen

---

z) Or, "Happy." See note at ch. 6:20.
a) A member of the tribe of Levi, which was chosen by God to serve Him in the tabernacle, Num. 3:12, 40-51. The Levites were substitutes, as it were, for the first-born males of Israel, who had been set apart by God to Himself, Exod. 13:2.
b) The Jews despised Samaritans. See note at ch. 9:53.
c) The text reads "two denarii." A denarius would be equivalent to twenty-five cents in mid-twentieth century U. S. currency. But what seems hardly more than a pittance now would have been ample for a stay of two days at an inn in the first century.
d) In some ancient manuscripts words and phrases from Matt. 6:9-13 are inserted here. Luke gives the essentials of the Lord's Prayer.

insistence,[e] and give him as much as he needs." [9]And I tell you, "Ask, and it will be given you; seek, and you will find; knock, and it will be opened to you; [10]for everyone who asks receives, everyone who seeks finds, and to everyone who knocks the door will be opened. [11]What father among you whose son [asks bread will give him a stone, or if he][f] requests a fish will instead hand him a snake, [12]or if he requests an egg will hand him a scorpion? [13]If you then, evil as you are, know enough to give good gifts to your children, how much more will the heavenly Father give the Holy Spirit to those who ask Him."

[14]He was expelling a demon that caused dumbness, and after the expulsion the dumb man spoke so that the crowds wondered; [15]but some of them said, "He expels demons through Beelzebul,[g] the prince of the demons." [16]Others by way of testing Him, asked Him for a sign from heaven. [17]Well aware what they were thinking, He told them, "Every kingdom divided against itself comes to ruin; so does the quarreling home go down. [18]And if Satan is divided against himself, how will his kingdom stand? For you say that I expel demons through Beelzebul. [19]But if I expel demons through Beelzebul, through whom do your sons cast them out? They therefore shall be your judges. [20]But if I expel demons by means of the finger of God,[h] then the kingdom of God has already reached you.

[21]"When a strong man fully armed guards his residence, his belongings are undisturbed; [22]but when one stronger than he attacks and overcomes him, he robs him of his armor on which he depended and distributes his plunder. [23]He who is not with Me is against Me, and he who does not gather with Me scatters.

[24]"When an unclean spirit leaves a person, it crosses dry places in search of a resting place and, not finding it, says, 'I will go back to the house I left.' [25]But on his arrival he finds it swept and orderly. [26]He then goes and fetches seven other spirits, meaner than himself; they enter and dwell there, and that person's final condition is worse than it was at first."

[27]In the course of His telling this, a woman in the crowd raised her voice and said to Him, "Blessed[i] is the womb that bore You and the breasts on which You nursed." [28]But He said, "More blessed still are those who hear and keep the word of God."

[29]As many people were crowding Him, He began to say, "This generation is an evil generation; it desires a sign, but none shall be granted it except the sign of Jonah,[j] [30]for as Jonah was a sign to the Ninevites, so will the Son of Man be to this generation. [31]The queen of the South[k] will rise up in the judgment with the men of this age and will condemn them; for she came from the ends of the earth to listen to Solomon's wisdom, and remember, something greater than Solomon is here. [32]The men of Nineveh will rise in the judgment with this generation and will condemn it, because they repented at Jonah's preaching, and remember, something greater than Jonah is here.

[33]"No one lights a lamp and puts it in a cellar or under the grain measure, but on top of a stand, so that those who come in may see the light. [34]Your eye is the body's lamp. When your eye is sound your whole body is illumined; but in case it is defective, your body is darkened. [35]See to it, therefore, that the light in you is not darkness. [36]If, however, your whole body is illumined, with no portion dark, then it is as perfectly lit as when a lamp illumines you with its beam."

---

e) Literally the Greek word, *anaideia*, means *shamelessness, impudence.*
f) The words enclosed in brackets are not found in the majority of the most reliable ancient manuscripts.
g) Beelzebul (or Baalzebub) was a pagan god of Ekron in Philistia, II Kings 1:2. In N.T. times Beelzebul was a name used for Satan, "the prince of the power of the air," Eph. 2:2.
h) "The finger of God" denotes divine efficiency by the Holy Spirit, *cf.* Matt. 12:28.
i) Or, "Happy." See note at ch. 6:20.
j) Jonah 1:17; Matt. 12:40.
k) II Chron. 9:1-12.

[37]During His discourse a Pharisee[1] invited Him home to dine with him, so He went in and sat[m] at the table. [38]But the Pharisee noticed and wondered that He had not washed before the meal. [39]The Lord said to him, "Now you Pharisees cleanse the outside of the cup and of the plate, but inside you are full of robbery and wickedness. [40]Fools! Did not He who made the outside make the inside too? [41]You had better bestow in kindness what is inside and everything will be clean for you. [42]But alas for you Pharisees, because you tithe mint and rue[n] and every vegetable, while disregarding justice and love for God. These things you should practice without omitting the other things.

[43]"Alas for you Pharisees, for you cherish the prominent pews in the synagogue, and the salutations in the markets. [44]Alas for you, because you are like unseen tombs over which people walk without being aware of them."

[45]One of the teachers of the Law replied to Him, "Teacher, when You say this, You insult us too." [46]But He said, "Alas for you teachers of the Law as well, because you pack the people with loads that are hard to carry, while you yourselves do not touch those burdens with one of your fingers. [47]Alas for you, because you build monuments for the prophets whom your fathers killed. [48]In that way you are consenting to your fathers' works; for they indeed killed them and you build their monuments. [49]"The wisdom of God therefore says, 'I will send them prophets and apostles, some of whom they will kill and persecute,' [50]so that the blood of all the prophets that has been shed from the foundation of the world may be charged against this generation, [51]from Abel's blood[o] to that of Zechariah,[p] who was murdered between the altar and the temple. Yes, I tell you, it will be charged against this generation.

[52]"Alas for you, teachers of the Law, for you have taken away the key to knowledge; you yourselves have not entered, and you have prevented those who were entering."

[53]Upon His leaving there the scribes and Pharisees began to heckle Him fiercely and to draw Him out by cross-questioning on many points, secretly [54]watching Him for the purpose of trapping Him with something from His lips.

12 MEANWHILE, WHEN COUNTLESS people were massed, so that they stepped on one another, He began to say, primarily to His disciples, "Guard yourselves against the yeast[q] of the Pharisees, that is, against hypocrisy. [2]Nothing is hidden that will not be shown, or secret that will not be brought to light. [3]So whatever you say in the dark will be heard in the light and what you whisper in the ear within a private room will be proclaimed on the roofs.

[4]"My friends, I tell you, have no fear of those who kill the body and afterward can do nothing more; [5]but I will show you whom to fear: fear Him who, after taking the life, has power to cast into hell.[r] Yes, I say to you, fear Him.

[6]"Are not five sparrows sold for two small coins?[s] Yet none of them is forgotten in God's presence. [7]And the very hairs of your head are all counted. Have no fear; you are worth more than flocks of sparrows.

[8]"I tell you further, whoever acknowledges Me in the presence of people, the Son of Man will acknowledge him in the presence of God's angels. [9]But whoever denies Me before

---

l) See note at Matt. 3:7   m) See note at Mark 2:15.
n) Rue is a European strong-scented herb with a somewhat bitter taste. Its seeds are used for flavoring. Rue is comparable to dill (anise), Matt. 23:23.
o) Gen. 4:1-15.
p) II Chron. 24:20-22.
q) That is, leaven.
r) The word here rendered "hell" is the accusative form of the Greek *geenna*, from which "Gehenna" is derived. See note at Mark 9:43.
s) The text reads "two assarions." An assarion was a small Roman copper coin worth one-sixteenth of a denarius. The value of a denarius would be equal to about twenty-five cents in mid-twentieth century U. S. currency. Thus two assarions are the equivalent of approximately three cents.

men, he will be denied before the angels of God. [10]Whoever will make a statement against the Son of Man, for him there is forgiveness; but for him who blasphemes against the Holy Spirit there will be no forgiveness.[t]

[11]"When they bring you to synagogues and rulers and authorities, do not worry how to defend yourself or what to say, [12]for the Holy Spirit will teach you at the very moment what you ought to say."

[13]One of the crowd said to Him, "Teacher, tell my brother to share the inheritance with me." [14]But He said to him, "Man, who appointed Me judge or distributor of your goods?" [15]He then said to the people, "Look out and be on guard against all greed, for one's life is not made up of the abundance of his possessions."

[16]Then He told them a parable: "The field of a certain rich man yielded abundantly, [17]so he considered within himself, 'What shall I do; for I have no room to store my crops?' [18]He said, 'I will do this; I will tear down my barns and build bigger ones, and there I will store all my produce and my goods, [19]and I will say to my soul, "Soul, you have much wealth laid up for many a year. Take it easy; eat, drink, enjoy yourself."'

[20]"But God said to him, 'Fool, this night your soul will be demanded of you, and what you have gotten ready, whose is it to be?' [21]Thus does the person fare who stores up treasure for himself and is not rich in relation to God."

[22]But to His disciples He said, "For this reason I tell you, do not worry about what you will eat, or about your body, what you will wear; [23]for life is more than nourishment and the body more than clothes. [24]Look at the ravens, how they neither sow nor harvest, have neither barn nor granary, and God feeds them. How far more valuable are you than the birds!

[25]"Who of you can add one moment to his life's course[u] by worrying? [26]So, if you cannot bring about that little, why be anxious about the rest? [27]Consider the lilies, how they grow; they do not spin, but I tell you that not even Solomon in all his glory was clothed like one of them. [28]And if God so clothes the grass that is in the field today and is thrown into the oven tomorrow, how much more will He clothe you, you of little faith!

[29]"Do not be seeking what to eat and what to drink, neither be anxious; [30]for the people of the world desire all these things, but your Father knows that you need them. [31]But seek His kingdom, and these things will be supplied you besides. [32]Do not fear, little flock, for your Father is pleased to give you the kingdom.

[33]"Sell what you have and give to charity; make purses for yourselves that never age — unfailing treasure in heaven where no thief approaches or moth ruins. [34]For where your treasure is, there too your heart will be.[v]

[35]"Keep your loins girded and your lamps burning; [36]be like persons who await their own master when he comes back from the wedding, so that when he arrives and knocks, they may instantly open the door for him. [37]Happy are those slaves[w] whom the master finds on the alert when he comes. I assure you that he will gird himself, will have them sit[x] at the table and will come and wait on them. [38]Whether he arrives in the second watch or in the third, if he finds them alert, they are fortunate. [39]But understand this: if the owner of the house had known at what time the thief would come, he

---

t) To blaspheme against the Holy Spirit is to ascribe to Satan the work of the Holy Spirit, *cf.* ch. 11:15. This is the only sin for which there is said to be "no forgiveness." For a man can resist God the Father and God the Son and yet in due course be turned about by the wooing of the Holy Spirit; but he cannot resist Father, Son and Spirit, going so far as to attribute to the devil the works of God by His Spirit, and be saved. Those who are concerned about having committed the "unpardonable sin" are the least likely to have been guilty of it, or they would not care. And if they have not already committed themselves to Christ as Lord and Savior, they can do so now.
u) "One moment to his life's course" could equally as well be rendered "one cubit to his stature," and some translations of the Bible read that way.
v) Compare ch. 18:18-27.
w) See note at Matt. 13:27.
x) See note at Mark 2:15.

would have watched and would not have permitted his house to be burglarized. 40So you be ready, for the Son of Man comes at an hour you are not anticipating."

41Peter asked Him, "Lord, are You telling this parable just to us or to everyone?" 42The Lord replied, "Who is indeed the faithful and thoughtful custodian whom the master appoints over his household to supply their food allowance at the proper time? 43Happy is that slave whom the master finds doing so when he arrives. 44I tell you truly, he will put him in charge of everything he has.

45"But if that slave says to himself, 'My master is putting off his arrival,' and starts to beat the menservants and the maids, and also to eat and to drink and to get drunk, 46that slave's master will come on an unexpected day and at an hour of which he has no idea, and will discharge him and will make him share the fate of the unfaithful.

47"The slave who knew what his master wanted and neither got ready nor did it, will be severely lashed; 48but he who was ignorant of it, who does what deserves flogging, will be punished lightly. For of every one to whom much is given, much will be required, and of him to whom much has been entrusted, people will demand the more.

49"I have come to cast fire on the earth, and how I wish it were already kindled! 50I have baptism to undergo and how great is My distress until it is finished! 51Do you suppose that I am here to bring peace on earth? Not at all, I tell you, but rather discord; 52for from now on five will be at odds in one home, three against two and two against three — 53father against son and son against father; mother against daughter and daughter against mother; mother-in-law against daughter-in-law and daughter-in-law against mother-in-law."y

54And to the crowds He said, "When you see a cloud coming up in the west, at once you remark, 'A shower is coming,' and so it is. 55And when the south wind blows, you say, 'It will be hot,' and it happens. 56You hypocrites! You know how to interpret the appearance of earth and sky; why then can you not evaluate this time?

57"Why do not you yourselves decide what is right? 58When you go with your opponent to the magistrate, take pains to come to a settlement with him on the way, so as to be freed from him, for fear he drags you before the judge, the judge hands you over to the jailor, and the jailor throws you in prison. 59I tell you, you will not get out of there until you have paid the last penny."z

13 JUST THEN SOME WERE PRESent who told Him about the Galileans whose blood Pilate had mixed with their sacrifices, 2and He said to them in reply, "Do you suppose, because they suffered this, that those Galileans were worse sinners than all their fellow Galileans? 3Not at all, I tell you, but unless you repent you will all similarly perish. 4Or those eighteen on whom the Siloam tower fell so that it killed them, do you suppose that they committed greater sin than all other dwellers in Jerusalem? 5Not at all, I tell you, but unless you repent you will all similarly perish."

c. A.D. 30

6He spoke this parable: "Someone had a fig tree that was planted in his orchard and came to look for fruit on it, but did not find any; 7so he said to the gardener, 'Look here! For three years now I have come to look for fruit on this fig tree and have not found any. Cut it down. Why should

---

y) This is simply a statement of what may happen when some in a non-Christian home are converted.

z) Quite often, as Jesus here implies, the one who opposes us may be in the right. The word "penny" is the Greek noun *lepton* which, in Mark 12:42, is translated "mites" in its plural form. *Lepton* means *small, thin, light*. Its value in the mid-twentieth century would actually be about one-eighth of a penny.

it use up the soil?' 8But he replied, 'Master, leave it yet for this year, till I dig around it and put in fertilizer; 9perhaps it will bear fruit next season — but if not, cut it down.' "a

10While He was teaching in one of the synagogues on the Sabbath, 11a woman attended who for eighteen years had suffered from a weakening spirit; she was bent double and could not straighten herself up fully. 12When Jesus saw her He called her to Him and said to her, "Woman, you are set free from your ailment." 13And He laid hands on her, and instantly she was made erect, and she praised God.

14But the ruler of the synagogue, indignant because Jesus healed on the Sabbath, said to the crowd, "There are six days when work should be done; so come to be healed on those days and not on the Sabbath day." 15But the Lord answered him, "You hypocrites! Does not every one of you on the Sabbath untie his ox or his donkey from the feeding trough and lead him away to drink? 16Ought not then this woman, a daughter of Abraham whom Satan has held bound these eighteen years, to be loosed from her bond on the Sabbath day?"

17At these words all His opponents were ashamed, while all the people were glad about all the wonderful things that were done by Him.

18Then He said, "What does the kingdom of God resemble and to what shall I compare it? 19It resembles a mustard seed which a man took and planted in his garden. It grew up into a tree and the birds of the air made their nests in its branches." 20He further said, "To what shall I compare the kingdom of God? 21It resembles yeastb which a woman took and mixed in three batches of flour until it was all raised."

22Making His way to Jerusalem, He went through towns and villages, teaching. 23Someone asked Him, "Lord, are only a few saved?" He told them,

24"Strain every nerve to enter through the narrow door; for many, I tell you, will try to enter and will be unable to. 25After the owner of the house has gotten up and has shut the door, you will begin to stand outside and knock at the door, calling, 'Lord, open for us!' But He will reply to you: 'I neither know you, nor where you come from.' 26Then you will begin to say, 'We ate and drank with You, and You taught in our streets.' 27But He will tell you, 'I do not know from where you are. Get away from Me, all you evildoers.' 28There will be wailing and grinding of teeth when you see Abraham, Isaac, Jacob, and all the prophets in the kingdom of God, but you yourselves thrown outside. 29And from east and west, north and south they will come and will be sittingc at the table of the kingdom of God. 30But, mind you, there are last who will be first, and there are first who will be last."

31At that time certain Pharisees approached Him, saying, "Get out of this place, for Herod intends to kill You." 32He replied, "You go and tell that fox that I shall expel demons and perform cures today and tomorrow, and on the third dayd I shall complete My work. 33However, I must travel on today and tomorrow and the next day; for it would not do for a prophet to perish outside Jerusalem.

34"O Jerusalem, Jerusalem, that kills the prophets and stones those sent to you! How often have I wanted to gather your children as a hen gathers her brood under her wings, and you were not willing. 35Behold, your home is left you destitute. I tell you that you will not see Me at all until you say, 'Blessed is He who comes in the name of the Lord.' "

14 WHEN HE ENTERED THE HOUSE of one of the rulers of the Pharisees to eat a meal on the Sabbath, they watched Him closely. 2For a man with dropsy was in front of Him. 3So

---

a) The Jews of Jesus' day, under the leadership of the Pharisees and the Sadducees, had experienced little spiritual care; their souls needed cultivation.
b) That is, leaven.
c) See note at Mark 2:15.
d) This is figurative language denoting a future date, though not in the distant future.

Jesus spoke to the teachers of the Law, and Pharisees, asking, "Is it right to heal on the Sabbath or not?" 4But they kept still. He then took hold of him, healed him, and let him go. 5He said to them, "Who of you has an ox or donkey that falls into a pit and you do not immediately pull him out on the Sabbath day?" 6And they could make no reply to this.

7To the guests, whom He noticed selecting the choicest places, He spoke this parable: 8"When you are invited by someone to a wedding banquet, do not sit^e in the most preferable place; for one more highly esteemed by your host than yourself may have been invited by him 9and, as your mutual host arrives, he may say to you, 'Make room for him,' and then feeling deeply embarrassed, you proceed to take the lowest place. 10Rather, when you are invited, go and sit in the lowest place so that, when your host arrives, he may say to you, 'Friend, move up higher.' You will then enjoy honor before all your fellow guests. 11For whoever makes himself prominent will be humbled, and whoever humbles himself will be set high."

12He further told His host, "Whenever you give a dinner or supper, do not invite your friends or your brothers or your relatives or your well-to-do neighbors; for they may invite you in their turn and so repay you. 13Instead, when you give a dinner, invite the poor, the maimed, the lame, and the blind; 14then blessing will be yours, for they have nothing to repay you, but you will be repaid at the resurrection of the just."

15One of the fellow guests who heard this, said to Him, "Blessed is he who will eat bread in the kingdom of God." 16But He told him, "A man gave a great supper and invited many. 17At the supper hour he sent his slave^f to tell those who were invited, 'Come, for everything is now ready.' 18But one by one they began making excuse. The first told him, 'I have bought a field and I simply must go to see it; I beg of you, have me excused.' 19Another said, 'I have bought five yoke of oxen and I am going to test them; I beg of you, have me excused.' 20Another said, 'I have married a wife and on that account I cannot come.'

21"The slave came and reported this to his master. Then, his anger aroused, the master of the house told his slave, 'Hurry out into the streets and alleys of the city and bring in here the poor, the maimed, the blind, and the lame.' 22When the slave said, 'Master, what you ordered has been done and still there is room,' 23the master instructed the slave, 'Go out to the roads and hedges and force them to come in, so that my house may be filled; 24for I tell you, none of those that were invited shall taste of my supper.'"

25Great crowds accompanied Him; so He turned and told them, 26"Whoever comes to Me without hating^g his father and mother and wife and children and brothers and sisters, yes, even his own life, cannot be My disciple. 27Whoever does not carry his own cross and come after Me cannot be My disciple.

28"For who of you, wanting to build a tower, does not first sit down to figure out the expense, whether he has enough to complete it? 29Or else, when the foundation has been laid and he cannot finish it, everyone who sees it begins to say in ridicule, 30'This man started to build and could not finish it.' 31Or what king marches against another king for war without first sitting down to consider whether with ten thousand men he will be able to cope with the enemy, who is marching against him with twenty thousand? 32For if not, he will send a delegation requesting terms for peace while the other is still at a good distance.

33"So with every one of you who will not part with all he has; he cannot be My disciple. 34Salt is good; but

---

e) See note at Mark 2:15.
f) See note at Matt. 13:27.
g) The Greek verb *miseo* is used here. It means nothing less than *to hate, detest, abhor.* Terms that express emotions are sometimes comparative and this must be the case in this instance. In a clash of claims Jesus must be first and everything and everyone else have a lesser claim.

when salt is tasteless, with what can it be seasoned? [35]It is fit neither for the soil nor for the manure pile; they throw it away. Whoever has ears to hear let him hear."

15 ALL THE TAX COLLECTORS AND sinners were crowding close to Him to hear Him, [2]and the Pharisees and scribes complained, "This person welcomes sinners and eats with them." [3]So He told them this parable: [4]"Who of you with a hundred sheep and losing one of them would not leave the ninety-nine alone in the wilderness to go after the lost one until he finds it? [5]And when he has found it, he lays it on his shoulders, [6]and, when he gets home, summons his friends and neighbors, to whom he says, 'Be glad with me, for I have found my lost sheep.' [7]I tell you that in such fashion there will be joy in heaven over one repentant sinner more than over ninety-nine righteous persons who stand in no need of repentance.

[8]"Or what woman with ten silver coins[h] does not, at losing one of them, light a lamp and sweep the house and search carefully till she finds it? [9]And when she has found it, she summons her friends and neighbors, saying, 'Be glad with me, for I have found the lost coin.' [10]I tell you that in like fashion there is joy before God's angels over one repentant sinner."

[11]He further said, "A certain man had two sons, [12]the younger of whom said to his father, 'Father, give me the share of the property that is coming to me.' So he apportioned to them his property. [13]After a few days the younger son collected all he had and traveled to a distant country, and there he squandered what he had in reckless living. [14]When he had run through everything a terrible famine visited that whole land and he began to lack; [15]so he went and hired himself out to a citizen of that country, who sent him into his fields to tend hogs. [16]He longed to have his stomach filled with bean pods which the hogs were eating, but no one gave him any. [17]But when he came to himself, he said, 'How many of my father's hired hands have more than they can eat, and here I am starving. [18]I will rise and go to my father and say to him, "Father, I have sinned against heaven and before you, [19]and I no longer deserve to be called your son; take me on as one of your hired hands."'

[20]"So he got up and went to his father; but when he was still a great way off, his father saw him and felt deeply moved and, running, fell on his neck and kissed him. [21]The son said to him, 'Father, I have sinned against heaven and before you; I no longer deserve to be called your son.' [22]But the father told his slaves, 'Hurry! Fetch the choicest robe and put it on him; put a ring on his hand and sandals on his feet; [23]bring the fatted calf too, and butcher it. Let us feast and be merry; [24]for this my son was dead and he has come to life again; he was lost and has been found.' So they began to be merry.

[25]"Now his older son was in the field and, as he came to the house, he heard music and dancing. [26]Then calling one of the servants, he asked what it was all about. [27]He told him, 'Your brother has come and, because he has received him back safe and well, your father has butchered the fatted calf.' [28]And he was stirred with anger and would not go in. His father came out and pleaded with him, [29]but he replied to his father, 'See here! I have worked for you all these years without ever neglecting an order of yours, but never have you given me so much as a kid, so that I might make merry with my friends. [30]But when this son of yours has come, after squandering your livelihood with prostitutes, you have killed for him the fatted calf.' [31]But he said to him, 'Son, you are always with me and all I have is yours. [32]We just had to make merry and be happy, for this

---

h) The word rendered "coins" is *drachmas*. A drachma was a silver Greek coin almost equivalent in value to the Roman denarius; it would be worth about twenty cents in mid-twentieth century U. S. currency. The purchasing power of a drachma in the first century would have been sufficient to cause its loss to be a matter of concern to a housewife.

your brother was dead and he has come to life; he was lost and has been found.'"

16 He also told the disciples: "There was a rich man who had a manager, and this manager was reported to him as wasting his belongings. [2]So he called him and asked him, 'What is this I hear about you? Hand in an account of your management; for you can no longer be manager.'

[3]"The manager said to himself, 'What shall I do, now that my employer is about to deprive me of my managership? I have not strength to dig; I am ashamed to beg. [4]I know what I shall do so that, when I am discharged from my management, they may welcome me in their homes.' [5]So, calling in each one of his master's debtors, he said to the first, 'How much do you owe my master?' [6]He replied, 'A hundred barrels[i] of oil.' The manager then said to him, 'Take your bill, sit down quickly and write, fifty.' [7]He then asked another, 'How much do you owe?' And he replied, 'A hundred sacks[j] of wheat.' To him he said, 'Take your bill and write eighty.'

[8]"The master commended his dishonest manager for acting shrewdly; for the sons of this world are more astute than the sons of light in their own generation. [9]And I tell you to use unrighteous wealth so that you win friends who, when it fails, may welcome you into eternal dwellings.

[10]"He who is faithful in the least is faithful also in much, while he who is unreliable in the least is unreliable in much also. [11]Therefore if you have not been faithful in matters of unrighteous riches, who will entrust to you the true riches? [12]And if you are not reliable with what belongs to another, who will give you anything for your personal possession?

[13]"No domestic servant can serve two masters; for either he will hate the one and love the other, or he will support the one and despise the other. You cannot serve God and mammon."[k]

[14]The Pharisees were listening to all this and were sneering at Him, for they were lovers of money. [15]So He told them, "You claim righteousness before human eyes, but God knows your hearts. What seems outstanding to men is abhorrent in the sight of God. [16]Until John there were the Law and the Prophets; since then the kingdom of God has been preached and everyone forces his way into it. [17]But it is easier for heaven and earth to pass away than for the smallest part of a letter of the Law to become invalid.

[18]"Whoever divorces his wife and marries another, commits adultery; and he who marries the divorcee commits adultery.

[19]"There was a rich man dressed in purple and fine linen, who enjoyed luxurious living every day. [20]In front of his gate a beggar named Lazarus was placed, covered with sores, [21]and hungering to be fed crumbs that fell from the rich man's table. Even the dogs came and licked his sores.

[22]The beggar died and was carried by the angels to Abraham's bosom. The rich man also died and was buried, [23]and, while suffering tortures in hades,[l] he looked up and from a distance saw Abraham with Lazarus in his bosom. [24]So he called out, 'Father Abraham, take pity on me and send Lazarus to dip his finger tip in water and cool my tongue, for I am tormented in this fire.' [25]But Abraham said, 'Son, remember that you enjoyed the good things in your lifetime while Lazarus had the bad things; now he is being comforted here but you are suffering anguish. [26]Besides, there is a great chasm fixed between you and us, so that those who want to cross from here to you are unable; neither can they cross from your side to us.'

[27]"He said, 'Then I plead with you, father, to send him to my father's house, [28]for I have five brothers; let him warn them so that they may not

---

i) Literally "baths." Each bath contained eight or nine gallons.
j) Literally "kors." Each kor was equal to about eleven bushels.
k) That is, riches. *Cf.* ch. 18:25.   l) The realm of the dead.

come to this place of torment.' 29But Abraham said, 'They have Moses and the Prophets; they may listen to them.' 30He replied, 'No, father Abraham; but should one risen from the dead go to them, they will repent.' 31Abraham said to him, "If they will not listen to Moses and the Prophets, they will not be convinced even if someone rises from the dead.' "

17 TO HIS DISCIPLES HE SAID, "Obstacles must inevitably come, but alas for the person who causes them! 2It would be to his advantage to have a millstone hung around his neck and to be thrown into the sea, rather than to be an obstacle to one of these little ones.

3"Be on your guard. If your brother sins, call him to task, and if he repents, forgive him. 4Even if he sins against you seven times a day and comes back to you seven times with the words, 'I am sorry,' forgive him."

5The apostles said to the Lord, "Give us more faith." 6The Lord said, "If you had faith the size of a mustard seed, you would say to this mulberry tree, 'Be uprooted and planted in the sea,' and it would obey you.

7"Who of you with a slave[m] plowing or herding sheep will say to him as he comes in from the field, 'Come at once and sit[n] at the table'? Will he not rather say to him, 8'Get something ready for my supper; put on your belt and wait on me while I eat and drink, and afterward you may eat and drink'? 9Is he thankful to the slave for doing what he was assigned? 10It should be the same with you; when you have done everything that was assigned you, you should say, 'We are undeserving servants; we have simply done our duty.' "

11On His way to Jerusalem He crossed between Samaria and Galilee, 12and as He entered a certain village ten lepers met Him. Standing at a distance, 13they raised their voices, crying, "Jesus, Master, take pity on us!" 14When He saw them He told them, "Go and show yourselves to the priests." And as they went they were cleansed.

15But one of them, when he observed that he was healed, came back, loudly praising God. 16He fell on his face at His feet, thanking Him. And he was a Samaritan.[o] 17Jesus said, "Were there not ten cleansed? Where are the nine? 18Was no one found to return and give thanks to God except this foreigner?" 19And to him He said, "Stand up and go. Your faith has saved you."

20Asked by the Pharisees when the kingdom of God would come, He answered them, "The kingdom of God does not come by looking for it, 21neither will they say, 'Look! Here it is,' or 'There it is!' for the kingdom of God is in your midst."[p]

22To His disciples He said, "The time is coming when you will long to see one of the days of the Son of Man, but in vain. 23They will say to you, 'Look, here He is!' or 'Look, there He is!' Do not go out or follow them; 24for as the lightning flashes from one end of the sky to the other, so will the Son of Man be in His day. 25But first He must undergo much suffering and be rejected by this generation.

26"In the days of the Son of Man it will be just as it was in the days of Noah[q] — 27they ate, they drank, they married, and they were being married until the day when Noah entered the ark; and then came the deluge and destroyed them all. 28It was similar, too, in Lot's[r] days — they ate and drank, they bought and sold, they planted and built; 29but on the day when Lot went out of Sodom[s] it rained fire and brimstone from heaven and destroyed them all.

---

m) See note at Matt. 13:27.
n) See note at Mark 2:15.
o) See note at ch. 9:53.
p) The translation "within you" is also possible. But "in your midst" or "among you" is preferable in this context.
q) Gen. 6, 7.
r) Gen. 19.
s) See note at ch. 10:12.

30"It will be the same on the day when the Son of Man will be revealed. 31A person on the roof that day, with his belongings inside the house, must not go down to fetch them, and similarly a person in the field must not turn back. 32Remember Lot's wife.t

33"Whoever seeks to preserve his life for himself will lose it, and whoever loses it will preserve it alive. 34I tell you, in that night two persons will be on one bed, the one will be taken and the other left; 35two women will be grinding together, the one will be taken and the other left. 36[Two will be in the field; the one will be taken and the other left.]"u

37In response they asked Him, "Where, Lord?" And He told them, "Where there is a corpse, there the vultures will flock."

18 HE TOLD THEM A PARABLE TO show that they must always pray and not lose courage: 2"There was a judge in a certain city with no reverence for God and no regard for man; 3and in that city there was a widow, who kept coming to him with the appeal, 'See to it that I get justice against my opponent.' 4For a while he would not; but later on he said to himself, 'Even though I have neither reverence for God nor regard for man, 5still, because this widow bothers me, I will see that she gets justice, so that she may not finally wear me downv by her continual coming.'"

6And the Lord said, "Listen to what the unfair judge says; 7and will not God procure justice for His own chosen, who cry to Him day and night? Will He delay long over them? 8I tell you, He will procure justice for them in short order. However, when the Son of Man comes, will He find faithw on the earth?"

9To those trusting in their own righteousness and looking down on the rest, He told this parable: 10"Two men went up to the temple to pray, the one a Pharisee and the other a tax collector. 11The Pharisee stood up and said this prayer to himself, 'God, I thank Thee that I am not like the rest of men — robbers, cheats, adulterers; or even like this tax collector. 12I fast twice a week; I pay tithes on everything I get.' 13But the tax collector, standing at a distance, would not even raise his eyes toward heaven, but struck his chest and said, 'God, be merciful to me, the sinner.' 14I tell you, it was he who went home forgiven, rather than the other; for whoever exalts himself will be humbled, but he who humbles himself will be exalted."

15They brought Him infants to touch; but when the disciples noticed it they reproved them. 16So Jesus called them to Him and said, "Allow the little ones to come to Me, and do not forbid them; for the kingdom of God belongs to their kind. 17I assure you, unless one receives the kingdom of God like a child, he shall not enter it at all."

18One of the rulers inquired of Him, "Good Teacher, what shall I do to inherit eternal life?" 19Jesus said to him, "Why do you call Me good? No one is good except One — God. 20You know the commandments,x 'Do not commit adultery; Do not commit murder;y Do not steal; Do not witness falsely; Honor your father and mother.'" 21He replied, "All these I have observed from childhood up." 22Hearing this, Jesus told him, "You still lack one thing. Sell everything you have and donate it to the poor and you will have riches in heaven, and come, follow Me." 23Hearing this, he became very sad, for he was extremely rich. 24When Jesus saw that he became sad, He said, "With what difficulty do those who have wealth enter the kingdom of God!

---

t) Gen. 19:26.
u) Verse 36, enclosed in brackets, is not found in the majority of the most reliable ancient manuscripts.
v) Literally, "strike me under the eye," "give me a black eye."
w) Literally "the faith."
x) That is, the Ten Commandments, Exod. 20:1-17. The five that Jesus cited to the rich man deal especially with man's relationship to his fellow man.
y) The Greek verb *phoneuo* means specifically *to commit murder;* and so the Hebrew verb, *ratsach,* in Exod. 20:13.

[25]For it is easier for a camel[z] to pass through a needle's[a] eye than for a rich person to enter the kingdom of God."

[26]His listeners said, "Then who can be saved?" [27]But He said, "Those things that are impossible on man's part are possible with God." [28]Peter said, "Lo, we have left our homes and have followed You." [29]He told them, "I assure you, there is no one who has given up home or wife or brothers or parents or children on behalf of the kingdom of God [30]who will not receive many times more in this age, and in the coming age eternal life."

[31]Taking the Twelve, He told them, "Look, we are going up to Jerusalem and all the writings of the Prophets about the Son of Man will be fulfilled; [32]for He will be handed over to the Gentiles and ridiculed and insulted and spit on, [33]and they will flog and execute Him, and on the third day He will rise again." [34]But they did not understand a word of it; the saying was hidden from them; they did not know what He was telling them.[b]

[35]As He was nearing Jericho a blind man was seated by the road, begging. [36]Hearing the crowd passing by, he inquired what it was all about, [37]so they informed him, "Jesus of Nazareth is coming by." [38]Then he shouted, "Jesus, Son of David, take pity on me!" [39]Those up front warned him to keep quiet; but he shouted the louder, "Son of David, take pity on me!" [40]So Jesus stopped and gave orders to bring him to Him. As he approached, [41]Jesus asked him, "What do you want Me to do for you?" He said, "Lord, let me get back my sight!" [42]Jesus said to him, "Receive your sight. Your faith has saved you." [43]Instantly he regained his sight and followed Him, praising God.

All the people saw it and gave God praise.

19 He entered Jericho and, as He was passing through it, [2]there was a man named Zacchaeus, a chief tax collector and wealthy, [3]who tried to see who Jesus was. But he could not on account of the crowd, because he was short. [4]So he ran ahead and climbed a sycamore tree to see Him; for He was about to pass that way.

[5]When Jesus reached the spot He looked up and said to him, "Zacchaeus, come down quickly, for I must stay at your home today." [6]He hurried down and heartily welcomed Him. [7]And all who looked on complained, "He has gone to be the guest of a sinner." [8]But Zacchaeus paused, and said to the Lord, "See, Lord, I will give half of my belongings to the poor, and if I have defrauded anyone of anything I will pay it back fourfold." [9]Jesus said, pointing to him, "Today salvation has come to this house, since this man, too, is a son of Abraham; [10]for the Son of Man came to seek and to save the lost."

[11]While they were listening to these things He went on to tell a parable, because they were near Jerusalem and supposed that the kingdom of God was to appear at once. [12]He said: "A certain nobleman went to a distant land to acquire a kingdom for himself and to return. [13]Summoning ten of his slaves,[c] he gave them two hundred dollars[d] and told them, 'Trade with this till I come back.' [14]But his townsmen hated him and sent a delegation after him to say, 'We do not want him to be king over us.'[e]

[15]"On his return, having acquired the kingdom, he ordered those servants to whom he had given the money

---

z) "Camel" is rendered properly from the Greek *kamelos*. The Syriac version uses *kamilos*, which means *a rope or a ship's cable;* but the Syriac is a version and not an original Greek manuscript nor a reliable Greek copy. Neither a camel nor a rope could pass through the eye of a common sewing needle. But all things are possible with God.
a) See note at Mark 10:25.
b) Here was a threefold affirmation by Luke of the apostles' inability at this time to understand Jesus.   c) See note at Matt. 13:27.
d) The text reads "ten minas" (Gk. *deka mnas*). A mina was the equivalent of 100 drachmas and would be worth about twenty dollars in mid-twentieth century U.S. currency. Each of the ten slaves was given twenty dollars, vss. 16, 18, 20 — the total amount was $200.
e) Archelaus, one of the sons of Herod, had such an experience when he went to Rome in 4 B.C. to be crowned as king of the Jews. The Jewish people did not want him as their king.

to be summoned so that he might ascertain what business they had transacted. 16Now the first one presented himself and said, 'Master, your twenty dollars has made two hundred dollars.' 17He said to him, 'Well done, good servant; because you were trustworthy in a very little, you will have authority over ten cities.'

18"The second also came and said, 'Master, your twenty dollars has made one hundred dollars.' 19He told this one, 'Have charge of five cities.'

20"The other one came and said, 'Here is your twenty dollars, sir, which I have kept in a napkin; 21for I was afraid because you are a harsh man. You take up what you did not lay down and you reap what you did not sow.' 22He told him, 'You good-for-nothing servant, I will convict you from your own mouth. You knew that I was a harsh man, taking up what I did not lay down and reaping what I did not sow? 23Then why did you not put my money in the bank, so that when I came I might have gotten it with interest?' 24Then he said to the bystanders, 'Take the twenty dollars from him and give it to the one with two hundred dollars.' They said to him, 25'Master, he has two hundred dollars.' 26'I tell you, to the one who has shall be given, but from one who has not shall be taken what he has. 27'Now for these enemies of mine, who did not want me for their king, fetch them here and execute them in my presence.'"

28After this message He went on ahead of them, going up to Jerusalem. 29And as they neared Bethphage[f] and Bethany,[g] at what is called the Mount of Olives, He dispatched two of His disciples 30saying to them, "Go to the village opposite you and, as you enter it, you will find a colt tied up, on which no one has ever ridden; untie it and bring it here. 31And if someone asks you, 'Why do you untie it?' you say, 'The Lord needs it.'"

32The messengers went off and found it exactly as He had told them. 33As they were untying the colt, its owners asked them, "Why are you untying the colt?" 34And they said, "The Lord needs it." 35Then they brought it to Jesus and, throwing their coats on the colt, they placed Jesus on it.

36As He rode along they spread their garments on the road. 37And when He approached the place of the descent of the Mount of Olives, the whole throng of disciples began to be joyful and sang praise to God with loud acclaim for all the miracles they had seen, 38saying, "Blessed be the King who comes in the name of the Lord! Peace in heaven and glory in the highest!"

39Some of the Pharisees in the crowd spoke to Him, "Teacher, rebuke Your disciples." 40And He answered them, "I tell you, if these keep silence the stones will cry out."

41When He came close to the city and viewed it, He wept[h] over it 42and said, "If you only knew even today how you might enjoy peace! But that is now hidden from your eyes. 43For the time is coming to you when your enemies will throw up ramparts around you and will encircle you and besiege you from every direction, 44and will level you and your children within you to the ground, and will not leave you one stone on another, because you did not understand when you were divinely visited."

45Entering the temple He began to expel the traders, to whom 46He said, "It is written,[i] 'My house shall be a house of prayer,' but you have made it a den of robbers."

47And every day He was teaching in the temple, while the chief priests, the scribes and the leaders of the people were seeking a way to destroy Him; 48but they discovered no way to do it, for all the people hung on His words.

---

f) Bethphage was situated at the foot of the Mt. of Olives between Bethany and Jerusalem. See note at Matt. 21:1.
g) See note at Matt. 21:17.
h) Luke alone reports that the Lord wept on this occasion. *Cf.* Matt. 21:1-11; Mark 11:1-11.
i) Isa. 56:7; *cf.* Jer. 7:11.

20 ONE DAY AS HE WAS INSTRUCting the people in the temple and preaching the gospel, the chief priests and the scribes came up with the elders ²and said to Him, "Tell us by what authority You are doing these things, or who gave You this authority?" ³He replied to them, "I shall ask you a question too, and you tell Me: ⁴Was John's baptism derived from heaven or from men?"

⁵They argued among themselves, "If we say 'From heaven,' He will say, 'Why then did you not believe in him?' ⁶But if we say, 'From men,' all the people will stone us, for they are convinced that John was a prophet." ⁷So they answered that they did not know from where it came. ⁸Jesus said to them, "Neither do I tell you by what authority I do these things."

⁹He began to tell the people this parable: "A man planted a vineyard and leased it to tenant farmers; then went away for a considerable period. ¹⁰At the harvest season he sent the workers a servant,ʲ whom they should give a share of the vineyard crop; but the tenants beat him and sent him off empty-handed. ¹¹He then dispatched another servant whom they beat and abused and sent off empty-handed. ¹²Again he sent yet a third whom also they wounded and expelled. ¹³Then the owner of the vineyard said, 'What shall I do? I shall send my beloved son; surely, they will respect him.'

¹⁴"But when the tenant farmers saw him they discussed it among themselves, 'This is the heir; let us kill him, so that the inheritance may become ours.' ¹⁵Accordingly they threw him out of the vineyard and killed him. What then will the owner of the vineyard do to them? ¹⁶He will come and destroy those tenants and will give the vineyard to others."

When they heard it they said, "May it never be!" ¹⁷But He looked at them and said, "What then does this Scriptureᵏ mean: 'The stone which the builders rejected has become the chief stone of the corner'? ¹⁸Whoever falls on that stone will be crushed and he on whom it falls will be pulverized."

¹⁹The scribes and chief priests tried to get their hands on Him right then, but they were afraid of the people; for they realized that He had told this parable with them in mind. ²⁰So they watched Him and sent spies who pretended to be honest in the hope of catching Him in some saying that they might hand Him over to the governor's control and jurisdiction.

²¹They asked Him, "Teacher, we know that You are right in what You say and teach; You are partial to no one but teach the way of God sincerely. ²²Is it lawful for us to pay tribute to Caesar or not?" ²³Well aware of their trickery, He said to them, ²⁴"Show me a coin. Whose likeness and inscription does it bear?" They said, "Caesar's." ²⁵He said to them, "Then pay to Caesar what belongs to Caesar and to God what belongs to God." ²⁶So they could not lay hold on what He said before the people and, marveling at His answer, kept quiet.

²⁷Then some of the Sadducees,ˡ who deny the resurrection, came up and asked Him, ²⁸"Teacher, Moses wroteᵐ for us, 'When a man's married brother dies childless, the brother shall take the woman and raise children for his brother.' ²⁹Now there were seven brothers, the first of whom took a wife and died childless. ³⁰The second also took her, ³¹and the third, and so did all seven of them, and they died childless. ³²At last the woman died too. ³³Whose wife then will she be in the resurrection? For all seven were married to her."

³⁴Jesus said to them, "The sons of this world marry and are given in marriage, ³⁵but those who are considered worthy of attaining yonder world and the resurrection from the dead neither marry nor are given in marriage; ³⁶for they cannot die again but are like the angels and as sons of the resurrection they are God's sons. ³⁷But that the

---

j) See note at Matt. 13:27.
k) Ps. 118:22. The Apostle Peter later quoted these important words, Acts 4:11; I Pet. 2:7, 8.
l) See note at Matt. 3:7.   m) Deut. 25:5, 6.

dead are raised Moses too made known in the passage[n] about the burning bush, where he calls the Lord 'The God of Abraham, the God of Isaac, and the God of Jacob.' [38]He is not the God of the dead but of the living; for to Him they are all alive."

[39]Some of the scribes remarked, "Teacher, You have spoken well." [40]For they did not dare to ask Him any more questions. [41]But He said to them, "How can people say that Christ is David's son, [42]when David himself says in the book of Psalms,[o] 'The Lord said to my Lord, Be seated at My right [43]until I make Thine enemies a footstool for Thy feet.' [44]So David calls Him Lord; then how is He his son?"

[45]And in the hearing of all the people He said to the disciples, [46]"Beware of the scribes, who like to walk around in long robes and love salutations in public places and front seats in the synagogues and choice places at banquets, [47]who make away with widows' houses and pray long for appearance' sake. They will receive a severer sentence."

21 LOOKING UP, HE SAW THE wealthy dropping their donations into the treasury. [2]He saw a poor widow put in two small copper coins[p] [3]and remarked, I tell you truly that this poor widow has put in more than all the rest; [4]for they all gave from their plenty, but she from her poverty has thrown in her entire livelihood."

[5]And as some were talking about the temple, how it was adorned with beautiful stones and votive gifts,[q] He said, [6]"As for these things that you see, the time is coming when not one stone will be left on another without being torn down." [7]They asked Him, "Teacher, when will this happen, and what sign is there to indicate when it is about to happen?" [8]And He said, "Be careful not to be misled; for many will come in My name, saying, 'I am He,'

and 'The time is near.' Do not go out after them. [9]And when you hear of wars and disturbances, do not be alarmed; for these things must first occur, but the end will not come at once."

[10]Then He told them: "Nation will rise against nation and kingdom against kingdom; [11]there will be severe earthquakes and plagues and famines in various places; horrors, too, and great signs from heaven. [12]Previous to all that they will arrest and persecute you, delivering you to synagogues and prisons and having you brought before kings and governors on account of My name. [13]These occasions will give you opportunities for testifying. [14]So make up your mind not to prepare your defense; [15]for I will grant you eloquence and wisdom that none of your opponents will be able to resist or refute.

[16]"You will also be betrayed by parents and brothers, by relatives and friends, and some of you will be executed. [17]You will be hated by everyone for confessing Me, [18]but not a hair of your head will be lost.[r] [19]In your steadfastness you will gain possession of your souls.

[20]"But when you see Jerusalem surrounded by armies, then be assured that her ruin is pending. [21]Then those in Judea should flee to the mountains, and those inside the city should escape, while those in the country should not enter her; [22]for those are the days of vengeance in fulfillment of all that has been written.

[23]"Alas for those who are pregnant and for those who are nursing children in those days, for terrible misery will be on the earth and anger will visit this people. [24]They will fall by the edge of the sword and will be carried off as prisoners to all nations. And Jerusalem will be trampled down by the Gentiles until the period of the Gentiles is completed.

[25]"There will also be signs in sun, moon and stars, with distress on earth

---

n) Exod. 3:1-14.
o) Ps. 110:1, which clearly intimates Christ's divine and human nature.
p) These copper coins were mites, worth about one-eighth of a cent each. See note at Mark 12:42.
q) Votive gifts are offerings made in fulfillment of a vow, gifts consecrated by a pledge of devotion.
r) Cf. Ps. 121:7.

among the nations, bewilderment at the roaring of sea and waves, 26men swooning from dread and apprehension about events that are about to take place in the world; for the powers of the heavens will be shaken. 27Then will they see the Son of Man coming in a cloud[s] with great power and glory. 28But when these things begin to occur, straighten up and lift up your heads, because your deliverance is near."

29He told them a parable: "Observe the fig tree and all the trees. 30When they are fully budding, you know by looking at them that summer is in the offing. 31Similarly when you notice these things taking place, be assured that the kingdom of God is near. 32I assure you that all this will happen before this generation[t] passes away. 33Heaven and earth will pass away, but My words will not pass away.

34"Be on your guard, so that your hearts are not overloaded with dissipation, drunkenness and worldly cares, and that day takes you by surprise like a trap; 35for it will come upon all the inhabitants of the globe. 36But you be vigilant and pray unceasingly so that you may have strength to escape all those impending events and to stand in the presence of the Son of Man."[u]

37During the day He taught in the temple, but at night He went out and stayed in the open at what is called the Mount of Olives. 38Early in the morning all the people resorted to Him in the temple to listen to Him.

22 THE FEAST OF UNLEAVENED Bread, called the Passover, was drawing near, 2and the chief priests and the scribes were seeking a way to kill Him; for they were afraid of the people. 3Then Satan entered Judas, called Iscariot, who was counted among the Twelve, 4and he went off to confer with the chief priests and officers how

he might deliver Him to them. 5They were delighted, and agreed to give him money. 6He consented and looked for a chance to betray Him to them away from the crowd.

7Then came the Day of Unleavened Bread, when the Passover must be sacrificed; 8so He sent Peter and John with instructions, "Go and get the Passover ready for us to eat." 9They asked Him, "Where do You want us to prepare it?" 10He replied, "As you enter the city, a man will meet you, carrying a pitcher of water. Follow him into the house he enters, 11and say to the owner of the house, 'The Teacher sends you word, "Where is the guest hall in which I may eat the Passover with My disciples?"' 12He will show you a large upper room all furnished; there make ready." 13So they went and found everything just as He had told them, and they prepared the Passover Supper.

14When the hour came, He and His disciples sat[v] together at the table, 15and He said to them, "I have longingly desired to eat this Passover with you before I suffer; 16for I tell you, I shall never eat it again until it is fulfilled in the kingdom of God."

17Taking the cup in His hands, He gave thanks and said, "Take this and divide it among yourselves; 18for I tell you, I shall from now on never again drink the fruit of the vine until the kingdom of God comes."

19And taking the bread, He gave thanks, broke and gave it to them, saying,[w] "This is My body [given up for your sakes; do this in My memory." 20Similarly He gave the cup after supper, saying, "This cup is the new Covenant in My blood, poured out on your behalf][x]. 21However, the hand of My betrayer is with Me at the table; 22for the Son of man goes, indeed, as was determined, but alas for that man by whom He is betrayed." 23And they

---

s) Compare Acts 1:9-11, where Christ's ascension and His personal return to the earth are mentioned.
t) The word "generation" is translated from the Greek *genea* which means (1) *generation*, i.e., contemporaries living on earth or the span of an individual's lifetime; (2) *race;* and (3) *family.*
u) To stand in Christ's presence without fear of condemnation, because of trust in Him.
v) See note at Mark 2:15.   w) Here Jesus instituted the Lord's Supper. Cf. I Cor. 11:23-26.
x) The latter part of vs. 19 and all of vs. 20 which are enclosed in brackets do not appear in some of the most reliable ancient manuscripts.

started to inquire among themselves who of them might possibly be going to do this.

24There also was a controversy among them, who of them should be considered most important. 25But He told them, "The kings of the nations lord it over them and their authorities are called benefactors. 26But you are not to be that way. Instead, the most prominent among you must be as the youngest, and the leader as one who serves. 27For who is more important, the one who sits at the table or the waiter? Is it not the one who sits at the table? But I am among you as one who serves.y

28"You have been standing by Me through My trials 29and, just as My Father has assigned to Me a kingdom, so I assign to you 30that you may eat and drink at My table in My kingdom, and you will be seated on thrones judging the twelve tribes of Israel.

31"Simon, Simon, Satan has asked permission to sift all of you like wheat, 32but I have prayed for you that your faith may not fail; and when you return to Me, strengthen your brothers." 33Peter told Him, "Lord, I am ready to go to prison and to death for You." 34But He said, "I tell you, Peter, the rooster will not crow today before you have denied three times that you know Me."

35And He said to them, "When I sent you out without purse or bag or sandals, did you lack anything?" They answered, "Nothing." 36Then He told them, "But now he who has a purse, take it, and a bag too, and he who has no sword, sell your coat and buy one. 37For I tell you that what is writtenz has to be accomplished in Me, 'He was classed among criminals'; for what is written about Me is reaching conclusion." 38They said, "Lord, look, here are two swords." He said to them, "It is enough."

39He went out as usual to the Mount of Olives, and the disciples followed Him. 40When He reached the place, He told them, "Pray that you may not enter into temptation"; 41then He withdrew from them about a stone's throw, knelt down and prayed, 42"Father, if Thou art willing, remove this cup from Me; nevertheless, not My will but Thine be done." 43[And an angel from heaven appeared to Him to strengthen Him, 44and in agony He prayed yet more intensely, and His sweat fell to the ground like great drops of blood.]a

45Arising from prayer and going to the disciples, He found them asleep from sorrow, 46and said to them, "Why are you sleeping? Rise up and pray that you may not enter into temptation."

47While He was still speaking, there was a mob headed by one of the Twelve named Judas, who approached Jesus to kiss Him. 48Jesus said to him, "Judas, are you betraying the Son of Man with a kiss?" 49When those with Him saw what was coming, they said, "Lord, shall we strike with the sword?" 50And oneb of them struck the slavec of the high priest and cut off his right ear. 51But Jesus said, "Enough of this!" And touching the ear, He healed him.

52Then Jesus said to the chief priests, the temple officers and the elders who came to arrest Him, "Have you come out with swords and clubs as against a robber? 53When I was daily in the temple with you, you never put out a hand against Me. But this is your hour and the power of darkness."

54They arrested Him, led Him away and took Him inside the house of the high priest, while Peter followed from a distance. 55When they kindled a fire in the center of the courtyard and sat around it, Peter sat in their circle. 56Then a maid noticed him seated by the fire, took a good look at him and said, "This fellow was with Him too." 57But he denied, saying, "Woman, I do not know Him!" 58A little later another

y) For example, Jesus had washed the feet of the Twelve, John 13:1-17.
z) Isa. 53:12.
a) Verses 43 and 44, enclosed in brackets, do not appear in the majority of the most reliable ancient manuscripts.
b) This was Simon Peter, John 18:10.
c) See note at Matt. 13:27.

looked at him and said, "Yes, you are one of them." But Peter said, "Man, I am not!" 59About an hour had gone by when another insisted, "Unquestionably this fellow was with Him, for he is a Galilean also." 60But Peter said, "Man, I cannot make out what you are talking about!" And instantly, while he was still speaking, the rooster crowed. 61Then the Lord, turning round, looked at Peter and Peter remembered the Lord's warning, how He had said to him, "Before the rooster crows tonight you will disown Me three times." 62And going clear outside, he wept bitterly.d

63The men who were holding Jesus in custody ridiculed Him while flogging Him; 64they blindfolded Him, inquiring, "Prophesy! Who struck You?" 65And they made many more insulting remarks to Him.

66With break of day the elders of the people, both chief priests and scribes, got together and had Him brought into their Sanhedrin.e 67They said, "If You are the Christ, tell us." But He said to them, "You will not believe if I tell you; 68neither will you answer if I question you. 69But from now on the Son of Man will be seated at the right hand of God Almighty." 70They all said, "Are You then the Son of God?" He said to them, "You say that I am." 71They said, "What need do we still have of testimony? We have personally heard it from His own lips."

23 THEN THEY ROSE UP IN A BODY and conducted Him to Pilate. 2And they started to accuse Him, "We found this fellow perverting our nation and forbidding them to pay taxes to Caesar, claiming that He Himself is Messiah, a king."

3And Pilate asked Him, "Are You the king of the Jews?" He answered him, "You say so." 4Then Pilate told the chief priests and the crowd, "I find nothing criminal in this man." 5But they strongly insisted, "He stirs up the people by teaching all over Judea, beginning from Galilee and coming to this place."

6Hearing that, Pilate asked if the man were a Galilean and, 7having learned that He came under Herod's jurisdiction, he sent Him back to Herod, who was himself in Jerusalem during those days.

8Herod was very pleased to see Jesus, for he had wanted for a long time to see Him, for he had been hearing about Him, and he hoped to see Him perform some miracles; 9but though he questioned Him at length, Jesus never answered him.f 10Meanwhile the chief priests and scribes stood there accusing Him with all their might. 11Then Herod, with his soldiers, made light of Him and mockingly put resplendent attire on Him, then sent Him back to Pilate. 12On that day Herod and Pilate became friends, for they had previously been enemies.

13Pilate then summoned the chief priests and the rulers and the people, 14to whom he spoke: "You brought me this man as inciting the people to rebellion. I have examined Him in your presence and have found the man not guilty of any of your accusations against Him; 15neither, in fact, has Herod, for he sent Him back to us. Observe that He has done nothing deserving death; 16so, after a scourging I will let Him go." 17[For he had to release them one convict at the feast.]g 18But they all shouted as one voice, "Away with Him! Release Barabbas for us!" 19He had been thrown in prison on account of a

---

d) In contrast with Judas, who suffered remorse at his betrayal of Christ and then hanged himself, Peter truly repented of his denial of the Lord Jesus. His tears were the first sign of repentance. See John 21:15-19.
e) The Sanhedrin, composed of seventy-one members, was the highest Jewish council under the jurisdiction of the Roman procurators. Its powers of administration of the government and justice were extensive throughout all Judea. It had its own police force, with power of life and death, though apparently no authority to execute the death penalty, which action had to be submitted to the review of the Roman authorities. The seventy regular members of the Sanhedrin, or council (corresponding to the seventy elders of Moses' time), had to be Israelites whose descent was unquestionable. The seventy-first member, the Sanhedrin's president, was the high priest.
f) Isa. 53:7.
g) Verse 17, enclosed in brackets, is not found in the majority of the most reliable ancient manuscripts.

riot that had occurred in the city, and for murder. 20Again Pilate, because he wanted to release Jesus, called out to them; 21but they roared, "Crucify, crucify Him!" 22For the third time he said to them, "What wrong, then, has He done? I find nothing in Him that deserves death; so after a scourging I will let Him go."

23But with loud voices they urged their demand that He be crucified, and their shoutings won the day. 24Pilate pronounced sentence, that what they asked should be done. 25He released the one they wanted, who had been thrown in prison for riot and murder, and handed Jesus over to their wishes.h 26And as they led Him away, they took hold of Simon, a Cyrenian,i who was coming from the country, and laid the cross on him to carry it behind Jesus.

27A vast host of people followed Him and women too, who beat their breasts and bewailed Him. 28Turning to them Jesus said, "Daughters of Jerusalem, do not weep for Me; instead, weep for yourselves and for your children; 29for be sure the time is coming when they will say, 'Happy are the childless, the wombs that never gave birth and the breasts that never nursed babies.' 30Then they will begin to say to the mountains,j 'Fall on us!' and to the hills, 'Hide us!' 31For if they do this to the green wood, what will happen to the dry?"k

32Two others, criminals, were also led away with Him to be crucified. 33And when they reached the place called The Skull,l there they crucified Him and the criminals, one at His right and the other at His left. 34And Jesus said, "Father, forgive them, for they do not know what they are doing." And they divided His clothes among themselves by casting lots.

35And the people stood staring, while the leaders sneered, "Others He saved; let Him save Himself, if He is the Christ of God, His Chosen!" 36The soldiers, too, ridiculed Him, coming up and offering Him vinegar, 37saying, "If You are the king of the Jews, save Yourself!" 38For there was an inscription above Him, THIS IS THE KING OF THE JEWS.

39One of the criminals that were hanged reviled Him, "Are You not the Christ? Save Yourself and us!" 40But the other reproved him and told him, "Do you not fear God, when you are suffering the same punishment? 41We, however, are suffering justly; we are getting what we deserve for our misdeeds, but He has done nothing amiss." 42Then he said, "Jesus, remember me when You come into Your kingdom." 43Jesus said to him, "I assure you, today you will be with Me in Paradise."

44It was then about twelve o'clock, and darkness came over the whole land, which lasted until three in the afternoon, 45due to the sun's eclipse. And the veilm of the temple was torn in two. 46With a loud voice Jesus cried, "Father, into Thy hands I entrust My spirit!" And with these words He died.

47When the centurion saw what had happened, he praised God, saying, "Truly this man was innocent." 48And when all the crowds that had gathered for this spectacle saw what had occurred, they went back, beating their breasts. 49All His acquaintances too, and the women who had come along with Him from Galilee, observed it all, standing at a distance.

50Now there was a man named Joseph, a member of the council, a good and upright man, 51who had not voted for the council's plan and action; a native of Arimathea, one of the Judean towns, he lived in expectation of the kingdom of God. 52He went to Pilate and asked for the body of Jesus;

---

h) Pilate, who as governor was the supreme judge of the Jewish subjects in Jerusalem, had no right to condemn Jesus on the charges that had been made against Him, and he knew it.
i) See note at Matt. 27:32.
j) Rev. 6:16; *cf.* Hos. 10:8.
k) Here Jesus used what was evidently a current proverb, meaning that if the Romans had mistreated and condemned Him to death (the green tree — i.e., an innocent person), what would they later do to the guilty (the dry tree)?
l) This place is generally known as Calvary, from the Latin word *calvaria* meaning *skull.*
m) This was the curtain that hung in the temple between the Holy of holies and the holy place.

53which he took down and wrapped in linen, then laid in a rock-hewn tomb where nobody had yet been laid. 54It was preparation day with the Sabbath drawing near. 55And the women, who had accompanied Him from Galilee followed and saw the tomb and how His body was laid. 56Then they went back to prepare spices and perfumes, and rested on the Sabbath in obedience to the commandment.n

24 ON THE FIRST DAY OF THE week at early dawn they went to the tomb taking the spices they had prepared. 2They found the stone rolled away from the tomb, 3and going inside they did not find the body of the Lord Jesus. 4They were greatly perplexed about this when, lo, two men stood by them in dazzling clothing. 5Frightened, the women bowed their faces to the ground, but the men said to them, "Why do you look for the living among the dead? 6He is not here, but He has risen! Remember how He toldo you while He was still in Galilee, 7that the Son of Man must be delivered into the hands of sinful men and be crucified and rise again on the third day."

8Then they recalled His sayings 9and, returning from the tomb, they told everything to the Eleven and to all the rest. 10They were Mary Magdalene, and Joanna,p and Mary,q the mother of James; they and the rest of the women told these things to the apostles. 11But these reports seemed nonsense to them; they did not believe the women. 12[Peter got up, though, and ran to the tomb and, stooping down, saw the linen clothes lying by themselves; then he went away wondering at what had happened.]r

13That same day two of them were walking to a village called Emmaus, about seven miles from Jerusalem, 14and they were talking to each other about all these occurrences. 15During their conversation and discussion, Jesus Himself caught up with them and walked along with them, 16but their eyes were kept from recognizing Him. 17He said to them, "What are these things you are discussing as you walk?" Looking downcast, they stopped, 18and one of them, named Cleopas, answered Him, "Are You the lone visitor in Jerusalem who does not know the things that have happened there during the past few days?" 19He asked, "What things?" They said to Him, "About Jesus of Nazareth, who was a mighty prophet in deed and word before God and all the people, 20and how the chief priests and our leaders gave Him over to be sentenced to death and had Him crucified. 21But we had hopes that He was the one who would deliver Israel. Moreover, three days have already passed since all those events occurred.

22"Some of our women, though, astounded us. Early this morning they went to the tomb 23and, not finding the body, came back to tell us that they had seen a vision of angels, who said that He is alive. 24Some of our group then went to the tomb and found it just as the women had said; but Him they did not see."

25Jesus said to them, "O fools, with hearts so slow to believe everything the prophets have spoken! 26Did not Christ have to suffer all this and enter into His glory?" 27Then, beginning at Mosess and through all the Prophets He explained to them in all the Scriptures what referred to Himself.

28They drew near to the village to which they were going, and He behaved as if He were going on, 29but they urged Him, "Stay with us, for it is toward evening and the day is already declining." So He went in to stay with them. 30And as He satt at the table with them, He took bread, gave thanks, and broke it, and handed

---

n) Exod. 20:8-11.   o) Chapter 9:22.
p) Joanna was the wife of Chuza, Herod's steward, ch. 8:3.
q) See note on the four Marys of the Gospels, Matt. 1:16.
r) Verse 12, enclosed in brackets, does not appear in the majority of the most reliable ancient manuscripts.
s) That is, from Genesis through the whole Old Testament. This is one of the most important of all passages relating to Bible study because it shows that Christ is at the center of the Scriptures.
t) See note at Mark 2:15.

it to them. 31Then their eyes were opened and they recognized Him. And He vanished from their sight.

32They said to one another, "Did not our hearts burn within us while He was talking to us on the road and opening the Scriptures to us?" 33Rising at once, they went back to Jerusalem and found the Eleven and their friends all congregated, 34saying, "The Lord is risen indeed and appeared to Simon!" 35Then they related their own experience on the road and how they had recognized Him in the breaking of the bread.

36While they were talking of those things, He Himself stood in their midst and said to them, "Peace to you." 37They were startled and terrified, imagining that they saw a ghost; 38but He asked them, "Why are you disturbed and why are such doubts arising in your hearts? 39Look at My hands and My feet. It is I Myself. Touch Me and see; for a ghost does not have flesh and bones as you see Me have." 40[And when He said this, He showed them His hands and feet.]u

41Since they still were unable to believe for sheer joy, and marveled, He asked them, "Do you have any food on hand?" 42And they gave Him a piece of broiled fish, 43and He took and ate it.

44Then He said to them, "These are My teachings which I spoke to you while I was still with you, that everything written in the Law of Moses and in the Prophets and Psalms about Me must take place." 45Then He opened their minds to understand the Scriptures. 46He said to them, "So it is written, that the Christ should suffer and rise from the dead on the third day, 47and that repentance, leading to forgiveness of sins, should be preached in His name to all nations beginning at Jerusalem.

48"You are witnesses of these things, 49and I will send out upon you what was promised by My Father.v But you wait here in the city until you are clothed with power from on high."

50Then He conducted them out as far as Bethanyw and, raising His hands, He blessed them. 51While He blessed them He was parted from them and taken up into heaven.

52They worshiped Him and went back to Jerusalem with great joy. 53And they were constantly in the temple, praising God.x

---

u) Verse 40, enclosed in brackets, does not appear in the majority of the most reliable ancient manuscripts.
v) That is, the Holy Spirit who now takes charge.
w) Bethany is at the foot of the Mt. of Olives. Thus Acts 1:12 is in accord with the statement here.
x) Luke continues his record of Christ's ministry in The Acts where he tells of the coming of the Holy Spirit, the beginnings of the church, and its early witness.

THEME OF LUKE:

SEGMENT DIVISIONS

		CHAPTER THEMES
		1
		2
		3
		4
		5
		6
		7
		8
		9
		10
		11
		12
		13
		14
		15
		16
		17
		18
		19
		20
		21
		22
		23
		24

Author:

Date:

Purpose:

Key Words:

kingdom of God

Son of Man

mark every reference to the devil or demons

covenant

JOHN

God in the flesh! What would He be like? What would He do? How would He live in relationship to the Father once He came to earth? How would people know He was God? Would He force people to believe in Him? And what about those who refused to believe He is God?

And what of those who believed, who followed Him? What would God in the flesh expect from them? And what if they failed?

God in the flesh. It would be hard for some to believe, but their belief or unbelief would be a matter of life or death.

Three other Gospels had been written, and years had passed. One more Gospel was needed, one which would answer these questions and more, one which would illuminate the shadows of doubt. So the apostle John answered God's call to write a fourth and final Gospel to explain the One who came to reveal the Father. It was about A.D. 85.

THINGS TO DO

1. Although the author of John is not identified by name, tradition holds that it was the apostle John. Read John 21:20–25 and note how the author identifies himself. You might want to put this reference or information under "Author" on the JOHN AT A GLANCE chart following this Gospel.
2. To understand the purpose of John read John 20:30, 31. Record John's purpose on JOHN AT A GLANCE.

Chapters 1–12

1. Carefully read this segment chapter by chapter, observing what the author includes to accomplish his purpose.
   a. As you read these chapters, look for and mark the following key words and their synonyms: *believe, life, sign (signs), judge (judgment), witness (testify), true (genuine, truth),* and *king (kingdom).*
   b. You will find it helpful to write down the key words on an index card to use as a bookmark. Mark the words on the card in the same way you want to mark them in your Bible.
   c. Also mark any other repeated key words that are pertinent to the message of the chapter.
2. As you read each of the first twelve chapters, ask the five W's and an H: Who? What? Where? When? Why? and How? Look specifically for the following, recording whatever facts you find in each chapter in the margin. As you move your findings to the margin, use the headings set in italics below as your headings in the margins.
   a. *Events:* What is happening? For example, "Nicodemus visited Jesus by night."
   b. *Geographic locations:* Where is this event taking place? For example, John was baptizing on the other side of the Jordan.
   c. *Timing of events:* When is this

event taking place? For example, "on the third day," or "before the Passover." In the margin next to the text, note these mentions of time by drawing an appropriate symbol. When you read of Jesus attending a feast, record that fact on the JOHN AT A GLANCE chart.

d. *Portrayals of Jesus Christ:* How is Jesus pictured or described? For example: "the Word," "the Lamb of God," etc.

e. *Signs and Miracles:* The signs that John recorded were for the purpose of leading people to believe that Jesus is the Christ, the Son of God. Look for these signs or miracles. For example, Jesus turned water into wine. The text says this was "the earliest of His signs."

f. *References that show the deity of Jesus* (references that show that Jesus is God): Look for verses that show Jesus is God. For example, John 10:33 says, "We would not stone You for a good act but for blasphemy, because You, a human being, make Yourself God."

g. *Witnesses:* Throughout his Gospel, John refers to those who bear witness to Jesus. Who are these witnesses and what is their witness? For example, John said, "I did see it and I testify that He is the Son of God" (John 1:34).

3. Determine the main subject or theme of each chapter and then record it just above the chapter number and on JOHN AT A GLANCE.

Chapters 13–17

1. This segment brings a change in Jesus' ministry as He draws away with the disciples in order to prepare them for what is to come. Make a new list of key words on a bookmark: *believe,*

love, works (deeds, activities), commands (orders), fruit, abide, ask, truth (true), and *devil (Satan, ruler of this world).* (Go back to chapter 12 and mark the reference to *ruler of this world.)*

2. Mark in the text in a distinctive way all references, including pronouns, to God, Jesus, and the Holy Spirit. Then list in the margin everything you learn about the Holy Spirit. This is especially important in chapters 14 through 16.

3. List in the chapter margins any specific instructions or commands that Jesus gives the disciples.

4. Record the main theme of each chapter in the space at the beginning of the chapter.

Chapters 18–21

1. The final chapters of John give an account of the events surrounding the arrest, trial, crucifixion, resurrection, and the postresurrection appearances of Jesus Christ. As you read each chapter:

a. Mark the following key words and their synonyms: *testify, believe, love, truth (true), life,* and *king (kingdom).*

b. Following the Gospel of John you will find two charts: THE ARREST, TRIAL, AND CRUCIFIXION OF JESUS CHRIST and THE ACCOUNT OF JESUS' RESURRECTION. Record on the appropriate chart the progression of events from Jesus' arrest through His resurrection and postresurrection appearances. Note chapter and verse for future reference. (It would be good to do this on notebook paper before recording it on the chart.) Also remember that since Luke gives the consecutive order of events, it becomes a plumb line for the other Gospel records.

2. Once again determine the theme of each chapter and record it as you have done previously.

3. Also following the Gospel of John you will find a chart WHAT THE GOSPELS TEACH ABOUT THE KINGDOM OF GOD/THE KINGDOM OF HEAVEN. Compile what John teaches about the King and the kingdom on this chart. (Compile your information on notebook paper before you write it on the chart, and note chapter and verse of insight.)

4. Complete JOHN AT A GLANCE by doing the following:

   a. Review your chapter themes of John and determine the theme of the book. Record this in the appropriate place on JOHN AT A GLANCE.

   b. You will notice a section titled "Segment Divisions" and two lines where you can record "Signs and Miracles" and "Portrayals of Jesus Christ." Review the information you have recorded in the margins. Record your observations on the appropriate segment division line. For example, in chapter 1 Jesus is referred to as "the Lamb of God." Record that fact at chapter 1 under "Portrayals of Jesus Christ." This will give you a visual picture of the structure of John.

THINGS TO THINK ABOUT

1. Do you really believe that Jesus is God? Do you live accordingly?

2. Do you know how to take another person through the Scriptures to show him that Jesus is God?

3. Do people know that you are a disciple of Jesus Christ because of your love for others and because you have continued in His Word?

4. Are you relying on the Spirit of God to comfort you, help you, bear witness through you, do the work of God through you, and guide you into all truth?

5. Do you look at other Christians and wonder why God deals differently with you than He does with them? Do you need to hear His words to Peter in John 21:22, "If I want him to remain until I come, what is it to you? You follow Me"? Are you willing to follow Jesus wherever He leads, even if you have to do it alone? Are you telling others about Him?

Life of Christ Showing Coverage by Luke (Shaded Area)

PREPARATION	PUBLIC MINISTRY			SACRIFICE

OBSCURITY (VANISHING)   **POPULARITY** (DECLINING)   **OPPOSITION** (INCREASING)

ASCENSION

40 days

RESURRECTION
DEATH

TRIUMPHAL ENTRY
Matthew 21:1

2 months

CONCLUDING MINISTRIES

3 months — PEREAN

BEYOND JORDAN
John 10:40

3 months — LATER JUDEAN

TO FEAST OF TABERNACLES
John 7:10

SPECIALIZED MINISTRIES

6 months — LATER GALILEAN

TO TYRE AND SIDON
Matthew 15:21

EXTENDED MINISTRIES

10 months — MIDDLE GALILEAN

JESUS ORDAINS THE TWELVE
Luke 6:12ff

4 months — EARLY GALILEAN

JESUS RETURNS TO GALILEE
Mark 1:14

EARLY MINISTRIES

8 months — EARLY JUDEAN

JESUS CLEANSES TEMPLE
John 2:13ff

OPENING EVENTS

4 months

JOHN INTRODUCES JESUS
John 1:19ff

BIRTH

5 B.C.

ANNUAL PASSOVERS

FIRST YEAR	SECOND YEAR	THIRD YEAR
John 2:13	John 5:1 John 6:4	John 11:55

Luke 1   Luke 4:13   Luke 4:14   Luke 6:12   Luke 9:17   Luke 9:18   Luke 9:51   Luke 13:22   Luke 19:28   Luke 24

Used by permission. Jensen, Irving L. Luke: A Self-Study Guide. Chicago: Moody Press, 1970.

THE GOSPEL ACCORDING TO

JOHN

1 IN THE BEGINNING WAS THE Word,[a] and the Word was with God, and the Word was God. [2]This is the One who was in the beginning with God. [3]Through Him everything came into being and without Him nothing that exists came into being. [4]In Him was Life, and the Life was the Light of men. [5]The Light shines in the darkness and the darkness did not overcome it.

[6]There was a man named John, sent from God. [7]He came to be a witness to testify regarding the Light, so that everyone might believe through him. [8]He was not himself the Light, but he came in order to testify regarding the Light.

[9]The true Light that illumines every person was coming into the world. [10]He was in the world and the world came into being through Him, yet the world did not know Him. [11]He came to His own home and His own people did not receive Him. [12]But to those who did receive Him He granted authority to become God's children, that is, to those who believe in His name, [13]who owe their birth neither to human blood, nor to physical urge, nor to human design, but to God. [14]And the Word became man and lived for a time among us, and we viewed His glory — such glory as an only son receives from his father — abounding in grace and truth.

c. A.D. 26

[15]John testified about Him and cried out, "This was the One of whom I said, 'He who comes after me ranks ahead of me because He was before me.'" [16]For from His abundance all of us have received more and more grace; [17]for while the Law was given through Moses, grace and truth came through Jesus Christ. [18]No one has ever seen God; the begotten Son who abides at the Father's side has made Him known.

[19]And this is John's testimony when the Jews sent priests and Levites[b] from Jerusalem to inquire of him, "Who are you?" [20]He admitted without denial and frankly confessed, "I am not the Christ." [21]They asked him, "Then who are you? Elijah?" He said, "No, I am not." "Are you the prophet?"[c] He answered, "No." [22]Then they said to him, "Who are you, so that we may have an answer for those who sent us? What have you to say about yourself?"

[23]He said, "I am the voice of one shouting in the desert, 'Prepare the way of the Lord,' just as Isaiah the prophet said."[d] [24]Now the messengers were from the Pharisees[e] [25]and they asked him, "Then why do you baptize, if you are neither the Christ nor Elijah, nor the prophet?" [26]John answered them, "I baptize with water, [27]but there is One who stands among you, whom you do not recognize, the

---

a) Greek *Logos* meaning *Word*. Christ is the Word of God, that is, He is not only a divine messenger but the exact expression in Person, life and speech of God Himself, Heb. 1:3. What God is, Christ is.
b) See note at Luke 10:32.
c) Deut. 18:15; John 6:14; 7:40.
d) Isa. 40:3.
e) See note at Matt. 3:7.

One who will come after me and whose sandal-strings I am not fit to untie."

28These things occurred at Bethany[f] beyond the Jordan, where John was baptizing.

c. A.D. 27

29The next day he saw Jesus approaching him and said, "There is the Lamb of God who takes away the sin of the world! 30He is the One of whom I said, 'After me comes a Man who ranks ahead of me, for He was before me.' 31I did not recognize Him; but I have come to baptize with water, so that He may be made known to Israel."

32John testified further, "I saw the Spirit come down from heaven like a dove and remain on Him, 33and although I did not know Him, He who sent me to baptize with water told me Himself, 'On whom you see the Spirit descend and remain, He is the One who baptizes with the Holy Spirit.' 34And I did see it and I testify that He is the Son of God."

35Again the following day John was standing with two of his disciples,[g] 36when he looked at Jesus as He was walking along, and he said, "There is the Lamb of God." 37Hearing him say this, the two disciples followed Jesus. 38Then Jesus turned and, noticing that they were following Him, said to them, "What are you looking for?" They said to Him, "Rabbi (which means Teacher) where are You staying?" 39He told them, "Come and see." They went and saw where He was staying and remained with Him that day — it was then about ten in the morning.

40Andrew, the brother of Simon Peter, was one of the two who listened to John and who followed Him. 41He first found his own brother, Simon, and told him, "We have found the Messiah" (which means the Christ), 42and brought him to Jesus. Looking

at him Jesus said, "You are Simon, the son of John; you will be called Cephas"[h] (which means Peter).

43The next day Jesus decided to go to Galilee and found Philip, to whom He said, "Follow Me." 44Philip came from Beth-saida,[i] the town of Andrew and Peter. 45Philip found Nathanael[j] and told him, "We have found the One of whom Moses wrote in the Law as did the Prophets also, Jesus of Nazareth, the son of Joseph." 46Nathanael said to him, "Can anything good come out of Nazareth?" Philip replied, "Come and see."

47Jesus saw Nathanael approaching Him and said of him, "There, truly, is an Israelite without deceit in him." 48Nathanael asked Him, "How do you know me?" Jesus replied, "I saw you under the fig tree before ever Philip called you." 49Nathanael replied, "Rabbi, You are the Son of God; You are the king of Israel." 50Jesus further replied to him, "Do you believe because I told you I had seen you under the fig tree? You will see greater things than that." 51He then said to him, "Truly I assure you all, you will see heaven opened and the angels of God ascending and descending on the Son of Man."

2 ON THE THIRD DAY THERE WAS A wedding at Cana in Galilee, at which Jesus' mother was present, 2and Jesus, with His disciples, was invited to the wedding. 3When the wine gave out, Jesus' mother said to Him, "They are out of wine." 4Jesus said to her, "Woman,[k] what right do you have to tell Me? My hour is not yet here." 5His mother told the servants, "Do whatever He tells you."

6Now there were six stone water jars standing there for the Jewish rites of purifying; each would hold from twenty to thirty gallons. 7Jesus said to them, "Fill the jars with water." So they filled them to the brim. 8Again

---

f) See note at Matt. 21:17.   g) John and Andrew.
h) *Këphas*, from an Aramaic word meaning *rock* which is equivalent to the Greek *Petros*, that is Peter.   i) See note at Mark 8:22.
j) Nathanael is called Bartholomew in Matt. 10:3; Mark 3:18; Luke 6:14; Acts 1:13.
k) As a form of address "Woman" was a title of respect in that day. Jesus spoke the same word to His mother at the cross, John 19:26.

He told them, "Now take some out and carry it to the table steward." They carried it [9]and when the steward tasted the water that had become wine, and did not know where it came from (though the servants who had drawn the water knew), [10]he called the bridegroom and told him, "Everyone serves the good wine first and the poorer when men have drunk freely; but you have retained the good wine until now."

[11]Jesus performed this earliest of His signs in Cana of Galilee, thereby displaying His greatness. And His disciples believed in Him.

[12]Following this He and His mother and brothers and His disciples went down to Capernaum[1] and stayed there for a few days.

[13]The Jewish Passover was near, so Jesus went up to Jerusalem. [14]There He found seated in the temple dealers in cattle, sheep, and pigeons; also money-changers; [15]so, making a whip out of cords, He drove them all out of the temple, as well as the sheep and cattle, poured out the money-changers' coins and overturned the tables. [16]And to the pigeon dealers He said, "Take these outside; do not make My Father's house a house of business."

[17]His disciples recollected that it was written,[m] "Passion for Thy house will consume me."

[18]The Jews then said to Him, "What sign[n] will You show us for Your doing these things?" [19]Jesus replied, "Destroy this temple and in three days I will rebuild it." [20]Then the Jews remarked, "This temple has been in process of building for forty-six years, and will You rebuild it in three days?"[o] [21]But He was speaking about His bodily temple; [22]so, when He had risen from the dead, His disciples recollected that He had said this; they believed the Scripture and the message which Jesus spoke.

[23]While He was at Jerusalem during the Passover Feast, many who observed the signs which He did believed in His name. [24]But Jesus would not entrust Himself to them, because He understood them all [25]and did not need any one's evidence about people, for He knew what was in the human heart.

3 AMONG THE PHARISEES THERE was a man named Nicodemus, a ruler of the Jews, [2]who visited Jesus by night and said to Him, "Rabbi, we know that You are a teacher who has come from God; for no one can work the signs You work unless God is with him."

[3]Jesus answered him, "Truly I assure you, unless a person is born from above he cannot see the kingdom of God." [4]Nicodemus said to Him, "How can a man be born when he is old? Can he enter his mother's womb a second time and be born?" [5]Jesus replied, "Truly I assure you, unless one's birth is through water and the Spirit[p] he cannot enter the kingdom of God. [6]What is born of the flesh is flesh[q] and what is born of the Spirit is spirit.

[7]"Do not be surprised because I told you, 'All of you need to be born from above.' [8]The wind blows where it pleases and, though you hear the sound of it, you neither know whence it comes nor where it goes. It is the same with everyone who is born of the Spirit." In response, [9]Nicodemus asked Him, "How is that possible?" [10]Jesus replied, "You are a teacher of Israel and ignorant of this? [11]I truly assure you that we speak of what we know and we testify to what we have seen; but you do not accept our evidence. [12]If I told you earthly things and you

---

1) See note at Matt. 4:13.
m) Ps. 69:9.
n) The Greek word *sĕmeion* means *a sign* or *a distinguishing mark* by which a person or thing is known; *a token; a miracle.* The words "sign" and "miracle" are used interchangeably in the New Testament. The sign that the Jews wanted from Jesus was as an evidence of His divine authority and hence a proof of His messiahship.
o) Herod began to rebuild the temple in 19 B.C. This remark was made in about A.D. 27.
p) Water as a token of repentance on our part; the Spirit for the new birth — this is God's part. Water is also a symbol for the Word of God, Eph. 5:26.
q) The usual meaning of the word "flesh" in the N.T. is the whole human being apart from the influences of the Holy Spirit.

do not believe, how will you believe if I tell you heavenly things?

[13]"No one has gone up to heaven except He who came down from heaven, the Son of Man [whose home is heaven].[r] [14]And just as Moses lifted up the serpent in the wilderness, so the Son of Man must be lifted up, [15]so that whoever believes in Him may not perish but have life eternal.

[16]"For God so loved the world that He gave His only Son,[s] so that whoever believes in Him should not perish, but have everlasting life. [17]For God did not send His Son into the world to condemn the world but in order that the world might be saved through Him.

[18]"He who believes in Him is not condemned; but he who does not believe is already condemned, because he has not believed in the name of the only Son of God. [19]And this is the verdict, that the light has come into the world, and people have loved darkness more than light because their deeds were wicked. [20]For every one who practices evil hates the light and keeps away from the light, in order that his activities might not be exposed. [21]But one who practices the truth wants light on it, so that it will be perfectly clear that he is working in union with God."

[22]After this, Jesus and His disciples came into the Judean district, where He remained with them and baptized. [23]John also was baptizing at Aenon near Salim,[t] for there was plenty of water there and a continual stream of people came and were baptized. [24]For as yet John had not been put into prison.

[25]A dispute then arose between some of John's disciples and a Jew about purification; [26]So they came to John and told him, "Rabbi, the One who was with you on the other side of the Jordan, whom you gave testimony to —

He is baptizing and everyone is flocking to Him."

[27]John replied, "No man is able to lay claim to anything unless it has been given him from heaven. [28]You bear me out that I said, 'I am not the Christ,' but 'I am sent ahead of Him.' [29]The one who has the bride is the bridegroom. But the bridegroom's friend, who stands near and listens to him, is very happy over the bridegroom's voice; so this joy of mine is complete. [30]He must increase and I must diminish.

[31]"He who comes from above is above everyone, while one who originates from the earth belongs to the earth and speaks from an earthly standpoint. He who comes from heaven is higher than they all. [32]He testifies to what He has seen and heard, yet nobody accepts His testimony. [33]Whoever does accept His testimony attests that God is true; [34]for He whom God has sent speaks the words of God, for God grants the Spirit in unlimited measure. [35]The Father loves the Son and has committed everything into His hands. [36]He who believes in the Son has eternal life, but he who disobeys the Son will not see life but God's wrath remains upon him."

c. A.D. 28

4 WHEN THE LORD KNEW THAT THE Pharisees had heard, "Jesus is making and baptizing more disciples than John" ([2]although Jesus Himself did not baptize, but His disciples did), [3]He left Judea and went away again into Galilee. [4]He found it necessary to pass through Samaria [5]and arrived at a Samaritan town called Sychar, near the tract of land[u] that Jacob had presented to his son Joseph. [6]And Jacob's well was there. So Jesus, wearied by His travel, sat down just as He was by the well. It was about six in the evening.

[7]A Samaritan woman came to draw

---

r) The words enclosed in brackets are not found in the majority of the most reliable ancient manuscripts.
s) Christ is the unique Son of God, eternally One with the Father and the Spirit, yet truly man in His perfect humanity.
t) The precise locations of Aenon and Salim have not yet been identified. The context suggests that they were in the Jordan Valley. According to at least one lexicographer "Aenon" means *fountain* or *spring*.
u) Gen. 33:18, 19; *cf.* 50:22.

water, to whom Jesus said, "Let Me have a drink." [8]For His disciples had gone off into the town to buy food. [9]The Samaritan woman said to Him, "How is this that You, a Jew, should ask me, a Samaritan woman, for a drink?" For Jews do not associate with Samaritans.[v]

[10]Jesus answered her, "If you knew God's gift and who really asked you, 'Give Me a drink,' you would have requested Him and He would have given you living water." [11]The woman said to Him, "Sir, You have no rope and bucket, and the well is deep. Where do You get that living water? [12]You surely are not superior to our father Jacob, who gave us the well; and he and his sons and his cattle drank from it?" [13]Jesus answered her, "Whoever drinks from this water will be thirsty again; [14]but whoever drinks the water I shall give him will never thirst again, but the water I shall give him will become a well of water within him that bubbles up for eternal life."

[15]The woman said to Him, "Sir, give me this water, so that I will not get thirsty nor have to come all the way here to draw water." [16]He said to her, "Go, call your husband and come back here." [17]The woman replied, "I do not have a husband." Jesus said to her, "You say correctly, 'I have no husband,' [18]for you have had five husbands and the one you are now living with is not your husband; in saying this you told the truth." [19]The woman said[w] to Him, "I perceive, Sir, that You are a prophet. [20]Our fathers worshiped on this mountain, and You say that Jerusalem is the proper place to worship."

[21]Jesus said to her, "Believe Me, woman, the time has come when you will worship the Father neither in this mountain nor in Jerusalem. [22]You worship what you do not know; we worship what we know, for salvation comes from the Jews. [23]But the hour is coming — and is now — when genuine worshipers will worship the Father in spirit and truth; for the Father is looking for such as His worshipers. [24]God is a Spirit and His worshipers must worship Him in spirit and in truth."

[25]The woman said to Him, "I know that the Messiah, the One who is called Christ, is coming, and when He comes, He will make everything plain to us." [26]Jesus told her, "I who am talking to you, am He."

[27]Upon this His disciples came and were astonished that He was talking with a woman; however, no one asked, "What are You seeking?" or, "Why are You talking with her?" [28]Then the woman left her pitcher and, going off to town, told the people, [29]"Come, see a man who told me everything I have done! Is not He the Christ?"

[30]They went out from town and were going to Him. [31]Meanwhile, the disciples urged Him, "Rabbi, eat." [32]But He said to them, "I have nourishment of which you have no idea." [33]So the disciples said to one another, "Surely, no one has brought Him anything to eat?" [34]Jesus said to them, "My nourishment is that I do the will of Him who sent Me and completely do His work. [35]Do you not say, 'Four months more and the harvest will be here'? Look, I tell you; raise your eyes and look at the fields, how they are white for harvest. [36]Already the reaper receives his wage and gathers the crop for life eternal, so that the sower and the reaper may rejoice together. [37]For the saying, 'One sows and another reaps,' is verified here; [38]I sent you to reap a crop on which you have not worked; others toiled and you step in to benefit from their work."

[39]Numerous Samaritans from that town believed[x] in Him on account of the woman's testimony, "He told me

---

v) See note at Luke 9:53.
w) When the conversation probed her life, the woman suddenly changed the subject. But Jesus used her attempted diversion to lead her to see who He was.
x) *Pisteuo*, the N.T. word for believing in Christ, is related to the Greek noun *pistis*, meaning *faith*. To have saving *faith* in Christ is to trust Him personally as one's Lord and Savior. It is significant that in John's Gospel the noun "faith" is never used, but the verb "believe" (*pisteuo*) is employed ninety times, more than in the other three Gospels together. The purpose of John's Gospel is to lead men to believe in Jesus Christ, ch. 20:31. Thus it is the good news concerning active, living faith in Him.

everything I did." 40So when the Samaritans met Him they invited Him to stay with them, and He remained there two days. 41A good many more believed on account of His message, 42and said to the woman, "We no longer believe just because of your story; for we have heard Him ourselves and we know that He truly is the Savior of the world."

43At the end of the two days He left there and went to Galilee; 44for Jesus Himself affirmed, "A prophet has no honor in his native town." 45So, on His arrival in Galilee the Galileans, because they had seen everything He had done at the feast in Jerusalem, welcomed Him, for they also had attended the feast.

46Jesus went once more to Cana in Galilee, where He had changed the water into wine, and there a courtier, whose son lay ill in Capernaum, 47when he learned that Jesus had come to Galilee from Judea, came to Him and begged Him to come down and heal his son, who was at the point of death. 48Jesus then said to him, "Unless you see signs and wonders you will not believe at all." 49The courtier replied, "Sir, do come down before my boy dies." 50Jesus said to him, "Go your way; your son lives." The man believed what Jesus told him and went his way. 51But while he was going down to Capernaum, his slavesʸ met him and announced that his boy had recovered; 52so he asked them at what time he began to improve. They told him, "Yesterday at seven o'clock the fever left him." 53Then the father knew that it was the very hour when Jesus had said to him, "Your son lives." And he and his entire household became believers.

54This, then, was the second sign Jesus performed when He came from Judea into Galilee.

5 LATER ON THERE WAS A FEASTᶻ OF the Jews, and Jesus went up to Jerusalem. 2Now there is in Jerusalem, by the sheepgate, a bathing pool called in Hebrew, Bethzath, with five entrances 3in which a crowd of invalids lay— blind, lame and paralyzed [waiting for the stirring of the water. 4For at intervals an angel descended into the pool and stirred the water. Whoever got in first after the agitation of the pool enjoyed healing, no matter what ailment he suffered].ᵃ

5One man there had suffered from an infirmity for thirty-eight years. 6When Jesus noticed him lying there, He asked him, knowing he had been there for a long time, "Do you want to get well?" 7The invalid replied, "I have no one, Sir, to put me into the bathing pool right after it has been disturbed; while I am going another gets in ahead of me." 8Jesus told him, "Get up, pick up your mat and walk." 9Instantly the man was well; he picked up his mat and walked. Now that was on the Sabbath day.

10So the Jews said to the healed man, "This is the Sabbath and you have no right to carry your mat." 11He told them, "The one who healed me, He Himself said to me, 'Pick up your mat and walk.'" 12They questioned him, "Who is the person who told you to pick it up and walk?" 13But the healed man did not know who it was; for Jesus had withdrawn because there was a crowd in the place. 14Afterward Jesus came across him in the temple and said to him, "You are now enjoying health; stop sinning or something worse will happen to you." 15The man went off and told the Jews it was Jesus who had healed him.

16For this reason the Jews persecuted Jesus because He did these things on the Sabbath. 17But He answered them, "My Father works till now and so I work." 18For this the Jews were more eager than ever to kill Him, since He not only broke the Sabbath but also called God His own Father and thus made Himself equal to God. 19Then Jesus replied to them, "I truly assure

y) See note at Matt. 13:27.
z) If this was a Passover Feast our Lord's ministry lasted three years and three months, *cf.* chs. 2:13; 6:4; 13:1.
a) The manuscript evidence for the words in vss. 3 and 4 that are enclosed in brackets is so slight that it is virtually certain that they were not in the original Greek text.

you that, the Son is not able to do anything by Himself, but only what He sees the Father doing; whatever He does, the Son does in the same way. 20For the Father loves the Son and shows Him everything that He Himself does, and He will show Him still greater deeds than these, so that you will marvel; 21for just as the Father raises the dead and makes them live, so the Son makes alive whom He wills. 22The Father does not even sentence anyone but has given all judgment to the Son, 23so that all may honor the Son just as they honor the Father. Whoever does not honor the Son does not honor the Father who sent Him.

24"Truly I assure you that he who listens to My message and believes Him who sent Me has eternal life; he comes under no sentence but has passed over from death into life. 25Truly I assure you, the hour is coming — and it is here — when the dead will hear the voice of the Son of God, and those who hear will live.b 26For as the Father has life in Himself, 27so has He granted the Son to have life in Himself and has given Him authority to act as judge because He is the Son of Man.c 28Do not be astonished about this, for the time is coming when all who are in the graves will hear His voice 29and will come out, those who have done good to the resurrection of life, and those who have practiced evil to the resurrection of condemnation.

30"I can do nothing independently; I judge as I am informed and My judgment is fair; for I am not looking out for My will but for the will of Him who sent Me. 31If I testify about Myself, My testimony is not accepted as true; 32but another is testifying about Me and I know that His testimony concerning Me is true. 33You sent messengers to John and he bore witness to the truth. 34However, I do not rest My claim on human testimony; I only say this in order that you may be saved. 35He was a lamp, shining and burning, and for a while you were willing to be happy in his light; 36but I have a greater witness than John, for the works which My Father has given Me to accomplish — the activities in which I am engaged — these are My evidence that the Father has sent Me. 37And the Father who sent Me has Himself testified on My behalf; only His voice you never yet heard, neither have you seen His form, 38nor do you even have His message living within you, because you do not believe the One whom He sent.

39"You investigate the Scriptures, because you suppose that you have eternal life in them, and yet they bear witness to Me; 40yet you do not want to come to Me in order to have life. 41I reach for no human fame; 42but I know you, that you do not have love for God in you. 43I have come in My Father's name and you do not receive Me; if another comes in his own name, you will accept him. 44How can you believe when you welcome praise from one another and do not seek praise from the only God?

45"Do not imagine that I shall accuse you before the Father; your accuser is Moses, in whom you are hoping. 46For if you believed Moses you would believe Me, since He wrote about Me. 47But if you do not believe his writings, how will you believe My teachings?"

c. A.D. 29

6 LATER ON JESUS WENT TO THE other side of the Sea of Galilee or Sea of Tiberias.d 2A great multitude followed Him, because they saw the signs He performed for the sick. 3But Jesus went up the mountain and there sat down with His disciples. 4The Passover, the Jewish feast, was near.

5Looking up and observing that a vast host was coming to Him, Jesus said to Philip, "Where shall 'we buy food, so that they may eat?" 6But He said this to test him, for He knew

b) Eternal life for the believer begins at his new birth, ch. 3:3, 16, 36. The resurrection of the believer's body is a consequence of his possessing the new life in Christ.
c) See note at ch. 3:16.
d) See note at Luke 5:1.

what He was going to do. [7]Philip replied, "Fifty dollars' worth[e] of bread would not suffice for each to receive even a little." [8]Andrew, Simon Peter's brother, one of His disciples, told Him, [9]"There is a lad here with five barley cakes and two fish; but what are these for so many?" [10]Jesus said, "Have the people sit[f] down." Now there was plenty of grass in the place, so the men, numbering about five thousand, sat down.

[11]Then Jesus took the loaves, gave thanks, and had them served to those who were seated, and the same with the fish, as much as they wanted. [12]When they were satisfied, He told His disciples, "Gather up the fragments that are left over, in order that nothing may be wasted." [13]So they gathered them and filled twelve baskets with pieces from the five barley cakes left over by those who had eaten.

[14]When the people saw the sign He performed, they said, "This surely is the prophet[g] who is to come into the world." [15]Then Jesus, aware that they intended to come and seize Him in order to make Him king, withdrew again into a mountain by Himself alone.

[16]As evening fell, His disciples went down to the sea, [17]boarded a boat and crossed the sea toward Capernaum. Darkness had overtaken them and Jesus had not yet come to them, [18]while the sea was mounting under a strong wind. [19]They had sailed about three or four miles when they saw Jesus walking on the sea and getting close to the vessel, and they were afraid. [20]But He said to them, "It is I; have no fear." [21]Then they were quite ready to take Him into the boat and at once the boat was at the shore to which they were sailing.[h]

[22]The next day the crowd that was standing on the other side of the sea realized that there was only the vessel which the disciples had used and that Jesus had not gone along with them into the boat, but the disciples had left by themselves. [23]However, craft from Tiberias did land near the place at which they had eaten after the Lord's thanksgiving. [24]So when the crowd noticed that neither Jesus nor His disciples were there, they themselves embarked in little boats and sailed for Capernaum in search of Jesus. [25]When they found Him across the sea, they asked Him, "Rabbi, when did You get here?" [26]Jesus answered them, "Truly I assure you, you are not looking for Me because you saw signs, but because you ate of the loaves and were filled up. [27]Do not work for the food that spoils but for the food that lasts to life eternal, such as the Son of Man will furnish you; for God the Father has placed His seal of approval on Him."

[28]Then they said to Him, "What should we do to accomplish the works of God?"[i] [29]Jesus replied, "This is God's work, that you believe in Him whom He sent." [30]They then said to Him, "What sign then will You work, so that we may see and believe You; what work will You do? [31]Our ancestors ate manna in the desert as it is written,[j] 'He gave them bread from heaven to eat.'" [32]Then Jesus told them, "Truly I assure you, Moses did not give you the bread from heaven, but My Father gives you the real, heavenly food; [33]for what comes down from heaven and furnishes life to the world, that is the Bread of God."[k]

[34]Then they said to Him, "Lord, give us this bread all the time." [35]Jesus replied, "I am the Bread of life. He who comes to Me will never hunger

---

e) The text reads "two hundred denarii's worth." A denarius would be worth about twenty-five cents in mid-twentieth century U.S. currency.
f) See note at Mark 2:15.
g) Deut. 18:15; John 1:21; 7:40.
h) No miracle is intimated. However, observe that with Jesus aboard they sailed smoothly, *cf.* vs. 18.
i) As always, it proved difficult to trust in Him, however they might be convinced of His miraculous power. Very humanly they wanted to be saved, not by faith but by works. Yet it is characteristic of human nature to expect to do something for salvation — to earn it as a reward for works whereas it can be received only by divine grace through believing. See v. 29; Eph. 2:8, 9.
j) Deut. 8:3; *cf.* Exod. 16:4-22.
k) That is, Christ Himself as the truth and the life.

and he who believes in Me will never thirst. [36]But as I told you, you have seen Me and yet you will not believe. [37]Every one whom the Father has given Me will come to Me, and I will certainly not cast out anyone who comes to Me; [38]for I came down from heaven, not to do My will but the will of Him who sent Me. [39]And this is the will of Him who sent Me, that of all that He gave Me I shall lose nothing but shall raise it up at the last day. [40]For this is My Father's will, that every one who sees the Son and believes in Him will have eternal life, and I shall raise him up at the last day."

[41]The Jews were grumbling about Him for saying, "I am the Bread that came down from heaven." [42]They remarked, "Is not this Jesus, the son of Joseph, whose father and mother we know? Now how can He say, 'I have come down from heaven'?" [43]Jesus replied to them, "Stop grumbling one to another. [44]No one is able to come to Me unless the Father who sent Me draws him, and I will raise him up at the last day.

[45]"It is written[1] in the Prophets, 'And they will all be taught by God.' Every one who has listened to and has learned from My Father comes to Me. [46]This does not mean that anyone has seen the Father except Him who is from God; He has seen the Father. [47]Truly I assure you, he who believes has eternal life. [48]I am the Bread of life. [49]Your ancestors ate the manna in the desert and they died. [50]This is the Bread that comes down from heaven, so that anyone who eats of it may not die. [51]I am the living Bread that came down from heaven. If anyone eats of this bread, he will live forever. And the bread which I will give for the life of the world is My flesh."

[52]Then the Jews argued with each other, "How can this person give us His flesh to eat?" [53]So Jesus said to them, "Truly I assure you, unless you eat the flesh of the Son of Man and drink His blood, you have no life in you. [54]He who eats My flesh and drinks My blood[m] has eternal life and I shall raise him up on the last day; [55]for My flesh is genuine food and My blood is genuine drink. [56]He who eats My flesh and drinks My blood remains in Me and I in him. [57]Just as the life-giving Father sent Me and I live because of the Father, so he who feasts on Me will live because of Me. [58]This is the Bread that came down from heaven, not such as your fathers ate and then died; he who eats this bread will live forever."

[59]These sayings He uttered as He was teaching in a Capernaum synagogue. [60]Therefore many of His disciples who were listening said, "This is a difficult message. Who can bear to listen to it?" [61]Aware within Himself that His disciples were grumbling about it, Jesus said to them: "This gives offense to you? [62]Suppose you should see the Son of Man ascending to where He was previously? [63]The Spirit is the life-giver; the flesh does not benefit at all. The words I have spoken to you are spirit and life, [64]but there are some of you who fail to believe." For Jesus knew from the beginning who were the unbelievers and who would be His betrayer. [65]He further said, "For this reason I have told you that no one is able to come to Me unless it is granted him by the Father."

[66]From then on many of His disciples turned back and no longer walked with Him. [67]Then Jesus said to the Twelve, "You do not want to leave too?" [68]Simon Peter answered Him, "Lord, to whom shall we go? You have the words of eternal life, [69]and we have believed and have grown certain that You are the Holy One of God." [70]Jesus answered them, "Have I not chosen you twelve? Yet one of you is a devil." [71]He meant Judas, son of Simon Iscariot, for he, although one of the Twelve, was going to betray Him.

---

l) Isa. 54:13.
m) The Christian is to be completely joined with Christ in thought, word, and deed so that Christ lives His life in him, *cf.* Gal. 2:20.

7 FOLLOWING THIS JESUS WENT about Galilee; for He did not want to go around in Judea because the Jews were seeking to kill Him. [2]However, the Jewish Feast of Booths[n] was near, [3]so His brothers told Him, "Get away from here and go off to Judea, so that Your disciples will see the works You do; [4]for no one who seeks to be in the limelight does things where they are not observed. Since You do these things, show Yourself to the world." [5]For his brothers had no faith in Him either.

[6]Jesus said to them, "My time has not yet arrived, but your time is always opportune. [7]The world cannot hate you; but it hates Me because I testify about it, that its works are wicked. [8]You go up to the feast; I am not going up to this feast yet, for My time is not yet completed."

[9]With these remarks to them He remained in Galilee. [10]But after His brothers had gone up to the feast then He went also, not publicly but privately.

[11]At the feast the Jews were looking for Him and inquired: "Where is He?" [12]There was considerable dispute about Him also among the crowd, some saying, "He is good," and others, "No, but He misleads the people." [13]No one, however, expressed himself openly about Him, because of fear of the Jews.

[14]By the time the feast was half over, Jesus went up to the temple and began to teach. [15]Then the Jews were astonished; they said, "How does this person know the Scriptures without an education?" [16]Jesus replied to them, "My teaching is not Mine but His who sent Me. [17]If anyone wills to do His will he will understand[o] the teaching, whether it is from God or whether I speak from Myself. [18]He who speaks from himself seeks his own honor; but he who seeks the honor of him who

sent him is sincere and in him there is no unrighteousness. [19]Has not Moses given you the Law? Yet none of you practices the Law. Why are you seeking to kill Me?"

[20]The crowd replied, "You have a demon! Who is seeking to kill You?" [21]Jesus answered them, "I have done a single deed and you all marvel about it. [22]Because Moses established circumcision among you — though it did not come from Moses but from previous ancestors — you circumcise a person even on the Sabbath. [23]If a person receives circumcision on the Sabbath so as to prevent Moses' Law from being broken, are you enraged at Me for making a man entirely well on the Sabbath?[p] [24]Do not judge superficially, but judge fairly."

[25]Then some of the people of Jerusalem said, "Is not He the one they seek to kill? [26]Here He stands talking in public and nothing is said to Him. The rulers surely have not discovered that He is the Christ! [27]But we know where this person is from. When the Messiah comes no one will know where He is from."

[28]So Jesus called out as He taught in the temple, "Do you know Me and do you know where I am from? I have not come self-appointed; but He who sent Me is true. You do not know Him. [29]I know Him because I am from His presence and He is the One who sent Me."

[30]So they[q] were seeking to arrest Him, but no one laid hands on Him, for His hour had not yet come. [31]Besides, many of the people believed in Him and said, "When the Christ comes, will He perform more signs than this one did?"

[32]The Pharisees heard the crowd whispering these things about Him, so the chief priests and the Pharisees dispatched officers to arrest Him. [33]Then Jesus said, "I will be with you a little

---

n) The Feast of Booths is identical with the Feast of Tabernacles, Lev. 23:34; Deut. 16:16. It was so named because, during its celebration, the Israelites lived in booths or tents. From the occasion of vs. 2 until the Feast of Dedication, ch. 10:22, Jesus conducted His final Judean ministry.
o) This means that whoever is willing to find out God's will and to act on it, will surely know the reality of Jesus' teaching about Himself and His work. Here Jesus faces man with the necessity of submitting his human will to the will of God, *cf.* I John 2:17.
p) *Cf.* ch. 5:5-16.   q) The Jewish leaders.

while longer and then I go to Him who sent Me. 34You will look for Me without finding Me and where I am, you will not be able to come."

35The Jews talked among themselves, "Where is He intending to go, so we cannot find Him? He surely does not plan to visit the Dispersion among the Greeks and to teach the Greeks? 36What does He mean by saying, 'You will seek Me and will not find Me,' and 'Where I am you cannot come'?"

37On the final and most important day of the feast, Jesus stood and called out, "Whoever is thirsty, let him come to Me and drink. 38He who believes in Me, just as the Scripture says,r streams of water will flow from his innermost being." 39He said this concerning the Spirit whom those who believe in Him were about to receive. For as yet the Spirit was not given, because Jesus was not yet glorified.

40When they listened to these teachings there were those in the crowd who said, "This really is the prophet."s 41Others said, "This is the Christ." Others questioned, "But the Christ does not come from Galilee, does He? 42Does not the Scripture say that the Christ comes from the offspring of David and from Bethlehem,t the town where David lived?" 43So, on account of Him there was disagreement among the people 44and some of them wanted to seize Him, but no one laid hands on Him.

45When the officers of the chief priests and Pharisees returned, they were asked, "Why did you fail to bring Him?" 46The officers replied, "No man ever spoke as this man speaks." 47The Pharisees replied, "Surely you are not misled too? 48Have any of the authorities believed in Him? Or of the Pharisees? 49But this crowd that does not know the Law — they are accursed."

50Nicodemus, one of their number who had previously called on Him, said to them, 51"Our Law does not condemn a person without giving him a hearing and finding out what he is doing, does it?" 52They replied to him, "Are you also from Galilee? Investigate and see that no prophet is to arise from Galilee."

53[Each went to his own home, but Jesus went to the Mount of Olives.

8 EARLY IN THE MORNING He went 2back to the temple and when all the people came to Him, He sat down and taught them.

3The scribesu and the Pharisees brought a woman caught in the act of adultery and, placing her in the center, 4they said to Him (they were talking to test Him so they might trump up a charge against Him), "Teacher, this woman was caught in the very act of adultery. 5Now Moses ordered in the Law to stone such as she, so what do You say?"

6But Jesus stooped down and wrote with His finger on the ground; 7and when they kept on questioning Him He raised Himself and told them, "Let the sinless one among you throw the first stone at her." 8Stooping down again, He wrote with His finger on the ground. 9But they, on hearing it, went away conscience-stricken, one after the other, beginning from the oldest to the last, until Jesus was left alone with the woman as she stood there.

10Jesus raised Himself and asked her, "Woman, where are your accusers? Has no one condemned you?" She said, 11"No one, Lord." So Jesus told her, "Then I do not condemn you either. Go, and from now on do not sin any more."]v

12Then Jesus spoke to them again, "I am the Light of the world; the one who follows Me will not walk in darkness but will have the light of life." 13So the Pharisees said to Him, "You are witnessing concerning Yourself; Your testimony is not valid." 14Jesus answered them, "Even if I do testify

---

r) Isa. 58:11.   s) Deut. 18:15; chs. 1:21; 6:14.
t) See note at Matt. 2:1.   u) See note at Matt. 2:4.
v) The episode recorded in ch. 7:53-8:11 is not found in any of the important ancient manuscripts. In some less authoritative manuscripts it appears either here or at the end of John's Gospel, or, with certain variations in the text, following Luke 21:38. Yet the incident is so in accord with Jesus' character that the church has been reluctant to dispense with it.

concerning Myself, My testimony is valid, for I know from where I come and where I go; but you neither know where I am from nor where I am going. 15You judge by human standards; I judge no one. 16And in case I do judge, My judgment is true, for I am not alone, but the One who sent Me is with Me. 17It is written in your Law that the evidence of two persons is valid; 18I am a witness concerning Myself, and My Father who sent Me witnesses concerning Me."

19Then they said to Him, "Where is Your Father?" Jesus replied, "You know neither Me nor My Father; if you know Me, you would know My Father as well."

20These words He uttered in the treasury, as He taught in the temple, but no one got hold of Him, for His hour had not yet come.

21Once more He told them, "I go away and you will look for Me; but you will die in your sin. Where I am going you cannot come." 22Therefore the Jews said, "He is not going to kill Himself, is He, because He says, 'Where I am going you cannot come'?" 23He further said to them, "You are from below and I am from above. You are from this world; I am not from this world, 24so I told you that you would die in your sins. For if you do not believe that I am He,w you will die in your sins.x

25They said to Him, "Who are You?" Jesus replied, "I am exactly what I tell you. 26I have much to say and to judge about you, but He who sent Me is reliable and what I have learned from Him I tell the world."

27They did not perceive that He was speaking to them about the Father, 28so Jesus said, "When you have lifted up the Son of Man, then you will realize that I am He and that I do nothing of My own accord, but tell things just as the Father has taught Me. 29He who sent Me is with Me; He has not left Me alone, for I always do what pleases Him."

30As He said these things many be-lieved in Him. 31Therefore Jesus said to the Jews who had come to believe in Him, "If you adhere to My teaching, you will truly be My disciples; 32you will know the truth and the truth will set you free."

33They replied to Him, "We are Abraham's progeny, and we have never been slaves to anyone. What do You mean by, 'You will become freemen'?" 34Jesus answered them, "Truly I assure you, every one who commits sin is a slave to sin. 35But the slave does not forever stay in the home; the son re-mains forever. 36So if the Son liberates you, then you are really free. 37I know that you are Abraham's offspring; but you look for means to kill Me, for you have no use for My teaching. 38I tell of what I have seen at the Father's side, and you behave as you have learned from your father."

39They retorted, "Abraham is our father"; to which Jesus replied, "If you were Abraham's children, you would do what Abraham did; 40but here you are seeking to kill Me, a Man who has told you the truth which He learned from God. Abraham did not act that way. 41You are doing your father's works." They said to Him, "We are not born illegitimately; God is our one Father." 42"If God were your Father," Jesus rejoined, "you would love Me, for I came and am here from God; neither did I come of My own accord, but He sent Me. 43Why do you not understand My language? Because you cannot bear to listen to My message. 44You have the devil for your father and you wish to practice the desires of your father; he was a murderer from the beginning and he could not stay in the truth because there is no truth in him. When he tells a lie he talks naturally; for he is a liar and its father; 45but because I speak the truth, you do not believe Me. 46Who of you con-victs Me of sin? If I tell the truth, why do you not believe Me? 47He who is from God listens to the words of God. Because you are not from God you do not listen."

---

w) The Redeemer-Messiah.
x) Such unbelief would deprive them of eternal fellowship with Christ.

48"Do we not say rightly," the Jews replied to Him, "that you are a Samaritan and have a demon?" 49Jesus answered, "I have no demon, but I honor My Father, and you dishonor Me. 50I do not desire My own glory; there is One who investigates that and who judges. 51With assurance I tell you, anyone who observes My teaching will never see death."

52"Now we know that You have a demon. Both Abraham and the prophets died and You say, 'If anyone observes My teaching he will never see death.' 53You are not superior to our father Abraham, who died, are You? And the prophets died. Whom do You make Yourself?" 54Jesus replied, "If I should ascribe glory to Myself, My glory would be worthless. My Father, whom you call 'our God,' ascribes glory to Me. 55You do not know Him, but I know Him, and if I said, 'I do not know Him,' I would be a prevaricator like yourselves. But I know Him and observe His word.

56"Your father Abraham was extremely happy in the prospect of seeing My day,y and he did see it and rejoiced." 57Then the Jews said to Him, "You are not yet fifty years old, and have You seen Abraham?" 58Jesus said to them, "Truly I assure you, before Abraham's birth I am."

59Then they picked up stones to hurl at Him; but Jesus concealed Himself and passed out of the temple.

9 AS HE WENT ON HIS WAY, HE NOticed a man who had been blind from his birth, 2and his disciples asked Him, "Rabbi, who sinned, this fellow or his parents, that he was born blind?"z 3Jesus answered, "This has not happened because he has sinned or his parents, but that in him God's works should be displayed. 4As long as daytime lasts we must do the works of the One who sent Me; night approaches when no one can work.

5While I am in the world, I am the Light of the world."

6When He had said this, He spat on the ground and made mud with the saliva, daubed the mud on the blind man's eyes 7and told him, "Go out and wash them in the pool of Siloam" (which means Sent). So he went and washed and returned enjoying sight.

8Then the neighbors and those who had seen him before as he begged, remarked, "Is not he the one who sat and begged?" 9Some said, "Yes, he is the one." Others said, "No, but he looks like him." He himself said, "I am the one." 10They asked him, "Then how were your eyes opened?" 11He replied, "A man by the name of Jesus made some mud and daubed my eyes and told me to go to Siloam and wash; so I went and washed and I was able to see." 12They asked him, "Where is He?" "I do not know," he said.

13They brought the man who previously had been blind to the Pharisees. 14The day on which Jesus had made the mud and opened his eyes was the Sabbath. 15Then the Pharisees asked once more how he came to see; but he told them, "He applied mud to my eyes, and I washed them and I see." 16Some of the Pharisees then remarked, "This man is not from God; for He does not observe the Sabbath." Others said, "How can a sinful man perform signs?" So there was disagreement among them.

17Then they asked the blind man again, "What do you say about Him, since He has opened your eyes?" He said, "He is a prophet." 18The Jews, however, did not believe that he had been blind and had gained his sight until they summoned his parents 19and asked them, "Is this your son, who you say was born blind? How is it that he now sees?" 20His parents replied, "We know that this is our son and that he was born blind; 21but we do not know

---

y) Abraham saw this by faith in the promises of God. In this passage moral rather than genealogical relationship is under discussion.
z) Man's fall through sinning, Gen. 3, was responsible for whatever suffering the world knows. However, whereas God sometimes chastens His own people, suffering is not always chastisement for sin. Verse 3 makes this clear.

how he now sees, neither do we know who opened his eyes. Ask him; he is of age; he will speak for himself." [22]His parents said this because they were afraid of the Jews; for the Jews had already agreed that every confessor of Christ should be debarred from the synagogue. [23]For that reason his parents said, "He is of age; ask him."

[24]So for the second time they summoned the man who previously was blind and told him, "Give God the praise; we know that this man is a sinner." [25]He then replied, "Whether He is a sinner I do not know. One thing I do know, that I was blind and now I see." [26]They asked him, "What did He do to you? How did He open your eyes?" [27]He answered them, "I have already told you and you did not listen; why do you want to hear it again? You too do not want to become His disciples, do you?" [28]They abused him and said, "You are His disciple; but we are Moses' disciples.[a] [29]We know that God spoke through Moses; but this fellow — we do not know where He hails from."

[30]The man replied to them, "This is the marvel of it: you do not know where He hails from, yet He opened my eyes. [31]We know that God does not respond to sinners, but He does hear one who reveres Him and does His will. [32]Through the ages this has never been heard of, that someone opened the eyes of one born blind. [33]If He were not from God, He could do nothing."

[34]They retorted, "You, altogether born in sins — would you teach us?" And they expelled him.

[35]Jesus learned that they had expelled him and, having found him, said, "Do you believe in the Son of Man?"[b] [36]He answered, "Who is He, Sir, so that I may believe in Him?" [37]Jesus told him, "You have looked at Him; in fact, He is talking with you now." [38]He said, "Lord, I believe!" and worshiped Him.

[39]Jesus said, further, "For judgment I have come into this world, so that the sightless may see, and those who see may become blind." [40]Certain of the Pharisees near Him asked Him, when they heard that, "We too are not blind, are we?" [41]Jesus said to them, "If you were blind you would be blameless; but since you claim to have sight, your sin remains.

10 "TRULY I ASSURE YOU, HE WHO does not enter the sheepfold through the door but climbs up from elsewhere is a thief and a robber, [2]but he who enters through the door is the shepherd of the sheep. [3]To him the doorkeeper opens and the sheep listen to his voice; he calls his own sheep by name and leads them out. [4]When he has led out all that belong to him, he walks ahead of them and the sheep follow him; for they know his voice. [5]They will not follow a stranger but will run away from him, because they do not recognize the voice of strangers."

[6]Jesus used this figure of speech for them, but they did not catch the meaning of what He said to them. [7]So Jesus spoke again, "Truly I assure you, I am the door for the sheep. [8]All who came before Me are thieves and robbers,[c] but the sheep did not listen to them. [9]I am the Door. Whoever comes in through Me will be saved; he will go in and out and find pasture. [10]The thief's only purpose in coming is to steal, to slaughter and destroy. I have come so they may have life and have it abundantly.

[11]"I am the Good Shepherd.[d] The good shepherd lays down his life for the sheep. [12]The hired man, who is not the shepherd, who does not own the sheep, deserts the sheep and runs when he sees the wolf coming; then the wolf tears and scatters them. [13]The hired man runs away because he is a hired man and does not care about the sheep.

[14]"I am the Good Shepherd and I

---

a) As loyal disciples of Moses they would enforce the Law of the Sabbath as they interpreted and enlarged it.
b) Some ancient manuscripts read "Son of God."
c) Not God's prophets but pretenders.
d) Jesus identifies Himself with the shepherd of Ps. 23 and thus affirms His Deity.

know My own. My own in turn know Me, [15]just as the Father knows Me and I know the Father; and I lay down My life on behalf of the sheep. [16]I have other sheep also that are not in this fold; those I must lead as well, and they will listen to My call, so that there will be one flock, one Shepherd.

[17]"For this reason My Father loves Me, because I lay down My life in order that I may take it up again. [18]No one snatches it from Me, but I voluntarily lay it down. I have authority to lay it down and I have authority to take it up again. I received this command from My Father."

[19] Once more a disagreement arose among the Jews due to these teachings. [20]Many of them said, "He has a demon; He is out of His mind. Why do you listen to Him?" [21]O t h e r s said, "These are not the remarks of a demoniac. A demon cannot open the eyes of the blind, can he?"

[22]The Feast of Dedication came in Jerusalem. [23]It was winter and Jesus walked inside the temple in Solomon's cloister. [24]So the Jews encircled Him and asked Him, "How long will You keep our minds in suspense? If You are the Christ, tell us plainly!"[e] [25]Jesus replied to them, "I have told you and you do not believe. The works that I do in My Father's name bear Me witness, [26]but you do not believe because you do not belong to My sheep. [27]My sheep listen to My call; I know them and they follow Me. [28]I give them eternal life and they will never perish, and no one will snatch them out of My hand. [29]My Father, who gave them to Me, is mightier than all and no one can wrest them out of My Father's hand. [30]I and the Father are One."[f]

[31]Again the Jews picked up stones to stone Him. [32]Jesus answered them, "I have shown you many good deeds from the Father; for which of them would you stone Me?" [33]The Jews replied, "We would not stone You for a good act but for blasphemy, because You, a human being, make Yourself God." [34]Jesus answered them, "Is it not written[g] in your Law, 'I said, you are gods'? [35]If it calls them gods, to whom the word of God came (and the Scripture cannot be broken[h]), [36]do you say to One whom the Father dedicated and sent into the world, 'You blaspheme,' because I said, 'I am God's Son'? [37]If I do not accomplish My Father's work, do not believe Me; [38]but if I do, then, though you do not believe Me, believe the things done, so that you may know and understand that the Father is in Me and I am in the Father."

[39]Then they tried again to get hold of Him, but [40]He escaped from their hands and went once more to the place beyond the Jordan, where John first had baptized, and there He stayed. [41]Many came to Him and said, "While John did no sign, yet everything John said about this man was true." [42]And many there believed in Him.

c. A.D. 30

11 A MAN BY THE NAME OF Lazarus, of Bethany, the village of Mary and her sister Martha, was ill. ([2]The Mary, whose brother Lazarus was ill, was the one who anointed the Lord with perfume and wiped His feet with her hair.) [3]So the sisters sent Him a message: "Lord, the one you love is ill." [4]Hearing it, Jesus said, "This illness is not to end in death, but is for the glory of God, so that through it the Son of God may be glorified."

[5]Now Jesus loved Martha and her sister and Lazarus. [6]Therefore, when He heard that he was ill, He stayed at the place where He was two more days [7]and after that He said to the disciples, "Let us go back into Judea." [8]The disciples told Him, "Rabbi, the Jews were just now seeking to stone

---

e) Although Jesus did not fit the expectations of the religious leaders He was indeed the Christ, the Messiah, and He came according to O.T. prophecy.
f) Our Lord here refers to more than moral unity, and they caught the allusion to His Deity. None but He could truly say this.
g) Ps. 82:6; *cf.* Exod. 22:28.
h) Here Jesus asserts the full reliability of Scripture.

You, and You are going back there?" [9]Jesus replied, "Are there not twelve hours in the day? If one walks during the day he does not stumble, for he sees the world's light; [10]but if he walks during the night, he stumbles because in him there is no light."

[11]He said this to them and then added, "Our friend Lazarus is asleep, but I am setting out to wake him up." [12]The disciples remarked to Him, "Lord, if he is sleeping, he will recover." [13]Jesus had spoken of his death; but they supposed that He had spoken about the repose of sleep. [14]Then Jesus told them plainly, "Lazarus is dead; [15]and for your sakes I am glad I was not present so that you may believe. But let us go to him."

[16]Thomas, called the Twin, then said to his fellow disciples, "Let us go too, so that we may die with Him."

[17]When Jesus arrived, He found that Lazarus had already been buried for four days. [18]Now Bethany is near Jerusalem, about two miles distant, [19]and many of the Jews had gone out to Martha and Mary to console them about their brother. [20]As soon, then, as Martha learned that Jesus had come, she went to meet Him; but Mary was sitting in the house.

[21]Then Martha said to Jesus, "Lord, if You had been here, my brother would not have died, [22]and I know that even now whatever You ask of God, He will grant You." [23]Jesus said to her, "Your brother will rise again." [24]Martha replied, "I know that he will rise again in the resurrection on the last day." [25]Jesus said to her, "I am the Resurrection and the Life;[i] He who believes in Me will live even when he dies, [26]and no one who lives and believes in Me will ever die. Do you believe this?" [27]She responded, "Yes, Lord, I have faith that You are the Christ, the Son of God, who was to come into the world."

[28]When she had said this she went off and called her sister Mary privately, saying, "The Teacher is here and He is calling you." [29]Hurriedly Mary arose when she heard it and went to Him. [30]Jesus had not yet entered the village; He was still at the place where Martha had met Him.

[31]When the Jews who were with her in the house to comfort her noticed that Mary got up quickly and left, they followed her, supposing that she was going to the tomb to weep there. [32]Mary, however, when she arrived at the place where Jesus was and saw Him, fell at His feet with the words, "Lord, if You had been here, my brother would not have died." [33]Then Jesus, when He saw her weeping, and the Jews who had come with her weeping also, was deeply moved in spirit and disquieted.[j]

[34]He asked, "Where have you laid him?" They told Him, "Lord, come and see." [35]Jesus wept. [36]The Jews then remarked, "Notice how He loved him." [37]But some of them said, "Could not He who opened the blind man's eyes have prevented this man's death?"

[38]Again deeply moved inwardly, Jesus approached the tomb. It was a cave with a stone laid against it. [39]Jesus said, "Remove the stone." Martha, the sister of the deceased, said to Him, "Lord, by now there is an odor, for it is four days since his death." [40]Jesus said to her, "Did I not tell you that if you will believe you will see the glory of God?" [41]So they removed the stone.

Then Jesus raised His eyes upward and said, "Father, I thank Thee for having heard Me, [42]and I know that Thou dost always hear Me; but on account of the people around here I said this, so that they may believe that Thou hast sent Me."

[43]When He had said this He called out in a loud voice, "Lazarus, come out!" [44]Out came the one who had died, feet and hands tied with graveclothes and his face wrapped in a towel. Jesus told them, "Unbind him and let him go."

[45]Then many of the Jews, who had

---

i) Without a risen Christ there would be no resurrection for any man.
j) Death is an enemy which Christ came to conquer, I Cor. 15:55-57. Ultimately death and its realm are doomed, Rev. 20:14.

come to Mary and had seen what He had done, believed in Him; [46]but some of them went off to the Pharisees and informed them of Jesus' activities. [47]So the chief priests and the Pharisees summoned the Sanhedrin[k] and said, "What shall we do? For this man performs numerous signs. [48]If we let Him go on this way, everyone will believe in Him, and the Romans will come to take away from us our holy place and our nation." [49]But one of them, Caiaphas, the high priest that year,[1] said to them, "You do not know anything; [50]you do not reason out that it is better for you to have one person die on behalf of the people, rather than to have the whole nation ruined."

[51]He said this not of his own initiative but, being the high priest that year, he foretold how Jesus was to die for the nation, [52]and not alone for the nation, but to gather into one all the scattered children of God.

[53]From that day on, therefore, they laid plans to kill Him. [54]So Jesus no longer went around openly among the Jews but withdrew to the country near the wilderness, to a town called Ephraim,[m] and there He stayed with the disciples.

[55]The Jews' Passover was approaching, and many went up from the country to Jerusalem to consecrate themselves for the Passover, [56]and they looked for Jesus and remarked, as they were standing together in the temple, "What do you think? Is He not coming to the feast?" [57]The chief priests and the Pharisees had given orders that, if anyone knew where He was, he should report it so that they might arrest Him.

12 SIX DAYS BEFORE THE PASSOVER Jesus came to Bethany, where Lazarus lived, whom Jesus had raised from the dead. [2]There they prepared a supper for Him[n] and Martha served the meal, while Lazarus was among those sitting[o] at the table with Him.

[3]Then Mary, taking a pound of costly perfume made of purest nard, anointed the feet of Jesus and dried His feet with her hair. So the house was filled with the fragrance of the perfume.

[4]But Judas Iscariot, one of His disciples (who was to betray Him) said, [5]"Why was not this perfume sold for seventy-five dollars[p] and the money donated to the poor?" [6]He did not say this because he cared for the poor, but because he was a thief; he had charge of the money-bag and pilfered the collections. [7]Then Jesus said, "Let her alone. Let her keep it for the day of My burial. [8]For you always will have the poor with you, but you will not always have Me."

[9]When a great crowd of Jews learned that He was there, they came not merely on account of Jesus but also to see Lazarus whom He had raised from the dead. [10]But the chief priests made plans to kill Lazarus also; [11]for many of the Jews went away on his account believing in Jesus.

[12]The next day a large crowd of people who had come to the feast heard that Jesus was on the way to Jerusalem; [13]so they took palm branches and went out to meet Him, and began to shout, "Hosanna![q] Blessed is He who comes in the name of the Lord, the King of Israel." [14]And, finding a young donkey, Jesus rode it, as it is written,[r] [15]"Have no fear, daughter of Zion! Behold, your king is coming, seated on an ass's colt." [16]At first His disciples did not understand this, but when Jesus had been glorified they remembered that this had been written of Him and that they had done this to Him.

[17]The people who were with Him

---

k) See note at Luke 22:66.   l) Caiaphas was the high priest A.D. 18-36.
m) Ephraim was situated about seventeen miles northeast of Jerusalem.
n) At the home of Simon, the leper, Mark 14:3.   o) See note at Mark 2:15.
p) The text reads "three hundred denarii." A denarius would be the equivalent of about twenty-five cents in mid-twentieth century U. S. currency, so that the figure of seventy-five dollars is substantially correct.
q) "Hosanna" means *save now* or *salvation.* The expression is somewhat similar to "God save the king." The people were quoting from Ps. 118:25, 26. Although they greeted Jesus as the Messiah, even the disciples did not seem to catch the real significance.
r) Zech. 9:9.

when He called Lazarus from the tomb and raised him from the dead bore witness about it, [18]and for that reason the crowd went out to meet Him; for they heard that He had performed this sign. [19]Then the Pharisees said among themselves, "You see how you are getting nowhere. Look, the world has gone after Him."

[20]Among those going up to worship at the feast were certain Greeks [21]who came to Philip of Beth-saida[s] of Galilee and said to him, "Sir, we want to see Jesus." [22]Philip came and told Andrew; then Andrew and Philip went and told Jesus. [23]Jesus answered them, "The hour has come for the Son of Man to be glorified. [24]Truly I assure you, unless a grain of wheat drops into the earth and dies, it remains single, but if it dies, it produces a rich yield. [25]The one who loves his life will lose it, but the one who hates his life in this world will preserve it to eternal life. [26]If anyone serves Me, let him follow Me; then where I am, there also will My servant be. If anyone serves Me, the Father will honor him.

[27]"Now My soul is disturbed, and what shall I say? Father, save Me from this hour? But for this reason I came to this hour. [28]Father, glorify Thy name."

Then a voice came from heaven, "I have glorified it and will glorify it again." [29] The people that stood and listened said, "It thundered." Others said, "An angel spoke to Him." [30]Jesus replied, "This voice did not come for My sake but for yours. [31]Now is this world's sentence; now the ruler of this world will be expelled; [32]and I, when I am lifted up from the earth, will draw everyone[t] to Myself." [33]This He said signifying what kind of death He was to die.

[34]The crowd answered Him, "We have learned from the Law that the Christ remains forever, and how can You say that the Son of Man must be lifted up? Who is this Son of Man?" [35]So Jesus told them, "For a little while

the Light still shines among you; walk while you have the Light, so that darkness may not overtake you. One who walks in darkness does not know where he is going. [36]While you have the Light, put faith in the Light so you may become sons of the Light."

After saying this Jesus went away and hid Himself from them. [37]In spite of all the signs that He had done in their presence, they put no faith in Him, [38]in order that the saying[u] of Isaiah the prophet might be fulfilled, "Lord, who has believed our message and to whom has the arm of the Lord been revealed?" [39]For this reason they could not believe, for again Isaiah said,[v] [40]"He has blinded their eyes and has calloused their hearts, so that they may neither see with their eyes nor understand with their hearts and repent and I should heal them." [41]Isaiah said this, for he saw His glory and spoke of Him.[w]

[42]Nevertheless even many of the leaders believed in Him but, because of the Pharisees, failed to confess it so that they might not be put out of the synagogue; [43]for they preferred men's esteem to divine approval.

[44]But Jesus called out in a loud voice, "He who believes in Me does not believe in Me but in Him who sent Me, [45]and he who sees Me sees Him who sent Me. [46]I am a light which has come into the world, so that no one who believes in Me may remain in the dark. [47]And if anyone hears My teachings and fails to observe them, I pass no sentence on him; for I did not come to judge the world but to save the world. [48]He who rejects Me and does not accept My teachings has his judge: My spoken word will judge him on the last day. [49]For I have not spoken of My own accord, but the Father who sent Me, He has given Me a command what I should say and what I should speak. [50]I know too, that His command is eternal life; so what I say is just what the Father has told Me to say."

---

s) See note at Mark 8:22.   t) Gentile as well as Jew.
u) Isa. 53.1.   v) Isa. 6:9, 10.
w) Here the reference is to Isaiah's great vision of the glory of the Lord, Isa. 6:1-8.

13 BEFORE THE PASSOVER FEAST Jesus, aware that the time had come for Him to leave this world to go to the Father, showed His own who were in the world that He loved them to the end. ²At supper time, when the devil had already put the purpose into the heart of Judas Iscariot, Simon's son, to betray Him, ³Jesus, conscious that the Father had placed everything into His hands and that He came from God and was going to God, ⁴rose from the table, laid aside His robe and, taking a towel, girded Himself. ⁵Then He poured water into the basin and began to wash the feet of the disciples and to dry them with the towel with which He was girded.

⁶So He came to Simon Peter, who said to Him, "Lord, You are going to wash my feet?" ⁷Jesus answered him, "Just now you do not understand what I do, but you will know later on." ⁸Peter said to Him, "You shall never wash my feet!" Jesus replied, "If I do not wash you, you are not sharing with Me." ⁹Simon Peter said to Him, "Lord, not only my feet but also my hands and my head!" ¹⁰Jesus said to him, "A bathed person does not need to be washed, except his feet, but is completely cleansed; and you are cleansed, but not all of you." ¹¹For He knew who His betrayer would be; so He said, "Not all of you are cleansed."

¹²After washing their feet and taking His garment, He sat^x at the table again and said to them, "Do you understand what I have done to you? ¹³You call Me 'Teacher' and 'Lord,' and rightly so, because I am. ¹⁴Then if I, your Lord and Teacher, have washed your feet, you surely ought to wash one another's feet. ¹⁵For I have set you an example so that you might do just as I did to you. ¹⁶I assure you with all truth, a slave^y is not superior to his master nor one who is sent to the one who sent him. ¹⁷If you know these teachings, blessed are you if you practice them.

¹⁸"I am not speaking of you all; I know those I have chosen; but the Scripture^z is to be fulfilled, 'The one eating my bread has raised his heel against me.' ¹⁹Right now I tell you this, before it occurs, so that when it does occur you may believe that I am He. ²⁰With assurance I tell you that he who welcomes whom I send, welcomes Me, and he who welcomes Me, welcomes the One who sent Me."

²¹When Jesus had said this He was inwardly disturbed and testified, "Most assuredly I tell you that one of you will betray Me." ²²The disciples looked at each other, undecided as to whom He referred. ²³One of His disciples, whom Jesus loved,^a was sitting^x next to Jesus; ²⁴so Simon Peter nodded to him, "Ask whom He means." ²⁵Then he, leaning closer to Jesus' side, asked Him, "Lord, who is it?" ²⁶Jesus replied, "The one to whom I give the bit of bread after I have dipped it." So He took and dipped the mouthful and gave it to Judas Iscariot, Simon's son. ²⁷And after the mouthful, Satan entered into him. Then Jesus said to him, "Do quickly what you are going to do." ²⁸But none of those at the table knew why He told him that. ²⁹Some had an idea, since Judas had charge of the money-bag, that Jesus said to him, "Buy what we need for the feast," or, "Give something to the poor." ³⁰Then at once, after taking the bit of bread, he went out. It was then night.

³¹When he had left, Jesus said, "Now the Son of Man is glorified, and in Him God is glorified. ³²If God is glorified in Him, then God will in Himself glorify Him and will glorify Him at once. ³³Little children,^b I am with you but a little longer. You will be looking for Me and, as I told the Jews so I tell you now, where I go you cannot come. ³⁴I give you a new command,^c 'Love one another.' Just as I

---

x) See note at Mark 2:15.   y) See note at Matt. 13:27.   z) Ps. 41:9.
a) This probably refers to John himself, *cf.* ch. 20:20-24.
b) "Little children" is a term that was dear to John, *cf.* I John 2:1, 12, 28.
c) From the Lord's command that His followers should love one another, exemplified by the washing of the feet, comes the name Maundy Thursday, the day before Good Friday. "Maundy" is from the Latin verb *mandare* meaning *to command*.

have loved you, so you should love one another. 35By this everyone will recognize that you are My disciples, if you love one another."

36Simon Peter asked Him, "Lord, where are You going?" Jesus replied, "Where I am going you cannot follow Me now, but later on you will follow Me." 37Peter said to Him, "Lord, why can I not follow You now? I will lay down my life for You."d 38Jesus replied, "Will you lay down your life for Me? Truly I assure you, the rooster will not crow until you have denied Me three times.

14 "LET NOT YOUR HEARTS BE troubled; believe in God, believe also in Me. 2In My Father's house are many dwelling places. If this were not so, I would have told you. For I am going away to prepare a place for you. 3And when I have gone and have prepared a place for you, I will come again and take you to Myself so that where I am, you also will be. 4And where I am going, you know the way."

5Thomas remarked to Him, "Lord, we do not know where You are going. How do we know the way?" 6Jesus said to him, "I am the Way and the Truth and the Life; no one comes to the Father except through Me. 7Had you recognized Me, you would have known My Father as well. From now on you do know Him; yes, you have seen Him."

8Philip said to Him, "Lord, show us the Father and it is enough for us." 9Jesus replied, "How long have I been with you without your knowing Me, Philip? He who has looked on Me has seen the Father. What do you mean by saying, 'Show us the Father'? 10Do you not believe that I am in the Father and the Father in Me? The words that I give to you all, I do not speak just from Myself; the Father who dwells in Me carries on His works. 11Believe Me that I am in the

Father and the Father in Me, and if not, then believe on account of the works themselves. 12Truly I assure you, the one who believes in Me will himself do the works I do, and do greater things than these, for I go to the Father. 13And I will bring about whatever you ask in My name, so that the Father may be glorified in the Son. 14I will do whatever you ask in My name.

15"If you love Me, keep My commands, 16and I shall ask the Father and He will give you another Helpere to stay with you forever, 17the Spirit of Truth whom the world cannot receive, because it neither perceives nor understands Him. You know Him, for He remains with you and will be within you.

18"I shall not leave you as orphans; I shall come to you. 19In a little while the world will no longer see Me; but you will see Me, for I live and you, too, will live. 20In that day you will know that I am in My Father, and you in Me and I in you. 21He who has My orders and observes them loves Me, and he who loves Me will be loved by My Father. I, too, shall love him and show Myself to him."

22Judas, not Iscariot, asked Him, "Lord, how does it happen that You are going to show Yourself to us and not to the world?" 23Jesus answered him, "If anyone loves Me, he will keep My word and My Father will love him and We shall visit him and make Our dwelling with him. 24The one who does not love Me does not keep My word — though the word you hear is not Mine but the Father's who sent Me.

25"I have been telling you this while I am still with you; 26but the Helper, the Holy Spirit, whom the Father will send in My name, He will teach you everything and will remind you of all that I have told you.

27"Peace I bequeath to you; My peace I give to you. I do not give you

---

d) Peter was sincere but too self-reliant.
e) The Greek noun *paracletos*, from which the English word "paraclete" is formed, means *advocate, comforter, consoler, counselor, helper, intercessor.* The Greek word is used in the N.T. to signify the Holy Spirit, who fulfils for the believer all the offices mentioned above.

gifts such as the world gives. Do not allow your hearts to be disturbed or intimidated. [28]You heard how I told you: 'I am going away,' and 'I am coming to you.' If you loved Me, you would be glad that I go to the Father, for the Father is greater than I.

[29]I have now told you this before it takes place so that when it does happen you may have faith. [30]I shall not talk over many things with you any more; for the world's ruler comes. He has no claim on Me; [31]but I act as I do in order that the world may learn that I love the Father and act in full agreement with His orders. Rise. Let us go from here.[f]

15 "I AM THE TRUE VINE AND MY Father is the Vinedresser. [2]Every branch in Me that bears no fruit He prunes away, and whatever bears fruit He prunes so that it may bear more fruit. [3]You are already clean through the word that I have spoken to you. [4]Remain in Me and I in you. Just as the branch cannot bear fruit by itself without staying on the vine, so you cannot without remaining in Me. [5]I am the Vine, you are the branches. He who remains in Me, and I in him, bears much fruit. For apart from Me you can do nothing.

[6]"Whoever does not remain in Me is thrown away as a branch and withers; people gather such branches, throw them into the fire, and they are burned. [7]If you remain in Me and My words remain in you, then you may ask what you wish and it will be done for you.

[8]"My Father is honored in this, that you produce much fruit; then you will be My disciples. [9]Just as the Father has loved Me so I have loved you; continue in this love of Mine. [10]You will remain in My love if you keep My commands, just as I keep My Father's commands and remain in His love.

[11]"I have talked these matters over with you so that My joy may be in you and your joy be made complete. [12]This is My command, that you love one another as I have loved you. [13]No one has greater love than this: to lay down his life for his friends. [14]You are My friends if you do what I command you. [15]I no longer call you slaves,[g] for a slave does not know what his master is doing, but I have called you friends because I have acquainted you with everything I heard from My Father. [16]You have not chosen Me, but I have chosen you and appointed you to go out and produce fruit and that your fruit should be permanent, so that whatever you ask the Father in My name He may grant you. [17]This is My command to you: 'Love one another.'[h]

[18]"If the world hates you, you know that it hated Me first. [19]If you belonged to the world, the world would love its own;[i] but because you are not of the world and I have selected you from the world, therefore the world hates you. [20]Remember what I said to you: a slave is not greater than his master. If they persecuted Me they will persecute you; if they observed My word, they will observe yours; [21]but they will do all this to you on account of My name, for they do not know the One who sent Me.

[22]"Had I not come and spoken to them, they would not be guilty; but now they have no excuse for their sin. [23]He who hates Me hates My Father as well. [24]Had I not accomplished the works among them which no other ever accomplished, they would not be guilty; but now they have seen and have hated both Me and My Father. [25]But they have done this so that the saying[j] in their Law might be fulfilled: 'They hated Me without just cause.'

[26]"When the Helper[k] comes, whom I will send you from the Father, the Spirit of Truth who comes from the

---

f) It appears that our Lord and the Eleven left the upper room in Jerusalem at this point. They may have passed through a vineyard as He told the parable of the vine and its branches.
g) See note at Matt. 13:27.
h) Verse 12.
i) Full commitment to Christ brings the opposition of the world.
j) Ps. 35:19; 69:4.　　k) Ch. 14:16.

Father, He will testify regarding Me; [27]but you too will testify, for you were with Me from the beginning.

16 "I HAVE TALKED THESE MATters over with you so that you may not be led astray. [2]They will exclude you from the synagogue; in fact the hour is coming when whoever kills you will think that he is rendering service to God. [3]And they will do these things because they know neither the Father nor Me. [4]But I have told you these things in order that, when the time comes, you may remember that I told them to you.

"I did not tell you this from the beginning, for I was with you; [5]but now I am going to Him who sent Me. Yet none of you asks Me, 'Where are you going?'[1] [6]Instead, your hearts are filled with sorrow because I told these things to you. [7]However, I tell you the truth: My going is for your benefit; for if I do not leave, the Helper will not come to you; but if I go, then I will send Him to you. [8]When He comes He will convict the world regarding sin and righteousness and judgment[m] — [9]regarding sin, because they do not believe in Me; [10]regarding righteousness, because I am going to the Father and you will see Me no more; [11]and regarding judgment, because the ruler of this world has been judged.

[12]"I have still many things to tell you, but you cannot bear them now. [13]When the Spirit of Truth comes, however, He will guide you into all truth; for He will not speak on His own account but will say whatever He hears, and He will make known to you what is to take place. [14]He will glorify Me, for He will take from what is Mine and will declare it to you. [15]Everything the Father has is Mine; therefore I said, He will take from what is Mine and declare it to you.

[16]"Just a little while and you will see Me no longer; then again a little while and you will see Me." [17]Then the disciples said to one another, "What does He mean by saying to us, 'A little while and you will not see Me, and again a little while and you will see Me,' and 'I am going to the Father'?" [18]So they said, "What does He mean by a little while? We have no idea what He is talking about."

[19]Jesus knew that they wanted to ask Him, and said to them, "You are questioning among yourselves about My saying, 'A little while and you will not see Me, and again a little while and you will see Me'? [20]Truly I assure you, you will be weeping and moaning while the world feels glad; you will be grieved, but your grief will turn to joy.[n] [21]The mother in childbirth has anguish because her time has come, but when she has borne the child she no longer remembers her affliction, because a human being has been born into the world. [22]So you have grief at present, but I shall see you again and your hearts will be glad, and no one will be able to deprive you of that joy.

[23]"At that time you will question Me about nothing. Truly I assure you whatever you ask the Father, He will grant you in My name. [24]Thus far you have asked nothing in My name. Ask and you will receive, so that your joy may be complete.

[25]"I have told you these things in figures of speech; a time approaches when I shall no longer talk to you in figures of speech but shall plainly inform you about the Father. [26]At that time you will pray in My name, and I do not say that I shall make request of the Father on your behalf, [27]for the Father Himself loves you, since you have loved Me and have believed that I came from the Father. [28]I did come from the Father and have entered

---

l) Earlier Simon Peter asked this same question, ch. 13:36, but evidently on the occasion recorded here the apostles' minds were so filled with sorrow, vs. 6, that they could not think clearly about other things.
m) Those who are acquainted with the Gospel face the inescapable decision of either accepting or rejecting Christ.
n) The apostles' grief would become joy after the Lord's resurrection and His appearances to them.

the world; again, I am leaving the world and am going to the Father."

²⁹His disciples said, "Now You are speaking plainly and not in figures of speech; ³⁰now we know that You know everything and do not need anyone to tell You. From this we believe that You came from God."

³¹Jesus replied, "You believe just now? ³²The hour is coming and it has arrived when you will be scattered each to his place and you will leave Me alone; but I am not alone, for the Father is with Me. ³³I have talked over these things with you so that in Me you may have peace. In the world you will have trouble; but have courage! I have overcome the world."ᵒ

17 Jesus said this, then raised His eyes toward heaven and said, "Father, the hour has come. Glorify Thy Son, so that the Son may glorify Thee, ²as Thou hast given Him authority over all mankind so that He may give eternal life to all whom Thou hast granted Him.

³"And this is eternal life, to know Thee, the only true God, and Jesus Christ whom Thou hast sent. ⁴I have glorified Thee on the earth; I have completed the task Thou gavest Me to do; ⁵ now glorify Thou Me, Father, with Thine own glory which I had in Thy presence before the world existed.

⁶"I have made Thy name known to the persons whom Thou gavest Me from the world; they were Thine and Thou gavest them to Me and they have kept Thy word. ⁷Now they have realized that all whom Thou hast given Me are from Thee; ⁸ for I have given them the words Thou gavest Me, and they have accepted them and have really understood that I came from Thee, and they have believed that Thou didst send Me.

⁹"I pray for them. I do not pray for the world but for those whom Thou hast granted Me, for they belong to Thee. ¹⁰Yes, all who are Mine are Thine, and Thine are Mine, and in them I am glorified. ¹¹My presence in the world is over, but these are in the world while I am coming to Thee. Holy Father, preserve in Thy name those whom Thou hast given Me, so that they may be one as We are. ¹²While I was with them I preserved and guarded them in Thy name which Thou gavest Me, and none of them perished except the son of perdition, so that the Scripture might be fulfilled. ¹³But now I am coming to Thee and say these things while I am still in the world, so that they may have My joy made complete in their hearts.

¹⁴"I have given them Thy word and the world has hated them, for they are not of the world, just as I am not of the world. ¹⁵I do not pray that Thou wilt take them out of the world but that Thou wilt preserve them from the evil one. ¹⁶As I am not of the world, so they are not of the world. ¹⁷Sanctify them by the truth. Thy word is truth.

¹⁸"As Thou hast sent Me into the world, so I have sent them into the world, ¹⁹and on their behalf I consecrate Myself, so that they, too, may be consecrated by truth.

²⁰"I am not praying only for them, but also for those who will believe in Me through their message, ²¹so that all may be one, as Thou Father art in Me, and I in Thee, so they may be in Us, and so that the world may believe that Thou hast sent Me.ᵖ ²²I have given them the glory which Thou hast given to Me, so that they may be one as We are one, ²³I in them and Thou in Me, so that they may be completed into one, that the world may recognize that Thou hast sent Me and hast loved them as Thou hast loved Me.

²⁴"Father, I would have those whom Thou hast given Me, to be with Me where I am, so they may see My glory which Thou hast given to Me, for Thou lovest Me before the founding of the world.

---

o) It seems evident that the conversations recorded in chs. 15 and 16 and the prayer of ch. 17 were spoken between the departure from the upper room in Jerusalem and the arrival at the Garden of Gethsemane, Cf. ch. 14:31; 18:1.
p) Here the Lord Jesus says that unity among believers on the exalted pattern of the unity of the Godhead leads the world to believe that the Father has sent Him.

25"Righteous Father, the world does not know Thee but I know Thee, and these know that Thou hast sent Me. 26I have made known and will make known to them Thy name, so that Thy love for Me as well as I Myself may be in them."

18 HAVING UTTERED THESE WORDS, Jesus went out with His disciples across the Kidron Brook to a garden which He and His disciples entered. 2But Judas, His betrayer, knew the spot; for Jesus often met there with His disciples. 3So Judas, getting a detachment[q] of soldiers and some attendants[r] from the chief priests and Pharisees, came there with torches, lamps, and weapons.

4Then Jesus, aware of everything that would befall Him, went out and asked them, "For whom are you looking?" 5They replied, "Jesus of Nazareth." Jesus told them, "I am He." And Judas, His betrayer, was standing with them.

6When He said to them, "I am He," they went backward and fell to the ground. 7Once more He asked them, "Whom do you seek?" And they said, "Jesus of Nazareth." 8Jesus replied, "I told you that I am He, so if you are after Me, let these others go." 9This took place so that the word[s] He had spoken might be fulfilled, "I did not lose any of those whom Thou hast given Me."

10Then Simon Peter, since he had a sword, drew it and struck the high priest's slave,[t] severing his right ear — the slave's name was Malchus. 11But Jesus said to Peter, "Sheathe your sword. The cup which My Father has given Me, shall I not drink it?"

12Then the detachment of soldiers and the commander,[u] together with the Jewish attendants, took hold of Jesus, bound Him 13and conducted Him first to Annas, for he was the father-in-law of Caiaphas, the high priest that year— 14the Caiaphas who advised the Jews that one man's death would benefit the people.

15Simon Peter followed Jesus with another disciple;[v] and as that disciple was acquainted with the high priest, he entered, along with Jesus, the high priest's courtyard, 16while Peter stood outside by the door. Then that other disciple, the high priest's acquaintance, came out to speak to the slave-girl who was in charge of the door, and brought in Peter.

17The girl in charge of the door then said to Peter, "Are you not one of that man's disciples too?" He replied, "I am not." 18The slaves had made a fire of charcoal and were standing by it and were warming themselves, for it was cold. And Peter also was standing with them and warming himself.

19Meanwhile the high priest asked Jesus regarding His disciples and about His teaching. 20Jesus answered him, "I have spoken openly to the world; I have been teaching right along in the synagogue and in the temple, where all the Jews gather, and I said nothing in secret. 21Why do you ask Me? Ask those who heard what I told them; they know what I said."

22When Jesus said this, one of the attendants standing by slapped Him in the face, saying, "Is this the way to answer the high priest?" 23Jesus answered him, "If I spoke wrongly, give evidence of the wrong; but if properly, why do you hit Me?" 24Then Annas sent Him bound to the high priest, Caiaphas.

25Simon Peter was standing and warming himself, so they said to him, "Are not you a disciple of His?" He denied it, saying, "I am not." 26One of the high priest's slaves, a relative of

---

q) The Greek word translated "detachment" is the one usually used for a Roman cohort of about 600 men, one-tenth of a legion. However, it may, as in this case, refer to less than a full cohort.
r) These were officers of the temple guard.
s) John 17:12.
t) See note at Matt. 13:27.
u) The literal meaning of the Greek word *chiliarchos*, rendered "commander" here, is *a leader of 1000 soldiers*; later it came to denote a commander of a cohort, which consisted of 600 men or less.
v) This is an allusion to John himself.

the one whose ear Peter had cut off, said, "Did not I see you in the garden with Him?" [27]Then Peter again denied it, and instantly the rooster crowed.

[28]Then they conducted Jesus from Caiaphas to the Praetorium.[w] It was early morning and they themselves did not enter the palace, so that they might not be defiled but might eat the Passover. [29]So Pilate went out to them and asked, "What charge do you bring against this man?" [30]They answered him, "If He were not a criminal, we would not have committed Him to you."[x] [31]Pilate told them, "You take Him and sentence Him according to your Law." The Jews said to him, "We have no right to execute anyone." [32]This happened so that the saying[y] of Jesus might be fulfilled that He had spoken showing what sort of death He was to die.

[33]Then Pilate entered the Praetorium again and summoned Jesus, whom he asked, "Are You the king of the Jews?" [34]Jesus replied, "Do you say this of your own accord or have others told you about Me?" [35]Pilate answered Him, "I am not a Jew, am I? Your own nation and the chief priests have handed You over to me. What have You done?"

[36]Jesus answered, "My kingdom is not of this world. If My kingdom were of this world, My attendants would have struggled to prevent My being delivered to the Jews. But as things now stand My kingdom is not of this world." [37]Pilate then said to Him, "You are a king, then?" Jesus replied, "You say that I am a king. For this purpose was I born and for this I entered the world, that I might testify to the truth. Everyone who loves the truth listens to My voice." [38]Pilate remarked to Him, "What is truth?"

When he had said this he went outside again to the Jews and told them, "I do not find Him guilty at all; [39]but it is your custom to have me set one free for you at the Passover. Do you

want me, therefore, to liberate for you the king of the Jews?" [40]Then they shouted again, "Not this fellow, but Barabbas." Yet Barabbas was a robber.

19 THEREUPON PILATE TOOK JESUS and had Him flogged. [2]And the soldiers wove together a crown of thorns and set it down on His head. They also dressed Him in a purple robe, [3]came up to Him and said, "Long live the King of the Jews!" And they slapped Him in the face.

[4]Once more Pilate came out and addressed them, "See! I am bringing Him out to you, so you may know that I do not find Him guilty." [5]Then Jesus came outside, wearing the thorny crown and the purple robe. Pilate said to them, "Here is the man!"

[6]When the chief priests and their attendants saw Him, they shouted, "Crucify Him! Crucify Him!" Pilate said to them, "You take Him and do the crucifying, for I find no guilt in Him!" [7]The Jews replied, "We have a Law and by that Law He ought to die, for He made Himself God's Son."

[8]At hearing that word, Pilate was still more alarmed. [9]Again he entered the Praetorium and asked Jesus, "Where are You from?" But Jesus gave him no answer. [10]Pilate said to Him, "You do not talk to me? Do You not know that I have power to liberate You and I have power to crucify You?" [11]Jesus replied, "You have no power whatever of your own, but only what is granted you from above. For this reason the one who betrayed Me has greater sin than you have."

[12]From then on Pilate kept seeking to set Him free, but the Jews kept shouting, "If you liberate Him, you are no friend of Caesar's. Whoever makes himself king rebels against Caesar."

[13]On hearing their words, Pilate led Jesus out and sat down in the judgment seat at a place called The Pavement,[z] or in Hebrew, Gabbatha.[a] [14]It

---

w) The Roman headquarters — in this case the palace that Herod had built.
x) This was not a legal charge but rather a confession that they had none.
y) Chs. 3:14; 12:32, 33; *cf.* Matt. 20:17-19.
z) Greek *Lithostrotos* which denotes *a stone pavement* or *a mosaic.*
a) This is an Aramaic word, Aramaic being a form of Hebrew used by many of the Jews at that time.

was the day of preparation for the Passover, about six in the morning. He said to the Jews, "This is your king." 15Then they cried out, "Away, away with Him! Crucify Him!" Pilate asked them, "Shall I crucify your king?" The chief priests answered, "We have no king except Caesar." 16Then he handed Him over to be crucified. So they took Jesus.

17And He went out carrying[b] His cross to the place called Skull, that is in Hebrew, Golgotha, 18where they crucified Him; and with Him two others, one on each side, with Jesus in the center. 19Pilate wrote a title and put it on the cross. It was written, JESUS, THE NAZARENE, THE KING OF THE JEWS. 20Many of the Jews read the title, for the place where Jesus was crucified was near the city, and it was written in Hebrew, Latin, and Greek.

21Then the chief priests of the Jews said to Pilate: "Do not write, 'The King of the Jews,' but that He said, 'I am the King of the Jews.'" 22Pilate answered, "What I have written, I have written."

23When the soldiers had crucified Jesus, they took His clothes and divided them in four parts, a part for each soldier; the tunic, too, but as it was seamless, woven all the way from top to bottom, 24they said to each other, "Let us not tear it but draw lots whose it will be." They did this so that the Scripture[c] might be fulfilled, "They divided my clothes among themselves and for my clothing they cast lots." So then the soldiers did this.

25By the cross of Jesus stood His mother, and His mother's sister, Mary[d] the wife of Clopas, and Mary Magdalene.[e] 26Then Jesus, seeing His moth-er and the disciple[f] whom He loved standing there, said to His mother, "Woman, there is your son." 27Then to the disciple He said, "There is your mother." And from that moment the disciple took her to his home.

28After this, since Jesus knew that everything was already completed, in order that the Scripture[g] might be fulfilled, He said, "I am thirsty." 29A vessel full of vinegar stood there, so they put a sponge soaked in vinegar on hyssop and held it to His mouth. 30When Jesus had taken the vinegar, He said, "It is finished!" Then, bowing His head, He yielded up His spirit.

31Now since it was preparation day, the Jews, in order not to have the bodies remain on the cross over the Sabbath, which was a specially important day, requested Pilate to have the legs broken and their bodies removed. 32So the soldiers came and broke the legs of the first and of the other who was crucified with Him; 33but when they came to Jesus and saw that He was already dead, they did not break His legs. 34However, one of the soldiers pierced His side with a spear and instantly blood and water came out. 35He[h] who saw it has testified and his testimony is true — he knows that he tells the truth — in order that you may believe. 36For these things happened so that the Scripture[i] might be carried out, "Not a bone of His shall be broken." 37And once more another Scripture[j] says, "They shall look on Him whom they have pierced."

38After this, Joseph of Arimathea, a disciple of Jesus, but secretly so for fear of the Jews, asked Pilate if he might remove the body of Jesus, and Pilate gave him permission; so he went and removed His body. 39Nicodemus,

---

b) At first Jesus carried the cross; then Simon of Cyrene was forced to carry it for Him, Matt. 27:32.
c) Ps. 22:18.
d) See note on the four Marys at Matt. 1:16.
e) Salome, the wife of Zebedee and the mother of James and John, was there also, Matt. 27:56.
f) The "disciple whom Jesus loved," here and in chs. 20:2; 21:7, 20, was John. See note at ch. 13:23.
g) Ps. 69:21.
h) This was John, who appears to have been the only one of the Twelve who was at the cross.
i) Concerning the Paschal lamb, which was typical of Christ, it was commanded that not a bone of it should be broken, Exod. 12:46; cf. Ps. 34:20; I Cor. 5:7.
j) Zech. 12:10; cf. Rev. 1:7.

who had earlier called on Him at night, also came and brought a mixture of myrrh and aloes, about a hundred pounds. [40]Then they took the body of Jesus and wrapped it with the spices in the linen clothes, as was the Jewish custom for burial.

[41]Now there was near the place where He was crucified a garden, and in the garden a new tomb in which none had ever yet been laid; [42]there they laid Jesus, because it was the Jews' preparation day and the tomb was close by.

20 EARLY ON THE FIRST DAY OF the week, when it was still dark, Mary Magdalene came to the tomb and saw that the stone was removed from the tomb. [2]Then she ran and went to Simon Peter and to the other disciple whom Jesus loved, and told them, "They have taken the Lord out of the tomb and we do not know where they have laid Him."

[3]Then Peter and the other disciple went and made their way to the tomb. [4]The two came running together; but the other disciple ran ahead, faster than Peter and arrived at the tomb first.[k] [5]When he stooped down, he saw the linen clothes lying; however, he did not go in. [6]Then Simon Peter came behind him, entered the tomb and saw the linen clothes lying, [7]and the handkerchief that had been around His head, not lying with the linen clothes but wrapped by itself in its particular place. [8]Then the other disciple, who had reached the tomb first entered also and saw and believed; [9]for as yet they did not understand the Scripture that He must rise from the dead. [10]Then the disciples went home again.

[11]But Mary[l] stood outside the tomb, weeping. While she was weeping, she stooped down to look into the tomb [12]and saw two angels in white sitting, one at the head and the other at the feet where the body of Jesus had lain. [13]They said to her, "Woman, why are you crying?" She told them, "Because they have taken away my Lord and I do not know where they have placed Him."

[14]On saying this, she turned around and saw Jesus standing there, but she did not recognize Him. [15]Jesus said to her, "Woman, why are you crying? Whom do you seek?" Supposing that He was the gardener, she said to Him, "Sir, if You have carried Him off, tell me where You put Him and I will remove Him." [16]Jesus said to her, "Mary!" Turning completely around, she said to Him in Hebrew, "Rabboni," (which means Teacher).

[17]Jesus told her, "Do not cling to Me, for I have not yet ascended to the Father; but go to My brothers and tell them that I am going to ascend to My Father and your Father, to My God and your God." [18]Mary Magdalene came, bringing the disciples news, "I have seen the Lord and He told me this."

[19]When it was evening that same first day of the week and, out of fear of the Jews the doors were shut where the disciples met, Jesus came and stood among them and said to them, "Peace to you." [20]Upon saying this He showed them His hands and side. Then the disciples were glad to see the Lord. [21]Then He said to them again, "Peace to you. Just as the Father sent Me forth, so I send you." [22]When He had said this, He breathed on them and said, "Receive the Holy Spirit. [23]If you forgive the sins of any, they are forgiven them; if you retain those of anyone, they are retained."[m]

[24]But Thomas, called the Twin, one of the Twelve, was not with them when Jesus came; [25]so the other disciples told him, "We have seen the Lord." But he replied, "Unless I see in His hands the print of the nails, and put my finger in the mark of the nails

---

k) John was younger than Peter; Peter was more impetuous than John.
l) Mary Magdalene, vs. 1.
m) In witnessing to Christ and proclaiming the Word of God in the power of the Holy Spirit Christ's disciples may be instrumental in bringing deliverance from sin. Since others aside from the apostles were present on this occasion, Luke 24:33, the church as a whole is included in this commission.

and thrust my hand into His side, I will not believe."

26A week later His disciples were again indoors and Thomas with them. Though the doors were shut, Jesus came and stood among them and said, "Peace to you." 27He then spoke to Thomas, "Reach your finger here and see My hands; reach and thrust your hand into My side; do not be faithless, but believe." 28Thomas answered Him, "My Lord and my God!" 29Jesus said to him, "You have believed because you have seen Me. Blessed are those who do not see and yet believe."

30Jesus did many other signs also in the presence of His disciples, which are not written in this book; 31but these are written so that you may believe that Jesus is the Christ, the Son of God, and that, believing, you may have life through His name.

21 AFTER THIS JESUS SHOWED Himself again to the disciples, by the Sea of Tiberias,n and this was the way He appeared. 2There were together Simon Peter, and Thomas called the Twin, and Nathanael of Cana in Galilee, the sons of Zebedee and two more of His disciples. 3Simon Peter said to them, "I am going fishing." They said, "We are coming with you." So they went off and got into the boat, and that night they caught nothing. 4Day had already dawned when Jesus stood on the shore. The disciples, however, did not know that it was Jesus. 5Then Jesus said to them, "Boys, have you caught anything?" They answered Him, "No." 6He told them, "Cast the net to the right of the boat and you will find some." So they cast the net and could not draw it up any more because of the great number of fish.

7The disciple whom Jesus loved then said to Peter, "It is the Lord!" So Simon Peter, hearing, "It is the Lord," wrapped his work jacket around him (for he was stripped) and flung himself into the sea. 8The rest of the disciples came with the boat — for they were near shore, only about a hundred yards away — hauling in the net of fish.

9When they got out on land they saw a charcoal fire there with fish on it, and bread. 10Jesus said to them, "Bring some of the fish you have just caught." 11Simon Peter got in the boat and hauled the net to shore; it was filled with a hundred and fifty-three large fish, and though there were so many, the net did not tear.

12Jesus said to them, "Come and have breakfast." None of the disciples dared ask Him, "Who are You?" for they knew it was the Lord.o 13Jesus came and took the bread and gave it to them, and also the fish. 14This was the third time Jesus appeared to the disciples after rising from the dead.

15When they had eaten breakfast, Jesus said to Simon Peter, "Simon, son of John, do you love Me more than these do?" He said to Him, "Yes, Lord, You know that I love You as a dear friend." He told him, "Feed My lambs." 16For the second time Jesus asked him, "Simon, son of John, do you love Me?" He replied, "Yes, Lord, You know that I love You as a dear friend." Jesus told him, "Tend My sheep." 17The third time He asked him, "Simon, son of John, do you love Me as a dear friend?"p Peter was distressed because He asked him for the third time, "Do you love Me?" and said to Him, "Lord, You know everything, You know that I love You as a dear friend." Jesus told him, "Feed My

---

n) See note at Luke 5:1.
o) The apostles knew that it was the Lord whom they saw, but still it must have been hard for them to believe their own eyes. Notice that, although the Lord was now in His resurrection body, His body was so like that in which they were used to seeing Him that they were able to recognize Him.
p) Two different Greek words for "love" are used in vss. 15-17: (1) *agapao*, denoting a very deep love, even divine love in ch. 14:21; and (2) *phileo*, signifying the love of friend for friend. The first and second time that the Lord Jesus asked Simon Peter, "Do you love Me?" *agapao* is the verb. In both instances Peter used the lesser word in his reply, "Yes, Lord, You know that I love You as a dear friend." The third time that Jesus asked Peter, "Do you love Me?" the verb *phileo* is employed. The distressed disciple acknowledged to the Lord that He knew all things and therefore knew that His apostle's love for Him was of the *phileo* kind.

sheep. [18]Truly I assure you, when you were young you girded yourself and went about where you wished; but when you grow old, you will hold out your hands and another will gird you and take you where you do not want to go."

[19]He said this to indicate by what kind of death he would glorify God. After saying this to him, He added, "Follow Me." [20]Peter turned around and saw following him the disciple[q] whom Jesus loved, who at the supper had leaned close to Jesus' side and said, "Lord, who is the one who will betray You?" [21]Noticing him, Peter asked Jesus, "Lord, what about him?" [22]Jesus told him, "If I want him to remain until I come, what is it to you? You follow Me."

[23]The word then went out among the brothers that that disciple would not die; however, Jesus did not say, "He will not die," but, "If I want him to remain till I come, what is it to you?"

[24]This is the disciple who testifies to these facts and has written them, and we know that his testimony is true.

[25]There are, besides, many other things that Jesus did, but if they were all described in detail, I suppose the world itself would not have room for the books that would be written.

---

q) This is John. See vs. 24 and note at ch. 19:26.

THEME OF JOHN:

SEGMENT DIVISIONS

PORTRAYALS OF JESUS CHRIST	SIGNS AND MIRACLES	MINISTRY	CHAPTER THEMES
		TO ISRAEL	1
			2
			3
			4
			5
			6
			7
			8
			9
			10
			11
		TO DISCIPLES	12
			13
			14
			15
			16
			17
		TO ALL MANKIND	18
			19
			20
		TO DISCIPLES	21

Author:

Date:

Purpose:

Key Words:

THE ARREST, TRIAL, AND CRUCIFIXION OF JESUS CHRIST

MATTHEW	MARK	LUKE	JOHN
		Luke gives consecutive	
		order of events in Jesus' life	
		(Luke 1:3)	

WHAT THE GOSPELS TEACH ABOUT THE KINGDOM OF GOD/THE KINGDOM OF HEAVEN

MATTHEW	MARK	LUKE	JOHN

The Account of Jesus' Resurrection

Matthew	Mark	Luke	John
		Luke gives consecutive order of events in Jesus' life (Luke 1:3)	

Postresurrection Appearances

Matthew	Mark	Luke	John

ACTS

I am going away."

The eleven heard nothing else. The promise of another Helper, the Holy Spirit, fell on deaf ears. The thought that they could do the works that Jesus had done—and even greater—must have seemed preposterous to them.

Jesus had died and been buried. But He had also risen! For over 40 days the disciples saw, heard, and touched the Word of Life as He spoke with them of things concerning the kingdom of God.

And then once again He was gone, taken away before their very eyes! He left with the promise to send the Spirit and He commissioned His disciples to reach the world.

Then came Pentecost and the acts of the apostles. Luke wrote Theophilus all about it. It was probably about A.D. 63.

THINGS TO DO

Chapters 1, 2

In the first two chapters of the book of Acts, Luke gives an account of Christ's ascension and the Holy Spirit's coming.

1. Read chapter 1, looking for Jesus' instructions and promises to the apostles.
   a. In a distinctive way mark in the text every occurrence of the key words (along with their synonyms and pronouns) listed on the ACTS AT A GLANCE chart following Acts. Record these key words on an index card that you can use as a bookmark while studying Acts.
   b. In the chapter margin list every-

thing you learn from the references to the Holy Spirit.
   c. In the margin list the instructions and the promises that Jesus gives to the apostles.
   d. Note the main events that occur in this chapter by either marking these events within the text or listing them in the margin.
2. The key verse for Acts is found in chapter 1. This verse also gives an outline for the book. See if you can identify it. When you do, put a box around it and in the margin write, "Key verse of Acts."
3. As you read chapter 2:
   a. Observe how much is taken from the Old Testament. You can see this by checking the footnotes.
   b. List in the margin the main events that occur. As you note them, ask the five W's and an H: Who? What? When? Where? Why? and How? For example, ask: Who was present on the day of Pentecost? What happened? Whom did it affect? What was their response? Why did they respond as they did? How did they hear?
   c. Mark key words. Also mark every reference to the Holy Spirit and to Jesus, including their synonyms or pronouns. Then list in the margin what you learn about each from this chapter. Watch the word *promise* and note its relationship to the Spirit. Compare this with Acts 1:4, 5.
   d. Mark every reference to time with

a symbol. Do this throughout the book of Acts whether the time is indicated by an event (such as a feast or the death of Herod) or by mentioning a certain period of months or years.

   e. List in the margin the main points in Peter's sermon on the day of Pentecost. Note what he emphasized in his sermon and the result.

4. Determine the theme of each of these chapters. Then record the themes on ACTS AT A GLANCE and in the space near the chapter number.

Chapters 3–7

1. As you study, do the following:

   a. Read each chapter in the light of the five W's and an H. Then in the margin note: What happens in that chapter? Where and when did it happen? Who is involved? How are things done or said?

   b. Mark every reference to the Holy Spirit and then list what you learn about the Holy Spirit, His ministry, and the results. Also mark in the text the other key words listed on ACTS AT A GLANCE. Remember to use your bookmark with the key words you wrote on it.

   c. If a message is proclaimed in these chapters, list in the margins the main points of that message. Also note the effect of the message on those who hear it.

2. Determine the theme of each chapter and then record the theme as before.

Chapters 8–12

1. Read Acts 8:1-8 and then Acts 1:8. What do you see happening in Acts 8 that is a change from the first seven chapters? Note this in the margin of chapter 8.

2. Read chapters 8 through 11 carefully, as significant events occur in these chapters. As you read:

   a. List the main events in each chapter. Who does what? When? Where is it done? What is said? What is the result? Who is affected? How does it happen? Don't add to the text, but simply observe it and list in the margin what you learn.

   b. Mark key words and list everything you learn about the Holy Spirit in the margin of each chapter. This is crucial to chapters 8, 10, and 11. To whom does the Holy Spirit come?

   c. Record the theme of each chapter in the text and on ACTS AT A GLANCE.

3. As you read and study chapter 12, keep in mind that this chapter is pivotal. At this point the focus of the book turns from Peter's ministry to that of Paul (Saul).

Chapters 13–28

1. Included in these chapters is an account of Paul's missionary journeys: Paul's first missionary journey in 13 through 14; Paul's second missionary journey in 15:36 through 18:22; and Paul's third missionary journey in 18:23 through 21:17.

   For easy reference, write and color code in the margin where each journey begins.

2. As you study these chapters, mark the key repeated words. Add the word *synagogue* to your list. Also keep in mind what you learned from Acts 1:8 and watch carefully the work of the Spirit throughout these chapters. In the margin note your insights.

   a. Examine each chapter with the five W's and an H. Note in the text who accompanies Paul, where they go, and what happens. On the map on the following page you can trace each of Paul's journeys.

b. Carefully observe each time the gospel is proclaimed, whether to an individual or a group. Watch how Paul reasons with Jews and Gentiles. Also note what their response is and how Paul handles it.

3. In several instances you will notice Paul giving his testimony. Compare each of these instances with Acts 9 and the account of Paul's conversion. This will give you a more complete picture of all that happened on that significant day.

4. Record the theme of each chapter on ACTS AT A GLANCE and in the text. Then determine the main subject for the book of Acts and record it. Then complete the chart. Record the ways you might segment the book of Acts according to its themes.

THINGS TO THINK ABOUT

1. What have you learned from Acts about the Holy Spirit and your responsibility to be a witness for the Lord Jesus Christ?

2. Based on what you saw in the sermons that were preached and the personal witnesses which were given, what would you include in your witness? Where would the emphasis be?

3. As you studied the lives of the early apostles and the commitment of the early church, how has God spoken to your heart? Stop and think about how they lived, and then think about how you are living. Do you have the Holy Spirit living inside you? Isn't He the same today, yesterday, and forever? If you are filled with the Holy Spirit and are not quenching Him, what should be happening in your life?

Paul's Missionary Journeys

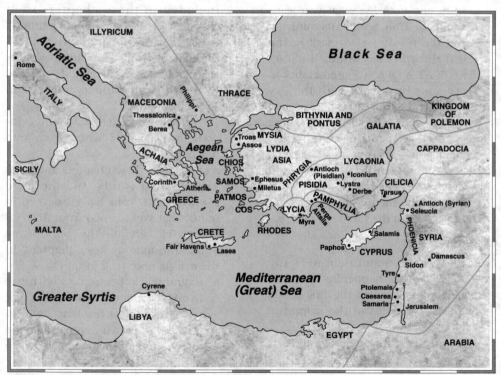

ACTS

OF THE APOSTLES

c. A.D. 62-63

1 THE FORMER NARRATIVE I composed, O Theophilus, regarding all that Jesus began to do and to teach ²until the day of His ascension, after giving His orders through the Holy Spirit[a] to the apostles, whom He had chosen ³and to whom He showed Himself alive after His suffering by many convincing proofs for forty days, appearing to them and discussing the kingdom of God.

⁴And as He met with them, He charged them, "Do not leave Jerusalem but await what the Father promised, which you have heard from Me; ⁵for whereas John baptized with water, after a few days you will be baptized with the Holy Spirit."

⁶So those who were meeting together asked Him, "Lord, will You at this time restore the kingdom to Israel?" ⁷He said to them, "It is not your affair to know times or seasons which the Father has placed under His own authority; ⁸but · you will receive power when the Holy Spirit comes upon you, and you will be My witnesses both in Jerusalem and in all Judea and in Samaria and to the remotest end of the earth."

c. A.D. 30

⁹Upon saying this and while they were looking on, He was taken up and a cloud carried Him up from their view. ¹⁰And as they kept gazing intently toward heaven as He was going away from them, two men in white clothing were standing by them, ¹¹who also said, "Men of Galilee, why do you stand gazing into heaven? This very Jesus, who was taken up from you into heaven, will come again in the same manner in which you have seen Him going to heaven."

¹²Then they went back to Jerusalem from the Mount of Olives, which is near Jerusalem, a Sabbath day's walk.[b] ¹³And when they arrived they went up to the upper room where they were staying — Peter and John, James and Andrew, Philip and Thomas, Bartholomew and Matthew, James the son of Alpheus and Simon the Zealot, and Judas the son of James. ¹⁴All these engaged constantly and with one mind in prayer, together with the women and Mary the mother of Jesus, and with His brothers.[c]

¹⁵In those days Peter arose among the brothers — there was a gathering of about a hundred and twenty persons — ¹⁶and said, "Brothers, the Scripture had to be fulfilled which the Holy Spirit foretold through the lips of David concerning Judas, who became guide to those who arrested Jesus; ¹⁷for he was counted with us

---

a) The saving work of Christ has been done; now the Holy Spirit will take charge. Throughout this book He is seen as directing believers in Christ.
b) In Josh. 3:4 it is shown that the distance which was to separate the Israelites from the ark of the covenant when they crossed the Jordan River was 2,000 cubits. This was thought to have been the distance between the tents of the people and the tabernacle in the wilderness and was as far as the Israelites were permitted to walk on the Sabbath day. A cubit equals about eighteen inches; thus 2,000 cubits would be 3,000 feet or a little more than half a mile.
c) Mary's other sons did not believe before the resurrection of Christ, her oldest Son, John 7:5.

and got his allotted share in this ministry." 18(Now this man bought a field from the wages of crime, and, falling headlong, he burst asunder and all his intestines gushed out, 19and it became known to the whole population of Jerusalem, so that they named that field in their own dialect, Akeldama, that is, Field of Blood.)

20"For in the book of Psalms it is written,d 'Let his dwelling be desolate and may no one live in it,' and, 'Let another take his office.' 21So then, of the men who accompanied us all the time that the Lord Jesus went in and out with us, 22beginning from the baptism of John and on to the day when He was taken up from us — one of these must be our fellow witness of His resurrection."e

23And they put up two names, Joseph called Barsabbas, who was surnamed Justus, and Matthias, 24and they prayed, "You, Lord, knower of all hearts, make clear which one of these two You have selected 25to take the position of this ministry and apostolate from which Judas turned aside to go to his own place."

26And they cast lots for them, and the lot fell on Matthias and he was added to the Eleven apostles.

2 WHEN THE DAY OF PENTECOST had fully come, they were all together in one place, 2when suddenly there came a roaring from heaven like the driving of a mighty wind, and it filled the whole house where they were sitting. 3There appeared to them tongues like flames that were distributed and that settled on each one of them. 4And they were all filled with the Holy Spirit and began to speak in foreign languages as the Spirit granted them expression.

5Now there were devout Jews staying at Jerusalem from every nation under heaven, 6and when this sound was heard the crowd collected and were confused, for each one heard them speak in his native language. 7Astonished and amazed, they said, "Are not all those who are speaking Galileans? 8How is it, then, that we each hear them in our native speech in which we were born? 9Parthians, Medes, Elamites, dwellers of Mesopotamia, of Judea, Cappadocia, Pontus, and Asia, 10Phrygia and Pamphylia, Egypt and the parts of Libya around Cyrene, visitors from Rome, both Jews and proselytes, 11Cretans and Arabs — we hear them telling in our own languages the excellencies of God."f 12They were all amazed and at a loss, remarking to one another, "What does this mean?" 13But others said sneeringly, "They had too much new wine."

14Then Peter arose together with the Eleven, and raising his voice, he addressed them: "Men of Judea and all you who dwell in Jerusalem, you should all understand this, so take note of what I say. 15These men are not drunk as you suppose, for it is only nine o'clock in the morning; 16but this is what was spokeng through the Prophet Joel: 17'It will be in the last days, says God, that I shall pour out My Spirit upon all flesh. Your sons and your daughters will prophesy and your youths will see visions; your elders shall dream dreams, 18and on My bond servants and My bondmaids I shall in those days pour out My Spirit and they will prophesy.h 19I shall present wonders, too, in heaven above and signs on the earth below — blood and fire, and smoky mist. 20The sun will be turned to darkness and the moon to blood before that great and conspicuous day of the Lord arrives. 21And it will be that whoever will call on the Lord's name will be saved.'

22"Men of Israel, listen to these words: Jesus the Nazarene, a Man divinely accredited to you through mighty works and wonders and signs

---

d) Ps. 69:25.
e) Here in vss. 21, 22 are apostolic qualifications that could be met in the first century only.
f) This was not a babbling in unknown tongues; their own languages were used by the worshipers.
g) Joel 2:28-31.
h) To prophesy is to declare the Word of God. It is not confined only to prediction.

which God did through Him in your midst, as you yourselves know, 23this Person you killed by nailing Him to the cross through the hands of lawless men, for He was delivered up in the determined will and foreknowledge of God — 24Him God raised up by setting Him free from the pangs of death; for He could not be held in its grip. 25For David says,[i] having Him in view, 'I saw the Lord constantly before me; for He is at my right hand that I may not be disquieted. 26For this my heart is gladdened and my tongue is jubilant; my flesh too will still have rest in hope; 27because Thou wilt not abandon my soul to the realm of the dead, neither wilt Thou permit Thy holy one to see corruption. 28Thou hast acquainted me with the ways of life; Thou wilt fill me with good cheer in Thy presence.'

29"Brothers, I may speak plainly to you about the patriarch David, that he died and was buried, and his tomb is with us to this day. 30Therefore, being a prophet and knowing that God had sworn to him with an oath to seat one of his descendants on his throne, 31he was looking ahead and spoke of the resurrection of Christ, that He would not be abandoned to the realm of the dead; neither would His flesh see corruption. 32This Jesus has God raised up; of this we all are witnesses.

33"So, lifted high at the right hand of God and receiving from the Father the promised Holy Spirit, He has poured out what you both see and hear. 34For David did not ascend to heaven; but he says,[j] 'The Lord said to my Lord, Sit at My right hand 35until I place Thy enemies for a footstool of Thy feet.'

36"Without a shadow of doubt, then, let the whole house of Israel know that God made Him both Lord and Christ — this Jesus whom you crucified."

37As they were listening, they were moved to the depths of their hearts; so they said to Peter and the rest of the apostles, "Brothers, what should we do?" 38Peter responded, "Repent and be baptized, each of you in the name of Jesus Christ for the forgiveness of your sins, and you will receive the gift of the Holy Spirit; 39for the promise is to you and to your children and to all those far away, as many as the Lord our God may call."

40With many other words he charged them earnestly and warned them: "Be saved from this crooked generation." 41Then those who welcomed his message were baptized, and there were added that day about three thousand souls.

42And they persevered in the apostles' teaching and in fellowship, in the breaking of bread and in prayers. 43But awe fell on every soul, as many wonders and signs took place in Jerusalem through the apostles.

c. A.D. 30-31

44The believers all met together and had everything jointly; 45they sold their property and their belongings, and distributed them to all, as anyone might have need. 46Daily they frequented the temple together and ate their meals at home together. So they received nourishment, 47praising God with happy and sincere hearts, and enjoying the good will of all the people, while daily the Lord added to the group those who were being saved.

3 NOW PETER AND JOHN WENT UP to the temple for the three o'clock hour of prayer 2and a man, lame from his birth, was being carried, whom every day they placed at the temple gate called Beautiful to beg alms from those frequenting the temple.

3When he saw Peter and John at the point of entering the temple, he asked for charity; 4but Peter fixed his eyes on him, and so did John, and said, "Look at us." 5So he watched them closely, expecting to get something from them; 6but Peter said, "I have neither silver nor gold, but I will give you what I have. In the name of Jesus Christ the Nazarene,[k] walk."

---

i) Ps. 16:8-11. This is a Messianic Psalm.
j) Ps. 110:1.   k) On Christ's authority.

7And gripping him by the right hand, he raised him up.

8Instantly his feet and ankles grew firm, he leaped up and stood, and began to walk and entered the temple[1] with them, walking and leaping and praising God.

9When the people all saw him walking around and praising God, 10and recognized him as the one who used to sit at the Beautiful Gate of the temple, they were completely overcome with awe and amazement at his experience. 11And as he kept clinging to Peter and John, all the people ran crowding toward them at the place called Solomon's Portico. 12And Peter, when he noticed it, addressed the people:

"Men of Israel, why are you surprised at this? And why are you staring at us as if we had made him walk through our own power or piety? 13The God of Abraham, Isaac and Jacob, the God of our fathers, has glorified His Servant Jesus, whom you delivered up and disowned before Pilate, when he had decided to set Him free. 14But you denied the Holy and Righteous One and requested that a murderer be granted you. 15You killed the Prince of Life, whom God raised from the dead — of this we are witnesses. 16By faith in His name this person, whom you see and recognize, has been strengthened, and faith in Him gave him this perfect health you all observe.

17"Now I know, brothers, that you behaved ignorantly just as your leaders did; 18but God has thus fulfilled what He made known beforehand through the lips of all the prophets, that His Christ[m] was to suffer. 19Repent and turn about, so that your sins may be wiped away and that seasons of refreshing may come from the presence of the Lord, 20and so that He may send the Christ, who has been appointed for you, Jesus, 21whom heaven had to receive until the times of universal restoration of which God spoke through the ages by the lips of His holy prophets. 22In fact Moses said,[n] 'The Lord God will raise up from among your brothers a prophet like me. Listen to everything he will tell you; 23and every soul that will not listen to that prophet will be utterly destroyed from among the people.'

24"So all the prophets that have spoken successively, from Samuel down, have announced these times of ours. 25You are the heirs of the prophets and of the covenant that God established with our fathers when He said[o] to Abraham, 'Through your posterity all the families on earth will be blessed.'

26"When God raised up His Servant, He sent Him to you to bless you, as each of you turns from his evil ways."

4 WHILE THEY[p] WERE SPEAKING TO the people, the priests, the captain of the temple guard and the Sadducees[q] approached them, 2chagrined because they taught the people and preached in the case of Jesus the resurrection of the dead. 3They seized them and, as it was already evening, they put them in custody until the next day. 4But many of those who had heard the message believed, and their number grew to about five thousand.

5The next day their rulers, as well as the elders and scribes,[r] gathered at Jerusalem 6with Annas[s] the high priest, and Caiaphas and John and Alexander and as many as belonged to the high priest's family, 7and placing them in the center, they inquired, "Through what power or by what name have you done this?" 8Then Peter, filled with the Holy Spirit, said to them, "Rulers and elders of the people, 9if today we are being called

---

l) The temple courts. Only the priests entered the sanctuary.
m) That is, Messiah, the Anointed One.   n) Deut. 18:15.   o) Gen. 12:3.
p) John must have spoken also, although no words of his are recorded here.
q) See note at Matt. 3:7.   r) See note at Matt. 2:4.
s) Annas had been high priest A.D. 7-14, but then was deposed by the Roman governor. The title still clung to him even though his son-in-law, Caiaphas, was then the high priest, Matt. 26:3; John 11:49.

to account for a good deed to a cripple, by what means he has been cured, ¹⁰then you and all the people of Israel should know that by the name of Jesus Christ of Nazareth whom you crucified, whom God raised from the dead, through Him this man stands before you in sound health. ¹¹He isᵗ 'The stone despised by you the builders, which became the head of the corner.' ¹²And there is salvation through no one else; for there is no other name under heaven given among men by which we must be saved."

¹³As they observed the fearlessness of speech on the part of Peter and John and understood that they were men without schooling or skill, they marveled and recognized them as having been with Jesus. ¹⁴Besides, looking at the man who had been healed standing with them, they had nothing to say against it. ¹⁵Ordering them to withdraw outside the Sanhedrin,ᵘ they consulted together, ¹⁶"What shall we do to these men? For that a notable sign has occurred through them is obvious to all the people of Jerusalem and we cannot deny it. ¹⁷However, so that this will not be spread further among the people, let us strongly warn them to speak no more to any person about this name."

¹⁸So they summoned them and gave orders not to refer to or to teach in the name of Jesus. ¹⁹But Peter and John replied to them, "Whether it is right in the sight of God to listen to you rather than to God is for you to judge; ²⁰as for us, we cannot refrain from telling what we have seen and heard."

²¹They threatened them still further and then freed them, as they saw no way to punish them, because of the people; for they were all praising God for what had happened. ²²For the man on whom this miracle of healing had been performed was over forty years old.

²³After their release they went to their own companions and related to them everything that the chief priests and elders had said. ²⁴Then those who heard it unitedly raised their voices to God and said: "Sovereign Lord, who hast made the heaven and earth, the sea and everything in them, ²⁵and who through the Holy Spirit saidᵛ by the lips of our forefather David Thy servant, 'Why do the Gentiles rage and the people devise vain things? ²⁶The kings of the earth got ready and the rulers mustered themselves against the Lord and against His Anointed'; ²⁷for they have actually gathered in this city against Thy holy Servant Jesus, whom Thou didst anoint—Herod and Pontius Pilate with the Gentiles and the peoples of Israel, ²⁸all doing what Thy hand and Thy purpose preordained to take place. ²⁹And now, Lord, notice their threats and endow Thy bond servantsʷ with fearlessness to speak Thy word ³⁰as Thou reachest out Thy hand to heal and to work signs and wonders through the name of Thy holy Servant Jesus."

c. A.D. 31-32

³¹And when they had prayed, their meeting place shook and they were all filled with the Holy Spirit, and fearlessly they gave utterance to God's message. ³²The host of believers were one in heart and soul; no one claimed his belongings just for himself,ˣ but everything was theirs in common. ³³And with great power the apostles bore witness to the resurrection of the Lord Jesus, and grace rested liberally on all of them. ³⁴Not one among them suffered need; for those who owned fields or houses sold them, brought the proceeds of the sale ³⁵and deposited the money at the feet of the apostles. Then it was distributed to each according to his need.

³⁶Joseph, a Cyprian Leviteʸ who was called Barnabas by the apostles,

---

t) Ps. 118:22; Matt. 21:42.   u) See note at Luke 22:66.
v) Ps. 2:1, 2.   w) See note at Matt. 13:27.
x) Christianity has its inescapable social outreach. Men are saved individually, but when they are saved they must live and serve in the communion (fellowship) of the saints. The sharing in the Early Church was not imposed, but was a voluntary expression of the believers' unity in Christ. In this instance the expectancy of Christ's early return gave stimulus to liberality.
y) See note at Luke 10:32.

which translated means Son of Consolation, to whom a field belonged, [37]sold it and brought the proceeds, which he deposited at the apostles' feet.

5 BUT A MAN NAMED ANANIAS, WITH Sapphira his wife, sold some real estate, [2]retained with his wife's knowledge some of the price, and brought a portion which he laid at the apostles' feet. [3]Then Peter said to him, "Ananias, why has Satan filled your heart to lie to the Holy Spirit[z] and misappropriate some of the field's price? [4]Could you not have kept the field for your own or, after the sale, have done with your proceeds as you pleased? Why did you devise such a thing? You did not lie to men but to God."

[5]Listening to these words Ananias fell down and died,[a] and great awe came over all who learned of it. [6]The young men then arose, wrapped his body, and carried it out for burial.

[7]About three hours had passed when his wife came in, ignorant of what had occurred, [8]and Peter asked her, "Tell me, did you sell the land for so much?" She said, "Yes, for so much." [9]Peter then asked her, "How did you agree together to test the LORD's Spirit? The feet of those who buried your husband are at the door, and they will carry you out also." [10]Instantly she fell at his feet and died; so the young men found her dead when they came in, carried her out, and buried her beside her husband. [11]And great awe fell upon the whole church and on all who learned of this.

[12]Many signs and wonders continued to be done among the people by means of the apostles, and they all met unitedly in Solomon's Portico. [13]None of the outsiders dared to join them, but the people held them in high esteem. [14]Moreover, throngs of men and women who believed in the Lord were increasingly added. [15]They went so far as to bring out their sick into the streets and to lay them on rugs and mats so that, as Peter passed by, at least his shadow might fall on some of them. [16]Even from towns outside Jerusalem the crowd came streaming in to bring the sick and those troubled with unclean spirits, and they were all cured.

[17]But the high priest and all those who were with him, and the Sadducean party arose, full of jealousy, [18]and seized the apostles and put them in the public jail. [19]But an angel of the Lord opened the prison doors at night, led them out, and said, [20]"Go, take your stand in the temple and tell the people all about this new life."

[21]Obediently they went into the temple at daybreak and began to teach. Now the high priest and his party summoned the Sanhedrin, even the whole senate[b] of the Israelites, and sent to the prison to bring the men. [22]But when the attendants arrived they failed to find them in jail and went back and reported, [23]"We found the prison securely locked and the sentries posted at the doors, but on opening them we found no one inside."

[24]When the captain of the temple guard and the chief priests heard this report, they were completely at a loss what had happened to them. [25]Someone came and announced to them, "The men you put in jail are standing in the temple teaching the people." [26]Then the captain went out with his officers and brought them, but not by force, for they were afraid the people might stone them.

[27]They brought them before the Sanhedrin, and the high priest asked them, [28]"Did we not strictly forbid you to teach in this name? And here you have filled Jerusalem with your doctrine and you want to bring upon us this man's blood."

[29]Then Peter and the apostles replied, "We must obey God rather than men. [30]The God of our fathers raised

z) The dealings of all believers in Christ, in the affairs of the church and elsewhere also, are with the Holy Spirit.
a) The verb rendered "died" is from the Greek *ekpsucho* meaning *to breathe one's last*, an expression used by medical writers of that day. Its use points to Luke, the physician, as the writer of The Acts.
b) This was another name for the Sanhedrin and was used when it met in full session.

Jesus, whom you put to death by hanging Him on a cross. [31]God exalted Him to His right hand as Leader and Savior, to grant to Israel repentance and forgiveness of sins. [32]And not only are we witnesses to these facts, but so is the Holy Spirit whom God bestows on those who obey Him."

c. A.D. 32-33

[33]As they listened they grew furious and determined to destroy them. [34]Then a Pharisee[c] named Gamaliel, a teacher of the Law who enjoyed the respect of all the people, arose in the Sanhedrin and ordered the men to be put outside for a few moments. [35]Then he addressed them, "Men of Israel, be careful what you intend to do to these men; [36]for in earlier days Theudas[d] appeared, claiming to be somebody, and about four hundred men adhered to him; but he was killed and all his supporters were dispersed, and they came to nothing. [37]After him Judas[e] the Galilean led an uprising at the time of the census, and raised a popular following, and he perished, too, and all his adherents were scattered. [38]So I advise you in this case to keep away from these men and leave them alone; for should this plan or movement be merely human, then it will go to pieces; [39]but if its source is God, then you will be unable to crush them. You might even find yourselves to be fighting against God."

[40]Persuaded by him, they called in the apostles, had them flogged, warned them not to talk in the name of Jesus, and let them go. [41]Then they went out from the presence of the Sanhedrin happy indeed for being thought worthy to suffer disgrace for His name. [42]They never stopped for a single day to teach and to preach Christ Jesus in the temple and at home.[f]

6 IN THOSE DAYS, AS THE NUMBER of disciples kept growing, there rose a complaint on the part of the Greek-speaking Jews against those who spoke Hebrew because their widows were overlooked in the daily charities. [2]So the Twelve summoned the assembly of the disciples and said, "It is not desirable that we should neglect the teaching of God's word to wait on tables; [3]therefore, brothers, look around for seven men among you of good reputation and full of the Spirit and of wisdom, whom we shall appoint for this duty, [4]while we continue to devote ourselves to prayer and the ministry of the word."

[5]The suggestion pleased the entire assembly and they selected Stephen, a man full of faith and of the Holy Spirit; also Philip, Prochorus, Nicanor, Timon, Parmenas, and Nicolaus, a proselyte of Antioch. [6]These they presented to the apostles who, with prayer, laid hands on them.

[7]So the word of God kept on spreading. The number of disciples in Jerusalem increased rapidly and even a large group of priests obeyed the faith.

[8]And Stephen, full of grace and power, did notable wonders and signs among the people; [9]but some from the so-called Synagogue of the Freedmen[g] and of the people of Cyrene and Alexandria, and of Cilicia[h] and Asia, undertook debating with Stephen [10]and could not successfully meet the wisdom and the Spirit by whom he spoke.

---

c) See note at Matt. 3:7.
d) Theudas is thought by some to have been one of the insurrectionists who led bands of men against Herod the Great. He was among the last of these, coming against the king in about 6 B.C. A man of lofty pretensions, Theudas died violently.
e) Judas the Galilean was also known as Judas the Gaulonite. He believed that the census under Caesar Augustus, taken when Quirinius was governor of Syria in about 5 B.C., Luke 2:1, 2, would bring the Jewish people to a place of rigid servitude to Rome. He was able to get some of his countrymen to join the revolt, but he lost his life and his followers soon disbanded.
f) Distinctive Christian teaching would probably have died within a century had not the Christian home become a Christian school, for the synagogues were closed to Christian children and pagan schools were subversive of Christianity.
g) Freedmen, sometimes called Libertines, are said to have been Jews whose fathers had been captured by the Romans and had afterward been set free. They built their own synagogue in Jerusalem.
h) Perhaps Saul of Tarsus in Cilicia, who later became Paul the apostle, was among them, cf. chs. 7:59; 13:9.

c. A.D. 36-37

[11]Then they instigated men to say, "We have heard him speaking blasphemous words against Moses and God." [12]Thus they stirred up the people, as well as the elders and the scribes; they attacked and grabbed him and brought him to the Sanhedrin. [13]They also produced false witnesses who said, "This man never quits uttering statements against the holy place and the Law; [14]for we have heard him say that this Jesus the Nazarene will demolish this place and will change the customs that were handed down to us by Moses."

[15]And all those seated in the Sanhedrin gazed at him and saw that his face shone like the face of an angel.

7 THE HIGH PRIEST ASKED, "ARE these statements correct?" [2]Then he said, "Brothers and fathers, listen: The God of glory appeared to our father Abraham when he was in Mesopotamia previous to his settling in Haran,[i] [3]and told[j] him, 'Get away from your country and your relations and come to the land I will show you.' [4]Then Abraham went out from the Chaldean country and settled in Haran; and from there, after his father's death, God transferred him to this land where you now live. [5]He gave him no heritable property in it, no, not a foot of it, but promised to give it for a possession to him and his offspring after him, though at the time he had no child. [6]But God spoke as follows:[k] 'Your offspring will be aliens in a foreign land and the people of that land will subject and ill-treat them four hundred years.[l] [7]And the nation whom they serve,' God said, 'I shall judge, and afterward they will come out and worship Me in this place.' [8]"He also gave him the covenant of circumcision, and he became the father of Isaac and circumcised him the eighth day; Isaac became the father of Jacob, and Jacob became the father of the twelve patriarchs.

[9]"The patriarchs, jealous of Joseph, sold him into Egypt, but God was with him. [10]He rescued him out of all his troubles and granted him favor and wisdom in the presence of Pharaoh, king of Egypt, who appointed him governor over Egypt and over his entire household.

[11]"Then a famine and great distress came over all Egypt and Canaan, so that our fathers failed to find nourishment; [12]but when Jacob learned that there was wheat in Egypt, he sent our fathers there on the first trip. [13]And on their second trip Joseph made himself known to his brothers, and Joseph's family was made known to Pharaoh.

[14]"Joseph then sent and invited his father Jacob and the whole family, comprising seventy-five souls. [15]So Jacob came down to Egypt, where he and our fathers died, [16]and they were removed to Shechem[m] and laid in the tomb that Abraham had bought from the sons of Hamor at Shechem for a sum of money.[n]

[17]But as the promised time approached, which God had announced to Abraham, the people grew and multiplied in Egypt [18]until another king, who knew nothing about Joseph, took the throne of Egypt. [19]He took advantage of our race and ill-treated our fathers, making them expose their infants, so that they might not survive.

[20]"In that period Moses was born, beautiful in God's sight, and was nurtured in his parental home three months. [21]And when he was exposed, the daughter of Pharaoh adopted him and brought him up to be her own son. [22]So Moses was educated in all

---

i) Haran was located about 125 miles east of the northeastern tip of the Mediterranean Sea and 200 miles northeast of Nineveh. It was not far from the source of the Euphrates River.
j) Gen. 12:1.
k) Gen. 15:13, 14.
l) The Exodus occurred a good four centuries after that promise. For the actual sojourn in Egypt four generations and four centuries seem to be used interchangeably, cf. Gen. 15:13, 16.
m) Shechem (now Nablus) is situated in Palestine west of the Jordan River and about 30 miles due north of Jerusalem.
n) Jacob was buried in the Machpelah cave purchased by Abraham at Mamre, Gen. 50:13; Joseph at Shechem, Josh. 24:32.

the science and learning of the Egyptians, and had ability in speech and in deeds. 23When he was forty years old he resolved to look after his brothers, the Israelites 24and, seeing one treated unfairly, he defended him and avenged the wronged person by slaying the Egyptian; 25for he supposed his brothers would understand that God would grant them deliverance through him; but they failed to understand.

26"The next day he appeared to them,° as they were fighting, and tried to reconcile them, saying, 'Men, you are brothers; why are you mistreating each other?' 27But the one who was mistreating his neighbor pushed him away with the words, 'Who appointed you ruler and judge over us? 28You want to kill me, perhaps, in the way you killed the Egyptian yesterday?' 29At this remark Moses fled and became an alien in the land of Midian, where he became the father of two sons.

30"And at the completion of forty years there appeared to him in the Mount Sinai wilderness an angel in the flame of a burning thornbush. 31When Moses saw it he marveled at the sight, and as he approached to look at it closely, the Lord's voice came saying,ᵖ 32'I am the God of your fathers, the God of Abraham, Isaac and Jacob.' Moses was so frightened that he did not dare to look.

33"The Lord saidq to him, 'Untie the sandals from your feet, for the place on which you are standing is holy ground. 34I have certainly observed the ill-treatment of My people in Egypt, and I have heard their groaning and have come down to deliver them. So come now, I will send you into Egypt.'

35"This Moses whom they disowned by saying, 'Who has appointed you a ruler and judge?' him God sent both to be a ruler and to be a redeemer with the help of the angel who appeared to him in the bush. 36It was he who led them out, performing wonders and signs in the land of Egypt, at the Red Sea, and in the wilderness forty years.

37"This is the same Moses who toldr the Israelites, 'God will raise up from your brothers a prophet like me.' 38This is the one who was in the congregation in the wilderness with the angel who spoke to him on Mount Sinai, and with our forefathers; he received the living messages to impart to us. 39To him our fathers did not want to submit; they pushed him aside and in their hearts turned back to Egypt, 40sayings to Aaron, 'Make us gods that will go before us; for this Moses who led us out of Egypt, we do not know what has befallen him.' 41They made a calf in those days and brought sacrifice to the image, and rejoiced in the works of their hands.

42"But God turned and abandoned them to worship the host of heaven, as it is writtent in the book of the prophets, 'O house of Israel, did you offer Me victims and sacrifices for forty years in the wilderness? 43You carried Moloch's tent and your god Romphan's star-idolu figures you made to worship them. So I shall deport you beyond Babylon.'

44"In the wilderness our fathers had the tent of testimony, just as He who spoke to Moses commanded him to make it according to the pattern he had seen. 45And our fathers received it and brought it in with Joshua into the territory of the nations, whom God drove out before our fathers. This tent remained until the time of David, 46who found favor before God and prayed that he might provide a house for the God of Jacob. 47But Solomon built Him a house. 48However, the Most High does not dwell in a build-

---

o) Two Hebrews.
p) Exod. 3:6.
q) Exod. 3:5.
r) Deut. 18:15.
s) Exod. 32:1.
t) Amos 5:25, 26.
u) Moloch was the idol of the Ammonites; Romphan (or Rephan), the Syrians' idol Saturn.

ing made with human hands, just as the prophet says,[v] 49'Heaven is My throne but the earth a footstool for My feet. What sort of house will you build Me, says the Lord, or what is My resting place? 50Has not My hand made all these things?'

51"You stiff-necked and uncircumcised in heart and ear, you have always resisted the Holy Spirit, the same as your fathers did![w] 52Which of the prophets have not your fathers persecuted? Yes, they killed those who announced beforehand the coming of the Righteous One whom now you have betrayed and murdered — 53you who received the Law through the mediation of angels and have not kept it."

54As they heard this they were enraged in their hearts and gnashed their teeth at him; 55but he, full of the Holy Spirit, looked up into heaven and saw the glory of God and Jesus standing at God's right hand, 56and said, "I see the heavens opened and the Son of Man standing at God's right hand." 57But they, shouting loudly and holding their hands to their ears, rushed upon him in a body 58and threw him out of the city and stoned him.[x] And the witnesses placed their clothes at the feet of a young man named Saul.

59So they stoned Stephen as he called upon the Lord, saying, "Lord Jesus, receive my spirit." 60Falling on his knees, he called out loudly, "Lord, do not hold this sin against them." And with these words he fell asleep in death.

8 SAUL WAS ALTOGETHER AGREED to his murder, and at that time a severe persecution broke out against the church in Jerusalem, so that all except the apostles were dispersed throughout the lands of Judea and Samaria. 2Devout men took charge of Stephen's funeral and made grievous lamentation over him. 3But Saul made havoc of the church and, forcing himself into homes and dragging out men and women, he put them in prison.

4Those who were dispersed were everywhere preaching the message of good news. 5So Philip[y] came down to a city of Samaria and preached Christ to them. 6The crowds unanimously attended to the teachings of Philip as they listened to him and observed the miracles he performed. 7For from many who were possessed, the unclean spirits went out, screaming with a loud voice, while many paralytics and lame too, were healed, 8so that there was much rejoicing in that city.

c. A.D. 37

9However, a man in that city, named Simon, had been astonishing the Samaritan nation by the practice of magic, claiming that he was a remarkable person. 10Everybody, young and old, paid attention to him and said, "He is what is called the Great Power of God." 11The reason they paid attention to him was that for a long time he had astonished them with magic arts.

12But when they believed Philip as he told the good news of the kingdom of God and of the name of Jesus Christ, they were baptized, men as well as women. 13Even Simon himself believed and, upon his baptism, kept close to Philip, amazed at the signs and mighty miracles he saw being performed.

14When the apostles in Jerusalem learned that Samaria had welcomed the message of God, they sent them Peter and John 15who, on coming down there, prayed for the believers to receive the Holy Spirit, 16for thus far they had been baptized only in the name of the Lord Jesus; the Spirit had not yet fallen upon any one of them. 17Then they placed their hands

---

v) Isa. 66:1, 2.
w) The burden of Stephen's address was that his listeners did to Jesus precisely what their fathers had done to their divinely appointed leaders.
x) It was not lawful for the Jewish people to execute anyone. It appears that there was no Roman retribution for their murder of Stephen because Pilate had been recalled and his immediate successor had not yet been appointed.
y) This man is known as Philip the Evangelist. He was one of the seven deacons appointed by the Jerusalem disciples to relieve the Twelve from ministering to the demands of many of the early Christians, ch. 6:1-6.

on them and they received the Holy Spirit.

18Now when Simon observed that through the laying on of the apostles' hands the Holy Spirit was conferred, he offered them money 19and said, "Give me this power, so that the person on whom I lay hands may receive the Holy Spirit." 20But Peter told him, "May your money go to perdition with you, because you thought you could buy the gift of God for money; 21you have neither share nor part in this message, for your heart is not right in God's sight. 22Repent of this wickedness of yours and plead with the Lord to forgive you for what you had in mind. 23For I see that you are in bitter gall and in fetters of wickedness."z

24But Simon answered, "Plead with the Lord for me yourselves, so that none of the things you have mentioned may befall me."

25Then after they had testified and spoken the Lord's message, they went back to Jerusalem, preaching the gospel to many Samaritana communities.

26But an angel of the Lord told Philip, "Rise up and about midday go down the road that runs from Jerusalem to Gaza — a lonely road." 27So he got up and went, and an Ethiopian eunuch, a high official of Candace, Queen of Ethiopia, who was in charge of all her finances and had come to worship in Jerusalem 28was on the way back and was sitting in his chariot reading the book of the Prophet Isaiah. 29Then the Spirit said to Philip, "Go up and join him in that chariot." 30And Philip ran up, heard him read the Prophet Isaiah, and said, "Do you understand what you are reading?" 31He said, "How could I, unless someone guides me?" And he invited Philip to climb in and be seated with him.

32Now the Scripture passage he was reading was this:b "As a lamb He was led to slaughter and as a sheep voiceless before his shearer, so He does not open His mouth. 33In His humiliation He was deprived of justice. Who can tell the story of His offspring? For His life was taken from the earth." 34The eunuch turned to Philip and said, "I beg of you, about whom does the prophet say this, of himself or of someone else?" 35Then Philip began to speak and, starting from that same Scripture, told him the good news about Jesus.

36Proceeding on the road, they came to some water and the eunuch said, "See, here is water. What is to prevent my being baptized?" 37[Philip assured him, "If you heartily believe, it is permitted." And he replied, "I believe that Jesus Christ is the Son of God."]c 38So he ordered the chariot to halt, and both Philip and the eunuch went down into the water and he baptized him.

39But when they came up from the water, the Lord's Spirit took Philip away and the eunuch did not see him any more; he went joyfully on his way. 40Philip, however, was found at Azotus,d and, as he passed through all the cities, he brought the good news all the way to Caesarea.e

9 BUT SAUL, STILL BREATHING OUT threat and murder against the Lord's disciples, called on the high priest 2and requested of him letters to the Damascusf synagogues, so that if he should find there any men or women who were of "the Way,"g he might bring them as prisoners to Jerusalem.

3But as he traveled and approached Damascus, a light from heaven suddenly shone all around him. 4He fell to

z) Because of this incident the sin of using religion for monetary purposes is still called Simony.
a) See note at Luke 9:53.   b) Isa. 53:7, 8.
c) So many reliable ancient manuscripts omit vs. 37, here enclosed in brackets, that it is practically certain that it was not part of the original text.
d) Azotus (now Ashdod) is situated on the eastern boundary of the Mediterranean Sea almost due west of Jerusalem.
e) Caesarea was founded by Herod the Great. Its site was a former coastal station called Strato's Tower. The location is on the Mediterranean shore a little more than 50 miles northwest of Jerusalem.
f) Damascus was and still is the principal city of Syria, located about 120 miles northeast of Jerusalem and approximately 30 miles from Caesarea Philippi.
g) "The Way" was a term used in the first century to denote Christianity, a new way of life, the Christian way of living.

the earth and heard a voice that spoke to him, "Saul, Saul, why do you persecute Me?" [5]He said, "Who are You, Lord?" He answered, "I am Jesus, whom you have been persecuting. [It is hard for you to kick against the goads." [6]Trembling and astonished, he asked, "Lord, what would You have me do?" The Lord said to him,][h] "Rise and enter the city and it will be told you what you must do."

[7]The men who were traveling with him stood speechless; they heard the voice well enough, but saw no one. [8]Saul got up from the ground, but when he opened his eyes he could see nothing. So they led him into Damascus. [9]And for three days he remained blind and neither ate nor drank.

[10]Now there was in Damascus a disciple by the name of Ananias, to whom the Lord said in a vision, "Ananias!" He said, "Here I am, Lord." [11]The Lord said to him, "Arise and go into the street called Straight and inquire at the home of Judas for one called Saul of Tarsus;[i] for he is there praying. [12]And he has seen a man named Ananias entering and laying hands on him so that he may see."

[13]Ananias replied, "Lord, I have heard from many about this man, how much he has hurt Your saints[j] in Jerusalem, [14]and here he has authority from the chief priests to put into chains every one who calls upon Your name." [15]But the Lord told him, "Go. For he is My choice instrument to carry My name before Gentiles and kings and the people of Israel. [16]For I will show him how much he will have to suffer on behalf of My name."

[17]So Ananias went and entered the house. Then placing his hands upon him he said, "Brother Saul, the Lord sent me — Jesus who appeared[k] to you

on the road you traveled — so that you may recover sight and be filled with the Holy Spirit." [18]Instantly it was as if scales fell from his eyes; he saw again. He arose and was baptized; [19]then, after eating something, he regained strength.

c. A.D. 37-40

For some time Saul remained with the Damascus disciples [20]and at once preached Jesus in the synagogues, that He is the Son of God. [21]All who listened were amazed and said, "Is not he the one who went about ravaging those in Jerusalem who called on this name, and who came here to take them as prisoners shackled to the chief priests?" [22]But Saul continued to gain in strength, and confounded the Jews who lived in Damascus by proving that this was the Christ.[l]

[23]After considerable time the Jews conspired to destroy him, [24]but Saul got wind of their plot. Day and night they watched the gates to kill him; [25]but his disciples took him and by night let him down over the wall in a basket.

c. A.D. 40

[26]On reaching Jerusalem he made efforts to associate with the disciples, but they were all afraid of him; for they did not believe that he was a disciple. [27]But Barnabas took him in, presented him to the apostles, and explained to them how Saul had seen the Lord on the road, how He had spoken to him, and how in Damascus he had fearlessly spoken in the name of Jesus.

[28]After that, Saul went in and out with them in Jerusalem, spoke boldly in the Lord's name, [29]and especially talked and argued with the Greek-

---

h) The words in vss. 5 and 6 that are enclosed in brackets are not found in the majority of the most reliable ancient manuscripts.
i) See note at ch. 11:25.
j) In the N.T. the word "saint" refers to one who has been set apart by God as His own and for His service. Such a person may not always be saintly in character or life, but in his standing before God he has been sanctified, that is, made a saint by virtue of Christ's atoning sacrifice, Heb. 10:10; 13:12. All believers in Christ are saints, even though they may not be as fully developed spiritually as they ought to be.
k) Paul testifies in I Cor. 15:8 of having seen the risen Christ.
l) It is probable that vss. 22-25 refer to a second ministry in Damascus, following a period of prayer and meditation in Arabia of which the apostle speaks in Gal. 1:16, 17. The "considerable time" of vs. 23 here corresponds with the "three years" of Gal. 1:18.

speaking Jews; but they undertook to murder him. ³⁰So when the brothers learned of it, they brought him down to Caesarea and sent him off to Tarsus.

³¹Then the church enjoyed peace all over Judea, Galilee and Samaria, strengthened within and progressing in reverence toward the Lord. And through the encouragement of the Holy Spirit there was increase in numbers.

³²As Peter was traveling about, his visits took him to the saints who lived at Lydda. ³³There he came across a man by the name of Aeneas, a paralytic who had been bedridden for eight years. ³⁴Peter said to him, "Aeneas, Jesus Christ heals you. Get up and make your bed." Instantly he got up, ³⁵and all the inhabitants of Lydda and Sharon saw him and turned to the Lord.

³⁶At Joppa there was a disciple named Tabitha, which means Dorcas,[m] a woman full of good deeds and acts of charity. ³⁷At about that time she fell ill and died; so they bathed the body and laid it out in an upper room.

³⁸Now since Lydda is near Joppa, the disciples, learning that Peter was there, dispatched two men begging him, "Do come over to us without delay." ³⁹So Peter got up and went with them. On their arrival they brought him to the upper room, where all the widows stood around crying and pointing at the garments and coats which Dorcas had made while she was with them. ⁴⁰But Peter put them all out, then kneeled down and prayed; and, turning to the body, he said "Tabitha, arise!" She opened her eyes and, seeing Peter, she sat up. ⁴¹Giving her a hand he lifted her up and called in all the saints and the widows, to whom he presented her alive.

⁴²This became known all over Joppa and many believed in the Lord. ⁴³It came about that Peter remained at Joppa for some time, the guest of Simon, a tanner.

10 NOW THERE WAS A MAN NAMED Cornelius living in Caesarea, a captain[n] of what was called the Italian Cohort,[o] ²who with his whole family was a devout person, one who feared God. He practiced liberal benevolences among the people and worshiped God constantly. ³He clearly saw in a vision at about three in the afternoon an angel of God entering his house and saying to him, "Cornelius." ⁴Gazing intently at him, he said in fear, "What is it, Lord?" He replied, "Your prayers and your alms have ascended as worthy to be remembered before God. ⁵Now then, sent men to Joppa and have them call for Simon, who is called Peter. ⁶He is lodging with one Simon, a tanner whose home is by the sea."

⁷As soon as the angel who spoke to him had left, he called two of his household servants, and a devout soldier who belonged to his personal attendants, ⁸explained everything to them, and dispatched them to Joppa.

⁹The next day, while they were on their journey and approaching the town, Peter went up on the roof about noontime to pray. ¹⁰However, he grew hungry and wanted to eat. But while they were preparing a meal, a trance came over him. ¹¹He saw heaven opened and something coming down like a wide sheet let down to earth by the four corners. ¹²In it were all sorts of four-footed beasts and reptiles and birds. ¹³And a voice came to him, "Rise, Peter, kill and eat." ¹⁴But Peter said, "By no means, Lord, for I have never eaten anything undedicated and unclean." ¹⁵Once more the voice came to him, "What God has purified you must not consider unclean." ¹⁶This happened three times; then immediately the thing was taken up into heaven.

¹⁷While Peter was inwardly puzzled about what the vision might mean, then and there the messengers of Cornelius, who had inquired for Simon's house, stood at the gate, ¹⁸calling out to inquire whether Simon, called Peter,

---

m) "Dorcas" means *gazelle*, an animal notable for its beautiful eyes.
n) A centurion, commander of 100 men.
o) A Roman cohort was the tenth part of a legion, or about 600 men. This captain was "of" the cohort and not necessarily in command of the full complement.

was a guest there. ¹⁹And as Peter was still pondering over the vision, the Spirit said to him, "There are three men looking for you. ²⁰Rise and go downstairs and go with them unhesitatingly, for I have sent them." ²¹So Peter went down and said to the men, "I am the one you are looking for. Why are you here?" ²²They said, "Captain Cornelius, a just and God-fearing man of good reputation among all the Jewish people, was instructed by a holy angel to have you brought to his house, and to hear what you have to say."

²³Then he invited them in and entertained them. The next day he got up and went with them, and some of the brothers from Joppa accompanied him.

²⁴On the following day they entered Caesarea. Expecting them, Cornelius had invited his relatives and intimate friends, ²⁵and as Peter entered, Cornelius met him, fell at his feet and paid him reverence. ²⁶But Peter raised him up with the words, "Get up. I am a human being too." ²⁷Conversing with him, he went in and found a large gathering ²⁸to whom he said, "You are aware how a Jew is not allowed to associate with or to visit one of another race; but God has shown me not to call any human being unhallowed or unclean.ᵖ ²⁹For this reason I came without hesitation when I was sent for. May I inquire for what reason you sent for me?"

³⁰Cornelius said, "Four days ago at about this time I was praying in my home at three o'clock in the afternoon, when a man stood before me in dazzling attire ³¹and said, 'Cornelius, your prayer has been heard and your charities are remembered before God. ³²Now then, send to Joppa and invite Simon, called Peter; he is a guest at the home of Simon the tanner by the sea.' ³³So I sent for you at once, and you have been good enough to come. Now then, we are all present here before

God to hear everything in which the Lord has instructed you."

³⁴Peter then opened his lips and said, "Now I thoroughly understand the truth that God is not partial, ³⁵but in every nation he who reveres Him and practices righteousness is acceptable to Him. ³⁶He sent this message to the Israelites, when through Jesus Christ He made the good news of peace known to them — He is Lord of all.

³⁷"You know what occurred up and down Judea, beginning from Galilee after the baptism that John preached, ³⁸how God anointed with the Holy Spirit and with power Jesus of Nazareth, who traversed the land doing good and healing all that were overpowered by the devil; for God was with Him. ³⁹And we are witnesses of everything He did, both in the country of the Jews and in Jerusalem — and they murdered Him, nailing Him to a cross.

⁴⁰"But God raised Him up on the third day and caused Him to appear, ⁴¹not to all the people but to witnesses who were previously selected by God, to us who ate and drank with Him after His resurrection from the dead. ⁴²And to us He gave orders to preach to the people and to bear solemn testimony that He is the God-appointed Judge of the living and of the dead. ⁴³To Him all the prophets bear witness, that all who believe in Him receive forgiveness of sins through His name."

⁴⁴While Peter was still saying these things the Holy Spirit fell upon all who listened to the message. ⁴⁵And the circumcised believers who had come with Peter were amazed that the gift of the Holy Spirit was poured out upon the Gentiles also, ⁴⁶for they heard them speaking in tongues and declaring the greatness of God.

⁴⁷Then Peter answered, "Would anyone refuse the water for their baptism, since they have received the Holy Spirit as we ourselves did?" ⁴⁸So he directed them to be baptized in the

---

p) This was the first appeal expressly to the Gentiles by any of the apostles and was due, of course, to Peter's response to his recent vision.

name of Jesus Christ.q Then they begged him to stay a few days.

c. A.D. 41

11 THE APOSTLES AND THE BROTH-ers who lived in Judea heard that the Gentiles had welcomed God's message; 2so when Peter came up to Jerusalem, those who insisted upon circumcision disputed with him 3with the charge, "You visited and ate with the uncircumcised." 4Peter, however, began to put the whole matter before them in order.

5"I was in the town of Joppa praying," he said, "and in a trance I saw a vision, something coming down like a large sheet let down from heaven by the four corners till it reached me. 6Looking into it, I noticed animals of earth and wild beasts and reptiles and birds. 7I also heard a voice saying to me, 'Rise, Peter, kill and eat.' 8But I said, 'By no means, Lord, for nothing undedicated or unclean has ever entered my mouth.' 9But for the second time the voice answered from heaven, 'What God has purified, you must not consider unholy.' 10This happened three times; then everything was taken up into heaven again.

11"At that very moment three men who had been sent to me from Caesarea stood at the house where we were staying, 12and the Spirit told me to go with them without any hesitation; so six of the brothers went with me and we entered the man's home. 13Then he declared to us how he had seen the angel in his house, who stood and said, 'Send to Joppa to bring Simon, called Peter; 14he will give you the message through which you and your family will be saved.' 15But at the beginning of my message the Holy Spirit fell upon them just as on us at the beginning; 16so I was mindful of the Lord's message, how He said, John did

indeed baptize with water, but you will be baptized with the Holy Spirit.' 17Now since God granted them the same gift that He gave us after believing in the Lord Jesus Christ, who was I that I could hinder God?"

18When they heard this, they quieted down and glorified God, saying, "Then God has granted to the Gentiles also the repentance that leads to life."

19Now those who were dispersed on account of the persecution that arose in connection with Stephen made their way as far as Phoeniciar and Cypruss and Antioch,t telling the message to none except Jews. 20However, there were some of the Cyprians and Cyrenians who arrived at Antioch and spoke to the Greeks as well, preaching the good news about the Lord Jesus. 21The Lord's hand was with them and a great number who believed turned to the Lord.

22When word of it came to the attention of the Jerusalem church, they sent Barnabas to Antioch, 23who, on his arrival, was happy to see the grace of God and who encouraged them all to remain loyal to the Lord with steady hearts — 24for he was a good man, full of the Holy Spirit and of faith — and a considerable number were added to the Lord.

c. A.D. 43

25Then he made a trip to Tarsusu to look for Saul 26and, on finding him, brought him to Antioch where for an entire year they met with the church and taught a large group. At Antioch, furthermore, the disciples were first designated as Christians.

27At about that time there came down prophets from Jerusalem to Antioch, 28one of whom, named Agabus, stood up and revealed through the Spirit that a terrible famine was to

---

q) This was probably the first Christian baptism of an uncircumcised group. It was all very astonishing to the Jewish believers in Christ because they had not grasped the full implications of Jesus' command to preach the Gospel to all the world.
r) Phoenicia was the name of a coastal territory on the Mediterranean Sea directly west of the Sea of Galilee. Tyre and Sidon were in Phoenicia
s) Cyprus, a large island in the Mediterranean Sea, is about 85 miles west of ancient Phoenicia.
t) Antioch in Syria is about 25 miles inland from the northeastern tip of the Mediterranean Sea.
u) Tarsus, the native city of the Apostle Paul, ch. 9:11, was situated in Cilicia no more than 12-15 miles north of the Mediterranean Sea.

come over the whole world — which occurred in the reign of Claudius.[v] [29]So the disciples determined to send a contribution to the brothers who lived in Judea, in which each of them would take part according to his ability. [30]And this they did: they sent it to the elders by Barnabas and Saul.

c. A.D. 44

12 AT ABOUT THAT TIME KING Herod[w] laid violent hands on some of those who belonged to the church. [2]He slew James, the brother of John, with the sword [3]and, noticing that it pleased the Jews, he proceeded also to arrest Peter. That was during the days of the Feast of Unleavened Bread. [4]Arresting him, he put him in prison and charged four squads of soldiers to guard him, intending to bring him out to the people after the Passover.

[5]So Peter was being kept in prison, but from the church prayer on his behalf was unceasingly made to God. [6]On the night before Herod intended to bring him out to the people, Peter was sleeping between two soldiers, bound with double chains, while sentries in front of the door guarded the prison. [7]Suddenly an angel of the Lord stood beside him, and a light shone in the cell; then, touching Peter on the side, he roused him and said, "Get up at once." The chains dropped from his hands [8]and the angel told him, "Put on your belt and your sandals," which he did. He added, "Put on your cloak, and follow me." [9]So he followed him out having no idea that the angel's activity was real, but imagining he was seeing a vision.

[10]They passed the first guard and the second, then reached the iron gate leading into the city, and it automatically opened for them. Walking out, they went along one block, when suddenly the angel departed from him. [11]When Peter came to his senses he said, "Now I know for certain that the Lord sent His angel and rescued me from the hand of Herod and from all that the Jewish people were expecting."

[12]When he got his bearings he went to the home of Mary, the mother of John, surnamed Mark, where a large number had gathered and were praying. [13]When he knocked at the door of the gate, a girl named Rhoda came to answer. [14]And, recognizing the voice as Peter's, she failed from sheer gladness to open the gate, but ran in to announce that Peter stood at the gate. [15]However, they told her, "You are raving." But she insisted up and down that it was so. Then they said, "It is his angel." [16]Peter meanwhile kept on knocking, and when they opened the door, they saw to their astonishment that it was he. [17]He motioned them with his hand to be silent and explained how the Lord had brought him out of the prison; and he said, "Let James[x] and the brothers know all this." Then he left and went to another place.

[18]With the break of day there was no little consternation among the soldiers as to what had really become of Peter. [19]When Herod sought for him and did not find him he had the guards executed, after examining them. He then left Judea for Caesarea where he resided.

[20]Now he was very angry with the Tyrians and the Sidonians;[y] so they came to him in a body, and winning over Blastus, the chief chamberlain, they pleaded for peace; for their country depended on the country of the king for its food.

[21]On the appointed day Herod, arrayed in his royal robes, took his seat on the throne and made a public address to them. [22]The mob shouted, "A voice of a god and not of a man!" [23]But instantly an angel of the Lord struck him, because he did not ascribe the

---

v) Claudius was the Roman emperor, A.D. 41-54.
w) This was Herod Agrippa I, a grandson of Herod I (Herod the Great) and King of Judea, A.D. 41-44.
x) James was a half brother of Jesus; he became the presiding officer of the Jerusalem church.
y) See note on Sidon at Matt. 11:21.

glory to God. He was eaten by worms, and died. [24]But the word of God kept on growing and multiplying.

[25]And Barnabas and Saul returned from Jerusalem, when they had finished their ministry there, and brought along John, surnamed Mark.

c. A.D. 47

13 NOW THERE WERE IN THE church that was at Antioch prophets and teachers, such as Barnabas, and Simon, known as Niger,[z] and Lucius of Cyrene; also Manaen, a childhood companion of Herod the Tetrarch, and Saul. [2]And as they were worshiping the Lord and fasting the Holy Spirit said, "Set apart for Me Barnabas and Saul for the work to which I have called them."[a] [3]Then, after fasting and prayer and laying on of hands, they sent them away.

[4]So they, as they were sent out[b] by the Holy Spirit, went down to Seleucia and from there they sailed to Cyprus. [5]Arriving at Salamis, they preached the word of God in the Jewish synagogues. And they had John[c] as their helper. [6]Traversing the entire island as far as Paphos, they came across a Jewish magician, a false prophet named Bar-jesus, [7]who was attached to the proconsul Sergius Paulus, an intelligent man who summoned Barnabas and Saul, seeking to hear the word of God. [8]But Elymas, the magician (for such is his name translated), opposed them by trying to turn the proconsul away from the faith.

[9]But Saul — also called Paul — filled with the Holy Spirit, looked straight at him [10]and said, "You son of the devil! You enemy of everything that is right, full of every deceit and villainy, will you never stop making crooked the straight ways of the Lord? [11]Now then the Lord's hand is on you. And you will be blind, not enjoying the sunlight for a time."

Instantly there fell on him a mist of darkness so that he groped around in search of someone to lead him by the hand. [12]Then the proconsul, when he saw what had happened, believed, for he was astonished at the teaching about the Lord.

[13]From Paphos Paul and his company sailed away to Perga in Pamphylia, where John separated himself from them and returned to Jerusalem; [14]but they went on from Perga and reached Pisidian Antioch.[d]

Entering the synagogue on the Sabbath, they took their seats; [15]but after the reading of the Law and the Prophets, the synagogue leaders sent them the message: "Brothers, if you have any word of encouragement for the people, speak up." [16]So Paul stood up and, motioning with his hand for silence, said:[e]

"Men of Israel and all you who reverence God, listen. [17]The God of this people Israel selected our fathers and made them a great nation, when they lived as foreigners in the land of Egypt; then with an uplifted arm He led them out from there. [18]For about forty years He endured their behavior in the wilderness; [19]then, destroying seven

---

z) "Niger" means *black.*
a) The title of this book, The Acts of the Apostles, appears to have been given it after the first century. Many have suggested that a better name would be The Acts of the Holy Spirit.
b) On Paul's first missionary journey, chs. 13:4-14:26, he was accompanied by Barnabas and for a while by John Mark, 13:5, 13. The party sailed from Seleucia, a Syrian port on the Mediterranean coast near Antioch, 13:1, 4, to the Island of Cyprus, 13:4, where they preached the Gospel from Salamis, at the eastern end of the island, as far as Paphos on the west, 13:5, 6. From Paphos they sailed to the region of Pamphylia in what is now southern Turkey. They must have landed at the seaport, Attalia, and gone immediately to nearby Perga, where John Mark left them, and then on to Antioch in Pisidia, 13:14. Paul and Barnabas traveled eastward from there to Iconium, 13:51, southward to Lystra, and from there southeast to Derbe in the Lycaonium region, 14:18. The two men retraced their steps to Lystra, Iconium and Antioch in Pisidia, 14:21, from which place they journeyed south to Perga and over to Attalia, where they set sail for their starting point, Antioch in Syria. The tour lasted about two years, A.D. 47-49.
c) That is, Mark, *Cf.* ch. 12:25.
d) Antioch in Pisidia (now Yalvac or Yalvaj in central Turkey) is about 300 miles northwest of Antioch in Syria, where the missionary journey began. Pisidian Antioch was originally a Greek city but became a Roman colony before the first century A.D.
e) There is a certain resemblance between the message that follows and Stephen's address in ch. 7. Of course Paul heard Stephen speak, 7:58-60. It was not that, however, that caused the resemblance but the fact that both men were expounding the Old Testament.

nations in the land of Canaan,[f] He distributed their land by lot — 20all of which took about four hundred and fifty years.[g]

"After that He gave them judges until the Prophet Samuel. 21At that time they asked for a king and God gave them Saul, the son of Kish of the tribe of Benjamin, for forty years. 22After deposing him, He raised up David for their king, of whom He testified,[h] 'I have found David, the son of Jesse, a man agreeable to My heart, who will fulfill all My desires.'

23"From his offspring God has brought Israel a Savior, even Jesus, according to the promise, 24after John had preached to all the people of Israel the baptism of repentance, preparatory to His coming. 25And as John was finishing, he said, 'Who do you suppose me to be? I am not He; but One is coming after me whose sandalstrings I am not fit to untie.'

26"Brothers, sons of Abraham's family and all among you who revere God, to us this message of salvation has been sent; 27for those who live in Jerusalem and their rulers, because they did not know Him, even though the words of the prophets are read every Sabbath, fulfilled them when they sentenced Him; 28and although finding no crime that deserved death, they requested of Pilate that He be executed. 29And when they fulfilled everything that is written about Him, they took Him down from the cross and laid Him in a tomb. 30But God raised Him from the dead, 31and for many days He appeared to those who had come up with Him from Galilee to Jerusalem, the very ones who are now His witnesses to the people.

32"So we are bringing you the good news of the promise 33which God has fulfilled to us their children by raising Jesus from the dead, as it is written in the second Psalm,[i] 'Thou art My Son; today I have become Thy Father.'

34But that He raised Him from the dead, never to return to decay, He has expressed this way,[j] 'I will give you the sacred blessings assured to David.'

35"For this reason He says in another passage,[k] 'Thou wilt not allow Thy Holy One to see corruption.' 36For David, after serving the purpose of God in his own generation, died and was buried with his fathers, and underwent decay; 37but He whom God raised did not experience decomposition.

38"It should be clear then to you, brothers, that through this One forgiveness of sins is announced to you. 39In Him every believer is absolved from everything from which you could not be absolved by the Law of Moses. 40So be careful that the prophetic utterance[l] does not become your experience, 41'Look, you scoffers, marvel and vanish; for in your time I will accomplish a deed such as you will never believe even if someone relates it to you.'"

42As Paul and Barnabas went out, the people begged to have the same things told them the next Sabbath, 43and when the synagogue was dismissed many of the Jews and of the devout proselytes followed Paul and Barnabas, who talked to them and persuaded them to continue in the grace of God.

44The next Sabbath nearly the whole city gathered to hear the word of God; 45but when the Jews noticed the crowds, they became terribly jealous. They contradicted what Paul had said, and talked abusively. 46Paul and Barnabas declared fearlessly, "God's message had to be told to you first, but since you reject it and do not consider yourselves worthy of eternal life, we are turning to the Gentiles. 47For so the Lord has commanded[m] us, 'I have appointed you to be a light to the Gentiles, to bring salvation to the ends of the earth.'"

---

f) The land now known as Israel.
g) That is, from the time of Abraham's call, Gen. 12:1.
h) I Sam. 13:14.
i) Ps. 2:7.
j) Isa. 55:3 and applied here as a Messianic promise.
k) Ps. 16:10.   l) Hab. 1:5.   m) Isa. 49:6.

48When they heard this, the Gentiles were glad; they acclaimed the Lord's message and as many as were appointed to eternal life believed. 49And the word of the Lord was carried all over the country. 50The Jews, however, stirred up the devout women of high repute and the outstanding men of the city, and instigated persecution against Paul and Barnabas and drove them out of their territory. 51But they shook the dust from their feet against them and went to Iconium, 52and the disciples were filled with joy and with the Holy Spirit.

c. A.D. 48

14 THE SAME THING HAPPENED AT Iconium. They went into the Jewish synagogue and so spoke that a large group both of Jews and of Greeks believed. 2But the unbelieving Jews stirred and embittered the minds of the Gentiles against the brothers. 3So they remained for a considerable time, speaking freely with reliance on the Lord, who witnessed to the message of His grace by granting signs and wonders to be performed by their hands.

4The population of the town was divided, some siding with the Jews and some with the apostles; 5but when both Gentiles and Jews with their rulers created a movement to mistreat and to stone them, 6and they grew aware of it, they fled to the Lycaonian towns of Lystra and Derbe and the surrounding area; 7where they went on preaching the good news.

8At Lystra there was a man seated who had no strength in his feet; he was lame from birth and had never walked. 9He heard Paul speaking, who in turn looked straight at him and, seeing that he had faith to be healed, 10said in a loud voice, "Stand up straight on your feet." He sprang up and began to walk.

11When the crowds saw what Paul had done, they shouted in Lycaonian, "The gods have come down to us in human form!" 12So they called Barnabas Zeus, and Paul Hermes,[n] because he was the principal speaker. 13In fact, the priest of Zeus, whose temple was in front of the city brought oxen and wreaths to the gates of the city to join the people in offering sacrifice.

14But when the apostles[o] Barnabas and Paul, learned of it, they tore their clothes and dashed forward among the crowds, 15shouting, "What is this you are doing, men? We are human, with emotions as yourselves. We are bringing you the good news to turn away from these useless things to the living God who made heaven, earth, and sea, and everything they contain. 16In days gone by He let all the nations go their own ways, 17though not leaving Himself without evidence as Benefactor; for He gave you rain from heaven and fruitful seasons and supplied you nourishment and enjoyment to your heart's content."

18Yet even though they spoke this way, they still had difficulty in stopping sacrificing to them. 19But Jews arrived from Antioch and Iconium, who influenced the crowds so that they stoned Paul, then dragged him out of the city supposing that he was dead. 20As, however, the disciples were encircling him, he got up and entered the city. And the next day he went with Barnabas to Derbe. 21They brought the good news to that city and, after gaining a considerable number of disciples, went back to Lystra, to Iconium, and to Antioch, 22reassuring the disciples spiritually and encouraging them to stand fast in the faith, and saying, "We must enter the kingdom of God by way of many afflictions."

23They also appointed elders for them in each church, whom they committed with prayer and fasting to the Lord in whom they had come to believe.

24After traveling through Pisidia,

---

n) Zeus was the chief of the Olympian gods; Hermes, reputedly the son of Zeus, was the herald of the gods. Zeus and Hermes are identified with the Roman gods Jupiter and Mercury.
o) Neither Paul nor Barnabas was of the Twelve, cf. ch. 1:13, 21-26, but they were apostles (from the Gk. verb *apostello* meaning *to send*). In the N.T. the word "apostle" seems to be used in a twofold sense: (1) strictly of those who were directly commissioned by Christ — the Twelve and Paul; and (2) more broadly of others who were not of the Twelve and Paul but were also called apostles, e.g. Barnabas, ch. 14:4, 14, and James, the brother of the Lord Jesus, Gal. 1:19.

they reached Pamphylia [25]and, when they had spoken the message at Perga, they went down to Attalia. [26]From there they sailed to Antioch, the place at which they had been entrusted to the grace of God for the work they had accomplished.

c. A.D. 49

[27]Upon their arrival, they called a church meeting and reported what God had done with them, and how He had opened a door of faith for the Gentiles. [28]And they spent a long time with the disciples.

c. A.D. 50

15 SOME WHO CAME DOWN FROM Judea were teaching the brothers, "If you are not circumcised after the Mosaic custom, you cannot be saved." [2]Since there was a great deal of dissension between Paul and Barnabas and these persons, it was arranged to have Paul and Barnabas and a few others of their number go up to the apostles and elders at Jerusalem about this dispute. [3]So then, sent on their way by the church, they passed through Phoenicia and Samaria, where they narrated in detail the conversion of the Gentiles, and thus made all the brothers very happy.

[4]When they arrived in Jerusalem they were welcomed by the church and the apostles and the elders, and they reported what God had done with them. [5]But some of the believers who belonged to the Pharisee[p] party got up and said, "They must be circumcised and ordered to observe the Law of Moses."[q]

[6]Then the apostles and the elders held a meeting to look into this question [7]and, after much debate, Peter arose and said to them, "Brothers, you will recall that a good while back God made choice among you, that through

my lips the Gentiles should hear the message of good news and believe, [8]and God, who knows all hearts, gave them evidence by granting them the Holy Spirit just as He did to us. [9]As He cleansed their hearts by faith, He did not at all discriminate between us and them. [10]Now then, why be a trial to God by placing a yoke on the neck of the disciples, which neither our fathers nor we have been able to carry? [11]Instead, we believe that we shall be saved through the grace of the Lord Jesus in the same way they are."[r]

[12]The entire assembly kept quiet and heard Barnabas and Paul tell the story of the signs and wonders which God had done among the Gentiles through them. [13]Then, after they had finished, James made reply, "Brothers, listen to me. [14]Symeon[s] has been telling how early God visited the Gentiles to take out a people for His name, [15]and the words of the prophets are in agreement with this, as it is written,[t] [16]'After this I will return and reconstruct David's tent that has fallen down and rebuild its ruins and restore it, [17]so that the rest of the people may search for the Lord, even all the nations over whom My name has been invoked, says the Lord who does these things, [18]which are known from eternity.'

[19]"It is my judgment, therefore, that we should not trouble those who turn to God out of the Gentiles, [20]but that we direct them to abstain from what is contaminated by idols[u] and from unchastity, and from the meat of strangled animals, and from blood. [21]For Moses has from earliest times in every city those proclaiming him, because he is read in the synagogues each Sabbath."

[22]Then it pleased the apostles and the elders, as well as the whole church, to select some of their men to be sent

---

p) See note at Matt. 3:7.
q) Not only the Ten Commandments but also all the ceremonial regulations of the Mosaic Law are referred to in this statement.
r) Peter and Paul are in complete agreement that salvation is by grace through faith and not by the works of the Law. Compare Peter's statement here with Paul's teaching in Gal. 2:16; Eph. 2:8, 9.
s) Simon Peter. "Symeon" is the Greek form of the name Simon.
t) Amos 9:11, 12.
u) By having been dedicated to those idols.

to Antioch with Paul and Barnabas — Judas known as Barsabbas, and Silas, who were leaders among the brothers, 23and they carried this letter:

"The brothers, including the apostles and elders, to the brothers from the Gentiles in Antioch, in Syria, and in Cilicia, greeting.v 24Since we have heard that some who came out there from among us but were not authorized by us have troubled you with messages and have unsettled your minds, 25we have unanimously thought it well to send you chosen men with our beloved Barnabas and Paul, 26men who have jeopardized their lives for the name of our Lord Jesus Christ. 27So we are dispatching Judas and Silas, who will themselves announce these things by word of mouth; 28for it seemed good to the Holy Spirit and to us to load you with no further burden except these essentials: 29that you abstain from food offered to idols, and from blood, and from strangled meat, and from unchastity. If you keep yourselves clear from these, you will get along splendidly. Farewell."

30So then, those who were dispatched went down to Antioch and, after gathering the entire body together, they delivered the letter; 31and when theyw had read it, they rejoiced because of its encouragement. 32Both Judas and Silas, who were themselves prophets, encouraged and strengthened the brothers with a long speech. 33When they had spent some time there the brothers sent them away with peace to those who had sent them, 34[though Silas decided to stay there.]x

35Paul and Barnabas remained at Antioch, teaching and preaching with many others the message of the Lord. 36But some time later Paul said to Barnabas, "Let us go back and look in on the brothers in every city in which we have preached the word of the Lord, to see how they are getting along." 37But Barnabas wanted to take along John, called Mark, 38while Paul considered it ill-fitting to take with them the man who had quit them in Pamphylia and had failed to accompany them to the work. 39The disagreement became so strong that they separated from each other, and Barnabas, taking along Mark,y sailed for Cyprus, 40while Paul, selecting Silas, set out, commended by the brothers to the grace of the Lord, 41and passed through Syria and Cilicia,z strengthening the churches.

16 HE CAME DOWN TO DERBE AND to Lystra, where a certain disciple named Timothy, the son of a believing Jewess and a Greek father, lived, 2who was well recommended by the brothers in Lystra and Iconium. 3Paul wanted him to go with him, so he took and circumcised him because of the local Jews who all knew that his father was a Greek.

4As they traveled from one city to another they delivered to them the regulations which the apostles and elders in Jerusalem had decided they

---

v) In letters written in the first century the signature was placed first; then the address and introductory greeting.
w) Christians at Antioch.
x) Verse 34, enclosed in brackets, is not found in the majority of the most reliable ancient manuscripts.
y) It is not revealed why Mark, who was Barnabas' cousin, left Paul and Barnabas at Pamphylia or exactly why Paul and Barnabas separated because of him. But that Luke reports this dispute shows his honesty as a historian. Later, although how it came to pass is not stated, Mark was fully reconciled to Paul and worked with him, Col. 4:10; II Tim. 4:11; Philem. 24.
z) On Paul's second missionary journey, chs. 15:36-18:22, he was accompanied by Silas, 15:4. Timothy joined the two men at Lystra, 16:1-3. The trip began at Antioch in Syria, 15:35, as did the first missionary tour. From Antioch Paul and Silas went by foot north into Cilicia, encouraging churches that were already in existence, 15:41. Then they moved on to places that Paul had visited on his first tour — Derbe, Lystra and Iconium, 16:1, 2 — and proceeded into the regions of Phrygia and Galatia, 16:6, which was located in Asia Minor in the area that is now Turkey. They stopped briefly in Troas, 16:7, 8, and from there went by sea to Philippi in Macedonia, evidently touching at Samothrace and Neapolis, 16:11, 12. After a powerful ministry in Philippi the apostles were beaten and imprisoned; but they were released and went on to Thessalonica, where they remained for about three weeks, 17:1. Again they met with opposition, so they moved on to Berea, 17:10. There they were well received. Visits to Athens and Corinth in Greece followed, 17:15-18:1; then back to Ephesus, 18:19, where Paul sailed for home. Landing at Caesarea, 18:22, he went to Jerusalem and then finally to Antioch where the long journey of more than three years' duration had begun, c. A.D. 50-53.

should observe. [5]Thus the churches were strengthened in the faith and daily their number increased.

[6]They traversed Phrygia and the Galatian country, since they were forbidden by the Holy Spirit to speak the word in Asia.[a] [7]On reaching Mysia they tried to enter Bithynia, but the Spirit of Jesus did not permit them; [8]so, by-passing Mysia, they came down to Troas.

[9]During the night a vision appeared to Paul — a Macedonian man who stood and pleaded with him, "Cross over into Macedonia and help us." [10]At once, when he had seen the vision, we[b] made attempts to enter Macedonia, for we concluded that God had called us to tell the good news to them. [11]So, sailing from Troas, we ran a straight course to Samothrace, and next day to Neapolis, and [12]from there to Philippi, a colony and chief city of the Macedonian district.

We stayed in this city a few days. [13]And on the Sabbath day we went outside the gate of the city by the riverside, where we supposed that there was a place of worship and, when we sat down, we talked to the women who gathered. [14]One woman, named Lydia, a purple-seller from the city of Thyatira, a worshiper of God, listened, and the Lord opened her heart to give attention to the things that Paul spoke. [15]When she and her family had been baptized, she begged us, "If you consider me faithful to the Lord, come to my home and stay with us." And she prevailed upon us to come.

[16]But it happened, as we were going to the prayer service, that a servant girl met us who was possessed of a clairvoyant spirit, whose fortunetelling brought in much money for her owners. [17]She followed Paul and us, shouting loudly, "These men are servants[c] of the Most High God; they are announcing to you the way of salvation." [18]For many days she kept this up; then Paul was annoyed and, turning to the spirit, said, "I order you in the name of Jesus Christ to come out of her." And that moment it left her.

[19]When her owners became aware that their hope for gains was gone, they grabbed Paul and Silas and dragged them before the authorities in the market place [20]and, bringing them to the magistrates, said, "These men are Jews and they are creating a disturbance in our city; [21]they are advocating ways of behavior which as Romans we ought neither to welcome nor observe."

[22]The crowd also joined against them, and the officials, after having them stripped, ordered them flogged; [23]then, after giving them a severe beating, they threw them into prison, charging the jailor to guard them securely.[d] [24]In view of this order he threw them into the inner prison and fastened their feet in the stocks.

[25]But about midnight Paul and Silas were praying and singing hymns to God, and the prisoners were listening to them. [26]Then suddenly a tremendous earthquake occurred, which shook the prison to its foundations. At once all the doors sprang open and everyone's chains fell off. [27]When the jailor awoke and saw the prison doors standing open, he drew his sword and was about to kill himself, supposing that the prisoners had escaped. [28]But Paul called out loudly, "Do not harm yourself, for we are all here!"

[29]Asking for a light, he rushed in and fell terror-stricken before Paul and Silas, [30]and when he led them out he said, "Sirs, what must I do to be saved?" [31]They said, "Believe on the Lord Jesus and you will be saved, and

---

a) The Asia of the N.T. was the southwestern province of what we now know as Asia Minor.
b) The use of the pronoun in the first person plural indicates that the author, Luke, a capable historian, joined Paul and his party here at Troas. Luke evidently left them at Philippi, for the "we" does not appear in the text again until ch. 20:5, when Paul returned to Troas with Luke. Thereafter "the beloved physician," Col. 4:14, accompanied the apostle all the way to Rome, ch. 28:16, and it seems that he was with Paul during at least the major portion of the apostle's imprisonment there, II Tim. 4:11.
c) See note at Matt. 13:27.
d) Despite Paul's Roman citizenship, cf. chs. 21:39; 22:27, 28, no opportunity was given him to plead his case, vs. 37.

your family also." [32]Then they told him, together with his whole family, the word of the Lord.

[33]At that very hour of the night the jailor took them and washed their wounds; and he was baptized then and there, he and all that were his. [34]Then, taking them up to his house, he set food before them and was extremely happy with all his loved ones because they had believed in God.

[35]With the break of day the magistrates sent their orderlies to say, "Let these men go." [36]So the jailor reported the message to Paul, "The magistrates have sent to release you; now then you may leave in peace." [37]But Paul told them, "After flogging us publicly without trial, though we are Romans, they threw us in prison, now will they put us out secretly? Not at all. Instead, let them come themselves and take us out."

[38]The orderlies reported these sayings to the magistrates, who grew alarmed at hearing they were Romans. [39]They came and apologized to them, and when they had brought them out, they begged them to leave the city. [40]So they left the prison and went to Lydia's house, and when they had seen the brothers, they encouraged them and then departed.

c. A.D. 51

17 PASSING THROUGH AMPHIPOLIS and Apollonia, they arrived at Thessalonica, where there was a Jewish synagogue [2]and, as was his custom, Paul went to meet with them. For three Sabbaths he argued with them out of the Scriptures, [3]explaining and pointing out that the Christ must suffer and then rise from the dead, saying, "This Jesus, whom I preach to you, is the Christ."

[4]Some of them were persuaded and associated themselves with Paul and Silas — a large group of devout Greeks, as well as a number of prominent women. [5]But the Jews grew jealous; they got hold of some unprincipled loungers of the market place and formed a mob to set the city in an uproar, and then attacked Jason's house seeking to bring them out to the mob. [6]And when they did not find them, they dragged Jason and some of the brothers before the city fathers, shouting, "These who have turned the world upside down have come here too; [7]Jason has taken them into his house as guests; they all oppose Caesar's ordinances, claiming there is another king — Jesus."

[8]The crowd and the magistrates were stirred up when they heard this, [9]and when they had taken security from Jason and from the rest, they let them go.

[10]At once the brothers sent away Paul and Silas, to Berea by night. Upon their arrival, they attended the Jewish synagogue. [11]But these were of a nobler attitude than those in Thessalonica; for they heartily welcomed the message and made a daily study of the Scriptures, whether these things were so. [12]Many of them, therefore, believed, including prominent Greek women and a number of men.

[13]But when the Jews of Thessalonica became aware that the word of God proclaimed by Paul in Berea also, they came there to agitate and stir up the crowds. [14]Then the brothers sent Paul off at once as far as the sea, but both Silas and Timothy remained there. [15]Those who were conducting Paul took him to Athens and returned with instructions to Silas and Timothy that they should join him as soon as possible.

[16]While Paul was awaiting them in Athens, his soul was deeply vexed when he observed the idol-filled city. [17]Accordingly, in the synagogue he discoursed with the Jews and the devout adherents, and daily in the market place with those he chanced to meet. [18]Some of the Epicurean[e] and of the Stoic[f] philosophers also encountered

---

e) The Epicureans, followers of Epicurus, 341-270 B.C., held that the end of all things was personal pleasure.
f) The Stoics, disciples of Zeno, 336-264 B.C., believed quite the opposite of the Epicurean philosophy, for they condemned desire for personal happiness as weakness, and taught self-repression and indifference to both pleasure and pain.

him, and some said, "What would this babbler be trying to say?" But others said, "He seems to be announcing foreign deities," because he told the good news of Jesus and the resurrection.

19They took hold of him, brought him to the Areopagus[g] and said, "May we know what this new teaching is, about which you are talking? 20For you are bringing some strange matters to our ears; we want to know just what they mean." 21For all the Athenians and the visiting foreigners spent their time in nothing else than to tell or to hear something novel.

22Standing in the center of the Areopagus, Paul said: "Men of Athens, I notice on every hand how religious you are; 23for as I went throughout your city and looked carefully at your sacred objects, I found even an altar with the inscription, TO AN UNKNOWN GOD. Now what you revere without knowing it, that I proclaim to you: 24The God who made the world and all it contains, who is Lord of heaven and earth, does not dwell in temples built by human hands, 25neither is He served by human hands as if He lacked anything — He, the Giver of life and breath and all things to every one. 26He has made from one person every nation of men to settle on the entire surface of the earth, definitely appointing the pre-established periods and the boundaries of their settlements, 27so that they might seek for God, if only they would feel for and find Him, although He is not far from each of us; 28for 'in Him we live and move and have our being.' As some of your own poets[h] have expressed themselves, 'For we are also His offspring.' 29Now then, since we have our being from God, we certainly should not have the idea that the Deity resembles gold or silver or stone or anything humanly manufactured or invented.

30"However, while God overlooked those times of ignorance, He is now summoning all people everywhere to repent, 31since He has fixed a day when He is to judge the world righteously through a Man whom He has destined for the task, having furnished proof to everyone by raising Him from the dead."

32Hearing of the resurrection from the dead, some scoffed, while others said, "We shall hear you again about this." 33So it was that Paul went out from among them. 34However, some men associated themselves with him and believed, of whom may be mentioned Dionysius, a member of the court of the Areopagus; also a woman called Damaris, and others besides them.

c. A.D. 51-53

18 AFTER THIS HE LEFT ATHENS and went to Corinth, 2where he met a Jew named Aquila, a native of Pontus, and Priscilla his wife, who had but recently migrated from Italy, because of Claudius' order that all Jews must leave Rome. He called on them, 3and, as they were of the same occupation, he stayed with them and worked with them; for they were tentmakers by trade. 4And every Sabbath he discoursed in the synagogue and won over both Jews and Greeks.

5When Silas and Timothy came down from Macedonia,[i] Paul was completely absorbed in preaching the message, strongly urging upon the Jews that Jesus was the Messiah. 6But since they kept opposing and defaming him, he shook out his garments against them and said to them, "Your blood be upon your heads! I am innocent. From now on I am going to the Gentiles."

7Then he left there and entered the house of a God-fearing man called Titius Justus, whose house adjoined the synagogue. 8But Crispus, the leader

g) "Areopagus" means *Hill of Ares,* Ares being the Greek god of war corresponding to the Roman god Mars. Mars Hill is a more familiar designation of the Areopagus than The Hill of Ares.
h) "In Him we live and move and have our being" is from the writings of the Cretan poet, Epimenides, seventh century B.C. "For we are also His offspring" is attributed to Cleanthes, a stoic philosopher. and also to Aratus, a Cilician poet, both third century B.C.
i) Macedonia was a dominant power in the fourth century B.C. when Alexander, its king, conquered Greece. Macedonia was situated in what is now northern Greece. Included in its territory were Philippi, Thessalonica and Berea.

of the synagogue, believed in the Lord with his entire family, and many of the Corinthians who listened believed and were baptized. [9]Then in a night vision the Lord said to Paul: "Have no fear, but speak and do not keep still, [10]because I am with you and none will attack you in order to harm you because I have many people in this city." [11]So he settled down among them for a year and six months, teaching the word of God.

c. A.D. 53

[12]When, however, Gallio[j] was proconsul of Achaia,[k] the Jews unitedly rose against Paul and led him before the court, [13]declaring, "This fellow advises the people to worship God in an unlawful way." [14]But as Paul was at the point of speaking, Gallio told the Jews, "If, O Jews, it were a matter of crookedness or a serious crime, it would be reasonable to put up with you; [15]but if it is a question of words and names and law among yourselves, then it is your own concern. I do not care to be judge of such matters." [16]And he drove them from the court.

[17]Then they got hold of the ruler of the synagogue, Sosthenes, and in front of the court gave him a beating; but Gallio paid no attention to any of these things.

[18]After staying several days more, Paul bade the brothers farewell and sailed for Syria, and with him Priscilla and Aquila. He had his hair cut short at Cenchrea, for he had made a vow.

[19]They arrived in Ephesus,[l] where Paul left them while he went himself to the synagogue to have a discussion with the Jews. [20]They requested him to remain for a longer time, but he did not consent. [21]Instead, he said goodby to them with the promise, "God willing, I shall come back to you." He then sailed from Ephesus [22]and landed at Caesarea;[m] then, after going up to greet the church,[n] he went down to Antioch.

c. A.D. 54

[23]After spending some time there, he took his leave and made his way[o] successively through the Galatian country and through Phrygia, strengthening all the disciples.

[24]Now there was a Jew named Apollos, a native Alexandrian, a man of learning, and powerful in the Scriptures, who came to Ephesus. [25]This man had been instructed in the way of the Lord and with a burning spirit he spoke and taught accurately of the things concerning Jesus, although he was acquainted only with the baptism of John. [26]He began to speak freely in the synagogue; but Priscilla and Aquila, after listening to him, took him aside and explained the way of God more accurately to him.

[27]And as he planned to cross over to Achaia, the brothers wrote the disciples, urging them to give him a hearty welcome. On his arrival he proved of great benefit to those who through grace were believers; [28]for

---

j) Gallio is said to have been the brother of Seneca, Roman philosopher and author who was one of Nero's teachers.
k) Achaia was located in the southern area of what presently is Greece. Corinth was Achaia's capital and Sparta an influential city.
l) Ephesus was the leading city of Ionia and lay on the west coast of what is now Turkey, i.e., on the eastern edge of the Ionian Sea.
m) See note at ch. 8:40.
n) The church at Jerusalem.
o) Paul's third missionary journey, chs. 18:23-21:15, began at Antioch, 18:22, as had the first two. He went north to the Roman province of Galatia in Asia Minor and then westward to a section of the province known as Phrygia, encouraging believers in all these areas, 18:23. At length he moved on to Ephesus in Ionia, where he spent about three years. After an unhappy experience in Ephesus, related to images of Artemis, 19:23-41, the apostle traveled farther west into Macedonia and from there southward into Greece, 20:1, 2, where he stayed for three months. Again opponents sought to seize him, 20:3, so that he went back to Macedonia, accompanied by seven men, 20:4, who evidently went on ahead to Troas in Mysia, Asia Minor. In Philippi Luke joined Paul, 20:6 (see note at ch. 16:10). They sailed from Troas, where Paul's seven friends met them, and spent a week there. From Troas the party went south by land and sea to Miletus, 20:13-15. There Paul said farewell to the elders of Ephesus, for whom he had sent, since he did not expect ever to see them again, 20:17-38. The apostle and his companions sailed from Miletus to Tyre, 21:1, where they spent a week, after which they journeyed by way of Ptolemais and Caesarea to Jerusalem, 21:15, where the trip of about four years ended, A.D. 54-58.

with power he publicly refuted the Jews, proving through the Scriptures that Jesus was the Messiah.

19 WHILE APOLLOS WAS IN CORinth, Paul, who had traveled overland, came down to Ephesus where he met some disciples, [2]whom he asked, "Did you receive the Holy Spirit on your becoming believers?" But they answered him, "Why, we have not even heard that there is a Holy Spirit." [3]He asked, "Into what, then, were you baptized?" They said, "Into John's baptism." [4]So Paul added, "John baptized the baptism of repentance, telling the people that they should believe in the One who was to come after him, that is, in Jesus."

[5]On hearing this, they were baptized in the name of the Lord Jesus. [6]And as Paul laid his hands upon them, the Holy Spirit came on them and they talked in tongues and prophesied. [7]Altogether there were about a dozen men.

[8]He also went into the synagogue and for three months he spoke with boldness, persuasively discussing the things concerning the kingdom of God. [9]When, however, some became stubborn, refusing to believe and denouncing the Way[p] before the people, he turned from them, taking the disciples with him and went on holding daily discussions[q] in the school of Tyrannus. [10]This kept up for two years, so that the whole population of the province of Asia, Jews as well as Greeks, heard the word of the Lord.

[11]God performed uncommon miracles, too, through the hands of Paul [12]to such an extent that people carried off to the sick handkerchiefs or aprons he had handled, and their illnesses were removed and the evil spirits cast out.

[13]But certain traveling Jews who practiced exorcism[r] undertook to name over those that had evil spirits the name of the Lord Jesus by saying, "I adjure you by the Jesus whom Paul preaches." [14]Seven sons of a certain Sceva, a Jewish chief priest, practiced this; [15]but the evil spirit replied to them, "Jesus I know and I am acquainted with Paul, but you, who are you?" [16]Then the man in whom the evil spirit dwelt, leaped on them, overpowered all of them and was so violent against them that they fled from that house stripped and wounded. [17]This became known to all the Jews and Greeks who lived in Ephesus, and awe fell on them all; and they extolled the name of the Lord Jesus.

[18]And many who believed came and made full confession and declaration of their magic practices, [19]and quite a number of those who had practiced magic arts collected the books into a pile and burned them before everybody. Counting up their value, they found them priced at ten thousand dollars.[s] [20]Thus mightily did the word of the Lord grow and become stronger.

[21]After these events took place Paul decided under the direction of the Spirit to travel to Jerusalem by way of Macedonia and Achaia, and said, "After I have been there, I must see Rome also." [22]So he sent two of his assistants into Macedonia, Timothy and Erastus, while he remained for some time longer in Asia.

c. A.D. 57

[23]At about that time considerable disturbance occurred regarding the Way. [24]For a certain Demetrius, a silversmith who made silver shrines of Artemis[t] and provided the artisans with a large income, [25]called them together along with the workmen of the same trade and said, "Men, you know that we are deriving a good living from

---

p) See note at ch. 9:2
q) Some ancient manuscripts add "from ten until three."
r) Exorcism is the practice of addressing evil spirits by magic or religious formulas, or trying to expel them by the employment of a holy name.
s) The text reads "fifty thousand pieces of silver." These silver coins were probably Greek drachmas. A drachma would be the equivalent of about twenty cents in mid-twentieth century U. S. currency.
t) Artemis, the Greek counterpart of the Roman Diana, was the mythological goddess of the moon and fertility.

this trade. 26Now you observe and hear how not only at Ephesus but in almost all Asia this Paul is alienating many people by persuading them that gods made by human hands are not real gods. 27So there is danger not merely that our trade will come into disrepute but also that the temple of the great goddess, Artemis, will be looked upon as nothing and her magnificent glory will come to an end — she whom all Asia and all the world worship."

28As they listened they became full of anger and shouted, "Great is Artemis of Ephesus!" 29Then the city was filled with confusion and, after dragging away Gaius and Aristarchus of Macedonia, fellow travelers of Paul, they pushed together into the theater. 30When Paul wanted to enter the assembly, the disciples did not permit him 31and even some of the deputies of the assembly who were his friends, sent him warning not to risk himself in the theater.

32Some were shouting this and others that; for the assembly was just a tumult and the majority had no idea why they had come together. 33Some of the crowd advised Alexander to speak, since he was pushed forward by the Jews, and Alexander motioned with the hand, as he wished to make his defense before the mob; 34but as soon as they recognized him as a Jew, the whole crowd as with one voice broke into a shouting that lasted two hours, "Great is Artemis of Ephesus!"

35But the town clerk quieted the mob and said, "Fellow Ephesians, where is there a person who does not know that Ephesus is the temple guardian of the great Artemis and of her image that fell from heaven? 36Since this is undeniable, you should compose yourselves and not do anything rashly. 37For you have brought these men here, who are neither temple destroyers nor insulters of our goddess. 38Now then, if Demetrius and his fellow craftsmen have a complaint against anyone, courts are in session and proconsuls are available; let them bring charges against each other. 39But if you have further complaint, then let it be straightened out in the legal assembly. 40For we are in danger of being accused of riot on account of to-day's affairs, since there is no reason whatever that we can offer for this disorderly gathering." 41And with these words he dismissed the gathering.

20 AFTER THE TUMULT HAD ceased, Paul sent for the disciples to see him, gave them encouragement, bade them farewell and left for Macedonia. 2Then, after traveling through those parts and encouraging the brothers in a long speech, he came to Greece, 3where he spent three months. When he was about to sail for Syria, he decided to return by way of Macedonia, because of a plot against him on the part of the Jews.

c. A.D. 58

4There accompanied him Sopater, son of Pyrrhus of Berea; Aristarchus and Secundus, both of Thessalonica; Gaius of Derbe, and Timothy; also Tychicus and Trophimus of Asia; 5and they went on ahead and awaited us[u] at Troas. Then, after the days of the Feast of Unleavened Bread, 6we sailed out from Philippi and reached them in five days at Troas, where we tarried for seven days.

7As we were gathered for the breaking of bread on the first day of the week, Paul talked with them and, since he intended to leave the next morning, he prolonged his message until midnight. 8There were numerous lamps in the upper room in which we met; 9and a young man named Eutychus was sitting in the window and, while Paul kept on talking heaviness of sleep proved too much for him; so as he sagged down in his sleep, fell from the third story and was picked up lifeless. 10However, Paul went down, stooped over him and embraced him, saying, "Have no anxiety, for his soul is in him." 11Then going up again,

---

u) Here Luke rejoined Paul. See note at ch. 16:10.

he broke the bread and ate, conversed at length even until daybreak and left just as he was. [12]They took the young man home alive, and were greatly encouraged.

[13]We went on ahead to the ship and sailed to Assos, intending to take Paul on board there; for so he had arranged it, intending himself to travel there on foot. [14]So, when he met us at Assos, we took him aboard and went to Mitylene. [15]The next day we sailed on from there to a point facing Chios; the next we crossed over to Samos and the day after we arrived at Miletus. [16]For Paul had decided to sail past Ephesus, so that he might lose no time in Asia, for he was hastening to be in Jerusalem on the Day of Pentecost if at all possible.

[17]From Miletus he sent messengers to Ephesus and called the elders of the church to him [18]and, when they arrived, he told them, "You are well acquainted with my behavior among you from the day I first set foot in Asia and ever since; [19]how I have served the Lord with all humility in tears and in trials that befell me because of the plottings of the Jews; [20]how I never failed to tell you what was for your benefit and to teach you publicly and in homes; [21]how I bore testimony to both Jews and Greeks that they should repent before God and have faith in our Lord Jesus.

[22]"And now I am bound by the Spirit to go to Jerusalem, and what is going to happen to me I do not know; [23]except that the Holy Spirit in one city after another testifies to me that bonds and affliction await me. [24]However, I am not concerned about anything; neither is my life dear to me except to finish my course and the ministry which I accepted from the Lord Jesus to bear witness to the gospel of the grace of God.

[25]"And now I know that you all, among whom I have gone in and out preaching the kingdom, will see my face no more. [26]For this reason I bear you witness today that I am guiltless of the blood of all of you; [27]for I have not fallen short at all of preaching to you the whole purpose of God. [28]Be on guard for yourselves and for the entire flock over which the Holy Spirit has appointed you overseers; shepherd the church of God,[v] which He has bought with His own blood.

[29]"For I know that after I have left, savage wolves will make their way to you, that have no mercy on the flock; [30]and from your own number also persons will arise who will teach distorted things to draw away the disciples after them. [31]Keep on the lookout, therefore, and remember how for three years with many tears I never stopped night and day giving each of you warning.

[32]"And now, I commit you to God and to the word of His grace, which is able to build you up and grant you the inheritance among all those made holy.

[33]"I have set my heart on no one's silver or gold or clothing. [34]You yourselves know that these hands supplied my needs and those of my companions. [35]I have in every way pointed out to you how, by working hard in this way, the needy must be assisted, and that we should remember the words of the Lord Jesus, how He said,[w] 'It is more blessed to give than to receive.' "

[36]Having so spoken, he bowed his knees and prayed with them all. [37]They all wept freely; they fell on Paul's neck and fervently kissed him. [38]They were grieved especially over the remark he made, that they would not see his face any more. Then they escorted him to the ship.

21 WHEN WE HAD TORN OURselves away from their embrace and put out to sea, we ran a straight course to Cos; the next day to Rhodes, and from there to Patara; [2]then, meeting with a ship that was crossing to Phoenicia, we embarked and set sail. [3]Sighting Cyprus and leaving it to

---

v) Some ancient manuscripts read "Lord," Gk. *kurios*. In the O.T. Septuagint translation the word is sometimes used of God; in the N.T. it usually refers to Christ, who is God.
w) The church is indebted to Paul for this information, for there is no record in the Gospels of Jesus having said it.

our left, we sailed on to Syria and docked at Tyre, for there the ship had to discharge the cargo.

4We looked up the disciples and stayed there seven days. They advised Paul through the Spirit not to go on to Jerusalem; 5but when the time was up, we left and went on our journey escorted by all the believers with their wives and children until we were outside the city. Kneeling on the beach, we prayed, 6then embraced one another and embarked. And they went back to their homes.

7When we had completed our voyage from Tyre, we arrived at Ptolemais, and we greeted the brothers and stayed with them for one day. 8The following day we departed and arrived at Caesarea, where we called at the home of Philip, the evangelist, one of the seven,[x] by whom we were entertained. 9He had four virgin daughters who prophesied.[y]

10We had stopped there for several days when a prophet named Agabus came down from Judea and called on us. 11He took Paul's belt and, tying his own feet and hands, he said, "Thus speaks the Holy Spirit: 'In this way the Jews in Jerusalem will bind the man who owns this belt and will deliver him to the Gentiles.'"

12On hearing this, both we and those who lived in that place urged him not to go up to Jerusalem. 13Then Paul replied,[z] "What are you trying to do by weeping and discouraging me? I am prepared not merely to be bound but also to die at Jerusalem on behalf of the Lord Jesus." 14And as he could not be dissuaded, we stopped trying to persuade him and said, "The Lord's will be done."

15So when these days were over, we got ready for the trip and went up to Jerusalem. 16Some of the Caesarean disciples, who went along with us, brought us to the home of Mnason of Cyprus, an early disciple by whom we were to be entertained.

17When we arrived in Jerusalem, the brothers welcomed us joyfully 18and the next day Paul called on James, and we went with him. All the elders were present and, 19after we greeted them he recounted to them step by step what God had done among the Gentiles through his ministry. 20As they listened to him, they gave glory to God and then said to him, "You see, brother, how many thousands of believers there are among the Jews, and they all remain zealous for the Law. 21But they have been informed about you, that you are teaching all the Jews who live among the Gentiles to turn away from Moses, telling them not to circumcise their children, neither to observe the ancestral customs. 22Now, how about it? For they will learn that you have arrived. 23So then, do as we tell you. We have here four men who have taken a vow. 24Take them along, be purified with them and take care of their expenses so that they can have their heads shaved. Then everyone will realize that there is no basis for the reports about you, but that you yourself order your life in observance of the Law.

25"With regard to Gentile believers, we have issued the resolution that they shall abstain from food offered to idols, and from blood, and from strangled meat and from unchastity."

26The following day Paul took the men along and, after undergoing the purification ritual with them, he entered the temple to announce the completion of the purification period, which would be when an offering had been made for each of them. 27But when the seven days were about completed, the Jews from Asia who had noticed him in the temple stirred up the whole crowd and grabbed hold of him, 28shouting, "You men of Israel, help! This is the man who teaches everyone everywhere against our nation, the Law, and this place, and besides, he has brought Greeks into the

---

x) The reference is to the seven deacons of ch. 6:1-16.
y) To prophesy is to declare the Word of God. Prophecy is not confined only to prediction of the future.
z) Divine guidance is a personal matter. *Cf.* chs. 19:21; 20:22; also I Kings 13:1-32.

temple and so defiled this holy place." [29]For they had on an earlier date seen Trophimus of Ephesus with him in the city and supposed that Paul had brought him into the temple.

[30]So the whole city became agitated; there was a rushing together of the people and, seizing Paul, they dragged him outside the temple, and instantly the doors were shut. [31]They were trying to kill him, when the report reached the commander of the cohort[a] that all Jerusalem was in an uproar. [32]At once he marched soldiers and their officers double-quick down to the mob which, on seeing the commander and the soldiers, stopped pommeling Paul. [33]The commander then advanced, took charge of him, ordered him bound with two chains, and inquired who he was and what he had done.

[34]Among the mob some shouted this and others that; so, unable to get at the facts because of the tumult, he ordered him taken to the barracks. [35]But when Paul got as far as the steps he had to be carried by the soldiers because of the violence of the mob; [36]for the multitude of people followed him, shouting, "Away with him!"

[37]At the point of being brought into the fortress, Paul said to the commander, "Am I permitted to have a word with you?" He said, "Do you know Greek? [38]Are not you the Egyptian[b] who recently stirred up the rebellion and led out four thousand cutthroats[c] into the wilderness?" [39]But Paul replied, "I am a Jew from Tarsus of Cilicia, a citizen of no insignificant city. I beg of you, please let me speak to the people." [40]With his permission Paul stood on the steps and motioned to the people and, when all of them were quiet, he addressed them in the Hebrew language[d] in these words:

22 "BROTHERS AND FATHERS, LISten to the defense I now make to you." [2]As soon as they heard him address them in Hebrew, they were still quieter, so he proceeded, [3]"I am a Jew, a native of Tarsus in Cilicia, but brought up in this city. At the feet of Gamaliel I have been educated with exacting care in our ancestral Law, with a zeal for God such as you all have today.

[4]"As such I persecuted this Way[e] to the death, binding and delivering to prison both men and women, [5]as the high priest and the whole council of elders can bear me out. For from them I received letters to the brothers in Damascus,[f] where I was going, to bring the believers there back as prisoners to Jerusalem for punishment.

[6]"But as I was nearing Damascus on my journey, suddenly at noonday an intense light from heaven shone around me, [7]and as I fell to the ground, I heard a voice saying to me, 'Saul, Saul, why do you persecute Me?' [8]But I answered, 'Who are You, Lord?' And He said to me, 'I am Jesus the Nazarene, whom you are persecuting.' [9]Now my companions saw the light, but they did not hear the voice of the One who spoke to me.

[10]"I said, 'Lord, what shall I do?' Then the Lord said to me, 'Rise and go on to Damascus. There you will be told about all the work that has been laid out for you to do.' [11]However, because of the brilliance of that intense light, I was blinded; so I entered Damascus guided by the hands of my companions.

[12]"Then a man named Ananias, a man devoted to the Law and well spoken of by all the Jews who lived there, [13]called on me, presented himself, and said to me, 'Brother Saul, re-

---

a) See note at ch. 10:1.
b) The historian Josephus tells of such an Egyptian who was one of many imposters at the time that Felix was governor of Jerusalem, *cf.* ch. 23:24. This man pretended to be a prophet. He predicted that the walls of Jerusalem would fall down and that he and his band could then enter and take the city. Felix sent an army to apprehend him, but he fled. It is not clear that the Egyptian of vs. 38 was the same man, for his rebellion may have been anterior to the governorship of Felix.
c) "Cutthroats" is translated from a Greek word, *sikarios* (nominative singular), which means literally *a man armed with a dagger,* therefore *an assassin.*
d) The language was the colloquial Aramaic that was used by the Jews of that period.
e) See note on "Way" at ch. 9:2.
f) See note on "Damascus" at ch. 9:2.

cover your sight,' and instantly I looked up at him. [14]He said further, 'Our fathers' God has prepared you beforehand to know His will, to see the Just One and to hear a message from His own lips; [15]for you will give testimony for Him to everyone concerning what you have seen and heard.[g] [16]Now then, why hesitate? Rise; be baptized and, calling on His name, be cleansed of your sins.'

[17]"Then when I returned to Jerusalem and was praying in the temple, I had a vision [18]and saw Him as He said to me, 'Hurry, get out of Jerusalem quickly, because they will not welcome your testimony about Me.' [19]I replied, 'Lord, they know well enough that I went from synagogue to synagogue, arresting and beating those who believed in You, [20]and, when the blood of Your martyr Stephen was shed, I myself was standing by and approving, and I watched over the clothes of those who killed him.' [21]And He said to me, 'Go, for I shall send you far away to the Gentiles.' "

[22]They listened to him up to that statement; then they shouted, "Away from the earth with such a fellow; for he is not fit to live!"[h] [23]While they were yelling, waving their clothes and throwing dust into the air, [24]the commander ordered him to be brought into the barracks and to be examined by means of flogging, so they might discover why they shouted at him that way. [25]But when they had tied him up to be flogged, Paul asked the captain in charge, "Is it legal to flog a Roman citizen without trial?" [26]On hearing that, the captain went to the commander and reported to him, with the remark, "What is to be done, for this man is a Roman?" [27]The commander then went to him and asked him, "Tell me, are you a Roman?" He said, "Yes." [28]The commander replied, "I have pur-

chased this citizenship for a large sum." Paul responded, "But I was actually born a citizen." [29]Then at once those who were to examine him kept their hands off, and the commander was afraid, on discovering that Paul was a Roman, because he had bound him.

[30]On the following day, with the purpose of finding out clearly why the Jews accused Paul, he unfastened him, ordered a session of the chief priests and the entire Sanhedrin,[i] and had Paul brought down to face them.

23 SO, WITH A STRAIGHT LOOK AT the council, Paul spoke. "Brothers, I have behaved myself in the presence of God with an altogether clear conscience to this very day." [2]But the high priest, Ananias, ordered the attendants to strike him on the mouth. [3]Then Paul said to him, "God is about to strike you, you whitewashed wall! You are sitting here to judge me according to the Law, and are you ordering me to be struck contrary to the Law?"

[4]The bystanders said, "You insult the high priest of God?" [5]Paul replied, "I did not know, brothers, that he was the high priest; for it is written,[j] 'You must not defame a ruler of the people.' "

[6]Paul, however, aware that one party was Sadducee[k] and the other Pharisee[l], shouted, right in the Sanhedrin, "Brothers, I am a Pharisee, a son of a Pharisee; concerning the hope of the resurrection of the dead I am accused." [7]At this saying a dispute arose between the Pharisees and the Sadducees, and there was division in the meeting. [8]For the Sadducees maintain there is neither resurrection nor angel nor spirit, while the Pharisees confess the one as well as the other. [9]So the outcry grew deafening. Some of the scribes of the Pharisees' party got up and argued, "We

---

g) Compare the testimony of Peter and John, ch. 4:20.
h) God promised Abraham that in him all the families of the earth would be blessed, Gen. 12:3. This promise was reaffirmed to Isaac, Gen. 26:4, and to Jacob, Gen. 28:14. In Jerusalem their descendants were not prepared to have the Gentiles, vs. 21, become recipients of that promise.
i) See note at Luke 22:66.
j) Exod. 22:28.
k) See note about the Sadducees at Matt. 3:7.
l) See note about the Pharisees at Matt. 3:7.

find nothing bad in this man; but if a spirit or an angel has spoken to him...."

[10]And the discord grew so bitter that the commander, afraid that Paul might be torn to pieces by them, ordered a detachment to march down and snatch him from their midst, and bring him into the barracks. [11]But that night the Lord stood by him and said, "Take heart! For as you have borne Me witness in Jerusalem, just so it is necessary for you to testify at Rome."

[12]At daybreak there were Jews who formed a plot and pledged themselves with an oath that they would neither eat nor drink until they had killed Paul. [13]More than forty formed this conspiracy. [14]Some of them went to the chief priests and the elders and said, "We have sworn ourselves to the liability of a curse, to taste of nothing until we have killed Paul. [15]Now then, you, in cooperation with the Sanhedrin, send word to the commander to have him conducted to you as if you wanted to determine more particularly about his case. Then we, before he comes anywhere near, are ready to do away with him."

[16]However, the son of Paul's sister got wind of the ambush; so he came along and entered the barracks and informed Paul about it. [17]Then Paul, after calling in one of the captains, said, "Take this young man to the commander, for he has something to tell him." [18]Accordingly he took him to the commander and said, "Paul, the prisoner, summoned me to request that I bring this young man to you, since he has something to tell you." [19]Then the commander, taking him by the hand, stepped to one side with him privately and inquired, "What is it you have to tell me?" [20]He said,[m] "The Jews have agreed to ask you that you bring Paul down tomorrow before the Sanhedrin, as if they were to investigate more particularly about him; [21]but do not give in to them, for more than forty of them are lying in wait for him and have pledged themselves with an oath neither to eat nor to drink until they have killed him, and right now they are in readiness, only waiting for your assent."

[22]The commander then dismissed the young man, cautioning him, "Divulge to no one that you informed me of this." [23]He then summoned two of his captains and said, "Have two hundred soldiers ready by nine tonight to march to Caesarea; also seventy cavalry and two hundred spearmen. [24]Provide animals, too, for mounts for Paul to ride, and conduct him safely to Governor Felix."[n]

[25]He wrote a letter with the following contents: [26]"Claudius Lysias to His Excellency Governor Felix — Greeting. [27]When this man was set upon by the Jews and was within an inch of being murdered by them, I went with my men and rescued him; for I learned that he is a Roman. [28]In the hope of discovering the reason for their accusation, I took him down to their Sanhedrin [29]and found that the complaint relates to questions of their Law, but without accusation of crime that deserves death or prison. [30]But when I was informed that there would be a plot against this man, I sent him to you at once and have directed his accusers to have their say to you."

[31]So the soldiers took Paul, according to their orders, and conducted him by night to Antipatris.[o] [32]The following day they returned to their barracks, leaving it to the cavalry to travel on with him. [33]When those men reached Caesarea, they delivered the letter to the governor and presented Paul to him.

[34]After reading it, the governor inquired from what province he was and, on learning that he was from Cilicia,

---

m) One does not need to be an ordained minister or a missionary to serve the Lord.
n) Felix was procurator of Judea at this time, holding the office from about A.D. 52-60, when he was succeeded by Festus, ch. 24:27. Felix, a former slave, was freed by the Emperor Claudius, who gave him his appointment in Palestine. He was a cruel and immoral man who, according to Josephus, seduced his wife Drusilla, a Jewess, from her lawful husband.
o) Antipatris was slightly more than half way to Caesarea from Jerusalem. It was formerly called Aphek, but when Herod the Great rebuilt the town he named it for his father, Antipater.

35said, "We shall give you a hearing whenever your accusers get here." He then gave orders to have him retained in Herod's palace.p

24 AFTER FIVE DAYS ANANIAS, THE high priest, with some of the elders and Tertullus, an orator, came down to present their evidence against Paul to the governor; 2and, after Paul had been called in, Tertullus began to bring charges as follows:

"Since we enjoy peace through you, most excellent Felix, and since reforms are being made for this nation through your provision, 3in every way and everywhere we welcome this with deep appreciation. 4However, not to take more of your precious time, I beg of you by your courtesy to listen briefly to us.

5"For we have found this man to be a veritable plague, stirring up, as he does, all the Jews on earth, and a ringleader of the sect of the Nazarenes. 6He even tried to defile the temple. So we seized him [and would have sentenced him by our Law; 7but the commander, Lysias, came and took him from us with great force. 8He ordered his accusers to present themselves to you].q If you will cross-question him yourself, you will be able to discover on what counts we accuse him."

9And all the Jews agreed and declared that all that he said was so. 10Then, at a motion from the governor, Paul made his answer:

11"Because I know that you have been judge over these people for many years, I find it easier to defend myself against these charges. It will be possible for you to ascertain that it is not more than twelve days since I went up to Jerusalem to worship, 12and neither did they find me arguing with anyone in the temple, nor raising a riot among the people, either in the synagogues or in the city. 13Neither can they produce any evidence to substantiate these charges.

14"I confess this to you, however, that according to the Way which they call heresy,r even so I worship the God of my fathers, believing in everything written in the Law and the Prophets; 15for I possess that hope in God which these men themselves hold as their own, that there is to be a resurrection of the just and unjust. 16And so I exert myself always to have a clear conscience in my relations with God and with men.

17"After many years I came to bring to my people alms and offerings, 18and while I was doing this they found me in the temple after I had completed the ceremony of purification — not at all with mobs or riots. 19But there were some Jews from Asia who should have been here to complain if they knew anything tangible against me. 20Or else let these men here say what wrong they found in me as I stood before the Sanhedrin, 21unless it is that one remark I expressed in their presence, 'I am being tried by you today concerning the resurrection of the dead.'"

22Since Felix understood the teachings of the Way quite well, he adjourned the case and said, "When the commander, Lysias, comes down I shall decide your case." 23He then gave orders to the captain to have Paul guarded, but with relaxed rigor, and that none of his friends should be prevented from rendering aid to him.s

c. A.D. 59

24After a few days, when Felix was present with his wife Drusilla, a Jewess, he sent for Paul and listened to him concerning faith in Christ Jesus. 25But as he discussed righteousness, the mastery of passions, and the coming judgment, Felix got frightened and responded, "You may go for now. When I can spare the time I will send for

---

p) In quarters reserved for prisoners.
q) The words in vss. 6-8 that are enclosed in brackets are not found in the majority of the most reliable ancient manuscripts.
r) The heresy was on the other side, for it was the Sadducees who were heretical in repudiating God's power to raise the dead.
s) Among Paul's friends in Caesarea were Philip and his family, ch. 21:8, 9.

you." 26Meanwhile he was hoping he might obtain money from Paul; so he summoned him frequently and talked things over with him. 27But after two years had gone by, Felix was succeeded by Portius Festus[t] and, to curry favor with the Jews, Felix left Paul imprisoned.

c. A.D. 60

25 THREE DAYS AFTER HE HAD ARrived in the province Festus went up from Caesarea to Jerusalem. 2The chief priests and the most prominent Jews appeared before him against Paul 3and requested of him and begged it as a favor to them that Paul be sent to Jerusalem — they planning to form an ambush and to murder him on the road.

4Festus replied that Paul was under guard at Caesarea, and that he himself would shortly go there. 5"Then," he went on, "those who are prominent among you may come along with me, and if the man has done anything wrong, bring your charges against him."

6After spending at the most from eight to ten days among them, he went down to Caesarea, took his seat the next day on the tribunal and ordered Paul to be brought in. 7At his arrival the Jews who had come down from Jerusalem stood around him and presented their charges — numerous and weighty, which they were not able to substantiate. 8Then Paul made his defense: "I have committed nothing wrong either against the Jewish Law, or against the temple, or against Caesar."

9Festus, however, desirous to curry favor with the Jews, answered Paul, "Are you willing to go up to Jerusalem and there be tried before me on these charges?" 10But Paul said, "I am standing at Caesar's tribunal, where I ought to be tried. I have in no respect wronged the Jews, as you understood well enough. 11In case I am guilty and have committed anything deserving death, then I am ready to die; but if there is nothing to their charges against me, then no one can surrender me to them. I make my appeal to Caesar." 12So, after conference with the council, Festus answered, "You have appealed to Caesar; to Caesar you shall go."

13When a few days had passed, King Agrippa and Bernice[u] arrived at Caesarea to bid Festus welcome; 14and after they had spent a good many days there, Festus acquainted the king with Paul's situation: "There is a prisoner left here by Felix, 15concerning whom, when I came to Jerusalem, the chief priests and the elders of the Jews made their appearance requesting sentence against him. 16I answered them that with Romans it is not customary to hand a man over until the accused has faced his accusers and has been given an opportunity to defend himself against the charges. 17So, when they assembled here, I lost no time in occupying the judgment seat on the next day, and I ordered the man brought in. 18When his accusers stood up they brought in no criminal charges against him such as I expected; 19but they had some controversies against him that concerned their own religion and a certain Jesus who had died, whom Paul asserted to be alive. 20As I felt uncertain about the proper investigation of such issues, I asked if he would be willing to go to Jerusalem and be tried there on these complaints; 21but

---

t) Portius Festus was the successor of Felix as procurator of Judea, taking office about A.D. 60. He did not have an easy time during his procuratorship, but his term of office was in favorable contrast with that of Felix. Festus reinvestigated Paul's case and was ready to try him in Jerusalem, but the apostle made an appeal to be tried before Caesar and this released Festus from any further obligation in the matter, ch. 25:20, 21.

u) King Herod (Herod Agrippa II) was the grandson of Herod the Great and son of Herod Agrippa I, whose oldest daughter was Bernice. Thus Bernice was the sister of King Herod. At one time she had been married to an uncle who was ruler of Chalcis; but he died and she came to live with her brother. There was some scandal about the brother-sister relationship. Later she became the mistress of Vespasian. Drusilla, the wife of Felix, 24:24, was also a daughter of Herod Agrippa I and therefore the sister of King Herod and Bernice.

since Paul appealed that his case be retained for a decision by Augustus,[v] I ordered him to be held until I send him on to Caesar."

22And Agrippa said to Festus, "I should like to hear the man myself." He replied, "Tomorrow you will hear him."

23Accordingly, on the following day Agrippa and Bernice arrived with great display and, accompanied by the chief military men and the prominent citizens of the city, entered the audience hall. At Festus' order Paul was led in 24and Festus said: "King Agrippa and all you men here present with us, you are looking at the person on whose account the whole constituency of the Jews have made complaint to me both in Jerusalem and here, shouting that he ought not to live any more. 25But I discovered nothing he has done that deserves death, and since he appealed to the emperor, I have decided to send him. 26I have nothing substantial to write His Majesty, and for this reason I have brought him before you, and particularly before you, King Agrippa, so that after due examination I may have something to report. 27For it seems to me odd to send on a prisoner without signifying the charges against him."

26 AGRIPPA SAID TO PAUL, "You are permitted to speak on your own behalf."[w] Then Paul extended his hand and made his defense:

2"Concerning all the charges against me by the Jews, I consider myself fortunate, O King Agrippa, that I am to defend myself before you; 3for you are thoroughly familiar with all the Jewish customs and problems. So, please listen to me with patience.

4"All the Jews are acquainted with my behavior from my youth up, both among my own people[x] and in Jerusalem. 5They are fully aware, if only they were willing to bear witness, how from the very first I have lived as a Pharisee in agreement with the strictest sect of our religion. 6And right now I am standing trial for the hope of the promise which God made to our fathers 7and which our twelve tribes expect to realize as they worship night and day. For this very hope, O King, I am accused by the Jews.

8"What? Is it considered incredible among you that God raises the dead? 9The fact is that I was possessed of the idea that I should in every way oppose the name of Jesus the Nazarene, 10and so I did in Jerusalem. Many a saint[y] have I shut up in prison, furnished as I was with authority from the chief priests; and when they were executed I cast my vote against them.[z] 11In all the synagogues I often forced them by torture to deny their religion. Yes, in my boundless rage against them I persecuted them as far as foreign cities.

12"With the authority and approval of the chief priests I was traveling to Damascus[a] for this purpose, 13when on the road at noon I saw, O King, a light from heaven, more brilliant than the sun, shining around me and my fellow travelers. 14And when we all fell to the ground I heard a voice saying to me in the Hebrew language, 'Saul, Saul, why do you persecute Me? It is hard for you to kick against the goads.'[b] 15But I said, 'Who are You, Lord?' And the Lord said, 'I am Jesus whom you are persecuting. 16But rise and stand on your feet; for I have appeared to you for this purpose, to appoint you a minister and witness both

---

v) Augustus was the personal name of the first Roman emperor, Augustus Caesar, Luke 2:1. He died in A.D. 14. The emperor at the time of Paul's defense was Nero, the fifth Roman emperor. The name Augustus was sometimes used for others of the Caesars.
w) Agrippa had no authority over Festus.
x) Paul's own people in Tarsus.
y) See note at ch. 9:13.
z) There are two views of Paul's reference to casting a vote for the execution of Christians prior to his own conversion to Christianity: (1) if his words are taken at face value, then he belonged to the Sanhedrin at that time; or (2) the reference may be a figurative expression of his opposition to Christians. The first interpretation seems more logical than the second. Since membership in the Sanhedrin was limited to married men, if Paul did cast his vote in the council he was a married man at the time.
a) See note at ch. 9:2.
b) A goad is a pointed rod used to urge a beast to move.

of the things that you have seen and of those in which I will still show Myself to you. [17]I will deliver you from your people and from the Gentiles, to whom I am sending you [18]for the opening of their eyes and their turning from darkness to light and from the authority of Satan to God, to obtain forgiveness of sins and their allotted portion among those made holy through faith in Me.'

[19]"Therefore, O King Agrippa, I was not disobedient to the heavenly vision, [20]but first to those in Damascus and in Jerusalem, and then all over Judea and among the Gentiles I preached that they must repent and turn to God and do works consistent with repentance.

[21]"For this reason the Jews seized me in the temple and tried to kill me. [22]So, as I have enjoyed the help of God until this day, I take my stand witnessing to both small and great, without saying anything, however, except what the prophets and Moses said would take place — [23]that the Christ was to suffer, and that He, as the first to rise from the dead, would proclaim light to our people and to the Gentiles."

[24]As he was thus making his defense, Festus called out loudly, "You are raving, Paul; your excessive study is driving you mad." [25]But Paul replied, "Most illustrious Festus, I am not mad but am giving utterance to words of truth and sane thinking. [26]The king knows about these matters, to whom I speak freely. I do not believe any of these things are unknown to him, for they have not occurred in a corner. [27]King Agrippa, do you believe the prophets? I know you believe."

[28]Agrippa turned to Paul, "You with a few words are trying to persuade me to be a Christian?" [29]Then Paul said, "I would pray to God that whether with a few words or with many not you alone but all who are now listening to me today might be in my condition — not including these shackles."

[30]The king then stood up, and the governor and Bernice and those who had been sitting with them [31]and, stepping to one side, they talked it over together and concluded, "This man has done nothing that deserves death or prison." [32]So Agrippa said to Festus, "This man could have been set free, if he had not appealed to Caesar."

27 WHEN IT WAS DECIDED THAT we should sail for Italy, they committed Paul and some other prisoners to a captain of the Augustan Cohort,[c] whose name was Julius. [2]Getting aboard an Adramyttiun ship that would make the ports along the coast of Asia, we sailed away, and Aristarchus,[d] a Macedonian of Thessalonica, was with us. [3]The next day we docked at Sidon,[e] where Julius, treating Paul kindly, allowed him to visit his friends and to be cared for.

[4]Putting to sea[f] from there we sailed along the south coast of Cyprus, because the winds were contrary; [5]then crossing the Cilician and Pamphylian waters, we landed at Myra in Lycia. [6]The captain found there an Alexandrian ship bound for Italy, and he transferred us to her. [7]After many days of slow sailing we arrived with difficulty off Cnidus; then, checked by the wind, we sailed south of Crete off Salmone, [8]and with difficulty coasted along it and reached a place called Fair Havens, near which the city of Lasea is located.

[9]As much time had been lost and navigation had grown dangerous — for the autumn fast was already over[g] — Paul warned them, [10]"Men, I discern that this voyage will involve damage and considerable loss not merely to the cargo and the ship but to our lives as well." [11]However, the centurion put confidence in the pilot and in the shipowner, rather than in Paul's words, [12]and because the harbor was poorly

---

c) See note at ch. 10:1.
d) Aristarchus appears to have been one of Paul's closest associates, chs. 19:29; 20:4, 6; Col. 4:10.
e) See note at Matt. 11:21.
f) This chapter is an illuminating source of information about seamanship in the first century.
g) That is, the Day of Atonement, celebrated early in October.

situated for wintering, the majority favored the plan of setting out again, so that they might possibly reach Phoenix, a harbor in Crete facing southwest and northwest, and winter there.

13With a light south wind coming up, they supposed that they were gaining their purpose, weighed anchor and ran close along the shore of Crete. 14But shortly after, a hurricane, known as a northeaster, came beating from the island, 15in which the ship was caught; so, unable to head against the wind, we gave way and were driven. 16Running under the lee of a small island called Clauda, we made the small boat secure only with the greatest difficulty 17and, having hoisted it, they undergirded the ship with ropes. Out of fear of being stranded on the Syrtis banks, they lowered the gear and so were driven. 18The next day, dangerously driven about as we were by the storm, they threw the cargo overboard 19and on the third day with their own hands they cast away the ship's tackle. 20For many days neither sun nor stars appeared; the storm kept raging strongly, so that the last vestige of hope of our being saved was snatched away. 21As they had gone without food for a long time, Paul stood among them and said, "Men, you should have listened to me and so spared yourselves this damage and loss, and not have put to sea from Crete. 22Even now I advise you to cheer up; for not a single person among you will perish — only the ship. 23For this night there stood by me an angel of God, whose I am and whom I serve. 24He said, 'Have no fear, Paul. You have to stand before Caesar, and be assured that God has granted you all that are sailing with you.' 25Therefore, be of good spirits, men; for I have faith in God that it will happen in accord with what was told me. 26But we have to be stranded on an island."

27On the fourteenth night of our drifting up and down the Adriatic,h

the sailors surmised at about midnight that they were bearing toward some shore; 28so, taking soundings, they found twenty fathoms, and at a little distance when they sounded again, they found fiteen fathoms.i 29Then, for fear that we might run aground on submerged rocks, they cast four anchors from the stern and longed for break of day.

30The sailors, however, tried to abandon the ship and, under pretense of going to cast anchor from the prow, they lowered the lifeboat into the sea; 31so Paul told the officer and the soldiers, "If these do not stay with the ship, you cannot be saved." 32Then the soldiers cut the boat's ropes and let her fall.

33With daybreak approaching, Paul urged them all to take some food. He said, "For fourteen days now you have been waiting expectantly without taking anything, 34so I implore you to eat something; it is necessary for your safety. For not a hair of your head will perish."

35Having said this, he took bread, gave thanks to God in the presence of them all and, breaking it, began to eat. 36Then they all were encouraged and partook of nourishment, — 37all told there were two hundred seventy-six of us on board.

38When they had eaten to their satisfaction, they lightened the ship by dumping the wheat into the sea. 39When day arrived, they did not recognize the coast, but they noticed an inlet with a beach into which they decided, if at all possible, to run the ship. 40After casting off the anchors and dropping them in the sea and meanwhile loosening the ropes that held the rudders, they hoisted the foresail to the wind and made for the beach. 41But as they hit a shoal where two seas met they grounded the ship; and the prow settled and stayed immovable, while the stern broke up under the force of the elements.

42It was then the soldiers' idea to

---

h) This was in the Ionian Sea which is south of what is now called the Adriatic Sea.
i) A fathom is approximately six feet.

kill the prisoners, so that they might not swim away and escape; [43]but the officer, wishing to save Paul, prevented their doing it. He ordered those who could swim to leap overboard first and make for shore, [44]and the rest to follow, some on boards and some on fragments of the ship. And so they all reached shore safely.

28 WHEN WE HAD ESCAPED, WE learned that the island was called Malta. [2]The natives showed us remarkable friendliness, for they lit a fire and welcomed all of us to it because of the rain that had set in and because of the cold. [3]When Paul had gathered a bundle of twigs and laid them on the fire, a viper crawled out on account of the heat and fastened to his hand. [4]When the natives observed the creature hanging from his hand, they remarked to each other, "Unquestionably this man is a murderer whom, though saved from the sea, Justice[j] will not allow to live." [5]But he simply shook off the creature into the fire and felt no hurt. [6]They, of course, expected him at any moment either to swell up or fall suddenly dead; so, after waiting for a long time and seeing nothing out of the way happen to him, they changed their minds and said, "He is a god."

c. A.D. 61

[7]Now in that part of the island there were pieces of land that belonged to the chief of the island, a man named Publius, who took us in and for three days entertained us courteously. [8]It so happened that Publius' father was laid up with fever and dysentery; so Paul went to visit him and, laying hands on him with prayer, he healed him. [9]When this had occurred, the rest of the islanders who had diseases came

and were healed. [10]They also showed us every kind of respect, and when we left they supplied all our needs.

[11]At the end of three months we put to sea in an Alexandrian ship, that had wintered in the island and had for her figurehead Castor and Pollux.[k] [12]We docked at Syracuse and tarried three days. [13]Then we tacked around and arrived at Rhegium. After one day a south wind came up and the following day we landed at Puteoli. [14]There we found some brothers and were invited to stay with them for seven days.

[15]Then we went on to Rome, and when the brothers there heard about us they came as far as the Market of Appius[l] and Three Taverns[m] to meet us. As soon as Paul saw them, he gave thanks to God and took courage.

[16]When we arrived in Rome [the officer delivered the prisoners to the captain of the guard; but][n] Paul was allowed to live by himself with a soldier to guard him.

[17]After three days he invited all the leading Jews to whom, when they gathered, he said, "Brothers, although I have committed nothing whatever against our people or against our fathers' customs, yet I was delivered to the Romans, a prisoner from Jerusalem. [18]Upon examination they wanted to set me free, because I am innocent of any act that deserves death; [19]but when the Jews objected, I was forced to appeal to Caesar—although I had no charge to bring against my nation. [20]For this reason I begged to see you and to talk to you. It is because of Israel's hope that I wear this encircling chain."

[21]They replied to him, "Neither have we received letters from Judea about you, nor have any of the brothers arrived with a bad report or any gossip about you. [22]But we desire to

---

j) "Justice" is here personified as a goddess. The Maltese, a mixture of Greeks, Romans, Carthaginians and Phoenicians, were a people of many cultures.
k) The text reads "the Dioscuri," from the Greek noun *Dioskouroi* meaning *Twin Sons,* the mythical children of Zeus and Leda. As a figurehead for this Alexandrian ship they were her patron deities.
l) The market place at Appius, a town situated about 43 miles from Rome, was known as the Appii Forum.
m) The Three Taverns was an inn that was evidently a travelers' way station. It was approximately 25 miles from Rome.
n) The words enclosed in brackets are not found in the majority of the most reliable ancient manuscripts.

hear from you what you have in mind; for so far as this heresy is concerned, we know that it is denounced everywhere."

23Arranging a date with him, they came to him at his lodging in large numbers, and he explained the matter to them from morning until evening, bearing witness about the kingdom of God, attempting to persuade them about Jesus, both out of the Law of Moses and from the Prophets. 24Some, indeed, were convinced by the things that he said, but others did not believe. 25So, since there was no agreement among them, they left when Paul spoke this one utterance. "The Holy Spirit spoke rightly to your fathers through Isaiah the prophet,o 26'Go to this people and say, "You will hear with your ears but will not catch the meaning. You will look with your eyes but will not see. 27For this people's heart is calloused and their ears are dull of hearing, and they have closed their eyes, so they may not see with their eyes and hear with their ears and understand with the hearts and turn about and I should heal them." ' 28Let it be clearly understood, then, that this salvation of God is sent to the Gentiles and they will listen."

29[After he had said this, the Jews went away and had considerable discussion among themselves.]p

30Paul remained for two whole years in his rented lodging and welcomed everyone who came to see him. 31He preached the kingdom of God and taught regarding the Lord Jesus Christ altogether openly and without hindrance.

o) Isa. 6:9, 10. Rejection reflected on them, not on the message.
p) Verse 29, enclosed in brackets, is not found in the majority of the most reliable ancient manuscripts.

THEME OF ACTS:

SEGMENT DIVISIONS

			CHAPTER THEMES
			1
			2
			3
			4
			5
			6
			7
			8
			9
			10
			11
			12
			13
			14
			15
			16
			17
			18
			19
			20
			21
			22
			23
			24
			25
			26
			27
			28

Author:

Date:

Purpose:

Key Words:

believe
(believed)

baptized
(baptism)

Spirit

witness
(witnesses)

word
(word of God)

saved

church

ROMANS

The gospel Paul preached, justification by faith alone, was under siege. While many directly opposed this gospel, others twisted it to suit their own preferences. The Judaizers said salvation might be by grace but the believer is "kept" by the law. They insisted that circumcision was necessary for salvation. At the other extreme, the antinomians taught that you could be saved by grace and still live any way you wanted—even continue in sin.

Only a clear explanation of the gospel could refute such errors. Eager to prove the gospel's power to save and sanctify both Jew and Gentile, Paul, like a wise lawyer, calls the gospel to the witness stand and examines it from every angle. The result is the book of Romans, a theological masterpiece written around A.D. 56 or 57.

THINGS TO DO

1. Romans is the constitution of the Christian faith. If you understand Romans you will have a plumb line for correctly interpreting any teaching on the gospel. It is a book you need to observe until you are so familiar with the text that its meaning is obvious.

    a. Read Romans in one sitting before you begin your study. If that is not possible, read it a chapter at a time. Every time you see the word *gospel (good news)*, mark it in a distinctive way so you can easily spot it in the text.

    b. Paul gives his reasons for writing Romans in the first and the last two chapters. Record these reasons in the appropriate place on the ROMANS OBSERVATIONS CHART following Romans.

    c. Watch for references to the recipients of this letter and record on the OBSERVATIONS CHART what you learn about them. Note whether Paul is writing to Gentiles, Jews, or both. Also as you read, find out as much as you can about Paul. Record your insights on the chart.

2. The book of Romans can be divided into four segments, each building on the previous one: chapters 1 through 5, 6 through 8, 9 through 11, and 12 through 16. Instructions for each segment follow. As you complete each one, return to these general instructions so you can see what else you are to do in each segment.

Chapters 1–5

1. Read Romans 1 through 5 a chapter at a time, observing and marking the text. Complete instructions on how to observe the text are in the observation section in the introductory pages of this New Testament.

    a. Mark each of the following key words and their synonyms: *grace, faith, law, justified (pronounce or make righteous, vindicate), righteous (righteousness), wrath (indignation, anger), judge (judgment), gospel (good news), believe (believers), sin, Gentiles,*

God, Jesus Christ, and *Spirit.*

    b. List these words on an index card to use as a bookmark when you study Romans. As you come to each new segment of Romans, add the next group of key words to your card. Mark or color code them on the card in the same way you plan to mark them in your Bible.

    c. Each chapter has key words or phrases which are unique to that chapter. Mark the following:

      1) In chapter 1 mark *altered* and *God gave them up (abandoned).* Note the progression of events as you observe what the people did and how God responded.

      2) In chapter 4 mark and observe *accounted.*

      3) In chapter 5 mark and observe *gift.*

      4) Mark any other key words that are pertinent to a chapter or to the book.

2. List in the margin what you learn from the text about each key word. For example, *sin* is a key word. What do you learn from the text about *sin*? About *wrath*? About *righteousness*? And so on.

3. From chapters 3 through 11 of Romans, Paul periodically asks an important question and then answers it. Mark each of Paul's questions. You might put a cloud like this around each question throughout the book. Carefully read each question and note how Paul answers it.

4. Watch for the word *therefore (then, so, since, for this reason)* and see what it is "there for." When Paul uses *therefore* he is making a point you will not want to miss.

5. When you finish observing each chap-

ter, record the theme of that chapter in the text just above the chapter number and on the ROMANS AT A GLANCE chart following Romans.

6. What do you see as the theme in this first segment of Romans? Write it (in pencil) on ROMANS AT A GLANCE in the first column under "Segment Divisions."

Chapters 6–8

1. Follow the same procedure as you did in the previous segment. Continue to mark the key words you marked in chapters 1 through 5, and in these chapters also mark the following words and their synonyms: *flesh (fleshly, human, human nature, earthly way), dead (died, death), life, reign (king), lordship (master), slave,* and *deliverance from sin (freed from sin).*

2. If it is significant, list in the margin what you learn from marking the prominent key words in this segment of Romans.

3. Mark Paul's questions and in the margin list the main points of his answers.

4. Record the theme of each chapter and of this segment as you did before.

5. On the ROMANS OBSERVATIONS CHART is a place to record everything you learn from chapters 5 through 8 regarding our position in Adam (before we were saved) and our position in Christ (after we were saved). Do not read anything into the text, but simply record what you learn.

Chapters 9–11

1. Follow the same pattern you used in the first segment and mark the same key words you marked in chapters 1 through 8. Also mark the following key words in this segment of Romans: *knew beforehand,* appointed*

beforehand,* choice (chosen, election), Israel (and its pronouns), unbelief (lack of faith, disobedience) saved (salvation—go back and mark it in Romans 1:16), and mercy.

*These words are used in Romans 8:29, 30. Go back and mark them, and in the margin note what you learn from the text.

2. In this section it is critical that you follow Paul's reasoning by marking each question and then listing in the margin the main points of Paul's answers. Do not read into the text meanings that aren't there. Let God speak as you listen. Meditate on Romans 11:33-36.

3. Record chapter and segment themes as before.

Chapters 12–16

1. At this point Paul makes a transition and changes from explaining the doctrinal aspect of the gospel to describing how to live it out practically. As Paul turns from doctrine to duty, note the *therefore* and how it would relate to what has been written in the first eleven chapters of Romans. Think about what Paul is asking you to do. Is it reasonable? Why? What do you need to do?

2. Read Romans chapters 12 through 16 and identify the main topic or subject of each chapter. Mark the following key words: *love, authority (magistrates), brethren (brother), Lord, Gentiles, minister (service, serving, servant), judge (feel contempt, find fault, censure),* and *weak (weaker).*

3. Complete ROMANS AT A GLANCE. Fill in the chapter themes and segment divisions and then record the theme of Romans. (Do not forget to record your chapter themes in the text, too.)

THINGS TO THINK ABOUT

1. Suppose someone accused you of not being a Christian. What proof could you give of the fact that you are a true child of God?

2. Do you know how to share the gospel with someone? How?

3. From your study of Romans, how is a person saved?

4. How will your relationships to those in authority over you and to those who are your brothers and sisters in the faith change as you apply the truth of Romans to your life?

5. Are you ready to defend the gospel? Can you refute modern-day Judaizers and/or antinomians?

THE EPISTLE OF PAUL TO THE

ROMANS

1 PAUL, A SLAVE[a] OF CHRIST JESUS, called to be an apostle, set apart for the good news from God, [2]which He promised in advance through His prophets in the sacred Scriptures [3]regarding His Son who, as to His human nature was descended from David and according to the Spirit of holiness [4]was openly designated as the Son of God with power when He was raised from the dead, even Jesus Christ, our Lord, [5]through whom we have received grace and apostleship, to promote among all the Gentiles in behalf of His name obedience to the message of faith, [6]among whom you also are included as those who have been invited by Jesus Christ; [7]to all God's loved ones in Rome, called to be saints:[b] Grace to you and peace from God our Father and the Lord Jesus Christ.

[8]To begin with, I certainly thank my God for all of you through Jesus Christ, because your faith is being mentioned all over the world. [9]For God, whom I serve with my spiritual self in the good news concerning His Son, bears me witness how constantly I mention you whenever I am at my prayers, [10]pleading that somehow by the will of God, I may some day be sped on my way to visit you. [11]For I am yearning to see you, so that I may bestow on you some spiritual gift for your confirmation — [12]I mean that we may be mutually strengthened by your faith and mine.

[13]But I do not want you to be unaware, brothers, that often I have planned to visit you, so that I might reap some harvest among you, just as I have among the other Gentiles, but thus far I have been prevented. [14]To both Greeks[c] and barbarians,[d] to both learned and unlearned I am a debtor; [15]so I am eager to preach the gospel to you in Rome as well. [16]For I am not ashamed of the good news; for it is God's power for salvation[e] to every believer, to the Jew first and to the Greek also. [17]For God's righteousness is disclosed in it through faith and leading to faith, as it is written,[f] "The one who is righteous through faith will live."

[18]On the other hand, God's indignation is revealed from heaven against all impiety and wickedness of men who through their wicked ways suppress the truth; [19]because whatever can be known regarding God is evident to

a) Greek *doulos*. See note at Matt. 13:27.
b) See note at Acts 9:13.
c) "Greeks" here is a broad term for all who had come under the influence of Hellenistic culture, including the Romans who had absorbed it; "barbarians" refers to all non-Greeks, i.e., foreigners. Together the two terms cover, according to the Greek point of view, the entire human race. To the Greeks all other people were barbarians; to the Jews all others were considered Gentiles. Elsewhere, I Cor. 1:23, 24, Paul classifies humanity as Greeks (Gentiles), Jews, and "the called," i.e., Christians ("both Jews and Greeks").
d) Compare Acts 28:2.
e) The word "salvation," when used in the Bible in a spiritual sense, embraces many facets of God's redemptive work, e.g. forgiveness, justification, propitiation, and redemption. Salvation is always the work of God in man; it is given to man by divine grace and through faith in the Son of God. Works that are pleasing to God follow faith in Him, Eph. 2:8-10.
f) Hab. 2:4; Gal. 3:11; Heb. 10:38.

them, for God has shown it to them. [20]From the creation of the world His invisible qualities, such as His eternal power and divine nature, have been made visible and have been understood through His handiwork. So they are without excuse. [21]Because, although they had knowledge of God, they failed to render Him the praise and thanks due to God. Instead, they indulged in their speculations until their stupid minds were all in the dark. [22]Claiming to be wise, they became foolish. [23]They even altered the glory of the immortal God into images in the form of mortal man and of birds, quadrupeds and reptiles.

[24]Therefore God gave them up[g] in the desires of their hearts to such impurity as dishonored their own bodies, [25]since they altered God's truth into falsehood, and revered and served the creature rather than the Creator, who is blessed forever. Amen.

[26]For this reason God abandoned them to shameful passions. Their women perverted natural functions for unnatural, [27]and similarly the men forsook their natural relationships with women and burned up with their lust for one another, men committing shamelessness with men and so acquiring in their persons the penalty that was coming to them on account of their wrong behavior. [28]Just as they did not see fit to acknowledge God any more, so God gave them over to depraved thoughts, to practice what is not decent, [29]because they have been filled with every sort of wickedness, immorality, depravity and greed; crammed with envy, murder, quarreling, deceit and malignity; [30]as gossips, slanderers, God-haters; insolent, proud, and boastful; inventors of evil; disobedient to parents; [31]without conscience, fidelity, natural affection or pity. [32]While knowing God's ordinance, that those practicing such things deserve death, they not only practice them but even give their approval to those who do them.

2 YOU CAN OFFER NO EXCUSE, O man,[h] whoever indulges in judging; for by passing judgment on another you condemn yourself, since you, who are passing judgment practice the same things. [2]We know that God's judgment rightly falls on those who practice such wrongs. [3]But do you imagine, O man, who condemn those practicing such evils and do them yourself, that you will escape God's judgment? [4]Or do you underestimate His wealth of kindness and tolerance and enduring patience, unmindful that God's kindness is meant to lead you toward repentance?

[5]But in line with your obstinacy and impenitence of heart you are treasuring up for yourself anger for the day of anger and the revealing of the righteous judgment of God, [6]who will reward each person according to his deeds.[i] [7]To those who with insistent good behavior seek glory, honor, and immortality, He awards eternal life; [8]but to those who are factious and disobedient to the truth but rather are obedient to wickedness, He awards indignation and fury. [9]Affliction and anxiety will be given to every human soul who does evil, to the Jew first and to the Greek as well. [10]But distinction and honor and peace will be given to all who do what is good, to the Jew first and to the Greek as well. [11]For God shows no favoritism.

[12]Those who sin without knowing the Law[j] will be lost without reference to the Law; while those who sin under the Law will be judged by the Law. [13]For not the hearers of the Law are righteous before God, but those who practice the Law will be pronounced righteous. [14]For when Gentiles who lack the Law do naturally practice it, they are for themselves a law, though they have none. [15]They

---

g) All divine restraint of evil seems to have been removed. *Cf.* vss. 26, 28.
h) The reference is to Gentiles and Jews, all who might read the epistle.
i) In this chapter Paul expresses the basic principles of God's impartial judgment, vs. 11. Here, vss. 6-8, he is not dealing with justification by faith, which he expounds specifically in chs. 3:21-5:21, but with God's general system of moral government.
j) The Law revealed through Moses, particularly the Decalogue, Exod. 20:1-17.

show that what the Law requires is written in their hearts, while their conscience also bears witness and their thoughts accuse or defend one another. [16]They will be judged on that day when God will judge the secrets of men through Christ Jesus in agreement with the good news I preach.

[17]But if you are termed a Jew and you rely on the Law and pride yourself in God [18]and know His will, and approve the things that really matter, because you have been instructed from the Law, [19]and you are convinced that you are a guide to the blind, a light to those who are in darkness, a trainer of the simple, [20]a teacher of the ignorant, since you possess in the Law the embodiment of knowledge and truth; [21]then, you who teach another, do you not teach yourself? You who preach against stealing, do you steal? [22]You who forbid adultery, do you commit adultery? You who detest idols, do you commit sacrilege?[k] [23]You who boast in the Law, do you dishonor God by its violation? [24]For "God's name," as has been written,[l] "is on your account maligned among the Gentiles."

[25]Circumcision, then, benefits only if you obey[m] the Law; but if you are a violator of the Law, then your circumcision becomes uncircumcision. [26]So, if the uncircumcised man observes the requirements of the Law, [27]will not his uncircumcision be accounted to him as circumcision? In fact, the physically uncircumcised, who carries out the Law, will judge you who, although you have the literally correct form of the Law and are circumcised, break the Law.

[28]For neither is one a Jew from his looks, nor is circumcision what shows in the body; [29]but a Jew is a Jew deep in his heart, and so circumcision is a matter of the heart, a spiritual observance rather than a mere literal observance of the Law. Such a person's praise[n] comes not from men but from God.

3 THEN WHAT ADVANTAGE HAS THE Jew, or what benefit has circumcision? [2]Considerable in every respect. Primarily, because they were entrusted with the utterances of God. [3]What if some failed to believe? Their unbelief surely does not nullify God's faithfulness, does it? [4]Not at all. Rather shall it be: God must be true though every man is a liar, as it is written,[o] "That You might be vindicated in Your sayings and might triumph when You are tried." [5]But if our wrongdoing brings out so strikingly the righteousness of God, what shall we say? Surely not that God is wrong — I speak humanly — when He inflicts punishment? [6]No indeed! Then how could God judge the world? [7]But if by my falsehood the truth of God abounds the more for His glory, then why am I condemned as a sinner? [8]Why not say then, just as by some we are being slandered and charged with saying, "Let us do evil, so that good may result"? Deservedly are such talkers condemned.

[9]Then what? Do we Jews have an advantage over the Gentiles? Not at all. For we have already charged both Jews and Greeks that they are all under sin's power, [10]as it is written,[p] "There is none righteous; not even one. [11]No one has understanding; no one is a searcher after God. [12]All have strayed; they have together become worthless. There is none doing right, not even one. [13]Their throats are open graves; with their tongues they deceive; venom of asps is behind their lips; [14]their mouths are full of cursing and bitterness. [15]Their feet are swift for shedding blood; [16]ruin and misery are in their ways [17]and they have not known the path of peace. [18]There is no reverence for God before their eyes."

[19]Now we know that whatever the Law says, it says to those who are under its control, so that every mouth may be shut and the whole world may become liable to divine retribution;

k) Not all, but some Jews, were guilty of such sins — witness the need of temple cleansing.
l) Isa. 52:5; Ezek. 36:20.
m) Obedience to the Law is to do the will of God.
n) "Jew," named for Judah, means *praise*, and Paul seems to play on the word.
o) Ps. 51:4.
p) Ps. 5:9; 10:7; 14:1-3; 36:1; 140:3; Prov. 1:16; Isa. 59:7.

20because not a single human being will be made righteous in God's sight through observance of the Law.q For through the Law comes the knowledge of sin.

21But now apart from the Law God's righteousness is revealed, as is witnessed to by the Law and the Prophets, 22namely, God's righteousness through faith in Jesus Christ for all believers. For there is no distinction, 23for all have sinned and fall short of God's moral excellence. 24We are justified freely by His grace through the ransom that Christ Jesus provided; 25whom God put forward as a reconciling sacrifice through faith in His blood. This was for the vindication of His righteousness in forgiving the sins that previously were committed under God's forbearance, 26and to vindicate His righteousness at the present time, that He is righteous and that He accepts as righteous him that has faith in Jesus.

27Where, then, does boasting come in? It is ruled out. Through what sort of law? Of works? No, indeed, but through the law of faith. 28For we come to the conclusion that a man is justified by faith without the works of the Law. 29Or is He God of the Jews only? Is He not also the God of the Gentiles? He is the Gentiles' God as well. 30Since there is but one God, He will justify the circumcised for their belief and the uncircumcised through their faith.

31Do we, then, abrogate the Law through faith? Not at all; instead, we uphold the Law.r

4 WHAT SHALL WE SAY, THEN, THAT Abraham, our human ancestor, has discovered? 2For if Abraham was justified on account of works, then he has something to brag about. But not before God; 3for what does Scripture say?s "Abraham believed God, and it was accounted to him for righteousness." 4Now, to a workman wages are not paid as a favor but as an obligation; 5while to the person who does not work by Law, but whose faith rests on Him who declares the ungodly righteous, to him his faith is accounted for righteousness.t 6Precisely as David mentionsu the blessedness of the man to whom God attributes righteousness apart from his works: 7"Blessed are they whose iniquities have been forgiven and whose sins have been covered. 8Blessed is the man of whose sin the Lord will take no account."

9Now, then, does this ascription of blessedness apply only to the circumcised, or to the uncircumcised as well? For this is our statement: Faith was accounted to Abraham for righteousness. 10Then how was it accounted? When he was circumcised, or when he was still uncircumcised? Not after, but before his circumcision; 11and he received the mark of circumcision as a seal of the righteousness of the faith which he had while he was still uncircumcised, so that he might be the father of all uncircumcised believers, that to them righteousness might be accounted, 12and also the father of those circumcised who are not merely circumcised but walk in the footsteps of the faith our father Abraham had when he was still uncircumcised.v

13The promise to Abraham or to his offspring to inherit the earth did not come through the Law but through righteousness because of faith; 14for if followers of the Law are the inheritors, then faith is futile and the promise is abrogated. 15Because the Law brings about wrath, but where there is no Law there is no transgression.

16For this reason it is a matter of faith, so that the promise may be made sure as a matter of grace to all his descendants; not only to the followers of the Law but also to those

---

q) The Law reveals sin but neither blots it out nor cleanses the sinner.
r) The righteous demands of the Law are revealed most clearly in Christ's death for sin.
s) Gen. 15:6.
t) James uses Abraham's obedience in offering Isaac as a sacrifice in illustration of how faith and works are harmonized in the believer's life, James 2:21-24; *cf.* Gen. 22:1-14.
u) Ps. 32:2.
v) Abraham demonstrated his faith by his works after the institution of circumcision, Gen. 17:10, but he believed God before that, Gen. 12:4. Thus Abraham became the father of all nations, and all believers are his spiritual descendants.

who share Abraham's faith, who is thus father to us all, [17]as it is written,[w] "I have appointed you a father of many nations" — all this in the presence of God, in whom he believed, who makes the dead live and calls into existence what has no being. [18]For Abraham kept hoping in faith, when hope was gone, that he would be the father of many nations, just as he had been told,[x] "So shall your offspring be." [19]And there was no weakening of his faith, even when he recognized the impotence of his own body at the age of one hundred, as well as Sarah's inability to bear.

[20]He did not in unbelief hesitate about God's promise but, empowered by faith, he rendered praise to God [21]in the complete conviction that He was able to make good His promise. [22]For this reason it was accounted to him as righteousness.

[23]This, however, was not written for him alone, "It was accounted to him," [24]but for us as well, to whom it will be accounted as believers in Him who raised from the dead our Lord Jesus, [25]who was put to death on account of our misdeeds and was raised on account of our justification.[y]

5 SINCE, THEN, WE HAVE BEEN PRO-nounced righteous through faith, let us have peace with God through our Lord Jesus Christ, [2]by whom we also obtain through faith entrance to this grace in which we stand firm, and rejoice in the hope of God's glory.

[3]Not this alone, but we glory in afflictions as well; for we know that affliction produces patience, [4]and patience develops a tried character, and character begets hope, [5]such hope as does not disappoint; for God's love is poured out into our hearts by means of the Holy Spirit who has been given to us.[z] [6]For when we were still helpless, Christ at the proper time died for the ungodly.

[7]Ordinarily one would hardly die for a righteous person; but still for a good person someone might perhaps bring himself to die. [8]But God proves His own love for us by Christ's dying for us when we were still sinners.

[9]Now then, as we have been declared righteous by His blood, how much surer is it that we shall be saved by Him from God's wrath. [10]For if as enemies we were reconciled to God through the death of His Son, surely much more shall we who have been reconciled be saved by His life. [11]And not only this, but we also exult in God through our Lord Jesus Christ, through whom we have now received the reconciliation.

[12]It is therefore as follows: through one man sin entered the world, and death through sin, and so death passed on to all persons in that all sinned. [13]To be sure, sin was in the world earlier than the Law; but, in absence of law, sin is not accounted. [14]Death, however, held rule from Adam to Moses over those who sinned but did not transgress a command in the way Adam, who foreshadowed the Coming One, had done.

[15]With the free gift, however, it is by no means as it is with the transgression; for if through the transgression of one person many die, far more richly did the grace of God and His gift, that comes through the favor of one man Jesus Christ, overflow to the many. [16]Nor is the gift similar in effect to that one person's sin; for the judgment of one man brings condemnation, but divine grace led to justification out of many transgressions. [17]For if, through that one person's transgression, death is king through that person, far more surely will those who receive the overflowing of grace and the gift of righteousness reign as kings in life through the One, Jesus Christ.

[18]So then, as through one transgression[a] condemnation came to all men, so through one righteous act[b] there is

---

w) Gen. 17:5.   x) Gen. 15:5.
y) Christ's resurrection was God's declaration that, with the work of atonement accomplished, believers are counted as righteous.
z) The gift of God's grace received in faith issues in Christlike behavior as the Spirit works in and through the believer.   a) That is, Adam's transgression.
b) Christ's sacrifice opens the door of grace to all who will enter it.

for all men justification and life. [19]For as through the disobedience of one man many were placed in the position of sinners, so through the obedience of the One many will be placed in the position of righteous ones.

[20]But Law slipped in to make the transgression more serious; yet where sin increased, grace was in greater abundance [21]so that, as sin[c] reigned in death, so grace might reign through righteousness to eternal life through Jesus Christ our Lord.

6 WHAT THEN ARE WE TO SAY? Shall we remain in sin to let grace become more plentiful? [2]Not at all! How shall we, who have died to sin, still live in it? [3]Or do you not realize that as many of us as were baptized in union with Christ Jesus were baptized in union with His death? [4]So we are buried with Him in death[d] through baptism in order that, just as Christ rose from the dead through the Father's glorious power, so we too shall conduct ourselves in a new way of living. [5]For if we have been united with Him in a death like His, then the same must be true of our resurrection with Him, [6]being aware of this, that our old self[e] was crucified with Him, so that the power of the sin-controlled body might be done away with and we should no longer be slaves of sin. [7]For a corpse is considered guiltless of sin.[f]

[8]If, then, we have died with Christ, we believe that we shall also live with Him, [9]well assured that Christ, once risen from the dead, will not die any more; death holds lordship over Him no longer. [10]The death He died was once for all to sin,[g] but the life He lives, He lives to God. [11]Similarly let us consider ourselves as actually dead to sin, but in Christ Jesus alive to God.

[12]Sin, then, must not be king in your mortal body, to have you yield to its passions, [13]neither must you offer the members of your body to serve sin as instruments of wickedness, but rather offer yourselves to God as living persons who rose from the dead, and present the members of your body to God as instruments of righteousness.[h] [14]Sin shall not be your master, for you are not governed by Law but by grace.

[15]Then what? Shall we sin because we are not governed by Law but by grace? Certainly not! [16]Do you not know that you are committed to obey as slaves[i] the one to whom you offer yourselves as obedient slaves, whether that be to sin that leads to death, or to obedience that leads to righteousness? [17]But thanks be to God that, though you were slaves of sin, you have become with all your hearts obedient to the standard of teaching to which you were introduced, [18]so that with deliverance from sin you were made slaves of righteousness.

[19]I speak in these human terms because of your human weakness. Just as you offered the members of your body in the service of impurity in one act of lawlessnes after another, so now offer your members in the service of righteousness for holy living. [20]For when you were slaves of sin, you were free from righteousness.[j] [21]And what good did you derive from things of which you are now ashamed? Death is their consequence. [22]But now, freed from sin and made slaves of God, the good you derive leads to holiness and the consequence is life eternal. [23]For the wages of sin is death, but the gift of God is eternal life in Christ Jesus our Lord.

7 DO YOU NOT KNOW, BROTHERS — for I address such as understand the Law — that the Law has authority over a person only during his lifetime? [2]The married woman is by law bound

c) Here and in chs. 6 and 7 "sin," which denotes man's natural state, is to be distinguished from "sins," which result from his possessing a sinful nature. Christ died for both sin and sins.
d) Christ died as our representative. In baptism believers become identified with His death and resurrection.
e) That is, the sinful nature in us, the inborn tendency to sin.
f) A dead body does not sin.
g) We died with Christ; therefore we also are dead to sin. Let us act that way, vs. 11.
h) Compare ch. 12:1, 2.
i) See note at Matt. 13:27.
j) That is, there was no relationship with righteousness.

to her husband while he lives; but when her husband dies, she is freed from the marriage law. [3]While her husband lives; she would be an adulteress in case she married another man; but if the husband dies, she is legally free and is no adulteress at all if she marries another man.

[4]In a similar way you, my brothers, were put to death to the Law by means of the body of Christ, so that you may belong to Another, to Him who was raised from the dead in order that we bear fruit[k] for God. [5]For when we lived our earthly way, our sinful passions, aroused by the Law, were active in our bodily organs to bear fruit for death. [6]Now, however, we are released from the Law; we have been dead to what once held us in its grip, so that now we serve in the new relationship of the Spirit and not in the old relationship of literalness.

[7]What, then, do we conclude? That the Law is sin? Far be it from our thoughts! Nevertheless, were it not for the Law, we should not have known sin. For instance, I should not have known about covetousness had not the Law said,[l] "Thou shalt not covet." [8]But sin, by grasping the opportunity through the commandment, effected in me all sorts of covetousness. For apart from the Law sin is dead.[m]

[9]I was once living in the absence of the Law, but with the coming of the commandment, sin took on new life — which to me meant death. [10]The commandment that was aimed to give life was found to mean death to me [11]because sin, by grasping the opportunity through the commandment, deceived me and killed me with it.[n] [12]So then, the Law is holy, and so is the commandment holy, just, and good.

[13]Did, then, what was good become death to me? Not at all! Instead, it was sin that must be shown up as sin, by working fatally for me through something good, so that through the commandment sin might become immeasurably sinful.

[14]For we know that the Law is spiritual; but I am fleshly, sold under sin's control; [15]for I[o] do not understand what I am doing. I do not do what I want to do but what I hate to do. [16]Now if I do what I do not want to do, I agree that the Law is good. [17]However, I am no longer the one who does the deed, but sin which is at home in me does it. [18]For I know that within me, that is within my flesh,[p] what is good is not at home; the personal willingness is there but not the accomplishing of what is right. [19]For I fail to do the good I want to do and I practice the bad that I do not want to practice.

[20]But if I do what I have no desire to do, then I am no longer doing it myself, but rather sin that makes itself at home in me. [21]Consequently, I discover a law that when I want to do right, wrong suggestions crowd in. [22]For in my inmost heart I agree with God's Law; [23]but in my whole natural make-up I observe another law, battling against the principles which my reason dictates, and making me a prisoner to the law of sin that controls my members.

[24]Miserable man that I am, who will rescue me from this body doomed to death? [25]Thanks be to God because of Jesus Christ our Lord! So then, with my mind I serve God's Law, but with my human nature I serve the principle of sin.

8 THERE IS THEREFORE NOW NO condemnation to those who are in

---

k) The fruit of the Spirit, Christian behavior, *cf.* Gal. 5:22, 23.
l) Exod. 20:17
m) Where there is no Law, there is no awareness of sin.
n) "Do and live," says the Law. But since man himself is incapable of living righteously, he cannot live the life that the Law demands. Only through faith in the crucified and risen Christ is a new life possible.
o) The Christian has two natures, the old one derived from Adam and the new one received at the new birth. In this profound passage, vss. 15-25, Paul uses "I" as referring sometimes to the old man and sometimes to the new man in Christ, as he portrays the struggle within the believer and finally recognizes that only in Christ can the believer be rescued from the domination of the old nature, vss. 24, 25; ch. 8.
p) "Flesh," as the word is used here, denotes man in his unregenerate state, not only subject to sin but also prone to sin. Only he who lives under the control of the Holy Spirit can be victorious over the control of the flesh, Gal. 5:16-18.

Christ Jesus; [2]for the life-giving principles of the Spirit have freed you in Christ Jesus from the control of the principles of sin and death. [3]For what the Law was unable to do, weakened as it was through the flesh, that God did by sending His own Son in the likeness of sinful flesh and on account of sin; He thus condemned sin in human nature [4]so that the Law's requirements might be completely met by us, who behave not in a fleshly but in a spiritual way.

[5]For those who are under control of the flesh are fleshly minded, but those who are under control of the Spirit are spiritually minded, [6]and to be fleshly minded means death, while spiritual-mindedness means life and peace, [7]because fleshly-mindedness is hostile to God; it is not submissive to God's Law, in fact it cannot be. [8]So those who are controlled by the flesh are unable to please God.

[9]You, however, are not controlled by the flesh but by the Spirit, if indeed the Spirit of God is at home in you. If, on the other hand, anyone does not have the Spirit of Christ, he does not belong to Him. [10]But if Christ is in you, then the body is dead on account of sin, but the spirit is alive on account of righteousness. [11]If, then, the Spirit of Him who raised Jesus from the dead dwells in you, then He who raised Christ Jesus from the dead will through the Spirit that dwells in you also make your mortal bodies live.[q]

[12]It follows then, brothers, that we are obligated, but not to our human nature to live under its control; [13]for if you live in a fleshly way, you will die. But if through the Spirit you put to death the deeds of the body, then you will live. [14]For as many as are guided by God's Spirit are sons of God. [15]Indeed, you receive no spirit that would re-enslave you to fear; instead, you receive the Spirit of sonship by which we cry, "Abba![r] Father!" [16]This Spirit bears witness with our spirits that we are God's children; [17]but if children, then heirs too; in fact, God's heirs together with Christ, presuming that we suffer together, so that we may also enjoy glory together.

[18]For I reason that this temporal suffering is not worth comparing with the glory that is to be revealed to us. [19]For the creation[s] eagerly awaits the revealing of the sons of God; [20]for the creation was subjected to frustration, not from choice but through Him who effected that bondage, and that with hope; [21]because creation itself will be liberated from its enslavement to decay into the glorious freedom of God's children.

[22]For we know that to this day the entire creation has been groaning and suffering agony together as if in childbirth, [23]and not merely so, but we ourselves, who have the Spirit as first fruits, we also groan within ourselves as we await our adoption as sons, that is, our bodily redemption. [24]In this hope are we saved; but hope within sight is not hope, for who hopes for what he sees? [25]But if we hope for what we do not see, then we keep on patiently awaiting it.

[26]In a similar way the Spirit joins in to help us in our weakness; for we do not know what and how we ought to pray, but the Spirit Himself intercedes on our behalf with sighs too deep for words.[t] [27]And the Searcher of hearts knows what the Spirit has in mind, for He pleads with God on behalf of the saints. [28]But we know that for those who love Him, for those called in agreement with His purpose, God makes all things work together for good.

[29]Because those whom He knew beforehand He appointed beforehand to share the likeness of His Son, so that He might be the First-born among many brothers. [30]But whom He predestined, those He also called; and

q) Not only does the word "live" speak of the resurrection body in heaven but it also relates to the new kind of life that the believer possesses now in his mortal body.
r) "Abba" is the Aramaic word for "father." It was frequently used in prayer and sometimes within a family to address the head of the household.
s) All nature suffered because of man's original sin. Thus creation as well as the creature looks forward to deliverance from the bondage of sin.
t) All true prayer originates from God the Holy Spirit.

whom He called, those He also made righteous; and whom He made righteous, those He also glorified. ³¹Then what conclusion do we draw? If God is for us, then who is against us? ³²He who did not even spare His own Son but gave Him up on behalf of us all, will He not also favor us with everything along with Him? ³³Who will enter a charge against God's chosen? God is the Acquitter; ³⁴who is the condemner? Christ Jesus is He who died; what is more, who rose again, who is at God's right hand, who also pleads on our behalf.

³⁵Who will separate us from Christ's love? Affliction? Or distress? Or persecution? Or famine? Or destitution? Or danger? Or sword? ³⁶Just as it is written,ᵘ "On Your account we are being killed all day long; we are considered sheep for slaughter." ³⁷But in all this we are more than conquerors through Him who loved us.

³⁸For I am convinced that neither death nor life, neither angels nor authorities, neither present nor future affairs, ³⁹neither powers of the heights nor of the depths, nor anything else created will be able to separate us from the love of God that is in Christ Jesus our Lord.

9 IN CHRIST I TELL THE TRUTH, I am not falsifying, as my conscience, fortified by the Holy Spirit, bears me witness, ²when I say that I have in my heart intense grief and unceasing distress; ³for I could wish myself banished from Christ for the sake of my brothers, my human kinsmen ⁴who are Israelites. Theirs are the sonship, the glorious Presence,ᵛ the covenants, the giving of the Law, the worship, and the promises. ⁵Theirs are the fathers, and from them Christ was

humanly descended, who is over all, God blessed forever. Amen.

⁶It is not as if God's message had failed, for by no means all who descend from Israel belong to Israel; ⁷neither are all Abraham's children because they are his offspring, butʷ "Through Isaac your offspring shall be named after you." ⁸This means that it is not his physical descendants who make up the children of God, but the children of the promise are considered his offspring. ⁹For this is the message of the promise,ˣ "At about this time next year I will come, and Sarah will have a son."

¹⁰But this is not all. When Rebecca had conceived by one man, our forefather Isaac, ¹¹and before the children were born or had done anything good or bad, even then, in order that the purpose of God's choice might prevail, which rests not on works but on His calling, ¹²it was said to her,ʸ "The older will serve the younger." ¹³As it is written,ᶻ "I loved Jacob, but I hated Esau."

¹⁴What shall we say then? Is there injustice with God? Perish the thought! ¹⁵For He saidᵃ to Moses, "I will have mercy on whom I will have mercy, and I will take pity on whom I will take pity." ¹⁶So then, it is not a matter of man's willing or running, but of God's mercy. ¹⁷As Scripture saysᵇ to Pharaoh, "For this very purpose I raised you up high, to show in you the evidence of My power, so that My name may be made known over the whole earth." ¹⁸So then, He shows mercy to whom He wills, and He hardens whom He wills.

¹⁹Then you will ask me, "Why does He still complain; for who is resisting His will?" ²⁰O man! who are you, anyway, to talk back to God? The thing that is being molded does not

---

u) Ps. 44:22.
v) The allusion is to the Shekinah cloud of glory that shone on the mercy seat in the tabernacle and temple, signifying the presence of the Lord, Exod. 40:34; Lev. 16:2; I Kings 8:10, 11.
w) Gen. 21:12.
x) Gen. 18:10.
y) Gen. 25:23. Obviously God endowed Jacob with latent resources superior to those of Esau, and Jacob made use of them.
z) Mal. 1:2, 3.
a) Exod. 33:19.
b) Exod. 9:16. In Exod. 8:15 it is stated that Pharaoh hardened his own heart, but Exod. 7:13, 14 ascribes the hardening to God. Because Pharaoh resisted the will of God, God caused his heart to become even harder than it had been before. Pharaoh became an instrument for God's purpose.

say to the one who molds it, "Why do you make me this way," does it? [21]Does not the potter have the right with the clay to make from the same lump one utensil for noble use and another for ignoble use? [22]What if God, wanting to show His anger and to evidence His power, with great patience endured the agents that deserve wrath and have been prepared for destruction, [23]so that He might make known the wealth of His glory to the recipients of mercy, whom previously He prepared for glory, [24]even us whom He has called not only from among the Jews but also from among the Gentiles?

[25]So, too, He says[e] in Hosea, "I will call those who were not[d] My people 'My people,' and her who was not loved [26]'My beloved,' and in the place where it was said to them, 'You are not My people,' there they will be called sons of the living God." [27]Isaiah, too, exclaims[e] regarding Israel, "Even though the number of Israel's sons were as the sand of the sea, only a remnant will be saved [28][for He will finish the work and round it out in righteousness]:[f] for thoroughly and with dispatch the Lord will execute His decree on the earth." [29]As Isaiah further foretold,[g] "Unless the Lord of hosts had left us offspring, we would have become like Sodom and would have been made like Gomorrah."

[30]Then what is our inference? That the Gentiles, who did not try to acquire righteousness, got hold of righteousness, that is, of the righteousness that comes through faith, [31]while Israel, pursuing a law for the securing of righteousness, failed to come up to it.[h] [32]And why? Because their principle was not by faith but by works; they stumbled over the stone that occasions stumbling, [33]as it is written,[i] "See, I am laying in Zion a stone that causes men to stumble, a rock that trips men up, and the believer in Him will not be shamed."

10 BROTHERS, THE DESIRE OF MY heart and my prayer to God for them is for their salvation; [2]for I will say for them, that they have enthusiasm for God, but not with correct understanding. [3]Ignorant of the righteousness that comes from God,[j] and trying to set up their own righteousness, they have not submitted to the righteousness of God. [4]For Christ brought the Law to completion so that everyone who believes in Him may be justified.

[5]Moses does indeed describe[k] the righteousness of the Law, "The man who practices it shall live by it." [6]The righteousness of faith, however, has this to say,[l] "Do not say to yourself, 'Who will ascend to heaven?' (which means, to bring Christ down), [7]or 'Who will descend into the depth?' (which means, to bring Christ up from the grave)." [8]But what does it say?[m] "The word is near you, in your mouth and heart." It is the message of faith which we preach, [9]that if you confess with your lips the Lord Jesus and believe in your heart that God raised Him from the dead, you will be saved. [10]For with the heart one believes so that he is made righteous, and with the mouth confession is made for salvation. [11]For the Scripture says,[n] "Whoever puts his trust in Him will not be put to shame."

[12]There is then no distinction between Jew and Greek, for they all belong to the same Lord, bestowing His riches on all who invoke Him; [13]for[o] "everyone who calls on the Lord's name will be saved."

[14]Now then, how can they invoke Him in whom they have no faith? And how can they believe in One of whom they have not heard? Again, how can they listen without a preacher? [15]But

c) Hos. 1:10; 2:23.　　d) That is, the Gentiles.　　e) Isa. 10:22, 23.
f) The words enclosed in brackets do not appear in the majority of the most reliable ancient manuscripts.
g) Isa. 1:9.
h) Gentile believers were better off than the Jews who tried to earn salvation by works; for salvation cannot be earned by any man, but is only by grace through faith in Christ.
i) Ps. 118:22; Isa. 8:14.　　j) Through the grace of Christ.　　k) Lev. 18:5.
l) Deut. 30:12, 13.　　m) Deut. 30:14.　　n) Isa. 28:16.
o) Joel 2:32, quoted by Peter at Pentecost.

how can they preach unless they are sent? Just as it is written,[p] "How lovely are the feet of those who publish the good news!"

[16]Not all, however, have heard the good news, as Isaiah says,[q] "Lord, who has believed our report?" [17]Faith, then, results from hearing, and hearing is through the message of Christ. [18]But I ask, Have they not heard? Yes, indeed,[r] "Their voice has gone forth over the whole earth and their words to the end of the world." [19]I ask further, Did not Israel understand? To begin with, Moses says,[s] "I will make you jealous of those who are not a nation, and I will infuriate you against a senseless nation." [20]Then Isaiah boldly expressed it,[t] "I have been found by those who did not seek Me; I have shown Myself to those who did not ask for Me." [21]But concerning Israel He says,[u] "All day long I have held out My hands to a disobedient and rebellious people."

11 I SAY THEN, HAS GOD REPUdiated His people? No, indeed! In fact, I myself am an Israelite, a descendant of Abraham and of Benjamin's tribe. [2]God has not repudiated His people whom beforehand He had in mind. Do you not know what the Scripture says concerning Elijah, how he appeals[v] to God against Israel, [3]"Lord, they have killed Your prophets; they have torn down Your altars; I alone am left and they are after my life"?

[4]Nevertheless, what divine response[w] is given him? "I have kept for Myself seven thousand men who have not bowed the knee to Baal." [5]Just so there is at present a remnant in accordance with His gracious choice. [6]But if it is by grace, then it is no longer an account of works; otherwise grace would no more be grace.

[7]Then what follows? Israel has not gained what it was seeking,[x] but those

who are chosen[y] have secured it, while the rest have grown callous; [8]as it is written,[z] "God has given them a spirit of stupidity — eyes that do not see and ears that do not hear, to this very day." [9]David also says,[a] "Let their table become a snare and a trap, a block and a retribution to them; [10]let their eyes be darkened so that they cannot see, and forever make them bend their backs."

[11]I say then, did they stumble so as to fall? Not at all! Instead, through their transgression salvation has come to the Gentiles to arouse Israel to jealousy. [12]But if their transgression means the world's enrichment, and their failure is the Gentiles' gain, then how much more will their fulfilling of the divine demand be.

[13]But I am speaking to you Gentiles. For the very reason that I am an apostle to the Gentiles, I take pride in my ministry, [14]trying if possible to rouse my own race to jealousy and save some of them. [15]For if the rejection on their part means the world's reconciliation, what must their acceptance mean but life from the dead? [16]If the first piece of dough is holy, so is the whole lump, and if the root is holy, so are the branches.

[17]If some of the branches have been broken off and you, a wild olive shoot, have been grafted in and are sharing the rich root of the olive tree, [18]do not boast against the branches, and if you do boast remember that you are not supporting the root; instead, the root supports you.

[19]You will reply, "The branches have been broken off so that I may be grafted in." [20]Well said! Through lack of faith they were broken off and through faith you remain in place. Be not haughty, but stand in awe. [21]For if God did not spare the natural branches, neither will He spare you. [22]So consider God's kindness and rigor — on the one hand His rigor applied to those who failed, and on the other

---

p) Isa. 52:7.   q) Isa. 53:1.   r) Ps. 19:4.   s) Deut. 32:21.
t) Isa. 65:1.   u) Isa. 65:2.   v) I Kings 19:10.   w) I Kings 19:18.
x) Righteousness was what Israel was seeking, but they sought it through self-effort, not by faith, ch. 10:3.
y) Righteousness is God's gift through Christ to His elect (chosen).
z) Deut. 29:4; Isa. 29:10. In both cases God was prepared to discipline His ancient people because of their disobedience.   a) Ps. 69:22.

hand God's kindness to you, provided you continue in His kindness; else you too will be cut away. [23]Besides they, if they do not persist in their unbelief, will be grafted in; for God is able to graft them in again. [24]And if you have been cut from a naturally wild olive tree and were grafted contrary to nature into a cultivated olive tree, then how much more readily will these natural branches be grafted into their own original tree.

[25]So that you might not be self-opinionated, brothers, I want you not to be ignorant of this secret: partial insensibility has come over Israel until the full number of the Gentiles come in, [26]and thus Israel will be saved, as it is written,[b] "From Mount Zion a deliverer will come; He will turn away ungodliness from Jacob; [27]and this is My covenant with them when I have taken away their sins."

[28]So far as the good news is concerned, they are enemies for your sakes; but so far as election is concerned, they are beloved because of the fathers. [29]For God's gifts of grace and His calling are irrevocable. [30]Just as you were once disobedient to God but now have received mercy, thanks to their disobedience, [31]so they have now been disobedient so that through the mercy you are enjoying they may now receive mercy. [32]For God has confined all men under the power of disobedience, so that He might have mercy on all men.

[33]O the depth of the wealth, the wisdom, and the knowledge of God! How inscrutable are His judgments and how untraceable His footsteps! [34]For[c] who has understood the Lord's mind, or who has become His counselor? [35]Or who has given anything to Him that it might be repaid him?" [36]For from Him, and through Him and to Him are all things. To Him be glory forever! Amen.

12 I BEG YOU, THEREFORE, BROTHERS, in view of God's mercies, that you present your bodies a living sacrifice, holy and acceptable to God, which is your reasonable service. [2]And do not conform to the present world system, but be transformed by the renewal of your mind, so as to sense for yourselves what is the good and acceptable and perfect will of God. [3]For through the grace that is granted me I warn each one among you not to value himself more highly than he should, but to think soberly as God has measured out to each his portion of faith.

[4]For just as in one body we have many members, but not all the members have the same function, [5]so the many of us form one body in Christ, while each is related to all others as a member. [6]But having gifts that differ according to the grace bestowed on us, if it is prophecy, let it be used in proportion to the measure of faith God has bestowed it; [7]if it is practical service, then employ such service in the same way — the teacher, in his teaching; [8]the one who admonishes, in his admonition; the contributor, in his liberality; the leader, in his deep interest; he who practices charity, in genuine cheerfulness.

[9]Let your love be sincere, clinging to the right with abhorrence of evil. [10]Be joined together in a brotherhood of mutual love, trying to outdo one another in showing respect, [11]never slacking in interest, serving the Lord, keeping spiritually aglow, [12]joyfully hoping as you endure affliction, persistent in prayer, [13]contributing to the needs of the saints,[d] practicing hospitality.

[14]Bless your persecutors; yes, bless and do not curse them. [15]Share the joy of those who are happy and the grief of those who grieve. [16]Live in harmony with others; do not aspire to eminence,[e] but associate yourselves with humble people; do not be conceited.

[17]In no case paying back evil for evil, determine on the noblest ways of

---

b) Isa. 59:20; *cf.* Ps. 14:7.   c) Compare Job 35:7; 41:11; Isa. 40:13*ff.*; Jer. 23:18.
d) See note at Acts 9:13.
e) Whatever honors may come to men are as a result of the grace of God, to whom all glory belongs, Ps. 96:7, 8; Mal. 2:2.

dealing with all people. [18]If possible, so far as it depends on you, live at peace with everyone. [19]Do not avenge yourselves, dear friends, but leave room for divine retribution; for it is written,[f] "It is Mine to punish; I will pay them back, says the Lord."

[20]Instead,[g] "if your enemy is hungry, feed him; in case he is thirsty, give him water to drink," for in doing so, you will pile burning coals on his head. [21]Be not overpowered by evil, but overcome evil with good.

13 LET EVERY PERSON RENDER obedience to the governing authorities; for there is no authority except from God, and those in authority are divinely constituted, [2]so that the rebel against the authority is resisting God's appointment.[h] Such resisters will incur judgment on themselves.

[3]For magistrates are not dread to the person who does right but to the wrongdoer. You do not want to fear the authority, do you? Do right, and you will earn its approval. [4]For it is God's agency for your welfare. But if you do wrong, then be alarmed, for it does not carry the sword without reason; it is God's agent to bring deserved punishment on the evildoer. [5]It behooves us, therefore, to be submissive, not because of punishment only but also for conscience' sake.

[6]Pay your taxes, therefore; for those who constantly attend to this task are God's agents. [7]Pay all of them their dues: tax to whom tax is due; customs duties to whom customs duties are due; respect to whom respect is due, and honor to whom honor is due. [8]Owe no one anything except that you love one another, for the person who loves his neighbor has fulfilled the Law. [9]Because,[i] "Do not commit adultery; do not kill; do not steal; do not covet," and

whatever other commandment there is, may be summarized in one word, and that is, "Love your neighbor as yourself." [10]Love works no harm to one's neighbor, so love meets all the Law's requirements.

[11]Observe this in consideration of our times, because the hour has struck for us to wake up, for our salvation is now nearer than when we first believed. [12]The night is well advanced and the day approaches; so let us put off the works of darkness and let us put on the armor of light. [13]Let us behave ourselves decently as befits the daytime, not in carousing and drinking, not in immorality and debauchery, not in quarreling and jealousy. [14]Instead, clothe yourselves with the Lord Jesus Christ; do not make provision for the flesh to gratify its cravings.

14 WELCOME THE WEAK BELIEVER, and do not criticize his views. [2]One person has faith that allows him to eat everything, but a weaker one confines himself to vegetables.[j] [3]The one who eats should not feel contempt for him who abstains, nor should the one who abstains censure him who eats; for God has accepted him.[k] [4]Who are you to censure another's servant? He will stand or fall with his own master. But he will stand, for the Lord will enable him to stand.

[5]One person gives preference to one day above another day, while another person esteems every day. Each person should be fully convinced in his own mind. [6]He who observes the day, observes it with the Lord in view. So who eats everything, eats with the Lord in mind, for he gives thanks to God. He who limits his eating refrains for the Lord's sake, and gives thanks to God.

---

f) Deut. 32:35; Prov. 20:22; *cf.* Prov. 24:29.
g) Prov. 25:21.
h) Paul here gives the norm for the Christian's relation to the state — namely, that he must be a law-abiding citizen. The apostle does not go into situations such as those when the government is so intolerable that it must be changed or when the authorities oppose God. *Cf.* Acts 5:29.
i) Exod. 20:13-15, 17.
j) In apostolic times there were some Christians of Jewish background who had conscientious scruples about eating meat which they feared might have been sacrificed to idols before being sold; these people Paul called "weak." Other "stronger" believers of Jewish background (like Paul himself) or Gentile Christians did not have such scruples, I Cor. 10:25. Christians also differed regarding the keeping of special days, vss. 5, 6.
k) Even a weak Christian is accepted by God because of his faith in the Lord Jesus Christ.

7For none of us lives to himself, and no one dies to himself; 8for in case we live, we live to the Lord, and in case we die, we die to the Lord; so whether we live or die, we belong to the Lord.[1] 9For this purpose Christ died and lives again, to be Lord both of the dead and of the living.

10But you, why do you find fault with your brother? Or you, why do you look down on your brother? For we shall all stand before God's tribunal, 11as it is written,[m] "As I live, says the Lord, to Me every knee shall bow and every tongue shall render acknowledgment to God." 12Accordingly, every one of us will give account of himself to God.

13So let us no longer censure one another, but let us rather decide not to place a hindrance or a stumbling block in our brother's way. 14In union with the Lord Jesus I know and am convinced that nothing is unclean[n] in itself; it becomes unclean to the person who considers it unclean. 15And yet, if your brother is harmed on account of your eating, then your behavior is no longer controlled by love. You would not by your eating ruin a person for whom Christ died, would you? 16Do not then allow what is wholesome for you to be spoken of as evil; 17for the kingdom of God does not consist in eating and drinking, but in righteousness and peace and joy in the Holy Spirit. 18Whoever serves Christ in this way is pleasing to God and is approved by men.

19So then let us definitely aim for everything that contributes to one another's peace and development. 20Do not on account of food tear down the work of God. Everything is clean, yet it is wrong for a man to make others stumble by what he eats. 21It is well to eat no meat and drink no wine, to do nothing that would make your brother stumble.[o]

22You have faith? Have it personally in the presence of God. Happy is the person who has no qualms of conscience in what he allows himself to do. 23But the person who entertains doubts, and nevertheless eats, stands condemned, because he is not acting from faith, and every act that does not spring from faith is sin.

15 WE WHO ARE STRONG OUGHT TO bear with the scruples of those who are weak. We should not please ourselves. 2But each of us should please his neighbor for his welfare, to strengthen him. 3For even Christ did not please Himself but, as it is written,[p] "The reproaches of those who reproached you fell on me."

4All those writings of long ago were written for our instruction, so that through the patience and encouragement of the Scriptures we might have hope. 5And may the God who gives patience and encouragement grant you such mutual understanding in agreement with Christ Jesus 6that together as with one voice you may praise the God and Father of our Lord Jesus Christ.

7Accept one another, therefore, just as Christ accepted you, for the glory of God. 8For I say that Christ became a servant to the circumcised on behalf of God's truth to verify the promises that had been made to our fathers, 9and also that the Gentiles should praise God for His mercy, as it is written,[q] "For this I will give You praise among the Gentiles and sing psalms to Your name." 10And again it says,[r] "Be glad, O you Gentiles, together with His people," 11and once more,[s] "Praise the Lord, all you Gentiles, and sing His praises, all you peoples." 12Isaiah further says,[t] "There will be a shoot from Jesse, even He who will stand up to rule the Gentiles; upon Him will the Gentiles rest their hope."

---

1) Compare ch. 12:5.   m) Isa. 45:23.
n) Under the Mosaic Law some meats were forbidden as unclean, Lev. 11; but the same God who gave this Law in the O.T. releases the Christian from it in the N.T., Acts 10. Observe, however, that in the same spirit as vss. 1-13 of this chapter in the Epistle to the Romans, the Early Church told the believers in Antioch that they should abstain from certain meats, Acts 15:28, 29.
o) Here is a guideline that Christians would do well to follow.
p) Ps. 69:9.   q) Ps. 18:49.   r) Deut. 32:43.   s) Ps. 117:1.
t) Isa. 11:10.

¹³So may God, the fountain of hope, fill you with all joy and peace in your believing, so that you may enjoy overflowing hope by the power of the Holy Spirit.

¹⁴I myself am convinced about you, my brothers, that you are full of goodness, amply furnished with knowledge, and competent to advise one another. ¹⁵But I have written to you very boldly in some matters so as to remind you, on account of the grace that God has granted me, ¹⁶that I should be a minister of Christ Jesus to the Gentiles, serving as a priest of the good news from God, whereby the Gentiles may become an acceptable offering, made holy by the Holy Spirit.

¹⁷In union with Christ Jesus, then, I take pride in my service for God; ¹⁸for I will not venture to speak of anything but what Christ has done through me to bring the Gentiles to the place of obedience by word and deed, ¹⁹by the power of signs and wonders, by the power of the Holy Spirit, so that from Jerusalem and everywhere as far as Illyricum,[u] I have fully preached the good news concerning Christ. ²⁰So I endeavored earnestly to preach only where the name of Christ was not yet known, in order not to build on the foundation of someone else, ²¹but as it is written,[v] "Those who have never been told of Him will see, and those who never heard will understand."

²²On this account also I have been frequently prevented from visiting you; ²³but now, since I have no more opportunities to do my work in this area, and with a longing extending over many years to visit you ²⁴whenever I might travel to Spain, I do hope to see you with my own eyes on passing through, and to have an escort from you on the way, after first having enjoyed your fellowship for a while.

²⁵Now I am on my way to Jerusalem[w] in a ministry for the saints;[x] ²⁶for Macedonia and Achaia have been pleased to make some contribution for the needy among the Jerusalem saints. ²⁷They themselves decided to do it, and they certainly owe it to them; for if the Gentiles shared in their spiritual possessions, then they owe them their service in material things.

²⁸When therefore I have finished this work and have turned over to them the full amount of the donation, I shall come by you on the way to Spain. ²⁹And I know that when I come to you I shall come in the abundant blessing of Christ.

³⁰But I plead with you, brothers, by our Lord Jesus Christ and the love of the Spirit, that you strive together with me in your prayers to God on my behalf, ³¹in order that I may be delivered from the unbelievers in Judea; also that my ministry for Jerusalem may be well received by the saints, ³²and that I may subsequently come to you with gladness by the will of God and enjoy a refreshing visit with you. ³³And may the God of peace be with you all. Amen.

16 MAY I PRESENT TO YOU OUR sister Phoebe, a deaconess of the Cenchreae[y] church, ²so that you may receive her in the Lord's name as saints deserve, and that you may assist her in whatever matter she may have need of you; for she has been a helper to many, including me.

³Give my greetings to Priscilla and Aquila, my fellow workers in Christ Jesus, ⁴who risked their own necks to save my life,[z] and to whom not only I but all the churches of the Gentiles are grateful. ⁵And include the church that meets in their house.[a]

My greetings to my dear Epaenetus,[b] the first convert to Christ in Asia. ⁶Greet Mary, who went through much

u) Illyricum was an extensive territory on the eastern coast of the Adriatic Sea and opposite a large area of Italy. Later Illyricum was called Dalmatia.
v) Isa. 52:15.
w) Twice Paul had been warned that he should not go to Jerusalem, Acts 21:4, 10-14, but he himself was compelled by the Holy Spirit to go there whatever might befall him. See note at Acts 21:13.   x) See note at Acts 9:13.
y) Cenchreae was the seaport of Corinth on the Aegean Sea.
z) This circumstance is not mentioned elsewhere in the N.T.
a) Priscilla and Aquila opened their house as a gathering place for the church, I Cor. 16:9; cf. Acts 18:26. The early Christians did not have church buildings.
b) This chapter contains the longest list of names of obscure Christians in the N.T. That this

trouble for you. 7Greet my relatives and fellow prisoners Andronicus and Junias; they are outstanding among the apostles and were Christians before I was one.

8Greetings to Amplias, my dear friend in the Lord. 9Greet Urbanus, our fellow worker in Christ, and my dear Stachys. 10Remember me to Apelles, one who is tried and true in Christ, and to those of Aristobulus' family. 11Greet my relative Herodion. Greet those of Narcissus' household that are in the Lord.

12My greetings to those Christian workers Tryphaena and Tryphosa. Greet that dear Persis, unwearied worker that she is in the Lord. 13Greetings to Rufus, chosen in the Lord, and to his mother, who is mine as well.

14My greetings to Asyncritus, Phlegon, Hermes, Patrobas, Hermas, and the brothers with them. 15Greet Philologus and Julia, Nereus and his sister, and Olympas and all the saints associated with them. 16Greet one another with a holy kiss. All the churches of Christ send you their greetings.

17But I warn you, brothers, to keep an eye on those who cause divisions and temptations, quite out of harmony with the doctrine you have been taught, and to keep away from them. 18For people of that type do not serve our Lord Christ but their own appetites, and by means of ingratiating talk and flattery they deceive the minds of the unsuspecting.

19The report of your obedience to Christ has reached everyone and makes me happy about you. But I want you to be wise when it comes to goodness, and innocent when it comes to evil. 20And the God of peace will shortly crush Satan under your feet.

The grace of our Lord Jesus be with you.

21Timothy, my fellow worker, sends you greetings, and so do my relatives Lucius, Jason, and Sosipater.

22I, Teritius, the writerᶜ of this letter, send you my greeting in the Lord. 23Gaius,ᵈ who is host to me and to the whole church, greets you. Erastus, the city treasurer, and brother Quartus send you their greetings.

24[The grace of our Lord Jesus Christ be with you all. Amen.]ᵉ 25Now to Him who is able to strengthen you according to the good news which I preach, the message concerning Jesus Christ, in accord with the revelation of the secretᶠ that was concealed for long ages 26but has now been disclosed and through the prophetic writings has been made known to all nations to bring about obedience to the faith, 27to the only wise God be the glory forever and ever through Jesus Christ. Amen.

---

profound exposition of the Gospel ends with Paul sending individual greetings to so many Christians, vss. 1-14, with others joining him in doing this, vss. 21-23, is a reminder that the truths Paul presented relate to persons, not only in his day but now also.

c) Tertius was the scribe or stenographer who wrote down the letter, probably under Paul's dictation. It is generally agreed that the Epistle to the Romans was written in Corinth at the time of the apostle's third visit to that city, *cf.* Acts 20:2, II Cor. 13:1.

d) Gaius was baptized by Paul himself, I Cor. 1:14.

e) Verse 24, enclosed in brackets, is found in only one ancient manuscript. It seems evident that it is an interpolation that some copyist repeated from the same words in v. 20.

f) The Greek word rendered "secret" is *musterion*, which is used in the N.T. of something that was formerly concealed but is now revealed, e.g. see Matt. 13:11, 34, 35; I Cor. 2:7, 8. It has thus become a kind of "open secret." In this verse the word relates to Christ and God's marvelous redemption in and through Him on behalf of all nations, Jews and Gentiles alike, *cf.* ch. 11:25-27; Eph. 1:9-12; 3:3-6; Col. 1:26, 27.

ROMANS OBSERVATIONS CHART

ABOUT PAUL

WHY HE WROTE

ABOUT THE RECIPIENTS

IN ADAM *(According to the flesh)*	IN CHRIST *(According to the Spirit)*

THEME OF ROMANS:

SEGMENT DIVISIONS

			CHAPTER THEMES
			1
			2
			3
			4
			5
			6
			7
			8
			9
			10
			11
			12
			13
			14
			15
			16

Author:

Date:

Purpose:

Key Words:

1 CORINTHIANS

*S*in abounded in the cosmopolitan city of Corinth, the chief city of Greece. Corinth overlooked the narrow isthmus that connected the Greek mainland with Peloponnesus and received ships in its two harbors. At one time it was home of at least twelve heathen temples. The Corinthians were intrigued by Greek philosophy and captivated by the disciplined training and athletic events held at the Isthmus. They desperately needed to hear the good news of Jesus Christ, the One crucified for sinners.

The worship ceremonies carried out by a thousand temple prostitutes connected with the temple of Aphrodite (the goddess of love) bred blatant immorality throughout Corinth—so much so that the Greek verb translated "to Corinthianize" meant to practice sexual immorality.

Prostitutes openly plied their wares and meat markets thrived on sales from the sacrifices offered in the temples. The Corinthians ate well, satisfied their sexual urges without condemnation, flirted with the wisdom of men, and did all they could to keep their bodies as beautiful as those of the Greek gods. They loved to listen to great orators. For the 250,000 citizens there were almost two slaves per person. What more did Corinth need? Freedom. Freedom from sin and death. God met that need by blocking Paul at every hand on his second missionary journey until he received the Macedonian call, "Come and help us."

After establishing the Corinthian church Paul eventually went to Ephesus, where he stayed for three years. From there he wrote his first epistle to the Corinthian believers, who so desperately needed help and correction. It was sometime between A.D. 52 and A.D. 56.

THINGS TO DO

Chapters 1–6

1. In chapter 1 note what Paul commends about the Corinthians. Make a list in the margin titled "Commendations."

2. Read chapters 1 through 6, one chapter at a time. As you read, keep in mind what you read in the introduction to this book. Do the following:

a. Note the problems Paul deals with in the text (as he writes). You can see these problems several ways.

1) As you read, ask the five W's and an H: Who? What? When? Where? Why? and How? Especially concentrate on the problems, subjects, or people mentioned. Ask questions such as: Why would Paul mention specific people by name in this chapter? Who is causing the problem? How did the Corinthians get this way? Why does Paul say what he does about himself or his ministry?

2) Mark the key words in the text. Key words help you see the main topics in a chapter. In 1 Corinthians they indicate what the problems are and what the solution is.

Write the following key words

for this segment on an index card and use it as a bookmark while you study chapters 1 through 6. They are: *God, Jesus (Christ, Lord), Spirit, factions (wranglings, dismembered, jealousy), spirit* (note whose spirit or what spirit), *power (strength), mind, wise (wisdom, intelligent, learned), preach, body,* and *church.*

    b. As you read each of the first six chapters, note the problems Paul deals with in each chapter. In the margin make a list of these with the heading "Problems."

3. As you read, look for and note on the OBSERVATIONS CHART following 1 Corinthians what you learn about the Corinthians, any commands directed to them, and the warnings Paul gives them.

4. As you finish each chapter, summarize the theme (subject) of that chapter and record it on 1 CORINTHIANS AT A GLANCE, and in the text just above the chapter number.

5. Two things prompted Paul to write to the Corinthians, and it is these two things which cause a natural division in his epistle. Read 1 Corinthians 1:10, 11, where Paul states his reason for writing. Record this reason on the 1 CORINTHIANS AT A GLANCE chart in the space under "Major Segment Divisions."

Chapters 7–16

1. The second division of 1 Corinthians is noted by a word which is repeated throughout the last segment of this book: *concerning (regarding)....* Read 7:1 and notice the transition. From this point on Paul deals with matters the Corinthians had questions on or issues that they needed to be instructed in.

2. Now look up the following verses and underline or mark in a distinctive way the words "concerning" or "regarding." As you mark these words, mark along with them the subject matter Paul is about to deal with. The verses are: 7:1; 7:25; 8:1; (in some translations 12:1 has this word); 16:1. In the same way also mark in 15:1 the words *I would further remind you, brothers, of the good news which I preached to you.* Marking these wordings will give you the topical divisions of this second segment of 1 Corinthians.

3. As you read through this last segment of 1 Corinthians, mark the following key words: *God, Jesus (Christ, Lord), Spirit, body, unbelieving (unbelievers), think (consider, fancies), church (churches), idols, knowledge (enlightenment, known), preach,* and *good news.* Make a new list of key words to use as a bookmark in this segment. (*Divisions* and *factions* each are used one more time in chapter 11. This is significant, since Paul again deals with problems while giving further instruction to the church.)

4. As you deal with each topic, ask questions such as: Why does the church have this question or problem? How are they behaving? What is their thinking? What are Paul's instructions regarding this subject? Why are they to do this? What are the consequences if they don't?

5. As Paul moves through these final matters of concern, he intermittently explains his position and ministry. Watch for these explanations and note if and how he ties them in with his subject matter.

6. Note on the OBSERVATIONS CHART what you learn from this segment

about the Corinthians and the commands and warnings Paul gives them.

7. Determine and record the theme of each chapter in the text just above the chapter number and on 1 CORINTHIANS AT A GLANCE.

8. Considering 7:1, give a title to the segment division for the second half of 1 Corinthians. Record your title on 1 CORINTHIANS AT A GLANCE.

9. Record the theme of 1 Corinthians and complete the 1 CORINTHIANS AT A GLANCE chart.

THINGS TO THINK ABOUT

1. Are you having any of the same problems in your own life or in your church that the Corinthians had? Do you think this letter has the answers for your problems or questions? How can you apply what you have learned?

2. According to the context of 1 Corinthians 3, what does it mean to be an unspiritual or worldly Christian? Remember, context rules over all accurate interpretation.

3. Are you untaught—ignorant—concerning spiritual gifts? Do you know about one or two of them but not the others? Have you believed or even taught others in accord with what the whole counsel of God has to say on the subject, or have you merely gone by your experience or reasoning? Do you appreciate other people's gifts even though they may be different from yours?

4. On what do you base your beliefs about marriage, divorce, and remarriage? What did you learn from 1 Corinthians 7 about these topics? Did this change your belief?

5. Is the preaching of the cross foolishness to you, or is it a demonstration of the power of God?

THE FIRST EPISTLE OF PAUL TO THE

CORINTHIANS

Date of writing: c. A.D. 56-57, at Ephesus

1 PAUL, CALLED BY THE WILL OF God to be an apostle of Christ Jesus, and our brother Sosthenes,[a] [2]to the church of God at Corinth,[b] those made holy in Christ Jesus and called to be saints,[c] together with all who in every place invoke the name of our Lord Jesus Christ, their Lord as well as ours: [3]Grace and peace to you from God our Father and from our Lord Jesus Christ.

[4]Always I thank my God for you, for the divine grace that has through Christ Jesus been granted you; [5]for in Him you have in every respect been enriched with full power of expression and full knowledge. [6]In this way our witnessing of Christ has been confirmed in you, [7]so that you are falling behind in no spiritual gift, while awaiting the appearing of our Lord Jesus Christ. [8]And He will establish you to the finish, so that no blame may be yours at the day of our Lord Jesus Christ. [9]God is trustworthy, through whom you were called into the companionship of His Son, our Lord Jesus Christ.

[10]But in the name of our Lord Jesus Christ I beg of you, brothers, that all of you agree, that you eliminate factions among you, and that you be united in mind and attitude. [11]For the Chloe family reports to me about you, my brothers, that there are wranglings among you. [12]I mean that each of you either says, "Paul certainly is my leader," or "But Apollos[d] is mine," or "But Cephas[e] is mine," or "But Christ is mine." [13]Is Christ dismembered? Paul was not crucified for you, was he? Or were you baptized in Paul's name?

[14]I am thankful to have baptized none of you except Crispus and Gaius, [15]so that none of you may claim baptism in my name. [16]Oh, yes, I baptized the Stephanas family, also, but I do not remember baptizing anyone else. [17]For Christ sent me, not to baptize but to preach the good news, and that not with verbal eloquence, so that the cross of Christ will not be made ineffectual.

[18]For the message of the cross is folly to those on their way to destruction, but to us who are being saved, it is God's power, [19]as it is written,[f] "I will render useless the wisdom of the learned and set aside the understanding of the intelligent." [20]Where is the wise man? Where is the scholar in the Law? Where is the debater of this time? Has not God shown the folly of worldly wisdom? [21]Inasmuch as in God's providence the world failed to know God by means of its wisdom,

---

a) Sosthenes was the ruler of the synagogue in Corinth, Acts 18:17.
b) Corinth, the principal city of the ancient Roman province of Achaia in southern Greece, is situated in close proximity to water on either side — The Gulf of Corinth on the west and nearby Cenchreae, Corinth's seaport on the Aegean Sea on the east.
c) See note at Acts 9:13.
d) Apollos was a Jew from Alexandria whom Paul met at Ephesus. He is said to have been "a man of learning and powerful in the Scriptures," Acts 18:24.
e) *Cephas* is the Aramaic equivalent of the Greek *Petros,* from which the name Peter comes. See note at Matt. 16:18.   f) Isa. 29:14.

God was pleased to save those who believe through the folly of the proclamation. 22And while Jews request signs and Greeks search for wisdom, 23we on our part preach the crucified Christ; a snare to the Jews and folly to the Gentiles, 24but to the called, both Jews and Greeks, Christ, God's power and God's wisdom. 25Because God's folly surpasses human wisdom and God's weakness surpasses human strength.

26Simply consider your own call, brothers; not many of you were wise, humanly speaking, not many mighty, not many noble, 27but God has chosen the world's foolish things to put to shame the learned; and God has chosen the weak in the world to shame the strong. 28God also has chosen the world's insignificant and despised people and nobodies in order to bring to nothing those who amount to something, 29so that nobody may boast in the presence of God.

30But from Him you have your existence in Christ Jesus, who became for us divine wisdom and righteousness and holiness and redemption, 31so that as has been written,g "Let the boaster boast in the Lord."

2 SO WHEN I CAME TO YOU, BROTHers, I came with no superiority of eloquence or of wisdom, when I announced to you God's revealed truth; 2for I determined to know nothing among you except Jesus Christ and Him crucified. 3And I was before you with a sense of weakness, with fear and considerable trepidation.

4My message and my preaching were not in persuasive, learned oratory, but rather in evidence of the Spirit and power, 5so that your faith might not rest on human wisdom but on divine strength.

6We do, indeed, express wisdom among the mature, but neither the wisdom of this world nor the rulers of this world, who are going to pass away. 7Instead, we give expression to divine wisdom in the form of a mystery,h wisdom that has been hidden,

which God before all time designed for our glory. 8None of this world's rulers has understood it, for had they understood they would never have crucified the Lord of glory. 9But as it is written,i "No eye has seen, nor ear has heard, neither has the human heart thought of what God has prepared for those who love Him."

10Through the Spirit, however, God has revealed it to us; for the Spirit fathoms everything, even the deep things of God. 11For among men who knows a person's thoughts, except the man's own inner spirit? Similarly, no one knows the thoughts of God except the Spirit of God. 12And we have received, not the spirit of the world but the Spirit that comes from God, in order that we may know the things which God has freely given us.

13Of these matters we speak, not in words taught by human wisdom, but in words taught by the Spirit — interpreting spiritual truth to spiritual persons. 14But the unspiritual person does not accept the things of the divine Spirit; to him they are folly and he cannot understand them, because they are evaluated from a spiritual standpoint. 15The spiritual person, on the other hand, judges the value of everything, while he is properly valued by none. 16For who has known the Lord's mind well enough to instruct Him? But we have the mind of Christ.

3 SO I WAS NOT IN POSITION, BROTHers, to speak to you as to spiritual persons but as to worldlings, as to babes in Christ. 2I gave you milk to drink, not solid food, because you were not yet strong enough. Neither, in fact, are you strong enough now, 3for you are still unspiritual. Insofar as you entertain jealousy and contentiousness, are you not unspiritual and do you not behave like the unconverted? 4When one says,j "I hold with Paul," and another, "I with Apollos," are you not unchanged men? 5Who is Apollos, anyway, and who is Paul, but ministers through whom, as the Lord gave each

g) Jer. 9:24; *cf.* II Cor. 10:17.
h) This mystery relates to "the deep things of God," vs. 10. *Cf.* note at Rom. 16:25.
i) Isa. 64:4.   j) Compare ch. 1:12.

his task, you came to believe? [6]I did the planting, Apollos did the watering, but God caused the growth, [7]so that neither the planter nor the waterer deserves credit, but God who causes the growth.

[8]The planter and the waterer, however, work as one, and each will receive his own reward in agreement with his particular labor. [9]For we are God's fellow workers. You are God's fields; you are the building which God is constructing.[10]Because of the grace of God which has been granted me, I have, as a wise master builder, laid a foundation on which another builds; and let each look out how he does the building. [11]For none is able to lay another foundation than the one already laid, which is Jesus Christ.

[12]In case one builds on this foundation gold, silver, precious stones, wood, hay, stubble, [13]each one's work will become evident, for the Day will bring it to light; it will be revealed by fire. Of whatever quality each one's work may be, the fire will test it. [14]In case one's construction survives, he will receive his pay. [15]In case one's work is burned down, he will be the loser; though he himself will be saved, yet only as in passing through fire.

[16]Do you not know that you are God's temple and that the Spirit of God dwells in you?[k] [17]If anyone destroys the temple of God, God will destroy him; for the temple of God is holy, and you are such a temple.

[18]Let no one fool himself. If someone among you seems to be wise in this age, let him become foolish in order to grow wise; [19]for the wisdom of this world is folly in God's estimation; as it is written,[l] "He snares the shrewd in their own cunning." [20]And again,[m] "The Lord knows the reasonings of the wise, how futile they are."

[21]Let none, therefore, boast in men, for everything is yours, [22]whether Paul or Apollos, or Cephas,[n] or the universe, or life, or death, or present things or future things, they are all yours, [23]while you are Christ's and Christ is God's.

4 PEOPLE SHOULD CONSIDER US AS servants of Christ and stewards of God's mysteries. [2]The prime requisite of stewards is fidelity. [3]To me it is of very little importance to be judged by you or by any human court; nor do I even judge myself, [4]for I am not vindicated because I am unconscious of wrong on my part. The One who judges me is the Lord. [5]So do not pass premature judgment before the Lord comes, who will bring to light the things hidden by darkness and will reveal the inner motives. Then will each one experience his approval from God.

[6]These suggestions, brothers, I have applied in a figure to myself and to Apollos for your sakes, so that from our experience you may learn not to go beyond what is written,[o] in order that you may not support one teacher against the other. [7]For who concedes you any superiority? What have you that you have not received? But if you received it, why do you boast as if it were not received? [8]Are you already satisfied? Are you already rich? Are you without us on the throne? How I wish you did reign, so we might reign with you!

[9]For I think that God has appointed us apostles last, as designed for death; for we have become an exhibition to the universe, to angels as well as to men. [10]On Christ's account we are fools, but in Christ you are intelligent; we are weaklings, but you are powerful. You enjoy honor, but we are despised.

[11]Up to this very hour we are hungry and thirsty; we are ill-clothed, roughly treated, and homeless. [12]We toil to exhaustion with our own hands. Being slandered, we bless; being persecuted, we patiently endure; [13]being defamed, we bring comfort. To this moment we are considered the scum of the earth, the off-scouring of all things.

---

k) The Holy Spirit resides in the heart of every believer in Christ, Rom. 8:9.
l) Job 5:13.
m) Ps. 94:11.
n) See note at ch. 1:12.
o) Everything is to be weighed by what God has revealed in His Word.

[14]I do not write these things to shame you, but to warn you as my dear children. [15]For although you have a myriad of tutors in Christ, you nevertheless have not many fathers; because in Christ Jesus I became your father by means of the good news concerning Christ. [16]Hence I urge you that you imitate me. [17]For this reason I am sending to you Timothy, my beloved and faithful son in the Lord, who will remind you of my principles of behavior in Christ Jesus, such as I teach everywhere in every church.[p]

[18]Some have grown inflated with pride, as though I were not coming to you. [19]But, the Lord willing, I shall come to you shortly, and then I shall discover, not the words of those conceited persons but their power; [20]for the kingdom of God is not a matter of words but of power.

[21]Which do you want? Shall I come to you to punish, or in love and in a spirit of gentleness?

5 IT IS ACTUALLY REPORTED THAT there is sexual immorality among you, and that of a kind which does not occur among the Gentiles — that a man has his father's wife.[q] [2]And you, rather than grieving about it enough to remove the person who committed such a deed, are you still puffed up? [3]As for me, present in spirit although absent in body, I have already, as if present, passed judgment on the one who thus behaved. [4]In the name of the Lord Jesus, when you are gathered together and my spirit[r] is present with you, together with the power of our Lord Jesus, [5]let such a person be handed over to Satan for the destruction[s] of the flesh in order that the spirit may be saved on the day of the Lord Jesus.

[6]Your boasting is not admirable. Are you not aware that a little yeast changes the whole batch? [7]Purge out the old yeast, so that you will be a fresh batch. You are in fact unleavened, for our Passover Lamb has been sacrificed, even Christ. [8]Let us therefore celebrate the feast, not with use of old yeast, certainly not with yeast of malice and vice, but with unfermented batches of purity and truth.

[9]I wrote you in that letter[t] not to associate with sexually immoral people; [10]not that in a public way you must have nothing whatever to do with the immoral of this world, or the avaricious and grasping, or the idolatrous, for then you must get out of the world altogether. [11]So I write you now that if a pretended brother is immoral or greedy or idolatrous or abusive or a drinker or a robber, you must not associate with him, nor even eat with one of that type.

[12]What business of mine is it to judge outsiders? Do you not have those within the church to judge? [13]But outsiders God will judge. Expel that wicked person from your own company.

6 DOES ONE WHO HAS A CASE against someone else dare to go to law before a pagan court and not before the saints?[u] [2]Are you not aware that the saints will judge the world? And if the world is to be judged by you, are you not competent to be judges of minor matters? [3]Do you not know that we shall judge angels, not to mention affairs of this life?[v]

[4]When, however, you do have an everyday case, do you appoint for judges those in the church who have no standing? [5]I say this to shame you. Is there really not a single wise person among you who is capable of deciding

---

p) Paul's life matched his teaching.
q) Not the man's actual mother but his stepmother, his father being still living, II Cor. 7:12.
r) Paul's spirit as led by the Holy Spirit.
s) The word rendered "destruction" is translated from the Greek *olethros*. It does not of necessity carry the thought of annihilation but rather defilement or ruin, the subject thus becoming unsuited for its original purpose. The believer who continues to sin, such as the man described in this passage, may be given over to Satan so that he may be brought under conviction of sin and turned back to the place of obedience to God. Sometimes even physical death comes as a result of offenses against the Almighty, ch. 11:30; *cf.* Acts 5:1-11; I John 5:16, 17.
t) No copy of this letter has been found.
u) See note at Acts 9:13.
v) Implicit in reigning with Christ is the responsibility of judging the world, Dan. 7:22; *cf.* Matt. 19:28; Luke 22:30.

between brothers, 6instead of one brother going to law against another brother and that before unbelievers?

7It means complete defeat for you when you have lawsuits among yourselves. Why do you not rather suffer injustice? Why not rather be defrauded? 8Instead, you practice injustice and fraud, and that on your brothers.

9Do you not know that the unrighteous will not inherit God's kingdom? Be not misled; neither profligates, nor idolaters, nor adulterers, nor partakers in homosexuality, 10nor thieves, nor the avaricious, nor drunkards, nor slanderers, nor robbers will inherit the kingdom of God. 11And some of you were just that; but you were washed and you were made holy and you were made righteous by the power of the Lord Jesus Christ and by the Spirit of our God.

12Everything is permitted me, but not everything is beneficial. Although everything is allowed me, I will not be mastered by anything. 13Food for the stomach and the stomach for food, but God will destroy both of them. The body is not for lust but for the Lord, and the Lord for the body; 14and as God raised up the Lord, so will He raise us up through His power.

15Are you not aware that your bodies are members of Christ? Shall I then take the members of Christ to make them members of a prostitute? No, never! 16Or do you not know that one who unites with a prostitute is one body with her? For "The two," He says,w "will become one flesh." 17But he who unites with the Lord is one spirit with Him.

18Shun sexual immorality. All other sin a person commits outside the body, but the immoral person sins against his own body. 19Or do you not know that your body is a temple of the Holy Spirit within you, whom you have from God, and that you do not belong to yourselves? 20For you were bought and paid for; then give God the glory with your body.

7 CONCERNING THE SUBJECTS OF your correspondence, it is good for a man to let a woman alone; 2but because of prevailing immoralitiesx let every man have his own wife and let every woman have her own husband. 3The husband must render to his wife the obligations that are due her, and similarly the wife to her husband. 4The wife does not have authority over her own body, but her husband does, and just so the husband does not have authority over his own body, but his wife does.

5Do not deprive each other, except by mutual agreement for a time to devote yourselves unhindered to prayer; and come together again, so that Satan may not tempt you on account of your lack of self-control.

6I say this by way of concession, not as a regulation. 7I wish all men were as I am, but each person has his own gift from God, the one in this direction, the other in that.

8To the single and the widows I say that it is good for them to remain as I am; 9but if they cannot restrain their passions, let them marry, for it is better to marry than to be consumed by passion.

10To the married couples I command — not really I but the Lord — that the wife must not leave her husband; 11and in case she does separate, she must either stay single or make up with her husband. And a husband must not divorce his wife.

12To the rest I say — but not as the Lord's commandy — if some brother has a wife who is not a believer but enjoys living with him, let him not divorce her. 13And if the wife has an unbelieving husband who enjoys living with her, let her not divorce her husband. 14For the unbelieving husband is dedicated through his wife, and the unbelieving wife is dedicated through her believing husband, else your children would be unholy, but now they are dedicated.

15In case the unbeliever wants to separate, let there be separation; the

w) Gen. 2:24.
x) Bear in mind that Paul's Epistle to the Romans was written in Corinth, in which letter see ch. 1:23-32.
y) Paul does not disclaim inspiration here but only disclaims a direct command of Christ.

brother or the sister is under such circumstances not tied down. But God has called you to enjoy peace. 16For how do you know, O wife, whether you will save your husband, or how do you know, O husband, whether you will save your wife?

17Certainly, as the Lord has assigned to each, as God has given each his calling, so keep on conducting yourselves; and this is my ruling in all the churches. 18Was a circumcised person called? Let him not try to efface it. Was an uncircumcised person called? Let him not be circumcised. 19Circumcision has no value, neither has uncircumcision, but the observance of God's commandments does count.

20Let each one stay in the station in life in which he received his call. 21Were you a slave when called? Do not let that worry you; but if you can gain freedom, you should avail yourself of the chance. 22It comes to this: the slave who is called by the Lord is the Lord's freedman; similarly he who is called while he is free is a slave of Christ. 23You were bought with a price; do not become slaves of men. 24Brothers, let each remain with God in the station in life in which he was called.

25Regarding the unmarried I have no divine injunction, but as one who has received mercy from the Lord to be trustworthy, 26I give my opinion. I consider, then, that in view of the impending distress it is good for a person to remain in his present situation. 27Are you united to a wife? Do not seek release. Are you unattached to a woman? Do not seek a wife. 28But in case you marry, you do not sin; nor does the unmarried woman sin if she marries. Such, however, will experience trouble in this life, and I would spare you that.

29I tell you this, brothers, the time is growing short. From now on let those who have wives behave as if they had none, 30and the mourners as if they were not mourning, and the joyful as if they did not rejoice; those who purchase as if they were not possessors, 31and those who make use of the world as if they had no use for it,z because the present world order is passing away.

32I would not have you worried. The single person is concerned with the Lord's affairs, how to please the Lord, 33but the married person is concerned with things of the world, how to please his wife; he has divided interests. 34The unmarried woman or the virgin is interested in the Lord's affairs, that she may be dedicated to Him in body and spirit; but the married woman is concerned with things of the world, how she may please her husband.

35I mention this for your own good, not to throw a rope around you but to promote proper behavior and undisturbed devotion to the Lord. 36If someone thinks he is not acting properly toward his virgin,a in case she is passing the bloom of youth and circumstances render it suitable, let him do as he pleases; it is no sin for them to marry. 37But he whose mind stands firm and who is under no compulsion, who has power over his own will and has determined in his own heart to preserve his virgin as a virgin, is doing right. 38So then, he who marries his virgin does well, and he who does not marry her does better.

39A wife is bound [by the law]b to her husband as long as he lives; but in case her husband dies, she is free to marry whom she pleases — only she should belong to the Lord.c 40It is my judgment, however, that she will be better off by remaining single. And I think also that I have God's Spirit.

8 WITH REGARD TO FOOD THAT HAS been offered to idols, we are aware that we all have knowledge. Knowledge puffs up, but love builds up. 2If anyone fancies he knows anything, he

---

z) Not worldly things but things that pertain to the kingdom of God must be the Christian's supreme interest.
a) Either one's daughter or fianceé, probably the latter.
b) The words enclosed in brackets are not found in the majority of the most reliable ancient manuscripts.
c) Compare II Cor. 6:14.

does not yet understand as he should; [3]but if anyone loves God, that person is known by Him.

[4]Now concerning food that has been dedicated to idols, we know that no idol really exists, that there is no God but one. [5]Even if there are so-called gods either in heaven or on earth, as indeed there are many gods and many lords, [6]for us there is one God the Father, from whom all things come and who is our goal; and one Lord Jesus Christ, through whom all things exist and through whom we are.

[7]This knowledge, however, does not rest with everyone. There are some so accustomed to still thinking in terms of idols, that they eat food as offered to idols,[d] and their conscience, weak as it is, becomes contaminated. [8]Of course food does not recommend us to God; we are none the better for eating nor any the worse for not eating. [9]But make sure that this freedom of choice of yours does not become a hindrance to those who are weak.

[10]For if someone sees you, with your knowledge, sitting[e] at the table in an idol temple, will not his conscience, weak as it is, encourage him to eat food offered to idols? [11]In consequence this weak brother, on whose behalf Christ died, is ruined by your enlightenment. [12]But as you thus sin against your brothers and hurt their weak consciences, you sin against Christ. [13]Therefore, if my eating causes my brother to stumble, I shall eat no meat forever, so that my brother will not be made to fall into sin.[f]

9 AM I NOT FREE? AM I NOT AN apostle? Have I not seen[g] our Lord Jesus? Are you not my work in the Lord? [2]If to others I am not an apostle, I certainly am to you; for in the Lord you are the certificate of my apostleship. [3]My reply to those who criticize me is this: [4]Do not we have the right to eat and to drink? [5]Do not we have the right to take along a Christian wife with us on our travels as the other apostles do, and the Lord's brothers, and Cephas?[h] [6]Or, are only Barnabas and I not entitled to freedom from manual labor?

[7]Who serves as a soldier at his own expense? Who plants a vineyard and does not eat its fruit? Or who herds a flock and does not enjoy its milk? [8]Am I saying this purely from a human standpoint, or does not the Law say the same thing? [9]For in the Law of Moses it is written,[i] "You must not muzzle a threshing ox." Is God thinking in terms of oxen, [10]or does He not certainly speak on our behalf? For our sakes it is written, because the plowman ought to plow in hope and the thresher thresh in expectation of his share.

[11]Inasmuch as we have sown spiritual seed among you, is it remarkable for us to reap material benefits from you? [12]Since others enjoy the right to share material benefits from you, do not we all the more? True, we did not avail ourselves of this right; instead, we endure everything so that we may furnish no obstacle to the good news concerning Christ.

[13]Are you not aware that those who conduct the temple service make their living from the temple, and that those who tend the altar share in the altar gifts? [14]In a similar way the Lord directed that those who preach the good news should live from the good news. [15]But I have not availed myself of any of these rights, nor am I writing this to have them granted to me. I would rather die than have anyone rob me of this reason for boasting.

[16]For preaching the good news I claim no glory, for I am under compulsion to do so. It is woe[j] to me if I do not preach the good news. [17]If I do this willingly I have my reward; but if I am compelled to do so, it is an of-

---

d) Since they keep thinking of idols as realities, their conscience is disturbed.
e) See note at Mark 2:15.
f) Here is a guide to Christians about engaging in certain doubtful practices.
g) On the Damascus Road, Acts 9:1-22; *cf.* I Cor. 15:8.
h) See note at ch. 1:12.
i) Deut. 25:4.
j) The word translated "woe," Greek *ouai*, is equivalent to "alas." It is an expression denoting displeasure or pain.

fice with which I am entrusted. [18]What then is my compensation? This, that in preaching I may offer the good news without cost; that I do not make full use of my authority as a preacher of the good news.

[19]Although I am free from every one, I have enslaved myself to all of them in order to win a larger number. [20]To the Jews I behave as a Jew to win Jews; to those under the Law as one who is under the Law — although I am not under the Law — to gain those who are under the Law. [21]To those who are without law I am as without law — although not lawless toward God but committed to Christ's Law — in order to win those who are without law. [22]To the weak I have become weak to win the weak. I have become everything to everybody so that by all means I may save some. [23]But I do it all to advance the good news, that I may have a share in it with you.

[24]Do you not know that those who race in the stadium all run, to be sure, but one receives the prize? So run your race that you may win it. [25]And everyone who enters the contest, practices self-control in every detail; he, indeed, does it to receive a perishable crown, but we an imperishable.

[26]Accordingly, I run straight ahead, not aimlessly; I thus box, not punching the air. [27]But I discipline my body and make it serve me, so that, while I am preaching to others, I myself may not be disqualified.

10 I WANT YOU TO KNOW, BROTH-ers, that although our fathers were all under the cloud, and all passed through the sea, [2]and all as followers of Moses were baptized in the cloud and the sea,[k] [3]and all ate the same spiritual food [4]and drank the same spiritual drink, for they drank from the spiritual rock which accompanied them, which rock was Christ.[l] [5]Nevertheless God was not pleased with the majority of them, for they were struck down in the wilderness.

[6]These things occurred as examples for us, so that we may not lust after evil as they lusted, [7]neither be idol-worshipers as some of them were, as it is written,[m] "The people sat down to eat and to drink and got up to dance." [8]Neither should we do immoral deeds as some of them did, when[n] twenty-three thousand fell in one day. [9]Neither should we become a trial to the Lord as some of them tried Him and were destroyed[o] by serpents. [10]Do not grumble, either, as some of them grumbled, and they were put out of the way[p] by the destroyer.

[11]These experiences came to them as a lesson for us and were written as a warning to us, on whom the end of the age has come.[q] [12]Therefore let him who feels sure of standing firm, beware of falling. [13]No temptation except what all people experience has laid hold of you, and God is faithful, who will not permit you to be tempted beyond your ability but will, at the time of temptation, provide a way out, so that you will be able to stand it. [14]For this reason, my dear friends, keep clear from idolatry.

[15]I appeal to your intelligence; judge for yourselves what I say. [16]Is not the blessed cup, which we consecrate, a fellowship in the blood of Christ? Is not the bread we break a fellowship in the body of Christ? [17]The many of us are one bread, one body, since we all participate in the one bread.

[18]Look at those of Israelite descent. Are not those who eat the sacrifice sharers of the altar? [19]What then am I saying? That an offering to idols amounts to anything, or that the idol itself is anything? [20]No, but that which they sacrifice, they are offering to demons and not to God, and I do not want you to have fellowship with demons. [21]You cannot drink the Lord's cup and the cup of demons. You can-

---

k) The Israelites identified themselves with Moses by sharing his experiences.
l) The rock was a symbol of Christ. A rock or stone is frequently employed figuratively of Him, e.g., Gen. 49:24; Deut. 32:4; II Sam. 23:3; Eph. 2:20; I Pet. 2:8.
m) Exod. 32:6.
n) Num. 25:1-9.
o) Num. 21:4-6.
p) Num. 16:41.
q) That is, particularly to those in the church in this present age.

not participate in the Lord's table and the table of demons. 22Or shall we provoke the Lord to jealousy? Are we mightier than He?

23Everything is allowed, but not everything is helpful. Everything is allowed, but not everything is constructive. 24Let none seek his own advantage but rather that of his neighbor. 25Eat whatever is sold in the meat market, without asking questions for conscientious scruples, 26for the earth and its fullness are the Lord's.

27In case an unbeliever invites you[r] and you wish to go, eat whatever is served you, without making conscientious inquiries. 28But if someone informs you, "This is food that has been offered to idols," then do not eat it, on account of the one who reminded you and for conscience' sake, — 29I mean not your own but the other person's conscience; for why should my freedom be unfavorably judged before another person's conscience? 30When I partake with gratitude, why should I be denounced on account of that for which I give thanks? 31So, whether you eat or drink or whatever you do, do it all to the glory of God.[s]

32Behave in such a way that you cause neither the Jews, nor the Greeks, nor the church of God to stumble, 33just as I myself please everyone in every way, not seeking my own advantage but that of the many, in order that they may be saved.

11 IMITATE ME, AS I IMITATE Christ. 2I commend you for remembering me in everything, and for observing the traditions I transmitted to you. 3But I want you to understand that Christ is the head of every man, that the man is the woman's head, and that God is the head of Christ. 4Any man who has his head covered while praying or prophesying dishonors his head, 5but any woman who has her head uncovered while praying or prophesying dishonors her head, for it is the same as if she were shaved. 6If a woman does not wear a veil,[t] let her hair be cut; but if it is disgraceful for a woman to have her hair cut off or her head shaved, then let her wear a veil.

7The man should not have his head covered, since he is the image and glory of God, but the woman is the man's glory. 8For man is not from woman but woman from man; 9neither was man created for the woman's sake, but woman for the man's sake. 10The woman, therefore, ought to have a token of authority on her head, because of the angels.[u] 11Nevertheless, in the Lord woman is not independent of man, and man is not independent of woman, 12for just as the woman is from the man, so the man is through the woman, and they all have their origin from God.

13Judge for yourselves. Is it becoming for a woman to worship God without covering for her head? 14Does not nature itself teach you that long hair is disgraceful for a man 15but glorious for a woman? For her hair is granted her for a covering. 16In case, however, anyone seems anxious to dispute the matter, we do not observe such a practice, neither do the churches of God.

17In giving these instructions, however, I do not commend you, because you do not meet together for the better but for the worse. 18For in the first place, I hear that as you meet as a congregation there are divisions among you, and to some extent I believe it. 19Indeed, there have to be factions among you, so that the genuine among you may be recognized.

20So when you meet, you do not come to eat the Lord's Supper, 21for in your eating each one goes ahead and takes his own supper, so that this one stays hungry and that one imbibes too freely. 22Do you not have homes for your eating and drinking? Or have you no respect for the church of God, and would you humiliate those who have nothing? What shall I tell you? Shall I commend you? In this matter I do not commend you.

r) For a meal with him.
s) Questionable practices should be examined by this test: can they be done to the glory of God?
t) That is, to cover her head.
u) Ministering angels, Heb. 1:14.

23For I have received from the Lord[v] what I also delivered to you, that the Lord Jesus, on the night in which He was betrayed, took bread, 24and when He had given thanks, He broke it and said, "This is My body, broken on your behalf; this do in remembrance of Me." 25Similarly also He took the cup, after they had supped, saying, "This cup is the new covenant in My blood. This do, as often as you drink it, in remembrance of Me." 26For as often as you eat this bread and drink the cup, you will proclaim the Lord's death till He comes.

27Whoever, therefore, eats the bread, or drinks the cup of the Lord in an unworthy manner, is a violator of the Lord's body and blood. 28But let a person look carefully at himself and in that spirit eat of the bread and drink from the cup; 29for whoever eats and drinks without due appreciation of the body[w] of Christ eats and drinks to his own condemnation. 30For this reason many among you are weak and sick, and a number have died.

31If, however, we scrutinized ourselves, then we should not be judged. 32And the judgments from the Lord serve to discipline us, so that we may not be condemned with the world. 33Accordingly, my brothers, when you come together to eat,[x] wait for one another. 34If anyone is hungry, let him eat at home, so that your meeting may not lead to judgment. The rest I will arrange[y] when I come.

12 I DO NOT WANT TO LEAVE YOU in the dark, brothers, about spiritual gifts. 2You know how in your days of paganism you were drawn away after dumb idols, in whatever way you were led. 3I therefore declare to you that no one who says, "Jesus be cursed!" is speaking by the Spirit of God; neither is any one able to say, "Jesus is Lord," except by the Holy Spirit.

4There are distinctive gifts of grace, but the same Spirit, 5and there are distinctive ministries, yet the same Lord. 6There also are varieties of things accomplished, but the same God does all the energizing in them all.

7To each is granted the evidence of the Spirit for the common welfare. 8To one person is given by the Spirit a message of wisdom and to another the utterance of knowledge according to the same Spirit; 9to a third faith is granted by the same Spirit; to yet another the gifts of healing by the one Spirit; 10to another miraculous powers; to this one prophecy, to that one discrimination between spirits, to a third variety of tongues, and to yet another the ability to interpret tongues. 11All these abilities one and the same Spirit energizes, distributing to each individual exactly as He pleases.[z]

12For just as the body is one and has many members, while all the numerous parts of the body compose one body, so it is with Christ. 13For by one Spirit we have all been baptized into one body, whether Jews or Greeks, whether slaves or free, and we have all been imbued with one Spirit.

14The body consists not of one but of many members. 15If the foot should say, "Because I am not a hand, I do not belong to the body," it would nevertheless remain part of the body. 16Or if the ear should say, "Because I am not an eye, I do not belong to the body," it is nevertheless part of the body. 17If the entire body were an eye, where would the hearing come in? Or if all were hearing, what of the smelling? 18As it is, however, God has

---

v) The way that the believers at Corinth had been observing the Lord's Supper was certainly not from the Lord. Paul, on the other hand, had received a direct revelation from the Lord concerning its commemoration.
w) The body of Christ is composed of all believers in Him.
x) On the night on which our Lord was betrayed He and the Twelve partook of the Passover Feast in the upper room before He instituted the Lord's Supper. In later years believers frequently held feasts of love before they broke the bread and poured the wine of communion. In Corinth the feast of love, cf. Jude 12, had become out of hand and, as a result, the Lord's Supper was partaken of in an unworthy manner. One needs to scrutinize his own life before he meets with God, lest he be judged.
y) I Cor. 7:17.
z) Every Christian has a gift from the Holy Spirit. Each must discover what his gift is, and then use it for the glory of God.

placed the members in the body, each particular one of them just as He saw fit.

19If they were all one member, where would the body be? 20As it is there are many members to form one body. 21The eye cannot say to the hand, "I do not need you"; nor again the head to the feet, "I do not need you." 22What is more, those seemingly delicate members of the body are indispensable, 23and on those that are considered ignoble we bestow additional honor. Our unpresentable members are also given more than usual modesty, 24such as our presentable members do not require. In fact, God has so constituted the body with the inferior members the more richly endowed, 25that there may be no discord in the body, but instead the members may have the same concern one for another. 26When one member suffers, all the members share the suffering. When a member is honored, they all share the joy.

27But you are Christ's body and individually members of it. 28And God has appointed in the church first apostles, next prophets,a third teachers, then miracle workers, then gifts of healing, helping, administering, speaking in tongues. 29Not all are apostles, are they? Not all are prophets, or teachers, or miracle workers, 30or possessing the gifts of healing, or speaking in tongues, or being able to interpret, are they? 31But earnestly desire the more valuable spiritual gifts. And I shall show you a still more excellent way.

13 EVEN THOUGH I SPEAK IN human and angelic language and have no love,b I am as noisy brass or a clashing cymbal. 2And although I have the prophetic gift and see through every secret and through all that may be known, and have sufficient faith for the removal of mountains, but I have no love, I am nothing. 3And though I

give all my belongings to feed the hungry and surrender my body to be burned, but I have no love, I am not in the least benefited.

4Love endures long and is kind; love is not jealous; love is not out for display; 5it is not conceited or unmannerly; it is neither self-seeking nor irritable, nor does it take account of a wrong that is suffered. 6It takes no pleasure in injustice but sides happily with truth. 7It bears everything in silence, has unquenchable faith, hopes under all circumstances, endures without limit.

8Love never fails. As for prophesyings, they will pass away; as for tongues, they will cease; as for knowledge, it will lose its meaning. 9For our knowledge is fragmentary and so is our prophesying. 10But when the perfect is come then the fragmentary will come to an end.

11When I was a child I talked like a child, thought like a child, I reasoned like a child, but on becoming a man I was through with childish ways. 12For now we see indistinctly in a mirror,c but then face to face. Now we know partly, but then we shall understand as completely as we are understood.

13There remain then, faith, hope, love, these three; but the greatestd of these is love.

14 MAKE LOVE YOUR GREAT QUEST; then desire spiritual gifts, and especially that you may prophesy. 2For whoever speaks in a tonguee does not speak to men but to God; no one catches the meaning; he is uttering secret matters in the Spirit. 3But he who prophesies gives people a constructive, encouraging and comforting message.

4He who speaks in a tongue improves himself, but he who prophesies builds up the church. 5I wish you might all speak in tongues, but I would

---

a) Prophets declare the full revelation of God and not simply predictions about the future.
b) The Greek noun for "love" in this chapter and 14:1 is *agape* (verb *agapao*) which denotes a very deep love such as Christ's love to man, John 13: 34. See note at John 21:15.
c) Most mirrors in apostolic times were made of metal. The images they reflected were not clear but blurred.
d) Love is greatest since it will endure throughout eternity, whereas faith and hope are temporal.
e) That is, an unknown tongue or unfamiliar language, and so in the verses that follow.

rather have you all prophesy. He who prophesies is more important than he who speaks in tongues, unless he should interpret so that the church may enjoy edification.

6If, for instance, I should come to you, brothers, speaking in tongues, what good would I do you unless I presented to you some revelation or information or prophecy or instruction? 7Unless musical instruments, such as a flute or a harp, produce distinct tones, how will anyone know what is being played? 8In case the trumpet emits an indistinct call, who will get ready for battle? 9Just so you, unless with your tongue you contribute an intelligent message, how will your speech be understood? You will be talking into empty space.

10There are who knows how many languages in the world, and none without meaning. 11If, then, I do not catch the significance of an expression, I shall seem a foreigner to the one who addresses me, and so will the one who speaks seem a foreigner to me. 12And you are in a similar situation. Since you are eager for spiritual gifts, seek to excel in the upbuilding of the church.

13The person, therefore, who speaks in a tongue, should pray for ability to interpret. 14For in case I pray in a tongue, my spirit prays but my mind is unproductive. 15Then what about it? I shall pray with my spirit, but I shall pray also with my understanding. I shall sing with my spirit, but I shall sing also with my understanding. 16Else, when you in the Spirit render thanks, how will one not gifted with tongues say "Amen" to your thanksgiving, since he does not know what you say? 17To be sure, you are giving thanks well enough, but the bystander is not edified.

18Thanks be to God, I speak in tongues more than all of you; 19but in the congregation I would rather speak five words intelligibly to instruct others than a myriad of words in a tongue.

20Brothers, do not be children in your thinking; be children in wicked-ness, but in your thinking be mature. 21It is writtenf in the Law, "I shall speak to this people through strange languages and through alien lips, and even so they will not listen to me, says the Lord." 22So then tongues are for a sign, not for believers but for unbelievers, while prophecy is not for unbelievers but for believers. 23Suppose at an assembly of the whole church they should all speak with tongues, and uninstructed or unbelieving persons came in, would they not say that you are demented? 24But suppose they all prophesied, and some unbelieving or uninstructed person came in, he would be convicted by all; he would be called to account by all. 25The secrets of his heart would become evident and so, falling face down, he would worship God, declaring that in very truth God is among you.

26What then, brothers? When you meet together, each one contributes his part — a song, a lesson, a revelation, a tongue, an interpretation of it; everything should be constructive. 27If someone speaks in a tongue, let there be two or at the most three, each in his turn, and let one give an interpretation. 28But in case there is no interpreter, let them keep still in the church; let each of them speak to himself and to God. 29So, two or three prophets may speak while the rest pay attention. 30But if a revelation comes to another who is sitting by, then let the first one be silent; 31for it is possible for all to prophesy, each in his turn, so that all may learn and all may receive encouragement. 32And the spirits of the prophets are in subjection to the prophets; 33for He is not the God of disorder but of peace, as in all the churches of the saints. 34Let the women keep silent in the churches, for they are not allowed to speak. Instead, they must, as the Law says,g be in subordination. 35If they wish to learn something, let them inquire of their own husbands at home; for it is improper for a woman to speak in church. 36Or did God's message get its start

---

f) Isa. 28:11, 12; *cf.* Deut. 28:49. The "Law" sometimes denotes not the Law of Moses only or the Pentateuch but all of the O.T.
g) Gen. 3:16.

from you? Or did it come to you alone? [37]If anyone considers himself a prophet or inspired, let him understand that what I write to you is the Lord's injunction; [38]but if anyone disregards it, he is to be disregarded. [39]To conclude, my brothers, earnestly desire to prophesy, but do not hinder the speaking with tongues. [40]Let everything be done with propriety and in orderly fashion.

15 I WOULD FURTHER REMIND you, brothers, of the good news which I preached to you, which you welcomed, in which you stand, [2]and by which you are saved, if you keep hold of my message to you — unless, indeed, you believed in vain.

[3]For I transmitted to you as of first importance what I also received, that Christ died for our sins in accordance[h] with the Scriptures, [4]that also He was buried, and that He rose on the third day in accordance[i] with the Scriptures; [5]that also He was seen by Cephas,[j] then by the Twelve. [6]Later He appeared to more than five hundred brothers simultaneously, of whom the majority are still alive; but some have died. [7]Afterward He appeared to James,[k] then to all the apostles, [8]and last of all He appeared to me[l] also, as to one whose birth was like a miscarriage. [9]For I am the least of the apostles, not deserving the name of apostle because I persecuted the church of God.

[10]By divine grace, however, I am what I am, and His grace toward me was not ineffective. In fact, I have worked harder than any of them — that is, not really I but the grace of God that is with me. [11]So, whether I or they, such is our preaching and such is what you believed.[m]

[12]But if Christ is preached, that He was raised from the dead, how is it that some of you claim there is no resurrection of the dead? [13]If there is no rising of the dead, then Christ has not been raised; [14]but if Christ has not been raised, then our preaching amounts to nothing and your faith is futile. [15]Then we are discovered to be false witnesses of God because we have testified about God that He raised Christ, whom He did not raise if no dead are actually raised. [16]For if no dead are raised, then neither has Christ been raised. [17]But if Christ has not been raised, then your faith is futile; you are still in your sins. [18]And what is more, those who have died in Christ perished. [19]If we have hope in Christ for this life only, then of all people we are most to be pitied.

[20]But the fact is that Christ has been raised from the dead, the first fruits of those who have died. [21]For inasmuch as death came through a man, the resurrection from the dead is also through a Man. [22]For just as in Adam all die, so in Christ shall all[n] be made to live; [23]each, to be sure, in his turn: Christ first; then His own at His coming. [24]After that the end will come, when He hands over the kingdom to God the Father, after abolishing every ruler and all government and power. [25]For He must be King until He puts all His enemies under His feet.

[26]The last enemy to be subdued is death, [27]for "He has put everything under His feet." But when it says,[o] "All things are subjected to Him," it is clear that the One who does the subjecting of all to Him is excepted. [28]However, once everything is subjected to Him, then the Son, too, will subject Himself to the One who put all things in subjection under Him, so that God may be all in all.

[29]Otherwise, if the dead do not rise at all, what are they to do who are baptized for the dead?[p] And why are

---

h) Ps. 22; Isa. 53.
i) Ps. 16:10.
j) See note at ch. 1:12.
k) This was Jesus' half brother, the son of Mary and Joseph, *cf.* Gal. 1:19.
l) On the Damascus Road, Acts 9:8, 17.
m) Without exception they preached the risen Christ.
n) All believers in Christ, called "His own" in the next verse, and not just everybody.
o) Ps. 8:6; *cf.* Heb. 2:8.
p) Perhaps the allusion is to those who bravely identified themselves in baptism with others who had been martyred for Christ's sake. *Cf.* vs. 30.

they baptized for them? [30]Besides, why do we live dangerously every moment? [31]Every day I face death, as surely as I take pride in you, brothers, through Christ Jesus our Lord. [32]From a human standpoint, what good is my fighting against beasts in Ephesus?[q] If the dead are not raised, "let us eat and drink, for tomorrow we die."[r] [33]Do not be misled. Bad associations corrupt good morals. [34]Return to sober-mindedness as you should, and quit sinning. For I say to your shame, some have no sense of the presence of God.

[35]"But," someone will ask, "how are the dead raised? And with what body do they come?" [36]You simpleton! What you sow does not come to life unless it dies. [37]Nor is what you sow the body that is to be; it is a mere kernel, either of wheat or of some other grain. [38]But God gives it a body as He plans, and to each seed its particular body. [39]All flesh is not the same; but one kind is human, another is animal, another is fowl, and another fish. [40]There are heavenly bodies and also earthly bodies; but the radiance of the heavenly is one kind and that of the earthly is another kind. [41]The sun is radiant in one way and the moon is another way; the stars in still a different way. So does one star differ in radiance from another.

[42]So too is the resurrection from the dead. The body is sown in dissolution; it is raised in immortality. [43]It is sown in dishonor; it is raised in glory. It is sown in weakness; it is raised in power. [44]It is sown a natural body; it is raised a spiritual body. There is a spiritual as well as a physical body. [45]So it is written,[s] "The first man, Adam, became a living soul"; the last Adam became a life-giving Spirit.

[46]However, the spiritual was not first, but the physical; then the spiritual. [47]The first man, from the earth, was made of dust; the second Man is from heaven. [48]Those who are of the dust are like the one who was made of the dust,[t] and those who are of heaven are like the One from heaven. [49]And just as we have borne the likeness of the earthly one, so we shall bear the likeness of the heavenly One.

[50]But I make this statement, brothers, that flesh and blood cannot inherit the kingdom of God, neither does the perishable inherit the imperishable. [51]Take notice; I am telling you a secret. We shall not all die but we shall all be changed, [52]in a moment, in the twinkling of an eye, at the last trumpet call. For the trumpet will sound and the dead will be raised imperishable, and we shall be changed. [53]For this perishable must put on imperishability and this mortal must put on immortality. [54]And when this perishable has put on imperishability and this mortal has put on immortality, then shall the written word be fulfilled,[u] "Death is swallowed up in victory. [55]Death, where is your victory? Death, where is your sting?"

[56]The sting of death is sin, and the power of sin is the Law.[v] [57]But thanks be to God, who gives us the victory through our Lord Jesus Christ!

[58]Consequently, my beloved brothers, be steadfast, immovable, at all times abounding in the Lord's service, aware that your labor in the Lord is not futile.

16 WITH REGARD TO THE COLLECtion for the saints,[w] you should do as I commanded the churches of Galatia. [2]When the first day[x] of each week comes, let each of you set aside in proportion to what he has gained, so that there may be no collection when I arrive. [3]Then when I reach there, I will send those whom you approve with credentials to convey your gift to Jerusalem. [4]And if it is fitting for me to go, then they will accompany me.

[5]When I have crossed Macedonia, I shall make you a visit, for I shall pass

q) The identity of the "beasts in Ephesus" is not wholly clear. *Cf.* ch. 16:9.
r) Isa. 22:13.   s) Gen. 2:7.   t) That is, Adam.
u) Isa. 52:8; Hos. 13:14.
v) Sin gave death its power over man when he broke the Law.
w) See note at Acts 9:13.
x) A day of praise for Christ's resurrection. On this account the early church gathered for worship on Sunday, the first day of the week, rather than on the Sabbath, which is the seventh day of the week.

through Macedonia; 6but I am likely to stay a while with you, or even spend the winter, so that you may send me off, wherever I may go. 7For this time I do not want to see you merely in passing, but I hope, the Lord permitting, to stay with you for a while. 8I shall remain in Ephesus, however, until Pentecost; 9for a wide door is opening up for service, and there are many opponents.

10When Timothy arrives, see to it that his presence with you is free from embarrassment, for he does the Lord's work, just as I do. 11So let no one slight him, and whenever he returns to me, see him off safely, for I expect him along with the brothers.

12As for our brother Apollos, I have strongly appealed to him to visit you with the brothers, and find him quite unready to go now; but he will come whenever it is convenient.

13Be alert; stand firm in the faith; play the man; be strong. 14Let all that you do be done in love.

15I appeal to you, brothers (you know the Stephanas family, how it is the first fruits of the Achaia converts, and how they have devoted themselves to the service of the saints), 16that you obey such people as well as every fellow worker and earnest toiler. 17I am happy because of the arrival of Stephanas, Fortunatus, and Achaicus, for they have made up for your absence; 18they have refreshed my spirit and yours. It is to such people that you would do well to give recognition.

19The churches of Asia send you greetings. Aquila and Priscilla, together with the church in their house,y greet you heartily in the Lord. 20All the brothers send you greetings. Greet one another with a holy kiss.

21Here is my greeting in my own handwriting,z Paul's. 22Whoever does not love the Lord, he shall be accursed.a Our Lord, come!

23The grace of the Lord Jesus be with you. 24My love to you all in Christ Jesus.

---

y) Aquila and Priscilla were among the first believers in Corinth. Paul made his home with them when he was there, since he worked in the same craft as Aquila, tentmaking. Aquila and Priscilla later moved to Ephesus, where this letter was written by Paul.
z) Usually Paul dictated his letters, e.g. Rom. 16:22. Sometimes he added a kind of postscript by his own hand, e.g. here and in Gal. 6:11; Col. 4:18; II Thes. 3:17.
a) In the Greek text *anathema*, referring to the object of a curse, is used here, followed by the Aramaic *marana tha*, meaning "Our Lord, come!"

Description of the Corinthians

_____
_____
_____
_____
_____
_____
_____
_____
_____

Commands to the Corinthians

_____
_____
_____
_____
_____
_____
_____
_____

Warnings to the Corinthians

_____
_____
_____
_____
_____
_____
_____
_____
_____
_____
_____
_____
_____
_____
_____
_____
_____
_____

Theme of 1 Corinthians:

Segment Divisions

Problems or Topics	Major Divisions	Chapter Themes
		1
		2
		3
		4
		5
		6
		7
		8
		9
		10
		11
		12
		13
		14
		15
		16

Author:

Date:

Purpose:

Key Words:

2 CORINTHIANS

Paul, the apostle to the Gentiles, was taught and appointed by Jesus Christ. Strong in faith, confident, and greatly used by God, Paul was loved by multitudes and hated by thousands. Determined that the grace of God would not prove vain, he labored more than anyone.

However, Paul's labor was not without cost. He endured conflicts without and fears within. Yet he persevered. What were his conflicts, his fears, his sufferings? Are they similar to yours? And how did he endure? What held him? As Paul writes his second epistle to the Corinthians from Macedonia, probably in the winter of A.D. 55, he lets us see the answers to these questions.

THINGS TO DO

General Instructions

1. Second Corinthians is different from Paul's other epistles. Watch the atmosphere or tone of this epistle. Paul is defending himself, which is unusual for Paul. As you read through the book, note the issues Paul addresses and what he says to the Corinthians, and you will understand what Paul is up against.

2. Study the OBSERVATIONS CHART following 2 Corinthians and see what you'll need to observe as you study 2 Corinthians chapter by chapter. Make a duplicate of this chart so you can use it as a worksheet. When you have completed it, record the information on the chart in your New Testament.

   a. As you read each chapter, list everything you learn about Paul. Be sure to note the afflictions he endured: What must he do in respect to the Corinthians? What has been done to him by the Corinthians? Ask God to show you Paul's character, his heart, his joys, and his sorrows.

   b. Note what you learn about the Corinthians. Remember to ask the five W's and an H: What are they like? What is their relationship with Paul like? What is going on in the Corinthian church at this time? What have they said about Paul? What problems has Paul had to deal with in respect to them?

   c. What is Paul's desire or goal for the Corinthians?

   d. Titus is mentioned several times in this letter. Record what you learn about him from 2 Corinthians.

3. As you read 2 Corinthians chapter by chapter, do the following:

   a. Mark in the text in a distinctive way the key words (and their synonyms and pronouns) listed on the 2 CORINTHIANS AT A GLANCE chart. Write these on an index card that you can use as a bookmark while you study 2 Corinthians. (Hint: If you mark every reference to Satan with an appropriate symbol it will be easy to spot.)

   b. As you come to specific chapters you will notice other key words which are not listed on 2 CORINTHIANS AT A GLANCE. Mark these also.

c. If there are several truths you learn from the use of a key word within a chapter, list in the margin what you learn from that word. For example, list all you learn about *affliction (distress, trouble)* and *suffering*. Record the heading "Affliction/Suffering" in the margin of each chapter where you mark these key words. Mark the heading in a distinctive way so you can spot its recurrence throughout 2 Corinthians. Then under it list what you learn from that chapter.

4. Look for the theme (subject) of each chapter and record it above the chapter number in the text and under "Chapter Themes" on 2 CORINTHIANS AT A GLANCE.

Chapters 1–7

1. In the midst of this very personal letter, Paul gives some important insights on several subjects. In the margin where they appear, list what you learn about each subject.

   a. Chapter 3 mentions the new covenant (which is grace) and the old covenant/testament (which is law). These are described as ministries, and then the ministries are contrasted according to the result of each: condemnation or righteousness. List in the margin what you learn about each from the text.

   b. In chapter 5 Paul talks about what will happen to our earthly bodies when we die. He also discusses the tribunal of Christ and our ministry of reconciliation. Identify how these relate to one another and what you learn about each from the text. Write your observations in the margins.

   c. In chapter 7 Paul deals with two kinds of sorrow and what they pro-

duce. Don't miss this. Take notes in the margin.

2. What is Paul writing about in chapters 1 through 7? Is there a theme which runs through these chapters? Remember that key words reveal the themes. What key words are repeated the most in this segment?

3. How does Paul begin and end this segment?

4. Record the theme for chapters 1 through 7 on 2 CORINTHIANS AT A GLANCE under "Segment Divisions."

Chapters 8, 9

1. What subject is Paul talking about in chapters 8 and 9? Note the use of the words *ministry, work,* and *service.* What ministry or work or service is he referring to?

2. Record this subject as the theme of this segment in the appropriate space on 2 CORINTHIANS AT A GLANCE.

Chapters 10–13

1. Notice when the key word *boast* first appears in the text and what happens when it appears. Note what or whom the boasting is in and what you learn.

2. In the margin of chapter 11 list what you learn about Satan and spiritual warfare from these four chapters.

3. What does Paul seem to be doing in chapters 10 through 13? What opposition is there to Paul, and what is the opposition saying about him? What is his response to this opposition? Record the theme of this segment under "Segment Divisions" and complete the chart.

THINGS TO THINK ABOUT

1. What is the purpose of affliction? When you need to be comforted, do you turn to people or to God?

2. Is it always wrong to feel sorrow, to be hurt, or to have a broken heart? Is

it always wrong to cause sorrow, to hurt, or to break another person's heart?

3. How do you deal with those who oppose you? How do you minister to those who are caught in the middle of a conflict and don't know who to believe?

4. Paul was human just like us; he had feelings just like we do. What can we learn from him about how we are to live and respond in spite of our feelings? When is the time to give a defense of one's self, of one's ministry?

5. Are you prepared to stand before the tribunal of Christ?

6. What place does the ministry of giving play in your life?

7. If you were to examine yourself, would you find your Christianity genuine?

THE SECOND EPISTLE OF PAUL TO THE

CORINTHIANS

Date of writing: c. A.D. 57,
in Macedonia, probably Philippi

1 PAUL, BY THE WILL OF GOD AN apostle of Christ Jesus, and brother Timothy,[a] to the church of God at Corinth,[b] and to all the saints[c] throughout Achaia: [2]Grace to you and peace from God our Father, and from the Lord Jesus Christ.

[3]Blessed be the God and Father of our Lord Jesus Christ, the Father of mercies and God of all comfort, [4]who consoles us in our every trouble, so that we may be able to encourage those in any kind of distress, with the consolation with which we are divinely sustained. [5]For as we experience richly the sufferings of Christ, so we enjoy through Christ an abundance of consolation.[d]

[6]When we are troubled, it is for your comfort and salvation. When we are comforted, it is for the encouragement that you experience in the enduring of the same sufferings we endure. [7]And our hope for you is unshaken in view of the fact that you are sharing as well in the sufferings as in the consolation.

[8]So we want you to know, brothers, about the trouble that came to us in Asia,[e] how we were weighed down beyond all possible endurance, so that we really despaired of life. [9]Indeed, we passed the sentence of death on ourselves, but it was in order that we might not rely on ourselves but on God, who raises the dead. [10]He rescued us from so perilous a death and will rescue us again; we hope in Him, for He will yet deliver us, [11]while you also cooperate by your prayer for us, so that thanks may be given by many on our behalf for the blessings that came to us through many.

[12]The reason for our pride is the witness of our conscience that we have behaved in the world generally, but especially toward you, with devout motives and godly sincerity; not with worldly wisdom but by divine grace. [13]For the meaning of what we write you is not different from what you read and understand perfectly, [14]just as you have partly understood us, to the effect that we are your reason for pride, as well as that you are ours in the day of our Lord Jesus.

[15]It was with this assurance that I planned to visit you first, so that you might enjoy a double blessing, [16]visiting you on the way to Macedonia and again on the trip from Macedonia to you, and to be sent by you on my way to Judea. [17]Since I intended this, did I act with fickleness; or did I plan in a worldly way what I had in mind, so that on my part yes, yes equals no, no? [18]As God is trustworthy, our word to you is not yes and no, [19]because Jesus Christ, the Son of God whom we preached to you, Silvanus and Timothy

---

a) See note at I Tim. 1:2.
b) See note at I Cor. 1:2.
c) See note at Acts 9:13.
d) Paul faced persecutions, divisiveness, and lack of discipline within the church. Yet in these trials he was consoled through Christ by the God of all comfort, vss. 3-5.
e) An example of Paul's troubles in Asia is recorded in Acts 19:23-41.

and I,[f] was not yes and no, but in Him it is yes. [20]In Him all the promises of God are yes. For this reason we also say through Him "Amen" to God for His glory through us. [21]But He, who makes us steadfast with you in joint fellowship with Christ and has anointed us, is God, [22]who also stamped His seal on us and deposited in our hearts the first installment of the Spirit.

[23]I call upon God as my soul's witness, that to spare you I have delayed my coming to Corinth. [24]Not that we lord it over your faith, but rather that we work with you for your happiness, for by faith you stand firm.

2 I MADE UP MY MIND NOT TO MAKE you another distressing visit, [2]for if I grieve you, who may make me happy except those whom I grieve? [3]I wrote this so that when I came I might not be grieved by those who should make me happy; for I was confident that my confidence would be shared by every one of you. [4]For in deep distress and with a heart of anguish, yes, with many tears I wrote you, not in order to grieve you but in order that you might know the love I so richly bear you.

[5]If someone[g] has caused grief, he has not simply grieved me but, to some extent at least — not to exaggerate — all of you. [6]For such a one this censure by the majority suffices; [7]so, instead of further rebuke, you should forgive and comfort him, else he may be overwhelmed by despair. [8]I therefore beg you to reinstate him in your affection. [9]For this purpose I wrote, to know your attitude, whether you were altogether obedient. [10]But whom you forgive, him I also forgive, and what I forgive is forgiven for your sakes in the presence of Christ, [11]lest Satan should take advantage of us; for we are not ignorant of his schemings.[h]

[12]When I arrived at Troas for the good news concerning Christ, although there was a door opened for me in the Lord, [13]yet I enjoyed no peace of mind because I did not find my brother Titus; so I left them to go into Macedonia. [14]But thanks be to God, who invariably leads us on triumphantly in Christ and evidences through us in every place the fragrance that results from knowing Him. [15]For to God we are Christ's fragrance for those who are being saved and for those who are perishing; [16]to the one a fatal aroma that brings death, but to the other a vital aroma that brings life.

[17]And who is qualified for these things? Are not we? For we do not, like so many, peddle an adulterated message of God, but from the purest motives before God we speak in Christ as those sent from God.

3 ARE WE BEGINNING AGAIN TO RECommend ourselves? Or do we, like some people, stand in need of letters of recommendation to you or from you? [2]You are our letter of recommendation, written in our hearts, acknowledged and read by everyone, [3]making it obvious that you are Christ's letter delivered by us, written not with ink but with the Spirit of the living God, not on tablets of stone but on human tablets of the heart.[i]

[4]In God's presence I have such confidence through Christ, [5]not because we possess self-sufficiency to regard anything as from ourselves, but because our sufficiency is God-given. [6]And He has qualified us to be ministers of a new covenant, not of written Law but of the Spirit; for the letter kills[j] but the Spirit makes alive. [7]Yet if the ministry of death, engraved in letters of stone, was inaugurated with such splendor that the Israelites were not able to gaze intently at the face of Moses, because of the radiance of his face, which after all faded away, [8]how much more glorious must be the ministry of the Spirit? [9]If there is glory in the administration that announces condemnation, how infi-

---

f) Three accordant witnesses, *cf.* ch. 13:1.
g) The Corinthians would know that Paul was referring to the erring brother of I Cor. 5:1.
h) Christians must be aware constantly of Satan's evil designs.
i) Jer. 31:33.
j) The Law, which points to man's sinfulness, condemns him; the Holy Spirit gives the believer life through Christ.

nitely more glory must there be in the administration that declares righteousness! [10]In view of the surpassing glory, what was once glorious retains no glory at all. [11]If what passed away had its splendor, how much more that which is permanent!

[12]Possessed of such hope we speak quite unreservedly, [13]not as Moses did, who put a veil over his face to keep the Israelites from gazing at the end of something that was fading away. [14]In fact, their minds were dulled. To this very day, when the Old Testament is being read, that same veil remains, not lifted because only by Christ is it removed. [15]Yes, until now, whenever Moses is being read, a veil lies over their hearts; [16]but whenever one turns to the Lord, the veil is removed. [17]For the Lord is the Spirit, and where the Spirit of the Lord is there is liberty.

[18]But we all, as with unveiled face we see as in a mirror the Lord's glory reflected, are changed into the same likeness[k] from one degree of glory to another, derived as it is from the Lord, who is the Spirit.

4 THEREFORE, BEING ENGAGED IN this service through divine mercy, we are not despondent, [2]but we have renounced underhanded ways of which one should be ashamed. We do not behave craftily, nor do we falsify the word of God, but by clear announcement of the truth we commend ourselves in the presence of God to every human conscience. [3]If the good news that we preach has been obscured, it has been obscured in the case of those who are perishing, [4]in whom the god of this world[l] has blinded their unbelieving minds, to prevent the illumination of the good news concerning the glorious Christ, who is the likeness of God, from penetrating their hearts.

[5]For we do not proclaim ourselves but Christ Jesus as Lord, and ourselves your servants for Jesus' sake, [6]because God, who commanded[m] that light should shine out of darkness, has made it shine in our hearts so as to show forth the knowledge of the glory of God in the face of Christ.

[7]This treasure, however, we possess within utensils of clay — an evidence that the unparalleled power is from God and not from us. [8]We are hedged in from every side, but we do not live cramped lives; we are perplexed, but we do not despair; [9]we are persecuted but not deserted; struck down but not destroyed, [10]all the while bearing about in the body the dying[n] of Jesus, so that by our bodies the life of Jesus may also be shown. [11]In the midst of life we are constantly handed over to death for Jesus' sake, so that the life of Jesus may yet be evidenced through our mortal flesh. [12]Accordingly, death is active in us, but life in you.

[13]We have, nevertheless, that same spirit of faith as he had of whom it is written,[o] "I have believed; therefore have I spoken." We, too, believe and therefore we speak, [14]assured that He who raised up the Lord Jesus will raise us up with Jesus and will have us stand with you before Him. [15]For all this is for your sakes in order that grace which is multiplying with the thanksgiving of the many may abound for the glory of God.

[16]For this reason we are not discouraged, but even though our outer nature suffers decay, our inner self is renewed day after day. [17]For this slight momentary trouble is producing for us an everlasting weight of glory that exceeds all measures, [18]because we do not fasten our eyes on the visible but on the unseen; for the visible things are transitory, but the unseen things are everlasting.

5 FOR WE KNOW THAT, IF OUR earthly tent in which we are living should be dismantled, we have a God-

---

k) The likeness of Christ, which grows stronger with spiritual maturity.
l) Satan, *cf.* John 12:31; 14:30; 16:11; Eph. 2:2.
m) Gen. 1:3.
n) Paul bore in his body scars that proved his sufferings for Christ's sake, Gal. 6:16; *cf.* II Cor. 11:24-27.
o) Ps. 116:9-11.

given dwelling, a house in heaven not made by hands, that will last forever. 2So it is that in this dwelling we sigh with longing to be clothed with our dwelling from heaven, 3since with such clothing we shall not be found naked.p 4For we sigh deeply while in this tent, not because we want to be stripped of it but rather to be further clothed, so that what is mortal may be absorbed by life.

5For this experience God, who granted us the first installment of the Spirit has prepared us, 6so we always keep confident, knowing well enough that being at home in the body means being absent from the Lord; 7for we walk by faith, not by sight. 8But we have courage, and we prefer to be absent from the body and at home with the LORD. 9Therefore we make it our aim to be pleasing to Him, whether absent or present; 10for we must all appear before the tribunal of Christ,q so that each may receive as his due what he practiced while in the body, whether good or bad.

11Knowing, therefore, what it means to revere the Lord,r we seek to win people over. Our motives are clear to God and I hope they are made clear as well to your consciences. 12This is no repeated commendation of ourselves to you, but it is providing you with an incentive to feel proud of us, so that you may reply to those who are proud of a person's position and not of his heart. 13If we are beside ourselves, it is for God. If we are thoughtful, it is for you. 14For the love of Christ lays hold of us and brings us to this conclusion: one died for all, so that they all died; 15and He died for all so that all who live may no longer live for themselves but for Him who died and rose for them.

16Consequently, from now on we think of no one just in terms of his human nature. Even if we had thought of Christ in that way, we now no longer know Him just in terms of His human nature.s 17Accordingly, if any one is in Christ he is a new creation. The old is gone; lo, the new has come. 18But all things come from God, who has reconciled us to Himself through Christ, and has given us the ministry of reconciliation, 19which is that God was in Christ reconciling the world to Himself, not counting up their sins against them, and committing to us the message of reconciliation.

20On behalf of Christ, then, we are ambassadors, God as it were making the appeal through us. We beg you for Christ's sake, be reconciled to God. 21God made Him who knew no sin to be made sin on our behalf, so that in Him we might share the righteousness of God.

6 AS GOD'S FELLOW WORKERS, however, we appeal to you not to accept the grace of God without using it; 2for He says,t "At a welcome time I have heard you and on a day of salvation I have helped you." Observe that now is a specially welcome time, that now is the day of salvation — 3and we put no obstacle whatever in anyone's way, so that our ministry may not be discredited. 4Rather, we prove ourselves in every respect as servants of God, by great endurance, in afflictions, distresses, and hardships; 5in lashes, imprisonments, and disturbances; in toils, sleepless nights, and without food; 6through purity, knowledge, and endurance of wrongs; through kindness, by the Holy Spirit, in genuine love; 7with a message of truth, by the power of God; by means of the weapons of righteousness for attack and defense; 8through honor and shame; through blame and praise; considered impostors when we are honest, 9and unknownu when we are well known; thought of as dying when, you see, we are alive, and as disciplined but not put to death; 10as deceived and yet always joyful; as poor but making many wealthy; as having nothing and yet in possession of everything.

11O Corinthians, we address you

---

p) That is, as disembodied spirits.
q) Rom. 14:10.
r) Sensing awe in view of the great Judge, our Lord Jesus Christ, John 5:22.
s) Having known Christ on earth is not as important as knowing Him now. *Cf.* John 20:29.
t) Isa. 49:8.   u) Compare Matt. 13:57.

frankly with wide-open hearts. 12You are not hedged in by us, but you are cramped in your own affections. 13In exchange — I am speaking as to children — open wide your hearts in the same way.

14Be not yoked unequally with unbelievers; for what common ground is there between righteousness and lawlessness, or what association is there between light and darkness? 15Or what harmony is there between Christ and Belial,ᵛ or what partnership between a believer and an unbeliever? 16What agreement has God's temple with idols? For we are the temple of the living God, as God has said,ʷ "I will dwell in them and walk among them, and I will be their God and they shall be My people." 17For that reason,ˣ "Come out from their midst and be separate, says the Lord, and do not touch anything unclean. 18Then I will receive you and I will be a Father to you, and to Me you shall be sons and daughters. The Lord Omnipotent speaks."

7 IN POSSESSION OF THESE PROMises, beloved, let us cleanse ourselves from every defilement of flesh and spirit, and complete our dedication in reverence of God.

2Allow us room in your hearts. We have wronged no one; we have ruined no one; we have exploited no one. 3I am not censuring you, for, as I previously said, you are in our hearts to die and to live together. 4My confidence in you is strong; my pride in you is great; I am filled with comfort; in all our trouble I am overjoyed.

5For as we reached Macedonia, our bodies enjoyed no respite at all, but there was trouble at every turn, quarrels outside and fears within. 6But God, who encourages the downhearted, encouraged us by the arrival of Titus,ʸ 7and not merely by his arrival but by the encouragement he received from you; for he reported how you are longing for us, your sorrow, your zeal for me, all of which turned out for my greater joy.

8If I have grieved you with my letter, I do not regret it, and although I did regret it — for I observe how that particular letter did, though only momentarily, give you grief — 9I am glad of it now, not because you were grieved but because your grief led to repentance. For your grief was such as God desired, so that you suffered no loss from us. 10For the sorrow that God approves works out a repentance that leads to salvation such as is never regretted, while the world's sorrow produces death.

11For see how earnest this godly grief has made you; how apologetic; longing for me; how zealous; how ready to vindicate me. In every way you have proved yourselves cleared in the matter. 12So although I wrote you as I did, it was not on account of the offender or of the one offended, but so that your devotion for us might be revealed to you before God. 13On this account we have been comforted.

Added to our own consolation there was the enjoyment of Titus' happiness, because his spirit was refreshed by all of you, 14and I was not ashamed of my boasting to him about you; but just as everything we told you was true, so our boasting to Titus proved true. 15His feelings go out to you the more as he remembers the obedience of all of you, as with fear and trembling you receive him. 16I am glad I can have full confidence in you.

8 WE WANT YOU TO KNOW, BROTHers, of the divine grace that has been granted the Macedonian churches:ᶻ 2how, under a terrible ordeal of affliction their great happiness, combined with their deep poverty, has overflowed into a wealth of their generosity; 3how up to their ability — yes, and I bear them testimony, beyond their ability — they voluntarily have given, 4most urgently begging of us the favor of taking part in this service to the saints.ᵃ 5They did not do simply what we hoped for, but they gave themselves first to the Lord and so, in

---

v) Greek *Beliar*, meaning *worthlessness*. It is a name that was frequently applied to Satan.
w) Lev. 26:12.   x) Compare Isa. 52:11.
y) Titus had visited the church at Corinth and had reported conditions there to Paul, *cf.* ch. 8:6.
z) For example, Philippi, Berea, and Thessalonica.   a) See note at Acts 9:13.

keeping with the will of God, also to us.

6So we urged Titus to complete this gracious work among you, since he began it. 7But just as you are ahead in everything, in faith, in expression, in knowledge, in diligence of every sort, and in your love for us, so be foremost in this gracious work also.

8I am not issuing an order, but I would test the genuineness of your love by the eagerness of others. 9For you know the grace of our Lord Jesus Christ, how, although He was rich, yet He became poor for your sakes, so that you by His poverty might become rich.b 10Let me advise you in this matter. It is to your interest, because a year ago you were not only the first to act but also to want to do so. 11Now then, complete the enterprise, so that your readiness in desiring it may be equaled by the task accomplished to the measure of your means. 12For if there is present a willing mind, the gift is appreciated in proportion to what one possesses, not to what one does not possess.

13In order to afford relief to others, you need not put a heavy burden on yourselves; 14rather share fairly. Let your abundance at this time make up for their shortage, so that their surplus may go toward your lack, and thus conditions may become equalized, 15as it is written,c "The one who got much had nothing over and the one who got little did not lack."

16Thanks be to God, who planted in the heart of Titus the same devotion for you, 17for he welcomed my appeal and is so deeply interested in you that he went off to you of his own volition. 18But we are sending the brotherd along with him whose commendable ways in the things pertaining to the good news are known through all the churches. 19Besides, as an appointee of the churches, he travels with us in this ministry of grace for the Lord's own glory and for expediting our work.

20We take this precaution, so that no one may find fault with us in our handling of this liberal collection; 21for we intend to do the right thing not only before the Lord but also before men.

22Along with them we are sending our brother whose zeal we have frequently put to the test and who is now all the more zealous because he has so much confidence in you. 23As to Titus, he is my associate and your fellow worker in serving you; as to our brothers, they are messengers of the churches, an honor to Christ. 24Show them proof, then, of your love and of our boastings about you, such as will be evidenced before the churches.

9 IT IS SUPERFLUOUS FOR ME TO write you about this ministering to the saints, 2for I know of your willingness, and I boast about you to the Macedonians, saying that Achaiae has been ready since last year, and your zeal has stirred up a large number of them. 3I am sending these brothers so that our pride in you may not in this instance be an empty boast, but that you may be as fully ready as I told them. 4Or else, if any Macedonians should come with me and find you unprepared, we — not to say you — should be humiliated because of our confidence. 5I considered it therefore necessary to request these brothers to visit you in advance and to have your promised bountiful gift all made up, so it will be ready to hand, a real thank offering and not something extorted from you.

6I say this, that he who sows sparingly will also reap sparingly, while he who sows liberally will also reap liberally. 7Let each one give as he has planned in his heart, neither grudgingly nor by compulsion; for God loves a happy giver. 8And God is able to pour out on you richly every possible grace, so that you will always and under all circumstances have plenty for your own need and an abundance for every good work, 9as

b) Christ is the supreme example of the believer's wealth.
c) The allusion is to the gathering of manna, Exod. 16:18.
d) No clue is given concerning this man's identity or of the man mentioned in vs. 22.
e) Achaia here may denote other cities in the province, e.g. Cenchreae, the seaport of Corinth, but the reference is particularly to the church at Corinth. The Macedonians would include the believers in Philippi, Berea, and Thessalonica.

it is written,[f] "He has scattered abroad; he has given to the poor; his righteousness never fails."

10Now He who provides seed to the sower and food to eat will also supply and multiply your store of seed and will increase the harvest of your righteousness. 11You will be enriched in every respect for all kinds of generosity, and your liberality, as it is worked out through us, will cause thanksgiving to God. 12For the rendering of this service not only supplies amply the wants of the saints, but it also abounds in causing many thanksgivings to God; 13because of the proof of this service they are praising God for your loyalty to the good news about Christ which you confess, and for the liberality of your contribution for them and for all. 14And they feel a yearning for you in their prayer because of the unusual measure of divine grace that has come upon you. 15Thanks be to God for His unspeakable Gift.[g]

10 I, myself, Paul, appeal to you on the basis of Christ's gentleness and considerateness — I who am so meek when face to face with you and so bold toward you from a distance. 2I beg you not to force such boldness on me when I am with you as I intend to assume toward some who entertain the notion that we behave from merely human motives. 3For while we spend our life in a body of flesh, we do not war with carnal weapons. 4For the weapons of our warfare are not physical, but they are powerful with God's help for the tearing down of fortresses, 5inasmuch as we tear down reasonings and every proud barrier that is raised up against the knowledge of God and lead every thought into subjection to Christ. 6We are prepared also to punish all disobedience, when your obedience is fully expressed.

7Take a look at what you are facing. If someone is confident that he belongs to Christ, let him ponder this, that we are Christ's as well as he. 8Even if we do boast excessively about our author-ity, which the Lord granted us for your establishment and not for your destruction, I shall not be put to shame; 9neither would I appear as wanting to terrify you with my letters. 10For, "His letters," they say, "are weighty and forceful, but his physical presence is insignificant and his speech is contemptible."

11Let such people consider this, that what we are when absent through the message of our letters, that we are in action when present. 12For we do not venture to count ourselves among or to compare ourselves with some who commend their own qualities. However, when they make themselves their standard of measurement and judge their own value from comparisons with each other, then they do not behave wisely. 13On our part, we shall not boast extravagantly but rather stay within the limit of the sphere which God has allotted to us, the boundary of which stretches far enough to include you.

14We are not overextending ourselves, as if we did not reach as far as you, for we were the first to reach you with the good news about Christ. 15Neither are we boasting unduly about fields in which others are serving[h] but we entertain the hope that your growing faith may enlarge our sphere of influence so greatly with your help, 16that we may evangelize those beyond you, rather than brag about labor that has been accomplished in another's field. 17The person who boasts should boast in the Lord; 18for not he who commends himself, but whom the Lord commends, stands approved.

11 bear with me a little in this foolishness of mine. Yes, you will have to tolerate me; 2for I am jealous for you with a divine jealousy, because I gave you in marriage to one Husband to present you as a pure virgin to Christ. 3Only I am afraid that, just as the serpent beguiled Eve with his craftiness, so your thoughts may be corrupted from a sincere and

---

f) Ps. 112:9.   g) That is, Christ.
h) Paul would not assume credit for work done by other men.

pure devotion to Christ. [4]In fact, if someone comes along and preaches another Jesus, whom we have not preached, or if you receive a different spirit from what you received, or a gospel different from what you accepted, you put up with it quite easily.[i]

[5]Nevertheless I consider myself not inferior to the most eminent apostles. [6]Even if I lack skill in speaking, I certainly do not lack knowledge, which we have in every way made perfectly clear to all of you. [7]Or have I erred by humbling myself so that you might be exalted, when I preached to you the good news of God without compensation? [8]I robbed other churches, taking support from them in order to minister to you; [9]and when I was with you and ran short of funds, I imposed on none of you, for the brothers that came from Macedonia supplied my needs. Thus I invariably kept myself from being a burden to you, and so I plan to keep myself.

[10]As sure as Christ's truth is in me, this boast of mine shall not be stopped in the Achaia districts. [11]And why? Because I do not love you? God knows I do. [12]What I do, however, I shall do to remove the occasion from those who want it in order that in the work of which they boast they may appear as equal with us.[j] [13]For such are false apostles, deceptive workers. wearing the masks of apostles of Christ; [14]and no wonder, for Satan himself masquerades as an angel of light. [15]So it is nothing extraordinary if his servants disguise themselves as servants of righteousness, whose destiny will be in agreement with their actions.

[16]Once more I tell you, let no one consider me a fool; but if you do, then tolerate me as a fool, so that I too may do a bit of boasting. [17]What I say, I do not speak from the Lord but in a foolish mood in this boastful confidence. [18]Since many boast in a worldly way, I too will boast; [19]for you, being so wise, will gladly tolerate fools. [20]You stand for it when someone enslaves you, or imposes on you, or exploits you, or snubs you, or slaps you in the face. [21]To my shame I admit that we were too lacking in force along those lines.

[22]But in whatever line someone may boast — I talk foolishly — I dare to match him. Are they Hebrews? So am I. Are they Israelites? So am I. Are they Abraham's offspring? So am I. [23]Are they ministers of Christ? I more so — I say it as if I were out of my mind — in measureless toils and imprisonments, in floggings beyond count and facing death frequently. [24]Five times I received from the Jews forty lashes minus one,[k] [25]three times I was beaten with rods,[l] once I was stoned, three times I was shipwrecked, for a night and a day I have been adrift at sea. [26]In my many travels I have been in dangers of rivers and robbers, of Jews and Gentiles, of city, desert, and sea; in dangers among false brothers; [27]in wearying work and hardship through many a sleepless night; in hunger, thirst, and often without food; in cold and lack of clothing.

[28]Besides these experiences from the outside, there is the daily responsibility for the churches.[m] [29]Who is weak without my being weak? Who is led into sin without my burning with indignation? [30]If I must boast, I shall boast of matters that show my weakness. [31]The God and Father of the Lord Jesus, who is to be praised forever, knows that I am not lying. [32]In Damascus the governor under King Aretas had the city of Damascus guarded to arrest me, [33]and through a window I was let down in a basket over the wall and escaped from his hands.

12 THERE HAS TO BE BOASTING, ALthough nothing is gained by it;

---

i) Although not so clearly as in Galatians, Paul seems to be referring to Judaizers, Christians who insisted upon circumcision and all the burdens it involved.
j) The Corinthians, who allowed Paul to earn his own living while he was preaching and teaching there, provided a living for false apostles.
k) Forty lashes was a punishment dealt to Jewish offenders by temple or synagogue officials. The O.T. Law prescribed forty strokes, Deut. 25:1-3, a number that was not to be exceeded. Therefore, lest while inflicting punishment according to the Law, the Law itself should be broken, only thirty-nine lashes were administered.
l) This penalty was adopted from the Romans.
m) Paul not only preached to these people but he also had a pastoral ministry among them.

so I will go on to visions and revelations from the Lord. [2]I know a man[n] in Christ who fourteen years ago — whether in the body or out of the body I do not know, God knows — was caught up as far as the third heaven. [3]I also know of the same man — whether in the body or out of the body I do not know, God knows — [4]how he was caught up into Paradise and heard words too sacred to tell, which no human being is allowed to repeat.

[5]Of such an instance I will boast, but not about myself — unless it be about my weakness. [6]Should I wish to boast, however, I should not be acting the fool, for I should be telling the truth. But I will refrain, so that no one may ascribe to me more than he observes in me or hears from me.

[7]In order that I might not swell with pride because of the extraordinary great revelations, there was given me a thorn[o] in the flesh, a satanic messenger[p] to strike me, that I might not be too elated. [8]Three times I invoked the Lord about this, to have it removed from me, [9]and He told me, "My grace is sufficient for you, for My strength comes to perfection where there is weakness." Therefore I am happy to boast in my weaknesses, so that the power of Christ may abide upon me. [10]I delight, then, in weaknesses, in insults, in needy circumstances, in persecutions and troubles, all on account of Christ. For when I am weak, then I am strong.

[11]I have become a fool. You forced me to it, for I ought to be recognized by you. In fact, though I am nobody, I am not in the least inferior to these super-apostles.[q] [12]The signs of the apostle were demonstrated among you by patience of every sort in the working of signs and miracles and acts of power. [13]In what respect, then, were you inferior to the other churches, except that I myself was not a burden to you? Pardon me this unfairness.

[14]Here I am ready for my third visit to you, and I shall be no burden to you, for I am not after your possessions but after you. For the children should not accumulate wealth for their parents, but the parents for their children. [15]So I shall gladly spend and be spent on behalf of your souls. If I love you excessively, am I loved the less?

[16]But let that be! I have not burdened you. But being crafty did I take you in by cunning? [17]I have not exploited you through anyone I sent to you, have I? [18]I urged Titus to go and sent along the brother. Did Titus exploit you? Have we not behaved in the same spirit and walked in the same tracks?

[19]You have been supposing all the while that we are apologizing to you? We are speaking in the presence of God as Christ's representatives, and it is all done, dear friends, for your upbuilding; [20]for I am afraid that perhaps when I arrive I may not find you in the condition I should like to find you; neither may you find me as you might desire.

There may be strife, jealousy, ugly temper, sectarianism, slander, gossiping, conceit, disharmony. [21]I am fearful that on my return my God may humble me before you, and I may be saddened over many who have continued in their former sins and have not repented of the impurity, immorality, and sensuality which they have practiced.

13 THIS IS MY THIRD VISIT TO YOU. "In the mouth[r] of two or three witnesses every statement will be confirmed." [2]I said previously, when I was there on my second visit, and I say it now in advance while I am still absent, to those who have sinned and to all the rest, that when I come once more I shall not spare them, [3]since you are looking for proof of Christ's

---

n) Paul is here speaking of himself.
o) A bodily ailment. Its nature is not disclosed, perhaps so that all Christians who suffer persistent physical distress may take comfort in the apostle's response to his thorn in the flesh.
p) Paul was under God's protective care, as all believers are. God permitted Satan to test the apostle in this way for Paul's own good.
q) A term used by Paul to designate those of his opponents who were false apostles.
r) Deut. 19:15.

speaking through me, Christ who is not feeble toward you but mighty in you. 4For whereas He was crucified out of weakness, yet He lives through divine power, and we, too, are weak in Him; but we shall live with Him for your benefit through the power of God.

5Test yourselves, whether you are in the faith; examine yourselves. Or do you not recognize by yourselves that Christ Jesus is within you, unless you fail to pass the test? 6But I hope you will acknowledge that we do not fail.

7But we pray to God that you may do no wrong; and our purpose is not that our integrity may be shown, but that you may do what is right, even though we may appear to have failed. 8For we have no ability against the truth, but only on behalf of the truth. 9We are happy to be weak when you are strong. And this is the object of our prayer, that you may reach full spiritual maturity.

10For this reason I write this in my absence, so that, when I am present, I need not be severe in the exercise of the authority which the Lord has granted me for constructive and not for destructive purposes.

11Finally, brothers, farewell. Mind your ways, accept admonition, agree in your thinking, preserve peace, and the God of love and peace will be with you.

12Greet one another with a holy kiss.s 13All the saintst greet you.

14The grace of the Lord Jesus Christ, and the love of God, and the fellowship of the Holy Spirit be with you all.u

s) This was a ceremonial kiss in the early churches, apparently reflecting a custom in the synagogue.
t) See note at Acts 9:13.
u) Verse 13 is sometimes called The Apostolic Benediction.

2 Corinthians Observations Chart

Paul

His character	His afflictions	His conflict with the Corinthians

The Corinthians

Their strengths	Their weaknesses	Their problems with Paul

Paul's desire for the Corinthians	Insights on Titus

THEME OF 2 CORINTHIANS:

SEGMENT DIVISIONS

		CHAPTER THEMES
		1
		2
		3
		4
		5
		6
		7
		8
		9
		10
		11
		12
		13

Author:

Date:

Purpose:

Key Words:

comfort
(comforted,
encourage,
consolation)

afflicted
(affliction,
suffer,
sufferings)

sorrow(ful)

boast

confidence

commend
(commendation,
recommend)

death

life

heart

joy (happy,
happiness,
enjoyment,
glad)

ministry
(service)

grace

Titus

mark
references
to the enemy
(warfare,
serpent, Satan,
as well as rela-
tive pronouns
and synonyms)

GALATIANS

The gospel introduced the Jews to a new way of life—that of grace rather than law. The old covenant with all of its regulations was made obsolete by the new covenant (Hebrews 8:13). This transition was difficult for some Jewish believers to handle, and a group called the Judaizers sprang up. The Judaizers embraced Christianity but said that some of the old covenant rites, including circumcision, still must be observed.

As Paul, God's apostle to the Gentiles, went on his missionary journeys sharing the gospel of grace, many of these Judaizers followed him, teaching the necessity of keeping the law to one degree or another. They even went to Galatia. That is why Paul wrote what he did to the churches in Galatia.

There is some uncertainty about whether Galatians was written after Paul's first or second missionary journey, and so the exact date of his writing is not known. The debate centers on whether Paul was writing to the northern or southern churches of Galatia. If Paul wrote to the northern churches, the epistle would have been written sometime between A.D. 53 and 57, but if the letter was written to the southern churches, this would have been between A.D. 48 and 49.

However, the date does not affect the message of this critical letter. The truths in this epistle will liberate you to walk in that glorious freedom of a righteous life in the Spirit—truths you can glean through careful observation. Therefore, devote your energies to discovering these truths rather than to debating when Galatians was written.

The more you read and observe the text of this book, the more you will understand Paul's words: "I no longer live as I myself, but Christ lives within me; the life I now live in the flesh I live by faith in the Son of God, who loved me and gave Himself for me" (Galatians 2:20).

THINGS TO DO

1. Read Acts 13 and 14, then look at the map in the introduction to Acts to acquaint yourself with the cities in this area. Also review the chart in the introduction to Ephesians showing the sequence of events in Paul's life after his conversion.

2. As you read, mark in the text the key words (and their synonyms and pronouns) that are listed on the GALATIANS AT A GLANCE chart following Galatians. Mark any other key words you see as you read.

    a. The key words will help you see the theme of this epistle. The best way to see and absorb the book's message is to read through Galatians as many times as possible. Familiarity with the text and careful observation of what is being said is crucial when you study the Bible.

    b. After you mark the key words make a list of everything you learn from the text about the key words. This will give you great insights into Paul's message to the church-

263

es. You may want to record these lists in the margin for future reference.

c. Jesus Christ is mentioned over 30 times in Galatians. List everything you learn about Him from this book.

3. Record the chapter themes on GALATIANS AT A GLANCE and in the text. Record the theme of the book and complete the chart.

4. As you read through the book, note Paul's emphasis in the first two chapters and then how the focus changes in chapter 3.

a. Look for the questions Paul asks the recipients of this letter. Watch for words such as *brothers, you,* and *thoughtless Galatians.* Make a list of these things on the chart PAUL'S CONCERN FOR THE CHURCHES AT GALATIA. (You may want to list these on separate paper before you write them in your New Testament.)

b. Think about why Paul said all he did about himself in those first two chapters. What does this have to do with what follows in the rest of his epistle?

c. Notice the progression of events in Paul's life as presented in these chapters. (There is a chart of the chronology of these events in the introduction to Ephesians.)

d. Trace Paul's travels on the map in the introduction to Acts.

5. In chapter 3 mark *promise*. Note what the promise is; the text will tell you.

6. Fill in the segment divisions on GALATIANS AT A GLANCE.

THINGS TO THINK ABOUT

1. Are you living under grace or under law? Have you accepted the grace of God for your salvation but still put yourself under the law for daily living?

2. According to Galatians 5:16–21, if you live under grace, under the control of the Spirit of God, you will not be able to live a life habitually controlled by the flesh, producing the works of the flesh. Evaluate your walk according to these verses.

3. What do you boast in?

4. As you look at Paul's life, what do you learn for your own life?

THE EPISTLE OF PAUL TO THE

GALATIANS

Date of writing: c. A.D. 52-55

1 PAUL, AN APOSTLE (SENT NEITHER from men nor through man[a] but through Jesus Christ and God the Father who raised Him from the dead) [2]and all the brothers here with me, to the churches of Galatia:[b] [3]Grace to you and peace from God our Father and from the Lord Jesus Christ, [4]who gave Himself for our sins, to rescue us out of this present evil world in agreement with the will of God our Father, [5]to whom be glory forever and ever, Amen.

[6]I am amazed that you are so readily turning away from Him who called you by the grace of Christ, to another gospel, [7]which is really not another; except that some are troubling you and want to distort the good news concerning Christ. [8]But even if we or an angel from heaven should preach to you a gospel that differs from what we have preached to you — a curse on him! [9]As we said before and repeat right now, if anyone evangelizes you with a gospel that varies from what you have received — a curse on him!

[10]Am I now trying to win men's favor, or God's? Or do I seek to please men? If I were still pleasing men I would not be a slave[c] of Christ. [11]For I declare to you, brothers, that the good news that is preached by me is no human affair; [12]for neither did I receive it from a human being nor was I taught it, but it came through a revelation of Jesus Christ.

[13]You have heard of my previous career in Judaism, how violently I persecuted the church of God and devastated it; [14]how in devotion to Judaism I went further than many of my age among my people, so fanatically zealous was I for the traditions of my ancestors. [15]But when it pleased Him who before my birth had set me apart and had called me through His grace, [16]to reveal His Son in me, so that I might preach Him to the Gentiles, I did not at once confer with any human being, [17]neither did I go up to Jerusalem to those who were apostles before I was, but I went away into Arabia and came back to Damascus. [18]Then after three years I went up to Jerusalem to get acquainted with Cephas[d] and stayed in his company for fifteen days; [19]but I saw no other apostle except James,[e] the brother of the Lord. [20]Now what I am writing to you I say in the presence of God, that I am not lying.

[21]Then I went into the regions of Syria and of Cilicia myself [22]but I was unknown to the Christian churches of Judea. [23]They only learned it from hearsay, "Our erstwhile perse-

---

a) Paul plunges at once into a chief reason for his writing — the denial of his apostleship by his opponents for the purpose of weakening the force of his ministry.
b) Galatia was a Roman province covering a large area in the central part of what is now Turkey. Antioch of Pisidia, Iconium, Lystra, and Derbe were in this region. Paul's ministry in Galatia is mentioned in Acts 13; 14; 16:1-6.
c) See note at Matt. 13:27.
d) That is, Peter. See note at I Cor. 1:12.
e) James, a half brother of Jesus, was the leader of the church in Jerusalem, Acts 15:13; 21:18, and the writer of the epistle that bears his name, James 1:1.

cutor now preaches the faith he once was trying to destroy." [24]And on my account they glorified God.

2 FOURTEEN YEARS LATER I WENT up once more to Jerusalem along with Barnabas, taking Titus with us. [2]And I went up in response to a revelation and laid before them the good news I preach among the Gentiles, but privately before the leaders, lest I might be running or had run my course uselessly.

[3]But Titus, who was with me, although he was a Greek, was not obliged to be circumcised [4]to gratify the false brothers that had gotten in underhandedly, who stole in to spy on our freedom which we enjoy in Christ Jesus, and who planned to enslave us.[f] [5]Not for a moment did we yield in submission to them, so that the truth of the good news might continue for you.

[6]But from those who enjoyed a reputation — whatever they amounted to makes no difference to me; God does not regard human appearance — nothing additional was contributed to me by those of reputation. [7]On the contrary, when they observed that I was entrusted with the good news for the uncircumcised, as Peter was for the circumcised — [8]for He who worked through Peter to make him an apostle to the circumcised also worked through me to make me an apostle to the Gentiles — [9]so, acknowledging the grace that had been given me, James and Cephas and John, who were considered as pillars, gave me and Barnabas the right hand of fellowship that we should serve the Gentiles and they the circumcised. [10]Only they wanted us to remember the needy, which I myself was eager to do.

[11]But when Cephas came to Antioch[g] I opposed him to his face, because he was at fault; [12]for until certain people arrived from James, he ate with the Gentile converts, but when they came, he withdrew and separated himself for fear of the circum-

cision party. [13]So the rest of the Jews acted hypocritically along with him, with the result that even Barnabas was carried away by their hypocrisy. [14]But when I saw that they were not walking in line with the truth of the good news, I said to Peter in everyone's presence, "If you, who are a Jew, live like a Gentile and not like a Jew, how can you require Gentiles to live like Jews?" [15]We are Jews by nature and not sinners of the Gentiles; [16]but since we know that a person is not made righteous through the works of the Law but only through faith in Christ Jesus, we have believed in Christ Jesus in order that we might be made righteous by faith in Christ and not through works of the Law; for by works of the Law no person will be justified.

[17]If then, seeking to be justified in Christ, we also are found to be sinners, is Christ a minister of sin?[h] Not at all! [18]Indeed, when I reconstruct the very things I have torn down, then I demonstrate that I am a wrongdoer. [19]For through the Law I died to the Law in order that I may live to God; [20]I have been crucified with Christ; I no longer live as I myself, but Christ lives within me; the life I now live in the flesh I live by faith in the Son of God, who loved me and gave Himself for me. [21]I do not nullify the grace of God; for if righteousness were through Law, then Christ died to no purpose.

3 O THOUGHTLESS GALATIANS, WHO has bewitched you, before whose eyes Jesus Christ was so graphically presented as crucified? [2]I want to learn from you only this: did you receive the Spirit from works of Law or from faith in the message? [3]Are you that foolish, that you would now come to perfection with the flesh after beginning with the Spirit? [4]Have you experienced so much for nothing? If indeed for nothing!

[5]Is He, then, who endued you with the Spirit and does wonderful works among you, doing so because of the

---

f) In the early days of the Christian faith some of the Jews could not believe that Christianity could exist apart from the regulations of the O.T. Law.
g) Antioch of Syria.
h) If salvation is gained through the Law, then Christ did not need to die for our sins, *cf.* vs. 21.

works of the Law or by faith in the message? [6]Just as Abraham[i] "had faith in God and it was credited to him for righteousness." [7]You see therefore, that those who are sons of Abraham are his sons by faith. [8]And in anticipation that God would justify the Gentiles through faith, the Scripture foretold the good news to Abraham in the promise,[j] "In you will all the nations be blessed," [9]so that they are blessed through faith with believing Abraham.

[10]Those who depend on the works of the Law live under a curse, for it is written,[k] "Cursed is every one who does not abide by all that is written in the book of the Law so as to do it." [11]But that no one is made righteous in God's presence through the Law is evident, for[l] "He who is righteous through faith will live." [12]The Law, however, does not rest on faith, but[m] "He who does these things will live by them."

[13]Christ has ransomed us from the curse of the Law inasmuch as He became a curse for us, for it is written,[n] "Cursed is every one who hangs on a tree," [14]in order that in Christ Jesus the blessing of Abraham might be realized for the nations and that we through faith might receive the promise of the Spirit.

[15]Speaking in terms of human relationships, brothers, no one sets aside or adds to a person's last will when it has been ratified. [16]But the promises were spoken to Abraham and to his offspring. It does not say,[o] "And to the offsprings," in the plural, but in the singular, "And to your offspring," which is Christ. [17]This is the point: the Law, that came four hundred thirty years later, cannot invalidate a covenant that had previously been ratified by God, so as to annul the promise. [18]If the inheritance is by the Law, then it is no longer by promise; but God

has given it to Abraham through a promise.[p]

[19]Why, then, was the Law given? It was added to show sins in their true light, until the Offspring should come concerning whom the promise was made. It was ordained through angels by means of a mediator. [20]But there is no call for an intermediary in case of one, and God is One.

[21]Is, then, the Law contrary to the promises of God? Not at all! If the Law had been as a power to produce life, then righteousness would in very truth have been by the Law; [22]but the Scripture has all men imprisoned under sin,[q] so that the promise might be given to those who believe, through faith in Jesus Christ.

[23]Before faith came, we were confined under the Law, awaiting in custody faith that was yet to be revealed, [24]so that the Law served as our custodian[r] until Christ came, in order that we might be justified by faith. [25]But with the coming of faith we are no longer under a custodian; [26]for through your faith in Christ Jesus you are all sons of God. [27]As many of you as have been baptized into Christ have clothed yourselves with Christ. [28]There is neither Jew nor Greek, there is neither slave nor freeman, there is neither male nor female, because you are all one in Christ Jesus. [29]But if you are Christ's, then you are the offspring of Abraham; you are heirs in agreement with the promise.

4 NOW I AFFIRM THAT SO LONG AS the heir is a minor,[s] he differs in no way from a slave,[t] although everything belongs to him; [2]but he is under guardians and trustees until the time that was prearranged by his father. [3]This is our situation. While we were minors, we were subservient to the

---

i) Gen. 15:6.
l) Hab. 2:4; Rom. 1:17; Heb. 10:38.
j) Gen. 12:3; 18:18; 22:18.
k) Deut. 27:26.
m) Lev. 18:5.   n) Deut. 21:23.   o) Gen. 13:15.
p) Abraham's faith is emphasized because he did not live under the Mosaic Law but more than four centuries before the Law was given, vs. 17.
q) The Law shows man that he is a sinner. That knowledge may point him to the Savior, Christ.
r) The Greek noun is *paidagogos*, from which comes the English word "pedagogue." A *paidagogos* was a man, usually a slave, who guided a boy to and from school. The Law guided men and women until Christ came.
s) Jews under the old covenant and Gentiles under sin were like minors.
t) See note at Matt. 13:27.

world's elementary teachings; [4]but when the time was completed, God sent forth His Son, born of a woman, born under the Law [5]in order to redeem those who were under the Law, and that we might receive adoption as sons. [6]And because you are sons, God has sent forth the Spirit of His Son into our hearts, calling out, "Abba![u] Father!" [7]You are, therefore, a slave no longer, but through God a son, and if a son, then an heir as well.

[8]Previously, however, when you did not know God, you were enslaved to gods that essentially are not gods. [9]But now, when you know God, or better yet, are known by God, how is it that you are turning back again to those weak and beggarly rudiments to which you want to be enslaved all over again? [10]You observe days and months, festivals and years. [11]You make me fear that perhaps I wasted my efforts on you.

[12]I beg of you, brothers, become like me, for I became as you are. You have in no respect wronged me. [13]But you know how that the first time I evangelized you because of physical infirmity, [14]and though my physical condition was for you a trial, you neither scorned nor spurned me, but you welcomed me as an angel of God, as Christ Jesus.

[15]What has become of that blessed enjoyment? For I bear you witness that, if possible, you would have plucked out your eyes to give them to me.[v] [16]Did I become your enemy because I am sincere with you? [17]They[w] busy themselves about you to no good purpose; instead, they want to isolate you from us so that you may be infatuated with them. [18]But it is well to be zealously sought after always for a good cause and not merely when I am present with you. [19]My children, over whom I once more suffer birthpains until

Christ is formed within you, [20]I wish I might be present with you right now and try a new way of speaking, for I am perplexed about you.

[21]Tell me, you who want to be under the Law, do you not listen to the Law? [22]For it is written[x] that Abraham had two sons, one by the slave girl and one by the freewoman; [23]but while the one by the slave girl was born in a fleshly way, the one by the freewoman came on account of the promise. [24]All of which is allegorical,[y] indicating two covenants, one from Mount Sinai that generates slavery and is Hagar — Mount Sinai in Arabia. [25]It corresponds to the present Jerusalem; for she and her children are in servitude.

[26]But the Jerusalem that is above is free, which is our mother, for it is written,[z] [27]"Be cheerful, barren woman who does not bear; break out with shouting, you who have no birthpangs, because more numerous are the children of the desolate woman than of the one who has a husband." [28]And you, brothers, are like Isaac, children of the promise. [29]But just as then the one born in a fleshly way persecuted the one born in accord with the Spirit, so too at present. [30]But what does the Scripture say?[a] "Expel the slave girl and her son, for the son of the slave girl will not be heir with the son of the freewoman." [31]We therefore, brothers, are not children of the slave girl, but of the freewoman.

5 FOR THIS FREEDOM CHRIST HAS liberated us. Stand firm, then, and do not be held fast again by a yoke of servitude.

[2]Take note of what I, Paul, tell you: if you become circumcised, Christ will not benefit you in the least. [3]Once more I assure every person who gets circumcised, that he is obliged to practice the entire Law. [4]All of you who aim

---

u) "Abba" is a transliteration of an Aramaic word for "father." It was used within the family and frequently in addressing God in prayer.
v) Paul's affliction might have been poor sight, *cf.* ch. 6:11.
w) Paul's opponents who wanted to compel believers to observe the regulations of the Law, e.g. circumcision.
x) Gen. 16:15; 21:3.
y) Paul uses the situation as an allegory of the Jew and the gospel of Christ.
z) Isa. 54:1.
a) Gen. 21:10, 12.

at justification by the Law are severed from Christ; you have fallen away from grace. [5]But by the Spirit we earnestly anticipate the righteousness for which by faith we hope, [6]because in Christ Jesus neither circumcision nor the want of it has validity, but faith working through love.

[7]You were coming along splendidly. Who got in your way, so that you do not follow truth? [8]That persuasion is not from the One who called you. [9]A bit of yeast raises the whole lump of dough.[b] [10]I have confidence in you in Christ, that you will not be otherwise minded; but that troubler of yours whoever he may be, will have to bear his punishment.

[11]As for me, brothers, if I still preach circumcision, why am I still perse-cuted? Then the offensiveness of the cross has been removed. [12]I wish those who are unsettling you would go so far as to make themselves eunuchs.

[13]You have been called to enjoy liberty, brothers; only, do not let the liberty be an opportunity for the flesh; instead, serve one another through love. [14]Because the entire Law is summed up in this one statement,[c] "Love your neighbor as yourself." [15]If, however, you tear at and consume one another, look out or you will be destroyed by each other.

[16]But I say, behave in a spiritual way; then you will not carry out your fleshly cravings. [17]For the longings of the flesh are contrary to the Spirit, and those of the Spirit are contrary to the flesh; they are in opposition to each other, so that you do not do what you want to do. [18]But if you are guided by the Spirit, then you are not under the Law.

[19]Now the deeds of the flesh are evident, such as immorality, impurity, sensuality, [20]idolatry, magic arts, animosities, strife, jealousy, bad temper, outbreaks of selfishness, dissensions, factions, [21]envy, drunkenness, carousings and everything of the kind, of

which I warn you as I did previously, that those who practice such things will not inherit the kingdom of God.

[22]But the Spirit's fruition is love, joy, peace, forbearance, kindness, generosity, fidelity, [23]gentleness, self-control. There is no law against these.

[24]Now those who belong to Christ have crucified the flesh with its passions and desires.[d] [25]If we live by the Spirit, let us also be directed by the Spirit; [26]let us not become vain-glorious so as to compete with each other and to envy one another.

[6] BROTHERS, IN CASE A PERSON IS caught in any misconduct, you spiritual persons should set him straight in a humble spirit, looking at yourself, so that you may not be tempted as well. [2]Carry one another's burden and thus fulfill the law of Christ; [3]for if anyone thinks he is somebody important and yet is of no account, he is deceiving himself. [4]Let each one put his own work to the test; then he will enjoy his personal satisfaction and not boast to another. [5]For each person has his own load to carry.[e]

[6]The person who is being taught should share all good things with him who teaches the word. [7]Make no mistake, God will not be mocked. What a person sows, that he will harvest as well. [8]The one who sows for his own flesh will harvest ruin from his flesh; while the one who sows for the Spirit will harvest eternal life from the Spirit. [9]Let us do what is right without tiring of it, for at its proper time we shall reap if we do not give up. [10]So then, as opportunity offers, let us practice what is beneficial for everyone, but particularly toward the members of the family of faith.

[11]Notice what large letters I write you in my own hand.

[12]Those who want to make a good showing in the flesh are the very ones who would force circumcision on you, for the simple reason that they may

---

b) Those who were disturbing the Galatian churches might corrupt all of the believers, as yeast raises the whole loaf.
c) Lev. 19:18; Matt. 22:39; Rom. 13:9.   d) This is spiritual circumcision.
e) Compare vs. 2, which speaks of burdens that can be shared, e.g. misfortune and sorrow. There are other burdens, e.g. painful duties, that the individual alone can bear. This kind is meant in vs. 5.

thus escape persecution on account of the cross of Christ. [13]For those who are circumcised do not themselves observe the Law, but they want to have you circumcised, that they may boast of your physical experience. [14]But for me, perish the thought that I should boast except in the cross of our Lord Jesus Christ, through whom the world has been crucified to me and I to the world. [15]For neither circum-

cision nor the lack of it is important, but a new creation is what counts, [16]and those who behave by this rule, peace and mercy be upon them, even on the Israel of God.

[17]From now on let no one make trouble for me, for I bear in my body the marks[f] of Jesus.

[18]The grace of our Lord Jesus Christ be with your spirit, brothers. Amen.

---

f) The bodily scars that Paul had as a result of persecution for Christ's sake, e.g. Acts 14:19; II Cor. 11:24, 25, were marks that revealed the Lord's ownership of him.

_____

_____

_____

_____

_____

_____

_____

_____

_____

_____

_____

_____

_____

_____

_____

_____

_____

_____

_____

_____

_____

_____

_____

GALATIANS AT A GLANCE

THEME OF GALATIANS:

Author:

SEGMENT DIVISIONS

Date:

		CHAPTER THEMES
		1
		2
		3
		4
		5
		6

Purpose:

Key Words:
Paul
(and pronouns
relating to him)
gospel
(good news)
grace
law
Spirit
faith
promise
covenant
Christ (Jesus)
free (free man,
free woman)

EPHESIANS

phesus, the fourth-largest city in the Roman Empire, was the home of the temple of the goddess Artemis, sometimes referred to as Diana. Of all the deities in Asia, none was more sought after than Artemis.

But by the time of Paul, Ephesus's position as a center of trade was lost because the harbor became unnavigable. From that point on, the worship of Artemis became the city's means of economic survival. The tourist and pilgrim trade associated with Artemis made many people in Ephesus wealthy. Silversmiths made their living selling images of this goddess and her temple. Innkeepers and restaurant owners grew rich from the large influx of worshipers who traveled great distances to see the temple of Artemis, one of the seven wonders of the world. Even the temple treasury served as a bank, loaning large sums of money to many, including kings. And since Artemis was the patroness of sex, prostitutes sold their bodies without condemnation in the two-story brothel on Marble Road.

Although Artemis was the main attraction, all sorts of magic and sorcery were conjured up and then documented. This documentation would later be referred to as *Ephesia grammata*.

Then God sent Paul to live in Ephesus and called out for Himself a church, a light to illumine the occult darkness of this city.

This brief glimpse into the historical and cultural setting of Ephesians should help you understand why Paul wrote what he did to the church in Ephesus. The message of this epistle is needed as much today as it was in A.D. 60 to 62, when Paul wrote it as a prisoner in Rome.

THINGS TO DO

General Instructions

1. Read Ephesians in one sitting before examining it chapter by chapter.
2. When you finish, read Acts 18:18–21 (Paul's first visit to Ephesus was on his second missionary journey). Then read Acts 19 for an account of Paul's second visit on his third missionary journey. This passage will help you understand why Ephesians deals with warfare and our position in Christ more extensively than any other epistle.

Chapters 1–3

Read Ephesians 1 through 3 one chapter at a time, doing the following:

1. Mark each reference to God, and in the margin list everything God does.
2. Mark distinctively each use of *in Christ* or *in Him* so you easily can spot it in the text. Then on the OBSERVATIONS CHART following Ephesians, under the heading "Our Wealth and Position in Christ," list what believers have *in Christ*. Pay particular attention to the phrase *in the heavenly spheres,* which is key to warfare. Note the chapter and verse from which the information comes when you make your list (e.g., 1:13). (You may want to list this information on separate paper before you record

it in your New Testament.)

3. Mark each reference to the Spirit or Holy Spirit. On the OBSERVATIONS CHART, under the heading "Our Relationship with the Holy Spirit," list what is taught about the person and work of the Holy Spirit.

4. Mark distinctively each occurrence of *rich* or *wealth*. Then in the margin list what you learn about this wealth. Remember to ask the five W's and an H: Who is rich and in what? How are these riches described? What is done with the wealth? And so on.

5. Mark each use of *previous* or *once*. Then on the OBSERVATIONS CHART under the heading "Our Previous Lifestyle and Walk," list what Ephesians says about how believers used to live before salvation.

6. Mark the other key words (with their synonyms and pronouns) listed on the EPHESIANS AT A GLANCE chart. Put these on an index card and use it as a bookmark. Then in the margin list what is said about each key word. Just record the facts.

Chapters 4–6

1. Read Ephesians 4 through 6 chapter by chapter, doing the following:

   a. Mark each occurrence of *live (conduct, behave)*. Then on the OBSERVATIONS CHART, under the heading "Our Conduct in Christ," list what is taught about the lifestyle of a believer. Also go back to 2:2, 10 and mark and list what these verses teach about the believer's lifestyle. Then ask yourself: How am I to live? Why am I able to live this way?

   b. Continue to mark in the text the key words listed on your bookmark. Also list what you learn from the uses of *previous (once)* in this section of Ephesians. Note the contrast between our former lifestyle and our conduct in Christ.

   c. Mark the following: *Holy Spirit, in Christ,* and *in the Lord*. Then list what you learn and think about it. This will help you see how to live in Him.

2. Record any other observations you have of the text as instructed in the observation section in the introduction to this New Testament.

3. On EPHESIANS AT A GLANCE:

   a. Record the theme of the book and of each chapter in the appropriate spaces. (Remember to go back and record each chapter's theme in the text above the chapter number.)

   b. As you have seen, there is a change of emphasis between chapters 3 and 4. Write down under "Segment Divisions" what best summarizes the content of chapters 1 through 3 and then chapters 4 through 6.

THINGS TO THINK ABOUT

1. Stop and review all you observed and listed about your position as a child of God. Go through chapter 1 again and note everything God has done for you. Watch for the personal pronoun *He*. Also note the phrase *according to (in agreement with, to the measure of)* and the word *will*. Think about what God has done for you and why. Then thank Him and tell Him you want to live accordingly.

2. Ephesians 2:8–10 are extremely important verses. Think about what God is saying to you and ask God to show you whether you are trusting in His grace or in your works to get you to heaven. But don't stop there. Think about the relationship of good works to the life of a believer. How are you living? Memorize these verses.

3. In your home do you live according to Ephesians 5:18 through 6:4?
4. Are you able to stand firm or are you defeated by the devil's schemes? Don't forget where you are seated. Think about the armor of God. Do you have it on and are you standing firm in truth, righteousness, peace, salvation, and faith? Are you able to use the Word of God as your offensive weapon?

Sequence of Events in Paul's Life after His Conversion*

*There are differing opinions on these dates. For continuity's sake this chart will be the basis for dates pertaining to Paul's life.

Year A.D.	Event
33-34	Conversion, time in Damascus
35-47	Some silent years, except we know that Paul:
	1. Spent time in Arabia and Damascus
	2. Made first visit to Jerusalem
	3. Went to Tarsus, Syria-Cilicia area
	4. Was with Barnabas in Antioch
	5. With Barnabas took relief to brethren in Judea—Paul's second visit to Jerusalem
	6. Returned to Antioch; was sent out with Barnabas by church at Antioch
47-48	First missionary journey: Galatians written(?)
49	Apostolic Council at Jerusalem—Paul visits Jerusalem (compare Acts 15 with Galatians 2:1)
49-51	Second missionary journey: 1 and 2 Thessalonians written
52-56	Third missionary journey: 1 and 2 Corinthians and Romans written
56	Paul goes to Jerusalem and is arrested; held at Caesarea
57-59	Appearance before Felix and Drusilla; before Festus; before Agrippa
59-60	Appeals to Caesar, sent from Caesarea to Rome
60-62	First Roman imprisonment: Ephesians, Philemon, Colossians, and Philippians written
62	Paul's release; possible trip to Spain
62	Paul in Macedonia: 1 Timothy written
62	Paul goes to Crete: Titus written
63-64	Paul taken to Rome and imprisoned: 2 Timothy written
64	Paul is absent from the body and present with the Lord
	(Others put Paul's conversion about A.D. 35, his death in A.D. 68.)

THE EPISTLE OF PAUL TO THE

EPHESIANS

Date of writing: c. A.D. 60-61, at Rome

1 Paul, an apostle of Christ Jesus by the will of God, to the saints[a] [in Ephesus],[b] the faithful in Christ Jesus: 2Grace to you and peace from God our Father and the Lord Jesus Christ.

3Blessed be the God and Father of our Lord Jesus Christ, who has blessed us with every spiritual blessing in the heavenly spheres[c] through Christ, 4even as He has chosen us in Him before the world was founded, to be holy and blameless in His presence. 5In love He predestined us in Jesus Christ to be His sons, in agreement with the kind intent of His will, 6for the praise of His glorious grace with which He has freely favored us in union with the Beloved. 7In Him we enjoy redemption through His blood, the forgiveness of our trespasses to the measure of the wealth of His grace, 8which He poured out on us, 9making known to us in all His wisdom and insight the secret of His purpose, according to His kind intention which He proposed in Christ, 10a plan to be brought to completion when the time fully comes, to bring everything together in Christ, things in heaven and things on earth.

11In Him we too were made His heritage, as foreordained according to His purpose, who works out everything in agreement with the design of His own will, 12so that we, the first to put our hope in Christ, might bring praise to His glory. 13In Him you also, after listening to the message of the truth, the good news of your salvation, have as believers in Him been sealed with the promised Holy Spirit, 14who is the guarantee of our inheritance, for a redemption through which you become God's property, and all to the praise of His glory.

15For this reason I too, on hearing about your faith in the Lord Jesus and your love for all the saints, 16never fail in giving thanks for you as I mention you in my prayers, 17that the God of our Lord Jesus Christ, the glorious Father, might grant you a spirit of wisdom and of revelation for an understanding of Himself, 18granting you eyes of the heart, so that you may know the nature of the hope to which you are called, and what is the wealth of His glorious inheritance in the saints, 19and how overwhelmingly great is His power for us believers. It is like the working of His mighty strength, 20which He exerted when He raised Christ from the dead and seated Him in the heavenly spheres at His right hand, 21high above all government and authority, power and lordship, and every name that is named,

a) See note at Acts 9:13.
b) The words enclosed in brackets do not appear in the majority of the most reliable ancient manuscripts. Since this letter is not, therefore, addressed specifically to the church in Ephesus, it has been surmised that it may be the letter to the Laodiceans mentioned in Col. 4:16. It is possible that what is known as the Epistle to the Ephesians was a joint communication to both Ephesus and Laodicea. Both cities were situated in what is now Turkey: Ephesus near the Aegean Sea; Laodicea, and Colossae also, not more than fifteen miles from each other, were about eighty miles directly east of Ephesus.
c) Literally "in the heavenlies," the spiritual realm of life with Christ; and so in vs. 20; 2:6; 3:10; 6:12.

not only in this but also in the future world.

22God has placed everything under His feet and has given Him as head over everything for the church, 23which is His body, the completeness of Him who fills the universe at all points.d

2 YOU TOO WERE DEAD IN YOUR trespasses and sins, 2in which you once conducted yourselves in line with the ways of this world system, controlled by the ruler of the kingdom of the air, the spirit of the one now working in disobedient people.e 3Among them we all once walked, as we indulged our fleshly desires and carried out the inclinations of our lower nature and our thoughts, and by nature we were objects of God's indignation, as were all the rest of mankind.

4But God is rich in mercy, so that on account of His great love with which He loved us, 5He made us who were dead in trespasses, alive with Christ — by grace you have been saved. 6And in Christ Jesus He caused us to rise, and seated us with Him in the heavenly spheres, 7so that He might show in the future ages the immeasurable wealth of His grace, by means of His goodness to us through Christ Jesus.

8For by grace you have been saved through faith, and that is not of yourselves; it is God's gift. 9It is not by works, so that no one may boast; 10for we are His handiwork, created in Christ Jesus for good works, which God previously prepared for us so that we should live in them.

11Keep in mind, therefore, that once you were physically Gentiles and were called uncircumcision by the so-called circumcision that is made with human hands in the flesh; 12that in those days you were separated from Christ, aliens without the right of Israel's citizenship, and strangers to the covenants of promise, living in the world without hope and without God. 13But now in Christ Jesus you, who were once far away, have been brought near by the blood of Christ. 14For He is our peace. Breaking down the barrier that separated Jews and Gentiles He united the two sections. By His own human nature He brought the hostility to an end, 15by abolishing the Law of commandments with its regulations, so that in Himself He might create the two into one new person and thus make peace, 16and through the cross reconcile them both in one body to God, bringing the hostility to an end by the cross.

17And He came and preached peace to you who were far away and peace to those who were near; 18because through Him we both have access to the Father by one Spirit. 19Therefore, you are no longer strangers and immigrants, but you are fellow citizens with the saints and members of God's household; 20you are constructed on the foundation of the apostles and prophets, of which the cornerstone is Christ Jesus. 21The whole building, framed together in Him, rises into a temple that is holy in the Lord, 22in whom you also are built up together for a dwelling of God in the Spirit.

3 BECAUSE OF THIS I, PAUL, THE prisoner of Christ Jesus on behalf of you Gentiles — 2you surely heard how the administration of divine grace to you was granted me,f 3how by revelation the secret was made known to me, as I wrote you briefly before.g 4A perusal of it will enable you to understand my insight into the secret of Christ, 5which was not made known to the sons of men in other generations as now it is revealed by the Spirit to His holy apostles and prophets, 6that the Gentiles are joint inheritors, share the same body, and are participants of the promise in Christ Jesus through the good news, 7of which I was made a minister by virtue of the gift of divine grace that was granted me in

---

d) There are two main interpretations of the words, "the completeness of Him who fills the universe at all points": (1) that Christ, who fills all things, so fills the church, His body, as to complete it; and (2) that, as a head without a body is incomplete, so Christ, who is the Head, is not complete without the church, His body. Possibly the latter view is preferable, although it must never be forgotten that spiritually Christ is the church's fullness.
e) Lit. "the sons of disobedience," an expression that denotes those who oppose God. In I Sam. 2:12 the same thought is expressed in the term "sons of Belial."
f) As the apostle to the Gentiles. g) Some think that the Epistle to the Colossians is meant.

agreement with the working of His power. [8]On me, the least of all saints, was this grace bestowed to preach to the Gentiles the fathomless wealth of Christ, [9]and to bring to light what arrangement was contained in the secret, that had through the ages been hidden with God, the Creator of all.

[10]Consequently, the many-sided wisdom of God may now be made known through the church to the rulers and the authorities in the heavenly spheres. [11]This is in accord with the eternal purpose which He carried out through Christ Jesus, our Lord, [12]in whom by faith in Him we enjoy the confidence of unreserved approach. [13]I pray, therefore, that you may not lose courage in these afflictions of mine for your sakes, for they serve to your honor.

[14]Because of this, I bow my knees[h] before the Father, [15]from whom every family in heaven and on earth takes its name, [16]that He may grant you, in keeping with the wealth of His glory, to be empowered with strength in the inner self by His Spirit; [17]that through faith the Christ may dwell in your hearts, that you may be rooted and grounded in love, [18]in order that you may have power to understand with all the saints what is the breadth, the length, the depth, and the height, [19]in fact to know the love of Christ which surpasses knowledge, so that you may be filled up to the whole fullness of God.

[20]Now to Him who is able according to the power that works within us to do everything immeasurably far beyond what we pray or think of, [21]to Him be glory in the church and in Christ Jesus through all generations for ever and ever, Amen.

4 SO I EXHORT YOU, PRISONER AS I am in the Lord, to conduct yourselves worthy of the calling you have received, [2]with unalloyed humility and gentleness, to bear patiently with one another in a loving way, [3]making every effort to preserve the unity of the Spirit in the bond of peace. [4]There is one body[i] and one Spirit, just as also you received your calling, with one hope; [5]one Lord, one faith, one baptism; [6]one God and Father of all, who governs all and pervades all and is in us all.

[7]But to each of us grace is granted and measured by the gift of Christ. [8]Thus it says,[j] "As He ascended on high, He led the captured[k] away into captivity; He gave gifts to men." [9]But what does "He ascended" mean, except that He also went down into the lower parts of the earth? [10]The One who descended is the very One who ascended far above all the heavens to fill the universe.

[11]So He has given some to be apostles and others to be prophets; some to be evangelists and others to be pastors and teachers, [12]to equip the saints for the task of ministering toward the building up of the body of Christ, [13]until we all may arrive at the unity of faith and that understanding of that Son of God that brings completeness of personality, tending toward the measure of the stature of the fullness of Christ. [14]As a result, we should no longer be babes, swung back and forth and carried here and there with every wind of teaching that springs from human craftiness and ingenuity for devising error; [15]but, telling the truth in love, we should grow up in every way toward Him who is the Head — Christ, [16]from whom the entire body is fitted together and united by every contributing ligament, with proportionate power for each single part to effect the development of the body for its upbuilding in love.

[17]So I tell you this and testify in the Lord: you must no longer behave like the Gentiles, whose lives are spent in the uselessness of their ways of thinking. [18]Their understanding has become darkened. Because of their ignorance and the obstinacy of their hearts, they have grown estranged from the divine life. [19]Troubled by no compunctions, they are the sort that have abandoned themselves to sensuality, so

---

h) Customarily the Jews stood when they prayed.
i) The body of Christ, that is the church, *cf.* I Cor. 12:13.   j) Ps. 68:18.
k) By His death and resurrection the Lord Jesus Christ conquered Satan, who had held men captive for such a long time, Heb. 2:14, 15.

as to practice with greediness all kinds of impurity.

20But this is not the way you have come to know Christ,[1] 21if, indeed, you have heard about Him and have been taught in Him according to the truth as it is in Jesus: 22that you are to rid yourself of the old nature[m] with your previous habits, corrupted as it is by deceitful lusts; 23that you be renewed in your mental attitude, 24and that you put on the new nature that is created in God's likeness in genuine righteousness and holiness.

25Therefore, laying all falsehood aside, speak truth each person to his neighbor, for we are one another's members. 26When you are angry, commit no sin; do not remain angry until sundown. 27Do not give the devil an opportunity. 28The thief must steal no more, but rather toil to earn a living with his own hands, so he may have something to give the person in need. 29Let no foul speech come out of your mouth, but only such as will build up where it is necessary, so as to add a blessing to the listeners. 30And never grieve God's Holy Spirit, by whom you have been marked with a seal for the day of redemption. 31Get rid of all bitterness among you — bad temper, anger, clamor, abusive language and all malice. 32Be kind toward one another, tenderhearted, forgiving one another, even as God has in Christ forgiven you.

5 BE THEREFORE IMITATORS OF God[n] as His beloved children, 2and live in love, as Christ also loved us and gave Himself for us, an offering and sacrifice to God as a fragrant scent.

3But immorality and every kind of impurity or greed should not so much as be mentioned among ·you; such is the proper way for saints.[o] 4Nor should there be indecency and foolish talking or low jesting; they are not fitting. Instead, let there rather be thanksgiving.

5For be sure of this, that none guilty of immorality or of impurity or of greed, which is idolatry, has an inheritance in the kingdom of Christ and of God.

6Let no one lead you astray with empty words,[p] for on account of such things the indignation of God comes on disobedient people.[q] 7Do not be sharing with them. 8For once you were darkness but now in the Lord you are light; live as children of light — 9for the fruition of the Light consists in all goodness, righteousness and truth — 10demonstrating what is pleasing to the Lord.

11Do not participate in the fruitless doings of darkness but rather expose them; 12for while it is a disgrace even to mention the things they do in secret, 13yet everything that is exposed by the light is made visible, and where everything is made visible there is light. 14Thus it says,[r] "Wake up, sleeper, and rise from the dead, and Christ will shine upon you."

15See to it, therefore, that you conduct yourselves carefully, not as foolish but as wise people 16who make the best possible use of their time, because these are evil days. 17Be not thoughtless, then, but gain insight in the Lord's will. 18And do not get drunk on wine, which leads to debauchery, but be filled with the Spirit, 19speaking one to the other in psalms and hymns and spiritual songs, singing heartily and making your music to the Lord, 20and at all times giving thanks for everything to God the Father in the name of our Lord Jesus Christ.

21Be submissive to one another out of reverence for Christ. 22Wives be subject to your husbands as to the Lord. 23For a husband is head of his wife as Christ also is Head of the church;[s] He is the Savior of the body. 24But as the church is submissive to Christ, so wives must in every respect be submissive to their husbands.

---

l) Not merely His teachings but Himself.
m) Literally "the old man," all that the Christian is apart from Christ. In vs. 24 it is "the new man" (lit.), that is, what the believer is in his new birth through Christ.
n) Compare Matt. 5:48.　　o) See note at Acts 9:13.　　p) That is, speech void of truth.
q) See note at ch. 2:2.
r) This appears to be an extract from an early Christian hymn. *Cf.* Isa. 26:19; 60:1, 2.
s) The husband and wife relationship dates from O.T. times as a spiritual symbol of the relationship of Jehovah and Israel, but the apostle is here speaking of Christ and the church, vs. 32.

[25]Husbands, love your wives, even as Christ loved the church and gave Himself for her, [26]in order that by cleansing her by means of the washing in water He may sanctify her through His word, [27]so that He may present the church to Himself gloriously, having no spot or wrinkle or any of such thing, but holy and blameless.

[28]In a similar way husbands ought to love their wives as their own bodies. One who loves his wife loves himself. [29]For no one ever hated his own flesh, but he nourishes and carefully protects it, just as Christ treats the church; [30]for we are members of His body. [31]"On[t] this account a man shall leave his father and mother and shall be joined to his wife, and the two shall become one flesh."

[32]There is a great, hidden meaning in this, but I am speaking about Christ and the church. [33]Nevertheless, let each of you love his wife as much as himself, and let the wife revere her husband.

6 CHILDREN, BE OBEDIENT TO YOUR parents in the Lord, for this is right. [2]"Honor your father and mother," which is the first commandment[u] with a promise, [3]"that it may be well with you and that you may enjoy great length of life on the earth."

[4]And fathers, do not arouse your children's anger, but bring them up in the instruction and admonition of the Lord.

[5]Slaves,[v] render obedience to your earthly masters,[w] with reverence and awe, with such unmixed motives as you feel toward Christ. [6]Do not be eye-slaves as men-pleasers, but as slaves of Christ carry out wholeheartedly the will of God, [7]rendering service with goodwill as to the Lord and not to men, [8]aware that whatever good each one may do he will be recompensed by the Lord, whether he is a slave or a freeman.

[9]And masters, treat your slaves in the same way. Dispense with threatening, as you keep in mind that their Master and yours is in heaven, and with Him there is no partiality.

[10]In conclusion, be strong in the Lord and in the strength of His might. [11]Put on the complete armor that God supplies, so you will be able to stand against the devil's intrigues. [12]For our wrestling is not against flesh-and-blood opponents, but against the rulers, the authorities, the cosmic powers of this present darkness, against the spiritual forces of evil in the heavenly spheres. [13]Take up, therefore, the whole armor of God so that you may be able to stand when you have done all the fighting.

[14]So stand your ground, with[x] the belt of truth tightened around your waist, wearing the breastplate of righteousness on your body, [15]with the readiness of the good news of peace bound on your feet; [16]above all taking up the shield of faith, with which you will be able to extinguish all the flaming arrows of the evil one. [17]And take the helmet of salvation and the sword of the Spirit, which is the word of God, [18]praying in the Spirit on every occasion with ceaseless prayer and entreaty, constantly alert to pray with all perseverance and entreaty for all the saints; [19]also for me, that, when I open my lips, the message may be given me that I may announce fearlessly the secret[y] of the good news [20]for which I am an ambassador in chains. Pray that I may present the good news freely, as it is my duty to speak.

[21]In order that you may know my affairs, how I am doing, Tychicus,[z] the beloved brother and faithful minister in the Lord, will give you all the information. [22]I have sent him to you for this very purpose, to let you know all about us, and that he may encourage your hearts.

[23]Peace to the brothers, and love joined with faith, from God the Father and the Lord Jesus Christ.[a] [24]Grace be with all who have a never-diminishing love for our Lord Jesus Christ.

---

t) Gen. 2:24. u) Exod. 20:12. v) See note at Matt. 13:27.
w) In principle this applies not only to slaves and their masters but also to employees and their employers. x) Isa. 11:5; 52:7. y) See note at Rom. 16:25.
z) Tychicus, who is mentioned also in Acts 20:4 and Titus 3:12, was Paul's courier who carried not only this letter but also the one to the Colossians, Col. 4:7.
a) God in Christ is the Source of Christian faith and love.

OUR WEALTH AND POSITION IN CHRIST

_____
_____
_____
_____
_____
_____
_____
_____
_____

OUR RELATIONSHIP WITH THE HOLY SPIRIT

_____
_____
_____
_____
_____
_____
_____
_____
_____

OUR PREVIOUS LIFESTYLE AND WALK   OUR CONDUCT IN CHRIST

_____
_____
_____
_____
_____
_____
_____
_____
_____

THEME OF EPHESIANS:

SEGMENT DIVISIONS

		CHAPTER THEMES
		1
		2
		3
		4
		5
		6

Author:

Date:

Purpose:

Key Words:
every reference to God, in Christ (in Him, in the Lord)

the (Holy) Spirit

rich (wealth)

in the heavenly sphere

previous (once)

grace

power (strength)

body (church)

redemption

live (conduct, behave)

mark every reference to the devil (including powers, rulers, authorities, etc.)

PHILIPPIANS

Blocked by the Spirit of God from going into Asia and Bithynia, Paul had a vision of a man from Macedonia asking him to come to Macedonia and help the churches there.

Confident that God had given him direction, Paul sailed with Timothy and Luke from Troas on a second missionary journey. Philippi, in Macedonia, basked in the fact that it was also a Roman colony which ensured its citizens all the benefits of Roman citizenship.

As was his custom, when Paul reached a city he sought out the Jews. While there were not enough Jews living in Philippi to form a synagogue, the Jews there met for prayer on the Sabbath. Little did Paul realize that he would end up in prison. God knew there was a Roman jailer and his family who needed Jesus.

The events of that day inaugurated the beginning of the church at Philippi, the church Paul addressed as he took pen in hand around the year A.D. 61 or 62.

THINGS TO DO

1. Familiarize yourself with the message of Philippians by reading the entire book in one sitting. As you read, look for the verses in chapters 1 and 4 which tell where Paul is as he writes.

2. To understand the historical setting of Philippians, read Acts 15:35 through 17:1, which records Paul's first visit to Philippi. After his third missionary journey, Paul went to Jerusalem, where he was arrested. From there Paul was taken by a Roman guard to Caesarea, the Mediterranean seaport where the Roman consulate often went to escape the heat and confines of Jerusalem. After remaining a prisoner in Caesarea for over two years, Paul, who as a Roman citizen had appealed to Caesar, was sent to Rome, where he lived under house arrest. Read Acts 28:14-31 and note how long Paul remained a prisoner at Rome. How does this compare with where Paul was when he wrote Philippians?

3. As you read Philippians chapter by chapter, do the following.

   a. Under "Author" on your OBSERVATIONS CHART following Philippians note where Paul is, why he is there, and what his attitude is in the midst of his difficult circumstances.

   b. In a distinctive way, mark in the text each key word (and its synonyms and pronouns) that is listed on the PHILIPPIANS AT A GLANCE chart. This will help you discover the themes (main subjects) of each chapter and of the book itself. Watch for other key words which are not listed but which may be emphasized in a particular chapter of Philippians.

   c. In the margin list what you learn from the text about each of the key words in Philippians.

   d. Record any other observations as instructed and demonstrated in the observation section in the introduction to this New Testament.

   e. List each of the instructions Paul gives to the Philippian saints on the chart PAUL'S INSTRUCTIONS TO THE PHILIPPIANS. As you list these instructions, evaluate your life in the light of each one.

4. On PHILIPPIANS AT A GLANCE:
   a. Fill in the theme for the book and for each chapter. (Be sure you also record the chapter theme in the text above the chapter number.)
   b. Under "Segment Divisions" record what you see to be Paul's example in each chapter. Remember, in Philippians 3:17 Paul tells his readers to follow his example.
   c. In the next column under "Segment Divisions" write down what each chapter says about who or what Jesus Christ is in relation to the believer.
   d. For another segment division, record a command to believers that correlates with the theme of each chapter.

THINGS TO THINK ABOUT

1. What have you learned from Philippians about your relationship to suffering as a Christian? How is it going to affect the way you respond to suffering?

2. Can you say with Paul, "For to me to live is Christ and to die is gain"? If you can't, think about what has replaced Christ's rightful place in your life.

3. What have you learned from Jesus' example that you can apply to your own life? Do you have the attitude of Christ in respect to God and others? Do you regard others as more important than yourself?

4. Do you allow your circumstances to affect your peace? What is keeping you from His peace? After reading Philippians 4 do you see any way to handle life's anxieties?

5. What have you learned about your own needs and sharing with others in need?

THE EPISTLE OF PAUL TO THE

PHILIPPIANS

Date of writing: c. A.D. 60, at Rome

1 PAUL AND TIMOTHY,[a] SLAVES[b] OF Christ Jesus, to all the saints[c] in Christ Jesus that live at Philippi[d] with the bishops and deacons:[e] [2]Grace to you and peace from God our Father and the Lord Jesus Christ.

[3]Every time I think of you I thank my God. [4]Every time I pray I make my petition for all of you, with joyfulness [5]for your fellowship in furthering the good news from the first day to this moment. [6]Of this I am convinced, that He who has begun a good work in you will bring it to completion in the day of Christ Jesus.[f]

[7]It is right for me to think of all of you in this way, because I have you in my heart, as all of you share with me in divine grace, whether it be in my imprisonment or in the defense and confirmation of the good news. [8]For God is my witness how I yearn for all of you with the affection of Christ Jesus.

[9]And this is my prayer, that your love may grow ever richer and richer in real knowledge and all discernment, [10]that you may test the things that are better, that you may be unsullied and blameless as you face the day of Christ, [11]abounding in the fruits of righteousness[g] which come through Jesus Christ to the glory and praise of God.

[12]I want you to understand, brothers, that what has happened to me has turned out for, rather than against the advance of the good news, [13]so that throughout the imperial guard[h] and everywhere else it has become known that my imprisonment is because I belong to Christ. [14]And the majority of the brothers in the Lord have been encouraged by my imprisonment to be far more daring in telling the divine message fearlessly.[i]

[15]Some, to be sure, are preaching Christ out of jealousy and rivalry, but others out of good will; [16]some, indeed, are preaching out of love, knowing that I am destined for the defense of the good news, [17]but others preach Christ out of party spirit and not from pure motives. They intend to add distress to my bonds.

[18]Well, what of it? Anyhow, in any event, whether from pretense or from pure motives, Christ is preached and I am glad of that; yes, and I shall be glad, [19]for I know that this will turn out for my deliverance through your prayer and the provision that comes from the Spirit of Jesus Christ. [20]For I eagerly desire and hope not to be

---

a) See note at I Tim. 1:2.   b) See note at Matt. 13:27.   c) See note at Acts 9:13.
d) Philippi was a Roman colony in Macedonia, an area which is now a part of northern Greece. The city was within a mile or two of the Aegean Sea and lay along the Egnatian Way that ran from the east coast of the Adriatic Sea to Byzantium, which bordered on the Bosporus.
e) The church at Philippi was organized in accordance with N.T. practice, cf. Titus 1:5-9. For notes on bishops and deacons see I Tim. 3:1 and 8 respectively.   f) The day of His return.
g) Compare Gal. 5:22, 23.
h) The headquarters of the imperial guard was the governor's palace. There were several thousand soldiers in the guard who may have heard the message of salvation in Christ.
i) Paul's courage under adversity fortified the courage of other believers.

put to shame at all,[j] but that with perfect boldness as always, so now Christ may be honored in my body, either through living or through dying. 21For to me to live is Christ and to die is gain.[k]

22If, however, to continue to live means fruitful service for me, then I cannot tell which to choose. 23So I feel the pressure from both sides: I have a yearning to take my leave and to be with Christ, for that would be far better, 24but on your account it is more necessary that I remain in the body. 25And since I am confident of this, I know that I shall stay and continue with all of you, that you may progress and have the joy that comes with faith, 26so that through my coming to you again your pride in Christ Jesus because of me may become greater.

27Only conduct yourselves in a manner worthy of the good news concerning Christ, so that whether I come and see you or am absent, I may hear that you are standing firm in one spirit and one mind, as you are joined in conflict for the faith of the good news, 28not for a moment intimidated by your antagonists. For them this implies destruction, but for you deliverance, and that from God. 29For you have been privileged on behalf of Christ not only to believe in Him but also to suffer for Him; 30so you are experiencing the same conflict you have seen me wage and which you now hear that I am having.

2 IF, THEREFORE, IN RELATIONSHIP with Christ there is any encouragement, if there is any persuasive appeal of love, if there is any fellowship in the Spirit, if any affections and compassion,[l] 2then make my joy complete by being in agreement, having the same love, being united in spirit, having the same attitude, 3doing nothing out of selfishness or conceit, but with humility regarding others superior to yourselves. 4Neither must each be looking out only for his own interests but also for those of others.

5Let this mind be in you which was also in Christ Jesus 6who, though existing in the form of God, did not consider His equality with God something to cling to, 7but emptied Himself[m] as He took on the form of a slave[n] and became like human beings. 8So, recognized in appearance as a human being, He humbled Himself and became obedient to death; yes, death by the cross.

9God, therefore, has lifted Him on high and has given Him the name that surpasses every name,[o] 10so that at the name of Jesus every knee should bow, of those in heaven, of those on earth, and of those under the earth, 11and that every tongue should confess that Jesus Christ is Lord to the glory of God the Father.

12Consequently, my beloved, just as you have always obeyed, not only when I was with you but even more so now that I am absent from you, cultivate your own salvation with reverence and trepidation, 13for it is God who is at work within you, so as to will and to work for His good pleasure.

14Do it all without grumbling and objections, 15so that you may be blameless and innocent, God's faultless children in the midst of a crooked and perverted generation, among whom you shine like stars in the world, 16thus holding fast to the message of life as to be my pride on the day of Christ, because I shall neither have run nor labored in vain. 17In fact, even if my lifeblood must be poured out for a drink offering upon the sacrifice of your faith, I am glad of it and am glad together with all of you. 18Equally so be glad and share happiness with me.

19But, trusting in the Lord Jesus, I hope to send you Timothy shortly, so

---

j) Paul would have been ashamed had he failed to live and speak for Christ.
k) On earth Christ was everything to Paul. But it would be to his gain to be in heaven and thus in Christ's presence, *cf*. vs. 23; II Cor. 5:8.
l) The four "ifs" of this verse have the force of "since," i.e., *since* these things are so, "then make my joy complete," etc.
m) Not of His Deity, but of some marks of His divine glory that might have obscured His perfect humanity as described in vss. 7, 8.   n) See note at Matt. 13:27.
o) After the ascension, which Paul refers to here, Christ took back to heaven the added glory of His perfect humanity; for on His return He was not only the Son of God but also the Son of man.

that I too may be cheered by news from you; 20for I have no one else who shares my own attitude with such genuine interest in your affairs. 21They are all looking out for their interests, not for those of Christ Jesus. 22But you know his sterling worth, how as a son with his father he has served with me for the good news. 23So I hope to send him as soon as I see how things go with me. 24But I have confidence in the Lord that soon I too shall come.

25I have considered it necessary to send you my brother and fellow worker and fellow soldier, Epaphroditus, whom you sent as your messenger to minister to my wants, 26inasmuch as he is yearning for all of you and is distressed, because you heard that he was ill. 27And he was ill indeed, even to the verge of death; but God took pity on him, and not only on him but on me as well, so that I might not experience one grief after another. 28I am, therefore, sending him the more eagerly, so that you may be glad to see him again and that I may feel more relieved. 29Therefore, welcome him with all joyfulness in the Lord, and hold such persons in high esteem, 30for on account of the work of Christ he came to the brink of death and endangered his life, to make up for the service you could not render me.

3 FINALLY, MY BROTHERS, BE GLAD in the Lord. Repetition in my writing you is not irksome to me and for you it is safe. 2Look out for those dogs; look out for those wicked workers; look out for the mutilation faction.p 3For we who worship God through the Spirit and pride ourselves in Christ Jesus, and do not confide in the flesh, we are the truly circumcised.

4I have, however, some basis for confidence in the flesh. If anyone else imagines that he has some basis for confidence in the flesh, I am ahead of him: 5circumcised on the eighth day, a native Israelite of the tribe of Benjamin,

a Hebrew of Hebrews, as to the Law a Pharisee, 6as to zeal a persecutor of the church, as to legal righteousness without blame.

7But everything that was gain for me I have considered loss for Christ's sake. 8And, what is more, I regard everything as loss in comparison with the supreme value of knowing Christ Jesus my Lord. For His sake I have incurred the loss of all things and consider them rubbish, in order to gain Christ 9and to be found in Him, not having my own righteousness, based on the Law but, through faith in Christ, the righteousness that comes from God on the basis of faith, 10that I may know Him, and the power of His resurrectionq and the sharing of His sufferings, becoming like Him in His death,r 11in order that I might arrive at the resurrection from the dead.

12Not that I have already made this my own or have already reached perfection, but I am pressing onward in the hope of making it my own because Christ Jesus has made me His own. 13Brothers, I do not imply that I have made it my own, but one thing I do — forgetting what is behind and reaching out for what lies ahead, 14I push on to the goal for the prize of God's heavenly call in Christ Jesus.

15Let those of us, then, who are matures have this in mind, and if your views differ in any respect, God will make this clear also to you. 16But we must hold on to what we have attained.

17Join with me as followers, brothers, and observe those who behave as you have it exemplified in us. 18For many are living, of whom I have often told you and I say it now with tears, who are enemies of the cross of Christ, 19whose end is destruction, whose god is their stomach, whose boast is in their shame, whose interests are centered on earthly matters. 20For our citizenship belongs in heaven, from which also we expect the Lord Jesus Christ as De-

---

p) The allusion is to those who insisted upon Gentile converts' abiding by Mosaic regulations, particularly circumcision.
q) Because Christ arose, believers may know His power in this life, Rom. 6:4, and have assurance that they will be raised also, Rom. 8:11.
r) Christians ought to live as having died with Christ, Rom. 6:6, 8.
s) That is, mature in Christian living.

liverer, 21who will change the fashion of our humiliated body so that it will resemble His glorious body by the power that enables Him to subject everything to Himself.

4 NOW THEN, MY BROTHERS, BEloved and longed for, my joy and my crown,ᵗ in this way stand firm in the Lord, dear friends. 2I appeal to Euodia and I appeal to Syntycheᵘ to agree in the Lord. 3Yes, and I beg of you also, my genuine yokefellow, to lend these women a hand; for they struggled side by side with me in the proclamation of the good news, along with Clement and the rest of my fellow workers, whose names are in the Book of Life.

4Be joyful in the Lord always; again I say, Rejoice. 5Be known by all the people for your considerateness; the Lord is near. 6Entertain no worry, but under all circumstances let your petitions be made known before God by prayer and pleading along with thanksgiving.ᵛ 7So will the peace of God, that surpasses all understanding, keep guard over your hearts and your thoughts in Christ Jesus.

8Finally, brothers, whatever is true, whatever is honorable, whatever is just, whatever is pure, whatever is lovely, whatever is kindly spoken, whatever is lofty and whatever is praiseworthy — put your mind on these. 9And what you have learned and received and heard and seen in me, that put into practice. And the God of peace will be with you.

10I was uncommonly happy in the Lord because of late your thoughtfulnessᵂ toward me came to life again, a matter in which you were interested but lacked opportunity. 11Not that I mention this because of need, for I have learned to make ends meet in whatever situation I am. 12I know how to live simply and I know how to enjoy prosperity. I am acquainted with all circumstances: to be filled up and to be hungry, to have abundance and to suffer want. 13I have strength for every situation through Him who empowers me.

14At the same time you did well by sharing with me in my trouble. 15And you Philippians know, too, how in the early preaching of the good news, when we took our departure from Macedonia, not a single church except yourselves went into partnership with me with regard to giving and receiving; 16for even when I was in Thessalonica you more than once sent me something to meet my needs. 17Not that I am after the gift, but I am after the fruition that is multiplying to your credit.

18Now that I have received from Epaphroditus what you sent, a fragrant perfume, an acceptable offering that pleases God, I have enough and to spare; I am amply supplied. 19And my God will fully supply all your needs according to His abundant wealth so glorious in Christ Jesus. 20And to God our Father be glory forever and ever. Amen.

21Greet every saintˣ in Christ Jesus. The brothers who are with me send you greetings. 22All the saints greet you, especially those of Caesar's household.

23The grace of the Lord Jesus Christ be with your spirit.

---

t) In the N.T. a crown is used as a figure for reward, *cf.* I Cor. 9:25; I Thess. 2:19; II Tim. 4:8; James 1:12; I Pet. 5:4.
u) Euodia and Syntyche were two women in the church at Philippi who apparently had a strong disagreement. Although Paul rebuked them kindly with this appeal, his regard for them was not lessened because of their dissent. Observe how frequently the apostle expressed affection for "all of you," chs. 1:4, 7, 8, 25; 2:17; 4:23.
v) The prayer of faith contains gratitude. See e.g. Christ's prayers, Matt. 11:25; John 11:41.
w) When Paul wrote this letter he needed the material help of fellow believers, for he was a prisoner in Rome. In the past he had worked with his own hands at his trade of tent making, *cf.* Acts 18:1-3; 20:34; I Cor. 4:12.   x) See note at Acts 9:13.

PHILIPPIANS OBSERVATIONS CHART

AUTHOR: *Look for both pronouns and direct references*

THE RECIPIENTS: *Look for* saints, brothers, beloved, you, *or any other ways Paul addresses those to whom he is writing. Remember to keep asking the five W's and an H: How does Paul describe the Philippians? What are their problems? What is his concern for them? Why is Paul writing to the Philippians?*

Paul's Instructions to the Philippians

Philippians at a Glance

Theme of Philippians:

Segment Divisions

Command to:	Jesus is:	Paul's Example	Chapter Themes
	1:21 My Life		1
			2
3:17 Follow Paul's Example			3
		4:11 Learned to be Content in his Circumstances	4

Author:

Date:

Purpose:

Key Words:

Christ Jesus

joy (glad)

mind (attitude)

good news

COLOSSIANS

Colossae was located twelve miles from Laodicea and about a hundred miles east of Ephesus in the valley of the Lycus River in the southern part of ancient Phrygia, the adopted home of Oriental mysticism. Many Jews, Phrygians, and Greeks came to Colossae because it was on a main trade route. The mixture of backgrounds made the city an interesting cultural center where all sorts of new ideas and doctrines from the East were discussed and considered.

With all these ungodly influences, it is no wonder that the Christians at Colossae were on Paul's heart during his imprisonment in Rome. He may never have seen their faces, but they belonged to his Christ and he was one with them in spirit. Physically he might be bound by chains, but he could reach them by letter. This was one way he could protect them from the wolves who were out to devour God's flock.

Paul wrote sometime around A.D. 62. This letter to the faithful saints at Colossae was one whose message would be needed down through the ages. Maybe that is one of the reasons God didn't let Paul deliver this message in person.

THINGS TO DO

1. As you read Colossians chapter by chapter, learn all you can from the text about the author and the recipients and discover why the author writes what he does to this particular church. This will give you the key to understanding Colossians. Following this simple procedure will help:

   a. As you read, ask the five W's and an H: Who? What? Where? Why? When? and How? Ask questions such as: Who wrote this? To whom? Where were they? What were these people like? What were their situations? What were their problems? When was this written? What seemed to be going on? Why did the author say what he did?

   Asking questions like these—answered only from what the text says—gives insight into a book of the Bible and helps you to understand the context and purpose of the book and to keep its teachings and truths in their proper context.

   b. As you read, watch for every reference to the author(s) (including names and pronouns such as *I, my, we, us*). Keep asking the five W's and an H and record your insights on the OBSERVATIONS CHART following Colossians.

   c. Look for pronouns such as *you* and note the relationship between the author and the recipients. Ask questions such as: How did the gospel get to the Colossians? Who preached the gospel to them? What was the author's main concern for the Colossians? The answers will help you understand why this letter was written. Record your insights on the OBSERVATIONS CHART.

2. Now read through Colossians again, a chapter at a time. As you read:
   a. Mark in the text the key words and

phrases that are listed on the COLOSSIANS AT A GLANCE chart. Be sure to mark the synonyms and pronouns for each key word, and also mark every reference to Jesus: *with Him, for Him, through Him,* and so on.

b. In the margin, list what you learn from marking *in Him*, and from marking other key words.

c. Also record any other observations of the text as instructed in the observation section in the introduction to this New Testament.

3. When you get to chapter 2, note the warnings in this chapter by looking for the phrases *beware, allow no one,* and *let no one.*

a. Record these warnings along with any instructions on the OBSERVATIONS CHART.

b. With these warnings in mind, you will understand the threat of gnosticism in the Colossian church. Gnostics emphasized a philosophical "enlightenment" that divided the "enlightened ones" from ordinary Christians, and they taught that certain material things could spiritually defile a person. They also believed that Christ was not fully divine and fully human.

4. Proceed through chapters 3 and 4, adding pertinent information to your OBSERVATIONS CHART.

5. Be sure to record the theme of the book and of each chapter on the COLOSSIANS AT A GLANCE chart. Remember to record the chapter theme in the text above the chapter number. Also fill out the date the book was written, the name of the author, and his purpose for writing.

THINGS TO THINK ABOUT

1. What are you pursuing? Does it have eternal value? Is it drawing you closer to God or keeping you from time alone with God in prayer and in studying the Word? Are you seeking things above or earthly things?

2. Are you being deluded with any modern-day philosophies or traditions which contradict the Word or aren't in the Word? Any legalistic rules which are not clearly taught in the New Testament? Any mystical teachings or prophecies that can't be supported in the Word of God or that have a tendency to add something which isn't there or which seem to be only for an elite group of people?

3. Inductive Bible study is not easy. The enemy will do all he can to keep you from knowing God and His Word intimately, for it is your major defense and offense in spiritual warfare. Are you going to make it your goal to let the Word of Christ richly dwell within you and to walk in its precepts?

4. Are you proclaiming the Lord Jesus Christ and holding firmly to all He is and all that you have in Him as He is presented in Colossians?

5. As you have studied Colossians, have you seen any areas in your life in which you are falling short or simply walking in disobedience to God's Word? What are you going to do about these?

THE EPISTLE OF PAUL TO THE

COLOSSIANS

Date of writing: c. A.D. 60-61, at Rome

1 PAUL, AN APOSTLE OF CHRIST Jesus by the will of God, and our brother Timothy[a] [2]to the consecrated and faithful brothers in Christ at Colossae[b]: Grace to you and peace from God our Father [and the Lord Jesus Christ].[c]

[3]We constantly give thanks to God, the Father of our Lord Jesus Christ, as we are praying for you; [4]for we have heard of your faith in Christ Jesus and the love you cherish for all the saints,[d] [5]because of the hope that is stored up for you in heaven. You first heard of this hope in the message of the truth concerning the good news that reached you, [6]as it has come also to the whole world, with fruitful results which are spreading abroad, as is the case among you ever since you heard and came to know in truth the grace of God.

[7]So you learned from Epaphras,[e] our dear fellow bondslave,[f] who is a faithful minister of Christ for you; [8]and he has also pointed out to us the love you cherish through the Spirit. [9]We have, therefore, from the day we heard it, never neglected praying and petitioning for you, that you might be filled with all spiritual wisdom and insight so as to understand His will clearly, [10]and to live in a way worthy of the Lord and to His entire satisfaction, by producing results in all sorts of good work, and by growing in the knowledge of God. [11]We pray that you may be invigorated with complete power in accordance with His glorious strength, for the cheerful exercise of unlimited patience and perseverance, [12]with thanksgivings to the Father, who has qualified you for your share in the inheritance[g] of the saints in the light.

[13]He has rescued us from the domain of darkness,[h] and has transferred us into the kingdom of His Beloved Son, [14]in whom we have redemption [through His blood],[i] the forgiveness of sins; [15]who is the likeness[j] of the invisible God, the first-born of all creation. [16]For through Him[k] all things were created in heaven and on earth, the visible and the invisible, whether thrones or lordships or rulers or authorities; they are all created through Him and for Him, [17]and He is Himself before all, and in Him all things hold together.[l]

[18]He also is the Head of the body,

a) See note at I Tim. 1:2.
b) Colossae, like Laodicea and Hierapolis, ch. 4:13, was situated in Phrygia, the western area of what is now known as Turkey. The three cities were close together.
c) The words enclosed in brackets are not found in the majority of the most reliable ancient manuscripts.   d) See note at Acts 9:13.
e) Epaphras, who may be identical with Epaphroditus of Phil. 2:25-30, had visited Paul in Rome, vs. 7; Philem. 23.   f) See note at Matt. 13:27.
g) As the Hebrews had once inherited the Promised Land.
h) The realm that is controlled by Satan and his emissaries, Luke 22:53; Eph. 6:12.
i) The three words enclosed in brackets are not found in the majority of the most reliable ancient manuscripts. Unquestionably they are an interpolation taken over from Eph. 1:7, where they are authentic.   j) It is in Christ that men can see what God is like, John 1:18; I Tim. 3:16; Heb. 1:3.
k) The Son of God.
l) As the Apostle John revealed, "through Him everything came into being," John 1:3; cf. Gen. 1:1; Heb. 11:3.

the church; He is its beginning, the first-born from the dead, so that in every respect He might have first place. [19]For God was pleased to have all His fullness dwell in Him, [20]and through Him to reconcile all things to Himself, those on earth as well as those in heaven, as through Him God made peace by means of the blood of His cross.

[21]You, too, who once were estranged and of a hostile attitude with your evil activities, [22]He has now reconciled in His human body through His death, to introduce you into His presence holy and blameless and irreproachable — [23]if you remain grounded and settled in the faith and are not moved away from the hope inspired by the good news to which you listened, which has been preached to every creature under heaven[m] and of which I, Paul, became a minister.

[24]I am now glad amid my sufferings for you, and am making up in my own life on behalf of His body, which is in the church, what I am still lacking of afflictions for Christ. [25]I have become a minister of the church by divine appointment that was given me, to preach fully to you the word of God, [26]the secret[n] that was hidden from ages and generations, but which now has been revealed to His saints, [27]to whom God has chosen to make known what is the wealth of this glorious secret among the Gentiles, which is Christ in you, the hope of glory.

[28]Him we proclaim, while warning every person and instructing every individual in all wisdom, so that we may present every person complete in Christ. [29]And for this I toil, wrestling according to His energy which is powerfully at work in me.

2 FOR I WANT YOU TO KNOW IN HOW great a struggle[o] I am engaged for you and for the Laodicean brothers, and for those who have not personally seen my face, [2]so that their hearts may be encouraged, welded together in love, to attain all the riches that the full assurance of insight brings, with a knowledge of Christ, the secret of God,[p] [3]in whom all the treasures of wisdom and knowledge lie hidden.

[4]I mention this, so that no one may confuse your thinking by specious argument; [5]for while I am physically absent, I am nevertheless with you in spirit, as I observe with joy your good order and the firmness of your faith in Christ.

[6]So, as you accepted Christ Jesus as Lord, live in union with Him, [7]rooted and built up in Him and confirmed in the faith, just as you have been taught. And be overflowing with the giving of thanks.

[8]Beware of anyone carrying you captive through philosophy and empty deceitfulness along lines of human tradition and the world's elementary principles and not according to Christ. [9]For in Him all the fullness of the Godhead dwells bodily,[q] [10]and in Him, who is the head of all rule and authority, you are enjoying fullness of life. [11]In Him, too, you were circumcised — not with a physical circumcision — in stripping off your fleshly body in Christ's circumcision, [12]when you were buried with Him in baptism and thereby raised to life with Him through faith in the working of God, who raised Him from the dead.

[13]And you, who were dead in your trespasses and your lack of physical circumcision, He made alive together with Him, as He forgave us all our trespasses, [14]canceled the record of debt that stood against us, with its requirements, and took it out of the way, when He nailed it to the cross. [15]Disarming the rulers and authorities[r] He publicly exposed them to disgrace as He triumphed over them by means of the cross.

[16]Allow no one, therefore, to be your judge in regard to eating and drinking, or the observance of a festival or a new moon or a Sabbath. [17]These

---

m) That is, to every conceivable rank and condition of men.
n) For the meaning of the word "secret" in vss. 26, 27, chs. 2:2; 4:3, see note at Rom. 16:25.
o) That is, in prayer and in writing this letter and the one to the Laodicean church, ch. 4:16.
p) The marvelous revelation of God's plan for man, ch. 1:27.
q) The incarnation continues; the verb is in the present tense.   r) That is, those of demonic type.

are shadows of things to follow, but the body is Christ. [18]Let no one defraud you of salvation's prize, no one who indulges in assumed humility and the cult of angel-worship[s] who brags of visions and is puffed up without cause by his fleshly mind, [19]instead of keeping hold of that Head from which the whole body, supported and held together by ligaments and sinews, grows with divine growth.

[20]If with Christ you have become dead to the elementary principles of the world, why allow regulations to be imposed on you as if you were living under the world's control: [21]Don't touch this! Don't taste that! Don't handle the other! [22]All these are destined to wear out; they are governed by human injunctions and instructions, [23]such as have, to be sure, a suggestion of wisdom by self-imposed worship and humiliation and unsparing severity of the body, but are of no value in combating fleshly indulgence.[t]

3 IF, THEN, YOU HAVE BEEN RAISED with Christ,[u] seek the things which are above, where Christ is seated at God's right hand. [2]Apply your mind to things above, not to things on earth; [3]for you have died, and your life is hidden with Christ in God. [4]When Christ, who is our life, makes His appearance, then we also will appear in glory with Him.

[5]Therefore put to death whatever in your nature belongs to the earth[v] — immorality, impurity, passion, evil desire, and greediness, which is idolatry. [6]On account of them God's anger will come [on disobedient people].[w] [7]And at one time you were addicted to them, when your life was spent in such ways. [8]But now you must also put all these things away — anger, bad temper, malice, slander, shameful language. [9]Do not lie to one another, since you have stripped off the old nature

with its practices [10]and have put on the new self who is being renewed in a full knowledge in the likeness of Him who created him. [11]You are where there is no difference between Greek and Jew, circumcised and uncircumcised, barbarian, Scythian,[x] slave, and freeborn, but Christ is all and in all.

[12]Therefore, as God's chosen, set apart and enjoying His love, clothe yourselves with tenderness of heart, kindliness, humility, gentleness, patient endurance. [13]Bear with one another and forgive each other in case one has a grievance against another. Just as the Lord has forgiven you, so do you. [14]But crown it all with love, which is the perfect bond of union. [15]And let the peace of Christ, to which you were called in one body, arbitrate in your hearts. And be thankful.

[16]Let the enriching message of Christ have ample room in your lives as you instruct and admonish one another in all wisdom with psalms and hymns and spiritual songs that are sung in a thankful spirit in your hearts toward God. [17]And whatever you do by word or deed, do it all in the name of the Lord Jesus, through whom you are offering thanks to God the Father.

[18]Wives, be submissive to your husbands, as it is becoming in the Lord to do. [19]Husbands, love your wives and do not be harsh toward them. [20]Children, be obedient to your parents in every respect, for this is pleasing to the Lord. [21]Fathers, do not irritate your children, that they may not lose heart.

[22]Servants,[y] obey your earthly masters in every way, not as men-pleasers when working under their eyes, but with unmixed motives out of reverence for the Lord. [23]Whatever you do, work heartily as for the Lord and not for men, [24]for you know that from the Lord you will receive the reward of the inheritance. It is Christ the Lord

s) The humility of these people was actually dishonoring to God; for in attempting to approach Him through worshiping angelic beings they were denying the only access available to them, that is, through Christ, John 14:6.
t) All these afford merely human satisfaction.
u) Christ died and rose again as representative of us. v) Compare Matt. 5:29; Mark 9:43-47.
w) The words enclosed in brackets are not found in the majority of the most reliable ancient manuscripts. The expression is found elsewhere in the N.T., however, e.g. Eph. 5:6.
x) The Scythians were an uncivilized people who lived north of the Black Sea.
y) See note at Matt. 13:27.

for whom you are working. 25For the wrongdoer[z] will get what is coming to him for his wrongdoing; there will be no partiality.

4 MASTERS, TREAT YOUR SERVANTS with justice and fairness, well aware that you also have a Master in heaven.

2Keep persevering in prayer; attend to it diligently with the offering of thanks, 3praying for us also, that God may open for us a door to tell the message of the secret[a] of Christ on account of which I am in prison, 4so that I may make this known in the way I am obliged to tell it.

5Conduct yourselves wisely toward outsiders, using your time to the best possible advantage. 6Let your speech always be gracious and so well reasoned out that you will know how to reply to each individual.

7Tychicus,[b] our beloved brother, faithful minister, and fellow servant in the Lord, will tell you all about my affairs. 8I have sent him to you for this very purpose, to let you know our circumstances, and to encourage your hearts.[c] 9He is accompanied by Onesimus, our faithful and beloved brother who is one of your own. They will acquaint you with everything that is going on here.

10Aristarchus,[d] my fellow prisoner, sends you greeting; so does Mark,[e] the cousin of Barnabas, about whom you received instructions — if he comes to you, welcome him. 11Also Jesus who is called Justus. These are the only ones of the circumcision who serve as co-workers for the kingdom of God; they have become a comfort to me.

12Epaphras,[f] one of your own, a slave of Christ Jesus, wants to be remembered to you. He is always wrestling for you in his prayers, that you may stand firm, mature, and thoroughly convinced in all the will of God. 13For I bear him witness how deeply concerned he is about you and the brothers at Laodicea[g] and Hierapolis.

14Luke,[h] the beloved physician, sends greetings, and so does Demas.[i] 15Extend our greetings to the brothers in Laodicea; also to Nympha and the church that meets at her home.

16When this letter has been read in your presence, arrange that it may also be read by the Laodicean church, while you read the letter from Laodicea.[j] 17And say to Archippus:[k] See to it that you fulfill the ministry which you have received in the Lord.

18My greeting in my own, Paul's, handwriting. Remember my bonds. Grace be with you.

---

z) That is, the abusive master.
a) See note at Rom. 16:25.
b) Tychicus, a native of Corinth, joined Paul there on his last missionary journey, Acts 20:4, 5, and remained with the apostle and served him for many years, Eph. 6:21; II Tim. 4:12; Titus 3:12.   c) Philem. 10.
d) Aristarchus was a native of Thessalonica, Acts 20:4. Like Tychicus, vs. 7, Aristarchus was a companion and fellow worker with Paul for a long time, Acts 19:29; 27:2; Philem. 24.
e) This was John Mark of Jerusalem, who with Barnabas accompanied Paul on his first missionary journey but not the second, Acts 12:25; 15:37-39. He later served Paul in various ways, II Tim. 4:11. It was to the home of John Mark's mother that Peter went when he was miraculously released from prison, Acts 12:12. Mark was the author of the Second Gospel.
f) See note at ch. 1:7.
g) For the location of Laodicea and Hierapolis see note at ch. 1:7. It was in Laodicea, mentioned in ch. 2:1, that one of the seven churches of Rev. 2-3 was situated, Rev. 3:14.
h) Luke, the author of the Third Gospel and The Acts, joined Paul at Troas during the apostle's second missionary journey, Acts 16:10 (where see note), and was with him almost constantly until Paul's martyrdom, II Tim. 4:11. i) See note at Philem. 24.
j) It was evidently customary in N.T. times to exchange letters among the churches. Some think that "the letter from Laodicea" was the one that is now known as the Epistle to the Ephesians.
k) Philem. 2.

AUTHOR

_____

_____

_____

_____

_____

_____

_____

RECIPIENTS

_____

_____

_____

_____

_____

_____

_____

WARNINGS AND INSTRUCTIONS

_____

_____

_____

_____

_____

_____

_____

_____

_____

_____

_____

_____

_____

_____

_____

Colossians Observations Chart

Colossians at a Glance

Theme of Colossians:

Segment Divisions

	Chapter Themes
	1
	2
	3
	4

Author:

Date:

Purpose:

Key Words:

wisdom
knowledge
(insight)
understanding
fullness
all
complete
faith
secret
in Him
(or before Him,
through Him,
etc.)

1 THESSALONIANS

Timothy joined Paul and Silas (Silvanus) while they were in Lystra on Paul's second missionary journey. Since his father was a Greek, Timothy hadn't been circumcised. There was no sense in causing any unnecessary conflicts with the Jews who were in those parts, so Paul had Timothy circumcised. Things went smoothly until Paul had his vision of a man from Macedonia appealing to him to come and help them.

Believing this call was of God, the three went to Philippi—and the persecution began. Paul and Silas were beaten with rods and thrown into prison. Undaunted and convinced of their heavenly commission, the trio traveled on through Amphipolis and Apollonia and came to Thessalonica. There they found a Jewish synagogue, where for three Sabbaths Paul reasoned with the Thessalonians from the Scriptures. Jews and Greeks, including a number of leading women, heard and believed. The other Jews became furious. Once again there was opposition, but this time the persecution was not directed only to the trio, but also to those who had believed.

Consequently, the Thessalonian believers sent Paul, Silas, and Timothy to Berea by night where again the gospel bore fruit. When the Jews of Thessalonica heard what happened in Berea, they couldn't bear it. They went to Berea to persecute the men who were upsetting the world.

From Berea Paul went to Athens, and from Athens to Corinth. But the church at Thessalonica was on his heart. How were they doing in the midst of such adamant opposition? Paul had to find out. So about A.D. 51, while in Corinth, Paul sat down to write his first epistle to the church at Thessalonica.

THINGS TO DO

1. Read 1 Thessalonians chapter by chapter. Record the information from the questions below on the OBSERVATIONS CHART following 1 Thessalonians. (Be sure to take your answers from the text.)
   a. List what you learn about the author(s). Look for the relationship of the author(s) to the recipients. In chapter 2, what comparisons are drawn to show how the author(s) feel about those to whom they are writing? Don't miss it.
   b. List everything you learn about the recipients. Who had they been serving? What happened when they heard and believed the gospel? What were they enduring?
   c. Note the different problems or concerns that are addressed in the letter.

2. Read through the book and mark in the text the key words (along with their synonyms and pronouns) listed on the 1 THESSALONIANS AT A GLANCE chart. As you observe the key words, list in the margin everything you learn from the text about each word. List what you learn about *the coming of the Lord* in one place in the margin.

3. In chapters 4 and 5 are several truths

about those "who have died" and "the living who remain." List what you observe from the text about each of these on the second page of the OBSERVATIONS CHART. As you do, note the progression of events in 1 Thessalonians 4:13–18. Ask the five W's and an H of the text: Who is involved? What will happen? Where will they meet the Lord? When? Why are they not to sorrow? How will all this happen?

4. Watch what you learn about "the day of the Lord" in chapter 5. Record this information on THE DAY OF THE LORD chart following Revelation.

5. On 1 THESSALONIANS AT A GLANCE, record the theme of the book. Then record the theme of each chapter on the chart and in the text above the chapter number. Fill in any additional information under author, date, purpose, etc.

6. Often you will be able to note a turning point in the book because the subject being addressed will change. These topical changes divide the book into segments. Think through the following questions to see if you can determine a segment division in 1 Thessalonians.
    a. Where does the main subject of the book change?
    b. What is the topic in the first three chapters of the book?
    c. What does the subject become in the last two chapters?
    d. Title each segment of the book by thinking of the theme or subject discussed in the first three chapters and then in the last two. Record your segment divisions on 1 THESSALONIANS AT A GLANCE.

THINGS TO THINK ABOUT

1. In this book Paul pours his life into other men who could carry on the work of the gospel. Are you spending time imparting the things God has done in your life to another person who can in turn minister to others?

2. It is sometimes hard to give thanks in all things, yet that is the will of God. Go back over the last few days and think of the things that have happened in your life for which you have not given thanks. Determine in your heart to obey this command.

3. Are the circumstances in your life difficult? How are you responding? What will others say about your response? Can people imitate your walk with God?

4. Are you abstaining from sexual immorality? Are you defrauding others sexually in any way at all? Do you realize that if you are acting on your sexual passions in a way contrary to God's Word, God will act as the avenger against you?

5. Do you pray unceasingly (5:17) for those in your life who don't know the Lord? Do you boldly approach the Lord for answers to your problems? Do you pray consistently for others?

THE FIRST EPISTLE OF PAUL TO THE

THESSALONIANS

Date of writing: c. A.D. 51, at Corinth

1 Paul and Silvanus[a] and Timothy,[b] to the church of the Thessalonians[c] in God the Father and the Lord Jesus Christ:[d] Grace to you and peace.

2 We offer thanks to God always for all of you as we make mention of you in our prayers, 3 and constantly recall in the presence of God and our Father your active faith, your labor prompted by love, and your enduring hope that rests on our Lord Jesus Christ.

4 Brothers, beloved of God, we know His choice of you; 5 for our good news reached you not only in words but also in power and in the Holy Spirit and with sound conviction, even as you well know in what way we conducted ourselves among you for your sakes. 6 You also became followers of us and of the Lord when, with joy derived from the Holy Spirit, you welcomed the message under great affliction,[e] 7 so that you became an example to all who believe in Macedonia and Achaia. 8 For not only did the Lord's message echo from you in Macedonia and Achaia, but the fact of your faith in God has been made known everywhere, so that we do not need to say anything.

9 For they voluntarily tell about us, what remarkable introduction we had to you and how you turned to God from idols, to serve the living and true God 10 and to await His Son from heaven, whom He raised from the dead — Jesus who delivers us from the coming wrath.

2 FOR YOU YOURSELVES ARE AWARE, brothers, how our entrance among you was not futile, 2 but after the sufferings and ill-treatment we experienced, as you know, at Philippi,[f] we took great courage by the help of our God to tell you amid severe struggle the good news from God. 3 For our appeal springs neither from delusion, nor from impure motives, nor from deceit, 4 but precisely as we have been divinely approved to be entrusted with the good news, so we tell it, not to ingratiate ourselves with men but to please God, who tests our hearts. 5 For we never indulged in flattery, as you well know, neither did we use a pretext to satisfy our greed — to which God is witness — 6 neither did we seek the plaudits of men, either from you or from others, though as Christ's apostles we were in position to claim authority. 7 Instead, we were mild-mannered in your circle, like a nurse tenderly fostering her own children. 8 Thus being strongly drawn to you, we were joyfully willing not only to impart to you

---

a) Silvanus, called Silas in The Acts, is first mentioned in Acts 15:22. Evidently he was a member of the Jerusalem church and as such was sent with Paul to inform the believers at Antioch of the decision of the Jerusalem council, Acts 15:27-29. Later he accompanied Paul on the apostle's second missionary journey, vs. 40, and was imprisoned with him at Philippi, Acts 16:19-40. Silvanus visited Thessalonica with Paul, Acts 17:4, and continued to help him in the work, II Cor. 1:19.   b) See note at I Tim. 1:2.
c) Thessalonica, now known as Salonica, is located in Greece on the northwestern coast of the Aegean Sea. In N.T. times it was the capital of Macedonia.
d) Notice that in this early epistle Christ shares an equal place with God the Father.
e) Acts 17:5-9.   f) See note at Phil. 1:1.

the good news from God but our own lives as well, because you had become dear to us.

9You will recollect, brothers, our toil and hardship as we worked night and day, so that we might be no burden to any of you while we preached to you the good news from God. 10You are witnesses, and so is God, how pure, fair, and irreproachable was our behavior toward you believers. 11You know how we, like a father toward his own children, appealed to each of you and encouraged you and charged you 12to conduct yourselves in a way worthy of the God who is calling you into His own kingdom and glory.

13On this account we also constantly thank God because, when you took hold of the divine message from us, you did not accept it as a human message but, as it truly was, a message from God, which also is effective in you who believe. 14For you, brothers, have become followers of the churches of God in Christ Jesus that are in Judea; because you also have suffered at the hands of your own countrymen just as they suffered from the Jews, 15who put to death the Lord Jesus as well as the prophets, and persecuted us. They are displeasing to God and opponents of all people; 16for they forbid us to tell the message of salvation to the Gentiles, so that they constantly fill up the measure of their sins. But divine indignation has overtaken them.

17But we, brothers, when we were deprived of you for a little while insofar as presence goes but not in heart, made the more intense efforts with great longing to see you face to face, 18because we wanted to come to you, I Paul indeed more than once, but Satan interfered with us.g 19For who except you is our hope or happiness or crownh of pride in the presence of our Lord Jesus at His coming?i 20For you are our glory and joy.

3 SO, WHEN WE COULD NOT STAND IT any longer, we thought it best to be left alone at Athens, 2and we sent Timothy, our brother and God's minister concerning the good news of Christ, to confirm you and encourage you in your faith, 3that no one may be disturbed by these afflictions. For you know yourselves that for this we were appointed; 4for when we were with you, we told you in advance that we were going to have trouble, exactly as you know it happened.

5And for this reason, when I could no longer stand it, I sent to make sure about your faith, whether perhaps the tempterj might have tempted you, and our work should be useless. 6Now, however, since Timothy has returned to us from you and has brought us the good news about your faith and love, and how you retain us constantly in loving remembrance, how you are yearning to see us, just as we are to see you, 7we have reason, brothers, to be encouraged about you on account of your faith, in spite of all our distress and affliction. 8Because now we truly live if you stand firm in the Lord.

9How can we ever repay God with enough thanksgiving for you in view of all the happiness we are enjoying because of you in the presence of our God? 10Night and day we keep praying earnestly to see you face to face and to supply what is lacking in your faith.

11May our God and Father Himself and our Lord Jesus direct our way to you. 12May the Lord make your love for one another and for everyone abundant and running over, just as ours is for you, 13so that your hearts may be made so steadfast that you will be spotless before God our Father at the coming of our Lord Jesus with all His saints.k

4 FINALLY THEN, BROTHERS, WE BEG of you and exhort you in the name of the Lord Jesus to continue living in the way you learned from us, a way that is pleasing to God (and as you are behaving), and that you keep on,

g) Apparently Satan did this by working through those who opposed Paul.
h) See note at Phil. 4:1.
i) Five times in this epistle the second advent of Christ is alluded to: chs. 1:10; 2:19; 3:13; 4:15, 16; 5:2, 3.   j) Satan.   k) See note at Acts 9:13.

doing still better. 2For you are aware what instructions we gave you by authority of the Lord Jesus.

3This is God's will — your sanctification,[1] that you keep yourselves from sexual immorality, 4that each of you learn how to take his own wife in purity and honor, 5not in lustful passion like the Gentiles who have no knowledge of God. 6Let no one overstep the bounds and take advantage of his brother in this matter, for the Lord is a punisher in all such cases, as previously we told and solemnly charged you. 7For God has not called us to an impure but to a holy life; consequently, 8the one who rejects this does not reject man but God, who has given us His Holy Spirit.

9It is not necessary to write you about brotherly love, for you yourselves are taught by God to love one another, 10and you are practicing it toward all the brothers throughout Macedonia. 11But we appeal to you, brothers, to keep advancing in it and to cherish ambition for a peaceful way of living; to mind your own affairs, and to work with your hands as we recommended to you, 12in order that your behavior toward the outsiders will be honorable and you need not depend on anyone.

13But we do not want you to be ignorant, brothers, about those who have died, so that you may not grieve as others do, who have no hope. 14For if we believe that Jesus died and rose again, in a similar way through Jesus God will bring with Him those who have died. 15We tell you this by the word of the Lord: we, the living who remain at the coming of the Lord, will not take precedence over those who have died. 16For with a shout, with the voice of the archangel and the trumpet of God, the Lord Himself will descend from heaven, and those who died in Christ will rise first. 17Afterward we, the living who remain, will be caught up along with them in the clouds to meet the Lord in the air. And so we shall forever be with the Lord. 18So then encourage one another with these words.

5 CONCERNING TIMES AND SEASONS, brothers, you need no writing from me,[m] 2for you are yourselves aware that the day of the Lord will come as a thief in the night. 3When they say, "Peace and safety," then sudden destruction will come upon them like the birthpangs of a pregnant woman, and there will be no escape.

4You, however, brothers, are not in the dark, so that the day should surprise you like a thief; 5for you are all sons of light and sons of the day. We belong neither to night nor to darkness. 6So then, let us not be asleep like the rest, but let us be on our guard and be sober. 7For those who sleep sleep at night, and the drunkards are drunk at night. 8But as we belong to the day, let us be self-controlled, equipped with faith and love for our breastplate, and the hope[n] of salvation for our helmet.

9For God has not destined us for His anger, but for the obtaining of salvation through our Lord Jesus Christ, 10who experienced death for us so that we, whether awake or asleep, might live together with Him. 11Encourage one another, therefore, and build up one another, as in fact you are doing.

12We beg of you, brothers, to recognize the workers among you, those who are leaders in the Lord and your advisers. 13Because of their work, hold them lovingly in highest regard. Enjoy peace among yourselves.

14But we appeal to you, brothers: warn the idle, encourage the fainthearted, give your support to the weak, exercise patience toward everyone. 15See to it that no one pays back evil for evil; instead, always try to be helpful to one another and to all people. 16Always be cheerful. 17Pray un-

---

l) Verses 3-12 describe some practical, moral outcomes of sanctification.
m) That Christ will come again is the important thing. How and when He will come is known by God alone. In His Word He has given some hints as to the manner and time of the event, but He has not revealed every detail concerning it.
n) Faith, hope, and love is a spiritual triad common to Paul's writings, e.g. ch. 1:3; I Cor. 13:13.

ceasingly.º ¹⁸Under all circumstances give thanks, for such is God's will for you in Christ Jesus.

¹⁹Do not stifle the Spirit. ²⁰Do not despise prophetic utterance, ²¹but test it all and retain what is good. ²²Keep away from evil in every form.

²³And may the God of peace Himself make you holy through and through. May your whole being — spirit, soul, and body — be kept blameless at the coming of our Lord Jesus Christ. ²⁴He who calls you is faithful and He will accomplish it.

²⁵Brothers, pray for us. ²⁶Greet all the brothers with a sacred kiss.

²⁷I solemnly charge you in the Lord's name to have this letter read to all the brothers.

²⁸The grace of our Lord Jesus Christ be with you.

---

o) Compare Luke 11:5-8.

AUTHOR(S)

Who wrote 1 Thessalonians?

RECIPIENTS

Who are they?

What relationship did these men have to one another?

What was their relationship to the author(s)?

What was their condition when the author(s) first ministered to them? Who were they serving?

Had they worked together before?

If so, where? How? Why?

What conditions were they in when the letter was written?

Describe the ministry these men had among the recipients

How strongly did the author(s) feel about the recipients?

Did they think of them often? How do you know?

What comparisons show the kind of love the author(s) feel for them?

What had the recipients become?

PROBLEMS/CONCERNS/STRUGGLES

1 Thessalonians 4:13–18

Those who have died	The living who remain	Progression of events

1 Thessalonians at a Glance

Theme of 1 Thessalonians:

Segment Divisions

		Chapter Themes
	1	
	2	
	3	
	4	
	5	

Author:

Date:

Purpose:

Key Words:

good news (word, message)

faith

love

hope

Lord Jesus Christ (any reference to Jesus)

God

Holy Spirit

affliction (trouble, suffering)

of the Lord

day of the Lord

2 THESSALONIANS

*I*t had been four to six months since Paul wrote his first epistle in A.D. 51 to the church at Thessalonica. Their persecution had not subsided, but much to Paul's joy, his labor had not been in vain; they had withstood the attacks of the tempter.

However, Paul was concerned about some things in the church. Once again, during his second missionary journey he had to take time to write—and put his distinguishing mark on this letter. The church had to know without a doubt that it was from him.

THINGS TO DO

1. If you haven't studied 1 Thessalonians, you should do so before you begin 2 Thessalonians. However, if you have worked through 1 Thessalonians, then read it once again. Observe what Paul says about the coming of the Lord Jesus. Also give special attention to 1 Thessalonians 4:13 through 5:11.
2. Now read 2 Thessalonians. Watch how 1 Thessalonians ties in with 2 Thessalonians. Look for the information below and record it on the OBSERVATIONS CHART following 2 Thessalonians.
   a. What do you learn about the author and the recipients of this letter? What are the circumstances of the recipients?
   b. Paul addresses several problems which need correction. List these in the margin and on the chart. This will help you see the author's

purpose in writing. Then note the instructions or commands related to each problem addressed. List these on your OBSERVATIONS CHART.
   c. Paul also praises the Thessalonians and encourages them about the things they are doing well. List the exhortations he includes in his letter.
   d. Be certain you record what happens to those who pay no attention to the good news.
   e. From what you have observed about the author and the recipients, why do you think Paul wrote this book? Record this on 2 THESSALONIANS AT A GLANCE under "Purpose."
3. Read through 2 Thessalonians again, a chapter at a time, and do the following:
   a. Mark in the text the key words (including their synonyms and pronouns) listed on 2 THESSALONIANS AT A GLANCE. Also watch for any words you feel are key but aren't listed.
   b. Now go back through the key words and in the margin make a list of what you have learned. Make one list for each word. In other words, you will have one list of everything these three chapters teach about *the coming of Christ,* one list for *affliction and suffering,* one list for *the day of the Lord,* and so on.
4. On the OBSERVATIONS CHART are two more headings: "When the Day of the Lord Comes" and "When the

Man of Sin Is Revealed."

a. Carefully read 2 Thessalonians 2:1-12 and list everything the chapter says must happen before the day of the Lord can come.

b. Do the same for the revelation of the man of sin.

c. Record your insights on the chart THE DAY OF THE LORD following Revelation.

5. Think through each chapter and record its theme on 2 THESSALONIANS AT A GLANCE and in the appropriate place in the text. Also record the theme of the book, author, and date.

THINGS TO THINK ABOUT

1. How do you react to trials? How do you respond to persecution? Does your response glorify God? Do people see your faith? Is His love evident in your life?

2. Do you lead a disciplined life? Does your lifestyle encourage laziness in others? Or can you say, "Follow my example"? Are you doing your share for the furtherance of the kingdom, or are you just waiting for Jesus to come back?

3. When the good you do doesn't seem appreciated or even noticed, how do you feel? For whom are you doing it? Will you persevere?

4. Does what you believe about prophecy or any other doctrine come from a careful, personal study of God's Word, or is it from what others teach you? Are you holding firmly to what you know of the Word of God, or are you easily persuaded by "faddish" teaching?

The Word Sounds Forth from Thessalonica

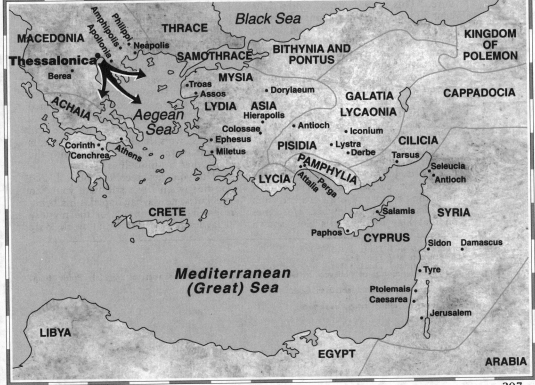

THE SECOND EPISTLE OF PAUL TO THE

THESSALONIANS

Date of writing: c. A.D. 51-52, at Corinth

1 PAUL AND SILVANUS[a] AND TIMO-thy[b] to the church of the Thessalonians[c] in God our Father[d] and the Lord Jesus Christ: [2]Grace to you and peace from God the Father and the Lord Jesus Christ.

[3]We are always bound[e] to give God thanks for you, brothers, as is befitting, because your faith is growing so splendidly and the love of each of you for one another is increasing, [4]so that we ourselves mention you with pride among the churches of God for your fortitude and faith amid all the persecutions and distresses which you endure. [5]This is evidence of God's righteous judgment, that you may be made worthy of the kingdom of God, on account of which you are suffering, [6]inasmuch as God considers it just to repay with affliction those who afflict you, [7]and to give relief along with us to you who are afflicted, when the Lord Jesus will be revealed from heaven with His mighty angels in a blaze of fire.

[8]He will inflict retribution on those who ignore God and who pay no attention to the good news concerning our Lord Jesus. [9]They will pay the penalty of everlasting ruin separated from the presence of the Lord and from His glorious power, [10]when He comes on that Day to have His glory shown in His saints[f] and to be admired in all those who believe, because our witnessing among you was believed.

[11]For this purpose we constantly pray for you, that our God may render you worthy of His call, and by His power may fulfill every desire for goodness and every faith-inspired effort, [12]so that the name of our Lord Jesus may be glorified in you and you in Him to the measure of the grace of our God and of the Lord Jesus Christ.

2 NOW WE BEG OF YOU, BROTHERS, with regard to the coming of our Lord Jesus Christ and our meeting together with Him, [2]not to allow your minds to be readily unsettled or disturbed, either by spirit, or by message, or by letter allegedly from us, as if the day of the Lord had arrived. [3]Let no one in any way deceive you; for the apostasy[g] is to come first, and the man of sin is to be revealed, the one doomed to hell, [4]the adversary who opposes and rises up against every so-called god and what is worshiped, so that he seats himself in the temple of God with the claim that he himself is God.

[5]Do you not recollect how I told you this when I was still with you? [6]So you know now what impedes his being revealed at this time; [7]for the mystery of lawlessness is already at work; only

---

a) See note at I Thess. 1:1.
b) See note at I Tim. 1:2.
c) See note at I Thess. 1:1.
d) The relationship of believers to God as His sons is through Christ in the Holy Spirit, Rom. 8:14-17.
e) Because of being indebted to God.
f) See note at Acts 9:13.
g) Literally, *falling away, departure.*

the one who is impeding now will do so until he is taken out of the way.[h] [8]Then will the lawless one[i] be revealed, whom the Lord Jesus will remove with the breath of His mouth, and bring to an end by the visible manifestation of His coming.

[9]The coming of the lawless one is according to Satan's working, with great power and signs and miracles, all of them false, [10]and with limitless deceit of wickedness for those who, because they did not welcome the love of truth for their salvation, are going to destruction. [11]And for this reason God visits them with a delusion that operates on them to believe the falsehood, [12]so that all who have not believed the truth but have taken pleasure in wickedness may be judged.

[13]But we are always bound to offer thanks to God for you, brothers, beloved by the Lord as you are, because from the beginning God chose you for salvation by the Spirit's sanctifying work and by faith in the truth. [14]He called you for this purpose by means of the good news which we preached, that you might share the glory of our Lord Jesus Christ. [15]So then, brothers, stand firm and hold on to the traditions you learned of us, whether orally or by letter.

[16]And may our Lord Jesus Christ Himself and God our Father, who has loved us and has graciously given us eternal comfort and well-founded hope, [17]encourage your hearts and strengthen you in every good work and word.

3 FINALLY, BROTHERS, PRAY FOR US, that the word of the Lord may run its course and be glorified as it was among you, [2]and that we may be rescued from morally evil and malicious people;[j] for all men are not believers. [3]But the Lord is faithful, who will make you strong and guard you from the evil one. [4]So through the Lord we have confidence in you, that you are practicing and will practice what we command. [5]And may the Lord direct your hearts into the love of God[k] and into the patient expectation of Christ.

[6]But we charge you, brothers, in the name of the Lord Jesus Christ, to avoid every brother who, instead of observing the tradition you received from us, is living in idleness. [7]For you know yourselves how you should follow us, because we were not idle among you, [8]neither did we eat anyone's food without paying for it; instead, we worked and knew hardship night and day, so as not to impose on any of you. [9]Not that we did not have the right to support, but to furnish you ourselves as an example which you should follow.

[10]For while we were with you, we gave you this charge, "If anyone does not want to work, then he should not eat either."[l] [11]For we are hearing that some of you are living in idleness, not working but busy in other people's affairs. [12]Such persons we direct and charge in the Lord Jesus Christ that by doing their work quietly, they earn their own living.

[13]As for you, brothers, do not get tired of doing good. [14]If someone does not follow our instruction in this letter, note him well; do not associate with him, so that he may grow ashamed. [15]But do not consider him an enemy, but warn him as a brother.

[16]And may the Lord of peace Himself grant you peace at all times under all circumstances. The Lord be with you all.[m]

[17]The greeting in my own, Paul's handwriting; which is a sign in every letter. It is the way I write.[n]

[18]The grace of our Lord Jesus Christ be with all of you.

---

h) In vss. 6, 7 someone or something that impedes lawlessness is introduced. It is the view of some scholars that that which restrains iniquity is government, specifically Rome in the first century A.D., in the person of the emperor. Others believe that the Holy Spirit is meant and that His impeding influence will continue until He is taken out of the way as a restrainer at the return of Christ.　i) The Antichrist.
j) Paul had an unhappy experience in Thessalonica with men of this kind, Acts 17:5-9.
k) Divine love fostered in our hearts.
l) It appears that there were some people so sure that the Lord would return at any moment that they ceased from working for a living.　m) Cf. Matt. 28:20.
n) As a safeguard against false messages allegedly from him, cf. ch. 2:2. Paul signed this letter by hand.

Author	Recipients	Those Who Pay No Attention to the Good News

Problems/Concerns	Instructions	Exhortations

When the Day of the Lord Comes		When the Man of Sin Is Revealed

THEME OF 2 THESSALONIANS:

SEGMENT DIVISIONS

	CHAPTER THEMES
	1
	2
	3

Author:

Date:

Purpose:

Key Words:

affliction

suffering (persecutions)

coming of Jesus Christ (or synonymous references)

God

Spirit

glory

man of sin

idle (idleness)

day of the Lord (and relative pronouns)

truth

1 TIMOTHY

hirty years of labor for the good news had taken its toll on Paul. His body bore the brandmarks of a servant of Jesus Christ (see Galatians 6:17). However, the intensity of his sufferings was minor compared to the intensity of his love and concern for the churches etched upon his heart.

Undaunted by two years of house arrest in Rome, Paul pressed on toward the prize of the high calling in Christ Jesus. He intended to visit Asia, Macedonia, and possibly Spain. Spain had been on his heart before he became a prisoner of Rome.

He also was concerned about the church at Ephesus. Timothy, his faithful co-laborer, was pastoring that strategically important church. Possibly concerned that he might be delayed and that Timothy might need something in writing to set before others as an ever-present reminder, Paul took quill and ink, spread out the parchment, and wrote his first epistle to his beloved son in the faith, an epistle which would become a legacy for the church and a pillar and support of the truth. It was around A.D. 62.

THINGS TO DO

1. Read 1 Timothy. Note 1:3 and 3:14, 15 to see why Paul wrote this epistle. Keep this in mind as you read the book. On the 1 TIMOTHY AT A GLANCE chart, record Paul's purpose for writing.

2. Read 1 Timothy again, one chapter at a time. On your OBSERVATIONS CHART following 1 Timothy:

   a. Record how Paul describes himself. Note how he refers to himself, stating his position of authority which qualifies him to instruct Timothy in the matters described in this letter.

   b. Note how Paul describes Timothy, where Timothy is when the letter is written, and what his relationship is to Paul.

   c. Write down the commands and instructions Paul gives about specific groups of people or practices. Record what you learn about overseers ("elders" or "bishops") and deacons. Also record what you see about general groups of believers in the church. There is a designated space for each of these groups on the OBSERVATIONS CHART.

   d. Record the specific charges Paul gives Timothy as his representative in Ephesus and as the one who is organizing and instructing the church there.

3. As you read, mark in the text the key words (and their synonyms and pronouns) that are listed on 1 TIMOTHY AT A GLANCE. These key words give clues about the most important and most often-mentioned instructions.

4. In the margin of the chapter, list everything you learn from the text about these key words. You can learn much about what was important to the health of the church.

5. What do you think is the theme of 1 Timothy? Are there any problems or

concerns the author must address? How does the theme relate to these concerns? Record the theme of the book on 1 TIMOTHY AT A GLANCE and then list the theme of each chapter on the chart and also in the text. Finally, fill in any additional information under author, purpose, and so on.

THINGS TO THINK ABOUT

1. Do you operate in your own church according to these principles?
2. How do you esteem your local church leadership?
3. Do you pray on behalf of all people, including those in authority?

THE FIRST EPISTLE OF PAUL TO

TIMOTHY

Date of writing: c. A.D. 64

1 PAUL, AN APOSTLE OF CHRIST Jesus by order of God our Savior and Christ Jesus our hope, [2]to Timothy,[a] my genuine child in faith: Grace, mercy and peace from God the Father and Christ Jesus our Lord.

[3]As I requested of you when on my way to Macedonia, stay in Ephesus so that you may warn certain people not to teach any other doctrine, [4]neither to pay attention to legends and interminable genealogies such as cause disputes rather than divine training that is in faith. [5]The purpose of our instruction, however, is love that rises out of a pure heart, a clear conscience, and undisguised faith. [6]Swerving from this, some have strayed into empty talk, [7]wanting to be teachers of the Law without understanding what they say or about what they are making their confident assertions.

[8]But we know that the Law is admirable if one makes lawful use of it, [9]keeping in mind that a law is not laid down for an honest person but for the lawless and the rebellious, for the ungodly and sinful, for the impious and profane, for those who kill their fathers or mothers, for murderers, [10]for immoral people, for sexual perverts, kidnapers, liars, perjurers and whatever else is contrary to wholesome teaching [11]according to the glorious good news of the blessed God, with which I have been entrusted.

[12]I am grateful to Christ Jesus our Lord, who strengthened me; for He considered me to be faithful and appointed me for service — [13]me, although I was formerly a slanderer, a persecutor and an insulter. But I found mercy, for in unbelief I acted ignorantly[b]; [14]and the grace of our Lord was present in greater abundance with faith and love that rest in Christ Jesus.

[15]Trustworthy is the saying and deserving of wholehearted acceptance, that Christ Jesus came into the world to save sinners, of whom I am foremost. [16]But I found mercy, so that in me, the foremost of sinners, Jesus Christ might display His unlimited patience, that I might be an example to all who would put their trust in Him for life eternal. [17]Now to the King of the ages, immortal, invisible, the only God, be honor and glory forever and ever. Amen.

[18]I charge you with these instructions, Timothy my son, in agreement with the prophecies that were made long ago concerning you, that you may with their aid fight the good fight, [19]holding faith and a clear conscience. By rejecting their conscience some have shipwrecked their faith; [20]for instance, Hymenaeus[c] and Alexander,[d] whom I

a) Timothy (called also Timotheus) was a native of Lystra in Lycaonia, a part of modern Turkey. His father was a Greek, his mother a Jewess, Acts 16:1. A convert of Paul, vs. 2, Timothy was very close to the apostle and was his companion on Paul's second and third missionary journeys. That the two were often together in Rome is evidenced by their names being linked in Paul's prison epistles, Phil. 1:1; Col. 1:1; Philem. 1. At the time that I Timothy was written Timothy was in Ephesus, ch. 1:3, overseeing the church there. Paul's last letter, II Timothy, which was written shortly before his martyrdom in A.D. 67, was addressed to this young man.
b) With faith came mercy; there had been no purposed opposition to the Holy Spirit.
c) II Tim. 2:17.   d) Perhaps this man was the metalworker of II Tim. 4:14.

314

have surrendered to Satan, so that they may learn not to blaspheme.

2 FIRST OF ALL, THEN, I URGE THAT petitions, prayers, intercessions, and thanksgivings be made for all people, ²for kings and all who hold high positions, that with all reverence and dignity we may lead a quiet and undisturbed life. ³This is good and acceptable before God our Savior, ⁴who wants all persons to be saved and to come to the knowledge of the truth. ⁵For there is one God, and one mediator between God and men, the man Christ Jesus, ⁶who gave Himself a ransom for all, which was attested in due time. ⁷For this I was appointed a preacher and an apostle — I am telling the truth; I am not lying —a teacher of the Gentiles in faith and in truth.

⁸So it is my desire that the men everywhere should pray, as without anger and disputing they lift up dedicated hands.ᵉ ⁹In a similar spirit the women should dress themselves modestly and prudently in attire that is becoming, not adorned with braided hair and gold or pearls or expensive clothes ¹⁰but with good works, as is appropriate for women who profess reverence for God. ¹¹Let a woman learn quietly with complete submission. ¹²I do not allow a woman to teach, neither to domineer over a man; instead, she is to keep still. ¹³For Adam was first formed, then Eve. ¹⁴And Adam was not deceived, but the woman, since she was deceived, experienced the transgression. ¹⁵She will, however, be kept safe through the child-bearing, if with self-control she continues in faith and love and consecration.

3 TRUSTWORTHY IS THE SAYING, "Whoever aspires to the office of bishopᶠ desires to do a splendid work." ²The bishop, then, must be above reproach, the husband of only one wife, temperate, discreet, well-behaved, hospitable, qualified to teach; ³neither a drunkard nor a bully, but genial, conciliatory, not after money; ⁴presiding well over his own home, keeping his children under control with complete respect, ⁵for if a person does not know enough to manage his own home, how will he take care of God's church? ⁶He should not be a new convert, so that he may not become conceited and fall into the condemnation of the devil.ᵍ ⁷He must also enjoy a favorable reputation among the outsiders, so that he may not fall into disgrace and into the trap of the devil.

⁸Similarly deaconsʰ should be dignified, not gossips, not addicted to much wine, not greedy for gain, ⁹but with a pure conscience keeping hold of the secretⁱ of the faith. ¹⁰They should first be put on probation and then, if they are without blame, they may serve as deacons.

¹¹Their wives should also be serious-minded, not given to slandering, but temperate and altogether trustworthy. ¹²A deacon should be the husband of one wife only, managing his children and his own household well. ¹³Because those who have rendered helpful service gain a good standing for themselves and much confidence in the faith which is in Christ Jesus.

¹⁴I am writing you this in the hope of shortly coming to you so that, ¹⁵in case I am delayed, you may know how we should behave in God's household, which is the church of the living God, the pillar and bulwark of the truth. ¹⁶And, confessedly, the secret of our faith is great:

He who was revealed in the flesh
    was vindicated by the Spirit,
    seen by angels,
    preached among Gentiles,
    believed on in the world,
    taken up in glory.ʲ

---

e) Jews often lifted up their hands while praying.
f) "Bishop" is translated from the Gk. *episkopos*, meaning literally *overseer*. In the first century *episkopos*, bishop or overseer, and *presbuteros*, elder, ch. 5:17, 19, were used interchangeably, e.g. Titus 1:5 and 7, where both words refer to the same office. After the first century the office of bishop or overseer over that of elder developed.
g) It was pride that caused Satan's fall, Isa. 14:12-17.
h) "Deacon" is translated from the Gk. *diakonos*, meaning *servant, helper*, and in later years deacon, as referring to a church officer. The seven men who were chosen to help the apostles by being of service to believers in Jerusalem, Acts 6:1-6, were the first appointed deacons. The noun "ministration," Acts 6:1, is *diakonia*, and the verb "serve," vs. 2, is *diakonein*.
i) See note at Rom. 16:25.   j) These lines are probably a part of an early Christian hymn.

4 BUT THE SPIRIT SAYS DISTINCTLY that in later times some will fall away from the faith; they will yield to deluding spirits and demonic teachings [2]by hypocritical liars, whose own consciences are seared as with a branding iron. [3]They prohibit marriage and the enjoyment of foods which God has created to be partaken of with thanksgiving by those who believe and know the truth. [4]For everything which God created is good and nothing to be rejected when it is gratefully received, [5]for it is consecrated through the word of God and prayer.

[6]If you will present these matters to the brothers, you will be a good minister of Christ Jesus, being reared on the messages of faith and of the noble teachings to which you have been conforming your life. [7]But shun unholy legends that are suitable for old women only. Train yourself for godliness, [8]because while physical training is of a little benefit, godliness is beneficial in every way; it holds promise for this present and for the future life. [9]This is a trustworthy saying, deserving the acceptance of all. [10]For this purpose we labor and wrestle, because we have placed our hope in the living God who is the Savior of all people, particularly of those who believe.

[11]Command and teach these things. [12]Let no one think little of you because of your youth; instead, become in speech, in behavior, in love, in faith, in purity, an example before those who believe. [13]Till I arrive, devote yourself to the public reading, the preaching and the teaching. [14]Do not neglect the gift in you that was given to you through a prophetic utterance with the laying on of hands by the elders.[k] [15]Practice these matters, devote yourself so that your advance may be evident to everyone. [16]Look to yourself and to the teaching; keep right on in that, for in so doing, you will save yourself as well as your hearers.

5 DO NOT REBUKE AN OLDER MAN but plead with him as a father, and younger men as brothers, [2]older women as mothers, and the younger women as sisters, with absolute purity. [3]Honor widows who really are widows. [4]But if any widow has children or grandchildren, let them first learn to practice religion at home and so to make recompense to those who nurtured them; for so it is acceptable in God's sight.

[5]The real widow who is left alone has put her hope in God and is steadfast in her petitions and prayers night and day; [6]while one who lives in self-indulgence is dead while she lives.[l]

[7]Command these things so that they may live above reproach. [8]Whoever does not provide for his dependents, and especially for his own family, has denied the faith and is worse than an unbeliever.

[9]Do not enroll[m] a widow unless she is over sixty years of age, who was the wife of one husband, [10]one who has a reputation for good works and has reared children, has practiced hospitality, has washed the feet of the saints,[n] has relieved the afflicted, and has been devoted to all kinds of good works.

[11]But refuse to enroll younger widows, for when they feel sensuous impulses that alienate them from Christ, they want to marry, [12]and become guilty of breaking their first promise to Him. [13]Moreover, they acquire habits of idleness as they go around visiting the homes, and not merely are they idle but they are gossips and busybodies, saying things they should not. [14]So I would have younger widows marry again, bear children, manage their home, and afford the opponent no opportunity whatever for reviling. [15]For even now some of them have gone astray after Satan. [16]If any believing woman has widowed relatives, let her take care of them so that the church may not be burdened and may look after those who are really widows.

[17]The elders who govern well are worthy of double honor, particularly those who labor in preaching and teaching; [18]for the Scripture says,[o]

---

k) Gk. *presbuteriou*, from which the English word "presbytery" is derived. See note at ch. 3:1.
l) This is like the eternal existence of the unsaved. The kind of person described here is dead spiritually and in ruin but continues to exist. m) For some such office as deaconess.
n) See note at Acts 9:13. o) Deut. 25:4.

"Do not muzzle the ox while he is threshing," and,[p] "The worker deserves his wage."

19Do not recognize a charge against an elder unless it is supported by two or three witnesses.[q] 20In the presence of all, correct those who continue in sin, so that the rest may be awed.

21I charge you in the presence of God and of Christ Jesus and the elect angels,[r] that you observe these commands without discrimination, that you act with no favoritism. 22Lay hands of ordination on no one hastily; neither make common cause with the sins of others. Keep yourself pure.

23Do not any longer drink water only, but use a little wine for the good of your stomach and your recurring illness.

24The sins of some people are soon in evidence; they lead on to judgment. But in the case of others they dog their steps. 25Equally so are good works readily observed; while those which are otherwise cannot remain hidden.

6 LET THOSE WHO ARE UNDER THE yoke of slavery[s] regard their masters as deserving of all respect, so that the name of God and our teaching may not be reviled. 2But those who have believing masters must honor them no less because they are brothers; instead, they should serve them better because those who benefit by their service are believers and are loved.

3Teach and urge these matters. Whoever teaches differently and does not adhere to the wholesome sayings of our Lord Jesus Christ and to the teaching that is according to our faith, 4is conceited and without understanding, with a morbid craving for controversy and dispute about words, which result in envy, wrangling, slander, bad suspicions, 5perpetual contention between people of depraved minds and defrauded of the truth, who think of piety in terms of profit.

6Piety with contentment is great gain indeed; 7for we brought nothing into the world and, obviously, we can carry nothing out. 8When we have food and clothing, we shall be content with these. 9Those who are eager to be rich fall into temptation and a snare, and into numerous thoughtless and hurtful cravings that plunge people into destruction and ruin. 10For the love of money is the root of all evils.[t] In striving for it, some have wandered away from the faith and have pierced themselves with many sorrows.

11But you, O man of God, shun these things and go after righteousness, godliness, faith, love, patience, gentleness. 12Fight the good fight of faith; take hold of the eternal life to which you were called as you made a good confession in the presence of many witnesses.

13In the presence of God, who gives life to all things, and of Christ Jesus, who witnessed the good confession before Pontius Pilate,[u] 14I charge you to keep the commandment[v] stainless and irreproachable until the appearance of our Lord Jesus Christ, 15which in due time He will make known, the blessed and only Sovereign, the King of kings and Lord of lords, 16who alone possesses immortality, dwelling in unapproachable light, whom no human being has ever seen or is able to see. To Him be honor and dominion forever. Amen.

17Command those who are rich in this present world not to be haughty, neither to put their hope in the uncertainty of wealth but in God, who so richly provides us with everything for our enjoyment. 18Urge them to do good, to be rich in good works, to be generous givers, to practice sharing, 19and to treasure up for themselves a sound foundation for the future, so that they may take hold of the life that is really life.

20O Timothy, guard what has been entrusted to you. Keep away from ir-

p.) Luke 10:7.   q) Deut. 19:15; Matt. 18:16.
r) New Testament writers follow our Lord in the assurance that angels are all around us.
s) This applies to all who are employed and the relationships between them and their employers. See note at Matt. 13:27.
t) The love of money fosters such things as selfishness, pride, cruelty, and separation from fellow men and from God.   u) John 18:33-38.   v) Concerning Christian behavior.

religious and empty discussions and contradictions of what is falsely called knowledge, 21which some people have claimed to have, and so have missed the mark with regard to the faith.

Grace be with you all.

1 Timothy Observations Chart

Paul	Timothy	The Rich	Women

Overseers ("Bishops")	Deacons	Men

Slaves	Widows

(continued)

1 Timothy Observations Chart

Prayer	Charges and Instructions to Timothy

1 Timothy at a Glance

Theme of 1 Timothy:

Segment
Divisions

	Chapter Themes	Author:
1		Date:
2		Purpose:
3		Key Words:
4		teach faith doctrine (teaching)
5		godliness (reverence, piety)
6		

2 TIMOTHY

*P*aul now found himself in a new set of circumstances. It was about A.D. 64 (some say A.D. 67) and Timothy was heavy on his heart. Paul had to write one last letter to his disciple, reminding Timothy of crucial matters concerning the ministry and urging him to make every effort to come quickly—before winter.

THINGS TO DO

1. Read 2 Timothy. In chapters 1 and 2, and then in chapter 4, Paul refers to his circumstances: where he is and what is about to take place in his life. To help set the context of the letter, record on the OBSERVATIONS CHART following 2 Timothy what you learn about Paul's circumstances.

2. Read 2 Timothy again. Look for everything you learn about Timothy and record it on the OBSERVATIONS CHART.

3. As you read 2 Timothy you probably noticed the many commands and/or instructions Paul gave Timothy. An example of this is seen in 1:6: "Keep alive the flame of God's gracious gift."

   a. List the instructions and/or commands Paul gives Timothy throughout the letter on the OBSERVATIONS CHART. (Be sure to note the chapter and verse in which you find each.)

   b. As you look for these instructions and/or commands, mark in the text the key words (and their synonyms and pronouns) that are listed on 2 TIMOTHY AT A GLANCE.

Be sure to mark any reference to the good news (*teaching, word, Scripture, message,* etc.) and to suffering (*persecuted, hardship,* etc.).

4. Think back over the list of instructions and/or commands Paul gives Timothy and keep in mind the emphasis Paul places on the good news. What do you think is Paul's main message to Timothy in this second epistle? Record this as the theme of the book on 2 TIMOTHY AT A GLANCE.

5. Look at the book one chapter at a time and summarize the main teaching or theme of each chapter and then record it on 2 TIMOTHY AT A GLANCE and in the text above the chapter number. (Note: The theme of each chapter should relate to the general theme of the book.)

6. On 2 TIMOTHY AT A GLANCE you will see space to trace two themes, "Paul's Example" and "God's Provision," which run throughout the book. Doing this will give you additional insight into the practicality of 2 Timothy for your own life. Examine each chapter in the light of these two themes and record your insights on the appropriate space on the chart.

THINGS TO THINK ABOUT

1. What is your responsibility toward the good news? To what lengths will you go in order to carry out this responsibility?

2. What are you doing to make sure you

handle the Word of God accurately? Do you simply repeat what you have been taught or are you carefully studying the Word systematically?

3. Are you willing to suffer for the sake of those who would come to know the Lord Jesus Christ and receive salvation?

4. What kind of men and women do you need to beware of in these last days?

5. How are you living? Are you a coward or have you fought the good fight of faith?

6. Are you ready to die? How will you feel when you see Jesus Christ face-to-face?

THE SECOND EPISTLE OF PAUL TO

TIMOTHY

Date of writing: c. A.D. 67, at Rome

1 PAUL, AN APOSTLE OF CHRIST Jesus by the will of God in accordance with the promise of the life that is in Christ Jesus, [2]to Timothy[a] my beloved child: Grace, mercy and peace from God the Father and Christ Jesus our Lord.

[3]I am grateful to God whom, in line with my ancestors, I worship with a clear conscience as constantly I remember you night and day in my prayers. [4]When I remember the tears you shed, I yearn to see you, so that I might be perfectly happy. [5]I bring back to mind your sincere faith that lived first in your grandmother Lois and in your mother Eunice and, I am convinced, in you as well.

[6]On account of this I would remind you to keep alive the flame of God's gracious gift[b] that is in you through the laying on of my hands. [7]For God has not given us a spirit of cowardice, but of power and love and self-control. [8]Do not be ashamed, therefore, about bearing witness to our Lord or about me His prisoner, but share my suffering for the good news by virtue of the power of God, [9]who has saved us and called us with a call for dedication, not because of any doings of ours but according to His own purpose and the grace that has been granted us in Christ Jesus before time began. [10]But now it has been realized through the appearance of our Savior Christ Jesus, who rendered death ineffectual and brought life and immortality to light through the good news, [11]for which I am appointed a preacher and an apostle and a teacher.

[12]Therefore I suffer in this way; but I am not ashamed, for I know whom I have believed[c] and am convinced that He is able to guard safely my deposit, entrusted to Him against that Day.

[13]Hold to the pattern of wholesome teachings which you heard from me, in faith and love in Christ Jesus. [14]Guard, by the help of the indwelling Holy Spirit within us, that precious deposit[d] that was entrusted to you.

[15]Of this you are aware, that all those in the province of Asia have deserted me — Phygelus and Hermogenes[e] among them. [16]May the Lord grant favor to the family of Onesiphorus[f] for he often refreshed me and was not ashamed of my being a prisoner. [17]Instead, on arriving in Rome, he eagerly searched for and found me. [18]The Lord grant him to find mercy with the Lord on that Day. And what services he rendered in Ephesus you know very well.

2 SO YOU, MY SON, BE STRONG BY means of the grace that is in Christ Jesus. [2]And what you have heard from me through many witnesses, this commit to reliable men who will be able to teach others as well.

---

a) See note at I Tim. 1:2.
b) God-given qualities remain alive only when they are used. *Cf.* I Tim. 4:14.
c) Not intellectual knowledge but personal trust.   d) The truth of God's saving grace.
e) Many of Paul's acquaintances forsook him because of his imprisonment, *cf.* ch. 4:10, 16, but that he names these two men, and Demas also, makes it appear that their desertion was particularly distressing to him.   f) Ch. 4:19.

[3]As a good soldier of Christ Jesus share my hardship. [4]No soldier gets involved in affairs of everyday life, so that he may please the one who enlisted him. [5]Again, whoever competes in a game does not win the award unless he competes according to the rules. [6]The toiling farmer must have first share of the produce.

[7]Consider what I say, for the Lord will grant you understanding in everything. [8]Keep in mind Jesus Christ, risen from the dead, descended from David according to the good news that I preach, [9]in which I suffer punishment like a criminal even to shackles; but the word of God is not shackled. [10]I endure all this for the sake of the elect, so that they also may gain possession of the salvation which is in Christ Jesus, together with eternal glory.

[11]This is a trustworthy saying:

If we have died together with Him, we shall also live together with Him.

[12]If we endure, then we shall also reign with Him.

If we deny Him, then He Himself will also deny us.

[13]If we are unfaithful to Him, He Himself will remain faithful, for He cannot deny Himself.[g]

[14]Remind them[h] of these facts and charge them in the presence of God to indulge in no wars of words; it helps no one and it completely upsets the listeners. [15]Do your utmost to present yourself to God approved, a workman who has no cause to be ashamed, correctly interpreting the message of the truth. [16]But keep away from those godless, empty discussions, for they lead people further on into godlessness, [17]and their[i] teaching spreads like gangrene. Hymenaeus[j] and Philetus are of that group [18]that has gone astray from the truth when they say that the resurrection has already occurred, and are playing havoc with the faith of some. [19]God's foundation, nevertheless, stands firm[k] bearing this inscription,[l] "The Lord knows those who are His," and "Let everyone who names the Lord's name stand aloof from wickedness."

[20]But in a large house there are not only gold and silver utensils, but wooden and earthen too, and some are indeed for noble but others for ignoble use. [21]Therefore, whoever will cleanse himself from these things will be a utensil for noble use, set apart and useful for the Master, prepared for good service of every sort.

[22]But flee from the lusts of youth. Go in pursuit of integrity, faith, love, peace, in fellowship with those who call upon the Lord out of pure hearts. [23]Decline those foolish, stupid speculations, as you know they breed quarrels. [24]And a slave[m] of the Lord must not quarrel; instead, he must be affable toward everyone, skilled in teaching, willing to suffer wrong. [25]In a gentle way he must correct those who put themselves in opposition to him, in the hope that God may grant repentance that leads to acknowledgment of the truth, [26]and that they may come to their senses and escape from the snare of the devil under whom they had been taken captive, to do his will.

3 BUT UNDERSTAND THIS, THAT IN the last days[n] difficult times will come. [2]For people will be lovers of themselves, avaricious, boasters, haughty, abusive, disobedient to parents, ungrateful, irreverent, [3]without natural affection, relentless, slanderers, uncontrolled, brutal, with no love for the good, [4]treacherous, rash, conceited, lovers of pleasure rather than lovers of God. [5]While retaining a form of piety, they are strangers to its power. Turn away from such people.

[6]For from such people are those who worm their way into houses and captivate idle women loaded down with sins and controlled by all sorts of

---

g) Like I Tim. 3:16, vss. 11-13 probably constitute part of an early Christian hymn.
h) "Them" refers to believers, probably in Ephesus, cf. I Tim. 1:3.
i) "Their" points to those mentioned in vss. 17, 18. j) I Tim. 1:20. k) I Cor. 3:11.
l) Num. 16:5, 26; John 10:14, 27. m) See note at Matt. 13:27.
n) The days between Christ's ascension and His return.

impulses, 7forever trying to learn and never able to reach a knowledge of the truth.

8Just as Jannes and Jambres[o] opposed Moses, so do these men oppose the truth, corrupt thinkers as they are and counterfeits so far as faith is concerned. 9However, they will not get very far, for their folly will be obvious to everyone, as was the case with those mentioned above.

10But you have adhered to my teaching, my conduct, my purpose, my faith, my steadfastness, my love, my patience, 11my persecutions, my sufferings — all that happened to me in Antioch, in Iconium and in Lystra, such persecutions as I underwent and from all of which the Lord rescued me. 12In fact, all who want to live devotedly in Christ Jesus will be persecuted. 13But wicked men and impostors will go on from bad to worse, deceiving and being deceived.

14You, however, must remain faithful in what you have learned and are convinced of, aware from whom you learned, 15and how from childhood you have known the sacred Scriptures that are able to make you wise for salvation through faith in Christ Jesus. 16All Scripture is inspired by God[p] and is profitable for teaching, for reproof, for correction, for training in righteousness, 17so that the man of God may be well-fitted and adequately equipped for all good work.

4 I CHARGE YOU IN THE PRESENCE of God and of Christ Jesus, who is to judge the living and the dead, by His appearing and His kingdom: 2Preach the message; be at it when convenient and when not convenient; correct, exhort, rebuke with complete patience and teaching.

3For the time is coming when they will not tolerate wholesome instruction; instead they will, to satisfy their own desires, gather up teachers that will tickle their ears. 4They will turn away from listening to the truth and will wander off to hear myths. 5But amid it all, keep your head, endure hardship, do the work of an evangelist, discharge to the full your duties as a minister.

6For I am already being poured out as a drink offering and the time of my death has come. 7I have fought the good fight; I have finished the race; I have kept the faith. 8Beyond that there is laid away for me the crown[q] of righteousness which the Lord, the righteous Judge, will award me in that Day, and not to me alone, but to all who have loved His appearing.

9Do your best to visit me soon, 10for Demas[r] has deserted me for love of the present world and has gone to Thessalonica; Crescens has gone to Galatia; Titus[s] to Dalmatia. 11Luke[t] alone is with me. Get hold of Mark[u] and bring him along, for he is helpful to me in service. 12I have sent Tychicus[v] to Ephesus.

13When you come, bring along the travel-cloak I left at Troas with Carpus; also the books, and especially the parchments.

14Alexander,[w] the metalworker, has displayed considerable ill will toward me. The Lord will pay him back to the measure of his doings. 15You, too, beware of him, for he strongly opposed our messages.

16In my first defense no one supported me; instead, they all deserted me. May it not be counted against them! 17But the Lord stood by me and strengthened me, so that through me the message might be fully proclaimed and all the Gentiles might hear it. And I was rescued from the lion's jaws. 18Indeed, the Lord will rescue me from every evil act and will save me for His heavenly kingdom. To Him be glory forever and ever. Amen.

o) These two men were the leaders of the Egyptian magicians of Exod. 7. Their names are not given in the O.T. but are found in Jewish tradition.
p) The Gk. word *theopneustos*, translated "inspired by God," literally means God-breathed.
q) See note at Phil. 4:1.
r) Earlier Demas has been with Paul in Rome, Col. 4:14; Philem. 24.
s) See note at Titus 1:4.
t) Luke, the physician, author of the Third Gospel and The Acts. See note at Col. 4:14.
u) John Mark, author of the Second Gospel. See note at Col. 4:10.   v) See note at Col. 4:7.
w) I Tim. 1:20; *cf.* Acts 19:33, 34.

[19]My greetings to Priscilla and Aquila[x] and to the Onesiphorus family.[y] [20]Erastus stayed at Corinth. I left Trophimus[z] behind in Miletus; he was ill.

[21]Do your best to arrive before winter.

Eubulus, Pudens, Linus, Claudia and all the brothers, send you greetings.

[22]The Lord be with your spirit. Grace be with you all.

---

x) Acts 18:2.   y) Ch. 1:16.   z) Acts 20:4

2 Timothy Observations Chart

PAUL	TIMOTHY
Where is he?	How is he described?
Why is he there?	What is his relationship to Paul?
Who is with him?	What do you learn about him?
What is about to happen?	
How is he going to handle it?	

(continued)

PAUL'S INSTRUCTIONS TO TIMOTHY

2 TIMOTHY AT A GLANCE

THEME OF 2 TIMOTHY:

SEGMENT DIVISIONS

GOD'S PROVISION	PAUL'S EXAMPLE	CHAPTER THEMES
		1
		2
DELIVERED PAUL OUT OF PERSECUTIONS	ENDURED PERSECUTIONS	3
		4

Author:

Date:

Purpose:

Key Words:

good news

word (message)

suffer (suffering[s], persecutions)

endure

faith

ashamed

TITUS

When Paul sailed past Crete on his way to Rome he was not the master of his own ship. He was Rome's prisoner. How wise the centurion guard would have been had he followed Paul's urging to put ashore in Crete! Despite the winds, they sailed on under much duress. As Paul had predicted, the ship was lost in Malta, the island 58 miles south of Sicily.

Paul's ship sank to the bottom of the sea; Crete had sunk to the depths of sin. Broken to pieces morally by the incessant pounding of a godless lifestyle, Crete needed the good news of the gospel. Unlike the ship, however, it was not beyond redemption.

Whether Crete was on Paul's heart before his two years' house arrest in Rome, we don't know. We only know that once Paul was free from Rome's chains he apparently went with Titus to Crete and left him there.

As Paul wrote Titus, it was about A.D. 62. He didn't know he would return to Rome for one final imprisonment.

THINGS TO DO

1. Read through Titus without stopping so that you understand the general content and thrust of the letter.

2. Read Titus again, one chapter at a time. As you read each chapter:

    a. Look for the information about the author: who he is, how he describes himself, where he is, etc. Record your insights on the OBSERVATIONS CHART following Titus. Note the chapter and verse in which you find your information; it helps when you want to find something later.

    b. Mark in the text the key words listed on the TITUS AT A GLANCE chart. Be sure also to mark the synonyms and pronouns.

    c. In the margin of your New Testament, list the truths you learn from the text about each key word.

3. The commands, warnings, and instructions Paul includes in his letter to Titus help define Paul's purpose for writing. Read Titus again chapter by chapter and note each command, warning, or instruction Paul gives Titus. List these on the OBSERVATIONS CHART under "Instructions to Titus."

4. Note on the OBSERVATIONS CHART what you learn about Titus and his relationship to Paul. In chapter 1 Paul clearly tells us where Titus is and why he is there.

5. In his letter Paul mentions various groups of people. List what you learn about each of these groups under the designated heading on your OBSERVATIONS CHART.

6. Listing Paul's commands, warnings, and instructions to Titus probably has helped you see the dominant subject of Titus. There are two verses, one in chapter 2 and one in chapter 3, which summarize the thrust of Paul's letter. These will help you determine the theme of the epistle. Record it on TITUS AT A GLANCE.

    a. Now summarize the theme or main

message of each paragraph and then of each chapter and record these on TITUS AT A GLANCE. Also record the chapter theme in the text above the chapter number.

b. Fill in author, date, and purpose on the same chart.

THINGS TO THINK ABOUT

1. The world's lifestyle denies God. By your lifestyle and attitudes, do you deny ungodliness and worldly desires, or do you indulge the desires of your flesh?

2. It is difficult always to be considerate to everyone, isn't it? When did you last fail in this area? Have you determined afresh to be gentle and uncontentious even in the most difficult situation with the most difficult person? Your actions often will speak louder than your words ever can.

3. Your salvation was not based on performance but upon the mercy and grace of God. What has your heavenly Father saved you from? Think on His goodness that brought you from death into life and brought you out of the kingdom of darkness into the kingdom of His glorious light. Have you thanked Him lately for His mercy and grace? Why not do it now? Pray for those close to you who have yet to experience the saving grace of God.

THE EPISTLE OF PAUL TO

TITUS

Date of writing: c. A.D. 65

1 PAUL, A SLAVE[a] OF GOD, AND AN apostle of Jesus Christ, to foster the faith of God's elect and their knowledge of the truth which is according to godliness, [2]based on the hope of eternal life which God, who does not lie, promised before time began [3]and has at the proper time revealed as His message through the preaching entrusted to me by order of God our Savior, [4]to Titus,[b] my true child in our common faith: Grace and peace from God the Father and Christ Jesus our Savior.

[5]I left you in Crete for this reason, that you might correct the defects and appoint elders[c] in each town, as I gave you directions, [6]if a person is above reproach, the husband of one wife only, has believing children who are not charged with being profligate or unruly. [7]For the bishop must, as God's steward, be irreproachable, not self-willed or hot-tempered, or a drunkard, or pugnacious, or greedy for dishonest gain.

[8]Instead, he must be hospitable, in love with what is good, self-controlled, fair, of holy life, disciplined. [9]He must hold to the trustworthy message of the doctrine, so he may be able to encourage by his wholesome teaching, as well as to refute those who raise objections.

[10]For many are refractory, senseless talkers and deceivers, particularly among those of the circumcision.[d] [11]These must be silenced because they upset whole families by teaching for dishonest gain what they should not teach. [12]A prophet from their own people said[e] of them, "Cretans are always liars, wicked brutes, lazy gluttons."

[13]This testimony is true. For this reason correct them sternly, that they may be sound in the faith [14]instead of paying attention to Jewish fables and to commandments of people who turn their backs on the truth. [15]To the pure everything is pure, but to the contaminated and the unbelieving nothing is pure; but even their mind and their conscience are polluted. [16]They profess to know God but by their practices deny Him. They are detestable and disobedient and unfit for any good deed.

2 BUT YOU MUST SPEAK WHAT IS fitting for wholesome doctrine: [2]that the older men be temperate, ven-

---

a) See note at Matt. 13:27.
b) Although Titus is not mentioned in The Acts, he accompanied Paul on some of the apostle's missionary journeys, Gal. 2:3. He was a Gentile, a Greek, and may have been brought to faith in Christ by Paul, who speaks of him here as "my true child in our common faith," vs. 4. Titus was Paul's emissary to the difficult church at Corinth, II Cor. 2:13; 7:6, 16; 12:18, and was also sent by the apostle to Dalmatia, now part of Yugoslavia, II Tim. 4:10. As is shown in ch. 1:5, Titus was on the island of Crete to supervise the work of the churches there.
c) Regarding "elders," Gk. *presbuteros*, here and "bishop," Gk. *episkopon*, vs. 7, see note at I Tim. 3:1.
d) The Epistle to the Galatians has much to say about those who insisted that Gentile Christians should be circumcised and abide by Mosaic regulations. There were some in Crete who were troubling new converts to Christianity in the same way.
e) The statement is from the Cretan poet Epimenides, sixth century B.C.

erable, sensible, sound in faith, in love, and in patience; [3]similarly that the older women be reverent in their behavior, neither slanderers nor slaves to drink. They should be teachers of what is good, [4]that they may wisely train the young women to be loving wives and mothers, [5]sensible, chaste, good housekeepers, good-natured, submissive to their own husbands, so that the word of God may not be slandered.

[6]Urge the younger men as well to behave prudently, [7]and set in your own person an all-round example of doing what is good, manifesting in your teaching integrity and seriousness, [8]giving a wholesome, unobjectionable message that will shame the opponent because he has nothing evil to say about us.

[9]Tell slaves to be submissive to their own masters,[f] to please them in every way, not to talk back, [10]not to pilfer but to give evidence of such complete reliability that altogether they will beautify the teaching of God our Savior.

[11]For the saving grace of God has appeared for all people, [12]training us to renounce godlessness and worldly passions, and to live self-controlled, upright, and godly lives in this present world, [13]with expectation of that blessed hope, even the glorious appearance of our great God and Savior Jesus Christ, [14]who gave Himself for us to redeem us from all iniquity, and to purify for Himself a people all His own who are eager to do good works.

[15]Assert these things and exhort and reprove with full authority. Allow no one to think little of you.

3 REMIND THEM TO BE SUBJECT TO the ruling authorities, to be obedient, to be prepared for every good work, [2]not to slander anyone, not to be quarrelsome but gentle, showing complete mildness toward all people. [3]For once we ourselves were thoughtless, disobedient, led astray, slaves to passions and pleasures of all sorts, wasting our time in malice and envy, detestable, and hating one another.

[4]But when the goodness of God our Savior was shown and His love of men was evidenced, [5]not because of righteous works that we have done but in agreement with His mercy, He saved us through the washing of regeneration and a renewing by the Holy Spirit, [6]whom He has poured out richly on us through Jesus Christ our Savior, [7]so that, counted as righteous by His grace, we might be made heirs in accordance with our hope of eternal life.

[8]This is a trustworthy saying, and I would have you insist on these things with confidence, so that those who have become believers in God may be careful to apply themselves to good works, which are excellent and beneficial for all people.

[9]But avoid foolish controversies, genealogies, strife, and wranglings about the Law, for they are futile and purposeless. [10]Have nothing to do with a factious person after a first and second warning, [11]aware that such a person is perverted and goes on sinning, and is self-condemned.

[12]When I send Artemas or Tychicus,[g] then do your utmost to visit me at Nicopolis,[h] for there I have decided to stay for the winter. [13]Equip Zenas the lawyer and Apollos[i] carefully for their journey, so that they may lack nothing. [14]And have our own people learn to apply themselves to honorable work to meet the urgent needs, that they may not be unproductive.

[15]All those with me send you greetings. Greet those who love us in faith. [16]May grace be with you all.

---

f) See note at I Tim. 6:1. g) See note at Col. 4:7.
h) Nicopolis was on the west coast of Macedonia (Greece) almost directly across the Adriatic Sea from Rhegium in Italy. One of the reasons why Paul is thought to have had two imprisonments in Rome, with an interval between them, is his possible presence in Nicopolis when this letter to Titus was written, c. A.D. 65. For he was taken to Rome as a prisoner in about A.D. 60 and was martyred there in the year 67. i) Acts 18:24.

TITUS OBSERVATIONS CHART

PAUL	TITUS	INSTRUCTIONS TO TITUS
Where is he?	Where is he? Why?	
How does he describe himself?	What is his relationship to Paul?	
ELDERS (OVERSEERS)	OLDER MEN	
	CRETANS	OLDER WOMEN
	SLAVES	YOUNG WOMEN
YOUNGER MEN		

THEME OF TITUS:

SEGMENT
DIVISIONS

	PARAGRAPH THEMES	CHAPTER THEMES
	1:1–4	1
	1:5–9	
	1:10–16	
	2:1–15	2
	3:1–11	3
	3:12–15	

Author:

Date:

Purpose:

Key Words:

God

Jesus Christ

doctrine
(teaching)

truth

grace

work (works,
practices,
doing)

PHILEMON

Slavery was a fact of life in Paul's day—a fact Paul couldn't change. But Paul could show slaves and masters how they were to behave toward one another as those redeemed by Jesus, who had become a bondservant on their behalf. In his epistles Paul shared these principles.

Now, however, something else had come up. Paul had to appeal to Philemon, a believer from Colossae, about a very personal matter: One of Philemon's slaves had run away, and according to Roman law he could be put to death by his master. So at about the same time he wrote Colossians, Paul wrote to Philemon from his rented quarters, where as a prisoner of Rome he also could be put to death. It was about A.D. 61 or 62.

THINGS TO DO

1. Philemon is only one short chapter. Read it to gain an understanding of why this letter was written.
   a. When you finish reading, go back and note everything you learn about Paul on the OBSERVATIONS CHART following Philemon. Also watch for Paul's reason for writing and how he goes about achieving his purpose. Then record the reasons on the PHILEMON AT A GLANCE chart.
   b. Also note everything you learn about the recipients of Paul's letter and record this information in the appropriate section of the OBSERVATIONS CHART.
   c. Record on the OBSERVATIONS CHART everything you learn about Onesimus.
2. Carefully read the book again, marking in the text each of the key words (with their synonyms and pronouns) listed on the PHILEMON AT A GLANCE chart. Then in the margin list the truths you learn about each of these words from the text.
3. Record the theme of Philemon on PHILEMON AT A GLANCE and also in the text. Because Philemon is only one chapter, it is divided into paragraphs on the chart. Read the book paragraph by paragraph and record on the chart the theme of each paragraph. Then fill in the rest of the chart.

THINGS TO THINK ABOUT

1. Are you willing to appeal to someone on behalf of another person, to assume the role of an advocate?
2. What can you learn from Paul's example in the way he appealed to Philemon?
3. Is there someone you need to forgive and offer restoration?
4. Can someone appeal to you to do the right thing on the basis of your character, or does he have to force your hand through rules, regulations, or some sort of a "bribe"?

THE EPISTLE OF PAUL TO

PHILEMON

Date of writing: c. A.D. 60, at Rome

Paul, a prisoner of Christ Jesus, and our brother Timothy,[a] to Philemon, our beloved fellow worker, [2]and to our sister Apphia[b] and to our fellow soldier Archippus,[c] and to the church that meets at your home: [3]Grace to you and peace from God our Father and the Lord Jesus Christ.

[4]I always offer thanks to my God when I mention you in my prayers, [5]for I hear of the love and the faith you practice toward the Lord Jesus and to all the saints.[d] [6]I pray that by an understanding of all the good you enjoy among yourselves, the sharing of your faith may become effectual for Christ. [7]For I have enjoyed much pleasure and comfort over your love, because through you, brother, the hearts of the saints have been refreshed.

[8]Therefore, although in Christ I feel very free to give you directions as to your duty, [9]I prefer to make my appeal on the basis of love. Here I am, then, as Paul the old man,[e] yet now a prisoner of Christ Jesus, [10]appealing to you on behalf of my son, Onesimus, who became my son during my imprisonment.[f] [11]Once he was useless to you, but now he is helpful both to you and to me.

[12]I am sending him back to you and my heart with him. [13]I should like to retain him for myself, so that he might serve me instead of you during my imprisonment for the sake of the good news; [14]but I do not wish to do anything without your consent, so that your kind action may not be compulsory but voluntary. [15]For he was parted from you for a while perhaps for this very reason, that you might have him back forever, [16]no longer as a slave,[g] but better than a slave, a beloved brother, unquestionably to me but how much more so to you both personally and in the Lord.

[17]So, if I am your partner, then receive him as you would me. [18]And if he wronged you in any way, or is in debt to you, put it down to my account. [19]I, Paul, am writing with my own hand,[h] I will refund it — not to mention that, over and above, you owe me your very self. [20]Yes, brother, I should like to make some profit out of you in the Lord; buoy up my deepest feelings in Christ.

[21]I am writing you, confident that

---

a) See note at I Tim. 1:2. b) Apphia was Philemon's wife.
c) Archippus was probably Philemon's son. Paul, in writing his letter to Colossae, exhorted Archippus to be faithful in his service for the Lord, Col. 4:17. d) See note at Acts 9:13.
e) "Old man," Gk. *presbutes*. The addition of an "e" would make it read *presbeutes*, meaning ambassador. Some scholars think that the original text may have been written in this way. *Cf.* II Cor. 5:20; Eph. 6:20.
f) "Onesimus," Gk. *Onesimos*, means *useful*. Onesimus was a runaway slave who had probably robbed Philemon. Evidently he met Paul in Rome and was converted. This letter was written to persuade his master, Philemon, who lived in Colossae, to receive and forgive the runaway slave. Notice the play on words in vss. 10, 11. Once "Useful," he had become useless to Philemon; now he was useful to Philemon and Paul. g) See note at Matt. 13:27.
h) Here Paul signed, as it were, a promissory note to pay back to Philemon the debt Onesimus owed him. So Christ through His sacrifice of Himself paid the debt we owe to God because of our sins.

you will listen to me, and knowing you will do more than I request. [22]Meanwhile, you may prepare a guest room for me, for I hope through your prayers to be restored to you.

[23]Epaphras,[i] my fellow prisoner in Christ Jesus, sends you greetings. [24]So do Mark,[j] Aristarchus,[k] Demas,[l] and Luke,[m] my fellow workers.

[25]The grace of the Lord Jesus Christ be with your spirit.

---

i) See note at Col. 1:7.
j) See note at Col. 4:10.
k) Aristarchus, a Macedonian, was one of Paul's travel companions, Acts 19:29.
l) At the time this letter was written Demas was quite close to Paul as a fellow worker in the service of Christ. But he was unable to endure the afflictions connected with the ministry and left the apostle, while the latter was in prison, to go to Thessalonica. "For Demas has deserted me for love of the present world," II Tim. 4:10.   m) See note at Col. 4:14.

THE AUTHOR	THE RECIPIENTS	ONESIMUS

PHILEMON AT A GLANCE

THEME OF PHILEMON:

SEGMENT
DIVISIONS

		PARAGRAPH THEMES	Author:
	VERSES 1–3		Date:
	VERSES 4–7		Purpose:
	VERSES 8–20		Key Words:
	VERSES 21, 22		love
	VERSES 23–25		appeal
			slave

$\mathcal{H}$EBREWS

$\mathcal{P}$ersecution increased as the gospel spread. The persecution was especially intense for Jewish believers, because they had turned their back on the world and its ways and had abandoned the ordinances of the law which Jews had embraced since the time of Moses. This left them in a no-man's land. Jews as well as Gentiles who did not believe in the Lord Jesus Christ could not understand them, nor would many tolerate their newfound faith without challenge or attack.

Imagine yourself in a similar situation. What if you were wrong about Jesus Christ? What if He were not really the Messiah? And what about the new covenant? What if it didn't replace the old covenant? What if you really did need a continuing blood sacrifice for your sins? *What if?*

So that we could be secure in our faith, God moved an unknown author to take up pen and parchment and write the book we call Hebrews. No other book in the New Testament gives us what Hebrews gives us—the assurance that we have a High Priest who sympathizes with the feeling of our weaknesses, One who always lives to intercede for us.

Hebrews was probably written before A.D. 70, because the temple was still standing and the priests were still making religious sacrifices.

THINGS TO DO

1. Before you begin your study of Hebrews, read Hebrews 13:22 to discover the author's purpose for writing. Record this on the HEBREWS AT A GLANCE chart.
2. In order to grasp the truth of this book, you need to understand to whom the book is written. As you read Hebrews chapter by chapter:
   a. Learn all you can about the recipients of this letter. Look for and mark the words *we, you, friends,* and *brothers*. Then record what you learn about the recipients on the OBSERVATIONS CHART following Hebrews under "Recipients."
   b. Note on the OBSERVATIONS CHART what you learn from the text about the author.
   c. Keep in mind the author's purpose for writing. Throughout the book you will see him exhorting his readers. Most of his exhortations begin with "let us." Mark each *let us* and then list each exhortation on the OBSERVATIONS CHART.
   d. Observe how the author periodically warns his readers about certain things.
      1) Note each warning on the OBSERVATIONS CHART. An example of a warning is found in 2:1: "We must therefore pay the more careful attention to what we have heard, so that we may not let ourselves drift from it."
      2) As you note the warning, watch for and record the consequences of not heeding the warning. Also remember to whom the book is addressed. Let the text speak for

itself. Don't read into it—just let it say what it says.

3. As you study each chapter, do the following:

    a. Write the key words (including their synonyms and pronouns) listed on the HEBREWS AT A GLANCE chart on an index card and then mark them in a distinctive way in the text. (Beginning at chapter 7, mark every occurrence of the word *covenant.*) Use this card as a reminder of what you are looking for as you study the book of Hebrews.

    b. List in the margin what you learn from each key word.

    c. As you finish reading a chapter, decide on the theme or subject of that chapter and record it above the chapter number in the text and on HEBREWS AT A GLANCE.

4. To truly appreciate and understand the book of Hebrews, you need to do the following:

    a. Look back through your work and note all the times you marked *Jesus* and the pronouns referring to Him. Also look for the word *better (greater)*. Then make a chart on THE SUPREMACY OF JESUS and list what you learn from Hebrews about our Lord. (Or record this information in the margin of your New Testament.)

    b. There is much in Hebrews about the priesthood and about Jesus as our High Priest. Make a chart entitled THE PRIESTHOOD AND JESUS and list your information in three columns: "Insights into Priests and the Priesthood," "Insights into Jesus, Our Great High Priest," and "How This Applies to Me." Record your insights in the proper columns. (Or list this information in the margin.)

    c. Review what you learn from marking the word *covenant* and note what the text says on a chart you title A COMPARISON OF THE TWO COVENANTS: LAW AND GRACE AS TAUGHT IN HEBREWS. (Or in the margin next to chapters 7 through 10, list what you learn about the old covenant and law, and the new covenant and grace.)

5. Complete HEBREWS AT A GLANCE by doing the following:

    a. Look at each of your chapter themes in order to determine the theme of Hebrews and record it on the chart.

    b. Fill in the section titled "Segment Divisions."

       1) Segment divisions indicate a change in the thrust or topic of the book. One change in emphasis occurs at Hebrews 10:19, where the author stops dealing with the doctrinal aspects of the truth he is sharing and begins to address the practical aspects. Record this segment division on the chart in the appropriate space.

       2) Look again at the chapter themes and see if there are any other divisions you can record. If so, record them on the chart. Completing this exercise will help you find where a specific truth is covered in Hebrews.

THINGS TO THINK ABOUT

1. Meditate on the truths you learned about Jesus. Do you see Him as "better"? How supreme is He in your life?

2. As you press on to Christian maturity, are you noticing a new sense of confidence in your God? Is your faith being strengthened? Are you drawing near to God? Do you think Jesus under-

stands what you're going through? Can He really help?

3. Are you laying aside every encumbrance (every weighty thing that is slowing you down) and every sin, and running with endurance the race set before you? If not, what is holding you back?

4. How are your morals? Do you live in the light of the fact that God will judge immoral people and adulterers?

5. Are you continually presenting a praise offering? What are some things you can thank God for today?

THE EPISTLE TO THE

HEBREWS

Date of writing: c. A.D. 68

1 God of old spoke[a] to our fathers at various times and in many ways by means of the prophets. [2]But He has at the end of these days[b] spoken to us in His Son, whom He has appointed Heir of all things and through whom He made the world. [3]As the reflection of God's glory and the true expression of His being He sustains the universe by His almighty word. And when He had effected our cleansing from sin, He took His seat at the right hand of the Majesty on high.

[4]He became as much greater than the angels as the name He inherited was superior to theirs. [5]For to which of the angels did God ever say,[c] "Thou art My Son; today I have begotten Thee"? And again,[d] "I will be a Father to Him and He will be a Son to Me"? [6]Once more, when He introduces the First-born into the world, He says,[e] "And let all God's angels worship Him." [7]Referring to the angels He says,[f] "Who makes His angels winds and His ministers flames of fire"; [8]but as to the Son,[g] "Thy throne, O God, is forever and ever, and the scepter of Thy kingdom is a scepter of righteousness. [9]Thou hast loved righteousness and hast hated injustice; therefore God, Thy God, has anointed Thee with the oil of gladness rather than Thy companions."

[10]Further[h] "Thou, Lord, didst found the earth at the beginning and the heavens are the works of Thy hands. [11]They will perish, but Thou remainest. They will all wear out like a garment, [12]and like a mantle Thou wilt fold them up and they will be changed; but Thou art the same and Thy years will not come to an end."

[13]Besides, to which of the angels did He ever say,[i] "Be seated at My right hand until I put down your enemies as a footstool for your feet"? [14]Are they not all ministering spirits, sent for the assistance of those who are to inherit salvation?

2 We must therefore pay the more careful attention to what we have heard, so that we may not let ourselves drift from it.[j] [2]For if the message that was spoken through angels[k] has held true, and every transgression and disobedience received its just retribution, [3]how shall we escape if we neglect so great a salvation? It was first spoken by the Lord; it was confirmed to us by those who heard Him; [4]then it was corroborated by God with signs and wonders and a great variety of miraculous powers and gifts of the Holy Spirit, distributed according to His will.

[5]For He did not subject the future world of which we are talking under the control of angels, [6]but one has somewhere testified,[l] "What is man that Thou art mindful of him, or the son of man that Thou lookest after

---

a) The name of the author of this epistle is nowhere stated in the N.T. It was evidently written prior to the destruction of the temple in Jerusalem, ch. 10:11.   b) Since the Messiah came. c) Ps. 2:7.   d) II Sam. 7:14.   e) Deut. 32:43, *Septuagint.*   f) Ps. 104:4.   g) Ps. 45:6, 7. h) Ps. 102:25-27.   i) Ps. 110:1.   j) On a tide of unbelief.   k) Acts 7:53; Gal. 3:19. l) Ps. 8:4-(

him? 7For a little while Thou hast ranked him lower than the angels; with glory and honor hast Thou crowned him; 8all things hast Thou subjected underneath his feet."

In thus subjecting all things to him, nothing is left out that is not subjected; but at present we do not yet see all things subjected to him. 9But we see Jesus, ranked lower than the angels for a little while, crowned with glory and honor because of the sufferings of death, in order that by divine grace He might taste death for everyone. 10For it befitted Him, for whom and through whom the universe exists, in bringing many sons to glory, to perfect the Leader of their salvation by means of sufferings.

11For the One who makes holy and those who are being made holy all have one Father, for which reason He is not ashamed to call them brothers, 12when He says,m "I shall proclaim Thy name to My brothers; in the midst of the congregation I shall sing Thy praise," 13and again,n "I shall put My trust in Him," and once more,o "Here am I and the children God has given Me."

14Since, then, the children share flesh and blood, He Himself shared these things with them, so that by means of His death He might destroy the one who wields the power of death, namely the devil, 15and set free those who throughout life were held in slavery by fear of death.

16For it is surely not to the angels that He reaches out to help, but to the offspring of Abraham;p 17so He had to be made like His brothers in every respect in order to become a merciful and faithful High Priest in things related to God, for the atonement of the people's sins. 18For because He Himself suffered in being tempted, He is able to bring aid to those who are tempted.

3 SO THEN, HOLY BROTHERS AND sharers in the heavenly invitation, set your thoughts on Jesus, the Apos-

tle and High Priest of our confession. 2He was faithful to Him who appointed Him, just as Moses was in the whole household of God.q 3For He is entitled to greater honor than Moses to the degree in which the builder of a house enjoys more honor than the house itself. 4Of course every house is built by someone, but the Builder of all things is God. 5And while Moses was faithful in His whole household as a servant, to bear witness to things that would be spoken of later, 6Christ was faithful as a Son in charge of God's household. And we are that household, if we firmly maintain the confidence and pride in what we hope for.

7Therefore, as the Holy Spirit says,r "Today if you will hear His voice, 8do not harden your hearts as in the rebellion at the time when you put God to the test in the wilderness, 9where your fathers for forty years tried Me by putting Me to the test and saw what I did. 10So I became sorely displeased with that generation and said, 'They are always going astray in their hearts; they did not learn My ways.' 11As I swore in My anger, 'They shall not enter into My rest.'"

12Look out, brothers, so that there may not be a wicked, unbelieving heart in any of you that would lead you to fall away from the living God. 13Instead, give daily warning to one another so long as we may speak of today,s so that not one of you may be hardened through the delusion of sin.

14For only if we maintain firmly to the very end the original assurance,t then are we sharers of Christ, 15with this in mind, "Today, if you hear His voice, do not harden your hearts as in the rebellion."

16For who heard and yet were rebellious? Was it not all who went out of Egypt under Moses? 17And with whom was He provoked for forty years? Was it not with those who sinned, whose corpses fell in the desert? 18And to whom but the disobedient did He swear, "They shall not

m) Ps. 22:22.　n) Isa. 8:17, *Septuagint.*　o) Isa. 8:18.
p) All believers, Gal. 3:17; *cf.* Rom. 4:11, 12.　q) Num. 12:7.　r) Ps. 95:7-11.
s) The day of grace.　t) Of salvation through Christ.

enter into My rest"? [19]So we see that on account of unbelief they were not able to enter.

4 LET US THEN BE ON OUR GUARD so that, while the promise of entering into His rest still holds, none of you may be found to be delinquent, [2]for we have had the good news preached to us, just as they did. But the message they heard did not benefit them, because it was not united by faith to those who heard it. [3]For we who have believed enter into His rest, as He has said, "As I swore in My anger, they shall not enter into My rest"; although His works had been accomplished from the foundation of the world. [4]For somewhere He says[u] this about the seventh day, "And God rested on the seventh day from all His works," [5]and again in this passage, "They shall not enter into My rest."

[6]Since, then, it is reserved for some to enter it,[v] and those who previously received the good news did not enter because of disobedience, [7]He fixes a new "today," as He says in David so much later, and as we have mentioned before, "Today, if you will hear His voice, do not harden your hearts."

[8]For if Joshua had given them rest, God would not have spoken of another day later on. [9]Consequently there is a sabbath rest reserved for the people of God;[w] [10]for one who enters into his rest, also rests from his works, just as God did from His.

[11]Let us then exert ourselves to enter into that rest, so that none may fall on account of such disobedience as they exemplified; [12]for the word of God is living and effective, and sharper than any two-edged sword. It penetrates even to the dividing line of soul and spirit, of joints and marrow, and judges the desires and thoughts of the heart. [13]Not a creature exists that is hidden from Him, but all things lie bare and exposed before the eyes of Him with whom we have to reckon.

[14]Inasmuch then as we have a great High Priest, Jesus, the Son of God, who has passed through the heavens,[x] let us hold firmly to our confession. [15]For ours is not a High Priest who cannot sympathize with our weaknesses, but One who was in every respect tested as we are, yet without committing any sin. [16]Let us then approach the throne of grace with assurance, so that we may receive mercy and find grace to help us in time of need.

5 FOR EVERY HIGH PRIEST, CHOSEN as he is from among men, is appointed to represent the people in matters that pertain to God, to offer gifts and sacrifices for sins. [2]And he can deal gently with the ignorant and the wayward, since he is himself liable to weakness. [3]For this reason he is obliged to present offerings for his own sins as well as for the people. [4]No one appropriates the honor for himself, but he is called by God, just as Aaron was.

[5]So, too, Christ did not glorify Himself to become a high priest, but He who said to Him, "Thou art My Son; today I have begotten Thee," [6]as also He says elsewhere,[y] "Thou art a priest forever after the order of Melchizedek."

[7]In the days of His flesh He offered prayers and petitions with strong crying and with tears to Him who could save Him from death, and He was heard because of His humble devotion to God. [8]Although He was a Son, He learned obedience by what He suffered [9]and, when He was perfected, He became the Author of eternal salvation for all who obey Him; [10]so He was called by God a High Priest after Melchizedek's order.

[11]There is much to say about this, and it is difficult to explain, since you have grown hard of hearing; [12]for whereas by this time you ought to be teachers, you stand again in need of someone to teach you the elementary

---

u) Gen. 2:2.
v) Of those who came out of Egypt, only Caleb and Joshua, and perhaps some who were infants at that time, entered the land of promise.   w) In heaven.
x) Into the immediate presence of God the Father.   y) Ps. 110:4.

principles of God's lessons; you have come to need milk and not solid food. [13]Of course, anyone who feeds on milk is inexperienced in the matter of righteousness[z] for he is an infant. [14]But solid food is for the mature person, for those whose faculties have been trained by practice to distinguish between good and evil.

6 LET US LEAVE BEHIND THE ELEmentary teachings of Christ and advance toward maturity. Let us not again be laying the foundation of repentance from dead works[a] and faith in God, [2]of teaching on washings and the laying on of hands, of resurrection from the dead and eternal punishment. [3]God permitting we do this.

[4]For it is impossible to bring anew to repentance those who have once for all been illumined, have tasted the heavenly gift, have become participants of the Holy Spirit, [5]have tasted the goodness of the word of God and the powers of the world to come, [6]and have fallen away; for they repeat so far as they are concerned the crucifying of the Son of God and are exposing Him to public disgrace. [7]For the land that drinks the rain that often falls on it, and that grows vegetation useful to those for whom it is tilled, receives a blessing from God, [8]but if it produces thorns and thistles, it is worthless; it is facing a curse and ends up by being burned.

[9]Even though we speak this way, dear friends, we feel confident of better things about you, things that belong to salvation. [10]For God is not unjust so as to forget what you did and the love you showed for His name as you have ministered to the saints,[b] and are still ministering.[c] [11]It is our desire, however, for each of you to evidence the same earnestness all the way through, to enjoy the full assurance of your hope to the end, [12]so you may not become sluggish but imitate those who through faith and patience inherit the promises.

[13]For when God made His prom-ise to Abraham, He swore by Himself, since He could swear by none greater, [14]and said,[d] "I certainly shall bless you with blessings and multiply you abundantly." [15]So it was that after patient waiting he realized what had been promised.

[16]Men do indeed swear by one greater than themselves, and an oath serves for settlement beyond all dispute. [17]In this way God, in His desire to show the heirs of the promise the unchangeableness of His purpose, guaranteed it with an oath, [18]so that by two unalterable things in which it is impossible for God to lie, we who have taken refuge in Him may have strong encouragement to seize the hope that is placed before us. [19]To this hope we anchor the soul safely and securely, and it reaches on beyond the veil into the Holy of Holies, where [20]Jesus entered in for us in advance[e] for He has become a High Priest forever after the order of Melchizedek.

7 FOR THIS MELCHIZEDEK, KING OF Salem, priest of the Most High God, who met Abraham as he returned from the defeat of the kings and who blessed nim, [2]to whom Abraham also apportioned a tithe of all the spoil,[f] was first of all, as the name means, king of righteousness and then king of Salem, which means king of peace. [3]Without father or mother or ancestral line,[g] with no beginning of days nor ending of life, made to resemble the Son of God, he remains a priest forever.

[4]Observe his greatness, to whom the patriarch Abraham gave a tithe of the first spoils. [5]Those who are the descendants of Levi, who receive the priestly office, are commanded by the Law to take tithes from the people, which means their own brothers, although they have sprung from Abraham's loins. [6]But a person without their ancestral line took tithes from Abraham and blessed the possessor of the promises. [7]Yet the lesser is unquestionably blessed by the greater.

---

z) Before God.   a) The works of the Law.   b) See note at Acts 9:13.   c) *Cf.* ch. 10:32-34.
d) Gen. 22:17.   e) A third guarantee.   f) Gen. 14:18-20.
g) That is, insofar as priestly lineage is concerned.

[8]Furthermore, in this instance mortal men receive tithes, but in that case it was one of whom it is witnessed that he lives. [9]And one might say that through Abraham even Levi, who received tithes, paid tithes, [10]for he was still in his forefather's loins when Melchizedek met Abraham.

[11]Now if perfection had been possible by means of the Levitical priesthood — for on its basis the people received the Law — why was it required to have another priest appointed after the order of Melchizedek instead of choosing one of the Aaronic order? [12]For when the priesthood is changed, there comes necessarily a change of the Law. [13]He of whom this was said belonged to a different tribe, no member of which has officiated at the altar; [14]for obviously our Lord sprang from Judah, regarding which tribe Moses never mentioned priests. [15]This is still even plainer when another priest arises who resembles Melchizedek, [16]who has become such, not according to the norm of a law dependent on the physical life but by the power of an indestructible life. [17]For it is witnessed concerning Him, "Thou art a priest forever of the Melchizedek order."[h]

[18]On the one hand, a previous regulation is set aside because of its ineffectiveness and its uselessness ([19]for the Law brought nothing to perfection) and on the other hand, a better hope is introduced through which we draw near to God. [20]And it was not without an oath. [21]For the Levites became priests without an oath, but He with an oath by the One who said to Him, "The Lord has sworn and will not change His mind, Thou art a priest forever." [22]And because of this difference Jesus became surety of a better covenant.

[23]And those priests[i] were numerous because they were prevented by death from continuing; [24]but He, because He remains forever, holds a priesthood that is never transferred. [25]Hence, too,

He is able to save to the uttermost those who come to God through Him,[j] because He always lives to intercede for them.

[26]For such a High Priest also suited our need — holy, innocent, spotless, different from sinners and exalted above the heavens. [27]He does not, like those high priests, have daily need to offer sacrifices, first for his own sins and then for those of the people, because this He did once for all when He offered Himself as a sacrifice.[k] [28]For the Law appoints weak human beings to the priesthood, but the word of the oath, that came later than the Law, appoints the forever-perfect Son, who has been made perfect forever.

8 NOW THE MAIN POINT OF WHAT we have been saying is this: we have such a High Priest, who is seated at the right hand of the throne of the Majesty in the heavens, [2]as minister in the sanctuary; yes, of the true tabernacle, which the Lord pitched,[l] not man.

[3]For every high priest is appointed to offer gifts and sacrifices; so this One also must have something to offer. [4]If, then, He were still on earth, He would not be a priest at all; for here they offer the gifts as prescribed by the Law, [5]that serve as a copy and shadow the heavenly sanctuary, just as Moses was instructed when he was about to build the tabernacle. "See to it," He said,[m] "that you make everything according to the pattern that was shown you on the mountain."

[6]But now He has acquired a ministry as far superior as the covenant He mediates is better, enacted as it is upon more excellent promises. [7]For if that first covenant had been flawless, no place would have been sought for a second. [8]But, finding fault with it, He says,[n] "The days are coming, says the Lord, when I will make a new covenant with the house of Israel and with the house of Judah, [9]not like the covenant I made with their fathers the

---

h) This spells the end of the Levitical priesthood.   i) The successive line of high priests.
j) Cf. John 14:6.   k) Christ our High Priest was at the same time the offerer and the victim.
l) Num. 24:6, *Septuagint.*   m) Exod. 25:40.
n) Jer. 31:31-34.

day I took them by the hand to lead them out of the land of Egypt; because they did not remain faithful to My covenant. So I let them alone, says the Lord.

10"For this is the covenant which I will make with the house of Israel after those days, the Lord says, I will fix My laws into their minds and will write them on their hearts, and I will be their God and they shall be My people. 11No longer shall each citizen be teaching his neighbor and each person his brother, saying, 'Know the Lord,' because they shall all know Me from the least of them to the greatest of them. 12For I will be merciful toward their wrongdoings, and their sins I will no longer remember."

13By saying, "new," He has made the first out of date. But what is antiquated and obsolete approaches the vanishing point.

9 TO BE SURE, THE FIRST COVENANT had its worship regulations and its earthly sanctuary; 2for the first tabernacle was furnished in this way: in what is called the Holy Place were the lampstand and the table and the presentation loaves.[o] 3Behind the second curtain was the tabernacle called the Holy of Holies, 4containing the golden altar of incense[p] and the ark of the covenant completely covered with gold; inside it the golden jar of manna, Aaron's rod that sprouted,[q] and the tablets of the covenant. 5Above it were the cherubim of glory overshadowing the mercy seat, — about which we cannot now go into detail.

6With these things so arranged, the priests always enter the first tabernacle to perform their priestly duties, 7but into the second the high priest alone enters once a year — not without blood, which he offers for himself and for the thoughtless sins of the people.

8Through this the Holy Spirit evidences that the way into the Holiest[r] was not yet opened with the first tabernacle still standing. 9This is a symbol for the present time. It means that the gifts and offerings which are presented cannot make the worshiper's conscience perfect, 10as they consist only of food and drink and various ablutions — physical regulations that are in effect until the time of the new order.

11But when Christ appeared as High Priest of the good things that have come, He passed through the greater and more perfect tabernacle, not made with hands — no part, that is, of material creation. 12And not with blood of goats and calves, but with His own blood He entered once for all into the Holy Place, procuring eternal redemption. 13For if the blood of goats and bulls and the ashes of a heifer, as it sprinkles those who were defiled, renders them holy so far as physical purity is concerned, 14how much more will the blood of Christ, who through the eternal Spirit offered Himself a flawless sacrifice to God, cleanse your conscience from lifeless work for the service of the living God!

15For this reason He is the Mediator of a new covenant so that, with a death occurring for atonement of the transgressions under the first covenant, those who have been called may receive the eternal inheritance that was promised. 16For where there is a testament, the death of the testator needs to be established. 17A will is effective at death; it is not valid so long as the testator lives.

18Therefore, the first covenant was not ratified without blood. 19When Moses had spoken every commandment according to the Law to all the people, he took the blood of calves and goats along with water, scarlet wool, and hyssop, and sprinkled it on the Book and on all the people, 20saying,[s] "This is the blood of the covenant which God has commanded upon you." 21Similarly he sprinkled the

o) These loaves were dedicated to God and eaten by the priests as His representatives on earth.
p) In O.T. times the altar of incense was in the Holy Place outside the veil (curtain), Exod. 30:1-6. Here it is included among the furnishings that were within the veil, the Holy of holies. Perhaps the writer of Hebrews was speaking symbolically in relocating the altar inasmuch as Christ, the eternal sacrifice, was now in the presence of God. q) Num. 17:1-10.
r) Of heaven, vs. 12.
s) Exod. 24:8.

tabernacle and all the service utensils with the blood.[t]

[22]According to the Law almost everything is purified by blood, and without bloodshedding there is no forgiveness. [23]So it was necessary that the copies of the heavenly things be purified by these sacrifices; but the heavenly things themselves require better sacrifices than these. [24]For Christ has not entered into a sanctuary made by hands, a copy of the true one, but into heaven itself, now to appear on our behalf in the presence of God — [25]not to present Himself repeatedly as an offering, as the high priest enters annually into the sanctuary with blood not his own; [26]for if so, He must have suffered repeatedly since the world began. But as it is, He has appeared once for all at the close of the ages to put away sin by the sacrifice of Himself.

[27]And as it is reserved for men to die once for all with judgment following, [28]so will Christ, sacrificed once for all to bear the sins of many, appear the second time, with no reference to sin, to those who are eagerly looking for Him, and that for their salvation.

10 FOR WHILE THE LAW foreshadowed the promised blessings without expressing them in reality, it can never make perfect those who continually approach with the same sacrifices year after year. [2]Else, would they not have ceased bringing their offerings, since the worshipers, cleansed once for all, would no longer have any consciousness of sin? [3]But in those sacrifices there is a reminder of sins year after year; [4]for the blood of bulls and of goats is powerless to take away sins.

[5]When Christ comes into the world, He therefore says,[u] "Sacrifice and offering Thou hast not desired, but a body Thou hast prepared for Me.[v]

[6]In burnt and sin offerings Thou hast taken no pleasure. [7]Then I said, 'Here I come — it is written of Me in the roll of the Book — to do Thy will, O God.'"

[8]Saying as He does above, "Thou hast not desired nor taken pleasure in sacrifices, and offerings, and burnt and sin offerings," all of which are offered according to the Law, [9]then He says, "Here I come to do Thy will." He takes away the first in order to establish the second, [10]by which divine will we have been made holy by means of the offering up once for all of the body of Jesus Christ.

[11]Furthermore, every priest stands daily for services to offer the same sacrifices repeatedly, which have no power whatever to take away sins; [12]but this One, after offering for our sins one sacrifice forever, sat down at the right hand of God, [13]from then on anticipating until His enemies are placed as a footstool for His feet. [14]For with a single offering He has forever perfected those who are being made holy.

[15]The Holy Spirit also affirms it to us, for after He says,[w] [16]"This is the covenant I will make with them after those days, the Lord says, I will place My laws upon their hearts and inscribe them on their minds," [17]He adds, "Their sins and their lawless deeds I will no longer remember." [18]Now where sins have been forgiven there are no longer any offerings for them.

[19]Since, therefore, we have confidence, brothers, to enter the Holiest through Jesus' blood [20]by a new and living way, so recently made for us through the veil,[x] that is, His flesh, [21]and since we have a great Priest in charge of God's house, [22]let us draw near with honest hearts and full assurance of faith, our hearts sprinkled clean[y] from an evil conscience, and our bodies bathed with pure water. [23]Let

---

t) Exod. 29:16, 20-21; Lev. 16:14, 15, 18. u) Ps. 40:6-8.
v) The Word that was always with God was made flesh, i.e., He took upon Himself a body that was prepared for Him and in which He lived on earth, died, and rose again for us.
w) Ch. 8:10-12.
x) Cf. Matt. 27:51; Mark 15:38; Luke 23:45, where it is written that the veil (curtain) of the temple was torn from top to bottom when Christ died.
y) By Christ's atoning blood, just as priests were dedicated with blood.

us hold unwaveringly our grip on the hope we confess, for He who promised is faithful.

24Let us also be mindful to stimulate one another toward love and helpful activities, 25not neglecting to meet together, as is habitual with some, but giving mutual encouragement, and all the more so since you see the Day approaching. 26For if we go on sinning willfully after acquiring the knowledge of the truth, there is no longer left any sacrifice for sins, 27but some dreadful anticipation of judgment and of a fierce fire that is to devour those who oppose God.

28The person who disobeys the Law of Moses is put to death without mercy on the evidence of two or three witnesses. 29How much worse, do you suppose, will be the punishment he is judged to deserve, who tramples on the Son of God and considers the blood of the covenant, by which he was made holy, something unholy, and who outrages the Spirit of grace? 30For we know Him who said,[z] "Retribution rests with Me; I will pay back," and also,[a] "The Lord will judge His people." 31It is dreadful to fall into the hands of the living God.

32Call to mind those previous days when, after enjoying the light, you endured sufferings that involved great struggle. 33On the one hand you were publicly exposed to insults and affliction, and on the other you made common cause with those who were thus treated. 34For you sympathized with the prisoners and accepted cheerfully the plundering of your property, knowing well that you yourselves had better and lasting possession.

35Therefore, do not throw away your confidence; it carries a rich reward. 36For you need endurance to gain the promised blessing upon accomplishing what God wills.[b] 37"For it will be just a little while before the coming One will come and will not delay; 38but he whom I find righteous through faith will live,[c] and if he shrinks back, My soul will not be

pleased with him." 39However, we are not of those who shrink back so as to perish, but of those who have faith and save their souls.

11 BUT FAITH IS AN ASSURANCE OF what is hoped for, a conviction of unseen realities.[d] 2The men of old gained approval by it.

3By faith we understand that the universe was created at God's command, so that what we now see was made out of what cannot be seen.

4By faith Abel brought God a sacrifice superior to that of Cain, and through faith he was witnessed to as being righteous; for God acknowledged his gifts, and though he died, through his faith he is still speaking.

5By faith Enoch was taken up, so that he did not see death, and was not found because God took him up; for before God took him up, so it is recorded, he was pleasing to God. 6But without faith it is impossible to please Him; for he who comes to God must believe that He exists and that He is a rewarder of those who search for Him.

7By faith N o a h, when he was divinely instructed about things that were not yet in sight, devoutly constructed the ark for the saving of his family, through which he condemned the world, while he fell heir to the righteousness that springs from faith.

8By faith Abraham obeyed when he was called to go out to a place which he was to receive for an inheritance, and he migrated without any idea where he was going. 9By faith he lived in the land of promise as in a foreign country, living in tents, as did Isaac and Jacob who were joint heirs with him of the same promise. 10For he was looking for the city with foundations, whose Architect and Builder is God.

11Also by faith Sarah herself received power to conceive and that when she was past the normal age,[e] because she regarded the One who promised to be t r u s t w o r t h y. 12And so from one person, and he already

---

z) Deut. 32:35.
a) Deut. 32:36.   b) Hab. 2:3, 4.   c) Hab. 2:4; Rom. 1:17; Gal. 3:11.
d) This is not a precise definition of faith but rather a description of it.   e) Gen. 21:1, 2.

impotent, there were born descendants as the stars of heaven in numbers and countless as the sand on the seashore.

[13]These all died in faith without having received what was promised them, but they saw it from a distance and welcomed it, confessing that they were foreigners and exiles on the earth.

[14]For those who say such things make it plain that they are looking for a homeland, [15]and if they had in mind that country from which they went out, they would have had a chance to return. [16]But now they are longing for a better, that is, a heavenly country; accordingly, God is not ashamed of being called their God. In fact, He has prepared a city for them.

[17]By faith Abraham, when he was tested, brought Isaac as an offering.[f] Yes, the recipient of the promises offered his only son, [18]of whom it had been said,[g] "Through Isaac you are to have your descendants." [19]For he reasoned that God was able to raise him from the dead, from which in a figure, he did receive him back.

[20]By faith Isaac[h] gave Jacob and Esau his blessing for their future. [21]By faith Jacob, at the point of death, blessed each of Joseph's sons[i] and bowed in worship on the top of his staff. [22]By faith Joseph,[j] when he was dying, mentioned the exodus of the Israelites, and gave instructions regarding his bones.

[23]By faith Moses, when he was born, was hidden by his parents[k] for three months because they saw he was a beautiful child and they were not afraid of the king's order.

[24]By faith Moses,[l] when he reached maturity, refused to be called a son of Pharaoh's daughter, [25]and preferred sharing ill-treatment with the people of God rather than enjoying the short-lived pleasures of sin.[m] [26]He considered the reproach, such as came to Christ, greater wealth than the treasures of Egypt. For he fixed his eye on the final recompense.

[27]By faith he left Egypt, unafraid of the king's anger; for he persevered as if he saw Him who is invisible.

[28]By faith he instituted the Passover[n] and the sprinkling of the blood, so that the destroyer might not touch their first-born.

[29]By faith the Israelites[o] crossed the Red Sea as on dry land, and when the Egyptians tried it, they were drowned.

[30]By faith the walls of Jericho fell[p] down after the Israelites marched around them for seven days.

[31]By faith Rahab, the harlot,[q] did not perish with those who were disobedient; for she had received the spies in peace.

[32]And what more shall I say? For time would fail me to go on telling about Gideon,[r] Barak,[s] Samson,[t] Jephthah,[u] David,[v] and Samuel,[w] and the prophets, [33]who through faith overcame kingdoms, administered justice, procured promised blessings, shut the mouths of lions,[x] [34]quenched the power of fire,[y] escaped being killed by the sword, were made powerful when they had been weak, became mighty in war, turned to flight foreign armies.

[35]Women received back their dead by resurrection.[z] Others,[a] who refused release so that they might procure a better resurrection, were tortured. [36]Still others suffered mocking and flogging, and chains and imprisonment. [37]They were stoned; they were tempted to sin; they were sawed in two; they were killed with the sword. In sheepskins and in goatskins they roamed about, destitute, afflicted, ill-treated — [38]the world was not worthy of them, those wanderers in deserts and mountains and caverns and fissures of the earth.

[39]And all these, while winning divine approval through their faith, did not receive the promised blessing; [40]for God had in view something better for

---

f) Gen. 22:1-14.   g) Gen. 21:12.   h) Gen. 27:26-40.   i) Gen. 48.
j) Gen. 50:24, 25.   k) Exod. 2:1-3.   l) Exod. 2:11-15.
m) In sharing his people's lot Moses resembled Christ.   n) Exod. 12.   o) Exod. 14:13-31.
p) Josh. 6:1-20.   q) Josh. 2:1-21; 6:23.   r) Judg. 6:11; 7:1-25.   s) Judg. 4:6-24.
t) Judg. 13:24 – 16:31.   u) Judg. 11:1-29; 12:1-7.   v) I Sam. 16, 17.   w) I Sam. 7:9-14.
x) Dan. 6:22.   y) Dan. 3:23-28.   z) I Kings 17:8-24; II Kings 4:18-37.
a) Whereas through faith some escaped severe trials, others by faith were enabled to suffer torture and imprisonment.

us, so that without us they would not be made perfect.

12 SO THEN, ENCIRCLED AS WE ARE with such a great cloud of witnesses[b] all about us, let us get rid of every impediment and the sin that ensnares us so easily, and let us run steadily the course mapped out for us, [2]with our eyes on Jesus, the cause and completer of our faith who, in view of the joy that lay ahead for Him, submitted to the cross, thought nothing of the shame, and is seated at the right hand of the throne of God. [3]Compare your experience with His, who was willing to stand so much hostility from sinners against Himself, so that you may not become weary and despondent.

[4]In your struggle against sin you have not yet resisted so that it has cost you blood, [5]and you have been forgetful of the appeal that speaks to you as sons:[c] "My son, do not think lightly of the Lord's discipline, neither become discouraged under His reproof; [6]for the Lord disciplines the person He loves and punishes every son whom He receives." [7]You must endure for the sake of correction; God is treating you as sons. For what son is there whom the father does not discipline? [8]If you receive no correction, such as all sons share, then you are illegitimate children and not sons.

[9]Now, if we were corrected by our human fathers and respected them, shall we not far rather submit to our spiritual Father and live? [10]For while they for a few days disciplined us as they saw fit, He does it for our benefit, so that we may share in His holiness. [11]Of course, no discipline seems at the time enjoyable, but it seems painful; later on, however, it affords those schooled in it the peaceful fruitage of an upright life.

[12]So, lift up your drooping hands[d] and strengthen your shaky knees; [13]step out straight ahead with your feet,[e] so that which is lame may not be dislocated but rather be healed.

[14]Seek eagerly for peace with everyone and for holiness without which no one shall see the Lord. [15]See to it that no one falls short of divine grace; that no one cultivates a root of bitterness[f] to cause a disturbance by which many will be defiled; [16]that no one be immoral or profane like Esau, who for a single meal sold his own birthright. [17]For you know how afterward, when he wanted to inherit the blessing, he was rejected, because he found no opportunity to repent, although with tears he sought for the blessing.

[18]For you have not come up to a mountain that was not to be touched, a blazing fire and gloom, darkness and storm, [19]to trumpet sound and audible words, the hearers of which implored that no further message be brought them, [20]for they could not bear the command,[g] "Even if an animal touches the mountain it must be stoned." [21]And the phenomenon was so dreadful that Moses said,[h] "I am terrified and trembling."

[22]Instead, we have come up Mount Zion, the city of the living God, the heavenly Jerusalem, to ten thousands of angels in festal gathering, [23]and to the assembly of the first-born, whose names are enrolled in heaven, and to God the Judge of all, and to the spirits of the righteous who have been made perfect,[i] [24]and to Jesus, the Mediator of a new covenant, and to the sprinkled blood that tells of better things than that of Abel.[j]

[25]Be careful not to refuse to hear the One who is speaking; for if those people did not escape who refused to hear the person who spoke God's message on earth, how much less shall we, if we turn away from the One who speaks from heaven. [26]His voice then shook the earth, but now He has promised,[k] "Once more I will shake, not only the earth but heaven as well." [27]This phrase, "Once more,"

---

b) Translated from the Gk. *marturon,* from which comes the English word "martyr."
c) Prov. 3:11, 12.   d) Isa. 35:3.   e) Prov. 4:25, 26.   f) Deut. 29:18.   g) Exod. 19:12, 13.
h) Deut. 9:18, 19; *cf.* Acts 7:32.   i) The redeemed in heaven.
j) Gen. 4:10.   k) Hag. 2:6.

indicates the final removal of every-thing shaken — created things, so that the unshaken things may remain.[1]

28Let us, therefore, be grateful that the kingdom we have received cannot be shaken, and so let us serve God ac-ceptably with reverence and awe. 29For our God is a consuming fire.

13 LET BROTHERLY LOVE CON-tinue. 2Do not be negligent in showing hospitality, for in doing so some entertained angels without knowing it. 3Keep in mind those who are in prison as if you are in prison with them, and the ill-treated as though you are suffering physically yourselves.

4Let marriage be held in honor by all and the marriage bed unpolluted; for God will judge the immoral adul-terous.

5Let your conduct be free from the love of money. Be satisfied with what you have, for He has said,[m] "I will not give you up nor desert you," 6so that we may say boldly, "The Lord is my Helper, I will not fear. What can man do to me?"

7Bear in mind your leaders, who spoke to you God's message; observe how they closed a well-spent life, and copy their faith: 8Jesus Christ the same yesterday, and today, and forever.

9Be not led astray by all sorts of strange teachings; for it is well to have the heart strengthened by grace, rather than by ritualistic foods from which devotees derived no benefit. 10We have an altar of which those that serve in the tabernacle have no right to eat; 11for the bodies of those animals, whose blood was brought by the high priest into the Holiest for sin, were burned outside the camp.

12So Jesus, too, suffered outside the gate, that He might sanctify the peo-ple by His own blood. 13Accordingly, let us go out to Him outside the camp, bearing His reproach, 14for we have here no permanent city; instead, we are seeking the future one. 15Through Him, then, let us at all times present a praise offering to God, which is the fruit of lips that confess His name.

16Do not forget to do good and be generous, for with such sacrifices God is well pleased.

17Obey your leaders and yield to them, for they keep watch over your souls as persons who must give ac-count. Have them do so joyfully and not with regrets, for that would be hurtful to you.

18Pray for us, for we are confident of having a clear conscience. In every respect we want to behave honorably. 19I especially beg of you to do this, so that I may be restored to you the sooner.

20Now may the God of peace, who brought again from the dead our Lord Jesus, that great Shepherd of the sheep,[n] through the blood of the ever-lasting covenant, 21furnish you with everything good to do His will, work-ing within us through Jesus Christ what is well-pleasing in His sight. To Him be glory forever and ever. Amen.

22I call on you, brothers, to listen patiently to this message for your en-couragement, for I have written you briefly. 23You should know that our brother Timothy has been freed.[o] Along with him, if he comes here shortly, I will see you.

24Extend our greetings to all your leaders and to all the saints.[p] The Italian believers send you greetings. 25Grace be with you all.

---

l) The material things pass; the spiritual things remain.
m) Deut. 31:6.   n) John 10:11; I Pet. 5:4.
o This is the only reference in the N.T. to Timothy's imprisonment.
p) See note at Acts 9:13.

AUTHOR

_____

_____

_____

_____

_____

RECIPIENTS

_____

_____

_____

_____

_____

EXHORTATIONS

_____

_____

_____

_____

_____

WARNINGS/CONSEQUENCES

_____

_____

_____

_____

_____

_____

_____

_____

_____

_____

_____

_____

THEME OF HEBREWS:

SEGMENT DIVISIONS

		CHAPTER THEMES
		1
		2
		3
		4
		5
		6
		7
		8
		9
		10
		11
		12
		13

Author:

unknown

Date:

Purpose:

Key Words:

Jesus (Son)

God

angels

priest (priests, priesthood)

therefore (then, so)

faith (faithful)

greater

better

let us

perfect (perfected, perfection)

mark any reference to the devil

covenant

JAMES

What a turnaround from the day James told his half-brother what to do if He wanted to be known publicly! Full of unbelief and convinced that Jesus was nothing more than his eldest brother, James told Jesus to take His disciples and go up to the Feast of Booths and do His works there. Jesus might have found more disciples there, but James was not to be numbered as one of them—until Jesus rose from the dead (see 1 Corinthians 15:7).

Convinced from that point on that Jesus was the Christ, James would lay claim not to his physical relationship to Jesus but to his spiritual relationship as a bondservant of the Lord Jesus Christ.

James became a pillar of the church, a leader of the council of Jerusalem, and a friend of Peter and Paul. But most of all he was a friend of Jesus, a covenant friend for whom he would be martyred around A.D. 62.

Sometime before A.D. 50 or in the early A.D. 50s, James would write his one epistle to be included in the pages of Holy Scripture, an epistle that would show what the gospel is like when it is lived out in shoe leather.

THINGS TO DO

1. Read James in one sitting to familiarize yourself with the book as a whole. James structures his writing distinctively. Once you see the pattern he uses, you will better understand the flow of the book.
   a. First, James introduces a subject by making a statement or giving an instruction. For example, in James 1:2 he says to consider it a joy when you encounter various trials.
   b. He then usually follows with more instructions concerning that particular subject, *or* he gives an illustration pertaining to the subject, *or* he gives an explanation of it.

2. As you read back through James, mark in the text the key words (and their synonyms and pronouns) listed on the JAMES AT A GLANCE chart following James. (Key words help you see the subjects of the book.)
   a. Mark every use of *say (says)* and *works* in chapter 2.
   b. Don't miss marking *tongue* and its pronouns in chapter 3.
   c. You may find other key words which are not listed for you. Mark these and also mark *grace* and any reference to the devil (as you have done throughout your New Testament).

3. Read James chapter by chapter:
   a. List the subjects introduced by the author on the JAMES SUBJECT BY SUBJECT chart. Be sure to include the chapter and verse from which you took the information.
   b. Next, if the author gives instructions or illustrations regarding a particular subject, record that information in the appropriate column. See JAMES SUBJECT BY SUBJECT for an example of how to do this.

4. After you list the subjects in each chapter, determine the theme of each chapter and record these themes on

JAMES AT A GLANCE and in the space above each chapter number.

5. Finally, look for the theme of James. From the information gathered, determine if one subject is more predominant than the others or if there is a common denominator among the subjects. The more dominant or common subject will be the theme of James and points to the author's reason for writing. Record the theme of James on JAMES AT A GLANCE and complete the chart.

THINGS TO THINK ABOUT

1. How are you handling the trials in your life?
2. Are you a doer of the Word or a hearer only?
3. Do you show partiality in dealing with people? Are you a respecter of persons?
4. Is your faith seen by your works?
5. Are you a friend of the world?

THE GENERAL EPISTLE OF

JAMES

Date of writing: c. A.D. 48-50,
probably at Jerusalem

1 JAMES,[a] A SLAVE[b] OF GOD AND OF the Lord Jesus Christ, to the twelve tribes in the Dispersion,[c] Greeting.

2Consider it complete joy, my brothers, when you become involved in all sorts of trials, 3well aware that the testing of your faith brings out steadfastness. 4But let steadfastness have full play, so that you may be completed and rounded out with no defects whatever.

5If any one of you lacks wisdom, let him ask God, who gives to everyone without reserve and without reproach, and it will be granted him. 6But he should ask in faith with never a doubt; for one who doubts resembles a wave of the sea that is driven and tossed by the wind. 7Let not that man. imagine he will receive anything from the Lord; 8he is a double-minded man, unsteady in all his ways.

9Let the lowly brother, however, be proud of his high position, 10and the wealthy of his humble place, because he shall fade out like a wild flower. 11The sun rises with its searing heat and withers the grass; its flower drops off and its beauty disappears. So will the rich man fade away in his undertakings.

12Blessed is the man who stands up under trial; for when he has stood the test, he will receive the crown[d] of life that God has promised to those who love Him. 13Let no one who is tempted say, "I am tempted by God," for God cannot be tempted by evil, and He tempts no one. 14But each person is tempted when he is drawn away and enticed by his own desire. 15Then when the desire has conceived it gives birth to sin, and sin, when it reaches maturity, produces death.

16Do not be misled, my dear brothers. 17Every beneficent gift and every perfect present is from above; it descends from the Father of lights, with whom no variation occurs nor shadow cast by turning. 18Voluntarily He gave us birth by the word of truth,[e] so that we might be a kind of first fruits of His creatures.

19Understand this, my dear brothers: let everyone be quick to listen, slow to talk, slow to get angry; 20for man's anger does not promote God's righteousness. 21Therefore get rid of everything vile and the outgrowth of evil, and in humility receive the implanted word that is able to save your souls. 22But be doers of the word,[f] and not deluders of yourselves by merely listening; 23for whoever hears the message without acting upon it is similar to the man who observes his own face in a mirror; 24he takes a look

a) James, who was the leader of the church at Jerusalem, Acts 15:13; 21:17, 18, was a half-brother of Jesus, Matt. 13:55. Like his other brothers James did not believe in the Lord Jesus during His earthly ministry, John 7:5. It appears that he was converted after the risen Lord had appeared to him, I Cor. 15:7. b) See note at Matt. 13:27.
c) The Jews who had been driven out of Judea under persecution. See note at I Pet. 1:1.
d) See note at Phil. 4:2. e) The Spirit's instrument to reach the soul, cf. vs. 21.
f) As you accept Christian truth, put it into practice.

at himself and goes off and promptly forgets how he looks. 25But whoever gazes into the perfect law of liberty and continues in it, who is not a forgetful listener but an active worker, that person will be blessed in his work.

26Whoever supposes he is religious without bridling his own tongue but, instead, deceives his own heart, that person's religion is worthless. 27Pure and undefiled religion in the sight of God the Father is this: to look after orphans and widows in their trouble and to keep oneself unstained from the world.

2 MY BROTHERS, DO NOT COMBINE faith in Jesus Christ our glorious Lord with partiality. 2For should there enter into your gathering a man wearing a gold ring and splendid clothes, and there enter also a poor man shabbily clad, 3and you pay attention to the one who is well-dressed and say, "Have a good seat here," and say to the poor one, "You stand there," or "Sit down on the floor by my feet," 4have you not discriminated among your own and become judges with evil thoughts?

5Listen, my dear brothers. Has not God chosen the poor in the world to be rich in faith and to be heirs of the kingdom He has promised to those who love Him? 6But you have dishonored the poor. Do not the rich domineer you and drag you into the courts? 7Do they not slander the good name by which you are known? 8If you observe the royal law according to the Scripture,g "Love your neighbor as yourself," you behave well. 9But if you show partiality, then you are practicing sin; you stand convicted by the Law as culprits.

10For whoever observes the whole Law but slips in one point, becomes guilty in every respect.h 11For He who said,i "Do not commit adultery," also said,j "Do not kill." So, if you do not commit adultery but you kill, you have become a breaker of the Law. 12Speak and act in such a way as befits people who are to be judged by the law of liberty. 13For the judgment is merciless to those who have practiced no mercy, but mercy triumphs over judgment.

14What is the use, my brothers, for anyone to say he has faith, if he fails to act on it? His faith cannot save him, can it? 15If a brother or sister is poorly clad and lacks the day's nourishment, 16but one of you says to them, "Go away in peace; get warmed and get fed," without supplying them with their bodily needs, what is the use? 17Exactly so faith that does not issue in works is in itself dead.

18Someone, however, will say, "You have faith and I have works." Show me your faith without its works and I will show you my faith through what I do.k 19Do you believe there is one God? Very well; the demons believe, too, and they shudder. 20But do you want to know, O senseless man, how faith without works is useless? 21Was not our father Abraham made righteous by his works when he offered up his son Isaac on the altar? 22You see how his faith cooperated with his works and how faith was completed through his works. 23So the Scripture was fulfilled that says,l "Abraham believed in God and it was accounted to him as righteousness," and he was calledm the friend of God.

24You see that a person is pronounced righteous by his works and not on account of faith alone. 25Similarly, too, was not Rahab the harlot accounted righteous by her works, when she entertained the messengers and sent them away by a different road? 26For as the body is dead without the spirit, so faith also is dead without works.

3 NOT MANY OF YOU SHOULD BEcome teachers, my brothers, for you know we are assuming the more accountability; 2because we all make many mistakes. Whoever makes no mistake with the tongue is certainly

g) Lev. 19:18.   h) He is a lawbreaker.   i) Exod. 20:14.   j) Exod. 20:13.
k) The reality of a man's faith is shown by what he does. Christ said: "You will know them by the deeds they do," Matt. 7:16.   l) Gen. 15:6.   m) Isa. 41:8.

a perfect man, able as well to control his entire body. [3]When we put bits into horses' mouths to make them obey us, we guide their whole bodies. [4]Notice the ships, too, big as they are and driven by violent winds, how they are steered by a small rudder wherever the pilot wishes.

[5]So the tongue is a small organ and can speak big things. Think how great a forest ever so small a spark sets on fire. [6]The tongue also is a fire, a world of wickedness. Among the members of our body the tongue is situated where it taints the whole body and sets on fire the whole round of existence,[n] while it is kindled by hell.[o]

[7]Every kind of animal, of bird, of reptile and sea creature is tamed and has been tamed by mankind, [8]but no human being is able to tame the tongue, restless evil so full of deadly poison. [9]We praise the Lord and Father with it; with it we also curse men who have been made in the likeness of God. [10]From the same mouth blessing and cursing proceed. This is not right, my brothers; it must not be this way.

[11]The spring does not well up sweet and bitter water from the same cleft, does it? [12]Nor is it possible, is it, my brothers, for a fig tree to bear olives, or for a grapevine to bear figs? Neither can salt water produce fresh water.

[13]Who among you is wise and understanding? Let him show by his good behavior that his actions are carried on with unobtrusive wisdom.[p] [14]But if you cherish bitter jealousy and rivalry in your hearts, do not pride yourselves in this and play false to the truth. [15]Such wisdom does not come down from above; instead it is earthly, unspirited, demonic, [16]for where jealousy and rivalry exist, there will be confusion and everything base.

[17]But the wisdom from above[q] is first of all pure, then peaceable, courteous, congenial, full of mercy and good fruits, impartial, and sincere. [18]And the harvest, which righteousness yields to the peacemakers, comes from a sowing in peace.

4 WHERE DO CONFLICTS AND FIGHT-ings among you originate? Do they not spring from your passions that are at war in your members?[r] [2]You covet and do not have; you murder[s] and strive and cannot attain; you fight and battle, and do not possess, because you do not pray. [3]You ask and do not receive, because you ask wrongly; you want to spend it on your dissolute pleasures.

[4]Do you not realize, you adulteresses, that friendship with the world is enmity toward God? Therefore, whoever determines to be a friend of the world becomes God's enemy. [5]Or do you suppose the Scripture speaks to no purpose? The Spirit, who took up His abode in us, yearns jealously over us. [6]But He affords the more grace, for He says,[t] "God opposes the haughty, but He grants grace to the humbleminded."

[7]So then submit yourselves to God. Resist the devil and he will flee from you. [8]Draw near to God and He will draw near to you. Clean your hands, you sinners, and purify your hearts, you of divided interests. [9]Be miserable and grieve and cry. Let your laughing be turned to sorrow and your enjoyment to dejection. [10]Take a low position before the Lord and He will exalt you.

[11]Do not malign one another, brothers. One who maligns or criticizes his brother, maligns the Law and criticizes the Law, but if you criticize the Law you are not a doer of it but its judge. [12]There is one Lawgiver and Judge — He who has power to save and to destroy. But who are you to be judging your neighbor?

[13]Come on, you who say, "Today or tomorrow we shall go into this or that city and spend a year there to transact business and make money," [14]when you have no idea about tomorrow. What is your life? You are a

---

n) Unfit speech also reacts harmfully on the speaker, Matt. 7:15, 20, 23.
o) Greek *geenna*. See note at Mark 9:43.   p) Not only faith but also wisdom is shown by conduct.
q) God-given, therefore relating to life.   r) Cf. Rom. 7; Gal. 5:16-18.
s) In the realm of Christian ethics to hate is equivalent to committing murder, I John 3:15.
t) Prov. 3:34.

vapor that appears for a little while and disappears. [15]Instead you ought to say, "If the Lord wills and we live we shall do this or that." [16]But as it is, you boast in your arrogance, all of which boasting is wicked. [17]So, then, to the person who knows what is right to do and fails to do it, to him it is sin.

5 COME ON YOU WEALTHY, WEEP with loud wailings about the miseries that are coming upon you. [2]Your hoarded wealth has decayed and your clothes have become moth-eaten; [3]your gold and silver are covered with rust, and their rust will be evidence against you. As fire that you have stored up for the last days,[u] it will consume your flesh.

[4]See, the pay of the workmen that mowed your fields, which you have withheld from them, is crying out, and the cries of the reapers have entered the ears of the Lord of hosts. [5]You have been living an easy life on the earth; you have given yourselves up to pleasures; you have fattened your hearts in a day of slaughter.[v] [6]You have condemned, you have murdered the upright without his resisting you.

[7]Therefore, endure patiently, brothers, until the coming of the Lord. Take notice how the farmer awaits the precious produce of the soil, continuing to be patient until it gets the early and the late rains. [8]So you keep waiting patiently. Fortify your hearts, for the coming of the Lord is near.

[9]Do not complain against onè another, brothers, so you may not come under judgment. See, the Judge is standing at the door. [10]For an example

of ill-treatment that was patiently endured, brothers, take the prophets who spoke in the Lord's name. [11]We call blessed those who have endured. You have heard of the perseverance of Job, and you have seen the outcome which the Lord brought about, because the Lord is compassionate and merciful.

[12]Above all, my brothers, do not swear, either by heaven or by the earth or with any other oath; but let your yes be yes, and your no, no, so that you may incur no judgment.

[13]Is any of you suffering trouble? Let him pray. Is anyone feeling cheerful? Let him sing psalms. [14]Is anyone of you ill? Let him call the elders[w] of the church, and let them pray for him and in the name of the Lord anoint him with olive oil.[x] [15]The prayer of faith will restore the sick one, and the Lord will raise him up. And if he has committed sin, it will be forgiven him.

[16]Therefore, confess your sins to each other and pray for one another, that you may be cured.[y] The earnest prayer of a righteous person has great effect. [17]Elijah was a man of similar weaknesses with us, and he prayed an earnest prayer that it should not rain, and no rain fell on the earth for three years and six months. [18]Again he prayed earnestly, and heaven gave rain and the soil yielded its produce.

[19]My brothers, if one of you strays from the truth and someone brings him back, [20]let him be assured that he who turns a sinner back from the wandering of his way will save his soul from death and a great number of sins.[z]

---

u) The days just preceding Christ's return, vs. 8.
v) As animals are fattened, not for their own enjoyment but for the butcher.
w) See note at I Tim. 3:1.
x) The Lord's disciples anointed some sick people with oil, Mark 16:3. Oil is medicinal, cf. Isa. 1:6; Luke 10:34, but heartfelt prayer must accompany its application, vs. 15.
y) No confession to a priest or to a group is here intimated.
z) James does not mean that the prayer of faith covers the sins of him who prays but of him who is prayed for as he receives salvation. Spiritual health is more important than physical health. To pray for the salvation of souls and spiritual growth is an essential part of intercessory prayer.

SUBJECT	INSTRUCTION	ILLUSTRATION/EXPLANATION
Trials (1:2-8)	-consider it complete joy	
	-let steadfastness have	-trials produce steadfastness, which makes you
	full play	complete, rounded out, with no defects
	-ask God for wisdom	
	-ask in faith, without doubt	-doubter like wave of sea
		-doubter will not receive anything from the Lord

JAMES SUBJECT BY SUBJECT

SUBJECT	INSTRUCTION	ILLUSTRATION/EXPLANATION

JAMES AT A GLANCE

THEME OF JAMES:

SEGMENT DIVISIONS

		CHAPTER THEMES
	1	
	2	
	3	
	4	
	5	

Author:

Date:

Purpose:

Key Words:

brothers

faith

perfect (complete)

judge(s) (judged, judgment, criticize)

law

1 PETER

The hour had come for the Shepherd to be smitten and for the sheep to be scattered. Jesus chose to spend His final hours with His eleven, preparing them for the tribulation that would come.

Yet after Jesus' resurrection and ascension, the tribulation seemed to be relatively mild. The disgruntled Pharisees wanted to shut up the men who were turning Jerusalem upside down with their teaching and miracles, but nothing seemed life-threatening.

Then the first stone was thrown. Stephen, the first martyr, was brought to the ground. Saul watched him die. In hearty agreement with Stephen's death, Saul went to the high priest to gain permission to round up those of the Way who were spreading this gospel. Saul's purge was short-lived. Jesus saved Saul on the road to Damascus and changed his name to Paul. But the persecution of Christians continued. Herod the king became the adversary of believers, and Jews who had come to know Jesus as the Messiah were scattered abroad to other Roman provinces.

However, it wasn't until Nero that the persecution of Christians reached beyond the confines of Judah. Rumor had it that Nero had burned Rome so he could rebuild it as he wanted. Needing a scapegoat to divert attention from himself, Nero blamed the fire on the Christians and began the systematic persecution of God's children.

Jesus had prepared Peter for the world's tribulation; now Peter would prepare others. Peter wrote his first epistle on the eve of Nero's persecution, about A.D. 63 or 64.

Nero died in A.D. 68, but not before Rome put Peter to death.

THINGS TO DO

1. Read through 1 Peter and do the following:
   a. In the initial verses of the book Peter describes himself and states to whom he is writing, and in the last verses of the book, he tells why he wrote this epistle. Record your insights about the author and his purpose in writing on the 1 PETER AT A GLANCE chart following 1 Peter.
   b. Pay close attention to what you see about the recipients of 1 Peter. What is their condition? What is going on in their midst? Record what you learn about them on the OBSERVATIONS CHART following 1 Peter.
2. Read 1 Peter chapter by chapter, looking for and marking in a distinctive way the key words (and their synonyms and pronouns) that are listed on 1 PETER AT A GLANCE. Also remember to mark the words such as *grace* and references to the devil which you are marking throughout your New Testament. In the margin list the truths you learn from every mention of key words. This is imperative if you want to understand 1 Peter.
3. Peter gives the reader many commands or instructions about things to

do. You notice these by the construction of the sentence. The verb usually comes first and the "you" is implied. An example is seen in 1:13: "Brace up your minds for action."

a. Underline the instructions or commands that Peter gives throughout the book. Then list these under "General Instructions" on the OBSERVATIONS CHART.

b. As you evaluate these instructions and commands you will see that 1 Peter was written not only for the recipients but also for you. Think about how these instructions apply to your own life.

4. Peter also gives instructions to specific groups of people such as servants (slaves), wives, husbands, etc. List his instructions to each group under the proper heading on the OBSERVATIONS CHART.

5. From what you have read, why do you think the believers are to do these things? In other words, what future event is the motivation for living life in accordance with Peter's exhortations?

6. Finally, summarize the theme of each chapter and record these themes on 1 PETER AT A GLANCE and in the space above the chapter number. Don't forget to record the overall theme of 1 Peter.

THINGS TO THINK ABOUT

1. What have you learned about the way you are to live? How are you to respond to others, even when they are not living properly or treating you properly? What is Jesus' example in 1 Peter 2:21–25? Will you follow it?

2. As you think about what those believers were suffering, should you be surprised if you undergo the same? What will suffering accomplish in your life?

3. Even if you don't have a Nero in your life, is your adversary the devil still prowling about like a lion, seeking whom he may devour? What are you to do, according to 1 Peter?

4. When our Lord Jesus Christ returns, will you be found standing firm in the true grace that has been provided you? What must you do or change in order to be prepared to see Him face-to-face?

THE FIRST GENERAL EPISTLE OF

PETER

Date of writing: c. A.D. 65, at Babylon

1 PETER, AN APOSTLE OF JESUS
Christ, to the exiles of the Dispersion[a] in Pontus, Galatia, Cappadocia, Asia and Bithynia,[b] [2]chosen in
accordance with the foreknowledge of
God the Father, and consecrated by
the Spirit to be obedient to Jesus
Christ, and to be sprinkled with His
blood: Grace to you and peace in increasing measure.

[3]Blessed be the God and Father of
our Lord Jesus Christ who according
to His ample mercy has given us new
birth into a life of hope, through the
resurrection of Jesus Christ from the
dead, [4]to an inheritance imperishable,
unsullied, and unfading that is kept
safely in heaven for you [5]who by the
power of God are protected through
faith for a salvation that is ready to be
revealed in the last time.

[6]You rejoice in this, although now
for a little while, if it must be, you
are distressed by various trials, [7]so that
the testing of your faith, far more
precious than perishable gold that is
tested by fire, may prove to be for
praise and glory and honor when Jesus
Christ is revealed, [8]whom having not
seen, you love. In Him you have faith,
though now you do not see Him, and
you rejoice with inexpressible and
heavenly joy, [9]while you obtain the
salvation of your souls as the goal of
your faith.

[10]About this salvation the prophets,
who prophesied of the grace intended
for you, [11]made inquiry and research
to find out to whom or to what time
the Spirit of Christ within them
pointed, in predicting the sufferings
that would happen to Christ, and the
glory that would follow them. [12]It was
disclosed to the prophets that they
were rendering their ministries not for
themselves, but for you, concerning
the things which have now been declared to you by those who have
preached the good news to you by
means of the Holy Spirit sent from
heaven, things in which the angels
long to stoop and look.

[13]Brace up your minds for action,
therefore, and be alert, and fix your
hope fully on the grace that will be
coming to you when Jesus Christ is
revealed.[c] [14]As obedient children, do
not shape your lives by the passions
that controlled you in your previous
ignorance; [15]instead, as the One who
called you is holy, so you yourselves
should be holy in all your conduct;
[16]for it is written,[d] "You shall be holy,
because I am holy."

[17]Besides, if you address Him as
Father, who impartially judges according to each one's work, you need to
behave reverently during the time of
your exiles, [18]well aware that you have
been ransomed from your futile ways
such as traditionally came down from
your forefathers, not with perishable

a) The Dispersion, Gk. *diaspora*, relates to Israelites who, usually under persecution, *cf.* Jer. 25:34,
were driven out of their land as a result of national disobedience to God, Lev. 26:33; Deut.
4:25-28. In N.T. times some of these families had never returned to their land. There were others
who had been obliged to flee from Jerusalem because they believed in Jesus as their Messiah, Acts
8:1, 4; 11:19. See note at James 1:1. b) These five provinces were all in Asia Minor.
c) As Christ suggests for His return, *cf.* Luke 12:35, 36. d) Lev. 11:44.

things such as silver or gold, 19but with the precious blood of Christ as that of a flawless and spotless lamb, 20foreknown, to be sure, before the foundation of the world, but disclosed at the end of the times for your sakes, 21who through Him are believers in God, who raised Him from the dead and gave Him glory. So your faith and hope rest in God.

22With your souls purified by obeying the truth that issues in sincere love for the brothers, you should love one another fervently from the heart. 23For you have been born again, not from a perishable but an imperishable seed through the living and lasting message of God; for,e 24"All flesh is like grass and all its glory like the flower of the grass; the grass withers and the bloom drops off, 25but the word of the Lord endures forever." And this is the message of good news that has been preached to you.

2 THEREFORE, LAY ASIDE ALL malice and all deceit, all pretense, envy, and slander; 2like newborn babes, be thirsty for the unadulterated, spiritual milk, so that by its use you may grow up to salvation, 3presuming you have tasted how good the Lord is.

4Come to Him, a living Stone rejected by men, it is true, but chosen by God and precious, 5and be built up as living stones into a spiritual house, a dedicated priesthood, to offer spiritual sacrifices that through Jesus Christ are acceptable to God.

6It is therefore contained in Scripture,f "See, I place in Zion a chosen, precious cornerstone, and he who believes in Him will never be put to shame." 7To you, then, who believe, He is precious, but to the unbelieving, "the stone which the builders rejected, this has become the main cornerstone," 8andg "a stone to trip over and a rock to make them fall." They stub their toes because they disbelieve the message; they were destined for this. 9But you are a chosen race, a royal priesthood, a holy nation, a people of His acquisition, so that you may proclaim

the perfections of Him who called you out of darkness into His marvelous light, 10you who once were no people but are now the people of God, who once experienced no mercy but have now received mercy.

11I implore you, dear friends, as aliens and exiles to keep from gratifying fleshly desires such as war against the soul. 12Conduct yourselves well among the Gentiles so that, although they may defame you as criminals, they may see your good works and glorify God in the day of visitation.h

13Be submissive to every human institution for the Lord's sake, whether to the emperor as supreme, 14or to governors as commissioned by him to bring criminals to justice and to encourage the well-behaved. 15For this is God's will, that by behaving well you should silence the ignorance of thoughtless people. 16Enjoy liberty, not by employing freedom to cover up wickedness but as slavesi of God. 17Treat everyone honorably; have love for the brothers; revere God; respect the emperor.

18You domestic slaves should with unqualified respect be submissive to your masters, not only to the kind and considerate but also to those who are harsh; 19for this is meritorious, if with consciousness of God one endures the pain of unjust sufferings. 20For what merit is there in standing a beating for doing wrong? But if you bear patiently with suffering when you are doing right, this is pleasing to God.

21To such experience you have been called; for Christ also suffered for you and left behind an example, that you might follow in His footsteps. 22He committed no sin, neither was deceit found in His mouth, 23who did not return the insult when He was insulted; who did not threaten when abused, but committed Himself to the Righteous Judge. 24He Himself carried our sins in His own body on the cross, so that we might die to sins and live to righteousness. By His wounds you were healed.

25For then you were straying like

---

e) Isa. 40:6-8.   f) Isa. 28:16.   g) Verses 7, 8 are cited from Isa. 8:14; Ps. 118:22.
h) When God's judgment will fall.   i) See note at Matt. 13:27.

sheep, but now you have returned to the Shepherd and Guardian of your souls.

3 IN A SIMILAR WAY YOU WIVES should be submissive to your own husbands, so that if any of them will not be persuaded by the message, they may without message be won over by the conduct of their wives, ²as they observe your chaste and respectful behavior. ³Your adornment should not be outward — braided hair, putting on gold trinkets, or putting on robes;ʲ ⁴instead it should be the inner personality of the heart with the imperishable qualities of a gentle and quiet spirit, something of surpassing value in God's sight.

⁵For in this way the holy women of the past, who fixed their hope on God, adorned themselves, submissive as they were to their own husbands. ⁶Sarah, for instance, obeyed Abraham, whom she called "Master." You have become her daughters if you do right and are not terrorized by any fear.

⁷By the same token you husbands need to live understandingly with your wives as with a weaker vessel, rendering them honor as joint heirs with you of the grace of life, so that your praying may not be hindered.

⁸Finally, let all of you be harmonious, sympathetic, loving as brothers, compassionate, humbleminded, ⁹returning no evil for evil or cursing for cursing. Quite to the contrary you will bless in return, because you are called for this, so as to inherit a blessing. ¹⁰Forᵏ "he who wants to enjoy life and see happy days must keep his tongue from speaking evil and his lips from uttering deceit. ¹¹He must turn away from wrong and do right; he must search for peace and keep after it. ¹²For the Lord's eyes are on the righteous and His ears are attentive to their prayer, but the Lord's face is set against those who practice evil."

¹³And who will hurt you if you become eager for the right? ¹⁴But even if you suffer on account of righteousness, you will be blessed. Be neither terrified nor troubled by theirˡ threat, ¹⁵but revere Christ in your hearts as Lord and be always ready to make a defense to everyone who asks you for a reason of the hope that is within you; but do it gently and reverently. ¹⁶Maintain a clear conscience so that, in case you are slandered, those who falsely accuse your good Christian conduct may be ashamed; ¹⁷for it is better, if it is God's will, to suffer for doing right than for doing wrong.

¹⁸For Christ also once died for sins on your behalf, the just on behalf of the unjust, so that He might bring us to God, being put to death physically but made alive in the Spirit, ¹⁹in whom Heᵐ went and preached to the spirits in prison, ²⁰who were disobedient at the time when God's patience was waiting while Noah was constructing an ark in which a few, in fact eight souls, were brought safely through the water.

²¹Its counterpart, baptism, saves you now, not by removal of physical filth but the earnest seeking of a conscience that is clear in God's presence, through the resurrection of Jesus Christ, ²²who is at God's right hand; for He went to heaven, and angels, authorities, and powers are subject to Him.

4 SINCE CHRIST, THEN, HAS SUFfered physically, you also must arm yourselves with the same attitude; for he who has suffered physically has gained relief from sin, ²so that he no longer lives by human passions but for the rest of his natural life he lives by what God wills. ³For to have been practicing the ways of the Gentiles heretofore is quite enough, indulging in unbridled lusts, in passions, in drinking parties, in carousings, in dissipations and forbidden idolatries.

---

j) Obviously Peter is not forbidding attractive appearance but stressing the greater value of inner virtue. Sarah is used as an example of this kind of virtue, vs. 6. Sarah was certainly not unattractive in outward appearance or the princes of Pharaoh would not have commended her to him, nor would she have found favor in his sight had that been the case, Gen. 12:10-20. But above all Sarah possessed "imperishable qualities of a gentle and quiet spirit," vs. 4.   k) Ps. 34:12-15.
l) "Their" alludes to the enemies of righteousness.
m) It was by the Holy Spirit that Christ preached through Noah to men of his day who are now in prison because they rejected the message.

[4]They[n] are surprised that you are not sharing the same life of unbridled dissipation with them, and they are reviling you for it, [5]but they must render an account to Him who stands ready to judge the living and the dead. [6]For this reason the good news was preached to the dead,[o] so that, whereas they are judged as men, they might live with God spiritually.

[7]The end of all things is near; therefore be self-controlled so that you can pray. [8]Above all else, cherish intense love for one another,[p] for love covers up many sins. [9]Practice hospitality toward one another without grumbling. [10]Let each one serve one another to the measure of his endowment, as good stewards of God's richly varied grace. [11]If you are speaking, let it be as speaking God's messages; if you are serving, let it be with the strength that God supplies, so that in it all God may be glorified through Jesus Christ, to whom be the glory and the dominion forever and ever. Amen.

[12]Do not be surprised, dear friends, at the fiery test that is coming upon you, as if you were experiencing something unheard of. [13]Instead, be joyful that you are sharing to some degree the sufferings of Christ, in order that at the revealing of His glory you may be full of joy. [14]If you are defamed for the name of Christ, you are blessed, because the Spirit of glory, yes, the Spirit of God, is resting on you.

[15]Of course none of you should suffer as a murderer or a thief or a criminal or a meddler in others' affairs; [16]but if you suffer as a Christian, do not be ashamed, but praise God because you bear that name. [17]For the time has come for judgment to begin with God's household; and if it starts with us, what will be the destiny of those who disobey the good news from God? [18]And if the righteous person is saved with difficulty, what chance have the impious and sinful?

[19]For this reason let those who are suffering according to the will of God, entrust their souls to God, the faithful Creator, while they do what is right.

5 THEREFORE, AS A FELLOW ELDER[q] and a witness of Christ's sufferings, a sharer, too, in the glory that is to be revealed, I appeal to the elders among you: [2]shepherd God's flock that has been entrusted to you,[r] not because you have to but willingly, because God wants you to; not out of greed for gain but eagerly; [3]not lording it over those who are under your charge but being examples to your flock. [4]And with the appearing of the Chief Shepherd you will be awarded the never-fading crown[s] of glory.

[5]So also the younger men should defer to those who are older, while you all put on the apron of humility toward each other,[t] because[u] "God sets Himself against the arrogant, but He grants grace to the humble." [6]Humble yourselves, therefore, under the mighty hand of God, so that He may in due time raise you up. [7]Throw all your anxiety upon Him, for His concern is about you.

[8]Exercise self-control. Be on your guard. Your opponent, the devil, prowls around like a roaring lion in search of someone to devour. [9]Firm in your faith, resist him, aware that throughout the world, sufferings of this kind are imposed upon your brothers.

[10]But the God of all grace, who has called you to His eternal glory in Christ, will, after you have suffered awhile, Himself equip, stabilize, strengthen, and firmly establish you. [11]To Him be dominion forever and ever. Amen.

[12]I have written you this brief letter with aid of Silvanus,[v] your faithful brother as I esteem him, to encourage you and to testify that this is the true grace of God. Stand firm in it.

[13]She who is at Babylon,[w] who is

---

n) The unregenerated. *Cf.* ch. 3:14.   o) That is, to those who are now dead.
p) Such as God's love that forgives.   q) See note at I Tim. 3:1.
r) Compare Christ's commission to Peter, John 21:15-17.   s) See note at Phil. 4:2.
t) Peter has not forgotten the footwashing in the upper room, John 13:1-17, our Lord's example of humility.   u) Prov. 3:34; James 4:6.
v) Silvanus, sometimes called Silas, was one of Paul's frequent companions. See note at I Thess. 1:1.   w) Some scholars think that Babylon is used here figuratively for Rome.

chosen together with you, sends you greetings, and so does my son Mark.[x] [14]Greet one another with a kiss of love.

Peace to all of you who are in Christ Jesus.

---

x) See note at Col. 4:10.

AUTHOR

RECIPIENTS

GENERAL INSTRUCTIONS

INSTRUCTIONS TO

Wives

Husbands

Elders

Younger men

Slaves

THEME OF 1 PETER:

SEGMENT DIVISIONS

Author:

Date:

Purpose:

	CHAPTER THEMES
	1
	2
	3
	4
	5

Key Words:
suffering (and all its synonyms)

grace

glory

salvation

Jesus Christ

God

Holy Spirit

called

chosen

holy (dedicated)

2 PETER

A fisherman by trade, Peter had been captured and transformed by a Shepherd. Is it any wonder that even in Peter's darkest hour, the welfare of God's sheep was uppermost in his mind?

Ever since the day he stood with Jesus by a fire, the morning air full of the aroma of roasting fish, Peter had known the way he would die. But Peter would be faithful. His concern about his death and the way he would die would not override his concern for his Lord's sheep, the sheep Jesus had commissioned him to feed and shepherd. And so, sometime around A.D. 63 or 64, Peter writes "to those who have received a faith of the same kind as ours."

In A.D. 64, according to tradition, Peter was crucified upside down for the Lord he once denied knowing. How Peter had grown in the grace and knowledge of his God!

THINGS TO DO

1. To familiarize yourself with 2 Peter, read the book without stopping or taking notes. The message of this short book is easily seen in each of the paragraphs, so as you read, notice the content of each. You will see that Peter contrasts certain things. Based on this first reading, what major contrast is Peter making in this book?

2. Read 2 Peter again, looking for facts concerning the author (pronouns such as *I, we, us*) and the recipients (pronouns such as *you, your*). Mark these in a distinctive way in the text. Then on the OBSERVATIONS CHART following 2 Peter record the answers to the following questions: What does the author say about himself? When in his life is he writing? Who are the recipients? How are they described?

3. In a distinctive way, mark in the text the key words (and their synonyms and pronouns) which are listed on the 2 PETER AT A GLANCE chart. Then list in the margin the truths you learn by marking these key words. Be as thorough as possible because the lists will help you see the flow of the book.

4. Read through 2 Peter again and look for specific instructions that Peter gives the readers concerning their behavior and belief. Record these on the OBSERVATIONS CHART under "Instructions." Also look for and note any people or groups of people of which Peter warns them to beware.

5. In this book, Peter states specifically why he is writing. Look for and underline any verse in which Peter says, *"I am writing you."* Also, underline any other verses that indicate his purpose in writing. Record his purpose for writing on 2 PETER AT A GLANCE.

6. Summarize the message of each paragraph and record its theme on 2 PETER AT A GLANCE. Then determine the chapter themes and the book theme and record these in the appropriate places on the chart and in the text at the start of each chapter.

THINGS TO THINK ABOUT

1. What would it take to live your life so that you may be found spotless and blameless at Christ's coming?
2. Is there a danger today that false teachers will arise among the people, as in Peter's day? What do you need to know to be able to detect them?
3. How can you keep from falling from your own steadfastness? Practically, what do you need to do in order to grow in the grace and knowledge of Jesus Christ?

THE SECOND GENERAL EPISTLE OF

PETER

Date of writing: c. A.D. 66-67

1 SIMON PETER, A SLAVE[a] AND APOStle of Jesus Christ, to those who through the righteousness of our God and Savior Jesus Christ have been allotted a faith as precious as ours:[b] [2]Grace and peace be yours in abundance through knowledge of God and Jesus our Lord. [3]For His divine power has bestowed on us every requisite for life and godliness, through knowing Him who called us to His own glory and excellence. [4]Through these there have been granted us great and precious promised blessings, so that by means of them you might become sharers of the divine nature, having escaped from the corruption in the world that arises from passion.

[5]For this very reason do your utmost to supplement your faith with virtue, your virtue with knowledge, [6]your knowledge with self-control, your self-control with patience, your patience with piety, [7]your piety with brotherly affection, and your brotherly affection with love. [8]For if you possess these qualities increasingly, they will render your knowledge of our Lord Jesus Christ neither inactive nor unproductive, [9]while he who does not have these is blind, short-visioned, oblivious of the cleansing from his former sins.

[10]Exert yourselves the more then, brothers, to confirm[c] your calling and election, for if you practice these things you will never stumble, [11]for so an entrance into the eternal kingdom of our Lord and Savior Jesus Christ will be liberally provided for you.

[12]I will, therefore, always remind you of these matters, even though you are aware of them and are established in the truth now available. [13]Still, I think it my duty, so long as I remain in this human body, to arouse you by reminding you; [14]for I know that shortly my body will be put off, as our Lord Jesus Christ made clear to me.[d] [15]Besides, I will make every effort to enable each one of you to keep these things in mind after I am gone; [16]for when we made known to you the power and coming of our Lord Jesus Christ, we were not following cleverly devised fables. On the contrary, we were eyewitnesses of His majesty; [17]for when He received honor and glory from God the Father, a voice was borne to Him from the supreme Glory,[e] "This is My Son, My Beloved, in whom I am delighted." [18]And we heard this voice borne to us from heaven, when we were with Him on the sacred mountain.[f]

[19]So we have the prophetic message reaffirmed,[g] to which you do well to pay attention as you would to a light that shines in a dark place until the day dawns and the Daystar arises in your hearts, [20]with this most clearly understood, that no prophetic Scripture can be explained by one's unaided mental powers. [21]Because no prophecy

a) See note at Matt. 13:27.　b) Including, therefore, all believers in Christ.
c) That is to say, validate your faith by what you do.　d) John 21:18.　e) Matt. 17:1-5.
f) The mountain where Christ was transfigured in the presence of Peter, James, and John.
g) By the gospel of Christ which the writer has been preaching.

ever came by the will of man; instead men spoke from God as they were carried along by the Holy Spirit.

2 BUT THERE WERE ALSO FALSE prophets among the people, just as there will be false teachers among you — the kind that will shrewdly introduce ruinous heresies, even denying the Master who bought them and so bringing on themselves swift destruction. ²Many will follow along in their shameless ways, on whose account the way of truth will be maligned. ³Motivated by greed, they will exploit you with their counterfeit arguments.

From of old their sentence has been hanging over them and their destruction has not been dormant. ⁴For if God did not spare the angels who sinned but committed them to the black dungeons of hell[h] to be kept for judgment, ⁵and did not spare the ancient world but preserved Noah, a preacher of righteousness, and seven with him, when He brought a flood upon a godless world; ⁶and if He condemned the cities of Sodom and Gomorrah by turning them to ashes, an example to show the godless what is to happen to them, ⁷and if He rescued upright Lot, distressed as he was by the immoral behavior of the lawless ⁸(for day after day as that righteous man lived among them, his upright soul was tortured at seeing and hearing their lawless doings), ⁹then the Lord knows how to rescue the godly from temptation and to keep the wicked under punishment for the day of judgment.

¹⁰This is especially true of those who yield to fleshly desires, indulge in polluting passions, and despise authority. Bold, headstrong as they are, they have no qualms at libeling glorious beings, ¹¹whereas angels, far superior to them in strength and might, do not pronounce a defaming judgment against them before the Lord. ¹²These, however, like irrational brutes that are naturally born to be caught and killed, while maligning what they do not know, will also be destroyed in the same destruction; ¹³they will be punished with suffering for the suffering they caused.

Revelry during the day is their idea of enjoyment; they are foul blots and blemishes that revel in their lusts as they stuff themselves at your table. ¹⁴They have their eyes full of adultery and their appetite for sin is never satisfied. They lure unsteady souls. Their hearts are practiced in greed — accursed children! ¹⁵Leaving the straight path, they have strayed as they have followed in the tracks of Balaam,[i] the son of Bosor, who loved the wages of wickedness. ¹⁶But he was rebuked for his own misdeed; a dumb beast of burden, speaking[j] with human voice, restrained the prophet's madness.

¹⁷These are waterless wells, hurricane-driven winds for which the gloom of darkness is reserved. ¹⁸For as they utter arrogant nonsense, they entice, through appeal to immoral passions of the flesh, those who have barely escaped from those who live in error. ¹⁹While they promise them liberty they are themselves slaves of corruption; for a person is a slave to whatever overpowers him.

²⁰For if those who have escaped the contaminations of the world through the knowledge of our Lord and Savior Jesus Christ, are again entangled and overcome by them, then their last condition becomes worse than the first. ²¹For it would be better for them never to have known the way of righteousness than, after knowing it, to turn back from the holy commandment that was imparted to them.[k] ²²In their case the true proverb[l] is realized, "A dog returns to his own vomit, and the scrubbed sow to wallowing in the mire."

3 THIS, DEAR FRIENDS, IS NOW THE second letter I am writing you, to

---

h) Gk. *tartarosos.* The Greek Tartarus corresponds with the Hebrew Gehenna, the abode of the wicked and unbelieving dead. See note at Mark 9:43.
i) Balaam was a prophet of God, but he used his gift for personal gain, Num. 22:25. *Cf.* Jude 11; Rev. 2:14.　j) Num. 22:26-30.
k) Compare Peter's strong language in this chapter with our Lord's pronouncements against the scribes and Pharisees recorded in Matt. 23:13-36.　　l) Prov. 26:11.

arouse your pure minds by way of remembrance, [2]so that you may be mindful of the sayings that were spoken beforehand by the holy prophets, and the commands of the Lord and Savior spoken by your apostles.

[3]First of all you should understand that in the last days scoffers will come on the scene with their scoffing, behaving in accord with their own lusts, [4]and saying, "What about His promised coming? For ever since the forefathers fell asleep, everything has remained as it was from the beginning of creation."

[5]They willfully ignore the fact that long ago there were heavens by the word of God, and an earth standing partly above and partly amidst water, [6]by means of which the then existing world was destroyed, deluged as it was by water. [7]At present, however, the heavens and the earth are by the same word stored up for burning, and reserved for the day of judgment and the destruction of godless people.[m]

[8]But do not overlook this one fact, dear friends, that with the Lord one day is as a thousand years and a thousand years as one day.[n] [9]The Lord is not negligent about His promise as some think of negligence; instead, He is exercising patience with you, unwilling that any should perish, but that all should come to repentance.[o]

[10]But the day of the Lord will come like a thief. Then with a tremendous roar the heavens will pass away, the elements will be dissolved with fire, and the earth and the works in it will be burned up.

[11]Since all these things are to be dissolved in this manner, how consecrated and reverent your behavior should be, [12]as you are expecting and hastening on the coming of the day of God, because of which the heavens will be on fire and be dissolved, and the elements will meet with fire. [13]But in accord with His promise we are looking for new heavens and a new earth in which righteousness is at home.[p]

[14]Therefore, dear friends, since you have these expectations, do your utmost to be found at peace with Him — spotless and blameless. [15]And regard the continued patience of our Lord as salvation, as our dear brother Paul also has written you, according to the wisdom that has been granted him, [16]speaking of those things, as he does in all his letters. There are some statements in them which are hard to understand. The untaught and unsteady twist those writings, as they do the other Scriptures,[q] to their own ruin.

[17]You therefore, dear friends, forewarned as you are, be on your guard so that you may not be carried away by the error of the lawless, and lose your own stability; [18]but grow in the grace and knowledge of our Lord and Savior Jesus Christ, to whom be glory now and to the day of eternity. Amen.

m) Forgetting the Creator, they are unmindful of the Judge; insisting on license, they get themselves enslaved. *Cf.* Isa. 66:15; Dan. 7:9.   n) Ps. 90:4.
o) Grace, not judgment, is the dominant note in God's music.   p) *Cf.* Matt. 6:33.
q) The N.T. is here ranked with the O.T. as Scripture.

PETER

RECIPIENTS

INSTRUCTIONS

WARNINGS

THEME OF 2 PETER:

Author:

SEGMENT
DIVISIONS

Date:

		PARAGRAPH THEMES	CHAPTER THEMES
		1:1–4	1
		1:5–11	
		1:12–21	
		2:1–22	2
		3:1–7	3
		3:8–13	
		3:14–18	

Purpose:

Key Words:

prophecy
(prophet,
prophetic)

knowledge
(know,
knowing,
known)

remind
(remem-
brance)

true (truth)

do your utmost
(exert)

false

destroyed
(destruction)

promise

1 JOHN

As a boy, John may have thought of Jesus as just a cousin, one of the sons of Aunt Mary, his mother Salome's sister. Little did John realize that someday he would be chosen by God to be one of Jesus' twelve apostles.

He had been known as a "son of thunder" (Mark 3:17); but a transformation had taken place. Now he was called "the disciple whom Jesus loved."

Even though John's name is not mentioned in this epistle, there is much evidence that he is the author. John had been with Jesus. He had seen Him, heard Him, touched Him, and been filled with His love. This is evident as you hear John's fatherly heart for those who belong to Jesus. He loves the fathers, the young men, the dear children. Yet as he writes about the antichrists and deceivers, you can hear the rumble of thunder in the background.

We don't know when John wrote this first epistle. It may have been between A.D. 85 and 95, when he was in Ephesus before being exiled to the Isle of Patmos. Love—and thunder—compelled him to write. He had to protect his children from a deception that could darken their understanding if they were not warned about the brewing storm of gnosticism—a teaching which could keep them from having fellowship with him (1 John 1:3).

THINGS TO DO

1. If you want to handle a passage of Scripture accurately you must always interpret it in the light of its context. Context simply means that which goes "with" (con) the "text." Context must always rule when it comes to interpretation. Identifying the author's purpose for writing will help you discern the context of a passage. What the author says, he says in the light of his purpose for writing.

   In this particular letter the author tells us his purpose in seven different verses: 1:4; 2:1, 12–14, 21, and 26. Then in 1 John 5:13 he concludes by summarizing his purpose for writing. Read these verses and record his reasons for writing on the chart I AM WRITING TO YOU following 1 John. Then read 1 John 5:13 and record on the 1 JOHN AT A GLANCE chart the author's purpose for writing.

2. One of the major heresies the church would face was gnosticism. Gnosticism wasn't in full bloom in John's time, but the seeds had been sown. Understanding gnosticism will help you better understand why John concentrated on the truths contained in his writing. Gnosticism promoted a supremacy based on knowledge. It divided Christians into "spiritual ones" and ordinary believers, and it denied that Christ was fully divine and fully human.

3. Now read 1 John chapter by chapter and observe the text, using the instructions outlined in the observation section in the introduction of this New Testament.

   a. Mark in the text in a distinctive way each of the key words (and their synonyms and pronouns) listed on 1 JOHN AT A GLANCE. When you finish marking these words, go to the chart 1 JOHN KEY WORDS following 1 John and record the number of times each word is used in each chapter. Then add them up to see the number of times each word is used in 1 John. Doing this will help you see the main themes of 1 John.

b. John uses a number of contrasts in order to make his point: light/darkness; children of God/children of the devil; etc. Watch for these contrasts, and in the margin next to where they are found list what you learn from them.

c. When you finish your observations on each chapter:

1) List in the margin the truths you learn from each of the key words.

2) Remember, 1 John was written "in order that you may know." When you finish reading all five chapters, trace throughout 1 John the repeated use of the word *know* and record what you learn from the text on the chart WHAT I CAN KNOW and HOW I CAN KNOW IT following 1 John. As you make this list, watch the matters John deals with in respect to wrong behavior or wrong belief.

3) Keep a running list of everything you learn about God, Jesus Christ, and the Spirit from this book. Record it in the margin.

4. Record the theme of each chapter on 1 JOHN AT A GLANCE and in the text above the chapter number. Fill in any remaining information called for on the chart.

THINGS TO THINK ABOUT

1. Based on the criteria given in this book, how can you know whether or not you have eternal life?

2. What have you learned about sin from 1 John? Do you practice sin or righteousness?

3. Do you love the things of the world? Are you caught up in proud display, in boasting, or in desiring whatever your eyes see?

4. According to 1 John 3, what are you to do when your heart condemns you?

5. Does your belief about Jesus Christ match what 1 John teaches about Him?

THE FIRST EPISTLE OF

JOHN

Date of writing: c. A.D. 65-85

1 WE ARE WRITING TO YOU ABOUT the Word of Life: He was from the beginning;[a] we have heard Him, we have seen Him with our eyes, we have looked at Him, and our hands have touched Him. [2]Yes, the Life has been revealed and we have seen and are witnessing and are announcing to you the eternal Life who existed with the Father and has been revealed to us. [3]We saw Him and we heard Him and are telling you, so that you too may enjoy fellowship along with us. And this fellowship of ours is with the Father and with His Son Jesus Christ. [4]This we are writing you so that our joy may be complete.

[5]The message we heard from Him and announce to you is this: God is Light and in Him there is no darkness whatever. [6]If we say that we enjoy fellowship with Him while we are walking in the dark, we are lying and not practicing the truth. [7]If, however, we walk in the light, as He Himself is in the light, then we enjoy fellowship with one another, and the blood of His Son Jesus cleanses us from all sin.

[8]If we say, "We have no sin," we are deluding ourselves and the truth is not in us.[b] [9]If we confess our sins, He is faithful and just to forgive us our sins and to cleanse us from all unrighteousness. [10]If we say, "We have not sinned," we make Him out to be a liar and His word is not in us.

2 DEAR[c] CHILDREN, I WRITE YOU these things so you may not sin, and if anyone does sin, we have a counsel for our defense in the Father's presence, Jesus Christ the Righteous One. [2]He is Himself an atoning sacrifice for our sins, and not for ours only but also for the whole world.

[3]By this token we are sure that we know Him, if we observe His commands. [4]He who says, "I know Him," and does' not keep His commands, is a liar and the truth is not in him. [5]But whoever observes His word, in him the love of God has truly reached maturity. In this way we are sure that we are in Him: [6]one who claims to remain in Him ought himself to live the way He lived.

[7]Dear friends, I am writing you no new command, but only the old command which you have had from the beginning. The old command is the message you have heard. [8]On the other hand I am writing you a new command,[d] realized in Him and in you, because the darkness is passing and the true light is already shining. [9]He who claims to be in the light and hates

---

a) Compare John 1:1.
b) Light, life, sinlessness — all alike are God's and not ours, except as His gifts.
c) Here and sometimes elsewhere in the epistle John uses the diminutive form of the Greek word for children, *teknia*. He is writing to members of God's family in Christ and thus addresses them in this tender way, chs. 2:1, 12, 28; 3:7, 18; 4:4; 5:21.
d) A fresh presentation of the eternal principle of love, without which life, light, and sinlessness are inconceivable.

his brother is in darkness to this very hour. [10]He who loves his brother remains in the light and there is nothing within him to occasion stumbling. [11]But he who hates his brother is in the dark and walks in the dark; he does not even know where he is going, because the darkness has blinded his eyes.

[12]I am writing you, dear children, because for His name's sake your sins have been forgiven you. [13]I am writing you, fathers, because you know Him who is from the beginning. I am writing you, young men, because you have conquered the evil one. I have written you, children, because you have come to know the Father. [14]I have written you, fathers, because you have learned to know Him who is from the beginning. I have written you, young men, because you are vigorous; God's message stays in your hearts and you have conquered the evil one.

[15]Neither love the world nor the things in the world. Whoever loves the world has not the Father's love in his heart, [16]because everything in the world, the passions of the flesh, the desires of the eyes, and the proud display of life have their origin not from the Father but from the world. [17]And the world with its lust passes away, but he who does the will of God remains forever.

[18]Children, the final hour is here and, as you have heard that antichrist is coming, even now many antichrists have arisen, from which we gather certainly that it is the last hour. [19]They went out from us but they never belonged to us; for had they been ours, they would have remained with us. But it had to become clear that not all belong to us. [20]Besides, you have an anointing[e] from the Holy One and you know all things.[f] [21]The reason I am writing is not because you do not know the truth, but because you know it and that nothing false originates from the truth.

[22]Who is the liar if it is not the one who denies that Jesus is the Christ? He is the antichrist who denies the Father and the Son. [23]No one who denies the Son has the Father.[g] Whoever acknowledges the Son has the Father as well.

[24]What you heard from the beginning, let that stay with you. If what you heard from the beginning stays with you, then you will remain in union with the Son and with the Father. [25]And this is what He Himself has promised us, eternal life.

[26]I am writing you these things about those who are trying to mislead you. [27]As for you, the anointing you have received from Him remains within you, and you stand in no need of teaching from anyone; but as His anointing instructs you about everything and is true and is no lie, so keep in union with Him just as it was taught you.

[28]And now, dear children, remain in Him so that when He appears we may have confidence and may not shrink in shame from Him at His coming. [29]If you know that He is righteous, you also are sure that everyone who practices righteousness has been born of Him.

3 SEE WHAT A WEALTH OF LOVE THE Father has lavished on us, that we should be called the children of God. And we are. For this reason the world does not know us, because it did not know Him.

[2]Beloved ones, we are God's children now, and what we shall be has not yet been shown; but we know that when He appears we shall resemble Him, for we shall see Him as He is. [3]And everyone who has this hope resting on Him, purifies himself as He is pure.[h]

[4]Everyone who commits sin is guilty of lawbreaking; sin is lawbreaking. [5]You know, too, that He appeared to take away sins, and in Him there is no sin. [6]No one who remains in Him

---

e) Gk, *chrisma*, meaning *an unguent* or *oil* for anointing, and symbolic of the entering of the Holy Spirit into the heart.   f) Other ancient manuscripts read "you all know."
g) Because Christ is the Way to the Father, John 14:6.
h) The Spirit purifies; the believer in Christ cooperates.

practices sin.[1] Whoever practices sinning has neither seen Him nor known Him.

[7]Dear children, no one should deceive you. He who practices righteousness is righteous, just as He Himself is righteous. [8]He who practices sin belongs to the devil, for from the beginning the devil has sinned. For this purpose the Son of God appeared, to destroy the works of the devil.

[9]No one who has been born of God commits sin, for the nature of God remains within him; because he has been born of God, he cannot practice sinning. [10]By this the children of God and the children of the devil are differentiated: anyone who does not practice righteousness, or who does not love his brother, is not from God. [11]For this is the message you have heard from the beginning, that we should love one another, [12]and not be like Cain,[j] who belonged to the evil one and murdered his brother. And for what reason did he murder him? Because his own deeds were wicked and those of his brother were righteous.

[13]Do not be surprised, brothers, if the world hates you. [14]We know that we have moved out of death into life, because we love the brothers.[k] One who does not love his brother remains in death. [15]Everyone who hates his brother is a murderer, and you know that no murderer has eternal life within him.

[16]We understand the meaning of love from this, that He laid down His life on our behalf, and we ought to lay down our lives on behalf of the brothers. [17]Whoever possesses the world's resources and notices that his brother is in need and then locks his heart against him, how is the love of God in him?

[18]Dear children, let us not love in word and tongue, but in deed and truth. [19]In this way we shall become aware that we belong to the truth, and in His presence we shall set our hearts at rest. [20]For if our hearts condemn us, God is greater than our hearts, and He knows everything.

[21]Beloved ones, if our hearts do not condemn us, then we have confidence before God, [22]and whatever we ask we receive from Him, for we observe His commands and practice what is pleasing in His sight. [23]And this is His command, that we put our faith in the name of His Son Jesus Christ and that we love one another as He commanded us. [24]He who obeys His commands remains in Him and He in him. By this we know that He remains in us, through the Spirit whom He has given us.

4 BELOVED ONES, DO NOT BELIEVE every spirit, but put the spirits to the test whether they are from God; for many false prophets have gone out into the world. [2]By this we know the Spirit of God: [3]every spirit that acknowledges Jesus Christ as having come incarnate is from God, whereas every spirit that does not acknowledge Jesus, is not from God; it is the spirit of antichrist, of whose coming you have heard. Right now he is in the world.

[4]You are from God, dear children, and have defeated them,[l] because the One in you is greater than the one in the world. [5]They are from the world, so they talk from a worldly point of view and the world listens to them. [6]We are from God. Whoever knows God listens to us. Whoever is not from God does not listen to us. In this way we distinguish the spirit of truth from the spirit of error.

[7]Beloved, let us love one another, because love springs from God and whoever loves has been born of God and knows God.[m] [8]He who does not love does not know God; for God is love. [9]As for us, the love of God was revealed by the fact that God sent His only Son into the world, that through

---

i) In a Christian sinning is a contradiction. It is the new creature's nature not to sin, vs. 9. When we sin, as Paul and John agree we do, we betray our new birth in Christ.
j) Gen. 4:8. k) A never-failing criterion of the reality of our discipleship.
l) Antichristian teachers.
m) Chapter 4:13 shows that love of our brothers in Christ is under consideration throughout the epistle.

Him we might live. [10]Love is manifested in this, not that we loved God but that He loved us and sent His Son as an atoning sacrifice for our sins.

[11]Beloved ones, if God loved us so much, we ought to love one another also. [12]No one has ever seen God. If we love one another, God remains in us and His love has been perfected in us. [13]From this we know that we remain in Him and He in us, because He has imparted His Spirit to us. [14]And we ourselves have seen and are bearing witness that the Father has sent the Son as the Savior of the world.

[15]Whoever confesses that Jesus is the Son of God, God remains in him and he in God. [16]We have come to know and have believed the love which God has for us. God is love, and he who remains in love remains in God, and God remains in him.

[17]On our part love comes to completion in this, that we face the Judgment Day confidently because we are as He is in this world. [18]Love has no fear in it; instead, perfect love expels fear, for fear involves punishment. Therefore he who fears has not reached love's perfection. [19]We love because He first loved us.

[20]If someone says, "I love God," while he hates his brother, he is a liar; for he who does not love his brother, whom he has seen, is not able to love God, whom he has not seen. [21]And this command we have from Him, that he who loves God should love his brother also.

5 EVERYONE WHO BELIEVES THAT Jesus is the Christ[n] has been born of God, and everyone who loves the Father will love the one born of Him. [2]This is how we know that we love God's children: when we love God and obey His commands. [3]For true love of God means this, that we observe His commands, and His commands are not irksome. [4]Because everyone who has been born of God conquers the world, and this is the victory that triumphs over the world, the faith that we have. [5]Who is the world's victor if not he who believes that Jesus is the Son of God?[o] [6]That One is Jesus Christ, who came by water and blood; not by the water only but by the water and by the blood. The Spirit bears witness as well, because the Spirit is the truth. [7]So there are three witnesses, [8]the Spirit, the water, and the blood, and the three are one.

[9]If we accept human testimony, God's testimony is stronger, and God's witness is this which He testified regarding His Son. [10]The believer in the Son of God possesses the witness within himself. He who disbelieves God, makes Him out to be a liar, because he has not believed in the evidence God has given regarding His Son. [11]And this is the evidence: God has granted us eternal life, and this life is in His Son. [12]He who has the Son has that life; he who does not have the Son of God does not have that life.

[13]I am writing this to you who believe in the name of God's Son in order that you may know that you have eternal life. [14]And this is the confidence we have toward Him, that if we petition anything in agreement with His will, He hears us; [15]and if we know that He listens to us whatever we may petition, then the requests we ask of Him are assured us.

[16]If anyone sees his brother commit a sin, not fatal, he will petition and will obtain life for him, presuming it is no mortal sinning. [17]There is a sin that means death; I advise no prayer for that. Every wrong is sin,[p] and there is sin which does not involve death.

[18]We know that no one who has been born of God practices sin;[q] instead, He who was born of God keeps him, and the wicked one does not get a grip on him. [19]We know that whereas the whole world lies under the

---

n) A faith that appropriates Him as Lord and Savior.   o) Cf. John 16:33.
p) This appears obvious, but repeatedly believers have thought of seemingly plausible reasons for doing wrong.
q) Cf. ch. 3:6, 9. Certainly as a new creation one does not sin habitually.

dominance of the wicked one, we belong to God. [20]And we know that the Son of God has come and has given us insight to know the true One. And we are in union with the true One, with His Son Jesus Christ. He is the true God and life eternal.

[21]Dear children, keep yourselves from idols.

1 JOHN OBSERVATIONS CHARTS

I AM WRITING TO YOU

1:4	
2:1	
2:12	
2:13	
2:14	
2:21	
2:26	

1 JOHN KEY WORDS

Chapter	Fellowship	Remain (stay)	Sin	Know (sure, certain)	Love	Born of God	Write	Light	Truth
1									
2									
3									
4									
5									
Total									

WHAT I CAN KNOW	HOW I CAN KNOW IT

1 John Observations Charts

What I Can Know	How I Can Know It

1 John at a Glance

Theme of 1 John:

Segment Divisions

	Chapter Themes
	1
	2
	3
	4
	5

Author:

Date:

Purpose:

Key Words:

fellowship

remain

sin

know

love

born of God

light

truth (true)

write (writing)

mark every reference to the devil (or evil one)

2 JOHN

A caring father can't ignore something that threatens his children. So around A.D. 90 the paternal apostle John sat down to write yet another epistle. It is short, to the point, and needful—even today.

THINGS TO DO

1. Read through 2 John as you would a letter you had just received. Then read it again and:
   a. Mark in the text the key words listed on the 2 JOHN AT A GLANCE chart.
   b. List in the margin all you learn about the recipients of this letter. Note John's feelings toward them, his instructions (or commandments) to them, and his warnings. Note also the reason for his warnings.
2. Record the theme of 2 John in the appropriate space on 2 JOHN AT A GLANCE. Then record the theme of each paragraph and fill in any other pertinent information.

THINGS TO THINK ABOUT

1. What does this book say about someone who does not remain in the teaching of Christ? Do you know someone who could fit that description? What should you do?
2. According to verse 4 some of the children are walking in truth. Are you careful to walk in all the truth you know? Do you realize that before God you are responsible to live out the truth that has been entrusted to you?
3. According to this little epistle, what does it mean to walk in love? Are you doing this?

THE SECOND EPISTLE OF

JOHN

Date of writing: c. A.D. 65-85

THE ELDER[a] TO THE ELECT LADY[b] with her children, whom I truly love, and not I alone but all those who know the truth, [2]for the sake of the truth that remains in us and will be with us forever: [3]Grace, mercy and peace will be with us from God the Father and from Jesus Christ, the Father's Son, in truth and in love.

[4]I feel extremely happy to have found among your children those who live in a true way, just as we received instruction from the Father. [5]And now I beg of you, lady, not by way of writing you a new command but instead the one we have had from the beginning, that we love one another. [6]And this love consists in our behaving in agreement with His commands; this is the command, that you walk in love, as you heard from the first.

[7]For many impostors have gone out into the world, who do not confess Christ as having come incarnated. Such a person is the deceiver and the antichrist. [8]Look out for yourselves, so that you may not lose the results of what you worked for, but may obtain a full reward.

[9]Whoever assumes leadership and does not remain in the teaching of Christ,[c] does not have God. He who remains in the teaching has both the Father and the Son. [10]If anyone comes to you who does not bring this teaching, do not receive him in your home nor extend him your greeting; [11]for he who bids him welcome makes himself a sharer of those wicked works of his.

[12]Although I have many things to write you, I would rather not use paper and ink, but I hope to have a visit with you to talk with you by word of mouth, so that our happiness may be complete.

[13]The children of your elect Sister send you greetings.

---

a) See note at I Tim. 3:1.
b) As *ekklesia*, meaning *church*, is feminine, and the church is called the bride of Christ, "Lady," Gk. *kuria*, probably refers to a local congregation or perhaps the church at large. The possibility remains, however, that Kuria is the name of a woman of John's acquaintance. c) John 7:16, 17.

THEME OF 2 JOHN:

SEGMENT
DIVISIONS

		PARAGRAPH THEMES	*Author:*
	VERSES 1–3		*Date:*
			Purpose:
	VERSES 4–11		*Key Words:*
			truth
			love
			commands
			teaching
	VERSES 12, 13		walk
			remain
			deceiver

3 JOHN

$\mathcal{L}$ove cares about the individual. Love encourages. Love rebukes. Love walks in truth. And so, in love, John wrote a third epistle before he was exiled to Patmos, where he wrote Revelation. It was around A.D. 90.

THINGS TO DO

1. Read this short letter through once. Then read the book again, marking each of the key words listed on the 3 JOHN AT A GLANCE chart. List in the margin what you learn from the key words.
2. To whom is the book written? List in the margin everything you learn about him from this letter.
3. Other names are mentioned. Who is named and what is said about each person? List this information in the margin of the text. What do you learn as you observe the contrast between these people?
4. Make a list of the instructions and warnings John gives in this short epistle.
5. Complete 3 JOHN AT A GLANCE.

THINGS TO THINK ABOUT

1. What is your testimony before others? Are you known for your love of others or for your love of yourself? Do you share what you have with others? Do you listen to others? Do you have to be first?
2. According to what John says in this epistle, what does the way you live have to do with your relationship to God?
3. Are you quick to love, to exhort, and to stand for truth? What do you need to do?

THE THIRD EPISTLE OF

JOHN

Date of writing: c. A.D. 65-85

THE ELDER[a] TO THE ESTEEMED Gaius,[b] whom I truly love.

2Beloved friend, I pray that you may get along well in every way and may enjoy health, just as your soul is prospering. 3For I was extremely happy when the brothers arrived and gave testimony about your fidelity to the truth, as indeed you are living the true life. 4Nothing affords me more joy than to hear that my children are leading the true life.

5Beloved friend, you are acting faithfully when you do anything for the brothers, and specially for strangers. 6They have testified before the church about your friendship. You will do well to send them forward on their journey in a way befitting God's service, 7because on behalf of that Name they have gone out without accepting anything from the Gentiles.[c] 8So we ourselves ought to support such people in order to be fellow workers with them in the truth.

9I have written something to the church, but Diotrephes,[d] who loves to be prominent among them, does not accept our authority. 10For that reason I shall, on my arrival, call attention to his activities, casting reflections on us as he does with insinuating language. And not satisfied with that, he does not himself welcome the brothers, and he hinders those who are willing to do so, and expels them from the church.

11Dear friend, do not imitate evil, but good. The well-doer is from God; the evildoer has enjoyed no vision of God.

12Demetrius[e] enjoys a good reputation from everyone and from truth itself. We add our testimony, and you know that our testimony is true.

13I had many things to write you, but I do not wish to write you with pen and ink. 14But I hope to see you shortly, and we shall talk face to face. Peace to you. The friends send you greetings. Remember me to the friends personally.

---

a) See note at I Tim. 3:1.
b) Gaius, Gk. *Gaios*, was a fairly common name in the first century. There are several men called by that name in the N.T.: (1) a Macedonian who was one of Paul's companions in Ephesus, Acts 19:29; (2) Gaius of Derbe, who was with Paul on his third missionary journey, Acts 20:4, who may be the same as (1); and (3) a Corinthian whom Paul baptized, Rom. 16:23; I Cor. 1:14, probably the Gaius of this epistle. c) That is, unbelievers.
d) Unfortunately there are still those in the church who are like Diotrephes.
e) One likes to think that this might have been the silversmith of Ephesus, Acts 19:24-41, and that he had been converted.

THEME OF 3 JOHN:

SEGMENT
DIVISIONS

	PARAGRAPH THEMES
VERSE 1	
VERSES 2–4	
VERSES 5–8	
VERSES 9–12	
VERSES 13, 14	

Author:

Date:

Purpose:

Key Words:
  truth
  testimony
  good
  evil

JUDE

Jude had to speak up. He had intended to write one thing, but was compelled to write another. Jude wasn't an apostle and wasn't a pillar in the church, like his brother James. Although he was the half-brother of the Lord Jesus Christ, Jude did not claim any relationship to Jesus Christ other than that of being His bondservant.

Initially Jude didn't believe in Jesus (John 7:5), but finally he saw Jesus as He was—the Son of God—and then he understood: Jude had grown up in the presence of the One who came to save His people from their sins (Matthew 1:21). No wonder Jude had to write what he did!

THINGS TO DO

1. Though only one chapter in length, Jude is a pertinent book. Read it to familiarize yourself with the content.
2. Now read it again. This time find out what you can about the author, the recipients, and Jude's reason for writing. Mark in a distinctive way every reference to the recipients *(loved, friends, you)*.
   a. List what you learn about Jude and the recipients on the OBSERVATIONS CHART. As you do, note how Jude and the recipients are described. At this point *don't* list what the recipients are to do; instead, list only how they are described.
   b. When you discover Jude's purpose for writing, put it on the JUDE AT A GLANCE chart. If you don't see his reason immediately, you will by the time you have finished Jude.
3. Now read through Jude again.
   a. Mark every occurrence of *these people* and *these* in the same color or with the same symbol. Also mark in the same way the pronouns *(they, them)* which refer to *these people*.
   b. Who are "these people"? Read verse 4. If you think "these people" refers back to "certain people" in verse 4, then mark *certain people* in the same way you marked *these* and *these people*. Add what you learn from verse 4 to your list that describes "these people."
   c. Now read through Jude again marking every occurrence of the word *ungodly* or *impious*. Mark these references in the same color or way that you marked the references to *these, these people,* and *certain people*.
   d. Read through Jude one more time. From observing the text, if you believe that *these people* and the *ungodly* are the same people, then box in with a rectangle every reference to *these people* and to the *ungodly*, using a different color than you have already used.

   However, do not box the word *ungodly* or *impious* when it is used merely as an adjective to describe something other than a person. Also, if you think *scoffers* in verse 18 is another term used to describe *these people*, then mark it in the same colors or in the same way.

4. Read Jude again. Mark *destroyed* and *judgment*. Leave out *destroyed* in verse 10, since the literal meaning is "corrupted" and is different from the meaning of the other words.

5. Now that you have marked every reference to *these ungodly people*, fill in the portion of the OBSERVATIONS CHART that deals with them, listing what they do, what they are or are like, and what will happen to them.

6. There is a pattern in this letter. First Jude refers to "these ungodly people," then he uses Old Testament examples or illustrations to make a point. Read through Jude again, and watch for this pattern. You may want to underline every Old Testament incident or reference that Jude uses. As you study, watch what the Old Testament people do and note how God deals with them. Then, if you want to study Jude further, look up the cross-references in the footnotes to the Old Testament characters and illustrations and see what you learn from each. This will deepen your insight into these ungodly people.

7. On the OBSERVATIONS CHART list Jude's instructions to the "loved" recipients of this epistle by noting what they are to do. Also be sure to note what God will do for them.

8. Finally, write down the theme of Jude on JUDE AT A GLANCE. Now look at Jude paragraph by paragraph, choose a theme for each paragraph, and then record it in the designated place on this chart. Fill in any other information requested.

THINGS TO THINK ABOUT

1. Think about the promises to the "loved by God." Spend time in prayer, praising God for what He will do on your behalf. Then think of the responsibilities that are yours and talk with God about how you are to fulfill these within the sphere of your life.

2. Review the characteristics of the ungodly. Do you know of anyone who fits this description? How did God tell you to respond to these ungodly persons in verses 22 and 23? Are you willing to do so? Talk with God about it.

THE EPISTLE OF

JUDE

Date of writing: c. A.D. 68

JUDE,[a] A SLAVE[b] OF JESUS CHRIST and a brother of James, to those who have been called, loved by God the Father and kept by Jesus Christ: 2Mercy, peace, and love be increasingly granted you.

3Dear friends, while I was making every effort to write you about the salvation we have in common, I found it necessary to write you an appeal, that you vigorously defend the faith[c] which was once for all delivered to the saints.[d] 4For certain people have sneaked in, who for a long time have been marked out for this judgment, impious ones, who pervert the grace of our God into unbridled lust and deny Jesus Christ, our only Master and Lord.

5So I desire to remind you, although once you were quite familiar with all the facts, how the Lord, after rescuing the people from the land of Egypt, afterward destroyed those who did not believe. 6Then, too, the angels who did not maintain their own office[e] but abandoned their proper dwelling, He has reserved in everlasting chains under densest darkness for the judgment of the great day. 7Similarly, Sodom and Gomorrah with their neighboring towns, who in like fashion abandoned themselves to sexual immorality and were bent on perverted sensuality, are placed before us as a warning by suffering the punishment of eternal fire. Nevertheless, 8in that same way these deluded dreamers defile their bodies; they reject authority and libel glorious beings.[f]

9Yet, the archangel Michael, when in his encounter with the devil he argued about the body of Moses, did not venture to pronounce a reviling judgment against him, but said, "The Lord rebuke you." 10These people, however, revile what they do not understand, while whatever they do know sensually as reasonless brutes, by those things they are destroyed.

11Woe to them, because they are traveling the path of Cain,[g] and have given themselves up to Balaam's error[h] for the sake of gain; they have perished in Korah's revolt.[i]

12These are stains in your love feasts[j] as in your company they shamelessly gorge themselves; rainless clouds they are, carried along by wind; fruitless autumn trees, twice dead and uprooted; 13wildly raging waves of the sea that foam up their own disgrace; straying stars for whom the gloom of darkness is forever reserved.

14Enoch, in the seventh generation from Adam, prophesied about them

---

a) Jude was one of the half-brothers of Jesus, Matt. 13:55; Mark 6:3. In the Gk. text the name "Jude" is "Judas," which was an honored name up to the time of Christ, when Judas Iscariot's act of betrayal ruined it. As a result translators generally soften the name to "Jude."
b) See note at Matt. 13:27.
c) The essential doctrines taught the church by the apostles, cf. Acts 2:42.
d) See note at Acts 9:13. e) Fallen angels, or demons. f) That is, angels. g) Gen. 4:8-12.
h) See note at II Pet. 2:15. i) Num. 16:1-7; 23-25. j) See note at I Cor. 11:33.

too when he said,[k] "Behold, the Lord has come with His myriads of holy ones [15]to execute judgment against all, and to convict all the ungodly for all their impious activities which in their godlessness they have practiced, and for all the harsh words those godless sinners have spoken against Him."

[16]These are grumblers, complaining of their lot, who go along in accord with their passions, and whose mouths give vent to arrogant remarks, while they flatter to one's face in hope of gain.

[17]But you, dear friends, remember the predictions that were made by the apostles of our Lord Jesus Christ; [18]for they told you, "In the last time there will be scoffers, whose lives are guided by their own impious passions." [19]These are the agitators, the worldly, who lack the Spirit.

[20]You, however, beloved, as you build yourselves upon your most holy faith and pray in the Holy Spirit, [21]keep yourselves in the love of God, all the while awaiting the mercy of our Lord Jesus Christ for eternal life. [22]Convince some who doubt, but save others by snatching them from the fire; [23]on still others have pity mingled with great caution, loathing even the clothing that has been polluted by their sensuality.

[24]Now to Him who is able to keep you from stumbling and to present you faultless in the presence of His glory with abounding joy, [25]to the only God our Savior, through Jesus Christ our Lord, be glory, majesty, power and dominion before all time, and now, and forever. Amen.

---

k) The quotation is not from the O.T. but a pseudepigraphical book known as I Enoch, which is dated somewhere in the second century B.C.

JUDE

_____
_____
_____
_____
_____
_____
_____
_____

THE RECIPIENTS

What They Are Like: **What God Will Do for Them:**

(How They Are Described)

_____
_____
_____
_____
_____

What They Are to Do:

_____
_____
_____
_____

THE UNGODLY

What They Do:

_____
_____
_____
_____
_____
_____
_____

(continued)

What Will Happen to Them:

_____

_____

_____

_____

_____

_____

_____

What They Are or Are Like:

_____

_____

_____

_____

_____

_____

_____

_____

JUDE AT A GLANCE

THEME OF JUDE:

SEGMENT DIVISIONS

	PARAGRAPH THEMES	
	VERSES 1, 2	*Author:*
	VERSES 3, 4	*Date:*
	VERSES 5–16	*Purpose:*
	VERSES 17–23	*Key Words:*
	VERSES 24, 25	

REVELATION

*J*ohn, one of the sons of Zebedee, identifies himself in his Gospel not by his name, but as "the disciple whom Jesus loved." John walked in faith, taking Jesus at His word, and was secure in His love.

Therefore, when John was banished to the Isle of Patmos (and, according to tradition, submerged in a cauldron of hot oil), he remained steadfast in Jesus' love. He was faithful to his calling even in the midst of Nero's persecutions of Christians in A.D. 54 through 68, and then Domitian's in A.D. 81 through 96.

While John was on Patmos, God unveiled to him the coming of the Lord Jesus Christ and what soon would come to pass—a revelation unparalleled, the last to be given. It was about A.D. 95. With John's revelation the New Testament canon of Scripture would be complete. The church could be secure. Every prophecy would be fulfilled, just as God had said.

THINGS TO DO

Chapters 1–3

1. To familiarize yourself with the first two segments of the book of Revelation, carefully read 1:1 through 4:1 in one sitting. (*Revelation* is a translation of the Greek word *apokalupsis*, which means "an unveiling.")
2. Mark the following key words (along with their synonyms and pronouns) in chapter 1, and then list in the margin everything you learn from the text about these words: *Jesus Christ, God (the Father), Spirit (seven Spirits),* and *write.* Then transfer this information to the chart WHAT REVELATION TEACHES ABOUT GOD, JESUS, and THE HOLY SPIRIT following Revelation.
3. Revelation 1:19 gives an outline of the book of Revelation.
   a. List the three things John was to write:
      1) _____
      2) _____
      3) _____
   b. Now look at Revelation 4:1 and note how it relates to 1:19. Revelation 4 begins the third segment of Revelation. Chapter 1 describes what John saw, and chapters 2 and 3 are "what is now." What is the third segment that begins in 4:1?
   c. Using the terminology found in Revelation 1:19, record these three segments in the space for segment divisions on the REVELATION AT A GLANCE chart following Revelation. (The lines to divide the book into these sections are already drawn.)
4. Read Revelation 1 through 3 and do the following:
   a. Watch for key repeated phrases or words listed on REVELATION AT A GLANCE. Mark these in the text in a distinctive way so you can spot them immediately. In Jesus' messages to the churches, watch for a pattern as Jesus addresses each church.
   b. Now concentrate on Jesus' mes-

sages to the churches, one church at a time. Record what you learn about each church on the chart JESUS' MESSAGES TO THE CHURCHES following Revelation. When you see what is said regarding the victors, note how John describes victors in 1 John 5:4, 5. Add what you learn to the chart.

5. Record the main theme of each chapter in the text next to the chapter number and on REVELATION AT A GLANCE.

Chapters 4–22

1. In the last nineteen chapters of Revelation Jesus shows John "what must take place hereafter." Read Revelation 4 through 22 one chapter at a time, and for each chapter do the following:

   a. As you read, ask the five W's and an H: Who? What? Why? When? Where? and How? For example, if it is an event, ask: What is happening? Who is involved? When will this happen and where? Why is this happening? How will it happen? If it is a person or a personage: Who is this? What is this person like? What does he do? When? Where? Why? What are the consequences? How will he accomplish it? These are very critical questions. If these are answered carefully after thoroughly observing the text and apart from preconceived ideas, you will learn much. Make a list of what you learn, and then if it is information you wish to keep, record the essence of your insights in the margin of the chapter.

   b. Mark key repeated words (along with their synonyms and pronouns—*he, she, it, we, they, us,* and *you*) in a distinctive way.

Some key words are listed on REVELATION AT A GLANCE. Since it is a long list, write these on an index card, color code the words as you intend to mark them in the text, and use the card as a bookmark. When you finish marking these, list on a piece of paper what you learn from each one (unless you have been told to record that information on a chart). Then in the margins, record any information you learn from the key words that you want to have accessible in your New Testament.

   c. As you go through Revelation chapter by chapter, let the text speak for itself. Remember, truth is revealed gradually, so don't become impatient. Simply observe what is being said without adding your own interpretation. Stay in an attitude of prayer, asking God to open the eyes of your understanding.

2. Mark in a distinctive way all references to time. Then note what happens during that time. In Jewish reckoning 42 months, 1260 days, and time, times and half-a-time all refer to a period of 3 1/2 years. When you finish studying this segment of Revelation, you might want to list in the margin what happens and when, and how these time periods and events relate to one another, if at all.

   Also watch *when* something begins and ends—for example, the great day of God's wrath, when the mystery of God is finished, when God begins to reign. Noting the timing of these will help you understand Revelation better.

3. Babylon intermittently plays an important role from Genesis to Revelation. As you mark every reference to Babylon, carefully note whether it is refer-

ring to "the woman" or to the city. Then discern whether they are one and the same or two separate but somehow related entities. In chapters 17 and 18, where Babylon is preeminent, list in the margin of the chapter what you learn from marking each reference to Babylon. Then compile your information on the chart WHAT THE BIBLE TEACHES ABOUT BABYLON.

4. As you observe what happens during each of the seals, trumpets, and bowls, record your insights on the chart THE SEVEN SEALS, TRUMPETS, AND BOWLS following Revelation. Then consider whether the seals, trumpets, and bowls happen at the same time or follow one another.

5. As you study Revelation, watch for references to "the day of the Lord" and note them on the chart THE DAY OF THE LORD. See if there are any parallels between what you have observed in other books of the Bible and what you see in Revelation.

6. There is much to learn about the Godhead in this book that you will want to remember and meditate on. Record what you learn on the chart WHAT REVELATION TEACHES ABOUT GOD, JESUS, and THE HOLY SPIRIT.

7. When you finish going through Revelation, record the chapter themes in the space at the beginning of each chapter and on REVELATION AT A GLANCE, along with other pertinent information called for on the chart.

8. Finally, see how various chapters of the book group according to events, places, or persons. Use your chapter themes as a guide to see when these groupings occur. Record these groupings under "Segment Divisions" on REVELATION AT A GLANCE, placing them at the chapter numbers in which they occur.

THINGS TO THINK ABOUT
Chapters 1–3

1. As you look at the Lord's message to each church, do you think the message could be for the church today? Look back through Jesus' messages to the churches in chapters 2 and 3 and note what the Spirit is saying to him who has "an ear." To whom is the Spirit speaking? What does He want you to hear? To do?

2. Think about what you have learned about Jesus Christ from chapters 1–3 and then spend some time worshiping Him for who and what He is.

3. Are you a victor? How does it show? Is there anything you need to do that you are not presently doing so that when Jesus appears you won't be ashamed?

Chapters 4–22

1. Revelation gives insight into the judgment of God upon the wicked because of what they worship. It also gives a glimpse of the way the righteous worship. How would you compare your worship with the worship described in Revelation? You might want to go back through Revelation and look at the scenes where God is worshiped and use them as a pattern for worship.

2. Now that you have a better understanding of the wrath to come upon the unbeliever, what priority needs to be placed on sharing the gospel? Is witnessing a priority in your church? Is witnessing a priority in your personal life?

3. Are you sure that you are a child of God? If not, will you acknowledge the Lord Jesus Christ as God, receive His forgiveness for your sins, and let Him take full control of your life? Surely

you have seen that He is worthy—and trustworthy.

4. What have you learned about your God? In the light of this, are you living in anticipation of Jesus' coming?

Seven Churches of Asia

THE
REVELATION

OF JESUS CHRIST

Date of writing: c. A.D. 95

1 THE REVELATION OF JESUS CHRIST, which God granted Him to show His bond servants what must shortly take place. So through His angel He sent the communication to His slave[a] John, 2who bears witness to everything he saw as the message of God and the testimony of Jesus Christ.

3Blessed[b] is the reader,[c] and blessed are those who hear the words of the prophecy, who observe what is recorded in it, for the time is near.

4John to the seven churches in Asia: Grace and peace to you from Him who is and who was and who is coming, and from the seven Spirits[d] who are before His throne, 5and from Jesus Christ, the trustworthy Witness, the First-born from the dead and the Commander of the kings of the earth. To Him who loves us and has freed us from our sins by His own blood, 6and has made us a kingdom, priests to God, even His Father, to Him be the glory and the dominion forever and ever. Amen.

7Behold, He is coming on the clouds and every eye, even of those who pierced Him, will see Him, and all the tribes[e] of the earth will beat their breasts over Him. Truly so, Amen.

8"I am the Alpha and the Omega," says the Lord God, "who is and who was and who is coming, the All-Sovereign."

9I, John, your brother and partner in the distress and the kingdom and the endurance of Jesus, was on the island called Patmos on account of the message from God and the testimony of Jesus. 10On the Lord's day I was in the Spirit and heard behind me a voice as loud as a trumpet, 11that said, "Write what you see in a book and dispatch it to the seven churches[f] — to Ephesus, to Smyrna, to Pergamum, to Thyatira, to Sardis, to Philadelphia, and to Laodicea."

12I turned to see whose voice was addressing me, and on turning I saw seven golden lampstands, 13and in the center of the lampstands One like the Son of Man, dressed in a robe that reached to the feet and girded around the chest with a golden girdle. 14His head and hair were white as wool, white as snow; His eyes were like a flame of fire; 15His feet were like precious ore as it glows in the furnace, and His voice was like the sound of many waters.[g] 16In His right hand He held seven stars; from His mouth there issued a sharp, two-edged sword,

a) Gk. *doulois*. See note at Matt. 13:27.
b) Seven times in this book the word "blessed" is used, chs. 1:3; 14:13; 16:15; 19:9; 20:6; 22:7, 14. It is translated from the Gk. *makarios* and means *happy*. See note at Luke 6:20.
c) Audible reading may be referred to here, as implied by "those who hear the words."
d) The expression "the seven Spirits" is used also in chs. 3:1; 4:5; 5:6. It appears to allude to the Holy Spirit in His complete ministry, Isa. 11:2, seven often being employed in Scripture to imply perfection or completion.   e) Cf. Zech. 12:10-14.
f) These seven churches were all located in the western part of Asia Minor, now Turkey. It is to be assumed that the virtues and faults of these churches were common to all the churches of the latter part of the first century and generally to churches today. Certainly the repeated exhortation, "Whoever has an ear, let him hear what the Spirit says to the churches," chs. 2:7, 11, 17, 19; 3:6, 13, 22, is addressed to all men and women everywhere in every century.
g) Cf. Dan. 7:9; 10:6.

and His face shone as when the sun shines in its full strength.

[17]When I saw Him I fell at His feet as dead. Then He laid His right hand on me and said, "Do not fear. I am the First and the Last [18]and the Living One. I experienced death and behold, I am alive forever and ever, and I possess the keys of death and of its realm. [19]Therefore write what you have seen, both what is now and what will occur hereafter. [20]As to the mystery of the seven stars that you saw in My right hand, and of the seven golden lampstands, the seven stars are angels of the seven churches, and the seven lampstands are the seven churches.

2 "TO THE ANGEL OF THE CHURCH in Ephesus write: 'He, who holds the seven stars in His right hand and who walks among the seven golden lampstands, says this:

[2]" 'I know your activities, your toil, and your endurance, and how you cannot tolerate wicked men; how you have put to the test those who call themselves apostles though they are not, and you have found them to be impostors. [3]You have been patient and have been bearing up because of My name, and you have not become exhausted. [4]But I hold against you that you have given up your first love. [5]Therefore, call to mind from what you have fallen, and repent and practice what you did previously; or else, if you do not repent, I shall come to you and remove the lampstand from its place. [6]You have this, however, that you hate the doings of the Nicolaitans,[h] which I hate too. [7]Whoever has an ear, let him hear what the Spirit says to the churches. I shall grant the victor to eat from the tree of life that stands in the paradise of God." '

[8]"To the angel of the church in Smyrna write: 'This says the First and the Last, who died and became alive.

[9]" ' "I know your affliction and your poverty (but you are rich) and the slander of those who call themselves Jews but are instead a synagogue of Satan.[i] [10]Do not dread what you are to suffer. True, the devil is going to throw some of you into prison, so that you will be tested, and for ten days[j] you will have trouble. Be loyal, though it means your death, and I shall give you the crown[k] of life. [11]Whoever has an ear, let him hear what the Spirit says to the churches. The victor will suffer no hurt from the second death." '[l]

[12]"To the angel of the church in Pergamum write: 'He, who has the sharp, double-edged sword, says this:

[13]" ' "I know where you live; Satan's throne[m] is there. And you are holding onto My name; you have not renounced faith in Me even in the days when My faithful Antipas,[n] who witnessed for Me, was put to death among you, where Satan dwells. [14]I hold a few things against you, though; for you have those there who hold to the doctrine of Balaam,[o] who instructed Balak to throw a stumbling block before the sons of Israel, so that they might eat idol offerings and practice immorality. [15]Besides, you have as well those who adhere to the doctrine of the Nicolaitans.[p] [16]Therefore, repent. Otherwise I shall shortly come to you, and make war on them with the sword of My mouth. [17]Whoever has an ear, let him hear what the Spirit says to the churches. To the victor I shall give some of the hidden manna and I shall give him a white stone, and engraved on the stone a new name, which no one knows except the recipient." '[q]

[18]"To the angel of the church in Thyatira write: 'This says the Son of

---

h) "Nicolaitans" is the name of a sect that identified itself with Christianity but apparently countenanced loose living.
i) At Smyrna the Jews allied themselves with the pagans in persecuting the Christians.
j) Ten days is probably a figure for a short period.   k) See note at Phil. 4:2.
l) The soul's experience of eternal loss.
m) Pergamum's excessive paganism was symbolized by a magnificent altar-platform to Zeus.
n) An otherwise unknown Christian martyr. It is certain that his name is known in heaven.
o) See note at II Pet. 2:15.
p) What is described as "the doings of the Nicolaitans" in the church at Ephesus, vs. 6, was a teaching at Smyrna.   q) *Cf.* Isa. 62:6.

God, whose eyes are like a flame of fire and His feet are like white-hot metal:

[19]" "I know your doings, your love and faith and service and endurance, and that of late you are accomplishing more than at first. [20]But I hold against you that you tolerate that woman Jezebel,[r] who calls herself a prophetess and teaches my servants[s] deceitfully to practice immorality and to eat offerings made to idols. [21]I have given her time to repent, but she refuses to repent of her immorality. [22]Take note: I shall throw her on a sickbed, and those who commit adultery with her into great distress unless they repent of her practices, [23]and her children I shall put to death. Then all the churches will know that I am the Searcher of minds and hearts, who rewards each of you according to your works. [24]But I say to the rest of you in Thyatira, who neither adhere to this doctrine nor have explored the hidden things of Satan, as they put it, I shall place no further burden on you, [25]except that you hold on to what you have until I come. [26]To the victor and the one who takes my deeds to heart until the end I shall grant authority over the nations. [27]He will rule them with an iron rod as when clay jars are shivered to pieces, just as I received authority[t] from My Father. [28]I shall also give him the morning star. [29]Whoever has an ear, let him hear what the Spirit says to the churches." '

3 "TO THE ANGEL OF THE CHURCH in Sardis write: 'He who has the seven Spirits[u] of God and the seven stars says this:

" " 'I know your doings, that you are said to live but you are dead. [2]Be awake and invigorate the things that remain that are at the point of dying; for I have not found your works perfect before My God. [3]Call to mind, then, what you have received and heard; observe it and repent. If you do not keep wide-awake, I shall come like a thief and you will have no idea at what hour I shall come upon you. [4]You have a few persons in Sardis, however, who have not soiled their clothes.[v] They will walk with Me in white, because they are deserving. [5]Similarly the victor will be dressed in white robes and I shall not erase his name from the Book of Life; I shall confess his name before My Father and before His angels.[w] [6]Whoever has an ear, let him hear what the Spirit says to the churches." '

[7]"To the angel of the church in Philadelphia write: 'The Holy, the True, the One who holds David's key, who opens and no one shuts; who shuts and no one opens, says this:

[8]" " 'I know your doings. See, I have provided an opened door in front of you, one which no one is able to close; because, while possessing little strength, you have observed My word and have not renounced My name. [9]Take note: I shall make those of the synagogue of Satan, who claim to be Jews but are instead impostors — indeed I shall make them come and bow at your feet and acknowledge that I have loved you.[x] [10]Because you have observed the message of My endurance, I also shall preserve you from the hour of trial that is coming upon the whole inhabited world, to put to the test those who live on the earth. [11]I am coming soon. Hold fast to what you have, so that no one may rob you of your crown.[y] [12]As for the victor, I shall make him a pillar in the temple of My God; he will leave it nevermore. And I shall inscribe on him the name of My God and the name of the city of My God, the new Jerusalem that is coming down out of heaven from My God, as well as My new name. [13]Whoever has an ear let him hear what the Spirit says to the churches." '

[14]"To the angel of the church in Laodicea write: 'This says the Amen, the faithful and true Witness, the Beginning of the creation of God:[z]

---

r) I Kings 16:31, 32.   s) Gk. *doulous*. See note at Matt. 13:27.   t) Ps. 2:7-9.
u) See note at ch. 1:4.   v) That is, their Christian character.
w) *Cf.* Matt. 10:32, 33; Mark 8:38; Luke 12:8, 9.   x) *Cf.* Isa. 43:4; 60:14.
y) See note at Phil. 4:2.
z) That is, He was the source of creation.

15" ' "I know your doings, that you are neither cold nor hot. I wish you were either cold or hot. 16So, because you are lukewarm and neither hot nor cold, I am going to spew you out of My mouth. 17For you say, 'I am rich; I have grown wealthy; I need nothing,' and you do not know that you are wretched, pitiable, poor, blind, and naked. 18I advise you to buy from Me gold that has been tested in the fire, in order that you may be wealthy; and white clothes to put on, so that the shame of your nudity may not be shown; and salve[a] to put on your eyes, so that you may see. 19The ones I love I correct and discipline; so burn with zeal and repent. 20Behold, I stand at the door and knock. If anyone listens to My voice and opens the door, I shall come in to him and dine with him and he with Me. 21As for the victor, I shall grant him to sit beside Me on My throne, as I also conquered and sat down beside My Father on His throne. 22Whoever has an ear, let him hear what the Spirit says to the churches." ' "

4 AFTER THIS I LOOKED AND SAW A door standing open in heaven, and the voice I had first heard speaking to me like a trumpet, said, "Come up here, and I shall show you what must take place hereafter."

2Immediately I came under the Spirit's power and saw a throne standing in heaven, and One seated on the throne. 3The One[b] seated there resembled in appearance a jasper stone and a sardius. And a rainbow that looked like an emerald encircled the throne.

4Surrounding the throne there were twenty-four thrones with twenty-four elders[c] sitting on them, clad in white robes and with golden crowns[d] on their heads.

5Out from the throne issued lightnings and rumblings and thunderpeals. And seven torches of fire were burning before the throne, which are the seven Spirits[e] of God. 6Also in front of the throne it was like a glassy sea, as transparent as crystal.

Around the throne, on each side, there were four living beings[f] full of eyes in front and behind; 7the first living being was like a lion; the second, like an ox; the third, with a manlike face; and the fourth, like a flying eagle. 8Each of the four living beings had six wings, and each living being was full of eyes all around and within. Neither by day nor by night do they cease saying, "Holy, holy, holy, Lord God Almighty, who was, and who is, and who is coming."

9And whenever the living beings render praise and honor and thanksgiving to the Occupant of the throne, who lives forever and ever, 10the twenty-four elders fall down before the One seated upon the throne and worship Him who lives forever and ever, and they cast their crowns[g] before the throne, saying, 11"Thou art worthy, our Lord and God, to receive glory and honor and dominion, because Thou hast created all things, and by Thy will they were and have been created."

5 I ALSO SAW IN THE RIGHT HAND of Him who was seated on the throne a scroll with writing inside and outside, sealed with seven seals. 2I further saw a mighty angel, who was exclaiming in a loud voice, "Who is worthy to open the scroll and to break its seals?" 3And no one, either in heaven or on earth or under the earth, was able to open the scroll or to look inside it.

4So I cried bitterly because none was found worthy to open the scroll or to look inside it. 5And one of the elders said to me, "Do not weep. You see, the Lion out of the tribe of Judah, the Offspring of David, has conquered, so as to open the scroll and its seven seals."

6And I saw, standing midway between the throne and the four living

---

a) In Laodicea Phrygian powders of medicinal value for the eyes were made.
b) Cf. I Kings 22:19; Isa. 6:1; Ezek. 1:26-28; Dan. 7:9.   c) See note at I Tim. 3:1.
d) See note at Phil. 4:2.   e) See note at ch. 1:4.   f) Cf. the Cherubim, Ezek. 1:5, 18.
g) All that they are and have comes from God.

beings and among the elders, a Lamb as if it had been sacrificed. It had seven horns and seven eyes,[h] which are the seven Spirits[i] of God dispatched over the whole earth. [7]He came and took the scroll from the right hand of Him who was seated on the throne; [8]and when He took the scroll the four living beings and the twenty-four elders fell down before the Lamb, each of them having a harp, and holding golden bowls full of incense, which are the prayers[j] of the saints.[k]

[9]And they sing[l] a new song, saying, "Thou art worthy to take the scroll and to open its seals, because Thou wast sacrificed and hast bought them for God with Thy blood, out of every tribe and tongue and people and nation, [10]and hast made them a kingdom, and priests to our God, and they shall reign over the earth."

[11]Then I looked, and I heard the voice of many angels around the throne and the living beings and the elders, and they numbered myriads of myriads and thousands of thousands, [12]saying with a loud voice, "Worthy is the Lamb that was slain to receive power and wealth and wisdom and strength and honor and glory and blessing."

[13]Then I heard every creature in heaven and on earth and under the earth and on the sea, and everything in them, exclaiming, "To Him who is seated on the throne, and to the Lamb be blessing and honor and glory and dominion forever and ever."

[14]The four living beings said, "Amen," and the elders fell down and worshiped.

6 AND I SAW WHEN THE LAMB opened the first of the seven seals, and I heard one of the four living beings say with a voice like thunder, "Come!" [2]Then I looked and saw a white horse,[m] and its rider holding a bow. To him a crown was given, and

he went out conquering and to conquer.

[3]And when He opened the second seal I heard the second living being say, "Come!" [4]Then another horse, fiery red, went out, and its rider was empowered to take peace from the earth, so that people would kill one another, and a huge sword was given him.

[5]When He opened the third seal I heard the third living being say, "Come!" Then I looked and saw a black horse, and its rider had a pair of scales in his hand. [6]I also heard a voice in the center of the four living beings, that said, "A quart of wheat for a day's wage[n] and three quarts of barley for a day's wage, and do not damage the oil and the wine."

[7]When He opened the fourth seal I heard the voice of the fourth living being say, "Come!" [8]Then I looked and saw an ash-colored horse. The name of its rider was Death, and Hades followed him closely. Authority was granted them over a quarter of the earth, to kill with the sword, with famine, with plague, and by means of the wild beasts of the earth.

[9]When He opened the fifth seal I saw underneath the altar the souls of those who had been slaughtered for the sake of the word of God and the witness they bore. [10]With a loud voice they cried out, "How long, O holy and true Sovereign, before Thou wilt judge and avenge our blood on the inhabitants of the earth?"

[11]And to each of them was given a white robe[o] and they were told to rest for a little while longer, until the number of their fellow servants and of their brothers, who were to be killed as they had been, should be complete.

[12]When He opened the sixth seal I saw a tremendous earthquake occur. The sun turned as black as sackcloth and the full moon became like blood.[p]

---

h) The expression "seven horns and seven eyes" symbolizes perfect power and wisdom.
i) See note at ch. 1:4.   j) Incense symbolizes prayer.   k) See note at Acts 9:13.
l) The present tense suggests that the song remains forever fresh.   m) Cf. Zech. 6:1-3.
n) The Gk. word twice rendered "a day's wage" in this verse is *denariou*. A denarius would be worth about twenty-five cents in mid-twentieth century currency, a day's wage in the first century! The prices of wheat and barley in this passage suggest famine.
o) A costume that suggests the righteousness of God in Christ that is graciously given to God's believing people. Cf. ch. 7:14.   p) Cf. Joel 2:10, 31; Acts 2:19-21.

13The stars of heaven fell to the earth as when a fig tree, shaken by a violent wind, drops its unripe fruit. 14The sky retreated like a scroll that is being rolled up, and every mountain and island was dislodged.

15Then the kings of the earth and the nobles, the generals, the wealthy, the powerful, yes, everyone, slave and free, hid themselves in the caves and in the mountain rocks, 16and called to the mountains and to the rocks, "Fall on us and hide us from the presence of the One who is seated on the throne, and from the wrath of the Lamb; 17for the great day of Their wrath has come, and who is able to stand?"q

7 FOLLOWING THIS I SAW FOUR ANgels stationed at the four corners of the earth, restraining the four winds of the earth, so that no wind might blow on land or sea or on any tree. 2I also observed another angel ascending from the sunrise, holding a seal from the living God. He shouted with a loud voice to the four angels, who had been empowered to injure the earth and the sea: 3"Injure neither the earth nor the sea nor the trees until we have sealed the servantsr of our God upon their foreheads."

4And I heard the number of those sealed of every tribe of Israel's sons, one hundred forty-four thousand. 5Of the tribe of Judah twelve thousand were sealed; of the tribe of Reuben, twelve thousand; of the tribe of Gad, twelve thousand; 6of the tribe of Asher, twelve thousand; of the tribe of Naphtali, twelve thousand; of the tribe of Manasseh, twelve thousand; 7of the tribe of Simeon, twelve thousand; of the tribe of Levi, twelve thousand; of the tribe of Issachar, twelve thousand; 8of the tribe of Zebulon, twelve thousand; of the tribe of Joseph, twelve thousand; of the tribe of Benjamin, twelve thousand were sealed.

9After this I looked and there was a vast host that no one could count out of all nations and tribes and peoples and tongues, standing before the throne and before the Lamb, clothed in white robes and with palm branchess in their hands. 10And they shouted with a loud voice: "Salvation is due to our God, who is seated on the throne, and to the Lamb."

11Then all the angels stood surrounding the throne, the elders and the four living beings, and fell on their faces before the throne and worshiped God, 12saying, "Amen! Blessing and glory, wisdom and thanksgiving, honor, dominion, and power be to our God forever and ever. Amen."

13Addressing me, one of the elders then asked, "These who are wearing white robes, who are they and from where have they come?" 14I said to him, "Sir, you know." Then he told me, "These are the ones who have come out of the great tribulation, and they have washed their robes and have made them white in the blood of the Lamb. 15For this reason they are before God's throne, and day and night they serve Him in His temple,t while He who sits on the throne spreads His tent over them. 16They will nevermore either hunger or thirst, nor will the sun or any scorching heat whatever beat upon them; 17for the Lamb, who is in the center of the throne, will shepherd them and will lead them to springs of living water. And God will wipe away all tears from their eyes."

8 WHEN THE LAMB OPENED THE seventh seal, there was silence in heaven for about half an hour.

2Then I saw the seven angels who were standing before God, and they were given seven trumpets. 3Also another angel with a golden censer came and stood at the altar. A vast quantity of incenseu was given him, so that he might place it on the golden altar before the throne with the prayers of all the saints.v 4And the smoke of the incense arose before God from the angel's hand, with the prayers of the saints. 5Then the angel took the cen-

---

q) Isa. 2:19. r) Gk. *doulous.* See note at Matt. 13:27. s) In celebration of victory.
t) All believers are priests before God, chs. 1:6; 5:10.
u) In the temple the golden incense altar belonged in the Holy of Holies. v) See note at Acts 9:13.

ser and filled it with fire from the altar and poured it on the earth, and there followed thunderpeals, rumblings, lightning flashes, and an earthquake.

[6]And the seven angels with trumpets got themselves ready to blow them. [7]The first angel blew his trumpet, and there came hail and fire mixed with blood, that was poured on the earth, so that one-third of the earth and of the trees was burned up, and all the green grass.[w]

[8]Then the second angel blew his trumpet, and something like an immense mountain ablaze with fire was hurled into the sea, so that one-third of the sea turned to blood, [9]and a third of the living creatures in the sea died, and a third of the ships were destroyed.

[10]The third angel blew his trumpet, and a huge star, blazing like a torch, fell from the sky and came down on one-third of the rivers and on the water springs.[x] [11]The star's name is Wormwood, and one-third of the waters turned to wormwood. Many people died from the water, because it had turned bitter.

[12]The fourth angel blew his trumpet, and a blight fell on one-third of the sun, of the moon, and of the stars, so that a third part of them was darkened[y]; no light shone for a third of the day, nor for a third of the night.

[13]Then I looked, and I heard an eagle flying in mid-heaven, that cried with a loud voice, "Woe, woe, woe, for the inhabitants of the earth, because of the remaining trumpet blasts of the three angels who are about to sound."

9 THE FIFTH ANGEL BLEW HIS trumpet, and I saw a star[z] that had fallen to the earth from heaven, to whom was given the key to the pit of the abyss. [2]He opened the pit of the abyss, and smoke whirled upward from the pit like the smoke of a gigantic furnace, so that the sun and the air were darkened by the smoke from the pit.

[3]Out of the smoke locusts went forth on the earth, and such power was granted them as the earth's scorpions possess. [4]They were told not to damage the earth's grass, neither any vegetation, nor any tree, but only the persons who do not have the seal of God on their foreheads. [5]Power was granted them, not to kill them but for five months to torture them, and their torture was like that of a scorpion that stings a person. [6]During those days people will seek death without finding it; they will be anxious to die, but death evades them.

[7]The locusts looked like horses equipped for battle.[a] On their heads were something like golden crowns, their faces were like human faces, [8]their hair was like that of women, and their teeth were like lion's teeth, [9]their scales were like breastplates that seemed made of steel, and the drone of their wings was like the roar of many horse-drawn chariots charging into battle.

[10]They have tails with stings like scorpions, and power in their tails to hurt mankind for five months. [11]They have as king over them the angel of the abyss, whose name in Hebrew is Abaddon and in Greek Apollyon.[b] [12]The first woe is past; two woes are still to follow.

[13]The sixth angel blew his trumpet, and I heard a voice from the four horns of the golden altar[c] before God, [14]saying to the sixth angel with the trumpet, "Release the four angels that are bound at the great river Euphrates." [15]So the four angels, who were in readiness for that hour and day and month and year, were set free to kill one-third of mankind. [16]The number of their divisions of cavalry was two hundred million. I heard their number.

[17]In my vision the horses and their riders looked like this: the riders wore breastplates as red as fire, as blue as sapphire, and as yellow as sulphur. The horses' heads resembled lions'

---

w) Of the third of the earth that was burned up.   x) Supplying one-third of the rivers.
y) Isa. 13:10; Joel 2:31; Matt. 24:29; *cf.* Exod. 10:21-23.
z) The context shows this to be a person.   a) *Cf.* Joel 2:4-7.
b) "Abaddon," Gk. *Abaddon* from a Heb. noun, means *Destruction;* "Apollyon," Gk. *Apolluon,* means *Destroyer.*   c) The golden altar is associated with the prayers of the saints, ch. 8:2-4.

heads, and out of their mouths poured fire and smoke and sulphur.

18By these three plagues one-third of mankind was killed, by the fire, by the smoke, and by the sulphur that streamed out of their mouths. 19For the horses' power lies in their mouths and in their tails; their tails are like serpents; they have heads, and with them they do harm.

20But the rest of humanity, who were not killed by those plagues, did not repent from the works of their hands, so as to cease worshiping demons and the idols of gold, silver, bronze, stone, and wood, that can neither see nor hear nor walk. 21Nor did they repent of their murders, or of their magic arts, or of their immorality, or of their thefts.

10 THEN[d] I SAW ANOTHER MIGHTY angel descend from heaven, robed in a cloud, with a rainbow over his head. His face was like the sun; his legs resembled fiery pillars, 2and he held an opened little scroll in his hand. His right foot he placed on the sea, and his left foot on the land, 3while with a loud voice like the roar of a lion he gave a shout. And as he shouted, the seven thunders raised their voices.

4When the seven thunders had spoken, I was going to write; but I heard a voice from heaven that said, "Seal up what the seven thunders have spoken and do not write it."

5Then the angel whom I saw standing on the sea and on the land lifted his hand heavenward 6and swore by Him who lives forever and ever, who created the heaven and what it contains, also the earth and what is in it, and the sea with everything in it, "There shall be no further delay; 7but in the days of the seventh angel's trumpet blast, when he is at the point of blowing it, the mystery of God will reach completion in agreement

with the good news He gave His servants[e] the prophets."

8Then the voice from heaven which I heard, addressed me again and said, "Go and take the little, opened scroll that is in the hand of the angel who is standing on the sea and on the land." 9So I went to the angel, asking him to give me the little scroll.

He told me, "Take and eat it! It will be bitter in your stomach, but in your mouth it will be sweet as honey."[f] 10So I took the little scroll from the angel's hand and ate it, and in my mouth it was as sweet as honey, but when I had eaten it, my stomach was made bitter. 11Then he told me, "You must prophesy again about many peoples and nations and tongues and kings."

11 AND THERE WAS GIVEN ME A measuring reed like a rod, and I was told:

"Rise and measure the temple of God and the altar, and count those worshiping in it, 2but omit the outer court of the temple; do not measure it, because it has been given to the Gentiles. They will trample the holy city under foot for forty-two months.[g] 3And I shall allow My two witnesses to prophesy for twelve hundred sixty days, clad in sackcloth.

4"These witnesses are the two olive trees and the two lamps that are standing before the Lord of the earth.[h] 5If anyone wants to hurt them, fire issues from their mouths and consumes their enemies. Should anyone wish to injure them, he must be killed in that way.

6"These two have power to shut up the sky,[i] so that no rain may fall during the days of their prophecy; they also have power over the waters, to turn them into blood,[j] and to scourge the earth with every kind of plague as often as they desire.

7"When they shall have finished

d) An interlude between the sixth and seventh trumpets, chs. 10:1-11:13.
e) Gk. *doulous*. See note at Matt. 13:27.
f) *Cf.* Jer. 15:16; Ezek. 3:3. To "eat" the scroll symbolizes appropriating God's message.
g) Forty-two months; 1260 days; three and one-half years; a time, times, and half a time — all signify the same period of time. *Cf.* chs. 12:6, 14; 13:5; Dan. 9:27; 12:7.
h) *Cf.* ch. 1:12, 20; Zech. 4:2, 3. i) *Cf.* I Kings 17:1; James 5:17. j) *Cf.* Exod. 7:14-25.

their testimony, the beast[k] that comes up from the abyss will make war against them, and will conquer them and kill them. [8]Their dead bodies will lie in the streets of the great city[l] that is spiritually called Sodom and Egypt, where also their Lord was crucified. [9]And they of the peoples and tribes and tongues and nations will gaze at their dead bodies for three and a half days; they will not allow the bodies to be entombed. [10]Those dwelling on the earth will rejoice over them and will celebrate; they will send one another gifts, because the two prophets had been vexing the dwellers on the earth."

[11]And after the three and a half days the breath of life from God entered them, so that they rose to their feet; and great fear fell on those who saw them. [12]The two heard a loud voice calling to them from heaven, "Come up here." And they ascended in a cloud into heaven while their enemies saw them.

[13]At that very hour there was a tremendous earthquake; one-tenth of the city collapsed and seven thousand persons were killed in the earthquake. Then the survivors were terrified and ascribed glory to the God of heaven.

[14]The second woe is past. The third woe is speedily approaching.

[15]The seventh angel blew his trumpet, and there were loud voices in heaven: "The kingdom of the world has become that of our Lord and of His Christ, and He shall reign forever and ever."

[16]Then the twenty-four elders who were seated on their thrones before God, fell on their faces and worshiped God, [17]exclaiming, "We give Thee thanks, Lord God Almighty, who is and who was, because Thou hast assumed Thy great power and hast begun to reign. [18]The nations raged[m]

and Thy wrath has been realized; also the time for the judging of the dead and for the rewarding of Thy bond servants[n] the prophets and the saints[o] —in fact, all those who revere Thy name both small and great; also for the destruction of those who are destroying the earth."

[19]Then the temple of God in heaven was opened, and the ark of His covenant was seen in His sanctuary,[p] and there were lightning flashes, rumblings, peals of thunder, an earthquake, and a terrific hailstorm.

12

A GREAT PORTENT THEN APpeared in heaven: a woman robed with the sun, with the moon under her feet and a crown of twelve stars on her head, [2]was pregnant, and as she agonized in the pangs of her delivery, she cried out.

[3]Then another portent appeared in heaven. There was a gigantic, fiery-red dragon[q] with seven heads and ten horns, and on his heads seven diadems. [4]His tail swept away a third of the stars of heaven and hurled them to the ground.

The dragon then stationed himself in front of the woman, who was about to give birth, so he might devour her child as soon as it was born.

[5]She gave birth to a son, a male child, destined to rule all nations with an iron rod.[r] Her child was then snatched away up to God and to His throne, [6]while the woman[s] fled into the wilderness, where God had a retreat prepared for her to be cared for there during twelve hundred sixty days.

[7]Then war developed in heaven, Michael and his angels battling against the dragon, and the dragon with his angels waging war; [8]but they were defeated; there was no longer any place for them in heaven. [9]And the

---

k) Chs. 13; 17.   l) The scene is laid on earth, in Jerusalem.   m) Ps. 2:1-5.
n) Gk. *doulois*. See note at Matt. 13:27.   o) See note at Acts 9:13.
p) This may be a symbol of God's carrying through His covenant of grace to the end.
q) Satan, vs. 9.
r) The Messiah, of whom alone this is predicted, Ps. 2:7-9.
s) Identifications of the woman differ. An ancient interpretation, still held by many, is that she represents God's believing people in both the O.T. and N.T. Roman Catholics say that she is the virgin Mary. But many other commentators identify her with Israel, through which nation the Messiah came.

great dragon, the serpent of old, called the devil and Satan,[t] the deceiver of all humanity, was forced out and hurled to the earth, and his angels were flung out along with him.

[10]Then I heard a strong voice proclaiming in heaven, "Now have come the salvation, and the power, and the kingdom of our God, and the authority of His Christ, for the accuser of our brothers, who kept accusing them day and night in the presence of our God, has been thrown out. [11]And they have conquered him by means of the blood of the Lamb and by the word of their testimony; they have not loved their lives, even to the point of death. [12]Be joyful, therefore, you heavens and those who dwell in them. Woe to the earth and the sea, because the devil has come down to you with raging anger, well aware that he has but a short season."

[13]When the dragon saw that he had been hurled to the earth, he went in pursuit of the woman who had given birth to the male child; [14]but to the woman were granted two wings of a giant eagle, so that she might fly to her retreat in the wilderness where, away from the presence of the serpent, she will be cared for during a time, times, and half a time.[u]

[15]The serpent poured water like a river out of his mouth after the woman, that she might be swept away by the stream, but the earth came to the woman's aid; [16]the earth opened its mouth and swallowed the river which the dragon had poured from his mouth. [17]And the dragon, enraged at the woman, went off to wage war against the rest of her offspring, who observe the commands of God and adhere to the testimony of Jesus. And he[v] stood on the sandy seashore.

13

AND I SAW A BEAST COMING UP out of the sea with ten horns and seven heads, with ten diadems on his horns, and a blasphemous name upon his heads. [2]The beast I saw resembled a leopard, and his feet were like those of a bear, and his mouth like that of a lion. The dragon invested him with his power and his throne and great authority. [3]One of his heads seemed fatally wounded. His mortal wound was healed, however, and the whole earth followed the beast in wonder. [4]They worshiped the dragon, because he had bestowed authority on the beast; they also worshiped the beast, saying, "Who matches the beast, and who is able to war against him?"

[5]He was also given a mouth to speak proud words, to utter blasphemies, and he was granted the power to exercise authority for forty-two months. [6]So he opened his mouth to utter blasphemies against God, to blaspheme His name and His abode and those who dwell in heaven. [7]And he was allowed to make war against the saints[w] and to conquer them, and authority was given him over every tribe and people and language and nation.

[8]All those who live on earth, whose names are not recorded in the Book of Life of the Lamb that was slain from the foundation of the world, will worship him. [9]Whoever has an ear, let him hear. [10]Whoever is to be led into captivity will be led into captivity; whoever kills with the sword must be killed by the sword. In this way the saints exercise their endurance and their faith.

[11]Then I saw another beast who came up from the land. He had two horns like a lamb and spoke like a dragon. [12]He exercises the full authority of the first beast in his presence, and he makes the earth and those living in it worship the first beast, whose mortal wound had been healed. [13]He also performs impressive miracles; for instance, he causes fire to descend from heaven to the earth in the presence of the people. [14]By means of the wonders he is allowed to perform in the presence of the beast, he leads those living on the earth astray,

---

t) Although Satan fell from heaven when he sinned, *cf.* Isa. 14:12, 13; Luke 10:18, God has allowed him access to heaven and authority in the universe, Job 1:6; Zech. 3:1; Eph. 2:2. Satan's final judgment is stated in ch. 20:10.   u) *Cf.* vs. 6; ch. 13:5. See note at ch. 11:2.   v) Some ancient manuscripts read here, "And I stood," and place this sentence at the beginning of ch. 13. The most reliable Gk. texts place it here at the end of ch. 12.   w) See note at Acts 9:13.

telling the earth's inhabitants to erect a statue to the beast that had the wound by the sword and came back to life.

15He was further permitted to infuse breath into the beast's statue, so that the beast's image might speak and to bring it about that those who did not worship the beast's statue should be killed. 16He also compelled all, the small and the great, the rich and the poor, the freemen and the slaves, to have a mark put on their right hands or on their foreheads, 17so that no one might be able to buy or sell unless he bore the mark of the beast's name or the number corresponding to his name. 18Here intelligence comes in. Let him who has the mind for it calculate the number of the beast, for it is a man's number, and his number is six hundred sixty-six.x

14 THEN I LOOKED AND SAW THE Lamb standing on Mount Zion, and with Him one hundred forty-four thousand,y who had His name and His Father's name inscribed on their foreheads. 2And I heard a voice from heaven like the sound of many waters and like the peals of loud thunder. I then heard the music as of harpists playing on their harps.

3They were singing a new song before the throne and in the presence of the four living beings, and of the elders, and none was able to sing the song except the one hundred forty-four thousand who were redeemed from the earth. 4They are those who have not defiled themselves with women,z for they are celibates. They are those who follow the Lamb wherever He goes. These were redeemed from mankind as first fruits for God and for the Lamb. 5No lie was ever found on their lips; they are faultless.

6Then I saw another angel, flying in mid-air with everlasting good news to proclaim to those living on the earth — to every nation and tribe and tongue and people. 7With a mighty voice he said, "Revere God and ascribe to Him glory, for the hour of His judgment has arrived; so worship the Maker of heaven and earth and sea and watersprings."

8Another, a second angel, succeeded him, who said, "She is fallen, fallen, Babylona the great, who made all the nations drink of the wine of her passionate immorality."

9Then another angel, a third, followed them, who said with a loud voice, "Whoever worships the beast and his statue and receives the mark on his forehead or on his hand, 10shall drink of the wine of God's wrath that has been mixed undiluted in the cup of His anger, and he shall be tortured with fire and brimstone in the presence of the holy angels and of the Lamb." 11The smoke of their torture ascends forever and ever, and the worshipers of the beast and of his statue, as well as anyone with the mark of his name, will enjoy no rest day or night.b 12Here comes in the endurance of the saintsc who observe the commands of God and keep their faith in Jesus.

13I further heard a voice from heaven that said, "Write: Blessed are the dead who die in the Lord from now on." "Yes," says the Spirit, "that they may rest from their labors; for the results of their labors follow them."

14Then I looked and saw a white cloud, and One seated on the cloud, One like the Son of Man.d On His head He wore a golden crown, and in His hand was a sharp scythe. 15Another angel came out of the temple,e who shouted with a loud voice to the One seated on the cloud: "Thrust in your scythe and reap, for harvest time has come,f because the earth's harvest is overripe." 16So the One seated on the cloud swung his scythe on the earth, and the earth was harvested.

17Again, another angel came out

x) Since six falls short of number seven, which in Scripture implies perfection or completion, multiples of six magnify its connotation of failure.   y) Cf. ch. 7:4.
z) In the Bible marriage never implies defilement. Discipleship requires complete dedication to Christ in spiritual celibacy, however.
a) Not the Babel or Babylon of the O.T., Gen. 10:10; Isa. 13:1; Dan. 1:1, etc., but a symbolic name for Rome.
b) Contrast ch. 4:8.   c) See note at Acts 9:13.   d) In anticipation of chs. 19, 20.
e) That is, in heaven.   f) Cf. Jer. 51:33; Joel 3:13.

from the heavenly temple, who also had a sharp scythe. [18]Yet another angel came forth from the altar, who had authority over fire, and he called with a loud voice to the one with the sharp scythe, "Thrust in your sharp scythe, and harvest the clusters of earth's grapevines, for its grapes are overripe."

[19]So the angel swung his scythe on the earth and gathered the fruit of earth's grapevine, and threw it into the great wine press of God's wrath. [20]Outside the city the wine press was trodden and blood flowed out of the wine press, so that for two hundred miles it came up to the horses' bridles.

15 THEN I SAW ANOTHER PORTENT in heaven, great and marvelous — seven angels with seven plagues;[g] the last seven, because with them God's wrath is completed.

[2]And I saw something like a glassy sea mixed with fire, and those coming off victorious over the beast and over his statue and over the number corresponding to its name; I saw them standing on the sea of glass, holding the harps of God. [3]They sang the song of Moses,[h] the bond servant[i] of God, and the song of the Lamb:[j] "Great and marvelous are Thy works, Lord God the Omnipotent; just and true are Thy ways, O King of the nations. [4]Who will not revere and glorify Thy name, O Lord? For Thou alone art holy. For all the nations shall come and worship before Thee, because Thy sentences of judgment have been made known."

[5]After this I looked, and the sanctuary of the tent of witness in heaven was opened, [6]and out of the sanctuary came the seven angels holding the seven plagues. They were clad in pure, resplendent linen, and wore golden girdles around their chests.

[7]Then one of the four living creatures handed the seven angels seven golden bowls full of the wrath of God, who lives forever and ever, [8]and the tabernacle became filled with smoke from the glory and the power of God. And no one was able to enter the temple until the seven plagues of the seven angels were finished.

16 AND I HEARD A LOUD VOICE from the temple say to the seven angels, "Go your way and pour out on the earth the seven bowls of God's wrath." [2]So the first angel departed and emptied his bowl upon the earth. And a loathsome and malignant ulcer attacked the men who bore the mark of the beast and worshiped its statue.

[3]The second angel poured out his bowl upon the sea, so that it turned to blood as of a corpse, and every living creature that was in the sea died.

[4]The third angel poured out his bowl upon the rivers and the springs of waters, so that they turned to blood. [5]And I heard the angel of the waters say, "Thou who art and who wast, the Holy One, art just in Thy judgments. [6]Because they have poured out the blood of saints and prophets, Thou also hast given them blood to drink. They deserve it." [7]And from the altar I heard a response,[k] "Yes, Lord God Almighty, Thy judgments are true and just."

[8]The fourth angel poured out his bowl upon the sun, and it was permitted to scorch humanity with heat. [9]People were scorched with terrible heat and they blasphemed the name of God, who has control over these plagues. Yet they did not repent so as to give Him glory.

[10]The fifth angel emptied his bowl upon the throne of the beast; his kingdom was plunged in darkness, and people gnawed their tongues from pain. [11]They blasphemed the God of heaven for their sufferings and their sores, yet they did not repent of their practices.

[12]The sixth angel poured out his bowl upon the great river, the Euphrates, and its waters dried up, so that the highway of the kings from the east might be made ready. [13]Then I saw coming out of the

---

g) The third woe, composed of seven plagues.
h) Exod. 15:1-21, the song of Moses after Pharaoh's armies were engulfed in the Red Sea.
i) Gk. *doulou*. See note at Matt. 13:27.   j) A song of righteousness and mercy.
k) See ch. 6:9 for the source of this response.

mouth of the dragon and from the mouth of the beast and from the mouth of the false prophet,[1] three unclean spirits like frogs. [14]For they are spirits of demons that work miracles. They go out to the kings of the whole world to muster them for the war of the Sovereign God's great Day. [15]"See, I come like a thief. Blessed is the alert one who takes care of his clothes so that he will not go around naked and people see his shame." [16]So they mustered them at the place called in Hebrew, Armageddon.[m]

[17]The seventh angel emptied his bowl into the air, and a loud voice came out of the sanctuary from the throne, saying, "It is finished!" [18]Then there followed lightning flashes, rumblings and thunderpeals, and such a tremendous earthquake as had never occurred since man existed on the earth, so extensive and severe was it. [19]The great city split into three parts, and the cities of the nations fell. God remembered great Babylon,[n] and made her drink the cup of His furious wrath.

[20]Then every island fled, and mountains could not be found. [21]Hailstones, as big as hundredweights, fell down from the sky upon the people. And the people blasphemed God for the plague of the hail, because it was so fearful.

17 THEN ONE OF THE SEVEN ANgels with the seven bowls came and talked with me, saying, "Come this way. I shall show you the doom of the great harlot[o] who is seated on many waters. [2]The kings of the earth have committed fornication with her, and the inhabitants of the earth have become intoxicated with the wine of her immorality."

[3]So he carried me away in the Spirit into a wilderness. And I saw a woman seated upon a scarlet beast covered with blasphemous titles. It had seven heads and ten horns. [4]The woman was robed in purple and scarlet, and gilded with gold, a precious stone, and pearls. In her hand she held a gold cup, full of the abominations and impurities of her immorality. [5]On her forehead a symbolic title was inscribed, "Babylon, the great, the mother of the harlots and of the abominations of the earth."

[6]I saw the woman drunk with the blood of the saints and with the blood of those who witnessed for Jesus, and on seeing her I was utterly amazed. [7]But the angel said to me, "Why are you amazed? I will tell you the mystic meaning of the woman, and of the beast with the seven heads and the ten horns, that carries her. [8]The beast that you saw was and is not, and it is to ascend from the abyss and to go on to destruction. The dwellers of the earth, whose names are not inscribed in the Book of Life from the foundation of the world, will be amazed when they look at the beast because he was and is not and is coming.

[9]"Here is something for a mind having wisdom to ponder. The seven heads are seven hills on which the woman is seated. [10]They also are seven kings; five have fallen, one is reigning, the other has not yet come; and when he does come, he must stay for a little while. [11]The beast that was and is not, is himself an eighth king; he springs from the seven and goes on to destruction.

[12]"The ten horns you saw are ten kings,[p] who have not as yet received a kingdom; but for one hour they will receive royal authority along with the beast. [13]These have one purpose; they give over power and authority to the beast. [14]They will war against the Lamb, and the Lamb will conquer them, for He is Lord of lords and King of kings; while those with Him are called, chosen, and loyal."

[15]Then he said to me, "The waters you saw, where the harlot sits, are peoples and crowds and nations and languages. [16]The ten horns you saw and the beast, these will hate the harlot and will make her desolate and naked; they will consume her flesh

---

1) The false prophet seems to be identified with the beast of ch. 13:11.
m) Identical with Megiddo, Judg. 5:19; II Kings 9:27; 23:29.
n) Cf. chs. 14:8; 17:5, 18. Babylon is a symbolic name for Rome.   o) See vs. 18.
p) Subservient to the beast.

and will burn her up with fire. [17]For God has put into their hearts to work His purpose, and to act harmoniously in handing their kingdom to the beast until the words of God should be fulfilled. [18]And the woman you saw is the great city that has dominion over the kings of the earth."

18 AFTER THESE THINGS I SAW another angel descending from heaven, possessed of great authority, and the earth was illuminated by his splendor. [2]With a mighty voice he shouted out: "She is fallen, fallen, Babylon the great! She has become a resort for demons; a haunt for every unclean spirit; a refuge for every filthy and detested bird. [3]For all the nations have drunk of the wine of her passionate immorality, and the kings of the earth have committed fornication with her, and the merchants of the earth have grown rich on her abundance of wantonness."

[4]Then I heard another voice from heaven[q] say, "Come away from her, My people, that you may not participate in her sins, neither be visited by her plagues; [5]for her sins have piled up to reach heaven, and God has remembered her crimes. [6]Repay her as she has paid; give her even double for what she has done; in the cup she mixed, mix her a double potion. [7]As she has glorified herself and has lived in sensuality, to that measure impose on her torture and grief. Because in her heart she says, 'I sit as queen;[r] I am no widow, and I shall never see sorrow,' [8]therefore on a single day her plagues will be upon her, pestilence, mourning, and famine, and with fire she shall be burned up. For the Lord God, who judges her, is mighty.

[9]"The kings of the earth, who committed fornication and were wanton with her, shall weep and beat their breasts over her, when they look at the smoke of her conflagration.[s] [10]Standing at considerable distance because dreading her torture, they shall exclaim, 'Woe, woe, for the great city, for Babylon the mighty city; for

her judgment is come in a single hour.' [11]And the earth's merchants[t] will weep and mourn over her, because no one will any longer buy their cargo, [12]their cargo of gold, silver, precious stones, pearls, fine linen, purple, silk, and scarlet, besides all kinds of citron wood, all sorts of ivory articles and objects made of costly wood, of bronze, iron, and marble; [13]also cinnamon, spice, incense, perfume, frankincense, wine and olive oil, fine flour and wheat, cattle, sheep, horses and chariots, bodies and souls of men.

[14]"The fruit for which your soul longed is out of your reach; all the elegance and the glitter you enjoyed are lost to you and never again will they be found.

[15]"The merchants of these products, who grew rich from her trade, will stand a long way off in terror of her torture, weeping and mourning, [16]and exclaiming, 'Woe, woe, for the great city that was dressed in fine linen, purple and scarlet and gilded with gold and precious stones and pearls, [17]for in a single hour all this wealth has been laid waste.'

"Every pilot,[u] too, and all who sail the seas, mariners and all who work the sea for their living, stood at a distance [18]and cried out as they looked at the smoke of her conflagration, 'What city was as great as this?' [19]They threw dust on their heads[v] and shouted as they wept and mourned, 'Woe, woe, for the great city where all who had ships at sea grew wealthy from her great wealth! For in a single hour she has been laid waste.'

[20]"Rejoice over her, O heaven, and you saints[w] and apostles and prophets, for on your behalf God has passed judgment against her."

[21]Then a powerful angel picked up a stone like a big millstone and hurled it into the sea with the words, "With such violence shall Babylon, the great city, be hurled down and shall never again be found. [22]The music of harpists and musicians and flute players and trumpeters shall not be heard in you any more; neither shall a skilled

---

q) *Cf.* ch. 16:7.   r) *Cf.* Isa. 47:7-9.   s) *Cf.* Jer. 50:46.
t) *Cf.* Ezek 27:28-36.   u) *Cf.* Ps. 107:23, 24.   v) *Cf.* Ezek. 27:30.   w) See note at Acts 9:13.

artisan be found in you any more; nor shall the grinding of the millstone be heard in you any longer. 23And no light of a lamp shall shine in you any more, nor shall the voices of bridegroom and bride be heard in you any more.

"For your merchants were the earth's prominent men; by your magic charms all the nations were led astray. 24In her, too, was found the blood of prophets and of saints and of all who have been slaughtered on the earth."

19 AFTER THIS I HEARD WHAT sounded like the voice of a great throng in heaven that said, "Hallelujah! Salvation, glory, and power belong to God, 2because His judgments are true and just. For He has judged the great harlot, who corrupted the earth with her fornication, and He has required from her hand retribution for the blood of His servants."x 3And a second time they shouted, "Hallelujah! And her smoke will ascend forever and ever."

4Then the twenty-four elders and the four living beings fell down to worship God, who is seated upon the throne, exclaiming, "Amen! Hallelujah!" 5And a voice came forth from the throne that said, "Render praise to our God, all His servants who revere Him, both small and great!"

6And I heard what was like the voice of a mighty throng, like the sound of many waters, like the roar of thunders, saying, "Hallelujah, for the Lord our God the Omnipotent has begun to reign. 7Let us be joyful, and let us celebrate, and let us ascribe glory to Him because the wedding banquet of the Lamb has comey and His bride has gotten herself ready. 8It has been granted to her to be dressed in pure, resplendent linen." For the fine linen is the righteous deeds of the saints.

9Then the angel said to me, "Write: Blessed are those who are invited to the wedding banquet of the Lamb."

He also told me, "These are the true words of God."

10So I fell at his feet to worship him, but he said to me, "You must not do that! I am a fellow servant of yours and of your brothers who hold to that to which Jesus has borne witness. Worship God." For the testimony of Jesus is the spirit of prophecy.z

11Then I saw heaven open and a white horse appeared. Its ridera is called Faithful and True; justly He judges and wages war. 12His eyes are like a flame of fire,b and on His head are many diadems with a name inscribed which no one knows except Himself. 13The robe He is wearing has been dipped in blood, and the name by which He is called is The Word of God. 14On white horses and clothed in fine linen, white and pure, the heavenly armies follow Him.

15Out of His mouth issues a sharp sword with which to smite the nations. He will rule them with an iron rod; and He treads the winepress of the furious wrath of God the Almighty. 16On His robe and on His thigh He has His name inscribed: King of kings and Lord of lords.

17And I saw an angel standing in the sun, who shouted with a loud voice to all the birds that fly in midheaven, "Come, gather for God's great banquet, 18to feast on the flesh of kings, of commanders, of mighty men, of horses and of their riders, on the flesh of everyone, free and slave, small and great."c

19Then I saw the beast and the kings of the earth and their armies mustered to wage war against the One mounted on the horse and against His army. 20And the beast was seized, and with him the false prophetd who performed miracles in his presence, by means of which he led astray those who received the mark of the beast and who worshiped his statue. Both of them were flung alive into the lake of fire that burns with sulphur. 21The rest were put to death with the sword

---

x) Gk. *doulon*; vs. 5, *douloi*. See note at Matt. 13:27.
y) The banquet is still future but it is certain.
z) Christ is the center of prophecy just as He is the center of all Scripture.   a) Christ.
b) Ch. 1:14.   c) *Cf.* Ezek. 39:17-20.   d) Identical with the beast of ch. 13:11; *cf.* ch. 16:13.

that issued from the mouth of the One mounted on the horse. And all the birds gorged themselves on their flesh.

20 THEN I SAW AN ANGEL DEscending from heaven, holding in his hand the key of the abyss and an enormous chain. ²He seized the dragon, the serpent of old, who is the devil and Satan, and bound him for a thousand years. ³He hurled him into the abyss, which he shut and sealed above him, that he might lead astray the nations no more until the thousand years are completed. After that he must be released for a little while.

⁴Then I saw thrones that were occupied by such as received power to judge. I also saw the souls of those who had been slain for their testimony to Jesus and for God's message, and of those who had not worshiped either the beast or his statue, nor had received his mark on their foreheads or on their hands. They came to life and reigned with Christ a thousand years.

⁵The rest of the dead did not come to life until the thousand years were completed. This is the first resurrection. ⁶Blessed and holy is he who shares in the first resurrection. Over them the second death exerts no power; instead, they will be priests of God and of Christ, and will reign with Him a thousand years.

⁷When the thousand years have ended, Satan will be released from his prison ⁸and will go out to lead astray the nations in the four quarters of the earth, Gog and Magog,ᵉ to muster them for battle. Their number is as the sand of the seashore.

⁹They marched up over the breadth of the earth and surrounded the encampment of the saintsᶠ and the beloved city. And fire came down from heaven and consumed them. ¹⁰The devil, who had deceived them, was flung into the lake of fire and sulphur where also the beast and the false prophet were and they will be tortured day and night forever and ever.

¹¹Then I saw a great white throne and One seated upon it, from whose presence earth and heaven fled, and no room was found for them. ¹²I also saw the dead, great and small, standing before the throne, and scrolls were opened. Another scroll was opened, the Book of Life, and the dead were judged according to their conduct from the entries in the scrolls. ¹³The sea also gave up the dead persons it contained, and death and Hades gave up the dead in them, and each person was judged according to his works. ¹⁴Then were death and Hades hurled into the lake of fire. This is the second death — the lake of fire. ¹⁵And whoever was not found recorded in the Book of Life was cast into the lake of fire.

21 THEN I SAW A NEW HEAVEN and a new earth;ᵍ for the first heaven and the first earth had passed away, and no longer was there any sea.ʰ ²I also saw the holy city, the new Jerusalem,ⁱ descending out of heaven from God, made ready as a bride adorned for her husband. ³And I heard a loud voice from the throne say, "Behold, God's dwelling place is among men, and He will dwell with them; they shall be His people, and God Himself will be with them ⁴and shall wipe away every tear from their eyes. Death shall be no longer, nor mourning, nor crying, nor any further pain, because the former things have passed away."

⁵Then He who was seated upon the throne said, "Behold, I make all things new." He also said, "Write; for these words are trustworthy and true." ⁶And He told me, "It is done! I am the Alpha and the Omega, the Beginning and the End. To him who is thirsty, I will give him without charge from the fountain of the water of life. ⁷The victor shall inherit all this; I shall be his God and he shall be My

---

e) Cf. Ezek. 38:2, 14.   f) See note at Acts 9:13.
g) A realm of righteousness.
h) The sea symbolizes nations in their turmoil. But the old order comes to its end, vs. 4.
i) Earth has here become like heaven; it is once more God's home.

son. [8]As for the cowardly, however, and the unbelieving, and the depraved, the murderers, the immoral, those practicing magic arts, and idolaters, all liars — their lot is in the lake that burns with fire and sulphur. This is the second death."

[9]One of the seven angels who had the seven bowls full of the seven final plagues came to talk with me and said, "Come this way. I will show you the bride, the Lamb's wife." [10]He then conveyed me in the Spirit to a great and lofty mountain and showed me Jerusalem, the holy city, coming down out of heaven from God [11]with the glory of God.

Her luster resembled a most precious jewel, a jasper stone as clear as crystal. [12]It had a large, high wall with twelve gates and at the gates twelve angels, and on the gates the names inscribed of the twelve tribes of Israel's sons: [13]three gates on the east side, three gates on the north side, three gates on the south side, and three gates on the west side. [14]And the city wall had twelve foundation stones, and engraved on them were the twelve names of the Lamb's twelve apostles.[j]

[15]The one talking with me had a golden measuring rod to measure the city with its gates and its wall. [16]The city is laid out as a quadrangle, with its length equal to its width. With the rod he measured the city, about fifteen hundred miles[k] — the length, the width and the height exactly equal. [17]He measured its wall too, two hundred sixteen feet[l] by human measure, that is, by the angel's.

[18]Its wall was made of jasper, and the city was made of pure gold, as transparent as glass. [19]The foundation stones of the city wall were ornamented with every kind of precious stone: the first foundation stone was jasper; the second, sapphire; the third, agate; the fourth, emerald; [20]the fifth,

sardonyx; the sixth, sardius; the seventh, chrysolite; the eighth, beryl; the ninth, topaz; the tenth, chrysoprase; the eleventh, jacinth; and the twelfth, amethyst.

[21]The twelve gates were twelve pearls, each separate gate made of one pearl, and the street of the city was made of pure gold, as transparent as glass. [22]I saw no temple in it, for the Lord God Omnipotent is its temple, and so is the Lamb. [23]The city has no need of the sun or of the moon to shine on it, because God's glory illumines it and the Lamb is its light. [24]By its light the nations will walk and to it the kings of the earth will bring their splendor.[m] [25]Its gates shall not at all be closed during the day, for there will be no night there. [26]Into it they will carry the glory and the honor of the nations. [27]But nothing unclean nor anyone practicing immorality and falsehood shall ever enter it, but only those whose names have been recorded in the Lamb's Book of Life.

22 He then showed me the river of the water of life, as clear as crystal, flowing forth from the throne of God and of the Lamb, [2]and running through the middle of the street, and on this side and that side of the river, the tree of life, bearing twelve kinds of fruit, yielding its fruit every month. And the leaves of the tree are for the healing of the nations.[n]

[3]There shall no longer be anything accursed there, but the throne of God and of the Lamb shall be in it, and His servants[o] shall worship Him. [4]They shall look at His face and His name shall be on their foreheads. [5]And night shall be no more; they will need neither lamplight nor sunlight, for the Lord God will be their light, and they shall reign forever and ever.

[6]Then he said to me, "These words are trustworthy and true. The Lord,

j) *Cf.* Ezek. 48:30-34.
k) The text reads 12,000 stadia. A stadion (or stadium, Gk. *stadion*) is equivalent to 600, 607, or 625 feet, according to whether Greek, English, or Roman measurement is used. "About fifteen hundred miles" symbolizes the length, width, and height of the new Jerusalem.
l) The wall's thickness.
m) The new Jerusalem, the Lamb's bride, began with the first believers and will be completed when the full number of the redeemed is made up.   n) *Cf.* Ezek. 47:12.
o) Gk. *douloi*; vs. 6, *doulois*. See note at Matt. 13:27.

the God of the spirits of the prophets has sent His angel to show His servants what must shortly take place. [7]Behold, I come quickly." Blessed is he who observes the words of the prophecy of this book.

[8]I, John, am the one who saw and heard these things, and when I had heard and seen, I bowed down to worship at the feet of the angel who was showing me all this. [9]But he said to me, "You must not do that! I am a fellow servant of yours, and of your brothers the prophets, and of those who obey the messages of this book. Worship God."

[10]Then he said to me, "Do not seal up the words of the prophecy of this book, for the time is near. [11]Let him who does wrong do wrong still, and let the filthy still be filthy; let the righteous still do right, and let the saint[p] still be holy."[q]

[12]"Behold, I am coming soon and My reward is with Me, to render to each according to his doings. [13]I am the Alpha and the Omega, the First and the Last, the Beginning and the End. [14]Blessed are those who wash their robes, that they may have the right to the tree of life and to enter through the gates into the city. [15]Outside are dogs, sorcerers, immoral persons, idolaters, and everyone who loves and practices falsehood.

[16]"I, Jesus, have sent My angel to you to witness these things for the churches. I am the Root and the Offspring of David, the brilliant Morning Star."

[17]The Spirit and the bride[r] say, "Come!" And let him who hears say, "Come!" And let the thirsty come; he who desires it, let him take freely the water of life.

[18]I warn everyone who hears the words of the prophecy of this book: if anyone adds to them, God will add to him the plagues that are described in this book, [19]and if anyone takes away from the words of this prophetic book, God will take away his share in the tree of life and in the holy city as described in this book.[s]

[20]He who affirms this says, "Yes, I am coming very soon."

Amen, Come, Lord Jesus![t]

[21]The grace of the Lord Jesus Christ be with all.

---

p) See note at Acts 9:13.   q) Lev. 11:44; I Pet. 1:16.
r) The Spirit and the church unitedly, for believers are moved by the Holy Spirit.
s) The warning refers specifically to this book but is equally true concerning all divine revelation.
t) Christ and the church are agreed in desiring each other's company.

Jesus' Messages to the Churches

	Description of Jesus	Commendation to the Church	Reproof Given to the Church	Warnings and Instructions to the Church	Promise to the Victors
Ephesus					
Smyrna					
Pergamum					

JESUS' MESSAGES TO THE CHURCHES

	DESCRIPTION OF JESUS	COMMENDATION TO THE CHURCH	REPROOF GIVEN TO THE CHURCH	WARNINGS AND INSTRUCTIONS TO THE CHURCH	PROMISE TO THE VICTORS
THYATIRA					
SARDIS					
PHILADELPHIA					

JESUS' MESSAGES TO THE CHURCHES

	DESCRIPTION OF JESUS	COMMENDATION TO THE CHURCH	REPROOF GIVEN TO THE CHURCH	WARNINGS AND INSTRUCTIONS TO THE CHURCH	PROMISE TO THE VICTORS
LAODICEA					

WHAT REVELATION TEACHES ABOUT

GOD	JESUS	THE HOLY SPIRIT

THE SEVEN SEALS, TRUMPETS, AND BOWLS

	SEALS	TRUMPETS	BOWLS
1ST			
2ND			
3RD			
4TH			
5TH			
6TH			
7TH			

THEME OF REVELATION:

SEGMENT DIVISIONS

				CHAPTER THEMES
				1
				2
				3
				4
				5
				6
				7
				8
				9
				10
				11
				12
				13
				14
				15
				16
				17
				18
				19
				20
				21
				22

Author:

Date:

Purpose:

Key Words:

God

Jesus (Christ)

in the Spirit

church(es)

throne

mystery (mystic, symbolic)

repent

victor(s)

mark every reference to Satan (demons, devil, dragon)

after these things (after this, following this)

and I saw (looked)

angel(s)

seal(s)

nations

trumpet(s)

bowl(s)

plague(s)

wrath

beast

Babylon (woman)

earthquake, voices, thunder, lightning

What the Bible Teaches about Babylon*

Its First Description in Scripture	Location of Babylon
	    The City
	
	    The Babylonian Empire

Worship Connected with Babylon	Warnings Given about Babylon

*Use your concordance to find Old Testament references to Babylon.

PROPHECIES REGARDING BABYLON	DESTRUCTION OF BABYLON
	   HISTORY OF BABYLON'S DESTRUCTION
	     THE CITY.

	THE BABYLONIAN EMPIRE
	DETAILS CONCERNING BABYLON'S FINAL DESTRUCTION THE CITY
	THE BABYLONIAN SYSTEM

THE DAY OF THE LORD, THE DAY OF WRATH, THE DAY OF GOD*

REFERENCE	HOW IS IT DESCRIBED	WHAT HAPPENS IN NATURE	SIGNS OF BEGINNING OR END

*Use your concordance to find Old Testament references to these phrases.